THE ANNALS
OF
AMERICA

THE ANNALS OF AMERICA

Volume 8

1850 - 1857

A House Dividing

ENCYCLOPÆDIA BRITANNICA, INC.

Chicago London Toronto Geneva Sydney Tokyo Manila Johannesburg Seoul

The editors wish to express their gratitude for permission to reprint
material from the following sources:

Ray Allen Billington for Selection 57, from *Journal of Charlotte L. Forten,* ed. by Ray Allen Billington, New York: The Dryden Press, Copyright 1953 by Ray Allen Billington. Reprinted Collier Books, Inc., New York, 1961. Second printing 1967.

The Arthur H. Clark Company for Selections 15, 93, from *A Documentary History of American Industrial Society,* ed. by John R. Commons *et al.*

Harvard University Press for Selection 46, from *This Was America,* ed. by Oscar Handlin, Cambridge, Mass.: Harvard University Press, Copyright 1949 by the President and Fellows of Harvard College.

Teachers College Press for Selection 47, from *The Colleges and the Public 1787-1862,* ed. by Theodore Rawson Crane, New York: Teachers College Press, © 1963 by Theodore Rawson Crane.

CODED SOURCES IN THIS VOLUME

Allen
Cowboy Lore. Edited by Jules Verne Allen. San Antonio, 1933.

Commons
A Documentary History of American Industrial Society. Edited by John R. Commons *et al.* In 10 vols. Cleveland, 1910-1911.

Globe
Congressional Globe. A record of the proceedings of Congress from 1833 to 1873, arranged by number of Congress and by session. In 46 vols. Washington, 1834-1873.

Globe, App.
Appendix to the Congressional Globe. A supplement to the *Congressional Globe* (see above), paged separately and also arranged by Congress and session. Washington, 1835-1873.

19 Howard 393
Reports of Cases Argued and Adjudged in the Supreme Court of the United States. Edited by Benjamin C. Howard, Vol. 19, Washington, 1857, pp. 393ff.

Nicolay-Hay
Complete Works of Abraham Lincoln. Edited by John G. Nicolay and John Hay. New and enlarged edition in 12 vols. New York, 1905.

Richardson
A Compilation of the Messages and Papers of the Presidents 1789-1897. Edited by James D. Richardson. In 10 vols. Washington, 1896-1899.

Statutes
The Public Statutes at Large of the United States of America from the Organization of the Government in 1789, etc., etc. In 79 vols. as of August 1966. 1845 *et seq.* Vol. 9 edited by George Minat, Boston, 1851.

TWA
This Was America. Edited by Oscar Handlin. Cambridge, 1949.

Contents

1856

1857

A HOUSE DIVIDING
In Pictures

The Growing Cities 97-108

In the industrial cities of the East, particularly New York,
an already severe problem of congestion was being compounded by
the arrival of several hundred thousand immigrants a year. Such
explosive, unplanned growth served to magnify the difficulties
of political and social organization and the general debasement
of environment that still plague these same cities.

The Gold Rush 144-156

The discovery of gold in California in 1848 transformed
a trickle of emigrants moving west into a deluge. A few lucky
prospectors actually found gold, but the large fortunes were
made through land speculation, large-scale placer mining, or
catering to the needs of the new population at exorbitant prices.

Barnum to Thoreau 227-236

In the theater, in literature, in historiography, political
philosophy, and science the period expressed new depth and
maturity. But the self-assurance of the times was perhaps
personified by Phineas T. Barnum, the ultimate showman,
whose talent for spectacle and controversy coincided
with a public taste for extravagant entertainment.

American Images 317-327

Daguerreotypes and engraved views catch something of the
character of life for the vast majority of the population still
dependent on agriculture. Steamboats move the products of
Midwestern farms and Southern plantations to distant markets.
The harsh pioneer life has given way for many to a comfortable
prosperity, approximating the ideal of self-sufficiency.

Boom and Panic 355-364

The frantic pace of industrialization, primarily in the
complementary growth of railroads and heavy industry, often
overreached the country's resources of capital. The resulting
periodic financial panics hardly affected the speculative
fever, and stock companies continued to proliferate.

The Last Compromise 415-426

In 1850, the conflict of interests between North and South was
temporarily resolved in a settlement that coupled California's
admission as a free state with the passage of a new Fugitive
Slave Law. This last compromise before the Civil War treated
symptoms only and could not reach the underlying social and economic
causes. The national leadership was powerless against
the elemental intractability of the issues as violence increased and the
possibility of further compromise was foreclosed.

1850

1.

HENRY CLAY: Compromise Resolutions

The Mexican cession that was the final result of the Mexican War opened up once again the question of the expansion of slavery that had supposedly been settled by the Missouri Compromise of 1820. The problems of states' rights and of sectionalism that had been hotly disputed during the war became even more bitter after it was over. The session of Congress that opened in December 1849 found its members already embattled over these issues. President Zachary Taylor had taken the important step of asking California to draw up a constitution and apply for statehood. With California ready for admission (as a free state) and the areas later to be known as New Mexico and Utah ready for territorial organization, Congress was faced with the need to resolve several problems at once. Controversy was intense throughout the country as old party alignments were replaced by new ones: Northern Abolitionists, Northern moderates, states' righters, pro-slavery Northerners, anti-states' rights Southerners, the new Free-Soil Party — each advocated its own point of view, and attacked all the others. For the first time the secession of the entire South was being seriously proposed, with many Northerners in favor of the idea as a way of settling the question once and for all. But there were many who hoped that a way out could be found — a compromise that would keep the Union intact and yet give each faction what it most wanted. The leading exponent of compromise was Henry Clay of Kentucky, returned to the Senate after a long absence, who put the following resolutions before his colleagues on January 29, 1850, and supported them in a speech, part of which is reprinted here, on February 5 and 6.

Source: *Globe, App.,* 31 Cong., 1 Sess., pp. 115-127.

IT BEING DESIRABLE for the peace, concord, and harmony of the Union of these states to settle and adjust amicably all existing questions of controversy between them arising out of the institution of slavery upon a fair, equitable, and just basis: therefore,

1. *Resolved,* that California, with suitable boundaries, ought upon her application to be admitted as one of the states of this Union, without the imposition by Congress

of any restriction in respect to the exclusion or introduction of slavery within those boundaries.

2. *Resolved,* that as slavery does not exist by law, and is not likely to be introduced into any of the territory acquired by the United States from the Republic of Mexico, it is inexpedient for Congress to provide by law either for its introduction into or exclusion from any part of the said territory; and that appropriate territorial governments ought to be established by Congress in all of the said territory not assigned as the boundaries of the proposed state of California, without the adoption of any restriction or condition on the subject of slavery.

3. *Resolved,* that the western boundary of the state of Texas ought to be fixed on the Rio del Norte [Rio Grande], commencing one marine league from its mouth, and running up that river to the southern line of New Mexico; thence with that line eastwardly, and so continuing in the same direction to the line as established between the United States and Spain, excluding any portion of New Mexico, whether lying on the east or west of that river.

4. *Resolved,* that it be proposed to the state of Texas that the United States will provide for the payment of all that portion of the legitimate and bona fide public debt of that state contracted prior to its annexation to the United States, and for which the duties on foreign imports were pledged by the said state to its creditors, not exceeding the sum of $ —, in consideration of the said duties so pledged having been no longer applicable to that object after the said annexation, but having thenceforward become payable to the United States; and upon the condition also that the said state of Texas shall, by some solemn and authentic act of her legislature, or of a convention, relinquish to the United States any claim which it has to any part of New Mexico.

5. *Resolved,* that it is inexpedient to abolish slavery in the District of Columbia while that institution continues to exist in the state of Maryland, without the consent of that state, without the consent of the people of the District, and without just compensation to the owners of slaves within the District.

6. *But resolved,* that it is expedient to prohibit within the District the slave trade, in slaves brought into it from states or places beyond the limits of the District, either to be sold therein as merchandise, or to be transported to other markets without the District of Columbia.

7. *Resolved,* that more effectual provision ought to be made by law, according to the requirement of the Constitution, for the restitution and delivery of persons bound to service or labor in any state who may escape into any other state or territory in the Union; and,

8. *Resolved,* that Congress has no power to prohibit or obstruct the trade in slaves between the slaveholding states; but that the admission or exclusion of slaves brought from one into another of them, depends exclusively upon their own particular laws.

The first resolution, Mr. President, as you are aware, relates to California; and it declares that California, with suitable limits, ought to be admitted as a member of this Union, without the imposition of any restriction, either to interdict or to introduce slavery within her limits. Now, is there any concession in this resolution by either party to the other? I know that gentlemen who come from the slaveholding states say that the North gets all that it desires; but by whom does it get it? Does it get it by any action of Congress? If slavery be interdicted in California, is it done by Congress, by this government? No, sir; the interdiction is imposed by California herself.

And has it not been the doctrine of all parties that when a state is about to be admitted into the Union, that state has a right to decide for itself whether it will or will not have within its limits slavery? The great principle which was in contest upon the memorable occasion of the introduction of Missouri into the Union was whether it was competent or was not competent for Congress to impose any restriction which should exist after she became a member of the Union.

We who were in favor of the admission of Missouri contended that, by the Constitution, no such restriction could be imposed. We contended that whenever she was once admitted into the Union, she had all the rights and privileges of any preexisting state of the Union; and that of these rights and privileges one was to decide for herself whether slavery should or should not exist within her limits — that she had as much a right to decide upon the introduction of slavery, or upon its abolition, as New York had a right to decide upon the introduction or abolition of slavery; and that she stood among her peers equal and invested with all the privileges that any one of the original thirteen states, and those subsequently admitted, had a right to enjoy.

And so I thought that those who have been contending with so much earnestness and with so much perseverance for the Wilmot Proviso ought to reflect that, even if they could carry their object and adopt the Wilmot Proviso, it would cease the moment any state to whose territory it was applicable came to be admitted as a member of the Union. No one contends now — no one believes — that with regard to the Northwestern states to which the Ordinance of 1787 was applied — Ohio, Indiana, Illinois, and Michigan — no one now believes that any one of those states, if they thought proper to do it, has not just as much a right to introduce slavery within her borders as Virginia has a right to maintain the existence of slavery within hers. . . .

The next resolution of the series which I have offered, I beg gentlemen candidly now to look at. I was aware, perfectly aware, of the perseverance with which the Wilmot Proviso was insisted upon. I knew that every one of the free states of this Union — I believe without exception — had, by its legislative bodies, passed resolutions instructing its senators and requesting its representatives to get that restriction incorporated into any territorial bill that might be offered under the auspices of Congress. I knew how much — although I regretted how much — the free states had . . . put their hearts upon the adoption of this measure. In this second resolution I call upon them to waive persisting in it. I ask them, for the sake of peace, and in a spirit of mutual forbearance to other members of the Union, to give it up, and to no longer insist upon it — to see, as they must see if their eyes are open, the dangers which lie under it if they persevere in insisting upon it.

Well, when I called upon them in that resolution to do this, was I not bound to offer, for the surrender of that favorite measure of theirs, some compensation — not an equivalent by any means, but some compensation — as that spirit of mutual forbearance which animates the one side ought at the same time to animate the other side? What is it that is offered them? It is a declaration of what I characterize and must style, with great deference to all those who entertain the opposite opinion — I will not say incontestable, but to me clear, and I think they ought to be regarded as — indisputable truths. And what are they? The first is that by law slavery no longer exists in any portion of the acquisition made by us from the Republic of Mexico; and the other is that, in our opinion, according to all the probabilities of the case, slavery never will be introduced into any portion of the territories so acquired from Mexico. . . .

If, prior to your departure from your respective homes, you had had the opportunity of conversing with your constituents upon this great, controlling, and important fact of the adoption of a constitution excluding slavery in California, do you believe, senators and representatives coming from the free states, that if you had had the aid of this fact in a calm, serious, fireside conversation, your constituents would not have told you to come here and settle all these questions without danger to the Union? What do you want? What do you want, you who reside in the free states? Do you want that there shall be no slavery introduced into the territories acquired by the war with Mexico? Have you not your desire in California? And in all human probability you will have it in New Mexico also.

What more do you want? You have got what is worth more than a thousand Wilmot Provisos. You have nature on your side — facts upon your side — and this truth staring you in the face, that there is no slavery in those territories. If you are not infuriated, if you can elevate yourselves from the mud and mire of mere party contentions to the purer regions of patriotism, what will you not do? Look at the fact as it exists. You will see that this fact was unknown to the great majority of the people; you will see that they acted upon one state of facts, while we have another and far different state of facts before us; and we will act as patriots — as responsible men, and as lovers of liberty, and lovers, above all, of this Union. . . .

I think, entertaining these views, that there is nothing extravagant in the hope which I indulged at the time these resolutions were proposed — nothing extravagant in the hope that the North might content itself even with striking out these two declarations. . . . Of all the questions connected with or growing out of this institution of slavery which Congress is called upon to pass upon at this time, there are none so difficult and troublesome as this which relates to Texas; because Texas has the question of boundary to settle.

Possibly if the United States fixes it in a way contrary to the desire and rights of Texas, she might bring it before the Supreme Court of the United States and have the question again decided. . . . There are questions too large for any tribunal of that kind to decide — great political, national, and territorial questions, which transcend their limits and to which they are utterly incompetent. Whether this is one or not, I will not decide; but I will maintain that the United States are now invested solely and exclusively with that power which was in both nations — to fix, ascertain, and settle the western and northern limits of Texas.

Sir, the other day my honorable friend who represents so well the state of Texas [Mr. Rusk] said that we had no more right to touch the limits of Texas than we have to touch the limits of Kentucky; that the state is one and indivisible and that the federal government has no right to separate it. I agree with him that when the limits are certain and ascertained, they are undisputed and indisputable. . . .

But then I assume — what does not exist in the state of Texas — that this boundary was known, ascertained, and indisputable. On the contrary, it was open — it was unfixed and remains unfixed to this moment with respect to her western limits and north of the head of the Nueces. . . . But who is there that can say with truth and justice that there is no reciprocity, no concession in these resolutions made to Texas, even with reference to the question of boundary line? They give her a vast country, equal in amount nearly, I repeat, to what she indisputably possessed before — a country sufficiently large, with her consent hereafter, to carve out of it some two or three additional states, when the condition and number of the population may render it expedient to make new states. Well, sir, is not that concession, liberality, and justice?

But, sir, that is not all we propose to give. The second resolution proposes to pay a certain amount of the debt of Texas. . . .

I think that were you to give to Texas the large boundary that is assigned to her, when you take into view the abhorrence — for I think I am warranted in using that expression — with which the people of New Mexico east of the Rio Grande would look upon any political connection with Texas, and when you take into view the large amount of money, liberating and exonerating Texas from a portion of her public debts, equal to that amount — when you take all these circumstances into consideration, I think they present a case, with regard to which, I confess, I should be greatly surprised if the people of Texas themselves, when they come to deliberate upon this seriously, should hesitate a moment to accede. . . .

With this explanation of that part of the subject, I pass to the next resolution in the series which I had the honor to submit. It relates, if I am not mistaken, to this District:

> 5. Resolved, that it is inexpedient to abolish slavery in the District of Columbia while that institution continues to exist in the state of Maryland, without the consent of that state, without the consent of the people of the District, and without just compensation to the owners of slaves within the District. . . .

Mr. President, I said on yesterday that there was no one of these resolutions, except the first, which contained any concession by either party that did not either contain some mutual concession by the two parties, or did not contain concessions altogether from the North to the South. Now, with respect to the resolution under consideration, the North has contended that the power exists under the Constitution to abolish slavery here. I am aware that the South, or a greater portion of the South, have contended for the opposite doctrine. What does this resolution ask? It asks of both parties to forbear urging their respective opinions the one to the exclusion of the

other. But it concedes to the South all that the South, it appears to me, ought in reason to demand, inasmuch as it requires such conditions as amount to an absolute security for the property in slaves within the District — such conditions as will make the existence of slavery in the District coevil and coextensive with its existence in any of the states out of or beyond the District. The second clause of this resolution provides that it is expedient to prohibit within the District the trade in slaves brought into it.

Mr. President, if it be conceded that Congress has the power of legislation — exclusive legislation — in all cases whatsoever, how can it be doubted that Congress has the power to prohibit what is called the slave trade within the District of Columbia? My interpretation of the Constitution is this. . . . Congress has a power within the District equivalent to and coextensive with the power which any state itself possesses within its own limits. Well, can anyone doubt the power and right of any state in this Union — of any slaveholding state — to forbid the introduction as merchandise of slaves within its own limits? Why, almost every slaveholding state in the Union has exercised its power to prohibit the introduction of slaves as merchandise. . . .

Well, then, I really do not think that this resolution, which proposes to abolish that trade, ought to be considered as a concession by either class of states to the other class. . . . I am not going to argue the question whether if a man voluntarily carries his slave into a free state, he is or is not entitled to his freedom. . . . I think that the existing laws for the recovery of fugitive slaves, and the restoration and delivering of them to their owners, being often inadequate and ineffective, it is incumbent upon Congress (and I hope that hereafter, when a better state of feeling, when more harmony, and goodwill prevails among the various parts of this confederacy — I hope it will be regarded by the free states themselves as a part of their duty) to assist in allaying this subject, so irritating and disturbing to the peace of this Union. At all events, whether they do it or not, it is our duty to do it. It is our duty to make the laws more effective; and I will go with the furthest senator from the South in this body to make penal laws, to impose the heaviest sanctions upon the recovery of fugitive slaves, and the restoration of them to their owners. . . .

The last resolution declares:

> That Congress has no power to prohibit or obstruct the trade in slaves between the slaveholding states; but that the admission or exclusion of slaves brought from one into another of them depends exclusively upon their own particular laws.

This is a concession — not, I admit, of any real constitutional provision, but a concession — of what is understood, I believe, by a great number at the North to be a constitutional provision — from the North to the South, if the resolution be adopted. Take away the decisions of the Supreme Court of the United States on that subject and I know there is a great deal that might be said on both sides of the subject in relation to the right of Congress to regulate the trade between the states. But I believe the decision of the Supreme Court has been founded upon correct principles; and I hope it will forever put an end to the question whether Congress has or has not the power to regulate the slave trade between the different states. . . .

We are told now, and it is rung throughout this entire country, that the Union is threatened with subversion and destruction. Well, the first question which naturally arises is, supposing the Union to be dissolved — having all the causes of grievances which are complained of — how far will a dissolution furnish a remedy for those grievances? If the Union is to be dissolved for any existing causes, it will be dissolved because slavery is interdicted or not allowed to be introduced into the ceded territories, because slavery is threatened to be abolished in the District of Columbia, and because fugitive slaves are not returned, as in my opinion they ought to be, restored to their masters. These I believe will be the causes, if there be any causes, which can lead to the direful event to which I have referred. . . .

Mr. President, I am directly opposed to any purpose of secession, of separation. I am for staying within the Union, and defying any portion of this Union to expel or drive me out of the Union. I am for staying within the Union and fighting for my rights — if necessary, with the sword — within the bounds and under the safeguard of the Union. I am for vindicating these rights; but not by being driven out of the Union rashly and unceremoniously by any portion of this confederacy. Here I am within it, and here I mean to stand and die — as far as my individual purposes or wishes can go — within it to protect myself, and to defy all power upon earth to expel me or drive me from the situation in which I am placed. Will there not be more safety in fighting within the Union than without it? . . .

I think that the Constitution of the thirteen states was made not merely for the generation which then existed but for posterity, undefined, unlimited, permanent, and perpetual; for their posterity; and for every subsequent state which might come into the Union, binding themselves by that indissoluble bond. . . . The dissolution of the Union and war are identical and inseparable; they are convertible terms. . . .

I conjure gentlemen, whether from the South or the North, by all they hold dear in this world, by all their love of liberty, by all their veneration for their ancestors, by all their regard for posterity, by all their gratitude to Him who has bestowed upon them such unnumbered blessings, by all the duties which they owe to mankind and all the duties they owe to themselves, by all these considerations I implore them to pause — solemnly to pause — at the edge of the precipice before the fearful and disastrous leap is taken in the yawning abyss below which will inevitably lead to certain and irretrievable destruction.

2.

HORACE MANN: Slavery in the Territories

While the greatest debate in congressional history raged in the Senate over Henry Clay's compromise resolutions of January 29, 1850, the House of Representatives was also giving its attention to the problem of the expansion of slavery into the territories. Among those who spoke on the issue was Horace Mann, who had resigned his post as secretary to the Massachusetts Board of Education to take the seat of John Quincy Adams. Mann conceded his close relations with the Free-Soil Party, which had arisen in 1848 in opposition to the extension of slavery into any newly acquired territory, and he also admitted to being an Abolitionist. In his speech, given on February 15, he formulated many of the positions later developed by Lincoln in his debates with Stephen A. Douglas. Portions of the speech appear here.

Source: *Slavery: Letters and Speeches*, Boston, 1851, pp. 180-225.

EVER SINCE THE ORGANIZATION of this House, before its organization, and even in a preliminary caucus that preceded the commencement of the session, Southern gentlemen have pressed the cause, not only of human slavery but of slavery extension, upon us. From motives of forbearance, and not from any question as to our rights, we of the North have maintained an unbroken silence. The time has surely come when the voice of freedom should find an utterance. Would to God that on the present occasion it might find an abler defender than myself, although if my ability to defend it were equal to the love I bear it, it could ask no stronger champion.

I wish to premise a few words respecting the propriety and true significance of some of the epithets by which the parties to this discussion are characterized. The term "Free Soiler" is perpetually used upon this floor as a term of ignominy and reproach; yet I maintain that in its original and legitimate sense, as denoting an advocate of the doctrine that all our territorial possessions should be consecrated to freedom, there is no language that can supply a more honorable appellation. . . .

For myself, I will engage in any honorable measure most likely to secure freedom to the new territories. I will resist any and every measure that proposes to abandon them to slavery. The epithet "Free Soiler," therefore, when rightly understood and correctly applied, implies both political and moral worth; and I covet the honor of its application to myself. But what does its opposite mean? What does the term "Slave Soiler" signify? It signifies one who desires and designs that all soil should be made to bear slaves. . . .

And again; those of us at the North who resist slavery extension, who mean to withstand its spread beyond the limits where it now exists, are denounced as Abolitionists. This epithet is applied to us as a term of reproach and obloquy; as a brand and stigma upon our characters and principles. No distinction is made between those few individuals among us who desire to abolish the Constitution of the United States and that great body of the people who, while their allegiance to this Constitution is unshaken, mean also to maintain their allegiance to truth and to duty in withstanding the hitherto onward march of slavery.

Among the latter class, Mr. Collamer, the postmaster general, is called an Abolitionist. Mr. John Quincy Adams was denounced as an arch-Abolitionist. Every man who advocates the Jefferson proviso against the spread of slavery is so called; and if an unspeakable abhorrence of this institution, and the belief that it is the second greatest enormity which the oppressor, in his power, ever committed against the oppressed, in his weakness — being inferior only to that ecclesiastical domination which has trampled upon the religious freedom of man — I say, if this abhorrence of slavery and this belief in its criminality entitle a man to be denominated an Abolitionist, then I rejoice in my unquestionable right to the name. . . .

If we are Abolitionists, then, we are abolitionists of human bondage; while those who oppose us are abolitionists of human liberty. We would prevent the extension of one of the greatest wrongs that man ever suffered upon earth; they would carry bodily chains and mental chains — chains in a literal and chains in a figurative sense — into realms where even the half-civilized descendants of the Spaniard and the Indian have silenced their clanking. We would avert the impending night of ignorance and superstition; they would abolish the glorious liberty wherewith God makes His children free. In using this word, therefore, to calumniate us, they put darkness for light and light for darkness; good for evil and evil for good.

The constitutional right of Congress to legislate for the territories is still debated. Having presented my views on this subject before, I shall now treat it with brevity. In a speech by General Cass, which has lately been published, that distinguished senator, in order to prove that Congress has no power to legislate on the subject of slavery in the territories, has attempted to prove that it has no right to legislate for the territories at all. I refer to the senator from Michigan because he now stands before the country in the twofold character of being the head of the Democratic Party, which goes for the "largest liberty," and also of the extreme pro-slavery party, which goes for the *largest bondage.* He would sever all diplomatic relations between this country and Austria, because she has robbed the Hungarians of a part of their liberties, while he is drawing closer the political ties which bind him to the South, which has despoiled 3 million of the African race of all their liberties, and is now intent on propagating other millions for new despoliations. . . .

General Cass, in a speech that fills more than nineteen columns in the *Washington Union,* has reviewed the decisions of all the judges of the Supreme Court who have ever expressed any opinion on the subject of congressional power over territorial legislation; he has commented upon the views of all the jurists who have written upon it and of most of the speakers in both houses of Congress who have discussed it; he has surveyed the course of administration of all the presidents we have ever had; and has come to the clear conclusion that all of them — judges, jurists, legislators, and presidents — have systematically violated the Constitution of the United States, or commended its violation, on every practicable occasion for the last sixty years.

Omitting the hundred ways in which the absurdity of this conclusion can be exposed, let me subject it to one practical test. We have acquired territory from Mexico. General Cass voted to ratify the treaty of cession. Measures have been instituted for the formation of three separate governments in this territory — those of California, Deseret [the Colorado River Basin and the Great Basin], and New Mexico. The boundaries marked out by California and Deseret overlay each other to the amount of thousands of square miles. If they have the exclusive right of self-government, as General Cass declares, and Congress none, then they must settle this question of boundary themselves. They may declare war against each other, make alliances with foreign powers, equip armies, build fleets; while Congress can do nothing within their limits but sell land.

But what renders the argument of General Cass still more extraordinary is the fact that, according to his own doctrine, he has spent the greater part of his political life in violating the Constitution, while constantly repeating his oath to support it. As marshal of Ohio, as governor of Michigan, as Indian agent, he has appointed officers and magistrates, and executed laws, when, according to his own showing, he was a mere interloper and usurper; he has met territorial legislatures which had no more right to assemble than a mob; he has doubtless imprisoned, if not executed, many alleged offenders who had as good a legal right to execute or to imprison him; and he has received salaries for more than twenty years, to which the khan of Tartary was as much

entitled as he. Now, if he will refund the salaries he has unconstitutionally received; make reparation for the penalties or forfeitures he has wrongfully extorted; show some signs of contrition for the men whom he has unlawfully imprisoned or hung, it will remove the suspicions of many minds in regard to the sincerity, if not the soundness, of his argument.

I mention these facts from no personal feelings in regard to the senator from Michigan; but only to show to what desperate extremities men are driven in order to defend the right of spreading slavery from the Atlantic to the Pacific Ocean; and because this is the last reading of the Constitution which has been invented for the purpose.

Since the last session of Congress, the condition of a part of this territory has greatly changed. The unexampled velocity with which a living stream of men has poured into it within the last twelve months has reversed its condition and decided its destiny. In other countries, individuals seek their fortunes by changing their residence. Under the vehement action of our enterprise, cities migrate. The new residents of California have framed a constitution, have applied for admission into this Union, and their application is now pending before us. Of their own accord, they have excluded slavery from their borders by their fundamental law. Until the discovery of gold in that country, and until all incredulity in regard to that remarkable fact had been overcome, it was confidently anticipated at the South, and intensely feared at the North, that the whole region would be overrun with slaveholders and with slaves.

As far back as 1842, Mr. Wise, of Virginia, the administration leader in the House of Representatives, boldly declared that "slavery should pour itself abroad without restraint, and find no limit but the Southern Ocean." The war with Mexico was waged for the twofold purpose of robbing that republic of its territory, and then robbing that territory of its freedom. Congressional orators and the Southern press avowed that the object of acquiring territory was to extend the "divine institution." I could quote pages in proof of this assertion. The North had no hope, the South had no fear, if the territories were left without control, but that they would first be filled with slaveholders and would then incorporate slavery into their organic law.

While these prospects continued, the South insisted that the territories should be left untrammeled. Distinguished men in this House, Mr. Calhoun and other senators, the government organ, which was supposed to express the views of President Polk and his cabinet, all proclaimed that the territories should be left free to institute such government as they might choose. But since California has formed a *free* constitution, what a sudden change has taken place in the convictions of men! Within the present week we have had three most elaborate speeches in this House in which the admission of California, with her free constitution, is vehemently opposed on constitutional grounds. Yes, sir, did you know it? The Constitution of the United States has just been altered; or, what is intended to produce the same effect, without the trouble of an alteration in the manner prescribed by itself, its interpretation has been altered.

While California promised to be a slave state, all interference was unconstitutional. Now, as she desires to be a free state, it has become constitutional to interfere and repel her. Not only so, but, according to the gentleman from Alabama (Mr. Inge), in swearing to support the Constitution we have sworn to perpetuate, and not only to perpetuate but to extend slavery. "To those," he says, "who are disposed to resist my views, I commend a more attentive reading of that instrument. They will find that it not only guarantees slavery but provides for its extension." Or, as he says in another place, it makes provision "to extend the in-

stitution indefinitely." And, therefore, when a territory asks to be admitted as a free state, it is to be repulsed and virtually told, "If you will incorporate slavery into your constitution, you shall be admitted; if not, not." Had the man who first uttered the adage that "circumstances alter cases" foreseen our times, he would have said, "circumstances alter *principles*." . . .

It is further objected to the admission of California that its dimensions are too large for a single state. The force of this objection is somewhat abated when we reflect that it comes from men who were most strenuous for the admission of Texas. However, I shall not object very earnestly to the reduction of its limits. I will say in frankness, that the southern portion of California is understood to be even more attached to freedom than the northern. The result may, therefore, be, if this objection is persisted in and a division made, that we shall soon have two free states instead of one. It was said by the last administration that Mexico was to be dismembered in order "to extend the area of freedom." The most just retribution for that diabolical irony is to carry out the declaration literally.

But I now come to a more substantial part of this great question. The South rests its claims to the new territory upon the great doctrine of equality. There are fifteen slave states; there are only fifteen free states. The South contributed men and money for the conquest, not less than the North; hence, equal ownership and equal rights of enjoyment. This is the argument. In a long and most elaborate speech delivered in the Senate this week by one of the most eminent jurists in the Southern states (Judge Berrien), he founds the whole claim of the South on this doctrine of equality.

Now, I admit this principle in its fullest extent, and without hesitation. That country is equally free to all the people of the United States. The government can sell the lands not already covered by valid titles;

and any citizen who will comply with its terms can buy them. The people of each of the United States can go there and establish their domicile. The laws of Congress make no discrimination between them. The Constitution makes no such discrimination. The law of nature and of nations makes none. The North has no privilege over the South, and the South has none over the North. If the North has any greater right there than the South, the equality is destroyed. If the South has any greater right there than the North, the equality is equally destroyed.

And now, practically, what right has the North, or what right is claimed by the North, which the South has not to an equal extent? What article of property can a citizen of Massachusetts carry there which a citizen of Georgia *cannot* carry there? Can we carry any of our local laws there, even though all the inhabitants of the state should remove thither in a body? Certainly not. When we leave our state, we leave our local laws behind us. A citizen of Boston has a right to educate his children at school, at the public expense. In the Boston public schools, he can prepare his son to enter any college in this country, even though he is too poor to pay a cent for taxes and never has paid a cent for taxes. Has he any such right on arriving at San Francisco? If the city of Boston debars him of this right of educating his son at the public charge, he can institute a suit against it and recover full damages. Can he do the same thing at San Francisco or San Jose? Certainly not. He has left the laws and institutions of Massachusetts behind him. But, it is said, we can carry our property there, and you cannot carry your property there. I think those who use this argument, like the old Roman augurs, must smile at each other askance for the credulity or simplicity of those they beguile by it. Will not every man, even of the feeblest discernment, see the fallacy which is here covered up under the word "property"?

What is meant by this deceptive term "property"? If you mean silver, or gold, or seeds, or grains, or sheep, or horses, cannot you carry these there as freely as we can? But you have special laws — local and peculiar laws — laws contrary to the great principles of the common law by which you call men and women property. And then, forsooth, because we can carry property there, when property means grain and cattle, you can carry property there when it means human beings, perhaps your own brothers, or sisters, or children. Because we can carry our property there, when property means inanimate substances, you have only to call a human being property; you have only to call a creature, formed in the image of God, property, and then he can be smuggled in under the new name.

Why, sir, there is not a respectable village in the country where, if a juggler or mountebank were to attempt to palm off upon his audience so flimsy a trick as this, he would not be hissed from the stage. There are certain kinds of property and rights which we can carry with us to the territories, and other kinds which we cannot. We can carry movable property, but not immovable; a diamond or a library, but not a cotton factory nor a cotton field. . . .

The reason is that the law of slavery is a *local* law. Like lotteries, or polygamy, or infanticide, it can legally exist in no land where the principles of the common law prevail, until it is legalized and sanctioned by a special law. Then it is permitted on the simple ground that so much of the common law as secures liberty and property, the right of habeas corpus and freedom of speech to each individual, has been cut out and cast away. The Constitution proceeds upon this doctrine when it provides for the recapture of fugitive slaves. Why did it not provide for the capture of a fugitive horse or ox? Why did it not provide that, if a horse or an ox should escape from a slave state into a free state, it should be delivered up or be recoverable by legal process? Because horses and oxen are property by the common consent of mankind. It needed no law to make them property. They are property by the law of nations, by the English common law, by the law of every state in this Union, while men and women are not. An escaped slave could not be recovered before the adoption of the Constitution. The power to seize upon escaping slaves was one of the motives for adopting it.

These considerations demonstrate that slaves are not property, within the meaning of this word, when it is affirmed that if the North can carry its property into the territories, so can the South. As the Constitution, in terms, adopts the common law, it leaves slavery nothing to stand upon but the local laws of the states where it is established. Freedom is the rule, slavery is the exception. Judge Berrien's favorite doctrine of equality would, therefore, be destroyed if the exception should prevail over the rule. For, if slavery can be carried into any of our territories by force of the Constitution, it can into all of them; and if carried into all of them, the exception becomes the rule and the rule perishes. Ay, the rule ceases to be even so much as an exception to that which was its own exception. It is wholly swallowed up and lost.

I know it is said that the *fact* of slavery always precedes the *law* of slavery; that law does not go before the institution and create it, but comes afterward to sanction and regulate it. But this is no more true of slavery than of every other institution or practice among mankind, whether right or wrong. Homicide existed before law; the law came in subsequently and declared that he who took an innocent man's life without law should lose his own by law. The law came in to regulate homicide; to authorize the taking of human life for crime, just as we authorize involuntary servitude for crime; and it may just as well be argued that murder is a natural right because it existed before law as that slavery is a natural right because it existed before law. This argument appeals to the crime which the law was enacted to prevent, in order to establish the supremacy of the crime over the law that forbids it.

There is another fallacy in the arguments which Southern gentlemen use on this subject, which, though not as transparent as the preceding, is quite as unsound. They speak of the *rights* of the slaveholder in the new territories. They speak as though the collective ownership of the territories by the government were the ownership of the people in severalty; as though each citizen could go there and draw a line round a "placer," and say *this is mine;* and, then, because it is his, introduce his slaves upon it. But nothing is more clear than that there is no such individual right. The right of the government is first, a right of sovereignty and jurisdiction; and second, the right of ownership of all lands, navigable waters, etc., which have not been conveyed away by the preexisting government. Individuals retain their citizenship on going there, as they do on going to Great Britain or France; but a slave has just as much right to a portion of the public lands in California when he gets there as his master.

Again, if the master carries into California the legal right to hold slaves which he possessed at home, does not the slave also retain his legal rights when he is transferred there? The laws which govern slaves are as various as the states where they exist. In some states manumission is comparatively unobstructed. In Delaware, it is a penal offense even to sell a slave to a notorious slave dealer. In Georgia, the law forbids, or lately forbade, the importation of slaves for sale. Now, how can a Georgian import slaves into California from Georgia when the very laws of his own state, under which he claims to hold slaves and under which laws he claims to carry slaves with him, forbid their importation?

And, further, political franchises or privileges are just as much a part of a man's rights as any tangible commodity. In South Carolina, the ownership of ten slaves constitutes a property qualification for being a member of the legislature. On removing to California, will the citizen of South Carolina who owns ten slaves carry an eligibility to the legislature of California with him? Nay, this political privilege in South Carolina goes further. It is a right in every owner of ten slaves that no man who does not own ten slaves (or some legal equivalent) shall be a member of the legislature. The aspirant for office has a legal right in the limitation of the number of his competitors as much as in anything else. Can he carry this to California with him? The inference is inevitable that if the inhabitants of the fifteen slave states can carry slaves into California by virtue of the laws of their respective states, then they must also carry all the incidents of slavery known to their respective codes. For, how can the incident be separated from the principal? You might, therefore, have, in a neighborhood of fifteen families, fifteen slave codes in operation at the same time: a manifest absurdity.

The conclusion, then, is irresistible: that when you come to the boundary line between a slave state and a free state, you come to the boundary line of slavery itself. On one side of the line, down to the nadir and up to the zenith, the blackness of the slave code pervades all things; but, on the other side, as high above and as deep below, is the purity of freedom. Virginia cannot extend her laws one hairbreadth over the line into Pennsylvania or into Ohio, because their soil is beyond her jurisdiction. So neither Virginia, nor all the fifteen slave states combined, can extend their slave laws one hairbreadth into the new territories; and for the same reason: the territories are beyond their jurisdiction.

As to the argument that the Constitution of the United States recognizes slavery, and that, upon the cession of new territories, the Constitution, by some magical and incomprehensible elasticity, extends itself over them and carries slavery into them, I think I speak with all due respect when I say it does not come up to the dignity of a sophism. Where do strict constructionists, or even latitudinarian constructionists, find any clause, or phrase, or word which shows that the Constitution is anything but a compact between states? Where do they find anything that shows it to be a compact between territories, or between territories and states conjoined? On its very face, the Constitution meets this pretension with a denial.

The Preamble declares, "We the people of the United States," — not the people of the territories, nor the people of the states and territories — "in order to form a more perfect Union . . . do ordain and establish this Constitution for the United States of America." If the Constitution is a compact between the United States and the territories, then the people of the territories have all the rights under it which the people of the states have: the right to choose electors for President and Vice-President, etc., and to be represented in Congress by a member who can vote as well as speak. The only way in which the Constitution ever was extended, or ever can be extended over any part of the earth's surface outside of the "original thirteen," is this. The Constitution in express terms authorizes the admission of new states, and, therefore, when a new state is admitted, it becomes one of these "United States of America." The Constitution does not extend over the territories, but Congress, being the creature of the Constitution, is, when legislating for the territories, not only invested with constitutional powers but is limited by constitutional restrictions. . . .

But there is another consideration, one which appertains to the party supposed to be insulted rather than the party charged with the insult. In his *Theory of Moral Sen-*

timents, Adam Smith maintains that it is the judgment of men — the opinion of the bystanders — that gives us the pleasure of being approved, or the pain of being disapproved, on account of our conduct. Now, in this contest between the North and the South on the subject of extending slavery, who are the bystanders? They are the civilized nations of the earth. We, the North and the South, are contending in the arena. All civilized men stand around us. They are a ring of lookers-on. It is an august spectacle. It is a larger assemblage than ever witnessed any other struggle in the history of mankind; and their shouts of approbation or hisses of scorn are worthy of our heed.

And what do these spectators say, in the alternations of the combat? Do they urge on the South to mightier efforts, to the wider spread of slavery and the multiplication of its victims? Do they shout when she triumphs? When new chains are forged and riveted, when new realms are subdued by haughty taskmasters and overrun by imbruted slaves, do their plaudits greet your ears and rouse you to more vehement efforts? All the reverse; totally the reverse.

They are now looking on with disgust and abhorrence. They groan, they mock, they hiss. The brightest pages of their literature portray you as covered with badges of dishonor; their orators hold up your purposes as objects for the execration of mankind; their wits hurl the lightnings of satire at your leaders; their statute books abound in laws in which institutions like yours are branded as crimes; their moralists, from their high and serene seats of justice, arraign and condemn you; their theologians find your doom of retribution in the oracles of God.

England has abolished slavery. France, in one fervid moment of liberty, struck the chains from off all her slaves, as the bonds of Paul and Silas were loosed in the inner prison by the mighty power of God. Sweden has abolished it. More than twenty years ago, impotent, half-civilized Mexico did the same. Tunis, a Barbary state, and, I might add, a barbarous state, has abolished slavery. Mohammedanism precedes Christianity, and sets it an example of virtue. Liberia, a republic of emancipated slaves, the very brothers and sisters of those whom you now hold in bondage, has been acknowledged as an independent sovereignty and welcomed into the family of nations by two of the most powerful governments on the globe.

By this act, freedom secures a new domain on the Eastern continent, while you are striving to give a new domain to bondage on the Western. A monarchy hails the advent of a free nation in Africa, where slavery existed before; a republic is seeking to create 10,000 absolute despotisms in America, where freedom existed before.

Now, these are the bystanders and lookers-on in this grand and awful contestation. They are all agreed, as one man, in their opinions about it. They are unitedly visiting your course with execration and anathema. There is not a nation on the globe that has a printing press and a people that can read from which you can extort one token of approval. I would agree to submit the question now at issue between the North and the South to the arbitrament of any people on the face of the earth not absolutely savage, and to abide its decision. Nay, the wild tribes of the Caucasus and of Upper India, who have defended themselves so nobly against aggression, would spurn your claim and deride its pretexts. And yet you say you are insulted, dishonored, disgraced in the eyes of mankind if you are not permitted to bring down upon our heads, also, the curses they are pouring upon yours. So far is this from truth that if you would promptly and cheerfully consecrate the new territories to freedom, every nation in the world would send their plaudits of your conduct to the skies.

But gentlemen of the South not only argue the question of right and of honor; they go further, and they tell us what they will proceed to do if we do not yield to their demands. A large majority of the Southern legislatures have solemnly "resolved" that if Congress prohibits slavery in the new territories, they will resist the law "at any and at every hazard." And yet they say they do not mean to threaten us. They desire to abstain from all language of menace, for threats and menaces are beneath the character of gentlemen. Sir, what is the meaning of the terms "threats" and "menaces"? Mr. Troup, formerly governor of Georgia, speaking of us who are upon this floor, and of others who resist the extension of slavery, calls each of us a "fanatic." He says that it is only the dread of death that will stay our hands or stop our machinations; and then adds, "That dread you must present to him in a visible, palpable form." "If," he says in another place, "the Abolitionists resolve to force emancipation, or to force dishonor upon the Southern states by any act of Congress, then it is my decided opinion that, with the military preparation here indicated, conjoined to a good volunteer instead of a militia system, the state should march upon Washington and dissolve the government."

The gentleman from North Carolina [Mr. Clingman] forewarns us that if certain measures — and they are legal and constitutional measures which he indicates — are taken in order to carry on the business of legislation in this House, the House itself shall be the "Lexington" of a new revolution, and that "such a struggle would not leave a quorum to do business." I could occupy my hour in citing passages of a similar character from the Southern press and from Southern men. Now, if these are not threats — threats most gross, flagrant, and offensive — I know not the meaning of the word. Perhaps those who utter such sentiments are only practising an inversion of language equal to their inversion of ideas on this subject and would call them "enticements"; like the sailor who said he was enticed to join a mutiny, and being asked what arts had been used to entice him, said that the ringleader sprang at him with a handspike and swore if he did not join it he would knock out his brains.

And do those gentlemen who make these threats soberly consider how deeply they are pledging themselves and their constituents by them? Threats of dissolution, if executed, become rebellion and treason. The machinery of this government is now moving onward in its majestic course. Customhouses, post offices, land offices, Army, Navy are fulfilling their prescribed circle of duties. They will continue to fulfill them until arrested by violence. Should the hand of violence be laid upon them, then will come that exigency expressly provided for in the Constitution and in the President's inaugural oath, "to take care that the laws be faithfully executed." Mr. Chairman, such collision would be *war*. Such forcible opposition to the government would be *treason*. Its agents and abettors would be *traitors*. Wherever this rebellion rears its crest, martial law will be proclaimed; and those found with hostile arms in their hands must prepare for the felon's doom.

Sir, I cannot contemplate this spectacle without a thrill of horror. If the two sections of this country ever marshal themselves against each other and their squadrons rush to the conflict, it will be a war carried on by such powers of intellect, animated by such vehemence of passion, and sustained by such an abundance of resources as the world has never before witnessed. "Ten foreign wars," it has been well said, "are a luxury compared with one civil war." But I turn from this scene with a shudder. If, in the retributive Providence of God, the volcano of civil war should ever burst upon us, it will be amid thunderings above and earthquakes below and darkness around;

and when that darkness is lifted up, we shall see this once glorious Union — this oneness of government under which we have been prospered and blessed as Heaven never prospered and blessed any other people — rifted in twain from east to west, with a gulf between us wide and profound, save that this gulf will be filled and heaped high with the slaughtered bodies of our countrymen; and when we reawaken to consciousness, we shall behold the garments and the hands of the survivors red with fratricidal blood. . . .

In conclusion, I have only to add that such is my solemn and abiding conviction of the character of slavery that under a full sense of my responsibility to my country and my God, I deliberately say, better disunion — better a civil or a servile war — better anything that God in His Providence shall send, than an extension of the bounds of slavery.

3.

John C. Calhoun: Either Slavery or Disunion

As the great debate continued in the Senate over Clay's compromise resolutions, it was inevitable that the senior senator from South Carolina, the "grand old man of the South," should have his say. Calhoun worked for a month on his speech, but when the time came to deliver it he was too sick to stand — he died on March 31 — and it was read by a colleague, Senator James A. Mason of Virginia. For twenty years Calhoun had been the South's ablest spokesman and had fought to retain the delicate balance between slave and free states that was now threatened by the proposed admission of California. The speech enumerated the South's grievances and stated the demands that made the compromise resolutions unacceptable. It was read by Mason on March 4.

Source: *Globe*, 31 Cong., 1 Sess., pp. 451-455.

I HAVE, SENATORS, believed from the first that the agitation of the subject of slavery would, if not prevented by some timely and effective measure, end in disunion. Entertaining this opinion, I have, on all proper occasions, endeavored to call the attention of each of the two great parties which divide the country to adopt some measure to prevent so great a disaster, but without success. The agitation has been permitted to proceed, with almost no attempt to resist it, until it has reached a period when it can no longer be disguised or denied that the Union is in danger. You have thus had forced upon you the greatest and the gravest question that can ever come under your consideration: How can the Union be preserved?

To give a satisfactory answer to this mighty question, it is indispensable to have an accurate and thorough knowledge of the nature and the character of the cause by which the Union is endangered. Without such knowledge, it is impossible to pronounce, with any certainty, by what measure it can be saved. . . .

The first question, then . . . is: What is it that has endangered the Union? . . .

One of the causes is, undoubtedly, to be traced to the long continued agitation of the slave question on the part of the North and the many aggressions which they have made on the rights of the South during the time. . . .

There is another lying back of it, with which this is intimately connected, that may be regarded as the great and primary cause. That is to be found in the fact that the equilibrium between the two sections in the government, as it stood when the Constitution was ratified and the government put into action, has been destroyed. At that time there was nearly a perfect equilibrium between the two which afforded ample means to each to protect itself against the aggression of the other; but, as it now stands, one section has the exclusive power of controlling the government, which leaves the other without any adequate means of protecting itself against its encroachment and oppression. . . .

The result of the whole is to give the Northern section a predominance in every part of the government and thereby concentrate in it the two elements which constitute the federal government — a majority of states and a majority of their population, estimated in federal numbers. Whatever section concentrates the two in itself possesses the control of the entire government.

But we are just at the close of the sixth decade and the commencement of the seventh. The census is to be taken this year, which must add greatly to the decided preponderance of the North in the House of Representatives and in the electoral college. The prospect is also that a great increase will be added to its present preponderance in the Senate during the period of the decade by the addition of new states. Two territories, Oregon and Minnesota, are already in progress, and strenuous efforts are being made to bring in three additional states from the territory recently conquered from Mexico; which, if successful, will add three other states in a short time to the Northern section, making five states and increasing the present number of its states from fifteen to twenty, and of its senators from thirty to forty. On the contrary, there

is not a single territory in progress in the Southern section and no certainty that any additional state will be added to it during the decade.

The prospect, then, is that the two sections in the Senate, should the efforts now made to exclude the South from the newly acquired territories succeed, will stand before the end of the decade twenty Northern states to twelve Southern (considering Delaware as neutral), and forty Northern senators to twenty-eight Southern. This great increase of senators, added to the great increase of members of the House of Representatives and electoral college on the part of the North, which must take place over the next decade, will effectually and irretrievably destroy the equilibrium which existed when the government commenced.

Had this destruction been the operation of time, without the interference of government, the South would have had no reason to complain; but such was not the fact. It was caused by the legislation of this government, which was appointed as the common agent of all and charged with the protection of the interests and security of all.

The legislation by which it has been effected may be classed under three heads. The first is that series of acts by which the South has been excluded from the common territory belonging to all of the states as the members of the federal Union, and which had the effect of extending vastly the portion allotted to the Northern section, and restricting within narrow limits the portion left the South. And the next consists in adopting a system of revenue and disbursements by which an undue proportion of the burden of taxation has been imposed upon the South and an undue proportion of its proceeds appropriated to the North. And the last is a system of political measures by which the original character of the government has been radically changed.

I propose to bestow upon each of these . . . a few remarks with the view of showing that it is owing to the action of this government that the equilibrium between the two sections has been destroyed and the whole powers of the system centered in a sectional majority.

The first of the series of acts by which the South was deprived of its due share of the territories originated with the Confederacy which preceded the existence of this government. It is to be found in the provision of the Ordinance of 1787. Its effect was to exclude the South entirely from that vast and fertile region which lies between the Ohio and the Mississippi rivers now embracing five states and one territory. The next of the series is the Missouri Compromise, which excluded the South from that large portion of Louisiana which lies north of 36°30´, excepting what is included in the state of Missouri.

The last of the series excluded the South from the whole of the Oregon Territory. All these, in the slang of the day, were what are called slave territories and not free soil; that is, territories belonging to slaveholding powers and open to the emigration of masters with their slaves. By these several acts, the South was excluded from 1,238,025 square miles, an extent of country considerably exceeding the entire valley of the Mississippi.

To the South was left the portion of the territory of Louisiana lying south of 36°30´, and the portion north of it included in the state of Missouri; the portion lying south of 36°30´ including the states of Louisiana and Arkansas, and the territory lying west of the latter and south of 36°30´, called the Indian Country. These, with the territory of Florida, now the state, make, in the whole, 283,503 square miles. To this must be added the territory acquired with Texas. If the whole should be added to the Southern section, it would make an increase of 325,520, which would make the whole left to the South, 609,023. But a large part of Texas is still in contest between the two sections, which leaves it uncertain what will

be the real extent of the portion of her territory that may be left to the South.

I have not included the territory recently acquired by the treaty with Mexico. The North is making the most strenuous efforts to appropriate the whole to herself by excluding the South from every foot of it. If she should succeed, it will add to that from which the South has already been excluded 526,078 square miles, and would increase the whole which the North has appropriated to herself to 1,764,023, not including the portion that she may succeed in excluding us from in Texas.

To sum up the whole, the United States, since they declared their independence, have acquired 2,373,046 square miles of territory, from which the North will have excluded the South if she should succeed in monopolizing the newly acquired territories, from about three-fourths of the whole, leaving to the South but about one-fourth.

Such is the first and great cause that has destroyed the equilibrium between the two sections in the government.

The next is the system of revenue and disbursements which has been adopted by the government. It is well known that the government has derived its revenue mainly from duties on imports. I shall not undertake to show that such duties must necessarily fall mainly on the exporting states, and that the South, as the great exporting portion of the Union, has in reality paid vastly more than her due proportion of the revenue because . . . the subject has on so many occasions been fully discussed. Nor shall I, for the same reason, undertake to show that a far greater portion of the revenue has been disbursed at the North than its due share, and that the joint effect of these causes has been to transfer a vast amount from South to North, which, under an equal system of revenue and disbursement, would not have been lost to her.

If to this be added that many of the duties were imposed, not for revenue but for protection; that is, intended to put money, not in the Treasury but directly into the pocket of the manufacturers, some conception may be formed of the immense amount which, in the long course of sixty years, has been transferred from South to North. There are no data by which it can be estimated with any certainty, but it is safe to say that it amounts to hundreds of millions of dollars. Under the most moderate estimate, it would be sufficient to add greatly to the wealth of the North, and thus greatly increase her population by attracting emigration from all quarters to that section. . . .

That the government claims, and practically maintains, the right to decide in the last resort as to the extent of its powers will scarcely be denied by anyone conversant with the political history of the country. That it also claims the right to resort to force to maintain whatever power she claims, against all opposition, is equally certain. Indeed, it is apparent, from what we daily hear, that this has become the prevailing and fixed opinion of a great majority of the community. Now, I ask, what limitation can possibly be placed upon the powers of a government claiming and exercising such rights? And, if none can be, how can the separate governments of the states maintain and protect the powers reserved to them by the Constitution, or the people of the several states maintain those which are reserved to them, and, among others the sovereign powers by which they ordained and established, not only their separate state constitutions and governments but also the Constitution and government of the United States?

But, if they have no constitutional means of maintaining them against the right claimed by this government, it necessarily follows that they hold them at its pleasure and discretion, and that all the powers of the system are in reality concentrated in it. It also follows that the character of the gov-

ernment has been changed, in consequence, from a federal republic, as it originally came from the hands of its framers, and that it has been changed into a great national, consolidated democracy. It has, indeed, at present, all the characteristics of the latter and not one of the former, although it still retains its outward form.

The result of the whole of these causes combined is that the North has acquired a decided ascendancy over every department of this government, and through it a control over all the powers of the system. A single section, governed by the will of the numerical majority, has now in fact the control of the government and the entire powers of the system. What was once a constitutional federal republic is now converted, in reality, into one as absolute as that of the Autocrat of Russia, and as despotic in its tendency as any absolute government that ever existed.

As, then, the North has the absolute control over the government, it is manifest that on all questions between it and the South, where there is a diversity of interests, the interests of the latter will be sacrificed to the former, however oppressive the effects may be, as the South possesses no means by which it can resist through the action of the government. But if there was no question of vital importance to the South, in reference to which there was a diversity of views between the two sections, this state of things might be endured without the hazard of destruction to the South. There is a question of vital importance to the Southern section, in reference to which the views and feelings of the two sections are as opposite and hostile as they can possibly be.

I refer to the relation between the two races in the Southern section, which constitutes a vital portion of her social organization. Every portion of the North entertains views and feelings more or less hostile to it. Those most opposed and hostile regard it as a sin, and consider themselves under the most sacred obligation to use every effort to destroy it. Indeed, to the extent that they conceive they have power, they regard themselves as implicated in the sin and responsible for suppressing it by the use of all and every means. Those less opposed and hostile regard it as a crime — an offense against humanity, as they call it — and, although not so fanatical, feel themselves bound to use all efforts to effect the same object; while those who are least opposed and hostile regard it as a blot and a stain on the character of what they call the nation, and feel themselves accordingly bound to give it no countenance or support. On the contrary, the Southern section regards the relation as one which cannot be destroyed without subjecting the two races to the greatest calamity and the section to poverty, desolation, and wretchedness; and accordingly they feel bound by every consideration of interest and safety to defend it.

This hostile feeling on the part of the North toward the social organization of the South long lay dormant, but it only required some cause to act on those who felt most intensely that they were responsible for its continuance to call it into action. The increasing power of this government and of the control of the Northern section over all its departments furnished the cause. It was this which made an impression on the minds of many that there was little or no restraint to prevent the government from doing whatever it might choose to do. This was sufficient of itself to put the most fanatical portion of the North in action for the purpose of destroying the existing relation between the two races in the South.

The first organized movement toward it commenced in 1835. Then, for the first time, societies were organized, presses established, lecturers sent forth to excite the people of the North, and incendiary publications scattered over the whole South through the mail. The South was thoroughly aroused. Meetings were held everywhere and resolutions adopted calling upon the North to apply a remedy to arrest the threatened evil, and pledging themselves to adopt measures for their own protection if it was not arrested. At the meeting of Congress, petitions poured in from the North calling upon Congress to abolish slavery in the District of Columbia and to prohibit what they called the internal slave trade between the states, announcing at the same time that their ultimate object was to abolish slavery, not only in the District but in the states and throughout the whole Union.

At this period, the number engaged in the agitation was small and possessed little or no personal influence. Neither party in Congress had, at that time, any sympathy with them or their cause. The members of each party presented their petitions with great reluctance. Nevertheless, as small and as contemptible as the party then was, both of the great parties of the North dreaded them. They felt that, though small, they were organized in reference to a subject which had a great and commanding influence over the Northern mind. Each party, on that account, feared to oppose their petitions lest the opposite party should take advantage of the one who might do so by favoring their petitions. The effect was that both united in insisting that the petitions should be received and that Congress should take jurisdiction over the subject for which they prayed. To justify their course they took the extraordinary ground that Congress was bound to receive petitions on every subject, however objectionable it might be, and whether they had or had not jurisdiction over the subject.

These views prevailed in the House of Representatives, and partially in the Senate; and thus the party succeeded, in their first movements, in gaining what they proposed — a position in Congress from which agitation could be extended over the whole Union. This was the commencement of the agitation, which has ever since continued, and which, as is now acknowledged, has endangered the Union itself.

As for myself, I believed, at that early period, if the party who got up the petitions should succeed in getting Congress to take jurisdiction, that agitation would follow and that it would, in the end, if not arrested, destroy the Union. I then so expressed myself in debate and called upon both parties to take grounds against assuming jurisdiction; but in vain. Had my voice been heeded and had Congress refused to take jurisdiction, by the united votes of all parties the agitation which followed would have been prevented, and the fanatical zeal that gives impulse to the agitation, and which has brought us to our present perilous condition, would have become extinguished from the want of something to feed the flame. *That* was the time for the North to have shown her devotion to the Union; but, unfortunately, both of the great parties of that section were so intent on obtaining or retaining party ascendancy that all other considerations were overlooked or forgotten.

What has since followed are but the natural consequences. With the success of their first movement, this small, fanatical party began to acquire strength; and, with that, to become an object of courtship to both the great parties. The necessary consequence was a further increase of power and a gradual tainting of the opinions of both of the other parties with their doctrines, until the infection has extended over both, and the great mass of the population of the North who, whatever may be their opinion of the original Abolition Party which still preserves its distinctive organization, hardly ever fail, when it comes to acting, to cooperate in carrying out their measures. . . .

Unless something decisive is done, I again ask what is to stop this agitation before the great and final object at which it aims — the abolition of slavery in the South — is consummated? Is it, then, not certain that if something decisive is not now done to arrest it, the South will be forced to choose between abolition and secession? Indeed, as events are now moving, it will not require

the South to secede to dissolve the Union. Agitation will of itself effect it. . . .

It is a great mistake to suppose that disunion can be effected by a single blow. The cords which bind these states together in one common Union are far too numerous and powerful for that. Disunion must be the work of time. It is only through a long process, and successively, that the cords can be snapped, until the whole fabric falls asunder. Already the agitation of the slavery question has snapped some of the most important and has greatly weakened all the others. . . .

If the agitation goes on, the same force, acting with increased intensity . . . will snap every cord, when nothing will be left to hold the states together except force. But surely that can, with no propriety of language, be called a union, when the only means by which the weaker is held connected with the stronger portion is *force*. It may, indeed, keep them connected; but the connection will partake much more of the character of subjugation on the part of the weaker to the stronger than the union of free, independent, and sovereign states in one confederation, as they stood in the early stages of the government, and which only is worthy of the sacred name of Union.

Having now, senators, explained what it is that endangers the Union, and traced it to its cause, and explained its nature and character, the question again recurs: How can the Union be saved? To this I answer there is but one way by which it can be; and that is by adopting such measures as will satisfy the states belonging to the Southern section that they can remain in the Union consistently with their honor and their safety. . . .

The plan of the administration cannot save the Union, because it can have no effect whatever toward satisfying the states composing the Southern section of the Union that they can, consistently with safety and honor, remain in the Union. It is, in fact, but a modification of the Wilmot Proviso. It proposes to effect the same object: to exclude the South from all territory acquired by the Mexican treaty. It is well known that the South is united against the Wilmot Proviso and has committed itself, by solemn resolutions, to resist should it be adopted. Its opposition *is not to the name* but that which it *proposes to effect;* that the Southern states hold to be unconstitutional, unjust, inconsistent with their equality as members of the common Union and calculated to destroy irretrievably the equilibrium between the two sections.

These objections equally apply to what, for brevity, I will call the Executive Proviso. There is no difference between it and the Wilmot, except in the mode of effecting the object; and, in that respect, I must say that the latter is much the least objectionable. It goes to its object openly, boldly, and distinctly. It claims for Congress unlimited power over the territories, and proposes to assert it over the territories acquired from Mexico, by a positive prohibition of slavery. Not so the Executive Proviso. It takes an indirect course, and in order to elude the Wilmot Proviso, and thereby avoid encountering the united and determined resistance of the South, it denies, by implication, the authority of Congress to legislate for the territories, and claims the right as belonging exclusively to the inhabitants of the territories.

But to effect the object of excluding the South, it takes care, in the meantime, to let in emigrants freely from the Northern states and all other quarters except from the South, which it takes special care to exclude by holding up to them the danger of having their slaves liberated under the Mexican laws. The necessary consequence is to exclude the South from the territory just as effectually as would the Wilmot Proviso. The only difference in this respect is that what one proposes to effect directly and openly, the other proposes to effect indirectly and covertly.

But the Executive Proviso is more objectionable than the Wilmot in another and more important particular. The latter, to effect its object, inflicts a dangerous wound upon the Constitution by depriving the Southern states, as joint partners and owners of the territories, of their rights in them; but it inflicts no greater wound than is absolutely necessary to effect its object. The former, on the contrary, while it inflicts the same wound, inflicts others equally great and, if possible, greater. . . .

In claiming the right for the inhabitant, instead of Congress, to legislate over the territories, in the Executive Proviso it assumes that the sovereignty over the territories is vested in the former; or to express it in the language used in a resolution offered by one of the senators from Texas (General Houston, now absent), they have "the same inherent right of self-government as the people in the states." The assumption is utterly unfounded, unconstitutional, without example, and contrary to the entire practice of the government from its commencement to the present time. . . .

The recent movement of individuals in California to form a constitution and a state government, and to appoint senators and representatives, is the first fruit of this monstrous assumption. If the individuals who made this movement had gone into California as adventurers, and if, as such, they had conquered the territory and established their independence, the sovereignty of the country would have been vested in them as a separate and independent community. In that case they would have had the right to form a constitution and to establish a government for themselves; and if, afterward, they thought proper to apply to Congress for admission into the Union as a sovereign and independent state, all this would have been regular and according to established principles. But such is not the case. It was the United States who conquered California and finally acquired it by treaty. The sovereignty, of course, is vested in them and not in the individuals who have attempted to form a constitution and a state without their consent. All this is clear beyond controversy, unless it can be shown that they have since lost or been divested of their sovereignty.

Nor is it less clear that the power of legislating over the acquired territory is vested in Congress and not, as is assumed, in the inhabitants of the territories. None can deny that the government of the United States has the power to acquire territories, either by war or by treaty; but if the power to acquire exists, it belongs to Congress to carry it into execution. On this point there can be no doubt, for the Constitution expressly provides that Congress shall have power "to make all laws which shall be necessary and proper to carry into execution the foregoing powers" (those vested in Congress) "and all other powers vested by this Constitution in the *government* of the United States or in *any department* or *officer* thereof."

It matters not, then, where the power is vested; for, if vested at all in the government of the United States, or any of its departments or officers, the power of carrying it into execution is clearly vested in Congress. But this important provision, while it gives to Congress the power of legislating over territories, imposes important restrictions on its exercise by restricting Congress to passing laws necessary and proper for carrying the power into execution. The prohibition extends not only to all laws not suitable or appropriate to the object of the power but also to all that are unjust, unequal, or unfair; for all such laws would be unnecessary and improper and therefore unconstitutional.

Having now established beyond controversy that the sovereignty over the territories is vested in the United States — that is, in the several states composing the Union — and that the power of legislating over them is expressly vested in Congress, it follows that the individuals in California who have undertaken to form a constitution

and a state, and to exercise the power of legislating without the consent of Congress, have usurped the sovereignty of the state and the authority of Congress, and have acted in open defiance of them both. In other words, what they have done is revolutionary and rebellious in its character, anarchical in its tendency, and calculated to lead to the most dangerous consequences. Had they acted from premeditation and design, it would have been in fact actual rebellion; but such is not the case. The blame lies much less upon them than upon those who have induced them to take a course so unconstitutional and dangerous. They have been led into it by language held here and the course pursued by the executive branch of the government. . . .

Having now shown what cannot save the Union, I return to the question with which I commenced: How can the Union be saved? There is but one way by which it can with any certainty, and that is by a full and final settlement on the principle of justice of all the questions at issue between the two sections. The South asks for justice, simple justice, and less she ought not to take. She has no compromise to offer but the Constitution, and no concession or surrender to make. She has already surrendered so much that she has little left to surrender. Such a settlement would go to the root of the evil and remove all cause of discontent by satisfying the South that she could remain honorably and safely in the Union; and thereby restore the harmony and fraternal feelings between the sections which existed anterior to the Missouri agitation. Nothing else can, with any certainty, finally and forever settle the questions at issue, terminate agitation, and save the Union.

But can this be done? Yes, easily; not by the weaker party, for it can of itself do nothing — not even protect itself — but by the stronger. The North has only to will it to accomplish it; to do justice by conceding to the South an equal right in the acquired territory, and to do her duty by causing the stipulations relative to fugitive slaves to be faithfully fulfilled; to cease the agitation of the slave question; and to provide for the insertion of a provision in the Constitution, by an amendment, which will restore to the South in substance the power she possessed of protecting herself before the equilibrium between the sections was destroyed by the action of this government. There will be no difficulty in devising such a provision — one that will protect the South and which, at the same time, will improve and strengthen the government instead of impairing and weakening it.

But will the North agree to do this? It is for her to answer this question. But I will say she cannot refuse if she has half the love of the Union which she professes to have, or without justly exposing herself to the charge that her love of power and aggrandizement is far greater than her love of the Union. At all events, the responsibility of saving the Union rests on the North and not the South. The South cannot save it by any act of hers, and the North may save it without any sacrifice whatever, unless to do justice and to perform her duties under the Constitution should be regarded by her as a sacrifice.

4.

Daniel Webster: A Plea for Harmony and Peace

Daniel Webster, the senior senator from Massachusetts, was as eminent among Northerners as was Senator John C. Calhoun of South Carolina among Southerners. Prompted by the latter's speech of March 4, 1850, against Henry Clay's compromise resolutions, and deeply troubled by the now open threats of disunion and secession, Webster replied to Calhoun three days later. It was one of the last and probably the greatest of his orations. Though Webster had stood with the Northern Whigs against the further extension of slavery to the territories, he now lent his support to the compromise proposals, strong in his belief that the Union must be preserved at all costs. Webster stressed that peaceable secession was unthinkable and, to avoid war, urged his Northern colleagues to accept the compromise. He rallied considerable support for the resolutions, but many felt he had betrayed them and all who opposed slavery. Webster never regained the favor of the Whig Party.

Source: *Globe*, App., 31 Cong., 1 Sess., pp. 269-276.

Mr. President, I wish to speak today, not as a Massachusetts man, nor as a Northern man, but as an American and a member of the Senate of the United States. . . . I have a part to act, not for my own security or safety, for I am looking out for no fragment upon which to float away from the wreck, if wreck there must be, but for the good of the whole and the preservation of the whole; and there is that which will keep me to my duty during this struggle, whether the sun and the stars shall appear or shall not appear, for many days. I speak today for the preservation of the Union. "Hear me for my cause." I speak today out of a solicitous and anxious heart for the restoration to the country of that quiet and that harmony which make the blessings of this Union so rich and so dear to us all. . . .

Mr. President, in the excited times in which we live, there is found to exist a state of crimination and recrimination between the North and the South. There are lists of grievances produced by each; and those grievances, real or supposed, alienate the minds of one portion of the country from the other, exasperate the feelings, subdue the sense of fraternal connection and patriotic love and mutual regard. I shall bestow a little attention, sir, upon these various grievances produced on the one side and on the other.

I begin with the complaints of the South. I will not answer, further than I have, the general statements of the honorable senator from South Carolina that the North has grown upon the South in consequence of the manner of administering this government, in the collecting of its revenues, and so forth. These are disputed topics, and I have no inclination to enter into them. But I will state these complaints, especially one complaint of the South, which has in my opinion just foundation; and that is that there has been found at the North, among individuals and among the legislatures of the North, a disinclination to perform, fully, their constitutional duties in regard to the return of persons bound to service who have escaped into the free states. In that respect, it is my judgment that the South is right and the North is wrong.

Every member of every Northern legislature is bound by oath, like every other officer in the country, to support the Constitution of the United States; and this article of the Constitution which says to these states they shall deliver up fugitives from service is as binding in honor and conscience as any other article. No man fulfills his duty in any legislature who sets himself to find excuses, evasions, escapes from this constitutional obligation. I have always thought that the Constitution addressed itself to the legislatures of the states themselves, or to the states themselves. It says that those persons escaping to other states shall be delivered up, and I confess I have always been of the opinion that it was an injunction upon the states themselves. When it is said that a person escaping into another state, and coming therefore within the jurisdiction of that state, shall be delivered up, it seems to me the import of the passage is that the state itself, in obedience to the Constitution, shall cause him to be delivered up. That is my judgment. I have always entertained that opinion, and I entertain it now.

But when the subject, some years ago, was before the Supreme Court of the United States, the majority of the judges held that the power to cause fugitives from service to be delivered up was a power to be exercised under the authority of this government. I do not know, on the whole, that it may not have been a fortunate decision. My habit is to respect the result of judicial deliberations and the solemnity of judicial decisions. But, as it now stands, the business of seeing that these fugitives are delivered up resides in the power of Congress and the national judicature, and my friend at the head of the Judiciary Committee has a bill on the subject, now before the Senate, with some amendments to it, which I propose to support, with all its provisions, to the fullest extent. And I desire to call the attention of all sober-minded men, of all conscientious men in the North, of all men who are not carried away by any fanatical idea, or by any false idea whatever, to their constitutional obligations.

I put it to all the sober and sound minds at the North as a question of morals and a question of conscience: What right have they, in all their legislative capacity, or any other, to endeavor to get round this Constitution, to embarrass the free exercise of the rights secured by the Constitution, to the persons whose slaves escape from them? None at all — none at all. Neither in the forum of conscience nor before the face of the Constitution are they justified in any opinion. Of course, it is a matter for their consideration. They probably, in the turmoil of the times, have not stopped to consider of this; they have followed what seemed to be the current of thought and of motives as the occasion arose, and neglected to investigate fully the real question, and to consider their constitutional obligations, as I am sure, if they did consider, they would fulfill them with alacrity.

Therefore, I repeat, sir, that here is a ground of complaint against the North, well founded, which ought to be removed; which it is now in the power of the different departments of this government to remove; which calls for the enactment of proper laws authorizing the judicature of this government in the several states to do all that is necessary for the recapture of fugitive slaves and for the restoration of them to those who claim them. Wherever I go and whenever I speak . . . I say that the South has been injured in this respect and has a right to complain; and the North has been too careless of what I think the Constitution peremptorily and emphatically enjoins upon it as a duty. . . .

Mr. President, I should much prefer to have heard, from every member on this floor, declarations of opinion that this Union should never be dissolved than the declaration of opinion that in any case, under the pressure of any circumstances, such a dissolution was possible. I hear with pain, and anguish, and distress, the word "secession," especially when it falls from the lips of those who are eminently patriotic, and known to the country, and known all over the world for their political services.

Secession! Peaceable secession! Sir, your eyes and mine are never destined to see that miracle. The dismemberment of this vast country without convulsion! The breaking up of the fountains of the great deep without ruffling the surface! Who is so foolish — I beg everybody's pardon — as to expect to see any such thing? Sir, he who sees these states, now revolving in harmony around a common center, and expects to see them quit their places and fly off without convulsion may look the next hour to see the heavenly bodies rush from their spheres and jostle against each other in the realms of space without producing the crush of the universe. There can be no such thing as a peaceable secession. Peaceable secession is an utter impossibility.

Is the great Constitution under which we live here — covering this whole country — is it to be thawed and melted away by secession as the snows on the mountain melt under the influence of a vernal sun — disappear almost unobserved and die off? No, sir! No, sir! I will not state what might produce the disruption of the states; but, sir, I see it as plainly as I see the sun in heaven — I see that disruption must produce such a war as I will not describe, in its twofold characters.

Peaceable secession! Peaceable secession! The concurrent agreement of all the members of this great republic to separate! A voluntary separation, with alimony on one side and on the other. Why, what would be the result? Where is the line to be drawn? What states are to secede? What is to remain American? What am I to be? An American no longer? Where is the flag of the republic to remain? Where is the eagle still to tower? Or is he to cower, and shrink, and fall to the ground? Why, sir, our ancestors — our fathers, and our grandfathers, those of them that are yet living among us with prolonged lives — would rebuke and reproach us; and our children and our grandchildren would cry out, Shame upon us! if we of this generation should dishonor these ensigns of the power of the government and the harmony of the Union, which is every day felt among us with so much joy and gratitude. What is to become of the Army? What is to become of the Navy? What is to become of the public lands? How is each of the thirty states to defend itself?

I know, although the idea has not been stated distinctly, there is to be a Southern confederacy. I do not mean, when I allude to this statement, that anyone seriously contemplates such a state of things. I do not mean to say that it is true, but I have heard it suggested elsewhere that that idea has originated in a design to separate. I am sorry, sir, that it has ever been thought of, talked of, or dreamed of in the wildest flights of human imagination. But the idea must be of a separation, including the slave states upon one side and the free states on the other. Sir, there is not — I may express myself too strongly perhaps — but some things, some moral things, are almost as impossible as other natural or physical things; and I hold the idea of a separation of these states — those that are free to form one government, and those that are slaveholding to form another — as a moral impossibility.

We could not separate the states by any such line if we were to draw it. We could not sit down here today and draw a line of separation that would satisfy any five men in the country. There are natural causes that would keep and tie us together, and there are social and domestic relations which we could not break, if we would, and which we should not, if we could. Sir, nobody can look over the face of this country at the present moment — nobody can see where its population is the most dense and growing — without being ready to admit and compelled to admit that, ere long, America will be in the valley of the Mississippi. . . .

And now, Mr. President, instead of speaking of the possibility or utility of secession, instead of dwelling in these caverns of darkness, instead of groping with those ideas so full of all that is horrid and horrible, let us come out into the light of day; let us enjoy the fresh air of liberty and union; let us cherish those hopes which belong to us; let us devote ourselves to those great objects that are fit for our consider-ation and our action; let us raise our conceptions to the magnitude and the importance of the duties that devolve upon us; let our comprehension be as broad as the country for which we act, our aspirations as high as its certain destiny; let us not be pygmies in a case that calls for men. Never did there devolve on any generation of men higher trusts than now devolve upon us for the preservation of this Constitution and the harmony and peace of all who are destined to live under it. Let us make our generation one of the strongest, and the brightest link, in that golden chain which is destined, I fully believe, to grapple the people of all the states to this Constitution, for ages to come. It is a great, popular, constitutional government, guarded by legislation, by law, by judicature, and defended by the whole affections of the people.

No monarchical throne presses these states together; no iron chain of despotic power encircles them; they live and stand upon a government popular in its form, representative in its character, founded upon principles of equality, and calculated, we hope, to last forever. In all its history, it has been beneficent; it has trodden down no man's liberty; it has crushed no state. Its daily respiration is liberty and patriotism; its yet youthful veins are full of enterprise, courage, and honorable love of glory and renown. It has received a vast addition of territory. Large before, the country has now, by recent events, become vastly larger. This republic now extends, with a vast breadth, across the whole continent. The two great seas of the world wash the one and the other shore. We realize on a mighty scale, the beautiful description of the ornamental edging of the buckler of Achilles:

Now the broad shield complete the artist
  crowned,
With his last hand, and poured the ocean
  round;
In living silver seemed the waves to roll,
And beat the buckler's verge, and bound
  the whole.

5.

John Greenleaf Whittier: "Ichabod"

"Ichabod" appeared in the National Era, *of which Whittier was an editor, on May 2, 1850. The title derived from I Samuel 4:21: "And she named the child Ichabod, saying, The glory is departed from Israel." Ichabod, of course, was Daniel Webster, whose speech in the Senate two months before had dismayed antislavery men in the North. Whittier described the poem's inception in a famous note. The birth of the poem, he said, was "the outcome of the surprise and grief and forecast of evil consequences which I felt on reading the seventh of March speech of Daniel Webster in support of the 'compromise' and the Fugitive Slave Bill. No partisan or personal enmity dictated it. On the contrary my admiration of the splendid personality and intellectual power of the great senator was never stronger than when I laid down his speech, and, in one of the saddest moments of my life, penned my protest . . . in tones of stern and sorrowful rebuke."*

Source: *Complete Poetical Works*, Cambridge Edition, Boston, 1894.

❧ ICHABOD

So fallen! so lost! the light withdrawn
  Which once he wore!
The glory from his gray hairs gone
  Forevermore!

Revile him not — the Tempter hath
  A snare for all;
And pitying tears, not scorn and wrath,
  Befit his fall!

O, dumb be passion's stormy rage,
  When he who might
Have lighted up and led his age,
  Falls back in night.

Scorn! would the angels laugh, to mark
  A bright soul driven,
Fiend-goaded, down the endless dark,
  From hope and heaven!

Let not the land once proud of him
  Insult him now,

Nor brand with deeper shame his dim,
  Dishonored brow.

But let its humbled sons, instead,
  From sea to lake,
A long lament, as for the dead,
  In sadness make.

Of all we loved and honored, naught
  Save power remains —
A fallen angel's pride of thought,
  Still strong in chains.

All else is gone; from those great eyes
  The soul has fled:
When faith is lost, when honor dies,
  The man is dead!

Then pay the reverence of old days
  To his dead fame;
Walk backward, with averted gaze,
  And hide the shame!

6.

William H. Seward: A Higher Law than the Constitution

*Four days after Webster's seventh of March speech Senator William H. Seward, a
staunch Abolitionist from New York, denounced the compromise proposed by
Henry Clay. Invoking a "higher law than the Constitution," Seward urged his fellow
senators to consider not only the constitutional but also the moral implications of
slavery when they ruled on the status of the new territories. As an orator, Seward
was not a Senate favorite and thus addressed a less than full chamber. However,
his words were enthusiastically and sympathetically received by many in the North.
Portions of Seward's speech, delivered on March 11, are reprinted here.*

Source: *Globe, App.,* 31 Cong., 1 Sess., pp. 260-269.

Today, California is a state, more populous than the least and richer than several of
the greatest of our thirty states. This same
California, thus rich and populous, is here
asking admission into the Union, and finds
us debating the dissolution of the Union itself. . . .

Shall California be received? For myself,
upon my individual judgment and conscience, I answer, yes. For myself, as an instructed representative of one of the states,
of that one even of the states which is
soonest and longest to be pressed in commercial and political rivalry by the new
commonwealth, I answer, yes; let California
come in. Every new state, whether she
come from the East or from the West, every new state, coming from whatever part
of the continent she may, is always welcome. But California, that comes from the
clime where the West dies away into the
rising East; California, which bounds at
once the empire and the continent; California, the youthful queen of the Pacific, in
her robes of freedom, gorgeously inlaid
with gold, is doubly welcome. . . .

But it is insisted that the admission of
California shall be attended by a compromise of questions which have arisen out of
slavery. I am opposed to any such compromise, in any and all the forms in which it
has been proposed, because, while admitting the purity and the patriotism of all
from whom it is my misfortune to differ, I
think all legislative compromises radically
wrong and essentially vicious. They involve
the surrender of the exercise of judgment
and conscience on distinct and separate
questions, at distinct and separate times,
with the indispensable advantages it affords
for ascertaining truth. They involve a relinquishment of the right to reconsider in future the decisions of the present on questions prematurely anticipated; and they are
a usurpation as to future questions of the
province of future legislators.

Sir, it seems to me as if slavery had laid
its paralyzing hand upon myself, and the
blood were coursing less freely than its
wont through my veins, when I endeavor
to suppose that such a compromise has
been effected; and my utterance forever is
arrested upon all the great questions, social,
moral, and political, arising out of a subject
so important and as yet so incomprehensible. What am I to receive in this compro-

mise? Freedom in California. It is well; it is a noble acquisition; it is worth a sacrifice. But what am I to give as an equivalent? A recognition of a claim to perpetuate slavery in the District of Columbia; forbearance toward more stringent laws concerning the arrest of persons suspected of being slaves found in the free states; forbearance from the proviso of freedom in the charters of new territories. None of the plans of compromise offered demands less than two, and most of them insist on all of these conditions. The equivalent then is some portion of liberty, some portion of human rights in one region for liberty in another region. But California brings gold and commerce as well as freedom. I am, then, to surrender some portion of human freedom in the District of Columbia, and in East California, and New Mexico for the mixed consideration of liberty, gold, and power on the Pacific coast. . . .

There is another aspect of the principle of compromise which deserves consideration. It assumes that slavery, if not the only institution in a slave state, is at least a ruling institution, and that this characteristic is recognized by the Constitution. But slavery is only one of many institutions there — freedom is equally an institution there. Slavery is only a temporary, accidental, partial, and incongruous one; freedom, on the contrary, is a perpetual, organic, universal one, in harmony with the Constitution of the United States. The slaveholder himself stands under the protection of the latter, in common with all the free citizens of the state; but it is, moreover, an indispensable institution. You may separate slavery from South Carolina, and the state will still remain; but if you subvert freedom there, the state will cease to exist.

But the principle of this compromise gives complete ascendancy in the slave state, and in the Constitution of the United States, to the subordinate, accidental, and incongruous institution over its paramount antagonist. To reduce this claim for slavery to an absurdity, it is only necessary to add that there are only two states in which slaves are a majority, and not one in which the slaveholders are not a very disproportionate minority.

But there is yet another aspect in which this principle must be examined. It regards the domain only as a possession, to be enjoyed either in common or by partition by the citizens of the old states. It is true, indeed, that the national domain is ours; it is true, it was acquired by the valor and with the wealth of the whole nation; but we hold, nevertheless, no arbitrary power over it. We hold no arbitrary authority over anything, whether acquired lawfully or seized by usurpation. The Constitution regulates our stewardship; the Constitution devotes the domain to union, to justice, to defense, to welfare, and to liberty.

But there is a higher law than the Constitution which regulates our authority over the domain and devotes it to the same noble purposes. The territory is a part — no inconsiderable part — of the common heritage of mankind, bestowed upon them by the Creator of the universe. We are His stewards and must so discharge our trust as to secure, in the highest attainable degree, their happiness. . . .

This is a state, and we are deliberating for it, just as our fathers deliberated in establishing the institutions we enjoy. Whatever superiority there is in our condition and hopes over those of any other "kingdom" or "estate" is due to the fortunate circumstance that our ancestors did not leave things to "take their chance," but that they "added amplitude and greatness" to our commonwealth "by introducing such ordinances, constitutions, and customs as were wise." We, in our turn, have succeeded to the same responsibilities; and we cannot approach the duty before us wisely or justly except we raise ourselves to the great consideration of how we can most certainly "sow greatness to our posterity and successors."

And now the simple, bold, and even awful question which presents itself to us is this: Shall we, who are founding institutions, social and political, for countless millions — shall we, who know by experience the wise and the just, and are free to choose them, and to reject the erroneous and unjust — shall we establish human bondage, or permit it, by our sufferance, to be established? Sir, our forefathers would not have hesitated an hour. They found slavery existing here, and they left it only because they could not remove it. There is not only no free state which would now establish it but there is no slave state which, if it had had the free alternative as we now have, would have founded slavery. Indeed, our revolutionary predecessors had precisely the same question before them in establishing an organic law, under which the states of Ohio, Michigan, Illinois, Wisconsin, and Iowa have since come into the Union; and they solemnly repudiated and excluded slavery from those states forever. I confess that the most alarming evidence of our degeneracy which has yet been given is found in the fact that we even debate such a question.

Sir, there is no Christian nation, thus free to choose as we are, which would establish slavery. I speak on due consideration, because Britain, France, and Mexico have abolished slavery, and all other European states are preparing to abolish it as speedily as they can. We cannot establish slavery, because there are certain elements of the security, welfare, and greatness of nations, which we all admit, or ought to admit, and recognize as essential; and these are the security of natural rights, the diffusion of knowledge, and the freedom of industry. Slavery is incompatible with all of these, and just in proportion to the extent that it

prevails and controls in any republican state, just to that extent it subverts the principle of democracy and converts the state into an aristocracy or a despotism. . . .

This brings me to the great and all-absorbing argument, that the Union is in danger of being dissolved, and that it can only be saved by compromise. I do not know what I would not do to save the Union; and therefore I shall bestow upon this subject a very deliberate consideration. . . .

In any condition of society, there can be no revolution without a cause, an adequate cause. What cause exists here? We are admitting a new state; but there is nothing new in that we have already admitted seventeen before. But it is said that the slave states are in danger of losing political power by the admission of the new state. Well, sir, is there anything new in that? The slave states have always been losing political power, and they always will be, while they have any to lose. At first, twelve of the thirteen states were slave states; now only fifteen out of the thirty are slave states. Moreover, the change is constitutionally made, and the government was constructed so as to permit changes of the balance of power in obedience to changes of the forces of the body politic. . . .

Those who would alarm us with the terrors of revolution have not well considered the structure of this government and the organization of its forces. It is a democracy of property and persons, with a fair approximation toward universal education and operating by means of universal suffrage. The constituent members of this democracy are the only persons who could subvert it; and they are not the citizens of a metropolis like Paris, or of a region subjected to the influences of a metropolis like France; but they are husbandmen, dispersed over this broad land, on the mountain and on the plain and on the prairie, from the ocean to the Rocky

Mountains, and from the Great Lakes to the Gulf. And this people are now, while we are discussing their imaginary danger, at peace and in their happy homes, and as unconcerned and uninformed of their peril as they are of events occurring in the moon. Nor have the alarmists made due allowance in their calculations for the influence of conservative reaction, strong in any government and irresistible in a rural republic, operating by universal suffrage. That principle of reaction is due to the force of the habits of acquiescence and loyalty among the people.

No man better understood this principle than Machiavelli, who has told us, in regard to factions, that "no safe reliance can be placed in the force of nature and the bravery of words, except it be corroborate by custom." Do the alarmists remember that this government has stood sixty years already without exacting one drop of blood? That this government has stood sixty years, and treason is an obsolete crime? That day, I trust, is far off when the fountains of popular contentment shall be broken up; but whenever it shall come, it will bring forth a higher illustration than has ever yet been given of the excellence of the democratic system; for then it will be seen how calmly, how firmly, how nobly a great people can act in preserving their Constitution — whom "love of country moveth, example teacheth, company comforteth, emulation quickeneth, and glory exalteth."

When the founders of the new Republic of the South come to draw over the face of this empire, along or between its parallels of latitude or longitude, their ominous lines of dismemberment, soon to be broadly and deeply shaded with fraternal blood, they may come to the discovery then, if not before, that the natural and even political connections of the region embraced forbid such a partition, that its possible divisions are not northern and southern at all, but eastern and western, Atlantic and Pacific; and that

nature and commerce have allied indissolubly, for weal and woe, the seceders and those from whom they are to be separated; that, while they would rush into a civil war to restore an imaginary equilibrium between the Northern states and the Southern states, a new equilibrium has taken its place, in which all those states are on the one side and the boundless West is on the other.

Sir, when the founders of the new Republic of the South come to draw these fearful lines, they will indicate what portions of the continent are to be broken off from their connection with the Atlantic, through the St. Lawrence, the Hudson, the Delaware, the Potomac, and the Mississippi; what portion of this people are to be denied the use of the lakes, the railroads, and the canals now constituting common and customary avenues of travel, trade, and social intercourse; what families and kindred are to be separated and converted into enemies; and what states are to be the scenes of perpetual border warfare, aggravated by interminable horrors of servile insurrection. When those portentous lines shall be drawn, they will disclose what portion of this people is to retain the Army and the Navy and the flag of so many victories; and, on the other hand, what portion of the people is to be subjected to new and ominous imposts, direct taxes, and forced loans, and conscriptions to maintain an opposing army, an opposing navy, and the new and hateful banner of sedition. Then the projectors of the new Republic of the South will meet the question — and they may well prepare now to answer it — what is all this for? What intolerable wrong, what unfraternal injustice have rendered these calamities unavoidable? What gain will this unnatural revolution bring to us? The answer will be: All this is done to secure the institution of African slavery.

And, then, if not before, the question will be discussed: What is this institution of slavery that it should cause these unparalleled sacrifices and these disastrous afflictions? And this will be the answer: When the Spaniards, few in number, discovered the Western Indies and adjacent continental America, they needed labor to draw forth from its virgin stores some speedy return to the cupidity of the court and the bankers of Madrid. They enslaved the indolent, inoffensive, and confiding natives, who perished by thousands, and even by millions, under that new and unnatural bondage. A humane ecclesiastic advised the substitution of Africans, reduced to captivity in their native wars; and a pious princess adopted the suggestion, with a dispensation from the head of the church, granted on the ground of the prescriptive right of the Christian to enslave the heathen to effect his conversion. The colonists of North America, innocent in their unconsciousness of wrong, encouraged the slave traffic, and thus the labor of subduing their territory devolved chiefly upon the African race.

A happy conjuncture brought on an awakening of the conscience of mankind to the injustice of slavery, simultaneously with the independence of the colonies. Massachusetts, Connecticut, Rhode Island, New Hampshire, Vermont, New York, New Jersey, and Pennsylvania welcomed and embraced the spirit of universal emancipation. Renouncing luxury, they secured influence and empire; but the states of the South, misled by a new and profitable culture, elected to maintain and perpetuate slavery; and thus, choosing luxury, they lost power and empire.

When this answer shall be given, it will appear that the question of dissolving the Union is a complex question; that it embraces the fearful issue whether the Union shall stand, and slavery, under the steady, peaceful action of moral, social, and political causes, be removed by gradual, voluntary effort, and with compensation, or whether the Union shall be dissolved and civil wars ensue, bringing on violent but complete and immediate emancipation. We are now arrived at that stage of our national progress when that crisis can be foreseen — when we must foresee it. It is directly before us. Its shadow is upon us. It darkens the legislative halls, the temples of worship, and the home and the hearth. Every question, political, civil, or ecclesiastical — however foreign to the subject of slavery — brings up slavery as an incident; and the incident supplants the principal question. We hear of nothing but slavery, and we can talk of nothing but slavery.

And, now, it seems to me that all our difficulties, embarrassments, and dangers arise, not out of unlawful perversions of the question of slavery, as some suppose, but from the want of moral courage to meet this question of emancipation as we ought. Consequently, we hear on one side demands — absurd, indeed, but yet unceasing — for an immediate and unconditional abolition of slavery; as if any power except the people of the slave states could abolish it, and as if they could be moved to abolish it by merely sounding the trumpet violently and proclaiming emancipation, while the institution is interwoven with all their social and political interests, constitutions, and customs.

On the other hand, our statesmen say that "slavery has always existed, and, for aught they know or can do, it always must exist. God permitted it, and He alone can indicate the way to remove it." As if the Supreme Creator, after giving us the instructions of His Providence and revelation for the illumination of our minds and consciences, did not leave us, in all human transactions, with due invocations of His Holy Spirit, to seek out His will and execute it for ourselves.

Here, then, is the point of my separation from both of these parties. I feel assured that slavery must give way, and will give way, to the salutary instructions of economy and to the ripening influences of humanity; that emancipation is inevitable and is near; that it may be hastened or hindered; and that whether it be peaceful or violent depends upon the question whether it be hastened or hindered; that all measures which fortify slavery or extend it tend to the consummation of violence — all that check its extension and abate its strength tend to its peaceful extirpation. But I will adopt none but lawful, constitutional, and peaceful means to secure even that end; and nonesuch can I or will I forego.

Nor do I know any important or responsible body that proposes to do more than this. No free state claims to extend its legislation into a slave state. None claims that Congress shall usurp power to abolish slavery in the slave states. None claims that any violent, unconstitutional, or unlawful measures shall be embraced. And, on the other hand, if we offer no scheme or plan for the adoption of the slave states, with the assent and cooperation of Congress, it is only because the slave states are unwilling, as yet, to receive such suggestions, or even to entertain the question of emancipation in any form.

But, sir, I will take this occasion to say that, while I cannot agree with the honorable senator from Massachusetts in proposing to devote $80 million to remove the free colored population from the slave states, and thus, as it appears to me, fortify slavery, there is no reasonable limit to which I am not willing to go in applying the national treasures to effect the peaceful, voluntary removal of slavery itself.

I have thus endeavored to show that there is not now, and there is not likely to occur, any adequate cause for revolution in regard to slavery. But you reply that, nevertheless, you must have guaranties; and the first one is for the surrender of fugitives from labor. That guaranty you cannot have . . . because you cannot roll back the tide of social progress. You must be content with what you have. If you wage war against us, you can, at most, only conquer us, and then all you can get will be a treaty, and that you have already.

But you insist on a guaranty against the abolition of slavery in the District of Columbia, or war. Well, when you shall have declared war against us, what shall hinder us from immediately decreeing that slavery shall cease within the national capital?

You say that you will not submit to the exclusion of slaves from the new territories. What will you gain by resistance? Liberty follows the sword, although her sway is one of peace and beneficence. Can you propagate slavery, then, by the sword?

You insist that you cannot submit to the freedom with which slavery is discussed in the free states. Will war — a war for slavery — arrest, or even moderate, that discussion? No, sir; that discussion will not cease; war would only inflame it to a greater height. It is a part of the eternal conflict between truth and error — between mind and physical force — the conflict of man against the obstacles which oppose his way to an ultimate and glorious destiny. It will go on until you shall terminate it in the only way in which any state or nation has ever terminated it — by yielding to it — yielding in your own time and in your own manner, indeed, but nevertheless yielding to the progress of emancipation. You will do this sooner or later, whatever may be your opinion now; because nations which were prudent, and humane, and wise, as you are, have done so already.

Sir, the slave states have no reason to fear that this inevitable change will go too far or too fast for their safety or welfare. It cannot well go too fast, or too far, if the only alternative is a war of races. . . .

The Union, then, *is*, not because merely men choose that it shall be but because some government must exist here, and no other government than this can. If it could be dashed to atoms by the whirlwind, the lightning, or the earthquake, today, it would rise again in all its just and magnificent proportions tomorrow. This nation is a globe still accumulating upon accumulation, not a dissolving sphere.

I have heard somewhat here — and almost for the first time in my life — of divided allegiance, of allegiance to the South and to the Union, of allegiance to states severally and to the Union. Sir, if sympathies with state emulation and pride of achievement could be allowed to raise up another sovereign to divide the allegiance of a citizen of the United States, I might recognize the claims of the state to which, by birth and gratitude, I belong — to the state of Hamilton and Jay, of Schuyler, of the Clintons, and of Fulton — the state which with less than 200 miles of natural navigation connected with the ocean has, by her own enterprise, secured to herself the commerce of the continent and is steadily advancing to the command of the commerce of the world.

But for all this, I know only one country and one sovereign — the United States of America and the American people. And such as my allegiance is, is the loyalty of every other citizen of the United States. As I speak, he will speak when his time arrives. He knows no other country and no other sovereign. He has life, liberty, property, and precious affections, and hopes for himself and for his posterity, treasured up in the ark of the Union. He knows as well and feels as strongly as I do that this government is his own government; that he is a part of it; that it was established for him and that it is maintained by him; that it is the only truly wise, just, free, and equal government that has ever existed; that no other government could be so wise, just, free, and equal; and that it is safer and more beneficent than any which time or change could bring into its place.

You may tell me, sir, that although all this may be true, yet the trial of faction has not yet been made. Sir, if the trial of faction has not been made, it has not been because faction has not always existed and has not always menaced a trial but because faction could find no fulcrum on which to place the lever to subvert the Union, as it can find no fulcrum now; and in this is my confidence. I would not rashly provoke the trial, but I will not suffer a fear which I have not to make me compromise one sentiment — one principle of truth or justice — to avert a danger that all experience teaches me is purely chimerical.

Let, then, those who distrust the Union make compromises to save it. I shall not impeach their wisdom, as I certainly cannot their patriotism; but indulging no such apprehensions myself, I shall vote for the admission of California directly, without conditions, without qualifications, and without compromise.

For the vindication of that vote, I look not to the verdict of the passing hour, disturbed as the public mind now is by conflicting interests and passions, but to that period, happily not far distant, when the vast regions over which we are now legislating shall have received their destined inhabitants.

While looking forward to that day, its countless generations seem to me to be rising up, and passing in dim and shadowy review before us; and a voice comes forth from their serried ranks, saying:

Waste your treasures and your armies, if you will; raze your fortifications to the ground; sink your navies into the sea; transmit to us even a dishonored name, if you must; but the soil you hold in trust for us, give it to us free. You found it free, and conquered it to extend a better and surer freedom over it. Whatever choice you have made for yourselves, let us have no partial freedom; let us all be free; let the reversion of your broad domain descend to us unencumbered and free from the calamities and the sorrows of human bondage.

7.

HENRY CLAY: Slavery and Expansion

After four months of heated debate a solution to the problems posed by the new territories seemed no closer than when Congress convened in December. Upon the motion of Mississippi's Senator Henry S. Foote, a select committee was chosen on April 18, 1850, to review Clay's compromise resolutions. Comprised of seven Whigs and six Democrats, representing six free and seven slave states, the Committee of Thirteen drafted a bill based substantially on the resolutions. This Omnibus Bill, so named because it attempted to solve all the important territorial issues in one legislative act, was presented to the Senate by the committee's chairman, Clay, on May 8, and was supported by him in two important speeches on May 13 and May 21. Portions of the committee report and of Clay's address of May 13 appear below.

Source: *Globe*, 31 Cong., 1 Sess., pp. 944-947.
　　　　 Globe, App., 31 Cong., 1 Sess., pp. 567-573.

I.

Proposals of the Committee of Thirteen

I HAVE RISEN TO PRESENT to the Senate a report from the Committee of Thirteen, which was appointed some weeks ago. The report is of some length, sir, and there have been some erasures and alterations in it and, therefore, if the Senate will allow me . . . the views and recommendations contained in this report may be recapitulated in a few words:

1. The admission of any new state or states formed out of Texas to be postponed until they shall hereafter present themselves to be received into the Union, when it will be the duty of Congress fairly and faithfully to execute the compact with Texas by admitting such new state or states.

2. The admission forthwith of California into the Union with the boundaries which she has proposed.

3. The establishment of territorial governments without the Wilmot Proviso for New Mexico and Utah, embracing all the territory recently acquired by the United States from Mexico not contained in the boundaries of California.

4. The combination of these two last-mentioned measures in the same bill.

5. The establishment of the western and northern boundary of Texas, and the exclusion from her jurisdiction of all New Mexico, with the grant to Texas of a pecuniary equivalent; and the section for that purpose to be incorporated in the bill admitting California and establishing territorial governments for Utah and New Mexico.

6. More effectual enactments of law to secure the prompt delivery of persons bound to service or labor in one state, under the laws thereof, who escape into another state.

7. Abstaining from abolishing slavery; but, under a heavy penalty, prohibiting the slave trade in the District of Columbia.

If such of these several measures as require legislation should be carried out by suitable acts of Congress, all controversies to which our late territorial acquisitions have given rise, and all existing questions connected with the institution of slavery, whether resulting from those acquisitions or from its existence in the states and the District of Columbia, will be amicably settled and adjusted, in a manner, it is confidently believed, to give general satisfaction to an overwhelming majority of the people of the United States. Congress will have fulfilled its whole duty in regard to the vast country which, having been ceded by Mexico to the United States, has fallen under their dominion.

It will have extended to it protection, provided for its several parts the inestimable blessing of free and regular government adapted to their various wants, and placed the whole under the banner and flag of the United States. Meeting courageously its clear and entire duty, Congress will escape the unmerited reproach of having, from considerations of doubtful policy, abandoned to an undeserved fate territories of boundless extent, with a sparse, incongruous, and alien, if not unfriendly, population, speaking different languages and accustomed to different laws, while that population is making irresistible appeals to the new sovereignty to which they have been transferred for protection, for government, for law, and for order.

The Committee have endeavored to present to the Senate a comprehensive plan of adjustment, which, removing all causes of existing excitement and agitation, leaves none open to divide the country and disturb the general harmony. The nation has been greatly convulsed, not by measures of general policy but by questions of a sectional character, and, therefore, more dangerous and more to be deprecated. It wants repose. It loves and cherishes the Union. And it is most cheering and gratifying to witness the outbursts of deep and abiding attachment to

it which have been exhibited in all parts of it, amid all the trials through which we have passed and are passing.

A people so patriotic as those of the United States will rejoice in an accommodation of all troubles and difficulties by which the safety of that Union might have been brought into the least danger. And, under the blessings of that Providence who, amid all vicissitudes, has never ceased to extend to them His protecting care, His smiles, and His blessings, they will continue to advance in population, power, and prosperity, and work out triumphantly the glorious problem of man's capacity for self-government.

II.

Defense of the Proposals

I HAVE RISEN FOR THE PURPOSE of making some statements and an additional exposition relative to the report of the Committee, of their proceedings, and of their action upon the important subjects before you. . . .

The first measure which they reported, Mr. President, was that of the true exposition of the compact between the United States and Texas upon the occasion of the admission of that state into the Union. Upon that subject, as has been already announced in the report, I am happy to say there was an undivided opinion. . . .

I will now, Mr. President, approach that subject which in the Committee and the two houses of Congress has given most trouble and created the most anxiety of all the measures upon which the Committee has reported: I mean the admission of California into the Union. Against this measure there are various objections. . . .

Now, with regard to the limits of California. Mr. President, upon that subject an effort was made in the Committee to extend a line through California at 36°30′ of north latitude, and one member who was not satisfied with that line proposed 35°30'. A majority of the Committee, I believe, were in favor of that amendment; but, on the question being taken for the line of 35°30', a majority was found to be against it. Sir, is it not a little remarkable that this opposition to the line — this attempt to cut California in two by the line of 36°30', or 35°30', or by any other line — is a line not coming from the north at all from where we might suppose it would be proposed? . . . .

But how is it with California? . . . She has come here to ask for admission; and I ask again, as I had occasion to ask three months ago, whether she does not present herself with much stronger claims to admission than those states which had all the advantages of free governments which have come here to be admitted into the Union? I think, then, Mr. President, that with respect to the population of California, with respect to the limits of California, and with respect to the circumstances under which she presents herself to Congress for admission as a state into the Union, all are favorable to grant her what she solicits; and we can find neither in the one nor in the other a sufficient motive to reject her and to throw her back into the state of lawless confusion and disorder from which she has emerged.

Sir, with the Committee, I unite in saying on this occasion that all the considerations which call upon Congress to admit California as a state, and to sanction what she has done, and to give her the benefit of self-government, apply with equal force to the territories of Utah and New Mexico.

Mr. President, allow me, at this stage of the few observations which I propose to address to the Senate, to contrast the plans which have been presented for the settlement of these questions. One has come to us from a very high authority, recommending, as I understand it, the admission of California, and doing nothing more, leaving the question of the boundary unsettled between New Mexico and Texas, and leaving the people who inhabit Utah and New Mexico unprovided for by government.

Mr. President, I will take occasion to say that I came to Washington with the most anxious desire, a desire which I still entertain, to cooperate in my legislative position in all cases in which I could conscientiously cooperate with the executive branch of the government. I need not add, however, sir, that I came here also with a settled purpose to follow the deliberate dictates of my own judgment, wherever that judgment might carry me. Sir, it is with great pleasure that I state that we do cooperate with the President of the United States to the extent which he recommends. He recommends the admission of California. The Committee proposes this. There the President's recommendation stops, and there we take up the subject and proceed to act upon the other parts of the territory acquired from Mexico. Now, which of these two courses commends itself best to the judgment of those who are to act in the case? In the first place, if we do not provide governments for the other portion of the country acquired from Mexico, we fail to fulfill an obligation, a sacred obligation, contained in the treaty with Mexico. . . .

Is it right to say to the people of Utah, comprehending the Mormons, and to the people of New Mexico, deprived as they are of the benefit of the government they once had, the supreme authority of which resides at Mexico — is it right to say that we will leave them to themselves? It is said that they will "take care of themselves," and that "when they get ripe for state government — and when will they get ripe for state government? — after the lapse of many years, let them come forward and we will admit them as states." Sir, is that discharging our duty?

I will go further with reference to the

message in relation to California, which I am sorry it is my duty to contrast with the plan of the Committee now under consideration, and say that I have no doubt that there were strong, or at least plausible, reasons for the adoption of the recommendation contained in the message of the President at the time it was sent to Congress, at the beginning of the session. I have no doubt that it was apprehended at that time that it was impossible to pass any measure providing governments for the territories without producing in Congress scenes of the most painful and unpleasant character. I have no doubt it was believed, as indeed was stated in the message, that the distraction would be greatly aggravated; that differences of opinion would be carried to extreme lengths if, as the President believed at the time the message was sent in, any attempt should be made to extend the authority of the government over these territories. But, sir, I am happy to be able to recognize what all have seen, that since the commencement of the session a most gratifying change has taken place. The North, the glorious North, has come to the rescue of this Union of ours. She has displayed a disposition to abate in her demands.

The South, the glorious South (not less glorious than her neighbor section of the Union) has also come to the rescue. The minds of men have moderated; passion has given place to reason everywhere. Everywhere, in all parts of the Union, there is a demand — a demand, I trust, the force and effect of which will be felt in both houses of Congress — for an amicable adjustment of those questions, for the relinquishment of those extreme opinions, whether entertained on the one side or on the other, and coming together once more as friends, as brethren, living in a common country and enjoying the benefits of freedom and happiness flowing from a common government.

Sir, I think, if the President had at this time to make a recommendation to Congress, with all the lights that have been shed upon the subject since the commencement of the present session of Congress nearly five months ago, he would not limit himself to a recommendation merely for the admission of California, leaving the territories to shift for themselves as they could or might. He tells us in one of these messages (I forget whether in the one which was sent in December or January) that he had reason to believe that one of these territories, at least New Mexico, might possibly form a state government for herself, and might come here with an application for admission during the progress of this session. But we have no evidence that such an event is about to happen; and if it did, could New Mexico be admitted as a state? At all events, there has been such a change of circumstances from the period when the message was sent in down to the present time that I cannot but believe that the gentleman who now presides at the head of our public affairs, if he had had the benefit of all these lights, would have made the recommendation much more comprehensive, and much more general and healing in its character than a simple recommendation for the admission of California, leaving all the other questions unsettled and open to exasperate the feelings of opposing parties.

Sir, I have spoken of the abandoned condition of Utah and New Mexico, left without any authority of this government, acting locally to protect the citizens who come there to settle, or to protect those who are in transit through the country, without any authority connected with the supreme government here or any means of communicating from time to time the state of things as they exist there. To abandon these countries, in the face of our obligations contained in the treaty of Hidalgo, and other high obligations by which we are bound — to abandon them thus would not, as it appears to me, be comfortable to that duty which we are called upon to perform. Leave these territorial questions unsettled and the door of agitation is left wide open; settle them and it is closed, I hope, forever.

Well, then, there is the boundary question with Texas. Why, sir, at this very moment we learn through the public papers that Texas has sent her civil commissioners to Santa Fe, or into New Mexico, for the purpose of bringing them under authority; and if you leave the Texas boundary question unsettled, and establish no government for Utah and New Mexico, I venture to say that, before we meet again next December, we shall hear of some civil commotion, perhaps the shedding of blood, in the contest between New Mexico and Texas with respect to the boundary; for, without meaning to express at this time, or at any time, any positive opinion on that question, we know that the people of Santa Fe are as much opposed to the government of Texas, and as much convinced that they do not belong to Texas, that they constitute no portion of the territory of Texas, as we know Texas to be earnest in asserting the contrary and affirming her right to the country from the mouth of the Rio Grande to its uppermost sources. Is it right, then, to leave these territories unprovided for? Is it right to leave this important question of boundary between New Mexico and Texas unsettled? Is it right that it should be left unsettled to produce possibly the fearful consequences to which I have adverted?

Sir, on these questions I believe, though I do not recollect the exact state of the vote in Committee, that there was no serious diversity of opinion. We all thought we should establish governments for them if we could; that, at any rate, we should make the attempt; and if we failed, after making the attempt, we should stand irreproachable for any voluntary abandonment or neglect of them on our part. . . .

I will pass on, with a single observation on an amendment introduced by the Committee into the territorial bill. To that

amendment I was opposed, but it was carried in the Committee. It is an amendment which is to be found in Section 10 of one of the bills limiting the power of the territorial legislature upon the subject of laws which it may pass. Among other limitations, it declares "that the territorial legislature shall have no power to pass any law in respect to African slavery." I did not then and do not now attach much importance to the amendment, which was proposed by an honorable senator now in my eye, and carried by a majority of the Committee. The effect of that clause will at once be understood by the Senate. It speaks of "African" slavery. The word "African" was introduced so as to leave the territorial government at liberty to legislate as it might think proper on any other condition of slavery: "peon" or "Indian" slavery, which has so long existed under the Spanish regime.

The object was to impose a restriction upon them as to the passage of any law either to admit or exclude African slavery, or of any law restricting it. The effect of that amendment will at once be seen. If the territorial legislature can pass no law with respect to African slavery, the state of the law as it exists now in the territories of Utah and New Mexico will continue to exist until the people form a constitution for themselves, when they can settle the question of slavery as they please. They will not be allowed to admit or exclude it. They will be restrained, on the one hand, from its admission, and, on the other, from its exclusion.

Sir, I shall not enlarge on the opinion which I have already announced to the Senate as being held by me on this subject. My opinion is that the law of Mexico, in all the variety of forms in which legislation can take place — that is to say, by the edict of a dictator, by the constitution of the people of Mexico, by the act of the legislative authority of Mexico — by all these modes of legislation, slavery has been abolished there. I am aware that some other senators entertain a different opinion; but without going into a discussion of that question, which I think altogether unnecessary, I feel authorized to say that the opinion of a vast majority of the people of the United States, of a vast majority of the jurists of the United States, is in coincidence with that which I entertain; that is to say, that at this moment, by law and in fact, there is no slavery there, unless it is possible that some gentlemen from the slave states in passing through that country may have taken along their body slaves.

In point of fact and in point of law, I entertain the opinions which I expressed at an early period of the session. Sir, we have heard since, from authority entitled to the highest respect, from no less authority than that of the delegate from New Mexico, that labor can be there obtained at the rate of $3 or $4 per month; and if it can be got at that rate, can anybody suppose that any owner of slaves would ever carry them to that country, where he could only get $3 or $4 per month for them?

I believe, on this part of the subject, I have said everything that is necessary for me to say; but there remain two or three subjects upon which I wish to say a few words before I close what I have to offer for the consideration of the Senate.

The next subject upon which the Committee acted was that of fugitive slaves. The Committee have proposed two amendments to be offered to the bill introduced by the senator from Virginia [Mr. Mason] whenever that bill is taken up. The first of these amendments provides that the owner of a fugitive slave, when leaving his own state, and whenever it is practicable — for sometimes in the hot pursuit of an immediate runaway, it may not be in the power of the master to wait to get such record, and he will always do it if it is possible — shall carry with him a record from the state from which the fugitive has fled; which record shall contain an adjudication of two facts:

first, the fact of slavery, and, second, the fact of an elopement; and, in the third place, such a general description of the slave as the court shall be enabled to give upon such testimony as shall be brought before it. It also provides that this record, taken from the county court, or from the court record in the slaveholding state, shall be carried to the free state, and shall be there held to be competent and sufficient evidence of the facts which it avows. Now, sir, I heard objection made to this, that it would be an inconvenience and an expense to the slaveholder. I think the expense will be very trifling compared to the great advantages which will result. . . .

Mr. President, the only measure remaining upon which I shall say a word now is the abolition of the slave trade in the District of Columbia. There is, I believe, precious little of it. . . . I believe there has been no time within the last forty years when, if earnestly pressed upon Congress, there would not have been found a majority — perhaps a majority from the slaveholding states themselves — in favor of the abolition of the slave trade in this District. The bill which the Committee has reported is founded upon the law of Maryland, as it existed when this District was set apart and ceded to the United States. Maryland has since very often changed her laws. What is their exact condition at present I am not aware. I have heard that she has made a change at the last session, and I am told that they may again be changed in the course of a year or two.

Sir, some years ago it would have been thought a great concession to the feelings and wishes of the North to abolish this slave trade. Now, I have seen some of the rabid Abolition papers denounce it as amounting to nothing. It is nothing that slavery is interdicted in California! They do not care for all that. And will my friends, some of my friends on the other side of the House, allow me to say a word or two with respect to their course in relation to this measure? At the beginning of this session, as you know that offensive proviso called the "Wilmot Proviso" was what was the most apprehended and what all the slaveholding states were most desirous to get rid of.

Well, sir, by the operation of causes upon the Northern mind friendly to the Union, hopes are inspired, which I trust will not be frustrated in the progress of this measure, that the North, or at least a sufficient portion of the North, are now willing to dispense with the Proviso. When, the other day, on the coming in of the report to these measures, it was objected, by way of reproach, that they were simply carrying out my own plan, my honorable friend from North Carolina at the moment justly pointed out the essential differences between the plan, as contained in the resolutions offered by me, and that now presented by the Committee. At the time I offered those resolutions, knowing what consequences, and, as I sometimes feared, fatal consequences, might result from the fact of the North insisting on that proviso, by way of compensation, in one of the resolutions which I offered, the second one, I stated two truths, one of law and one of fact, which I thought ought to satisfy the North that it ought no longer to insist on the Wilmot Proviso. Those truths were not incorporated in the bill reported by the Committee, but they exist, nevertheless, as truths. I believe them both now as much as I did in February last.

I know there are others who do not concur with me in opinion. Every senator must decide for himself, as the country will decide for itself, when the question comes to be considered. Well, when our Southern friends found they were rid of the Proviso, they were highly satisfied, and I shared with them in their satisfaction. If I am not much mistaken, a great majority of them would have said, "If, Mr. Clay, you had not put those two obnoxious truths in them, we should have been satisfied with your series of resolutions." Well, sir, we have got rid of the Wilmot Proviso; we have got rid of the enactment into laws of the two truths to which I refer.

But I fear there are some of our Southern brethren who are not yet satisfied. There are some who say that there is yet the Wilmot Proviso, under another form, lurking in the laws of Mexico, or lurking in the mountains of Mexico, in that natural fact to which my honorable friend from Massachusetts adverted, as I myself did when I hinted that the law of nature was adverse to the introduction of slavery there. Now, as you find in the progress of events that all is obtained which was desired or expected three months ago, there is something further, there are other difficulties in the way of the adjustment of these unhappy subjects of difference, and of obtaining that which is most to be desired: the cementing of the bonds of this Union. . . .

Mr. President, after we have got rid, as I had hoped, of all these troubles — after this Wilmot Proviso has disappeared, as I trust it may, both in this and the other end of the Capitol — after we have been disputing two or three years or more, on the one hand, about a mere abstraction, and, on the other, if it were fraught with evil, not so much present as distant and future, when we are arriving at a conclusion, what are the new difficulties that spring up around us? Matters of form. The purest question of form that was ever presented to the mind of man: whether we shall combine in one united bill three measures, all of which are necessary and homogeneous, or separate them into three distinct bills, passing each in its turn if it can be done.

Mr. President, I trust that the feelings of attachment to the Union, of love for its past glory, of anticipation of its future benefits and happiness; a fraternal feeling which ought to be common throughout all parts of the country; the desire to live together in peace and harmony, to prosper as we have prospered heretofore, to hold up to the civilized world the example of one great and glorious republic fulfilling the high destiny that belongs to it, demonstrating beyond all doubt man's capacity for self-government; these motives and these considerations will, I confidently hope and fervently pray, animate us all, bringing us together to dismiss alike questions of abstraction and form, and consummating the act of concord, harmony, and peace in such a manner as to heal not one only but all the wounds of the country.

8.

ANONYMOUS: A Defense of the President's Plan for Compromise

The passage of legislation concerning the Mexican cession was hindered not only by partisan factions in Congress but also by President Zachary Taylor, who had formulated his own plan. Taylor had encouraged the citizens of California to draft a constitution and apply for admission as a free state, and now he called for a policy of "no action" in regard to the rest of the territories until they should also qualify for admission to the Union. The "compromisers" had rejected this plan, believing it was the constitutional duty of Congress to provide civil law for the territories. Henry Clay's speech before the Senate on May 21, attacking the President's position, prompted the following article in the New York Republic *six days later.*

Source: *New York Republic*, May 27, 1850.

IT IS NOW MORE THAN SIX MONTHS since the President of the United States, in a message to Congress transmitting information in answer to a resolution of the House of Representatives on the subject of California and New Mexico, pursuant to the provision of the Constitution which makes it the duty of the Executive from time to time to recommend to Congress such measures as he may deem necessary and expedient, pointed out the course of policy which, in his opinion, under all the circumstances of the case, it would be most wise to pursue in reference to the government of the territory acquired from Mexico by the Treaty of Guadalupe Hidalgo. To that subject, and that subject alone, did the recommendations contained in his message refer. To none other did he conceive it to be his duty, on that occasion, to call the attention of Congress. That the line of policy then recommended by him was, at the time, most favorably received by the people of the United States, and was generally accepted by them as satisfactory, and as probably the best which existing circumstances rendered practicable, we presume no one will pretend to deny.

After the President had recommended to Congress the plan of proceeding which he deemed best, various other plans were offered by individual members of the Senate, and more recently another has emanated from a committee of thirteen members of the Senate, to whom the subject had been referred. This is known as the Compromise. During the discussions which from day to day sprung up and were continued in the Senate, with regard to the relative merits of these plans, and to the best mode of disposing of the subject, it began to be rumored that the President had *changed his opinion* in regard to the policy originally recommended by him, and that he thought better of some other plan. Positive statements to that effect were made in the public prints, and began to obtain a very general credence.

Under these circumstances, it was alike due to the President, to the public, and, in a particular manner, to those members of Congress who preferred the line of policy recommended by him to any other, and who had from the beginning stood ready to support it, that the misapprehension should be corrected. He accordingly authorized us to say that no such change of opinion as that attributed to him had taken place, and that he was still firm in the belief that the policy recommended by him was, under all the circumstances of the case, the best that was practicable. This simple correction of current misapprehensions and misrepresentations, in relation to an alleged change of opinion by the President on the subject of a great measure of public policy which he had, on his official responsibility, recommended to Congress, and which had numerous supporters in that body — this mere enunciation of a truth which it was due to himself, to Congress, and to the people of the United States, should be made known, has, it appears, been singularly misconceived as to its object, and as strangely received in certain quarters. The *Union* newspaper, the sole organ in this city of the Democratic Party, construes it into an indication that the President is opposed to "the Compromise" — which means the Compromise in all its parts and provisions — and that he is "against the settlement of the slavery question."

The enunciation was also received, it appears, "with profound surprise and regret" by a distinguished Whig senator, Mr. Clay, who, the day after the enunciation, on Tuesday the 21st instant, in the discharge of "a painful duty," felt himself called upon to contrast the plan proposed by the President with the compromise plan. This he did by a "simile." "Here," said he, "are five wounds — one, two, three, four, and five — bleeding and threatening the well-being, if not the existence of the body politic. What is the plan of the President? Is it to heal all these wounds? No such thing. It is only to heal one of the five, and to leave the others to bleed more profusely than ever, by the sole admission of California, even if it should produce death itself." These five wounds the senator then proceeded to describe. "First," said he, "there is California; there are the territories, second; there is the question of the boundary of Texas, the third; there is the Fugitive Slave Bill, the fourth; and there is the question of the slave trade in the District of Columbia, the fifth. The President, instead of proposing a plan comprehending all the diseases of the country, looks only at one." Further on the senator says: "The recommendation of the President proposes the simple introduction of California as a state into the Union," and it "proposes to leave all else untouched and unprovided for."

In this contrast, which the senator proceeds to carry out at considerable length, it appears to us, and we doubt not it will so appear to the public, that he has done the President very great injustice. With all proper respect for the distinguished senator, we think he has not fairly presented the President's plan. To point out that injustice and unfairness, and to set the policy recommended by the President fairly and truly before our readers, is the object of these remarks; it is their *only* object, and we hope that the performance of this simple act of justice to the President on our part may not subject us to "misinterpretation" in any quarter.

The injustice of the contrast in part lies here — that while the course of policy recommended by the President had reference only to the government of the people of the territory acquired from Mexico; while he expressed no opinion, and was called upon to express no opinion, on the subject of the Fugitive Slave Bill and the question of the slave trade in the District of Columbia, that policy is held up by the senator as antagonistic to these last-mentioned measures. These two "wounds" the senator represents the President as proposing to leave open.

Now, where is the incompatibility between the President's recommendations, referring, as they do, expressly and solely to the territory acquired from Mexico, and the Fugitive Slave Bill and the question of the slave trade in the District of Columbia? Who has the shadow of a right to assume, from anything the President has anywhere said, that he is opposed or indifferent to the adoption of either of those measures? We are not aware that he has expressed an opinion favorable or adverse to those measures, or either of them. How can either be in anywise affected by the adherence of the President to his plan in respect to California and New Mexico? Could they not both as well go hand in hand with the policy recommended by him, in reference to our newly acquired Mexican territory, as with the policy recommended in "the Compromise" in reference to the same territory? These two "wounds," it may be sufficient here to say, the President did not open; he has not recommended that they should be left open; nor has he offered the slightest impediment to their being healed up.

The subjects of the government of the territories, and the question of the boundary of Texas — the second and third "wounds" in the order enumerated — we will consider together. These two subjects, or "wounds," the senator says, the President recommends should "remain and be left untouched, to cure themselves by some law of nature, by the *vis medicatrix naturae,* or some self-remedy, in the success of which I cannot perceive any ground of the least

Chicago Historical Society
Daguerreotype of Zachary Taylor

confidence." Elsewhere the senator says: "The President's plan proposes the admission of California. He proposes nonintervention as to slavery. But he proposes further nonintervention in the establishment of territorial government; that is to say, that we shall neglect to execute the obligation of the Treaty of Hidalgo — fail to govern those whom we are bound to govern — leave them without the protection of the civil authority of general government — leave Utah without any government at all, but that which the Mormons may institute — and leave New Mexico under the military government of a lieutenant colonel. His plan fails to establish the limits of New Mexico east of the Rio Grande, and would expose the people who inhabit it to civil war, already threatened, with Texas."

A formidable array of alleged defects and omissions in the President's plan! Let us turn for a few moments to the plan itself, and see whether it is justly liable to the grave objections urged by the senator. That plan contemplated the *immediate* formation of state constitutions by the people of California and New Mexico, and their early admission into the Union as states. With this view, the President states in his message, of the 21st of January, that he had not hesitated "to express to the people of those territories [California and New Mexico] my desire that each territory should, if prepared to comply with the requisitions of the Constitution of the United States, form a plan of a state constitution and submit the same to Congress, with a prayer for admission into the Union as a state."

California, accordingly, proceeded to form a state constitution, and is now applying to Congress for admission into the Union as a state. Nothing has existed, or now exists, to prevent New Mexico from following the example of California. She may, and probably will, do so before the close of the present session of Congress, unless she is deterred by the declaration of the senator that he will not vote for her admission into the Union at present as a state.

With what fairness and justice, then, can it be charged upon the President, that he proposes to leave New Mexico under the military government of a lieutenant colonel, without the protection of the civil authority of any general government, and in utter disregard of the obligation of the United States in the Treaty of Guadalupe Hidalgo? Leave them in that condition? For how long a period? For such brief space only as will be requisite for the formation of a state constitution, and their admission into the Union as a state. The President proposing to neglect to [execute] the obligation of the United States in the Treaty of Guadalupe Hidalgo! Why, he states expressly, in his message, that "with a view to the faithful execution of the treaty, so far as lay in the power of the Executive, and to enable Congress to act of the present session with as full knowledge and as little difficulty as possible," he sent certain persons to California and New Mexico, with instructions, among other things, to make known to the people of those territories his "desire that each ter-

ritory should, if prepared to comply with the requisitions of the Constitution of the United States, form a plan of a state constitution, and submit the same to Congress, with a prayer for admission into the Union as a state!" It will not be pretended, we suppose, that the people of New Mexico are not prepared to comply with all "the requisitions of the Constitution" in this respect.

Another of the objections of the senator to the President's plan is, as he alleges, that the President recommends that the subject, or "wound," of the Texas *boundary*, along with that of the territorial government, should remain and be left untouched, to cure itself by some law of nature — by the *vis medicatrix naturae*, or some self-remedy — in the success of which he cannot perceive any ground of the least confidence. And this in the face of the following extract from the message of the President:

A claim has been advanced by the state of Texas to a very large portion of the most populous district of the territory commonly designated by the name of New Mexico. If the people of New Mexico had formed a plan of a state government for that territory, as ceded by the Treaty of Guadalupe Hidalgo, and had been admitted by Congress as a state, our Constitution would have afforded the means of obtaining an adjustment of the question of boundary with Texas by a judicial decision. At present, however, no judicial tribunal has the power of deciding that question, and *it remains for Congress to devise some mode of adjustment.*

Is this express submission of the Texas boundary question to *Congress,* with whom the subject properly belonged, "to devise some mode of adjustment" — is this proposing to leave it "untouched, to cure itself by some law of nature, by the *vis medicatrix naturae,* or some self-remedy"? New Mexico being admitted into the Union as a state, the Supreme Court would then have jurisdiction over the question of boundary between that state and Texas, and its adjudication would be competent to heal that wound.

With regard to Utah, the people of that portion of the territory acquired from Mexico have emigrated thither of their own free volition, and now constitute an isolated people. They have adopted a provisional form of government, perhaps as well or better suited to their condition and wants than any which Congress could devise for them. They are in the full enjoyment of the great right of self-government. They are well armed, and, if we are correctly informed, abundantly able to protect themselves from the Indian tribes in the vicinity. Should they at any time need additional military protection, the President will no doubt take care that it be promptly extended to them. In reference to this people, no imputation of infidelity to the engagements of the United States in the Treaty of Guadalupe Hidalgo can arise, they having, for the most part, emigrated thither since the conclusion of that treaty, and never having been citizens of Mexico.

Speaking of the President's plan the senator says: "He [the President] recommends the admission of California. We are willing to admit California. We go with him as far as he goes, etc." With the utmost deference to the senator, we must say that we do not so understand the two plans. We understand the President to recommend something more than the admission of California. We understand him to recommend the reference of the question, whether the introduction of slavery shall or shall not be prohibited in the residue of the territory, to the people thereof when they shall come to form a state constitution or constitutions preparatory to their admission into the Union as a state or states, and that in the meantime Congress, *abstaining from the establishment of territorial governments,* should leave the people of the territory to be governed by their own local laws and customs, with such military protection from the

United States as their necessities shall require and the exigencies of the public service elsewhere will permit. *Early* admission into the Union as states, nonintervention by Congress in respect to slavery, and *nonaction by the same body in regard to the establishment of territorial governments,* constitute the policy recommended by the President.

Nonaction by Congress in respect to the establishment of territorial governments is an important feature in the President's policy. He is not in favor of the establishment of territorial governments, while the compromise plan insists upon their necessity. Now, without desiring or intending to assail any plan, we may be permitted, we hope, without offense, to examine this feature of the President's plan, in connection with the antagonistic feature in the compromise plan.

In recommending the course of policy he did, the President had in view the early and final settlement of the slavery question so far as it concerned the territory acquired from Mexico; his object was to put a stop to all agitation, in Congress and out of it, on the subject of the prohibition of the introduction of the institution of slavery into that territory, and to relieve Congress from the necessity of legislating on that subject at all. For, if that body legislated at all on the subject, it must needs bring itself into conflict with the passions, prejudices, and opinions of both sections of the Union.

Now, it was evident that no bill establishing territorial governments over the territory could pass Congress without bringing up the Wilmot Proviso question — if, indeed, any such bill could pass without having the Proviso incorporated into it. The mere discussion of that question in Congress, and the necessity of having to vote upon it, were to be deprecated and avoided, if possible, because such discussion, and such a vote, even if the Proviso should be voted down, would, in all probability, sow the seeds of future agitation and excitement broadcast over the whole of the free states. In the South, too, what evidence have we that there will be general acquiescence and satisfaction with so much of the Compromise as relates to the government of the territory acquired from Mexico? Are the Southern members of Congress united on that subject? It is well known that they are not. May not a fierce strife spring up in the South, in consequence of the opposing votes and conflicting views of the different members from that section on the Compromise? We do not say that such will be the case, but certainly the "signs of the times" point in that direction. So far, then, from there being any certainty that the manner in which the territorial question is proposed to be adjusted in the Compromise will allay agitation and restore permanent harmony to the country, it is more than probable, nay, it is almost sure to give rise to renewed and continued agitation, in both the North and the South. It is not so unequivocal in its terms as not to admit of contrary interpretations, North and South.

While at the South it is held by distinguished men to secure all that the South desires, other equally distinguished men in the same section maintain that it surrenders all that the South has contended for. Equally conflicting views of its effect are held at the North — some contending that it will open the whole of New Mexico and Utah to the admission of slavery; while its supporters from that section contend that slavery is now prohibited by the local law in those territories, which will not be abrogated by the Compromise, and thus that it will have all the effect of the Wilmot Proviso. Is it not, then, manifest that Northern men who support it will be arraigned for surrendering the principle of the Proviso, and that Southern men who support it will be arraigned for surrendering the rights of the South, for which they had pledged themselves to contend so strenuously? Can a measure like this give harmony and tranquillity to the country? Is it not rather to be feared that, if adopted, it will prove a prolific fountain, from which will flow continued agitation and discord?

That plan for the adjustment of this question is the best which takes the subject of slavery out of the political arena, and extinguishes it as a political issue in the party contests of the times. In this respect we humbly conceive the President's plan superior to any that has been suggested. The President's plan, if adopted and carried out, can be attended with no such consequences. It will leave nothing behind it to agitate about. It gives finality to this vexed question of the inhibition or admission of slavery into the territory acquired from Mexico, and in nowise conflicts with the other measures contemplated in reference to fugitive slaves and the slave trade in the District of Columbia — both of them subjects of high and grave importance, and neither of which is any more dependent upon the adoption of the territorial portion of the Compromise plan than it is upon the adoption of the President's plan.

Either or both may possibly be defeated, though the Compromise bill should pass. If the Compromise bill should pass, and the Fugitive Slave Bill be lost, will not the Southern supporters of the former impute bad faith to its Northern supporters? And if the bill respecting the slave trade in the District of Columbia should fail to become a law, will not those Northern members of Congress who support the Compromise as a whole, make loud complaints against its Southern supporters? Will there not, in either of these cases, be mutual imputations of bad faith, and mutual criminations and recriminations? Where, then, will be the harmony, the absence of which the senator from Kentucky so eloquently deplores? May there not, in either case, be a startling addition to the five bleeding wounds so graphically described by the senator?

Upon a full view of the whole question, and upon a candid consideration of the reasons on both sides, we are wholly unable to see that superior remedial potency in the Compromise plan over that of the President, which is claimed for the former by its supporters. Certainly such superiority, if it indeed exists, is not so manifest as to justify its supporters in *requiring* the President to abandon his own opinions, deliberately formed and expressed, and actively exert his influence to defeat the principle of adjust-ment which he has deliberately recommended, and which he still believes to be the best calculated to overcome all the difficulties growing out of our acquisition of territory from Mexico. Such a course, on his part, would be incompatible with self-respect, and could not fail to diminish the confidence of the country in his firmness and wisdom.

9.

Resolutions of the Nashville Convention

Early in June 1850 a convention of delegates from nine slaveholding states met at Nashville, Tennessee, to consider a course of action on the compromise measures over which Congress was still laboring. The Southerners who urged secession if slavery were restricted in any of the new territories were overruled by the moderates. Speaking for the moderate position, the presiding officer, Judge William L. Sharkey, declared that the convention had not been "called to prevent but to perpetuate the Union." Thus, the Nashville delegates, while they denounced the Omnibus Bill and reaffirmed the constitutionality of slavery, agreed to a "concession" whereby the geographic dividing line designated by the Missouri Compromise of 1820 would be extended to the Pacific Coast. Some of the convention's resolutions of June 10 and 11 appear below.

Source: *Resolutions and Address Adopted by the Southern Convention, held at Nashville, Tennessee, June 3-12, 1850*, Columbia, S.C., 1850, pp. 3-9.

1. *Resolved*, that the territories of the United States belong to the people of the several states of the Union as their common property. That the citizens of the several states have equal rights to migrate with their property to these territories, and are equally entitled to the protection of the federal government in the enjoyment of that property so long as the territories remain under the charge of that government.

2. *Resolved*, that Congress has no power to exclude from the territory of the United States any property lawfully held in the states of the Union, and any act which may be passed by Congress to effect this result is a plain violation of the Constitution of the United States.

3. *Resolved*, that it is the duty of Congress to provide proper governments for the territories, since the spirit of American Institutions forbids the maintenance of military governments in time of peace, and as all laws heretofore existing in territories once belonging to foreign powers which interfere with the full enjoyment of religion, the freedom of the press, the trial by jury, and all other rights of persons and property as secured or recognized in the Constitution of

the United States, are necessarily void so soon as such territories become American territories, it is the duty of the federal government to make early provision for the enactment of those laws which may be expedient and necessary to secure to the inhabitants of and emigrants to such territories the full benefit of the constitutional rights we assert.

4. *Resolved*, that to protect property existing in the several states of the Union, the people of these states invested the federal government with the powers of war and negotiation and of sustaining armies and navies, and prohibited to state authorities the exercise of the same powers. They made no discrimination in the protection to be afforded or the description of the property to be defended, nor was it allowed to the federal government to determine what should be held as property. Whatever the states deal with as property the federal government is bound to recognize and defend as such. Therefore it is the sense of this Convention that all acts of the federal government which tend to denationalize property of any description recognized in the Constitution and laws of the states, or that discriminate in the degree and efficiency of the protection to be afforded to it, or which weaken or destroy the title of any citizen upon American territories, are plain and palpable violations of the fundamental law under which it exists.

5. *Resolved*, that the slaveholding states cannot and will not submit to the enactment by Congress of any law imposing onerous conditions or restraints upon the rights of masters to remove with their property into the territories of the United States, or to any law making discrimination in favor of the proprietors of other property against them.

6. *Resolved*, that it is the duty of the federal government plainly to recognize and firmly to maintain the equal rights of the citizens of the several states in the territories of the United States, and to repudiate the power to make a discrimination between the proprietors of different species of property in federal legislation. The fulfillment of this duty by the federal government would greatly tend to restore the peace of the country and to allay the exasperation and excitement which now exist between the different sections of the Union. For it is the deliberate opinion of this Convention that the tolerance Congress has given to the notion that federal authority might be employed incidentally and indirectly to subvert or weaken the institutions existing in the states confessedly beyond federal jurisdiction and control is a main cause of the discord which menaces the existence of the Union, and which has well-nigh destroyed the efficient action of the federal government itself.

7. *Resolved*, that the performance of this duty is required by the fundamental law of the Union. The equality of the people of the several states composing the Union cannot be disturbed without disturbing the frame of the American institutions. This principle is violated in the denial of the citizens of the slaveholding states of power to enter into the territories with the property lawfully acquired in the states. The warfare against this right is a war upon the Constitution. The defenders of this right are defenders of the Constitution. Those who deny or impair its exercise are unfaithful to the Constitution; and, if disunion follows the destruction of the right, they are the disunionists.

8. *Resolved*, that the performance of its duties, upon the principle we declare, would enable Congress to remove the embarrassments in which the country is now involved. The vacant territories of the United States, no longer regarded as prizes for sectional rapacity and ambition, would be gradually occupied by inhabitants drawn to them by their interests and feelings. The institutions fitted to them would be naturally applied by governments formed on Ameri-

can ideas and approved by the deliberate choice of their constituents. The community would be educated and disciplined under a republican administration in habits of self-government and fitted for an association as a state, and to the enjoyment of a place in the confederacy. A community so formed and organized might well claim admission to the Union and none would dispute the validity of the claim.

9. *Resolved,* that a recognition of this principle would deprive the questions between Texas and the United States of their sectional character and would leave them for adjustment, without disturbance from sectional prejudices and passions, upon considerations of magnanimity and justice.

10. *Resolved,* that a recognition of this principle would infuse a spirit of conciliation in the discussion and adjustment of all the subjects of sectional dispute which would afford a guarantee of an early and satisfactory determination.

11. *Resolved,* that in the event a dominant majority shall refuse to recognize the great constitutional rights we assert and shall continue to deny the obligations of the federal government to maintain them, it is the sense of this Convention that the territories should be treated as property and divided between the sections of the Union, so that the rights of both sections be adequately secured in their respective shares. That we are aware this course is open to grave objections, but we are ready to acquiesce in the adoption of the line of 36°30′ north latitude, extending to the Pacific Ocean, as an extreme concession, upon consideration of what is due to the stability of our institution.

12. *Resolved,* that it is the opinion of this Convention that this controversy should be ended, either by a recognition of the constitutional rights of the Southern people or by an equitable partition of the territories; that the spectacle of a confederacy of states involved in quarrels over the fruits of a war

in which the American arms were crowned with glory is humiliating; that the incorporation of the Wilmot Proviso in the offer of settlement, a proposition which fourteen states regard as disparaging and dishonorable, is degrading to the country. A termination to this controversy by the disruption of the confederacy or by the abandonment of the territories to prevent such a result would be a climax to the shame which attaches to the controversy which it is the paramount duty of Congress to avoid. . . .

24. *Resolved,* that slavery exists in the United States independent of the Constitution. That it is recognized by the Constitution in a threefold aspect: first, as property; second, as a domestic relation of service or labor under the law of a state; and, last, as a basis of political power. And, viewed in any or all of these lights, Congress has no power under the Constitution to create or destroy it anywhere; nor can such power be derived from foreign laws, conquest, cession, treaty, or the laws of nations, nor from any other source but an amendment of the Constitution itself.

25. *Resolved,* that the Constitution confers no power upon Congress to regulate or prohibit the sale and transfer of slaves between the states.

26. *Resolved,* that the reception or consideration by Congress of resolutions, memorials, or petitions from the states in which domestic slavery does not exist, or from the people of said states, in relation to the institution of slavery where it does exist, with a view of effecting its abolition, or to impair the rights of those interested in it, to its peaceful and secure enjoyment, is a gross abuse and an entire perversion of the right of petition as secured by the federal Constitution; and, if persisted in, must and will lead to the most dangerous and lamentable consequences — that the right of petition for a redress of grievances as provided for by the Constitution was designed to enable the citizens of the United States to manifest

and make known to Congress the existence of evils under which they were suffering, whether effecting them personally, locally, or generally; and to cause such evils to be redressed by the proper and competent authority, but was never designed or intended as a means of inflicting injury on others, or jeopardizing the peaceful and secure enjoyment of their rights, whether existing under the Constitution or under the sovereignty and authority of the several states.

10.

The Compromise of 1850

The Compromise of 1850 comprised five separate statutes that became law in September of that year. The statutes, reprinted below, were strikingly similar to Henry Clay's original compromise resolutions, and resulted from nine arduous months of debate over the issue of the extension of slavery into the Western territories. The sudden death in July of President Zachary Taylor, whose veto had been feared by the "compromisers," and the willingness of many Northern and Southern leaders to relinquish their sectional differences to avert war, contributed to the final passage of the acts. The moderate forces in the Senate, which attempted at first to wrap all the issues into one Omnibus Bill, realized that it would be more expedient to vote on each issue separately. Thus, from September 9 to 20, the five bills were taken up one at a time. The Compromise of 1850 was at best a temporary truce between the slave and free states; and four years later its value was negated by the Kansas-Nebraska Act.

Source: *Statutes,* IX, pp. 446-458, 462-465, 467-468.

An act proposing to the state of Texas the establishment of her northern and western boundaries, the relinquishment by the said state of all territory claimed by her exterior to said boundaries, and of all her claims upon the United States, and to establish a territorial government for New Mexico.

Be it enacted by the Senate and House of Representatives of the United States of America in Congress assembled, that the following propositions shall be, and the same hereby are, offered to the state of Texas, which, when agreed to by the said state, in an act passed by the General Assembly, shall be binding and obligatory upon the United States and upon the said state of Texas. *Provided,* the said agreement by the said General Assembly shall be given on or before December 1, 1850.

First, the state of Texas will agree that her boundary on the north shall commence at the point at which the meridian of 100° west from Greenwich is intersected by the parallel of 36°30′ north latitude, and shall run from said point due west to the meridian of 103° west from Greenwich; thence her boundary shall run due south to 32° north latitude; thence on the said parallel of 32° north latitude to the Rio Bravo del Norte [Rio Grande] and thence with the channel of said river to the Gulf of Mexico.

Second, the state of Texas cedes to the United States all her claim to territory exterior to the limits and boundaries which she agrees to establish by Article 1. . . .

Third, the state of Texas relinquishes all claim upon the United States for liability of the debts of Texas and for compensation or indemnity for the surrender to the United States of her ships, forts, arsenals, customhouses, customhouse revenue, arms and munitions of war, and public buildings with their sites which became the property of the United States at the time of the annexation.

Fourth, the United States, in consideration of said establishment of boundaries, cession of claim to territory, and relinquishment of claims, will pay to the state of Texas the sum of $10 million in a stock bearing 5 percent interest, and redeemable at the end of fourteen years, the interest payable half yearly at the Treasury of the United States.

Fifth, immediately after the President of the United States shall have been furnished with an authentic copy of the act of the General Assembly of Texas accepting these propositions, he shall cause the stock to be issued in favor of the state of Texas, as provided for in Article 4 of this agreement. *Provided, also,* that no more than $5 million of said stock shall be issued until the creditors of the state holding bonds and other certificates of stock of Texas, for which duties on imports were specially pledged, shall first file at the Treasury of the United States releases of all claim against the United States for or on account of said bonds or certificates in such form as shall be prescribed by the secretary of the treasury and approved by the President of the United States. *Provided,* that nothing herein contained shall be construed to impair or qualify anything contained in Article 3 of the Section 2 of the "joint resolution for annexing Texas to the United States," approved March 1, 1845, either as regards the number of states that may hereafter be formed out of the state of Texas, or otherwise.

Section 2. *And be it further enacted,* that all that portion of the territory of the United States bounded as follows: beginning at a point in the Colorado River where the boundary line with the Republic of Mexico crosses the same; thence eastwardly with the said boundary line to the Rio Grande; thence following the main channel of said river to the parallel of 32° north latitude; thence east with said degree to its intersection with 103° longitude west of Greenwich; thence north with said degree of longitude to the parallel of 38° north latitude; thence west with said parallel to the summit of the Sierra Madre; thence south with the crest of said mountains to 37° north latitude; thence west with said parallel to its intersection with the boundary line of the state of California; thence with said boundary line to the place of beginning — be, and the same is hereby, erected into a temporary government, by the name of the Territory of New Mexico.

Provided, that nothing in this act contained shall be construed to inhibit the government of the United States from dividing said territory into two or more territories, in such manner and at such times as Congress shall deem convenient and proper, or from attaching any portion thereof to any other territory or state. *And provided, further,* that, when admitted as a state, the said territory, or any portion of the same, shall be received into the Union, with or without slavery, as their constitution may prescribe at the time of their admission.

Section 3. *And be it further enacted,* that the executive power and authority in and over said Territory of New Mexico shall be vested in a governor, who shall hold his office for four years, and until his successor shall be appointed and qualified, unless sooner removed by the President of the United States. . . .

Section 7. *And be it further enacted,* that the legislative power of the territory shall extend to all rightful subjects of legislation, consistent with the Constitution of the United States and the provisions of this act; but no law shall be passed interfering with the primary disposal of the soil; no tax shall be imposed upon the property of the United States; nor shall the lands or other property of nonresidents be taxed higher than the lands or other property of residents. All the laws passed by the legislative assembly and governor shall be submitted to the Congress of the United States, and, if disapproved, shall be null and of no effect. . . .

Section 17. *And be it further enacted,* that the Constitution, and all laws of the United States which are not locally inapplicable, shall have the same force and effect within the said Territory of New Mexico as elsewhere within the United States.

Section 18. *And be it further enacted,* that the provisions of this act be, and they are hereby, suspended until the boundary between the United States and the state of Texas shall be adjusted; and when such adjustment shall have been effected, the President of the United States shall issue his proclamation declaring this act to be in full force and operation, and shall proceed to appoint the officers herein provided to be appointed in and for said territory.

Section 19. *And be it further enacted,* that no citizen of the United States shall be deprived of his life, liberty, or property in said territory, except by the judgment of his peers and the laws of the land.

An act for the admission of the state of California into the Union.

Whereas the people of California have presented a constitution and asked admission into the Union, which constitution was submitted to Congress by the President of the United States, by message dated February 13, 1850, and which, on due examination, is found to be republican in its form of government:

Be it enacted by the Senate and House of Representatives of the United States of America in Congress assembled, that the state of California shall be one, and is hereby declared to be one, of the United States of America, and admitted into the Union on an equal footing with the original states in all respects whatever. . . .

Section 3. *And be it further enacted,* that the said state of California is admitted into the Union upon the express condition that the people of said state, through their legislature or otherwise, shall never interfere with the primary disposal of the public lands within its limits, and shall pass no law and do no act whereby the title of the United States to, and right to dispose of, the same shall be impaired or questioned; and that they shall never lay any tax or assessment of any description whatsoever upon the public domain of the United States, and in no case shall nonresident proprietors, who are citizens of the United States, be taxed higher than residents; and that all the navigable waters within the said state shall be common highways and forever free, as well to the inhabitants of said state as to the citizens of the United States, without any tax, impost, or duty therefor. *Provided,* that nothing herein contained shall be construed as recognizing or rejecting the propositions tendered by the people of California as articles of compact in the ordinance adopted by the convention which formed the constitution of that state.

An act to establish a territorial government for Utah.

Be it enacted by the Senate and House of Representatives of the United States of America in Congress assembled, that all that part of the territory of the United States included within the following limits, to wit, bounded on the west by the state of California, on the north by the Territory of Oregon, and on the east by the summit of the Rocky Mountains, and on the south by 37° north latitude, be, and the same is hereby, created into a temporary government, by the name of the Territory of Utah; and, when admitted as a state, the said territory, or any portion of the same, shall be received into the Union, with or without slavery, as their constitution may prescribe at the time of their admission. *Provided,* that nothing in this act contained shall be construed to inhibit the government of the United States from dividing said territory into two or more territories, in such manner and at such times as Congress shall deem convenient and proper, or from attaching any portion of said territory to any other state or territory of the United States.

Section 2. *And be it further enacted,* that the executive power and authority in and over said Territory of Utah shall be vested in a governor, who shall hold office for four years, and until his successor shall be appointed and qualified, unless sooner removed by the President. . . .

Section 5. *And be it further enacted,* that every free white male inhabitant above the age of twenty-one years, who shall have been a resident of said territory at the time of the passage of this act, shall be entitled to vote at the first election, and shall be eligible to any office within the said territory; but the qualifications of voters and of holding office at all subsequent elections shall be such as shall be prescribed by the legislative assembly. *Provided,* that the right of suffrage and of holding office shall be exercised only by citizens of the United States, including those recognized as citizens by the treaty with the Republic of Mexico concluded February 2, 1848.

Section 6. *And be it further enacted,* that the legislative power of said territory shall extend to all rightful subjects of legislation, consistent with the Constitution of the United States and the provisions of this act; but no law shall be passed interfering with the primary disposal of the soil; no tax shall be imposed upon the property of the United States; nor shall the lands or other property of nonresidents be taxed higher than the lands or other property of residents. All the laws passed by the legislative assembly

and governor shall be submitted to the Congress of the United States, and, if disapproved, shall be null and of no effect. . . .

Section 13. *And be it further enacted,* that a delegate to the House of Representatives of the United States, to serve during each Congress of the United States, may be elected by the voters qualified to elect members of the legislative assembly, who shall be entitled to the same rights and privileges as are exercised and enjoyed by the delegates from the several other territories of the United States to the said House of Representatives. . . .

Section 17. *And be it further enacted,* that the Constitution and laws of the United States are hereby extended over and declared to be in force in said Territory of Utah, so far as the same, or any provision thereof, may be applicable.

An act to amend, and supplementary to, the act entitled "An act respecting fugitives from justice, and persons escaping from the service of their masters," approved February 12, 1793.

Be it enacted by the Senate and House of Representatives of the United States of America in Congress assembled, that the persons who have been, or may hereafter be, appointed commissioners, in virtue of any act of Congress, by the Circuit Courts of the United States, and who, in consequence of such appointment, are authorized to exercise the powers that any justice of the peace, or other magistrate of any of the United States, may exercise in respect to offenders for any crime or offense against the United States, by arresting, imprisoning, or bailing the same under and by virtue of Section 33 of the act of September 24, 1789, entitled "An act to establish the judicial courts of the United States," shall be, and are hereby, authorized and required to exercise and discharge all the powers and duties conferred by this act.

Section 2. *And be it further enacted,* that the Superior Court of each organized territory of the United States shall have the same power to appoint commissioners to take acknowledgments of bail and affidavits, and to take depositions of witnesses in civil causes which is now possessed by the Circuit Court of the United States; and all commissioners who shall hereafter be appointed for such purposes by the Superior Court of any organized territory of the United States shall possess all the powers and exercise all the duties conferred by law upon the commissioners appointed by the Circuit Courts of the United States for similar purposes, and shall moreover exercise and discharge all the powers and duties conferred by this act.

Section 3. *And be it further enacted,* that the Circuit Courts of the United States and the Superior Courts of each organized territory of the United States shall from time to time enlarge the number of commissioners, with a view to afford reasonable facilities to reclaim fugitives from labor and to the prompt discharge of the duties imposed by this act.

Section 4. *And be it further enacted,* that the commissioners above named shall have concurrent jurisdiction with the judges of the Circuit and District courts of the United States, in their respective circuits and districts within the several states, and the judges of the Superior Courts of the territories, severally and collectively, in term time and vacation; and shall grant certificates to such claimants upon satisfactory proof being made, with authority to take and remove such fugitives from service or labor, under the restrictions herein contained, to the state or territory from which such persons may have escaped or fled.

Section 5. *And be it further enacted,* that it shall be the duty of all marshals and deputy marshals to obey and execute all warrants and precepts issued under the provisions of this act when to them directed; and should any marshal or deputy marshal refuse to receive such warrant, or other process, when tendered, or to use all proper means diligently to execute the same, he shall, on conviction thereof, be fined in the sum of $1,000, to the use of such claimant, on the motion of such claimant, by the Circuit or District court for the district of such marshal; and after arrest of such fugitive by such marshal or his deputy, or while at any time in his custody under the provision of this act, should such fugitive escape, whether with or without the assent of such marshal or his deputy, such marshal shall be liable, on his official bond, to be prosecuted for the benefit of such claimant, for the full value of the service or labor of said fugitive in the state, territory, or district whence he escaped.

And the better to enable the said commissioners, when thus appointed, to execute their duties faithfully and efficiently, in conformity with the requirements of the Constitution of the United States and of this act, they are hereby authorized and empowered, within their counties respectively, to appoint, in writing under their hands, any one or more suitable persons, from time to time, to execute all such warrants and other process as may be issued by them in the lawful performance of their respective duties; with authority to such commissioners, or the persons to be appointed by them, to execute process as aforesaid, to summon and call to their aid the bystanders, or *posse comitatus* of the proper county, when necessary to ensure a faithful observance of the clause of the Constitution referred to, in conformity with the provisions of this act; and all good citizens are hereby commanded to aid and assist in the prompt and efficient execution of this law whenever their services may be required, as aforesaid, for that purpose; and said warrants shall run, and be executed by said officers, anywhere in the state within which they are issued.

Section 6. *And be it further enacted,* that when a person held to service or labor in any state or territory of the United States has heretofore or shall hereafter escape into another state or territory of the United States, the person or persons to whom such service or labor may be due, or his, her, or their agent or attorney, duly authorized, by power of attorney, in writing, acknowledged and certified under the seal of some legal officer or court of the state or territory in which the same may be executed, may pursue and reclaim such fugitive person . . . and remove such fugitive person back to the state or territory whence he or she may have escaped as aforesaid. In no trial or hearing under this act shall the testimony of such alleged fugitive be admitted in evidence. . . .

Section 7. *And be it further enacted,* that any person who shall knowingly and willingly obstruct, hinder, or prevent such claimant, his agent or attorney, or any person or persons lawfully assisting him, her, or them, from arresting such a fugitive from service or labor, either with or without process as aforesaid, or shall rescue, or attempt to rescue, such fugitive from service or labor, from the custody of such claimant, his or her agent or attorney, or other person or persons lawfully assisting as aforesaid, when so arrested, pursuant to the authority herein given and declared; or shall aid, abet, or assist such person so owing service or labor as aforesaid, directly or indirectly, to escape from such claimant, his agent or attorney, or other person or persons legally authorized as aforesaid; or shall harbor or conceal such fugitive, so as to prevent the discovery and arrest of such person, after notice or knowledge of the fact that such person was a fugitive from service or labor as aforesaid, shall, for either of said offenses, be subject to a fine not exceeding $1,000 and imprisonment not exceeding six months, by indictment and conviction before the District Court of the United States for the district in which such offense may have been committed, or before the proper court of criminal jurisdiction, if committed within any one of the organized territories of the United States; and shall moreover forfeit and pay, by way of civil damages to the party injured by such illegal conduct, the sum of $1,000 for each fugitive so lost as aforesaid, to be recovered by action of debt in any of the District or Territorial courts aforesaid, within whose jurisdiction the said offense may have been committed.

Section 8. *And be it further enacted,* that the marshals, their deputies, and the clerks of the said District and Territorial courts shall be paid, for their services, the like fees as may be allowed to them for similar services in other cases; and where such services are rendered exclusively in the arrest, custody, and delivery of the fugitive to the claimant, his or her agent or attorney, or where such supposed fugitive may be discharged out of custody for the want of sufficient proof as aforesaid, then such fees are to be paid in the whole by such claimants, his agent or attorney. . . .

Section 9. *And be it further enacted,* that, upon affidavit made by the claimant of such fugitive, his agent or attorney, after such certificate has been issued, that he has reason to apprehend that such fugitive will be rescued by force from his or their possession before he can be taken beyond the limits of the state in which the arrest is made, it shall be the duty of the officer making the arrest to retain such fugitive in his custody and to remove him to the state whence he fled, and there to deliver him to said claimant, his agent or attorney. And to this end, the officer aforesaid is hereby authorized and required to employ so many persons as he may deem necessary to overcome such force, and to retain them in his service so long as circumstances may require. The said officer and his assistants, while so employed, to receive the same compensation and to be allowed the same expenses as are now allowed by law for transportation of criminals, to be certified by the judge of the district within which the arrest is made, and paid out of the Treasury of the United States.

An act to suppress the slave trade in the District of Columbia.

Be it enacted by the Senate and House of Representatives of the United States of America in Congress assembled, that from and after January 1, 1851, it shall not be lawful to bring into the District of Columbia any slave whatever for the purpose of being sold, or for the purpose of being placed in depot, to be subsequently transferred to any other state or place to be sold as merchandise. And if any slave shall be brought into the said District by its owner, or by the authority or consent of its owner, contrary to the provisions of this act, such slave shall thereupon become liberated and free.

Section 2. *And be it further enacted*, that it shall and may be lawful for each of the corporations of the cities of Washington and Georgetown, from time to time, and as often as may be necessary, to abate, break up, and abolish any depot or place of confinement of slaves brought into the said District as merchandise, contrary to the provisions of this act, by such appropriate means as may appear to either of the said corporations expedient and proper. And the same power is hereby vested in the Levy Court of Washington County, if any attempt shall be made within its jurisdictional limits to establish a depot or place of confinement for slaves brought into the said District as merchandise for sale, contrary to this act.

11.

Military Presidents

Zachary Taylor was the fourth military hero to become President. Popularity gained in the Mexican War was sufficient to obtain for him the Whig nomination in 1848, despite political inexperience and lack of familiarity with public issues. Taylor, whose administration lasted only sixteen months, barely perceived the complexity of the slavery issue that was convulsing the nation, suggested oversimplified solutions, and threatened to veto Clay's compromise resolutions. His lack of leadership virtually forced the Senate to take the dominant role it was to maintain in public policy until the election of Lincoln. The following editorial assesses Taylor's administration and questions the advisability of electing military men to high office. The editorial, reprinted here in part, appeared in June 1850, a month before Taylor died in office.

Source: *United States Magazine and Democratic Review*, June 1850.

MILITARY GLORY has ever been the idol of mankind — the subject on which poetry, tradition, and history have most delighted to dwell. Like beauty in women, it hides a multitude of faults and attracts by an irresistible fascination. Nor is it without reason that successful warriors are objects of such general admiration; for the man who has shown himself capable of defending or vindicating the rights and honor of his country in time of danger possesses the highest claim to its confidence and gratitude. Success in war, though it may sometimes be the result of accident or good fortune in a single instance, yet, if uniform and long continued, furnishes decided evidence of courage and capacity, at least in military affairs; and when earned in a righteous cause, merits the highest distinction among men.

But it does not follow that a man who has gained a victory, or a succession of victories, is for that reason qualified to govern the country he has defended. The duties of a civil magistrate are widely different from those of a military commander and require different qualifications. Military laws and regulations are in direct contrast to the civil rights of free citizens; and that principle of complete subordination which lies at the root of the one is totally incompatible with that freedom of action and political equality which constitute the basis of the other.

The President of the United States, although the nominal commander in chief of the Army and Navy, is not expected to take the field or go on a cruise to the distant regions of the earth; for he cannot do so without deserting his most important duties as a civil magistrate, and virtually abdicating his authority at home for the purpose of exercising it abroad. It is not, therefore, his military skill or capacity for leading armies but his civil courage, his qualifications as a statesman, and his experience in political affairs that are brought into requisition when placed in a position to give tone and character to the government. Military talent is not what we want in a president. We require a man versed in the foreign and internal policy of the country, and the character, the rights, and the interests of the people; who comes into office not to learn, but to teach; not to be governed, but to govern. We want a leader, not a tool; we want a unit, not a cipher.

Washington was a military man, but not exclusively so. Those who have read his letters to the old revolutionary Congress, governors of states, and distinguished contemporaries, during the progress of the great struggle for liberty, will at once perceive that he was a statesman as well as a soldier; that his counsel and suggestions influenced almost every act and measure of Congress; and that his wisdom in the cabinet was equal to his valor and conduct in the field. Through a period of eighty years of intestine war, he was at school, learning the art of government; and almost his first action after laying down the sword was as president of the Convention which framed the Constitution of the United States. Here, surrounded by statesmen, sages, and philosophers, he listened to discussions involving the great fundamental principles of civil and religious liberty, the rights of states, and of citizens, and the entire circle of political science. He came, therefore, into the presidency deeply imbued with a thorough comprehension of its duties and a clear perception of the great landmarks which were to direct him in the exercise of his high functions as chief executive officer of the United States. He had the chart before him and steered the ship accordingly; with what success, it is unnecessary to state. The history of the country is his best eulogium, and the admiration of the world his everlasting monument.

General Jackson is also principally known to the world as a military man. But he, too, like Washington, had been schooled in civil life before he undertook to direct the affairs of his country. He had sat on the bench; in Congress; and at two different periods, once in his youth and next in mature age, in the Senate of the United States. He was a judge and a legislator as well as a soldier, and did not spring at one bound from the camp to the cabinet. But even had not this been the case, Andrew Jackson was an extraordinary man; such a man as we see but once in an age, and sometimes in many ages. We never saw Washington, and it has always been a subject of deep regret that we could not embody from memory the form and features of one of the noblest beings that ever trod the earth. But we knew Andrew Jackson from having been domesticated with him at Washington during the winter immediately succeeding the war of 1814; and especially from sharing his hospitality for some weeks at the Hermitage, about two years before he became immortal in both worlds.

He was indeed an extraordinary man; the only man we ever saw that excited our admiration to the pitch of wonder. At the period in which we visited him at the Hermitage, he was in a state of great physical debility; but his intellect was as clear and bright as ever. He was but the shadow of a man, and it seemed that the only principle of vitality by which he was supported was the vigor of his mind. Tall, straight as an arrow, without flesh, and with a profusion of snow-white hair, his appearance was sublime; and his manner more kind, graceful, and benevolent than that of any man who has ever fallen under our observation. It was not the studied politeness of conventional habits but the courtesy of the heart; and his deportment toward his family, his guests, and his slaves was that of a patriarch of old presiding over his flocks, his herds, and his dependents. At this period he might be almost said to live without food, for he ate less than an infant. His long table was almost every day crowded by visitors from different quarters, who came from far and near to see him; and though he sat down with them and shared in the gay freedom of the hospitable board, he never tasted anything but a little rice and milk.

We cannot better indicate the character of his intellect than by saying he was a man to whom knowledge seemed entirely unnecessary. He saw intuitively into everything, and though he seemed never to take aim deliberately, was always sure to hit the mark. He had a shortcut by which he reached a conclusion while others were beating the bush for their game. His reasoning was impulse, and his impulses inspiration. His genius and his courage were his guides. One pointed out the path; the other prompted him in the pursuit. He never sought an object that he did not succeed in attaining and never fought a battle that he did not win. His political opponents ascribed his success to good fortune; but fortune, though she often does us a single good turn, soon becomes tired of tagging at the heels of imbecility and folly. To always win is the best proof of skill in the player.

He began his public career in Tennessee, where the men are all brave and the women handsome, and was one of the early settlers at a period when — as an old lady who came up with the first party to Nashville once told us — "there was neither law or gospel." In such a state of things, personal qualities give the law and courage assumes its proper rank as the first, because it is the great conservative of all the other virtues, which never are to be depended upon in any man who may be frightened out of them. Here he soon gained that ascendancy over the wild spirits he had to cope with, which he ever after maintained in his intercourse with his fellowmen. Many anecdotes are told in Nashville of his quick decision, his indomitable courage, and inflexible determination, but we forbear to give them in this brief sketch. It is sufficient to say that he became the master spirit among men who had no other master. There was nothing on earth he despised so much as cowardice, and his highest eulogium on his favorite, General Coffee, whose fine portrait hung up in the sitting room, was, "Sir, he was as brave a man as ever lived." When he returned home from the Battle of New Orleans, it was to inhabit a log house, which was still standing at the time of our visit, and occupied by two or three superannuated slaves, one of whom had been Mrs. Jackson's nurse.

As might be expected, the administration of such a man was brilliant and successful. He seized the helm at once. He did not shrink from the high functions delegated to him by the Constitution, and which no man has a right to shuffle off on others, but took the responsibility of his own acts on his own shoulders. He wrestled with and overcame the most potent engine of corruption that ever existed in the United States. He scattered to the winds its pensioned tools, in and out of Congress, for he rested for support on his own integrity, and that of an uncorrupted people who sustained him manfully, as they always have done and always will an honest and courageous ruler who does not shrink from that terror to weak and dishonest minds — "responsibility."

Of General Harrison it is unnecessary to speak as he died before his acts could give character to his administration.

The fourth military President is the gentleman who now occupies that high and unique station. We have, heretofore, spoken of the illustrious dead, and shall now speak of the illustrious living, we trust, with equal justice, though not with equal praise. As to General Taylor's military talents, we accord with the sentiment of the people who elected him; although we cannot help expressing an opinion that there is a certain contemporary of his who has equaled the first conqueror of Mexico in skill and valor, and far exceeded him in clemency and generosity, who, if military exploits in two wars are to be the tests, might well dispute the palm with the hero of Buena Vista. In saying this, we neither wish to elevate one nor undermine the other. Both well deserve the gratitude of their country; both were followed by armies of heroes; and both were worthy to lead them.

But General Taylor, though crowned with well-earned laurels, we fear is neither a Washington nor a Jackson. His whole life has been a series of military services, ending in a blaze of glory. He is, according to his own frank and honest declarations, utterly unskilled in matters of state and divested of all experience in civil affairs. Far be it from us to object to any man being President of the United States because he is not a hack-

neyed politician, initiated into all the mysteries of party squabbles and personal rivalries, from which men but too often learn nothing but paltry tricks and stratagems to overreach each other and become mere political pettifoggers. Still we cannot help thinking a man should know something besides marshaling a squadron in the field before he aspires to the presidency of the most powerful republic in the world. It is not every general who has gained a victory, or a series of victories, that is worthy of such exalted honors or capable of sustaining such stupendous duties. If he is not one of nature's most chosen productions, either self-made or self-taught, he should be matured by study and reflection, and, above all, experience in preparatory stations, to supply the absence of genius or innate capacity, else there may be great danger that the laurels reaped in the field will be withered in the cabinet.

Is General Taylor thus qualified by nature, or by study and experience? We are compelled to shake our heads and doubt, if not decide. It may be urged in reply to this that the President has as yet done nothing by which his capacity for the duties of his high station could be tested, and that our opinion is therefore premature. It is from the very fact of his having done nothing but look on that we are obliged to doubt his capacity to do anything else. He has been in office more than a year, during a great portion of which the country has been almost convulsed by internal sectional struggles, and when, if ever, the direct and vigorous exercise of all the executive wisdom and influence in allaying it was not only justifiable but obligatory on him, and what has he done? If he has not fed the fire or blown the coals of dissension, he has stood looking on as an idle spectator. So far from doing anything good, bad, or indifferent, it is universally understood that he has voluntarily divested himself of all power of action by abdicating his authority to those who it would appear are afraid or ashamed of the responsibility of its exercise in anything but removing officers and settling old accounts.

Nothing but an innate consciousness of incurable incompetency can justify a man, chosen by the free suffrages of a great people to administer the laws of the land and direct the foreign policy of their government, in thus throwing down his arms and surrendering at discretion to his ministers. A man so brave in the field as General Taylor should not exhibit such a cowardly will in the cabinet. The people require and have a right to require something from their chief magistrate, a little beyond the incarnation of King Log of the Fable. They bestowed certain powers on him and him alone; and for the exercise of these they expect him to be responsible. They don't want to be governed at second hand, and look to subordinates for what should be done by the principal or at least by his direction.

There is a little too much of royalty in this to be relished by republicans. It may do very well for a king by divine or hereditary right to shield himself from all responsibility for his acts of folly, caprice, or oppression by throwing it on his ministers, and thus securing himself from the just indignation of the people. But it won't do here. The President of the United States must stand before the people at full length, in his own proper person, and be judged like other men by his own acts, and not lag behind his corporals in the day of battle. There cannot be a more antirepublican policy than this, or one more directly calculated to undermine and destroy the force of public sentiment, when brought to bear on the acts and policy of the administration.

The public disapprobation, if thus excited, must concentrate itself not on the principal offender but his mere instruments, who thus become the scapegoats of him, by whom they are chosen and changed at pleasure. In

this way a President virtually evades all personal responsibility for his measures by laying the blame on his ministers for an unpopular act, and exemplifies the doctrine of legitimacy, that "the king can do no wrong," because of himself he does nothing.

Justice to a brave, and we fully believe an upright, man, compels us here distinctly to admit that in adopting this course of policy the President has deceived nobody and violated no pledges. When invited to become a candidate for the presidency, he frankly acknowledged his incapacity and entire want of experience in civil affairs; and if the people who elected him did not take him at his word, it is their fault, not his. He gave them fair warning that they must take him for better or for worse. He intimated to them pretty distinctly that they must make choice of two alternatives, namely: either of being governed by a man without a particle of the knowledge and experience necessary to the task, or by deputies for the wise and discreet selection of whom this same want of knowledge and experience in a great measure disqualified him. We are far from blaming the President for adopting this latter course. Necessity has no law; and what a man cannot do for himself, he must either leave undone or get others to do for him.

We, however, take leave respectfully to observe that, in our opinion, the President cannot be fully justified in aspiring to a station for which, according to his own acknowledgment, he was so eminently disqualified. He should have rested under the shade of his laurels and been content to pass onward to future generations as a gallant, successful warrior rather than an incompetent statesman. There is great wisdom in knowing where to stop and when to retire; and history is filled with examples of men who broke their necks by walking over a precipice for want of this saving discretion.

12.

Massachusetts Compulsory Schooling Law

Since early colonial times Massachusetts had led the other states in making education available to its citizens. But availability did not necessarily insure attendance. Many children worked at home, in factories, or as apprentices. Others simply did not go to school. To remedy this situation, the state legislature passed the following compulsory schooling law in 1850. In 1852 the act was amended to require formal education for all children between the ages of eight and fourteen for at least three months of the year.

Source: *Acts and Resolves Passed by the General Court of Massachusetts in the Years 1849, 1850, 1851*, Boston, 1851, pp. 468-469.

Section 1. Each of the several cities and towns in this Commonwealth is hereby authorized and empowered to make all needful provisions and arrangements concerning habitual truants and children not attending school, without any regular and lawful occupation, growing up in ignorance, between the ages of six and fifteen years; and also all such ordinances and bylaws respecting such children as shall be deemed most conducive to their welfare and the good order of such city or town; and there shall be annexed to such ordinances suitable penalties, not exceeding, for any one breach, a fine of $20. *Provided*, that said ordinances and bylaws shall be approved by the Court of Common Pleas for the county, and shall not be repugnant to laws of the Commonwealth.

Section 2. The several cities and towns availing themselves of the provisions of this act shall appoint, at the annual meetings of said towns, or annually by the mayor and aldermen of said cities, three or more persons who alone shall be authorized to make the complaints, in every case of violation of said ordinances or bylaws, to the justice of the peace or other judicial officer, who, by said ordinances, shall have jurisdiction in the matter; which persons, thus appointed, shall alone have authority to carry into execution the judgments of said justices of the peace or other judicial officer.

Section 3. The said justices of the peace or other judicial officers shall in all cases, at their discretion, in place of the fine aforesaid, be authorized to order children, proved before them to be growing up in truancy and without the benefit of the education provided for them by law, to be placed, for such periods of time as they may judge expedient, in such institution of instruction or house of reformation or other suitable situation, as may be assigned or provided for the purpose, under the authority conveyed by Section 1 of this act, in each city or town availing itself of the powers herein granted.

13.

Francis Wayland: Schooling Adapted to all Classes in Society

*American institutions of higher education were originally patterned after their
European counterparts both in curriculum and make-up of student body. But well
before the middle of the nineteenth century it had become evident that the nature
of American society was making previous educational methods unworkable. The
number of men who trained for the learned professions decreased, while more
and more Americans became involved in commerce, agriculture, and industry.
In a democratic society there was less prestige attached to scholarship and more
to an active life, which could lead as well to positions of eminence and respect.
To college presidents such as Francis Wayland of Brown University, it was clear
that the schools must broaden their appeal or they would lose both financial support
and students. The following selection from his* Report of March 28, 1850, *outlines
the plight of higher education and offers some remedies.*

Source: *Report to the Corporation of Brown University, on Changes in the
System of Collegiate Education,* Providence, 1850, pp. 20-61.

In the early history of New England, the colleges supported themselves. They had no endowments, there were no education societies, nor was there any provision for the support of indigent students. While these changes, however, were going forward in the course of education, it was found that the means of the colleges were diminishing. Their fees were unable to pay the instructors, and many of them were running in debt. This may, in part, have been owing to the increase of their number, occasioned by the differences in religious opinion which arose some thirty years since in New England. A more important reason, however, is found in the relative changes in the masses of society, which, within this period, have been rapidly going forward.

It is manifest to the most casual observer, that the movement of civilization is precisely in the line of the useful arts. Steam, machinery, and commerce, have built up a class of society which formerly was only of secondary importance. The inducements to enter the learned professions have become far less, and those to enter upon the active professions, vastly greater. The most coveted positions in society, seats in our highest legislative chambers, and even foreign embassies await the successful merchant or manufacturer, no less than him who has devoted his life to what is called a learned profession. And yet more; the number of those who consider a collegiate education indispensable to a profession, has, for some time, been rapidly decreasing. . . .

From these, or some other causes, it is the fact that, within the last thirty years or more, it has been found that the colleges of New England could not support themselves.

The fact is, they were originally schools for merely the learned professions, and the proportion of those who desired a professional education was growing less. It is true the sciences which relate to practical life were taught in them, but they were taught only in reference to the professions. The portion of time allotted to them, was merely sufficient to communicate that knowledge which was considered needful for a lawyer, or a clergyman; the physician pursued these studies in the regular course of his profession. The demand for the article produced in the colleges was falling off, not from the want of wealth . . . but really because a smaller number of the community desired it.

In this dilemma, two courses were again open before the colleges. The first was to adapt the article produced, to the wants of the community. Inasmuch as a less number desired to enter the learned professions, and those who were entering them, did not, in many cases, prefer this mode of preparation, the sources from which students were supplied to the colleges seemed to be drying up. But here were large and intelligent classes of citizens who needed education, though not such education as the colleges afforded. These institutions might then have been at once modified, and their advantages extended, not to *one class* merely, but to *every class* which needed a scientific and liberal education. In this manner, they might probably have been enabled still to support themselves. The other course was to appeal to the charity of the public, and thus provide funds by which the present system might be sustained.

The second course was adopted. Funds were contributed in behalf of most of the New England colleges, to a very large amount. These were at first, if we do not mistake, for the purpose of reducing the fees of tuition. When this was done for one college, it must soon be done for all, for students tend to the cheapest college, as certainly as purchasers repair to him who sells at the lowest price. But this was not found sufficient. Soon funds began to be provided, in addition to those granted by education societies, by which a large number of students might obtain *gratuitous* tuition. In some cases a portion of these beneficiaries also received room rent and furniture free.

Such is now the course to which nearly all the colleges in New England, to a greater or less degree, are tending. They determined to restrict a collegiate education to the instruction required in a preparation for the professions. The demand for this kind of education decreased. It could not be disposed of at cost. The first effort made was to provide the means for furnishing it below cost. When it could not be sustained at this reduction, the next effort made was to furnish a large part of it gratuitously. Hence, if it be desired to render a college prosperous, we do not so much ask in what way can we afford the best education, or confer the greatest benefit on the community, but how can we raise funds, by which our tuition may be most effectually either reduced in price, or given away altogether?

It deserves to be remarked, that to these calls in behalf of the colleges, the people of New England have responded nobly. An immense sum of money has, within the last thirty years, been contributed among us, for the purposes of collegiate education. . . . These endowments have been created by benevolent men deserving of all praise. . . .

The objects designed to be accomplished by endowments for the reduction of tuition and for furnishing it gratuitously in our colleges, have been, we suppose, the following:

First, to increase the number of educated men in the whole community.

Second, to raise the standard of professional learning, and thus increase its intellectual power.

Third, to increase the number of the ministers of the Gospel.

It will be granted that, in just so far as

Francis Wayland, president of Brown University

the present system has accomplished these objects, it has succeeded; and just insofar as it has not accomplished them, it has failed. . . . It appears then, that if the institution is to be maintained, some means must be adopted for its relief. The question to be considered is: What shall these means be?

In the first place, however, it is proper to inquire whether the instruction and discipline of the institution have rendered it less worthy than formerly of the favor of the public. If any fault exists here, the remedy is obvious. The present officers should be removed, and their places supplied by such persons as can command the confidence of the friends of the college. Should the corporation be of the opinion that no change in this respect is necessary, we must look for relief in some other direction.

If it be determined to sustain the institution, two methods of accomplishing this object present themselves. The first is, to continue it upon its present system, retaining the four years' course; considering the college as a mere preparatory school for the professions of Law, Medicine and Divinity; and adjusting the various branches of instruction in conformity with this idea. To accomplish this object, at our present rate of numbers, would probably require a fund of $50,000. This would enable the corporation to pay a more remunerating salary to the officers, and improve the condition of the college in several essential particulars. It would, however, do nothing, or very little, either to reduce the cost of tuition or render it gratuitous. It would not, therefore, increase the number of students. To accomplish this object, it is probable that a much greater outlay would be necessary.

But, if the views entertained in the previous part of this report be correct, it may be doubted whether this would be more than a temporary expedient. The reduction of tuition might avail, so long as our terms were lower than those of other colleges; but so soon as theirs were reduced to the same level, we must provide the means for still further reduction. It seems to your committee undesirable, that the colleges of our country should, by any contingency, be enlisted in a competition of this nature.

The question deserves to be considered, whether the funds necessary to accomplish this object could be raised. On this subject, your committee dare not speak with confidence. They are aware of the attachment of the graduates of this college to the place of their education; and they have confidence in the enlightened liberality of their fellow citizens. But of the degree in which this object would commend itself to their good offices, they are not prepared to determine. It is, however, obvious, that if the competition be determined by capital, this institution may as well decline it at the outset.

A second method of relieving the institution from its present embarrassments has been proposed, suggested from the view which your committee has been led to take by the present condition of collegiate education in New England.

If it be the fact that our colleges cannot sustain themselves but are obliged to make repeated calls upon the benevolence of the community, not because the community is poor and education inordinately expensive but because, instead of attempting to furnish scientific and literary instruction to every class of our people, they have furnished it only to a single class, and that by far the least numerous; if they are furnishing an education for which there is no remunerative, but even at the present low prices, a decreasing demand; if they are, not by intention but practically, excluding the vastly larger portion of the community from advantages in which they would willingly participate, and are thus accomplishing but a fraction of the good which is manifestly within their power, then it would seem that relief must be expected from a radical change of the system of collegiate instruction. We must carefully survey the wants of the various classes of the community in our own vicinity, and adapt our courses of instruction, not for the benefit of one class but for the benefit of all classes.

The demand for general education in our country is pressing and universal. The want of that science, which alone can lay the foundation of eminent success in the useful arts, is extensively felt. The proportion of our young men who are devoting themselves to the productive professions is great and annually increasing. They all need such an education as our colleges, with some modifications in their present system, could very easily supply. Is there not reason to believe that, if such an education were furnished, they would cheerfully avail themselves of it?

Were an institution established with the intention of adapting its instruction to the wants of the whole community, its arrangements would be made in harmony with the following principles.

1. The present system of adjusting collegiate study to a fixed term of four years, or to any other term, must be abandoned and every student be allowed, within limits to be determined by statute, to carry on, at the same time, a greater or lesser number of courses as he may choose.

2. The time allotted to each particular course of instruction would be determined by the nature of the course itself, and not by its supposed relation to the wants of any particular profession.

3. The various courses should be so arranged, that, insofar as it is practicable, every student might study what he chose, all that he chose, and nothing but what he chose. The faculty, however, at the request of a parent or guardian, should have authority to assign to any student such courses as they might deem for his advantage.

4. Every course of instruction, after it has been commenced, should be continued without interruption until it is completed.

5. In addition to the present courses of instruction, such should be established as the wants of the various classes of the community require.

6. Every student attending any particular course should be at liberty to attend any other that he may desire.

7. It would be required that no student be admitted as a candidate for a degree unless he had honorably sustained his examination in such studies as may be ordained by the corporation; but no student would be under any obligation to proceed to a degree unless he chose.

8. Every student would be entitled to a certificate of such proficiency as he may have made in every course that he has pursued.

The courses of instruction to be pursued in this institution might be as follows:

1. A course of instruction in Latin, occupying two years.

2. A course of instruction in Greek, occupying two years.

3. A course of instruction in three modern languages.

4. A course of instruction in pure mathematics, two years.

5. A course of instruction in mechanics, optics, and astronomy, either with or without mathematical demonstrations, 1½ years.

6. A course of instruction in chemistry, physiology and geology, 1½ years.

7. A course of instruction in the English language and rhetoric, one year.

8. A course of instruction in moral and intellectual philosophy, one year.

9. A course of instruction in political economy, one term.

10. A course of instruction in history, one term.

11. A course of instruction in the science of teaching.

12. A course of instruction on the principles of agriculture.

13. A course of instruction on the application of chemistry to the arts.

14. A course of instruction on the applicaton of science to the arts.

15. A course of instruction in the science of law.

Some of these courses would require a lesson or lecture every working day of the week, others only two or three in the week. Any professor might be allowed to conduct the studies of more than one course, if he could do it with advantage to the institution. Should this idea be adopted, and the instruction given in this college be arranged on these principles, it would be seen that opportunity would be afforded to modify it as experience should prove desirable. . . .

That such a change as is here proposed would add to the number of its pupils seems to your committee probable for several reasons.

1. The course of instruction will, it is hoped, present a better preparation for the learned professions than that pursued at present. There is no reason, therefore, why this class of pupils should be diminished.

2. Opportunity would be afforded to those who wished to pursue a more generous course of professional education to remain in college profitably for five or six years, instead of four as at present.

3. Many young men who intend to enter the professions are unwilling or unable to spend four years in the preparatory studies of college. They would, however, cheerfully spend one or two years in such study, if they were allowed to select such branches of science as they chose. This class would probably form an important addition to our numbers, and we should thus, in some degree, improve the education of a large portion of all the professions.

4. If we except the ancient languages, there are but few of the studies now pursued in college which, if well taught, would not be attractive to young men preparing for any of the active departments of life. If these several courses were so arranged as to be easily accessible to intelligent young men of all classes, it may reasonably be expected that many will desire to spend a term, a year, or two years under our instruction.

5. It is not probable that the courses of instruction in agriculture, or chemistry, or science applied to the arts, will, of necessity, occupy all the time of the student. Many of these persons will probably desire to avail themselves of the advantages so easily placed in their power. Another source of demand for the courses in general science would thus be created.

Should these expectations be realized, it will be perceived that the addition to our numbers will come from classes who now receive no benefit whatever from the college system as it at present exists. Our numbers would thus be increased without diminishing the number of students in other colleges in New England; and we should be carrying the blessings of scientific and literary education to portions of society from which they have thus far been practically excluded.

Perhaps it may not be inappropriate to add that if the above views be correct, any college in our country now able to support itself might easily adopt, to a considerable extent, the system we have ventured to recommend. Its means now are its funds and its fees for tuition. It is not supposed that the number of its students could be diminished by offering its advantages to vastly larger classes of the community. Supposing its numbers to be the same, it would have the same means of support as at present. There would seem, therefore, to be no particular risk in trying the experiment, since its resources will be increased by every student that it may attract from those classes of society that now yield it no income.

If reasons need be offered for attempting the changes in our collegiate system that have been here indicated, the following will readily suggest themselves.

1. It is just. Every man who is willing to pay for them, has a right to all the means which other men enjoy, for cultivating his mind by discipline, and enriching it with science. It is therefore unjust, either practically or theoretically, to restrict the means of this cultivation and discipline to one class, and that the smallest class in the community. . . .

We have in this country 120 colleges, 42 theological seminaries, and 47 law schools, and we have not a single institution designed to furnish the agriculturist, the manufacturer, the mechanic, or the merchant with the education that will prepare him for the profession to which his life is to be devoted. Our institutions of learning have generally been endowed by the wealth of the productive classes of society. It is surely unjust that a system should be universally adopted which practically excludes them from the benefits which they have conferred upon others.

2. It is expedient. The moral conditions being equal, the progress of a nation in wealth, happiness, and refinement, is measured by the universality of its knowledge of the laws of nature, and its skill in adapting these laws to the purposes of man.

Civilization is advancing, and it can only advance in the line of the useful arts. It is, therefore, of the greatest national importance to spread broadcast over the community that knowledge by which alone the useful arts can be multiplied and perfected. Every producer who labors in his art scientifically is the best of all experimenters; and he is, of all men, the most likely, by discovery, to add to our knowledge of the laws of nature. He is, also, specially the individual most likely to invent the means by which those laws shall be subjected to the service of man. Of the truth of these remarks, everyone must be convinced who will observe the success to which any artisan arrives, who, fortunately, by his own efforts (for at present he could do it in no other way) has attained to a knowledge of the principles which govern the process in which he is employed. . . .

Probably no country on earth can boast of as intelligent a class of mechanics and manufacturers as our own. Had a knowledge of the principles been generally diffused among them, we should already have outstripped Europe in all those arts which increase the comforts or multiply the refinements of human life. Perhaps, in the earlier history of our country, such knowledge would not have been adequately appreciated. That period, however, has now passed away. An impulse has been given to common school education, which cannot but render every man definitely sensible of his wants, and consequently eager to supply them. The time then would seem to have arrived when our institutions of learning are called upon to place themselves in harmony with the advanced and rapidly advancing condition of society.

3. It is necessary. To us, it seems that but little option is left to the colleges in this matter. Anyone who will observe the progress which, within the last thirty years, has been made by the productive classes of society, in power, wealth, and influence, must

be convinced that a system of education practically restricted to a class vastly smaller, and rapidly decreasing in influence, cannot possibly continue. Within a few years, the manufacturing interest has wrung the Corn Laws from the aristocracy of Great Britain. Let anyone recall the relative position of the professions and of the mercantile and manufacturing interests in any of our cities twenty years since, and compare it with their relative position now, and he cannot but be convinced that a great and a progressive change has taken place.

Men who do not design to educate their sons for the professions are capable of determining upon the kind of instruction which they need. If the colleges will not furnish it, they are able to provide it themselves; and they will provide it. In New York and Massachusetts, incipient measures have been taken for establishing agricultural colleges. The bill before the legislature of New York provides for instruction in all the branches taught in our colleges with the exception of languages. It is to be, in fact, an institution for giving all the education which we now give, agricultural science being substituted for Latin and Greek.

What is proposed to be done for the farmers must soon be done either for or by the manufacturers and merchants. In this manner, each productive department will have its own school in which its own particular branch of knowledge will be taught, besides the other ordinary studies of a liberal education. A large portion of the instruction communicated will thus be the same in all. Mathematics, mechanics, chemistry, physiology, rhetoric, moral and intellectual philosophy, and political economy will be taught in them all. The colleges teach precisely the same sciences, with the addition of Latin and Greek, in the place of the knowledge designed in these separate schools for a particular profession.

If the *prestige* of colleges should be thus destroyed and it be found that as good an education as they furnish can be obtained in any of those other schools, the number of their students will be seriously diminished. If, by this dissemination of science among all the other classes of society, the tendency toward the professions should be still farther arrested, the colleges will be deserted by yet larger numbers. They may become very good foundations for the support of instructors, but very few will be found to avail themselves of their instructions. . . .

Would it not seem desirable that they should so far modify their system as to furnish all the instruction needed by the various classes of society, who desire special professional teaching, and so arrange their courses of general knowledge that all, of every class, may with equal facility avail themselves of their advantages? In this manner the colleges will reap all the benefit arising from the diffusion and progress of knowledge. Pursuing any other course, they would seem to suffer injury from one of the most hopeful indications of the progress of civilization.

The cowards never started and the weak ones died by the way.
Slogan of the Society of California

Bring Me Men to Match My Mountains.
Inscription in the State Library, Sacramento, California

14.

Anonymous: Railroad Land Grants

Demands for better systems of transportation throughout the nation were met by government grants of public land for canal and railroad construction. The earliest large scale subsidy was initiated by Stephen A. Douglas, a congressman from Illinois, who managed to secure for his sponsors about two and a half million acres of land between Chicago and Mobile, Alabama, for the building of the Illinois Central Railroad. Congress was soon swamped with similar requests, and within the next twenty years much of the choicest land in the West was given or sold to railroad speculators. The strongest argument in support of federal grants was that the railway lines would encourage settlement in desolate areas not reached by natural waterways or other transportation routes. The following portion of an 1850 magazine article tells the value of a projected Pacific Railroad to the areas beyond the Mississippi River.

Source: *Western Journal*, October 1850.

In regard to the Pacific Railroad, the surveys of which have been in active progress during the whole of this season, the effect of the loss of this bill may be to delay its definite location for a time; but this delay, if it should occur, could not extend beyond the termination of the next session of Congress, on March 4, 1851. The commencement of construction at St. Louis, would necessarily experience a similar suspension. This short delay does not, however, represent all the evil which this enterprise may suffer from the rejection of the land bill, unless our citizens rally and take some steps to make their existence better felt at Washington.

In all undertakings of this kind, it is the few who clearly perceive the advantages to the state and to private property, and who tenaciously advocate and labor for it until their endeavors are successful. The many without whose aid they cannot proceed, flow to it with the flood which generally attends its first conception, but are equally ready to drop from it with every apparent

ebb. They have not equally studied its effects and creative properties; the conviction of its advantages is, with them, one of credit rather than personal examination, and any occurrence increasing the difficulties of the project, tends to excite their distrust and shake their confidence.

In the state of Missouri, all are so much interested in the commencement and vigorous prosecution of some one leading railroad, which shall at the same time give life to the resources of the section through which it passes, and encouragement and credit to similar roads in other sections of the state, that we may look for less hindrance from this timidity, than usually prevails in the commencement of works of the same extent. Its existence, however, more or less, is one of the discouraging features of all enterprises of this kind, and the present occasion is one to call it into life.

In connection with the Pacific Railroad, we have thus far been wonderfully exempt from it. The directors of that railroad must have felt encouraged and gratified, by the hearty support which they have received at every point coming within the influence of this proposed road. This land bill is the first discouragement that has appeared. It is an important but not an insurmountable one, and will call forth, we trust, that personal action which the occasion demands. Upon the successful progress of this, the first railroad enterprise which has been earnestly taken hold of by our citizens, hinges the general faith in our ability as a state, to work out, like other neighboring states, the relief of our internal resources, by a prudent and successful system of rapid communications through the leading sections of the state, settling and cultivating the idle lands, opening their produce to the markets of the south and east, enabling the capital now lying dormant in the mining districts to procure a return, creating new establishments for the reduction of the metals, and enlarging, vastly, the trade and commerce of our cities.

If this road languishes now, our more enterprising neighbors to the east of the Mississippi, will look northward, from Springfield toward Carthage and Kanesville, for a passage to the Western country, and a connection with the great railroad enterprise of modern days, beyond the limits of this state, for it cannot be possible that the railroad from Hannibal to St. Joseph will be constructed, if the Pacific Railroad, with the wealth and interest of St. Louis to back it, fails to be sustained.

But that it will be sustained admits of but little doubt, if our citizens and the friends of the road sufficiently value their own interests to secure the earnest advocacy of their just claims at the coming session of Congress, and thereby the passage of the land bill then, as the cornerstone, on which depends, in a measure, the speedy construction of their railroad. Failing in that, there remains, doubtless, in this city, and in the southern counties of the route, ample means to make up the deficiency and build the road — but will that means be forthcoming with the emergency. Will not rather the discouragement attending this loss, and the hope that another session may correct it, lead to sluggish and temporizing action, extending the time of construction over double the number of years necessary under better influences?

On the supposition that justice will, under proper representations prevail, and that a land bill in aid of the Pacific Railroad will yet become a law, we propose to make a few remarks on certain provisions of the land bills of the late session.

The broad principle of these bills disclaims the propriety of affording aid in the shape of lands to any railroad company, without providing for the return, in some shape, of an equivalent in value. The correctness of the principle is conceded, but the manner of its application to this road and to the Hannibal Road is objectionable. In strict fairness the government should not seek to secure more than an equitable consideration for the present money value of the lands granted, and in policy it could well afford to accept of less, for the sake of hastening the completion of any link of that westerly communication, which by bringing it near to the Pacific coast and to the intervening lands now in possession of the Indians, places within its immediate practical control, countries which are now all but beyond its efficient reach. This policy has been liberally acted on already, in the case of the lines of steamships to Chagres and to Europe.

By one clause of the bill, the government arranges for the payment of the lands donated, by doubling the price of the alternate sections reserved. These reserved sections are thus made to pay for the lands conferred. By another clause the government further pays itself by requiring of the company the transportation of any "property or troops of the United States," "free from toll or other charge." . . . This double payment shows, it must be confessed, a cautious protection of the money rights of the government, and cannot be attacked as a liberal encouragement of great public improvements.

We contend that in the case of this particular road and also of the Hannibal and St. Joseph Railroad, looking on both as forks of a great road yet to be made to the Pacific, the government could well afford to grant them lands without providing for any equivalent on the face of the bill, the advantage in the shape of rapid and convenient transport and communication, and of a speedy settlement of the public lands, forming ample compensation on the narrowest grounds of trading practice.

The liberality contended for is one which is clearly for the interest of the giver as well as the receiver. It is one, as regards the land which is familiar in both state and county legislation, where, in the construction of new roads, the benefit conferred by the road or railroad is directed to be considered, in estimating the value of the lands applied to the purposes of the road.

It is a common provision in railroad charters in the Eastern states, that the damage done to lands in passing over them shall be compared with the benefit accruing to the land, and payment made only where that damage shall appear to exceed the benefit, and this provision is constantly acted on in land appraisements there. It is true that the United States does not receive the whole of this benefit as in the case of the settler, but it receives a large share of it in two ways. In the rapid sale of land on either side of the railroad which would otherwise have remained unsold, and have been disposed of after a time at reduced rates, and in the reduction of the annual outlay attending the action of land offices and land agents.

But these considerations we look upon as entirely secondary to the more important one of placing the central government in prompt communication with its distant states and territories. And as the Pacific Railroad of Missouri fulfills to the extent of 300 miles the last condition, as a link or branch of the great road to San Francisco, we are led to speak of the proposed railroad to the Pacific Ocean, which, to distinguish it from the Pacific Railroad of this state, will be named here the California Railroad.

The one prominent difficulty attending the construction of a railroad is usually that of the ways and means. The capital once obtained, the other difficulties of execution gradually vanish. The California Railroad project presents *two* prominent difficulties, which discussion will doubtless by-and-by solve. The first is the immense capital required. The second is the organization of a company or companies, and a system of management and operation practically applicable to the construction of 2,500 miles of one continuous route of railroad.

We hold that when a fair remuneration can be demonstrated, or predicated on reasonably just grounds, capital will be forthcoming, and a close scrutiny of the statistics of the last two years in connection with California, taking into consideration the still undeveloped commerce of the Pacific Ocean, will probably satisfactorily show that a fair return for the capital required could be depended on.

The second difficulty, is at this moment the great difficulty of the project. With a liberal grant of land from Congress, and ample means provided for the construction of the railroad, the efficient application of the means under proper control and within a limited time, would still form the problem to be solved: A clear perception of a businesslike mode of going to work, would go far to untie the knot which at present, more than any other feature of this great project, perplexes businessmen.

Independent of the value of this project as a private enterprise, and its pressing importance to California and Oregon, the government in the execution of its bureau duties is deeply interested in its speedy accomplishment. It is on account of this interest of state, of convenience and of economy on the part of the government proper, that it can afford to make large concessions whether in the shape of public lands or otherwise, to secure through private means the execution of this project, and this without further return than the important facilities which the road will afford it.

A connection with two most important states and their sea border on the Pacific, of six days instead of six weeks; the means of concentrating troops on such short notice upon any one of the Indian tribes; the opening of lands now beyond the reach of settlement to emigrants, and the commerce and security resulting thence — Are not these benefits worth more than any land which has been proposed to be granted? The more closely the considerations indicated are scrutinized, the more clearly will they be perceived to be advantages cheaply procured at the expense of any donation of land which the government will consent to give.

The distance of California and Oregon from the seat of government must render its control over the operations of its agents there, very unsatisfactory, and must oblige it to trust them with a discretionary power about as extensive as if they were established in the Mediterranean instead of in the United States. At Washington, the evils attending the lapse of time in receiving answers to important communications must be constantly felt in the State Department and in the Army and Navy departments. When there is no remedy, such evils are submitted to — where a remedy is at hand at a reasonable expense it will be coveted and procured.

To knit herself to her colonies, and have prompt communication with them, England created a steam post office marine at great expense but with most satisfactory results. Her relation with the Canadas now as respects time, is as intimate, as has been hitherto the city of Washington with Pensacola or New Orleans during the winter months, and greatly more intimate that those of our government with the territories and states west of Missouri. Acting on the same principles, our own government has at great expense established lines of steamboats to Chagres, and on the Pacific to San Francisco, and has in this way placed herself within six weeks and two months of California and Oregon.

But when these states become more densely settled, and a mercantile marine belonging to the Pacific coast is established on the Pacific in communication with China and Australia, the inconvenience attending this lapse of time in corresponding with the seat of government will become very serious. Members of Congress from these states will practically know little of the movements of their constituents, or their constituents of their congressional action, and unless that mode of communication is by that time in operation, which only can remedy the evil and bring all parties into intimate relation, it will become the interest, and may become the inclination of the states and territories on the Pacific slope, to form a separate government to which they can have ready access and by which their peculiar interests can be more promptly furthered.

Considerations of this character will affect the interior of Nebraska, New Mexico, and Utah, as well as the extreme Western coast. These inland territories are even more beyond the reach of regular communication than the California coast.

It is evident then, that the government is as pressingly interested, as are the Pacific states, in the construction of a railroad across the continent to the California coast, and that this railroad may become the necessary key to the permanent connection of the Atlantic and the Pacific states.

15.

Hillside Ditches and Circular Plowing

The first half of the nineteenth century witnessed a great migration of planters from the Southeastern Seaboard, where the soil had been exhausted from overuse, to the fertile Alabama-Mississippi Black Belt area. There the great cotton plantations thrived once more. However, by 1850, the land along the Eastern Coast, which had been described a generation earlier as a "scene of desolation . . . worn out, washed and gullied, so that scarcely an acre could be found in a place fit for cultivation," was being renovated by new agricultural methods. The following editorial, which appeared in an April issue of a Georgia newspaper, described the results obtained by one farmer in Twiggs County.

Source: *Milledgeville Federal Union*, April 23, 1850 [Commons, I, pp. 132-133].

Two QUESTIONS present themselves. One is — Could this desolation have been prevented? And the other — Can it be repaired or modified? A few days since, in common with the great mass of agriculturists in Georgia, we should have answered both of these questions in the negative. A recent visit, however, to our friend General Tarver, in Twiggs County, and a minute examination of his plantations in the vicinity of his residence have materially changed our opinion.

His lands there are as hilly and broken as any of the tablelands of Georgia; yet upon none cleared within the last few years was there a single gully or red hill to be seen, and, what is more, none will ever be seen as long as his present system is practised. He has not only succeeded in rendering secure and permanent his fresh land but has also taken fields abandoned by their former owners, and which are trenched by gullies thirty and twenty feet wide and as many deep, and whose hillsides have been too poor to yield the poorest grasses, and he is resuscitating and restoring them to a condition in which they will again be productive, filling up the gullies, and by a process that is as simple and economical as it is successful.

All who know General Tarver know that he is one of the largest and most successful planters in the South. He indulges in no theory that will not by its practical results commend itself. The system by which he has perfected such wonders is simply in his fresh lands so to conduct the water by trenches as to prevent washing, and in his old land so to conduct it as to accomplish this end and at the same time to repair the washes occasioned by the former rush of the water.

Before we had examined General Tarver's plantation, we had read much about and seen something of hillside ditches and circular plowing, but had no conception of what could be accomplished by either the one or the other. His successful experiments have enlisted the admiration of his neighbors and all who have noticed them. He has demonstrated the truth and practicability of the theory that he has practised; and if, as it has been said, he is a public benefactor who can cause two straws to grow where before but one grew, General Tarver is entitled to that epitaph. None can visit his Twiggs plantation without being forcibly struck with what Georgia would now be had her lands been tilled by such agriculturists, or what she would yet be were they under the control of men of his energy and practical skill.

16.

LEMUEL SHATTUCK: A Plan for the Promotion of Public Health

Lemuel Shattuck, a founder of the American Statistical Association, was appointed by the Massachusetts legislature in 1849 to head a commission to survey the public health. The report that he wrote and presented to the legislature on April 25, 1850, was the most comprehensive investigation made up to that time of sanitary conditions in a single state. Of the fifty recommendations made, all were eventually carried out, although it was not until 1869 that Massachusetts had a state Board of Health. Portions of the 1850 report are reprinted below.

Source: *Report of a General Plan for the Promotion of Public and Personal Health,*
Boston, 1850, pp. 109-206.

I. *We recommend that the laws of the state relating to public health be thoroughly revised, and that a new and improved act be passed in their stead.*

We suppose that it will be generally conceded that no plan for a sanitary survey of the state, however good or desirable, can be carried into operation unless established by law. The legislative authority is necessary to give it efficiency and usefulness. The efforts, both of associations and individuals, have failed in these matters. We have shown that the present health laws of the state are exceedingly imperfect, even for the general object for which they were designed; that it is difficult, and perhaps impracticable, to ascertain what precise powers they confer and what duties they require; and that they are not adapted, in any way, to the purposes of a sanitary survey. This must be apparent to anyone who may examine them.

There are two remedies for these defects: one, to amend the existing laws; and the other, to combine such amendments as it would be desirable to make with such provisions of the existing laws as it would be desirable to retain, and to present the whole together in this amended form, as a complete health act, repealing such acts as are inconsistent with its provisions. We prefer the latter remedy. It will be better understood and more easily carried into practice by the people. Such legislation has been common, in this state and elsewhere, in relation to this and other matters.

Entertaining these views, we suggest that

a general health law should be passed which should be comprehensive in its design and simple in its provisions, be adapted to the present circumstances of the state, and be so framed that it might be clearly understood and carried into practical operation; and which, while it would answer all the purposes of a general health act, as heretofore understood, would, at the same time, accomplish all the purposes of a sanitary survey. . . .

II. *We recommend that a General Board of Health be established, which shall be charged with the general execution of the laws of the state, relating to the enumeration, the vital statistics, and the public health of the inhabitants.*

The act establishing the Board of Education was one of the most important acts relating to common schools ever passed in Massachusetts. That central agency, under the guidance of its late talented secretary, has given to the cause of public education an importance, and to the common schools a standard of elevation and usefulness, not before attained. The cause of public health needs a similar central agency to give to the whole sanitary movement a uniform, wise, efficient, economical, and useful direction. If different local authorities, or individuals — not always possessed of the best means of information — are left to originate plans for their own guidance, and anything is done, they will be more likely to make unintentional mistakes and create unnecessary expense than if wise and able minds were devoted to the subject, and suggested what ought to be done, and the best and most economical mode of doing it.

Such an agency would have an exact knowledge of the condition of every city and town in the state, and by these means of information would be able to suggest the measures best adapted to the different circumstances. They would prevent a wasteful expenditure of money in imperfect or inefficient measures. The advantages which would result to the whole state and to every part of it — to each and all of the inhabitants — from the establishment of such a central General Board of Health, composed of the best scientific counsel and the best practical experience which the state can afford, having constant access to the most enlightened intellects and to a knowledge of the labors of the best practical men in the world, and assisted by at least one mind wholly devoted to the object in view, are too great to be fully seen at once, and can scarcely be overstated or overestimated.

The duties of the Board are pointed out in the 4th Section of the act. They are to have the general direction of each census; to superintend the execution of the sanitary laws of the state; to examine and decide upon sanitary questions submitted to them by public authorities; to advise the state as to the sanitary arrangements of public buildings and public institutions; to give instructions to local boards of health as to their powers and duties; to suggest local sanitary rules and regulations; to recommend such measures as they may deem expedient for the prevention of diseases and the promotion of the public health; and to report their proceedings annually to the state.

III. *We recommend that the Board, as far as practicable, be composed of two physicians, one counselor at law, one chemist or natural philosopher, one civil engineer, and two persons of other professions or occupations; all properly qualified for the office by their talents, their education, their experience, and their wisdom. . . .*

The Board should . . . contain:

1. Two physicians, at least, of scientific attainments and of extensive practical experience in their profession, thoroughly understanding sanitary science and deeply feeling the importance of wise sanitary measures.

2. One counselor at law, who, besides the general knowledge of law and medical jurisprudence which he could bring to the

purposes of the Board, might especially be able to investigate any legal question that might arise.

3. One chemist or natural philosopher. Many questions relating to the influence of the elements on the production or prevention of disease may require the special investigation of an experienced chemical philosopher, and this important branch of science should be ably represented at the Board.

4. One civil engineer possessing competent knowledge to determine the best methods of planning and constructing public works and the best architectural sanitary arrangements of public buildings, workshops, and private dwelling houses would be an exceedingly valuable member.

5. Two other persons of acknowledged intelligence, good judgment, and of practical experience in the common business affairs of life, and capable of investigating and fully understanding the principles of sanitary science, might compose the remainder. . . .

IV. *We recommend that the Board be authorized to appoint some suitable and competent person to be the secretary of the Board, who should be required to devote his whole time and energies to the discharge of the duties of his office, and be paid a proper salary for his services.* . . .

V. *We recommend that a local Board of Health be appointed in every city and town, who shall be charged with the particular execution of the laws of the state, and the municipal ordinances and regulations relating to public health, within their respective jurisdictions.* . . .

In Boston, the mayor and aldermen are constituted health commissioners and they appoint, annually, a Committee on Internal Health, on External Health, on Streets, on Drains and Sewers, on Water, and on Burial Grounds, each consisting of three members, who examine into all complaints and matters affecting the public health in their respective departments. The City Council choose, annually, the following officers:

1. A superintendent of streets to have the general care of sweeping and cleansing the streets, lanes, alleys, public walks, squares, etc., of the city.

2. A superintendent of common drains and sewers to superintend the location and construction of these important aids to comfort and health.

3. A Water Board to superintend the distribution of the inestimable blessing to health, which is now furnished in all desirable quantities by the Boston Water Works.

4. A city physician

to examine into all nuisances, sources of filth, and causes of sickness which may be on board of any vessel at any wharf within the harbor of Boston, or in any article which may have been landed from any vessel on any wharf or other place, and, under direction of the mayor and aldermen, to cause the same to be removed and destroyed; . . . to vaccinate all persons who may apply to his office for the purpose, and to give certificates of vaccination, without charge; . . . to attend upon all cases of disease in the jail [and] . . . within the city, whenever he shall be called upon by the health commissioners or overseers of the poor.

5. A port physician to be the physician of the city establishments at Deer Island, and to superintend the quarantine of all vessels and passengers which arrive in the harbor of Boston.

6. Five consulting physicians

in case of an alarm of any contagious, infectious, or other dangerous disease occurring in the city or neighborhood, to give the mayor or either branch of the City Council all such professional advice and information as they may request, with a view to the prevention of the said disease, and at all convenient times to aid and assist with their counsel and advice in all matters that relate to the preservation of the health of the inhabitants.

7. A city registrar to record births, marriages, and deaths, and to superintend the interment of the dead.

8. A city marshal to act as health officer; "from time to time to pass through the streets, alleys, and courts of the city to observe nuisances, to receive complaints from the inhabitants," etc.

Each of these departments is independent of the others. The superintendent of streets collects the street dirt and house dirt, deposits it in an outer limit of the city, and sells it as wanted. He also collects the house offal and delivers it at a given place within the city to contractors, who remove it without the city, and who paid $8,000 for it in 1849. The night soil is removed under the direction of the city marshal, the householders paying $3 per load for its removal in summer and $1.50 in winter. . . .

XV. *We recommend that provision be made for obtaining observations of the atmospheric phenomena, on a systematic and uniform plan, at different stations in the commonwealth.*

The atmosphere or air which surrounds the earth is essential to all living beings. Life and health depend upon it; and neither could exist without it. Its character is modified in various ways; but especially by temperature, weight, and composition; and each of these modifications have an important sanitary influence. . . .

The atmosphere is corrupted in various ways. Man himself cannot breathe the same air twice with impunity. Every minute of every day he appropriates to the vitalization of his blood 24 cu.in. of oxygen, and supplies its place with 24 cu.in. of carbonic acid gas. When present in large quantities, from whatever cause produced, carbonic acid gas is destructive of life. Charcoal burned in a close room is an illustration. Some other gases are also very destructive. The experiments of Thenard and Dupuytren proved that birds perish when the vapors of sulfureted hydrogen and ammonia exist in the atmosphere to the extent of a fifteenth-thousandth part; that dogs are deprived of life when the air contains a thousandth part; and that man cannot live when the air he breathes is impregnated with a

three-hundredth part; and suffers in corresponding degree when a less proportion of these poisonous gases exists. Persons frequently fall dead when entering a well, vault, tomb, sewer, or other place filled with these gases, or with stagnated air in which are diffused emanations from decomposing animal, vegetable, or mineral substances.

Such are a few only of the facts which illustrate the important agency of the atmosphere in the animal economy. What that peculiar condition is which produces a specific disease, or what changes produce different diseases, are as yet unknown; it has not been ascertained,

> because meteorological science, as connected with the propagation and spread of disease, is as yet in its infancy. We have, indeed, some knowledge of the influence of two of the obvious conditions, namely, those of heat and moisture; but of the action of the subtler agents, such as electricity and magnetism, the present state of science affords us little information. Still, there are unequivocal indications that there is a relation between the conditions of the atmosphere and the outbreak and progress of epidemic diseases, though we are as yet ignorant of the nature of that relation. . . .

Although we are as yet uninformed on this subject, it is unreasonable to suppose that we shall always remain so. It opens a vast field for examination, which is as yet almost entirely unexplored; but it promises results of great value and importance to science and to human life. The meteorological observations which have hitherto been made in this country have been published rather as contributions to general science than to show their specific relation to health. . . .

XVIII. *We recommend that, in erecting schoolhouses, churches, and other public buildings, health should be regarded in their site, structure, heating apparatus, and ventilation.*

To provide for all public buildings where large numbers of people congregate, an abundant and constant supply of air in its pure, natural state and of a proper temperature is a very important though difficult matter. It is so, too, in regard to private dwellings. It has received much theoretical and practical attention, and very many schemes have been devised to attain the object. Which of them is to be preferred, or whether any one as yet known is unobjectionable in a sanitary view, we are unprepared to decide. If the measures here proposed should be adopted, the General Board of Health would become acquainted with the different methods of constructing and ventilating public and private buildings and would be able to recommend to the local Boards of Health, and to the people generally, those plans which seem best adapted to the circumstances of each case. Such information would be of great importance, whether regarded as contributing to the pecuniary or sanitary welfare of the people.

XIX. *We recommend that, before erecting any new dwelling house, manufactory, or other building, for personal accommodation, either as a lodging house or place of business, the owner or builder be required to give notice to the local Board of Health of his intention and of the sanitary arrangements he proposes to adopt.*

XX. *We recommend that local Boards of Health endeavor to prevent or mitigate the sanitary evils arising from overcrowded lodging houses and cellar dwellings.*

Such places are universally acknowledged to be incompatible with health. The hints already given have shown the destructive influence of corrupted air. Such air exists in these places, to a great extent, and its deleterious effects should by all proper means be avoided. This matter has attracted much though not the undeserved attention of different sanitary inquirers. Dr. James Stewart, of New York, in March, this year, procured a census of the cellar population of that city, and found that 18,456 persons lived in 8,141 rooms, in 3,741 separate basements. This is about 1 in 25, or 4 percent of the whole population of the city. The proportion of such inhabitants is believed to be nearly as great in Boston. In Lowell and other places in the state, the same evil also exists. We are pleased that the present legislature, on the 21st of March, thought the subject of so much importance as to pass the subjoined act. It gives all requisite legal authority to regulate the matter:

Whenever the Board of Health of any city or town shall be satisfied, upon due examination, that any cellar room, tenement, or building, occupied as a dwelling place within such city or town is unfit for that purpose and a cause of nuisance or sickness either to the occupants or to the public, such Board of Health may issue a notice in writing to such persons, or any of them, requiring them to remove from or quit such cellar room, tenement, or building within such time as the said Board of Health may deem reasonable. And if the person or persons so notified, or any of them, shall neglect or refuse so to remove and quit within the time mentioned, it shall be lawful for such Board of Health to remove them forcibly and to close up such cellar room, tenement, or building, and the same shall not be again occupied as a dwelling place without the consent in writing of the Board of Health, under a penalty of not less than $10 nor more than $50, to be recovered by indictment of the owner or owners, if they shall have knowingly permitted the same to be so occupied.

XXI. *We recommend that open spaces be reserved in cities and villages for public walks; that wide streets be laid out; and that both be ornamented with trees.*

Such an arrangement would have a good effect upon the beauty and social enjoyments of the place; but it would have a greater effect upon its general sanitary condition. Vegetation would absorb much of the carbonic acid gas which is produced in so great superabundance in populous places and thus render the air more fit for respiration. Open spaces also would afford to the artisan and the poorer classes the advantages of fresh air and exercise in their occasional hours of leisure. . . .

XXV. *We recommend that measures be taken to ascertain the amount of sickness suffered in different localities; and among persons of different classes, professions, and occupations.* . . .

There are several reasons why this subject should be fully and carefully investigated and that exact facts in relation to different populations, existing under different circumstances, should be known. We shall allude to two principal ones only:

1. *It would subserve a pecuniary purpose.* The wealth of a country consists in its capacity for labor. That people who enjoy the greatest vital force — the highest degree of health — and apply it most skillfully to the production of wealth are the most wealthy. It is their capital, their means of subsistence. Persons who sustain a low vitality only generally have little skill to apply what they possess, contribute little or nothing to the general welfare, and may, and often actually do, become a public burden. This is one view.

Another presents itself in the vast number of associations existing under the names of friendly societies, health insurance companies, Odd Fellows, and other titles, the object of which is, directly or indirectly, by the payment of a certain sum, to secure support to the members during the contingency of sickness. For the stability of these societies, and the security of the members themselves it is necessary that the rate of sickness under different circumstances should be definitely ascertained. So long as it is not known, no just rates of payment can be established.

Some of the health insurance companies in this state have closed their business because they have had to pay out more than they received. Some lodges of Odd Fellows have also been obliged to curtail their payments. All these institutions are now groping in the dark in regard to these matters,

and many of them, it is believed, cannot exist under the rates of payment proposed to be made. A misapprehension of the principles on which they should have been founded and managed is a principal cause of their failure. Health insurance might be so managed as to be a legitimate business of a useful character.

2. *It would subserve a sanitary purpose,* and show the exact condition of the people. . . .

XXVII. *We recommend that every city and town in the state be required to provide means for the periodical vaccination of the inhabitants.* . . .

XXX. *We recommend that measures be taken to prevent or mitigate the sanitary evils arising from the use of intoxicating drinks and from haunts of dissipation.*

That intemperance is an enormous evil is universally acknowledged. That it is the cause of a vast amount of direct sanitary suffering — of unnecessary sickness and of unnecessary death — to those who indulge in it; and of a still greater amount of indirect sanitary suffering and death to their associates, relatives, and dependents is equally true. The evil consequences are so great and so widely diffused that they have long since arrested public attention. Good citizens, moral reformers, religious teachers, and other classes of philanthropists have deplored the evil and devised various measures for its removal. It still exists, however, and fills the cup of suffering and provides a premature grave for many and many a person who might otherwise have lived to become a blessing instead of a curse to humanity. It is unnecessary, however, here to discuss the subject. Through thousands of channels it is brought to public notice. These channels should be widened and deepened, and the number should be increased, until all shall feel their influence. Local Boards of Health, by a careful observation of the sanitary evils of intemperance, and the local and personal circumstances under which they occur, and by adopting and enforcing such salutary regulations as will remove or mitigate them, may confer an immeasurable benefit upon the people.

XXXI. *We recommend that the laws for taking inquests upon the view of dead bodies, now imposed upon coroners, be revised.*

In our judgment, every matter relating to life, to health, and to death should, to some extent, come under the cognizance of Boards of Health. The cause of the death of every person who dies should be fully known to them; and in their offices records of inquests upon dead bodies should be preserved. These Boards, and especially the medical health officers, are presumed to be better informed than others in relation to such questions as present themselves in investigations of this kind; and hence they would be able to act more intelligently and correctly. It sometimes happens that inquests are held when there is no occasion for them, and unnecessary expenses are incurred. . . .

XXXII. *We recommend that the authority now vested in justices of the peace relating to insane and idiotic persons not arrested or indicted for crime be transferred to the local Boards of Health.*

By the present laws of the state, no insane or idiotic person other than paupers can be committed to any hospital or place of confinement except on complaint, in writing, before two justices of the peace, or some police court. Paupers may be committed by the overseers of the poor. By these proceedings, this unfortunate class of persons appear on the records as criminals while they are guilty of no crime, unless the possession of an unsound mind be considered one. A sanitary question, merely, is often the only one presented in such cases, and it has occurred to us that the local Boards of Health would be the proper tribunals before whom they should be brought and by whom they should be dis-

posed of. It may be supposed that such Boards will be better acquainted, generally, with the medical jurisprudence of insanity than justices of the peace; and their decisions will be, more than those of criminal courts, in accordance with the spirit of humanity which has been extended to that class of persons.

XXXIII. *We recommend that the general management of cemeteries and other places of burial and of the interment of the dead be regulated by the local Boards of Health. . . .*

XXXVI. *We recommend that measures be adopted for preventing or mitigating the sanitary evils arising from foreign emigration. . . .*

The state should pass suitable laws on the subject, and the general and local Boards of Health should carefully observe these evils in all their sanitary bearings and relations. We would, however, suggest:

1. That emigration, especially of paupers, invalids, and criminals, should, by all proper means, be discouraged; and that misrepresentation and falsehood, to induce persons to embark in passenger ships, should be discountenanced and counteracted.

2. That ship owners and others should be held to strict accountability for all expenses of pauper emigrants, and that existing bonds for their support should be strictly enforced.

3. That a system be devised by which all emigrants, or those who introduce them, by water or by land, should be required to pay a sufficient sum to create a general sinking fund for the support of all who may require aid in the state, at least within five years after their arrival.

4. That such a description of each emigrant be registered as will afford the means of identification of anyone, at any time, and in any place, within five or more years after arrival.

5. That encouragement be given to emigrate from places in this state where there is little demand for labor to other places; and

that associations be formed among the emigrants for settling on the public lands of the United States.

6. That efforts be made, by all proper means, to elevate the sanitary and social condition of foreigners and to promote among them habits of cleanliness and better modes of living.

7. That our system of social and personal charitable relief should be revised and remodeled, and that a general plan be devised which shall bring all the charities of the city, county, and state under one control and thus prevent injudicious almsgiving and imposition.

8. That an establishment for paupers, including a farm and workshops, be formed in each county in the state to which state paupers might be sent, and where they should be required to labor, as far as practicable, for their support.

17.

HERMAN MELVILLE: Hawthorne, Shakespeare, and a Great American Literature

After five successful novels, Herman Melville left New York for the Berkshires to produce, as he had promised his publishers, a book about whaling. During his struggle with Moby-Dick, *he became the friend of Nathaniel Hawthorne, at whose house in nearby Lenox he was a frequent visitor. "Nothing pleases me better," wrote Hawthorne's wife, Sophia, "than to sit and hear the growing man dash his tumultuous waves of thought up against Mr. Hawthorne's great, genial, silences."* Hawthorne and His Mosses *(part of which appears below), purporting to be by a Virginian spending July in Vermont, was written during this period but without Hawthorne's knowledge. The comparison of Hawthorne to Shakespeare is still considered an exaggeration, but "what everybody failed to realize," according to Perry Miller "— maybe even Melville — was that in the essay Melville was talking not about Hawthorne but about himself — himself in the midst of creating* Moby-Dick." *The publication in 1851 of* Moby-Dick *brought to an end Melville's public success as an author until the revival of his reputation in 1921.*

Source: *Literary World,* August 17, 1850.

IT IS THE LEAST PART OF GENIUS that attracts admiration. Where Hawthorne is known, he seems to be deemed a pleasant writer, with a pleasant style — a sequestered, harmless man from whom any deep and weighty thing would hardly be anticipated; a man who means no meanings. But there is no man in whom humor and love, like mountain peaks, soar to such a rapt height as to receive the irradiations of the upper skies; there is no man in whom humor and love are developed in that high form called genius; no such man can exist without also possessing, as the indispensable complement of these, a great, deep intellect, which drops down into the universe like a plummet. Or, love and humor are only the eyes through which such an intellect views this world. The great beauty in such a mind is but the product of its strength. . . .

Of all the Indian summer sunlight on the hither side of Hawthorne's soul, the other side — like the dark half of the physical sphere — is shrouded in a blackness, ten times black. But this darkness but gives more effect to the ever moving dawn that forever advances through it and circumnavigates his world. Whether Hawthorne has simply availed himself of this mystical blackness as a means to the wondrous effects he makes it to produce in his lights and shades; or whether there really lurks in him, perhaps unknown to himself, a touch of puritanic gloom, this I cannot altogether tell. Certain it is, however, that this great power of blackness in him derives its force from its appeals to that Calvinistic sense of innate depravity and original sin, from whose visitations, in some shape or other, no deeply thinking mind is always and wholly free. For, in certain moods, no man can weigh this world without throwing in something, somehow like original sin, to strike the uneven balance.

At all events, perhaps no writer has ever wielded this terrific thought with greater terror than this same harmless Hawthorne. Still more, this black conceit pervades him through and through. You may be witched by his sunlight, transported by the bright gildings in the skies he builds over you; but there is the blackness of darkness beyond; and even his bright gildings but fringe and play upon the edges of thunderclouds.

In one word, the world is mistaken in this Nathaniel Hawthorne. He himself must often have smiled at its absurd misconception of him. He is immeasurably deeper than the plummet of the mere critic; for it is not the brain that can test such a man; it is only the heart. You cannot come to know greatness by inspecting it; there is no glimpse to be caught of it, except by intu-

ition; you need not ring it; you but touch it and you find it is gold.

Now, it is that blackness in Hawthorne, of which I have spoken, that so fixes and fascinates me. It may be, nevertheless, that it is too largely developed in him. Perhaps he does not give us a ray of his light for every shade of his dark. But however this may be, this blackness it is that furnishes the infinite obscure of his background — that background against which Shakespeare plays his grandest conceits, the things that have made for Shakespeare his loftiest but most circumscribed renown, as the profoundest of thinkers. For, by philosophers, Shakespeare is not adored as the great man of tragedy and comedy.

"Off with his head; so much for Buckingham!" This sort of rant, interlined by another hand, brings down the house — those mistaken souls who dream of Shakespeare as a mere man of Richard-the-Third humps and Macbeth daggers. But it is those deep, faraway things in him; those occasional flashings-forth of the intuitive truth in him; those short, quick probings at the very axis of reality — these are the things that make Shakespeare, Shakespeare.

Through the mouths of the dark characters of Hamlet, Timon, Lear, and Iago, he craftily says, or sometimes insinuates, the things which we feel to be so terrifically true, that it were all but madness for any good man, in his own proper character, to utter or even hint of them. Tormented into desperation, Lear, the frantic king, tears off the mask and speaks the same madness of vital truth. But . . . it is the least part of genius that attracts admiration. And, so, much of the blind, unbridled admiration that has been heaped upon Shakespeare has been lavished upon the least part of him. And few of his endless commentators and critics seem to have remembered or even perceived that the immediate products of a great mind are not so great as that undeveloped and sometimes undevelopable yet dimly discernible greatness to which those immediate products are but the infallible indices.

In Shakespeare's tomb lies infinitely more than Shakespeare ever wrote. And if I magnify Shakespeare, it is not so much for what he did do as for what he did not do, or refrained from doing. For in this world of lies, truth is forced to fly like a scared white doe in the woodlands; and only by cunning glimpses will she reveal herself, as in Shakespeare and other masters of the great art of telling the truth — even though it be covertly and by snatches.

But if this view of the all-popular Shakespeare be seldom taken by his readers, and if very few who extol him have ever read him deeply or, perhaps, only have seen him on the tricky stage (which alone made, and is still making him, his mere mob renown) — if few men have time, or patience, or palate for the spiritual truth as it is in that great genius — it is then no matter of surprise that in a contemporaneous age Nathaniel Hawthorne is a man as yet almost utterly mistaken among men.

Here and there, in some quiet armchair in the noisy town or some deep nook among the noiseless mountains, he may be appreciated for something of what he is. But, unlike Shakespeare, who was forced to the contrary course by circumstances, Hawthorne (either from simple disinclination or else from inaptitude) refrains from all the popularizing noise and show of broad farce and blood-besmeared tragedy; content with the still, rich utterance of a great intellect in repose, and which sends few thoughts into circulation, except they be arterialized at his large, warm lungs and expanded in his honest heart.

Nor need you fix upon that blackness in him if it suit you not. Nor, indeed, will all readers discern it; for it is, mostly, insinuated to those who may best understand it and account for it; it is not obtruded upon everyone alike.

Some may start to read of Shakespeare and Hawthorne on the same page. They may say that if an illustration were needed, a lesser light might have sufficed to elucidate this Hawthorne, this small man of yesterday. But I am not willingly one of those who, as touching Shakespeare at least, exemplify the maxim of Rochefoucauld, that "we exalt the reputation of some in order to depress that of others" — who, to teach all noble-souled aspirants that there is no hope for them, pronounce Shakespeare absolutely unapproachable. But Shakespeare has been approached. There are minds that have gone as far as Shakespeare into the universe; and hardly a mortal man who, at some time or other, has not felt as great thoughts in him as any you will find in Hamlet.

We must not inferentially malign mankind for the sake of any one man, whoever he may be. This is too cheap a purchase of contentment for conscious mediocrity to make. Besides, this absolute and unconditional adoration of Shakespeare has grown to be a part of our Anglo-Saxon superstitions. The Thirty-Nine Articles are now forty. Intolerance has come to exist in this matter. You must believe in Shakespeare's unapproachability or quit the country.

But what sort of a belief is this for an American, a man who is bound to carry republican progressiveness into literature as well as into life? Believe me, my friends, that men, not very much inferior to Shakespeare, are this day being born on the banks of the Ohio. And the day will come when you shall say, "Who reads a book by an Englishman that is a modern?" The great mistake seems to be that even with those Americans who look forward to the coming of a great literary genius among us, they somehow fancy he will come in the costume of Queen Elizabeth's day; be a writer of dramas founded upon old English history or the tales of Boccaccio. Whereas great geniuses are parts of the times, they themselves are the times, and possess a corresponding coloring.

It is of a piece with the Jews who, while their Shiloh was meekly walking in their streets, were still praying for His magnificent coming; looking for Him in a chariot, who was already among them on an ass. Nor must we forget that in his own lifetime Shakespeare was not Shakespeare but only Master William Shakespeare, of the shrewd, thriving, business firm of Condell, Shakespeare, and Co., proprietors of the Globe Theatre in London; and by a courtly author, of the name of Chettle, was looked at as an "upstart crow," beautified "with other birds' feathers."

For, mark it well, imitation is often the first charge brought against real originality. Why this is so there is not space to set forth here. You must have plenty of sea room to tell the truth in; especially when it seems to have an aspect of newness, as America did in 1492, though it was then just as old and perhaps older than Asia; only those sagacious philosophers, the common sailors, had never seen it before, swearing it was all water and moonshine there.

Now I do not say that Nathaniel of Salem is a greater [man] than William of Avon, or as great. But the difference between the two men is by no means immeasurable. Not a very great deal more and Nathaniel were verily William.

This, too, I mean, that if Shakespeare has not been equaled, give the world time and he is sure to be surpassed in one hemisphere or the other. Nor will it at all do to say that the world is getting gray and grizzled now, and has lost that fresh charm which she wore of old, and by virtue of which the great poets of past times made themselves what we esteem them to be. Not so. The world is as young today as when it was created; and this Vermont morning dew is as wet to my feet as Eden's dew to Adam's. Nor has nature been all

over ransacked by our progenitors, so that no new charms and mysteries remain for this latter generation to find. Far from it. The trillionth part has not yet been said; and all that has been said but multiplies the avenues to what remains to be said. It is not so much paucity as superabundance of material that seems to incapacitate modern authors.

Let America, then, prize and cherish her writers; yea, let her glorify them. They are not so many in number as to exhaust her goodwill. And while she has good kith and kin of her own to take to her bosom, let her not lavish her embraces upon the household of an alien; for, believe it or not, England, after all, is in many things an alien to us. China has more bonds of real love for us than she. But even were there no strong literary individualities among us, as there are some dozens at least, nevertheless, let America first praise mediocrity, even in her own children, before she praises (for everywhere, merit demands acknowledgment from everyone) the best excellence in the children of any other land. Let her own authors, I say, have the priority of appreciation. I was much pleased with a hotheaded Carolina cousin of mine who once said, "If there were no other American to stand by in literature, why, then, I would stand by 'Pop' [Richard] Emmons and his *Fredoniad*; and till a better epic came along, swear it was not very far behind the *Iliad*." Take away the words and in spirit he was sound.

Not that American genius needs patronage in order to expand; for that explosive sort of stuff will expand though screwed up in a vise, and burst it, though it were triple steel. It is for the nation's sake, and not for her authors' sake, that I would have America be heedful of the increasing greatness among her writers; for how great the shame if other nations should be before her in crowning her heroes of the pen! But this is almost the case now. American authors have received more just and discriminating praise (however loftily and ridiculously giv-en in certain cases) even from some En-glishmen than from their own countrymen. There are hardly five critics in America; and several of them are asleep. As for patronage, it is the American author who now patron-izes his country, and not his country him. And if at times some among them appeal to the people for more recognition, it is not always with selfish motives but patriotic ones.

It is true that but few of them as yet have evinced that decided originality which merits great praise. But that graceful writer, who perhaps of all Americans has received the most plaudits from his own country for his productions — that very popular and amiable writer, however good and self-reliant in many things — perhaps owes his chief reputation to the self-acknowledged imitation of a foreign model and to the studied avoidance of all topics but smooth ones.

But it is better to fail in originality than to succeed in imitation. He who has never failed somewhere, that man cannot be great. Failure is the true test of greatness. And if it be said that continual success is a proof that a man wisely knows his powers, it is only to be added that, in that case, he knows them to be small. Let us believe it, then, once for all, that there is no hope for us in these smooth, pleasing writers that know their powers. Without malice, but to speak the plain fact, they but furnish an ap-pendix to Goldsmith and other English authors. And we want no American Gold-smiths; nay, we want no American Miltons. It were the vilest thing you could say of a true American author that he were an American Tompkins. Call him an American and have done, for you cannot say a nobler thing of him.

But it is not meant that all American writers should studiously cleave to national-ity in their writings; only this, no American writer should write like an Englishman or a Frenchman. Let him write like a man, for then he will be sure to write like an Ameri-can. Let us [do] away with this leaven of literary flunkeyism toward England. If ei-ther must play the flunkey in this thing, let England do it, not us. While we are rapidly preparing for that political supremacy among the nations which prophetically awaits us at the close of the present centu-ry, in a literary point of view, we are de-plorably unprepared for it; and we seem studious to remain so. Hitherto, reasons might have existed why this should be; but no good reason exists now. And all that is requisite to amendment in this matter is simply this: that while fully acknowledging all excellence everywhere, we should refrain from unduly lauding foreign writers, and, at the same time, duly recognize meritorious writers that are our own — those writers who breathe that unshackled, democratic spirit of Christianity in all things, which now takes the practical lead in this world, though at the same time led by ourselves — us Americans.

Let us boldly contemn all imitation, though it comes to us graceful and fragrant as the morning; and foster all originality, though at first it be crabbed and ugly as our own pine knots. And if any of our authors fail, or seem to fail, then, in the words of my Carolina cousin, let us clap him on the shoulder and back him against all Europe for his second round. The truth is that in one point of view this matter of a national literature has come to such a pass with us that in some sense we must turn bullies else the day is lost, or superiority so far beyond us that we can hardly say it will ever be ours.

And, now, my countrymen, as an excel-lent author of your own flesh and blood — an unimitating, and, perhaps, in his way, an inimitable man — whom better can I com-mend to you, in the first place, than Na-thaniel Hawthorne. He is one of the new and far better generation of your writers.

The smell of your beeches and hemlocks is upon him; your own broad prairies are in his soul; and if you travel away inland into his deep and noble nature, you will hear the far roar of his Niagara. Give not over to future generations the glad duty of acknowledging him for what he is. Take that joy to yourself, in your own generation; and so shall he feel those grateful impulses on him that may possibly prompt him to the full flower of some still greater achievement in your eyes. And, by confessing him, you thereby confess others; you brace the whole brotherhood; for genius, all over the world, stands hand in hand, and one shock of recognition runs the whole circle round.

In treating of Hawthorne, or rather of Hawthorne in his writings (for I never saw the man; and in the chances of a quiet plantation life, remote from his haunts, perhaps never shall); in treating of his works, I say, I have thus far omitted all mention of his *Twice Told Tales* and *Scarlet Letter*. Both are excellent but full of such manifold, strange, and diffusive beauties that time would all but fail me to point the half of them out. But there are things in those two books which, had they been written in England a century ago, Nathaniel Hawthorne had utterly displaced many of the bright names we now revere on authority.

But I am content to leave Hawthorne to himself and to the infallible finding of posterity; and however great may be the praise I have bestowed upon him, I feel that in so doing I have served and honored myself than him. For, at bottom, great excellence is praise enough to itself; but the feeling of a sincere and appreciative love and admiration toward it, this is relieved by utterance; and warm, honest praise ever leaves a pleasant flavor in the mouth; and it is an honorable thing to confess to what is honorable in others.

But I cannot leave my subject yet. No man can read a fine author, and relish him to his very bones while he reads, without subsequently fancying to himself some ideal image of the man and his mind. And if you rightly look for it, you will almost always find that the author himself has somewhere furnished you with his own picture. For poets (whether in prose or verse), being painters of nature, are like their brethren of the pencil, the true portrait painters, who, in the multitude of likenesses to be sketched, do not invariably omit their own; and, in all high instances, they paint them without any vanity, though at times with a lurking something that would take several pages to properly define.

I submit it, then, to those best acquainted with the man personally, whether the following is not Nathaniel Hawthorne; and, to himself, whether something involved in it does not express the temper of his mind — that lasting temper of all true, candid men — a seeker, not a finder yet:

> A man now entered, in neglected attire, with the aspect of a thinker, but somewhat too roughhewn and brawny for a scholar. His face was full of sturdy vigor, with some finer and keener attribute beneath; though harsh at first, it was tempered with the glow of a large, warm heart, which had force enough to heat his powerful intellect through and through. He advanced to the Intelligencer and looked at him with a glance of such stern sincerity that perhaps few secrets were beyond its scope.
> "I seek for Truth," said he. . . .

Here, let me throw out another conceit of mine. . . . May it not be that this commanding mind has not been, is not, and never will be individually developed in any one man? And would it, indeed, appear so unreasonable to suppose that this great fullness and overflowing may be, or may be destined to be, shared by a plurality of men of genius? Surely, to take the very greatest example on record, Shakespeare cannot be regarded as in himself the concretion of all the genius of his time; nor as so immeasurably beyond Marlowe, Webster, Ford,

Beaumont, Jonson, that these great men can be said to share none of his power?

For one, I conceive that there were dramatists in Elizabeth's day between whom and Shakespeare the distance was by no means great. Let anyone hitherto little acquainted with those neglected old authors for the first time read them thoroughly, or even read Charles Lamb's *Specimens* of them, and he will be amazed at the wondrous ability of those Anaks of men, and shocked at this renewed example of the fact that fortune has more to do with fame than merit; though without merit, lasting fame there can be none.

Nevertheless, it would argue too ill of my country were this maxim to hold good concerning Nathaniel Hawthorne, a man who already, in some few minds, has shed "such a light as never illuminates the earth save when a great heart burns as the household fire of a grand intellect."

The words are his, in the *Select Party;* and they are a magnificent setting to a coincident sentiment of my own, but ramblingly expressed yesterday in reference to himself. Gainsay it who will, as I now write, I am posterity speaking by proxy; and aftertimes will make it more than good when I declare that the American who up to the present day has evinced, in literature, the largest brain with the largest heart — that man is Nathaniel Hawthorne. Moreover, that whatever Nathaniel Hawthorne may hereafter write, *Mosses from an Old Manse*

will be ultimately accounted his masterpiece. For there is a sure though secret sign in some works which proves the culmination of the powers (only the developable ones, however) that produced them.

But I am by no means desirous of the glory of a prophet. I pray heaven that Hawthorne may *yet* prove me an impostor in this prediction. Especially, as I somehow cling to the strange fancy that in all men hiddenly reside certain wondrous, occult properties — as in some plants and minerals — which by some happy but very rare accident (as bronze was discovered by the melting of the iron and brass at the burning of Corinth) may chance to be called forth here on earth; not entirely waiting for their better discovery in the more congenial, blessed atmosphere of heaven.

Once more — for it is hard to be finite upon an infinite subject, and all subjects are infinite. By some people this entire scrawl of mine may be esteemed altogether unnecessary, inasmuch "as years ago" (they may say) "we found out the rich and rare stuff in this Hawthorne, whom you now parade forth, as if only *yourself* were the discoverer of this Portuguese diamond in your literature." But even granting all this — and adding to it the assumption that the books of Hawthorne have sold by the five thousand — what does that signify? They should be sold by the hundred thousand; and read by the million; and admired by everyone who is capable of admiration.

The parties in this conflict are not merely abolitionists and slaveholders — they are atheists, socialists, communists, red republicans, jacobins on the one side, and the friends of order and regulated freedom on the other. In one word, the world is the battleground — Christianity and atheism the combatants; and the progress of humanity the stake.

Rev. J. H. Thornwell, president of University of South Carolina, of the Compromise of 1850

18.

A. J. DOWNING: A Few Words on Rural Architecture

Andrew Jackson Downing was architect, landscape artist, and horticulturalist, and within these disciplines he exerted a wide influence in his brief lifetime. His talents were most directly brought to bear in the development of rural American architecture, the topic of the following essay published in the Horticulturalist *in July 1850. In 1851 Downing was commissioned to landscape the grounds around the Capitol, White House, and Smithsonian Institution, but he was unable to finish these projects before his death the following year.*

Source: *Rural Essays*, New York, 1853, pp. 205-208.

NO ONE PRETENDS that we have, as yet, either a national architecture or national music in America; unless our Yankee clapboard house be taken as a specimen of the first, and "Old Susannah" of the second fine art. But there is, on the other hand, perhaps, no country where there is more building or more "musicianing," such as they are, at the present moment. And as a perfect taste in arts is no more to be expected in a young nation, mainly occupied with the practical wants of life, than a knowledge of geometry is in an infant school, we are content with the large promise that we find in the present, and confidently look forward for fulfillment to the future.

In almost every other country a few landlords own the land, which a great many tenants live upon and cultivate. Hence the general interest in building is confined to a comparatively small class, improvements are made in a solid and substantial way, and but little change takes place from one generation to another in the style of the dwelling and the manner of living.

But in this country we are, comparatively, all landlords. In the country, especially, a large part of the rural population own the land they cultivate and build their own houses. Hence it is a matter of no little moment to them to avail themselves of every possible improvement in the manner of constructing their dwellings so as to secure the largest amount of comfort, convenience, and beauty for the moderate sum which an American landholder has to spend. While the rural proprietors of the other continent are often content to live in the same houses and with the same inconveniences as their forefathers, no one in our time and country who has any of the national spirit of progress in him is satisfied unless, in building a new house, he has some of the "modern improvements" in it.

This is a good sign of the times; and when we see it coupled with another, viz., the great desire to make the dwelling agreeable and ornamental as well as comfortable, we think there is abundant reason to hope, so far as the country is concerned, that something like a national taste will come in due time.

(Above) A. J. Downing, engraving dated 1859; (right) two illustrations from his book dealing with landscape gardening

[Fig. 3. View of a Country Residence, as frequently seen.]

[Fig. 4. View of the same Residence improved.]

What the popular taste in building seems to us to require, just now, is not so much *impulse* as right *direction*. There are numberless persons who have determined, in building their new home in the country, that they "will have something pretty"; but precisely what character it shall have, and whether there is any character, beyond that of a "pretty cottage" or a "splendid house," is not perhaps very clear to their minds.

We do not make this statement to find fault with the condition of things; far from it. We see too much good in the newly awakened taste for the beautiful to criticize severely its want of intelligence as to the exact course it should take to achieve its object — or perhaps its want of definiteness as to what that object is — beyond providing an agreeable home. But we allude to it to show that, with a little direction, the popular taste now awakened in this particular department may develop itself in such a manner as to produce the most satisfactory and beautiful results.

Fifteen years ago there was but one idea relating to a house in the country. It must be a Grecian temple. Whether 20 feet or 200 feet front, it must have its columns and portico. There might be comfortable rooms behind them or not; that was a matter which the *severe* taste of the classical builder could not stoop to consider. The roof might be so flat that there was no space for comfortable servants' bedrooms, or the attic so hot that the second story was uninhabitable in a midsummer's day. But of what consequence was that if the portico were copied from the Temple of Theseus, or the columns were miniature imitations in wood of those of Jupiter Olympus?

We have made a great step onward in that short fifteen years. There is, to be sure, a *fashion* now in building houses in the country, almost as prevalent and despotic as its pseudoclassical predecessor; but it is a far more rational and sensible one, and though likely to produce the same unsatisfactory effect of all other fashions — that is, to substitute sameness and monotony for tasteful individuality — yet we gladly accept it as the next step onward.

We allude, of course, to the Gothic or

English cottage, with steep roofs and high gables, just now the ambition of almost every person building in the country. There are, indeed, few things so beautiful as a cottage of this kind, well-designed and tastefully placed. There is nothing, all the world over, so truly rural and so unmistakably countrylike as this very cottage, which has been developed in so much perfection in the rural lanes and amid the picturesque lights and shadows of an English landscape. And for this reason, because it is essentially rural and countrylike, we gladly welcome its general naturalization (with the needful variation of the veranda, etc., demanded by our climate) as the type of most of our country dwellings.

But it is time to enter a protest against the absolute and indiscriminate employment of the Gothic cottage in *every* site and situation in the country — whether appropriate or inappropriate; whether suited to the grounds or the life of those who are to inhabit it, or the contrary.

We have endeavored, in our work on *Country Houses* just issued from the press, to show that rural architecture has more significance and a deeper meaning than merely to afford a "pretty cottage" or a "handsome house" for him who can afford to pay for it. We believe not only that a house may have an absolute beauty of its own, growing out of its architecture, but that it may have a relative beauty, no less interesting, which arises from its expressing the life and occupation of those who build or inhabit it. In other words, we think the home of every family possessed of character may be made to express that character, and will be most beautiful (supposing the character good) when, in addition to architectural beauty, it unites this significance or individuality.

We have not the space to go into detail on this subject here; and to do so would only be repeating what we have already said in the work in question. But the most casual reader will understand from our suggestion that if a man's house can be made to express the best traits of his character, it is undeniable that a large source of beauty and interest is always lost by those who copy each other's homes without reflection, even though they may be copying the most faultless *cottage ornée*.

We would have the cottage, the farmhouse, and the larger country house all marked by a somewhat distinctive character of their own so far as relates to making them complete and individual of their kind; and believing as we do that the beauty and force of every true man's life or occupation depend largely on his pursuing it frankly, honestly, and openly, with all the individuality of his character, we would have his house and home help to give significance to and dignify that daily life and occupation by harmonizing with them. For this reason, we think the farmer errs when he copies the filigree work of the retired citizen's cottage, instead of showing that rustic strength and solidity in his house which are its true elements of interest and beauty. For this reason, we think he who builds a simple and modest cottage in the country fails in attaining that which he aims at by copying, as nearly as his means will permit, the parlors, folding doors, and showy furniture of the newest house he has seen in town.

We will not do more at present than throw out these suggestions in the hope that those about to build in the country will reflect that an entirely satisfactory house is one in which there are not only pretty forms and details but one which has some *meaning* in its beauty, considered in relation to their own position, character, and daily lives.

19.

Anonymous: The Late Cuba Expedition

*President James K. Polk's offer to Spain, in 1848, to purchase Cuba for $100 million
was not unprecedented. The island, only ninety miles from Florida, had been under the
watchful eye of statesmen since Jefferson's time. It seemed logical to Americans that
Cuba would one day belong to the United States; the needs of defense and of commerce as
well as the promptings of Manifest Destiny seemed to make its acquisition inevitable.
As long as Spain refused to sell, the United States was determined that Cuba would never
be transferred to another foreign power. Between 1849 and 1851 private citizens were
encouraged to support an unofficial expedition to win Cuba from Spain. The expedition,
under the leadership of General Narciso López, after failure in 1849, reorganized in
1850 at New Orleans with strong support from Southerners who hoped to gain Cuba as
slave territory. This attempt also failed, as did a third the following year. The
expedition of 1850 is the subject of the following article, reprinted in part, from
De Bow's Review.*

Source: *De Bow's Review*, August 1850.

WHOEVER HAS FOLLOWED THE COURSE of the United States for the last half century without noting the growth of a *military spirit,* diffusing itself through all classes of society and ready, at any moment, to develop itself in every form of action, has observed to very little purpose. It was this spirit which almost defied the vigilance of Washington when Genet would have precipitated the West upon New Orleans — this which dictated the schemes of Burr, clamored for a part in the wars of Napoleon, and received with huzzas the proclamation of Mr. Madison's government of hostilities with England. Emboldened by the results of this brilliant war, the American eagle has plumed its pinions for a flight still nearer to the sun. Miniature West Points have sprung up in every state and on every hilltop, indurating young sinews for the toils of the camp and the battlefield, counseling discipline and strategy, and inspiring admiration for "nodding plumes" and "dazzling crests." . . .

How otherwise, in such a school, could American militia bayonets have else than bristled along the Maine frontier when the occupation of disputed territory was threatened by British soldiery? How otherwise but the genius of the wisest and the greatest statesman should be sorely taxed in preventing the execution, by force of arms, of the threat, "The whole of Oregon or none"? How otherwise, the call of Texas attracts legions of soldiers to her standard from our midst, and the proclamation of war with Mexico is received with illuminations and bonfires, and the tender, in a few months, as Mr. Polk is said to have admitted, of the *voluntary* services in the field of 200,000 men?

What have been the results of this Mexican War? They are but of yesterday, and we remember the intense excitement, from the Aroostook to the Columbia Valley; the illuminations, the bonfires, the banners, the shouts, the processions; the returning heroes, drawn in chariots over multitudes of heads, as great cities move from their foundations, in the figure of Cicero, to receive them on their triumphant advances; the muffled drum, the reversed arms, the toll of bells, the stifled sobs, the somber pageant, the eloquent Periclesian eulogiums, the insignia and the reward of the dead warrior, "from the field of his fame, fresh and gory." The people, in a delirium of joy, welcome the return of their champions and deem no chaplets of fame too glittering for their brows.

The warrior captain becomes the civil chief of the great nation; his immediate compatriots crown congressional, diplomatic, gubernatorial, and legislative seats; the subaltern and veriest soldiery have a potency at the ballot box, and distance all competition in the race for office! Shall not they who have borne the heat and burden of the day reap the greater reward? And the arm which was mighty to protect and defend in the hour of danger, must it not be guided by a heart pure and incorrupt, and earnestly solicitous of the public weal, in peace or in war? What higher preparation or fitness for office can be required than these?

"The curtain has fallen upon the first act of American history," said the great statesman who, but the other day, went down into his grave, "and, for the first time, all before me is dark." With the Mexican War the nation entered upon a new career which was predicted of her, and to which her institutions and position peculiarly inclined — one of *war and conquest!* Shall we essay to lift the curtain from the future? . . .

The military spirit of the country has been [aroused] and is rife for anything, and woe to the power that shall endeavor to stay it. Administrations will fall to pieces at its blow; statesmen will not dare the ostracism of its voice. The cry of war is flattering to our pride and our power, and they are either of them equal to that of any other nation, ancient or modern. The field before us is boundless, and the power that

broods over it grows every day in energy, in resources, and in magnitude, and will be as resistless in time as the whirlwind. Armed bands will sally from our ports, as in days of yore from the Northern hive, covertly, often openly, in the service of every power that shall offer emolument and glory. Our sympathies with freedom, everywhere, are first the incentive; but there will, in time, be other and less honorable incentives.

We have a destiny to perform, "a manifest destiny" over all Mexico, over South America, over the West Indies and Canada. The Sandwich Islands are as necessary to our Eastern, as the isles of the Gulf to our Western, commerce. The gates of the Chinese Empire must be thrown down by the men from the Sacramento and the Oregon, and the haughty Japanese tramplers upon the cross be enlightened in the doctrines of republicanism and the ballot box. The eagle of the republic shall poise itself over the field of Waterloo, after tracing its flight among the gorges of the Himalaya or the Ural Mountains, and a successor of Washington ascend the chair of universal empire! These are the giddy dreams of the day. The martial spirit must have its employ. The people stand ready to hail tomorrow, with shouts and enthusiasm, a collision with the proudest and the mightiest empire upon earth. The valley of the Mississippi alone will arm its half million of stout woodsmen, hardy hunters, deadly rifles, for any field where the cause of liberty and glory shall call. Thus is it.

Have a care how we trifle with this tremendous power, or unduly excite it, and let us not cease to admire the foresight of that Spanish minister, the Count of Aranda, who said, in 1783:

> The federal republic is a pygmy in its cradle; she has needed the support of two states, powerful like France and Spain, to obtain independence. The day will come when she will be a giant — a formidable colossus even in these parts.

She will forget the services received from those countries, and will only think of her own aggrandizement.

These reflections, rather too much extended perhaps, have been induced by the late attempt upon the island of Cuba by a party of adventurers under our flag and embarking from our ports. We are willing, at the outset, to accord to the leader of the expedition the highest motives of patriotism and honor, and to the hundreds who flocked around his standard many generous, though perhaps misdirected, impulses and sympathies, without questioning there were others, at the same time, moved by the most sordid considerations.

The signal failure of the enterprise and all the attendant circumstances of it have been such as to provoke derision rather than admiration or respect; and the parties having themselves braved the ordeal must be content with that obloquy which the want of success will ever inspire. The Abbé Raynal long ago laid down the principle with unerring precision: "I acknowledge that men accustomed to judge of things by the event call great and perilous resolutions heroism or madness, according to the good or bad success which attends them." Accordingly, in every part of the Union, denunciation grows pregnant, despite the evidences that the cause of the Cuba invaders and patriots was a few weeks ago a highly popular one, receiving the sympathies of the multitude and attracting, in the highest quarters, the most favorable consideration.

The movers and instigators are brought before the tribunals of the country for an infraction of its laws and the statute of 1818 attempted to be enforced against them. Now, although it be true, as we think not improbable, that this offense does not come within the *strict letter* of the statute, however its spirit be clearly isolated, yet, why were the agents of the government so fast asleep during the many weeks when it was notorious to the country that an armed expedition was in progress? Will it be maintained that the facilities of communication with Washington are less than with Cuba — the governor-general of which had timely notice of every movement, long, even, before the sailing of the expedition? Why not use the telegraph in arresting the parties and preventing this great infraction, as it is alleged, of our neutral duties? The telegraph was not idle at another stage of the business.

It is difficult to distinguish this case, *upon principle*, from that of the Texan revolution, when men and arms and ammunition were continually being thrown into that country from our ports, notwithstanding the loud protests of Mexico, with whom we were at peace and with whom we were bound by all the solemnities of treaty stipulations. The Cubans were not in arms, but revolution may begin long before a standard is erected or a sword drawn from its scabbard. Contributing money, conducting correspondence are as much overt acts of rebellion or treason as open revolt, and do not distinguish the parties, in the eye of the law and government, from those that are actually in the field. Were the Cubans so far committed? The evidences are not wanting that they were, and that contributions of money and the warmest protestations of sympathy and vows of hearty cooperation did emanate from that quarter to encourage and cheer the movement.

The rebutting circumstance is the cold reception which they gave to the men at Cardenas. We are bound, in our search after truth, to consider this of little weight. They must have been bold and hardy revolutionists, indeed — supposing that external aid was indispensable to their cause — to regard that which landed in the Creole as at all adequate to the exigence. A mere handful — where it is believed ten times the number had been expected — and a handful, too, whose movements had long before been known to the authorities of the island;

who, with extraordinary vigilance, were throwing armies of disciplined soldiers upon every assailable point and scouring the Gulf with their fleets. The landing at Cardenas could only have been considered a piece of American quixoticism, of which it seems we are capable when occasion requires.

It is not clear, at this moment, how far the interference of our government was in consonance with the letter and spirit of the treaty stipulations with Spain, or with the provisions of the act of 1818, intended to meet these cases. The instructions which were issued to the naval commanders dispatched in that quarter have not been officially communicated, and no doubt are misrepresented. That the President may have interdicted the sailing of the expedition is clear, and, in a high and liberal interpretation of our duties toward a friendly and weaker power, may have intercepted it afterward and prevented a hostile landing, ought not, perhaps, to be questioned. Any other construction would evidence a sort of Carthaginian faith, and that paltering, in a double sense, which would be at war with all international comity.

The power of the executive should be co-extensive with the evil intended to be remedied. Had the expedition landed, we may even go a step further and admit that reinforcements from our country might have been cut off, but it is a high and delicate trust and likely to be abused. Here the duties of neutrality would have been religiously observed and accomplished, and any expression of sympathy or incidental aid, even the slightest, extended toward the captain general in preventing or suppressing an intended revolt or in making captives, would be a gross and arbitrary assumption of power, which could be tolerated in no administration a single hour. There are no proofs of anything like this against the federal authorities, and we are to presume they did their duty. . . .

That this, the second unsuccessful attempt upon Cuba within a few months, is but the beginning of the end which looks to the acquisition of that island by the United States can hardly be a subject of debate. American and Spanish blood has been shed, and the bitter feelings of consequence engendered upon both sides will long survive the occasion, indulging itself in petty acts of jealousy — in ill-concealed hostility — incrimination and recrimination. Already the islanders loudly boast of their heroic onslaught upon the Buena Vista Yankees, and search their vocabulary for every term of opprobrium and contempt to heap upon their heads. Bravely, it must be admitted, almost chivalrously, as they did act, these glorifications are not likely to produce a pleasant tingle upon American ears unaccustomed to such sounds from others than themselves. It is not improbable that our citizens, now or hereafter in the island, will be subjected to vexatious restrictions growing out of these matters, and that, in the haughtiness of almost unexpected triumph, the authorities will be guilty of some infractions upon their rights and privileges. . . .

None can doubt that at this moment there is a well-fixed and almost universal conviction upon the minds of our people that the possession of Cuba is indispensable to the proper development and security of the country. We state the fact, without entering into the reasons of it or justifying it, that such a conviction exists. Call it the lust of dominion, the restlessness of democracy, the passion for land and gold, or the desire to render our interior impregnable by commanding the keys of the Gulf — the possession of Cuba is still an American sentiment, not to be sure a late but a growing and strengthening one. We trust, for the honor of humanity and the faith of treaties, it will lead us into nothing for which our history shall blush.

View of Broadway from Barnum's American Museum, located at Broadway and Ann

THE GROWING CITIES

In 1850 the great cities of the East — Boston, Philadelphia, and New York — were beginning to suffer the effects of explosive, chaotic growth. In New York, the largest city by far with a population of 515,394 in 1850, the problems were magnified. The city was the chief port of entry for immigrants (370,000 arrived in 1850) and had almost no arrangements to absorb them smoothly. Some of them would move west, but many stayed. By 1855, the foreign-born comprised half of New York City's population. Industrial expansion afforded jobs for some and many enterprising newcomers prospered by serving the needs of their fellow immigrants. But housing was inadequate and squalid shanty-towns contrasted with the fine mansions of the wealthy. The streets were congested with wagons and carriages, bringing forth proposals for pedestrian bridges and elevated trains to ease the problem.

A pedestrian bridge in New York in the 1850s

Broadway on a rainy day, 1859

New York from the steeple of
St. Paul's, looking south

An 1848 plan for an elevated railway and sewer. Work began on the elevated 20 years later

View of a street in Brooklyn from a painting executed sometime between 1840 and 1850

New York found it difficult to assimilate the waves of Irish and German immigrants. Newcomers were forced to accept inadequate and miserable housing conditions; the resulting exploitation and crime turned public opinion against the immigrants. As conditions worsened and the influx continued, a number of large squatters' communities developed on the outskirts of the city. One was Dutch Hill, a high bluff overlooking the East River; another, the area that was incorporated into Central Park in 1857. The nativists began to form anti-immigrant societies that later were to produce the Know-Nothing Party.

(Left) Daguerreotype portrait of a young girl; (below) view of Sixth Avenue between 55th and 57th streets looking west, showing horsedrawn public transportation

Interior of the Winter-Garden, a favorite gathering place of German immigrants

(Above) New York Police Court, from a magazine illustration, 1853; (left) a night rally of the Know-Nothing Party, an organization formed to combat the alleged menace of Catholicism and immigration

Photograph of the burning mills at Oswego, New York, during the great fire of 1853

Daguerreotype of the Oswego fire, which caused considerable financial loss in that community

American Museum of Photography

The Old Merchant's Exchange in Philadelphia in 1849

Philadelphia's "Newspaper Row" in 1842

Mrs. Ralph Mackay

A double portrait made around 1850

American Museum of Photography

(Top left) The Jayne Building in Philadelphia designed in 1849 reflects new building styles; (top right) a patent medicine ad of the Jayne Company

(Right) Photograph of Quaker sisters; (below) John McAllister, head of a ''philosophical instrument'' house in Philadelphia that made microscopes, telescopes, and other instruments

The brothers William and Frederick Langenheim

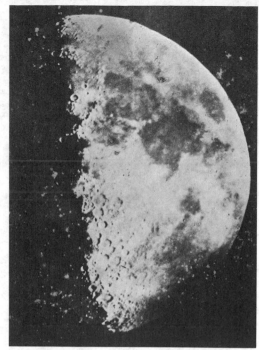

A daguerreotype of the moon taken in 1851

By the late 1840s photography was a big business in America. The Langenheim brothers in Philadelphia, Mathew Brady in New York, and Southworth and Hawes in Boston were using production line processing to meet the demand for portraits. The Langenheims were among the first successful users of a paper-print process developed in England. Brady's daguerreotype portraits won a prize at the Crystal Palace Exhibition as did Whipple's telescopic view of the moon (above).

Portrait of Albert S. Southworth

Portrait of Josiah Hawes

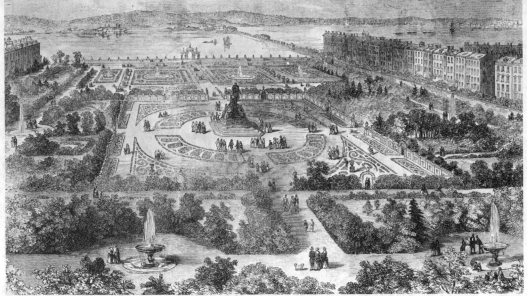

A plan for a public garden in Boston, from a magazine illustration of 1853

Massachusetts at this time produced many able spokesmen for reform. Arguments for abolition, temperance, the rights of women, humane treatment of the insane, and improved public education were eloquently stated in public discussion. Horace Mann, as the first secretary of the state's board of education, worked for principles of universal education which are fundamental to our modern view of public education. He advanced the ideas of compulsory education and support of nonsectarian schools with public funds.

(Left) Photograph of an elderly New England couple; (below) Smoker's Circle on the Boston Common

(Above) A daguerreotype of Massachusetts school children. Daguerreotypes of large groups were rare because of the long exposure times. (Left) The Emerson School; (below) double portrait of children

Daguerreotype portrait made c. 1855

(Above) Lemuel Shaw, Massachusetts chief justice, daguerreotype portrait by Southworth and Hawes; (below) Lajos Kossuth, Hungarian patriot who traveled in the U.S. in 1850

Daguerreotype portrait made c. 1850

20.

Millard Fillmore: A Golden Rule for Foreign Affairs

Because a republican form of government had been coupled in the United States with unprecedented economic, social, and scientific advances, many Americans were certain that similar results would obtain wherever there was a free government. They therefore applauded any attempt to overthrow despotism elsewhere in the world. But the expression of such sentiments was not always in accord with America's traditional policy of nonintervention in the affairs of other nations. President Millard Fillmore pointed this out in the following portion of his first annual message to Congress, December 2, 1850.

Source: Richardson, V, pp. 77-94.

BEING SUDDENLY CALLED in the midst of the last session of Congress by a painful dispensation of Divine Providence to the responsible station which I now hold, I contented myself with such communications to the legislature as the exigency of the moment seemed to require. The country was shrouded in mourning for the loss of its venerable chief magistrate and all hearts were penetrated with grief. Neither the time nor the occasion appeared to require or to justify on my part any general expression of political opinions or any announcement of the principles which would govern me in the discharge of the duties to the performance of which I had been so unexpectedly called. I trust, therefore, that it may not be deemed inappropriate if I avail myself of this opportunity of the reassembling of Congress to make known my sentiments in a general manner in regard to the policy which ought to be pursued by the government, both in its intercourse with foreign nations and its management and administration of internal affairs.

Nations, like individuals in a state of nature, are equal and independent, possessing certain rights and owing certain duties to each other, arising from their necessary and unavoidable relations; which rights and duties there is no common human authority to protect and enforce. Still, they are rights and duties, binding in morals, in conscience, and in honor; although there is no tribunal to which an injured party can appeal but the disinterested judgment of mankind and, ultimately, the arbitrament of the sword.

Among the acknowledged rights of nations is that which each possesses of establishing that form of government which it may deem most conducive to the happiness and prosperity of its own citizens, of changing that form as circumstances may require, and of managing its internal affairs according to its own will. The people of the United States claim this right for themselves, and they readily concede it to others. Hence it becomes an imperative duty not to interfere in the government or internal policy of other nations; and although we may sympathize with the unfortunate or the oppressed everywhere in their struggles for freedom, our principles forbid us from taking any part in such foreign contests.

We make no wars to promote or to prevent successions to thrones, to maintain any theory of a balance of power, or to suppress the actual government which any country chooses to establish for itself. We instigate no revolutions nor suffer any hostile military expeditions to be fitted out in the United States to invade the territory or provinces of a friendly nation. The great law of morality ought to have a national as well as a personal and individual application. We should act toward other nations as we wish them to act toward us, and justice and conscience should form the rule of conduct between governments, instead of mere power, self-interest, or the desire of aggrandizement.

To maintain a strict neutrality in foreign wars, to cultivate friendly relations, to reciprocate every noble and generous act, and to perform punctually and scrupulously every treaty obligation — these are the duties which we owe to other states, and by the performance of which we best entitle ourselves to like treatment from them; or, if that, in any case, be refused, we can enforce our own rights with justice and a clear conscience.

21.

DANIEL WEBSTER: America's Interest in Foreign Democratic Institutions

In 1849 an attempt by the people of Hungary to overthrow Austrian domination and establish a democratic government met with failure. The leader of the revolution, Lajos Kossuth, was acclaimed as a hero in the United States, which was enthusiastic in its support for a people that had shown the determination to resist oppression. The Austrian chargé d'affaires, Chevalier J. G. Hülsemann, expressed his government's displeasure at American support for the Hungarian uprising to Daniel Webster, then secretary of state. Webster's reply of December 21, 1850, portions of which appear below, justified American approval of foreign efforts to establish democratic principles and affirmed the right of the public to express its enthusiasm.

Source: *The Works of Daniel Webster*, 16th edition, Boston, 1872, Vol. VI, pp. 491-504.

THE UNDERSIGNED, SECRETARY OF STATE of the United States, had the honor to receive, some time ago, the note of Mr. Hülsemann, chargé d'affaires of His Majesty, the emperor of Austria, of the 30th of September. Causes, not arising from any want of personal regard for Mr. Hülsemann, or of proper respect for his government, have delayed an answer until the present moment. Having submitted Mr. Hülsemann's letter to the President, the undersigned is now directed by him to return the following reply.

The objects of Mr. Hülsemann's note are, first, to protest, by order of his government, against the steps taken by the late President of the United States to ascertain the progress and probable result of the revolutionary movements in Hungary; and, second, to complain of some expressions in the instructions of the late secretary of state to Mr. A. Dudley Mann, a confidential agent of the United States, as communicated by President Taylor to the Senate on the 28th of March last.

The principal ground of protest is founded on the idea, or in the allegation, that the government of the United States, by the mission of Mr. Mann and his instructions, has interfered in the domestic affairs of Austria in a manner unjust or disrespectful toward that power. The President's message was a communication made by him to the Senate, transmitting a correspondence between the executive government and a confidential agent of its own. This would seem to be itself a domestic transaction, a mere instance of intercourse between the President and the Senate, in the manner which is usual and indispensable in communications between the different branches of the government. It was not addressed either to Austria or Hungary; nor was it a public manifesto to which any foreign state was called on to reply. It was an account of its transactions communicated by the executive government to the Senate, at the request of that body; made public, indeed, but made public only because such is the common and usual course of proceeding. It may be regarded as somewhat strange, therefore, that the Austrian cabinet did not perceive that, by the instructions given to Mr. Hülsemann, it was itself interfering with the domestic concerns of a foreign state, the very thing which is the ground of its complaint against the United States.

This department has, on former occasions, informed the ministers of foreign powers that a communication from the President to either house of Congress is regarded as a domestic communication of which, ordinarily, no foreign state has cognizance; and, in more recent instances, the great inconvenience of making such communications the subject of diplomatic correspondence and discussion has been fully shown. If it had been the pleasure of His Majesty, the emperor of Austria, during the struggles in Hungary, to have admonished the provisional government or the people of that country against involving themselves in disaster by following the evil and dangerous example of the United States of America in making efforts for the establishment of independent governments, such an admonition from that sovereign to his Hungarian subjects would not have originated here a diplomatic correspondence. The President might, perhaps, on this ground, have declined to direct any particular reply to Mr. Hülsemann's note; but, out of proper respect for the Austrian government, it has been thought better to answer that note at length; and the more especially as the occasion is not unfavorable for the expression of the general sentiments of the government of the United States. . . .

The government and people of the United States, like other intelligent governments and communities, take a lively interest in the movements and the events of this remarkable age, in whatever part of the world they may be exhibited. But the interest taken by the United States in those events has not proceeded from any disposition to depart from that neutrality toward foreign powers which is among the deepest principles and the most cherished traditions of the political history of the Union. It has been the necessary effect of the unexampled character of the events themselves, which could not fail to arrest the attention of the contemporary world, as they will doubtless fill a memorable page in history.

But the undersigned goes further and freely admits that, in proportion as these extraordinary events appeared to have their origin in those great ideas of responsible and popular government on which the American constitutions themselves are wholly founded, they could not but command the warm sympathy of the people of this country. Well-known circumstances in their history, indeed their whole history, have made them the representatives of purely popular principles of government. In this light they now stand before the world. They could not, if they would, conceal their character, their condition, or their destiny. They could not, if they so desired, shut out from the view of mankind the causes which have placed them, in so short a national career, in the station which they now hold among the civilized states of the world. They could not, if they desired it, suppress either the thoughts or the hopes which arise in men's minds, in other countries, from contemplating their successful example of free government. . . . True indeed it is that the prevalence on the other continent of sentiments favorable to republican liberty is the result of the reaction of America upon Europe; and the source and center of this reaction has doubtless been, and now is, in these United States.

The position thus belonging to the United States is a fact as inseparable from their history, their constitutional organization, and their character as the opposite position of the powers composing the European alliance is from the history and constitutional organization of the government of those powers. The sovereigns who form that alliance have not infrequently felt it their right to interfere with the political movements of foreign states; and have, in their manifestoes and declarations, denounced the popular ideas of the age in terms so comprehensive as of necessity to include the United States and their forms of government. . . . The government of the United States heard these denunciations of its fundamental principles without remonstrance or the disturbance of its equanimity. This was thirty years ago.

The power of this republic, at the present moment, is spread over a region one of the richest and most fertile on the globe, and of an extent in comparison with which the possessions of the house of Hapsburg are but as a patch on the earth's surface. Its population, already 25 million, will exceed that of the Austrian Empire within that period during which it may be hoped that Mr. Hülsemann may yet remain in the honorable discharge of his duties to his government. Its navigation and commerce are hardly exceeded by the oldest and most commercial nations; its maritime means and its maritime power may be seen by Austria herself, in all seas where she has ports, as well as they may be seen, also, in all other quarters of the globe. Life, liberty, property, and all personal rights are amply secured to all citizens, and protected by just and stable laws; and credit, public and private, is as well established as in any government of continental Europe; and the country, in all its interests and concerns, partakes most largely in all the improvements and progress which distinguish the age.

Certainly, the United States may be pardoned, even by those who profess adherence to the principles of absolute government, if they entertain an ardent affection for those popular forms of political organization which have so rapidly advanced their own prosperity and happiness, and enabled them, in so short a period, to bring their country and the hemisphere to which it belongs to the notice and respectful regard, not to say the admiration, of the civilized world. Nevertheless, the United States have abstained, at all times, from acts of interference with the political changes of Europe. They cannot, however, fail to cherish always a lively interest in the fortunes of nations struggling for institutions like their own. But this sympathy, so far from being necessarily a hostile feeling toward any of the parties to these great national struggles, is quite consistent with amicable relations with them all.

The Hungarian people are three or four

times as numerous as the inhabitants of these United States were when the American Revolution broke out. They possess, in a distinct language and in other respects, important elements of a separate nationality, which the Anglo-Saxon race in this country did not possess; and if the United States wish success to countries contending for popular constitutions and national independence, it is only because they regard such constitutions and such national independence not as imaginary but as real blessings. They claim no right, however, to take part in the struggles of foreign powers in order to promote these ends. It is only in defense of his own government, and its principles and character, that the undersigned has now expressed himself on this subject. But when the people of the United States behold the people of foreign countries, without any such interference, spontaneously moving toward the adoption of institutions like their own, it surely cannot be expected of them to remain wholly indifferent spectators. . . .

Toward the conclusion of his note, Mr. Hülsemann remarks that

> If the government of the United States were to think it proper to take an indirect part in the political movements of Europe, American policy would be exposed to acts of retaliation and to certain inconveniences which would not fail to affect the commerce and industry of the two hemispheres.

As to this possible fortune, this hypothetical retaliation, the government and people of the United States are quite willing to take their chances and abide their destiny. Taking neither a direct nor an indirect part in the domestic or intestine movements of Europe, they have no fear of events of the nature alluded to by Mr. Hülsemann. It would be idle now to discuss with Mr. Hülsemann those acts of retaliation which he imagines may possibly take place at some indefinite time hereafter. Those questions will be discussed when they arise; and Mr. Hülsemann and the cabinet at Vienna may rest assured that, in the meantime, while performing with strict and exact fidelity all their neutral duties, nothing will deter either the government or the people of the United States from exercising, at their own discretion, the rights belonging to them as an independent nation, and of forming and expressing their own opinions, freely and at all times, upon the great political events which may transpire among the civilized nations of the earth.

Their own institutions stand upon the broadest principles of civil liberty; and believing those principles and the fundamental laws in which they are embodied to be eminently favorable to the prosperity of states — to be, in fact, the only principles of government which meet the demands of the present enlightened age — the President has perceived with great satisfaction that, in the constitution recently introduced into the Austrian Empire, many of these great principles are recognized and applied; and he cherishes a sincere wish that they may produce the same happy effects throughout His Austrian Majesty's extensive dominions that they have done in the United States.

I was born an American; I live an American; I shall die an American.
DANIEL WEBSTER, speech, July 17, 1850

22.

THEODORE PARKER: The State of the Nation

Among the most active reformers and Abolitionists in the North were clergymen whose calling led them to acts of civil disobedience in the name of social justice. One such was Theodore Parker, a Unitarian minister at Boston. Not only did he actively flaunt the Fugitive Slave Law by helping Negroes who had fled to the North but he also called for risings among the slaves. Parker failed to understand men like Webster, who placed the preservation of the Union above moral considerations, and was sympathetic to the Northern view that the nation might be better off without the "despotic" South. Parker's "State of the Nation" sermon, a portion of which is reprinted here, was delivered on Thanksgiving Day, 1850.

Source: *Discourses of Politics*, London, 1863, pp. 235-265.

WE COME TOGETHER TODAY, by the governor's proclamation, to give thanks to God for our welfare, not merely for our happiness as individuals or as families but for our welfare as a people. How can we better improve this opportunity than by looking a little into the condition of the people? And, accordingly, I invite your attention to a sermon of the state of this nation. I shall try to speak of the condition of the nation itself, then of the causes of that condition, and, in the third place, of the dangers that threaten, or are alleged to threaten, the nation.

First, of our condition. Look about you in Boston. Here are 140,000 souls living in peace and in comparative prosperity. I think, without doing injustice to the other side of the water, there is no city in the Old World of this population with so much intelligence, activity, morality, order, comfort, and general welfare, and, at the same time, with so little of the opposite of all these. I know the faults of Boston, and I think I would not disguise them; the poverty, unnatural poverty, which shivers in the cellar; the unnatural wealth which bloats in the parlor; the sin which is hid in the corners of the jail; and the more dangerous sin which sets up Christianity for a pretense; the sophistry which lightens in the newspapers and thunders in the pulpit — I know all these things, and do not pretend to disguise them; and still I think no city of the Old World of the same population has so much which good men prize and so little which good men deplore.

See the increase of material wealth; the buildings for trade and for homes; the shops and ships. This year Boston will add to her possessions some $10 million or $20 million, honestly and earnestly got. Observe the neatness of the streets, the industry of the inhabitants, their activity of mind, the orderliness of the people, the signs of comfort. Then consider the charities of Boston; those limited to our own border and those which extend further, those beautiful charities which encompass the earth with their sweet influence. Look at the schools, a monument of which the city may well be proud, in spite of their defects.

But Boston, though we proudly call it the Athens of America, is not the pleasantest thing in New England to look at; it is the part of Massachusetts which I like the least to look at, in spite of its excellence. Look further, at the whole of Massachusetts, and you see a fairer spectacle. There is less wealth at Provincetown, in proportion to the numbers, but there is less want; there is more comfort; property is more evenly and equally distributed there than here; and the welfare of a country never so much depends upon the amount of its wealth as on the mode in which its wealth is distributed.

In the state, there are about 150,000 families — some 975,000 persons, living with a degree of comfort which, I think, is not anywhere enjoyed by such a population in the Old World. They are mainly industrious, sober, intelligent, and moral. Everything thrives — agriculture, manufactures, commerce. "The carpenter encourages the goldsmith; he that smites the anvil, him that smootheth with the hammer." Look at the farms where intelligent labor wins bread and beauty, both out of the sterile soil and climate not overindulgent. Behold the shops all over the state; the small shops where the shoemaker holds his work in his lap and draws his thread by his own strong muscles; and the large shops where machines, animate with human intelligence, hold, with iron grasp, their costlier work in their lap and spin out the delicate staple of Sea Island cotton.

Look at all this; it is a pleasant sight. Look at our hundreds of villages, by river, mountain, and sea; behold the comfortable homes, the people well fed, well clad, well instructed. Look at the schoolhouses, the colleges of the people; at the higher seminaries of learning; at the poor man's real college further back in the interior, where the mechanic's and farmer's son gets his education, often a poor one, still something to be proud of. Look at the churches where, every Sunday, the best words of Hebrew and of Christian saints are read out of this Book, and all men are asked, once in the week, to remember they have a Father in heaven, a faith to swear by, and a heaven to live for, and a conscience to keep. I know the fault of these churches. I am not in the habit of excusing them; still I know their excellence, and I will not be the last man to acknowledge that. Look at the roads of earth and iron which join villages together and make the state a whole.

Follow the fisherman from his rocky harbor at Cape Ann; follow the mariner in his voyage round the world of waters; see the industry, the intelligence, and the comfort of the people. I think Massachusetts is a state to be thankful for. There are faults in her institutions and in her laws that need change very much. In her form of society, in her schools, in her colleges, there is much which clamors loudly for alteration, very much in her churches to be Christianized. These changes are going quietly forward and will in time be brought about.

I love to look on this state — its material prosperity, its increase in riches, its intelligence and industry, and the beautiful results that are seen all about us today. I love to look on the face of the people in halls and churches, in markets and factories; to think of our great ideas; of the institutions which have come of them; of our schools and colleges and all the institutions for making men wiser and better; to think of the noble men we have in the midst of us, in every walk of life, who eat an honest bread, who love mankind, and love God, who have consciences they mean to keep and souls which they intend to save.

The great business of society is not merely to have farms, and ships, and shops — the greater shops and the less — but to have men; men that are conscious of their manhood, self-respectful, earnest men, that have a faith in the living God. I do not think we have many men of genius. We have very few that I call great men; I wish there were more; but we have an intelligent, an industrious, and noble people here in Massachusetts which we may be proud of.

Let us go a step further. New England is like Massachusetts in the main, with local differences only. All the North is like New England in the main; this portion is better in one thing; that portion worse in another thing. Our ideas are their ideas; our institutions are the same. Some of the Northern states have institutions better than we. They have added to our experience. In revising their constitutions and laws, or in making new ones, they go beyond us, they introduce new improvements, and those new improvements will give those states the same advantage over us which a new mill, with new and superior machinery, has over an old mill, with old and inferior machinery. By and by we shall see the result and take counsel from it, I trust.

All over the North we find the same industry and thrift, and similar intelligence. Here attention is turned to agriculture, there to mining; but there is a similar progress and zeal for improvement. Attention is bestowed on schools and colleges, on academies and churches. There is the same abundance of material comfort. Population advances rapidly; prosperity, in a greater ratio. Everywhere new swarms pour fourth from the old hive and settle in some convenient nook far off in the West. So the frontier of civilization every year goes forward, farther from the ocean. Fifty years ago it was on the Ohio; then on the Mississippi; then on the Upper Missouri; presently its barrier will be the Rocky Mountains, and soon it will pass beyond that bar, and the tide of the Atlantic will sweep over to the Pacific; yea, it is already there!

The universal Yankee freights his schooner at Bangor, at New Bedford, and at Boston with bricks, timber, frame houses, and other "notions," and by and by drops his anchor in the smooth Pacific, in the Bay of St. Francis. We shall see there, ere long, the sentiments of New England, the ideas of New England, the institutions of New England; the schoolhouse, the meetinghouse, the courthouse, the townhouse. There will be the same industry, thrift, intelligence, morality, and religion; and the idle ground that has hitherto borne nothing but gold will bear upon its breast a republic of men more precious than the gold of Ophir or the rubies of the East.

Here I wish I could stop. But this is not all. The North is not the whole nation; New England is not the only type of people. There are other states differing widely from this. In the Southern states you find a soil more fertile under skies more genial. Through what beautiful rivers the Alleghenies pour their tribute to the sea! What streams beautify the land in Georgia, Alabama, Louisiana, and Mississippi! There genial skies rain beauty on the soil. Nature is wanton of her gifts. There, rice, cotton, and sugar grow; there, the olive, the orange, the fig all find a home. The soil teems with luxuriance. But there is not the same wealth, nor the same comfort. Only the ground is rich. You witness not a similar thrift.

Strange is it, but in 1840 the single state of New York alone earned over $4 million more than the six states of North and South Carolina, Georgia, Alabama, Louisiana, and Mississippi! The annual earnings of little Massachusetts, with her 7,500 square miles, are $9 million more than the earnings of all Florida, Georgia, and South Carolina! The little county of Essex, with 95,000 souls in 1840, earned more than the large state of South Carolina, with 595,000.

In those states we miss the activity, intelligence, and enterprise of the North. You do not find the little humble schoolhouse at every corner; the frequent meetinghouse does not point its taper finger to the sky. Villages do not adorn the margin of the mountain stream and sea; shops do not ring with industry; roads of earth and iron are poorer and less common. Temperance, morality, comfort are not there as here. In the slave states, in 1840, there were not quite 302,000 youths and maidens in all the schools, academies, and colleges of the South; but in 1840, in the free states of the North there were more than 2,212,000 in such institutions! Little Rhode Island has 5,000 more girls and boys at school than large South Carolina. The state of Ohio alone has more than 17,000 children at school beyond what the whole fifteen slave states can boast.

The permanent literature of the nation all comes from the North. Your historians are from that quarter — your Sparkses, your Bancrofts, your Hildreths, and Prescotts, and Ticknors; the poets are from the same quarter — your Whittiers, and Longfellows, and Lowells, and Bryants; the men of literature and religion — your Channings, and Irvings, and Emersons are from the same quarter! Preaching, it is everywhere, and sermons are as thick almost as autumnal leaves; but who ever heard of a great or famous clergyman in a Southern state; of a great and famous sermon that rang through the nation from that quarter? No man. Your Edwards of old time, and your Beechers, old and young, your Channing and Buckminster, and the rest, names which throng to every man's lips, all are from the North.

Nature has done enough for the South; God's cup of blessing runs over; and yet you see the result! But there has been no pestilence at the South more than at the North; no earthquake has torn the ground beneath their feet; no war has come to disturb them more than us. The government has never laid a withering hand on their commerce, their agriculture, their schools and colleges, their literature and their church.

Still, letting alone the South and the North as such, not considering either exclusively, we are one nation. What is a nation? It is one of the great parties in the world. It is a sectional party, having geographical limits; with a party organization, party opinions, party mottoes, party machinery, party leaders, and party followers; with some capital city for its party headquarters. There has been an Assyrian party, a British, a Persian, an Egyptian, and a Roman party; there is now a Chinese party, and a Russian, a Turkish, a French, and an English party; these are also called nations. We belong to the American party, and that includes the North as well as the South; and so all are brothers of the same party, differing among ourselves, but from other nations in this, that we are the American party, and not the Russian nor the English.

We ought to look at the whole American party, the North and South, to see the total condition of the people. Now, at this moment, there is no lack of cattle and corn and cloth in the United States, North or South, only they are differently distributed in the different parts of the land. But still there is a great excitement. Men think the nation is in danger, and for many years there has not been so great an outcry and alarm among the politicians. The cry is raised, "The Union is in danger!" and if the Union falls, we are led to suppose that everything falls. There will be no more Thanksgiving Days; there will be anarchy and civil war, and the ruin of the American people! It is curious to see this material plenty, on the one side, and this political alarm and confusion, on the other. This condition of alarm is so well known, that nothing more need be said about it at this moment.

Let me now come to the next point and consider the causes of our present condition. This will involve a consideration of the cause of our prosperity and of our alarm.

1. First, there are some causes which depend on God entirely; such as the nature of the country, soil, climate, and the like; its minerals and natural productions; its seas and harbors, mountains and rivers. In re-

spect to these natural advantages, the country is abundantly favored, but the North less so than the South. Tennessee, Virginia, and Alabama certainly have the advantage over Maine, New Hampshire, and Ohio. That I pass by; a cause which depends wholly on God.

2. Then again, this is a wide and new country. We have room to spread. We have not to contend against old institutions established 1,000 years ago; and that is one very great advantage. I make no doubt that, in crossing the ocean, our fathers helped forward the civilization of the world at least 1,000 years; I mean to say, it would have taken mankind 1,000 years longer to reach the condition we have attained in New England if the attempt had of necessity been made on the soil of the Old World and in the face of its institutions.

3. Then, as a third thing, much depends on the peculiar national character. Well, the freemen in the North and South are chiefly from the same race, this indomitable Caucasian stock; mainly from the same composite stock, the tribe produced by the mingling of Saxon, Danish, and Norman blood. That makes the present English nation, and the American also.

This is a very powerful tribe of men, possessing some very noble traits of character; active and creative in all the arts of peace; industrious as a nation never was before; enterprising, practical; fond of liberty, fond also of law, capable of organizing themselves into great masses, and acting with a complete concert and unity of action. In these respects I think this tribe, which I will call the English tribe, is equal to any race of men in the world that has been or is; perhaps superior to any race that has been developed hitherto. But in what relates to the higher reason and imagination, to the affections and to the soul, I think this tribe is not so eminent as some others have been. North and South, the people are alike of Anglo-Norman descent.

4. Another cause of our prosperity, which depends a great deal on ourselves, is this: the absence of war and of armies. In France, with a population of less than 40 million, half a million are constantly under arms. The same state of things prevails substantially in Austria, Prussia, and in all the German states. Here in America, with a population of 20 million, there is not one in a thousand that is a soldier or Marine. In time of peace, I think we waste vast sums in military preparations, as we did in actual war not long since. Still, when I compare this nation with others, I think we have cause to felicitate ourselves on the absence of military power.

5. Again, much depends on the past history of the race; and here there is a wide difference between the different parts of the country. New England was settled by a religious colony. I will not say that all the men who came here from 1620 to 1650 were moved by religious motives; but the controlling men were brought here by these motives and no other. Many who cared less for religious ideas came for the sake of a great moral idea, for the sake of obtaining a greater degree of civil freedom than they had at home. Now the Pilgrims and the Puritans are only a little way behind us. The stiff ruff, the peaked beard, the "Prophesying Book" are only six or seven generations behind the youngest of us. The character of the Puritans has given to New England much of its present character and condition. They founded schools and colleges; they trained up their children in a stern discipline which we shall not forget for two centuries to come. The remembrance of their trials, their heroism, and their piety affects our preaching today, and our politics also.

The difference between New England and New York, from 1750 to 1790, is the difference between the sons of the religious colony and the sons of the worldly colony. You know something of New York politics before the Revolution and also since the Revolution; the difference between New York and New England politics at that time is the difference between the sons of religious men and the sons of men who cared very much less for religion.

Just now, when I said that all the North is like New England, I meant substantially so. The West is our own daughter. New England has helped people the western part of the state of New York; and the best elements of New England character mingling with others, its good qualities will appear in the politics of that mighty state.

The South, in the main, had a very different origin from the North. I think few if any persons settled there for religion's sake, or for the sake of freedom in the state. It was not a moral idea which sent men to Virginia, Georgia, and Carolina. "Men do not gather grapes of thorns." The difference of the seed will appear in the difference of the crop. In the character of the people of the North and South, it appears at this day. The North is not to be praised nor the South to be blamed for this; they could not help it, but certainly it is an advantage to be descended from a race of industrious, moral, and religious men, to have been brought up under their training, to have inherited their ideas and institutions; and this is a circumstance which we make quite too little account of. I pass by that.

6. There are other causes which depend on ourselves entirely. Much depends on the political and social organization of the people. There is no denying that government has a great influence on the character of the people; on the character of every man. The difference between the development of England and the development of Spain at this day is mainly the result of different forms of government; for three centuries ago the Spaniards were as noble a race as the English.

A government is carried on by two agencies: the first is public opinion, and the next is public law, the fundamental law which is the Constitution, and the subsidiary laws which carry out the ideas of the Constitution. In a government like this, public opinion always precedes the laws, overrides them, takes the place of laws when there are none, and hinders their execution when they do not correspond to public opinion. Thus the public opinion of South Carolina demands that a free colored seaman from the North shall be shut up in jail at his employer's cost. The public opinion of Charleston is stronger than the public law of the United States on that point, stronger than the Constitution, and nobody dares execute the laws of the United States in that matter. These two things should always be looked at to understand the causes of a nation's condition: the public opinion, as well as the public law. Let me know the opinions of the men between twenty-five and thirty-five years of age and I know what the laws will be.

Now, in public opinion and in the laws of the United States, there are two distinct political ideas. I shall call one the democratic and the other the despotic idea. Neither is wholly sectional; both chiefly so. Each is composed of several simpler ideas. Each has enacted laws and established institutions. This is the democratic idea; that all men are endowed by their Creator with certain natural rights which only the possessor can alienate; that all men are equal in these rights; that among them is the right to life, liberty, and the pursuit of happiness; that the business of the government is to preserve for every man all of these rights until he alienates them.

This democratic idea is founded in human nature and comes from the nature of God who made human nature. To carry it out politically is to execute justice, which is the will of God. This idea, in its realization, leads to a democracy, a government of all, for all, by all. Such a government aims to give every man all his natural rights; it desires to have political power in all hands, property in all hands, wisdom in all heads, goodness in all hearts, religion in all souls. I mean the religion that makes a man self-respectful, earnest, and faithful to the infinite God, that disposes him to give all men their rights, and to claim his own rights at all times; the religion which is piety within you and goodness in the manifestation.

Such a government has laws, and the aim thereof is to give justice to all men; it has officers to execute these laws for the sake of justice. Such a government founds schools for all; looks after those most who are most in need; defends and protects the feeblest as well as the richest and most powerful. The state is for the individual and for all the individuals, and so it reverences justice, where the rights of all and the interests of all exactly balance. It demands free speech; everything is open to examination, discussion, "agitation," if you will. Thought is to be free, speech to be free, work to be free, and worship to be free. Such is the democratic idea, and such the state which it attempts to found.

The despotic idea is just the opposite: that all men are *not* endowed by their Creator with certain natural rights which only the possessor can alienate, but that one man has a natural right to overcome and make use of some other men for his advantage and their hurt; that all men are *not* equal in their rights; that all men have *not* a natural right to life, liberty, and the pursuit of happiness; that government is *not* instituted to preserve these natural rights for all.

This idea is founded on the excess of human passions, and it represents the compromise between a man's idleness and his appetite. It is not based on facts eternal in human nature, but on facts transient in human nature. It does not aim to do justice to all, but injustice to some; to take from one man what he ought not to lose, and give to another what he ought not to get.

This leads to aristocracy in various forms, to the government of all by means of a part and for the sake of a part. In this state of things political power must be in few hands; property in few hands; wisdom in few heads; goodness in few hearts, and religion in few souls. I mean the religion which leads a man to respect himself and his fellow men; to be earnest and to trust in the infinite God; to demand his rights of other men and to give their rights to them.

Neither the democratic nor the despotic idea is fully made real anywhere in the world. There is no perfect democracy nor perfect aristocracy. There are democrats in every actual aristocracy; despots in every actual democracy. But in the Northern states the democratic idea prevails extensively and chiefly, and we have made attempts at establishing a democratic government. In the Southern states the despotic idea prevails extensively and chiefly, and they have made attempts to establish an aristocratic government. In an aristocracy there are two classes: the people to be governed, and the governing class — the nobility which is to govern. This nobility may be movable, and depend on wealth; or immovable, and depend on birth. In the Southern states the nobility is immovable, and depends on color. . . .

Now it is not possible for these two ideas to continue to live in peace. For a long time each knew not the other, and they were quiet. The men who clearly knew the despotic idea thought, in 1787, it would die "of a rapid consumption." They said so; but the culture of cotton has healed its deadly wound, at least for the present. After the brief state of quiet, there came a state of armed neutrality. They were hostile, but under bonds to keep the peace. Each bit his thumb, but neither dared say he bit it at the other. Now the neutrality is over; attempts are made to compromise, to compose the difficulty. Various peace measures were introduced to the Senate last summer; but they all turned out war measures, every one of them. Now there is a trial of strength between the two. Which shall recede; which be extended? Freedom or slavery? That is the question: refuse to look at it as we will, refrain or refrain not from "political agitation," that is the question.

In the last Congress it is plain the democratic idea was beaten. Congress said to California, "You may come in, and you need not keep slaves unless you please." It said, "you shall not bring slaves to Washington for sale, you may do that at Norfolk, Alexandria, and Georgetown; it is just as well, and this 'will pacify the North.' " Utah and New Mexico were left open to slavery, and 50,000 or 70,000 square miles and $10 million were given to Texas lest she should "dissolve the Union," — without money or men! To crown all, the Fugitive Slave Bill became a law.

I think it is very plain that the democratic idea was defeated, and it is easy to see why. The three powers which are the allies of the despotic idea, were ready and could act in concert — the Southern slaveholders, the leading politicians, the rich and educated men of the Northern cities, with their appendages and servile adherents. But since then, the conduct of the people in the North, and especially in this state, shows that the nation has not gone that way yet. I think the nation never will; that the idea of freedom will never be turned back in this blessed North. I feel sure it will at last overcome the idea of slavery. . . .

I do not believe the South will withdraw from the Union, with 5 million freemen and 3 million slaves. I think Massachusetts would be no loser, I think the North would be no loser; but I doubt if the North will yet allow them to go, if so disposed. Do you think the South is so mad as to wish it?

But I think I know of one cause which may dissolve the Union — one which ought to dissolve it, if put in action — that is, a serious attempt to execute the Fugitive Slave Law, here and in all the North. I mean an attempt to recover and take back all the fugitive slaves in the North and to punish, with fine and imprisonment, all who aid or conceal them. The South has browbeat us again and again. She has smitten us on the one cheek with "protection," and we have turned the other, kissing the rod; she has smitten that with "free trade." She has imprisoned our citizens; driven off with scorn and loathing our officers sent to ask constitutional justice. She has spit upon us. Let her come to take back the fugitives and, trust me, she "will wake up the lion."

In my humble opinion, this law is a wedge — sharp at one end, but wide at the other — put in between the lower planks of our ship of state. If it be driven home, we go to pieces. But I have no thought that that will be done quite yet. I believe the great politicians who threatened to drive it through the gaping seams of our argosy will think twice before they strike again. Nay, that they will soon be very glad to bury the wedge "where the tide ebbs and flows four times a day." I do not expect this of their courage but of their fears; not of their justice — I am too old for that — but of their concern for property which it is the "great object of government" to protect.

The South, the poor South!

JOHN C. CALHOUN, last words, March 31, 1850

1851

23.

A. J. Downing: Country Churches

The small New England village churches built in the seventeenth and eighteenth centuries have often been praised as representative of one of the few early forms of architecture distinctly American in structure and style. However, a number of qualified observers of American church architecture, including A. J. Downing, believed that the stark simplicity and "meetinghouse atmosphere" of country churches did not properly reflect their purpose — the worship of God. The revival of Gothic architecture around 1850 reflected a desire for more elaborate structures. Downing urged the adaptation of the Gothic style to American churches in an essay of 1851.

Source: *Rural Essays*, New York, 1853, pp. 260-264.

WHAT, AMONG ALL THE EDIFICES that compose a country town or village, is that which the inhabitants should most love and reverence, should most respect and admire among themselves, and should feel most pleasure in showing to a stranger? We imagine the answer ready upon the lips of every one of our readers in the country, and rising at once to utterance, is the village church.

And, yet, are our village churches winning and attractive in their exterior and interior? Is one drawn to admire them at first sight by the beauty of their proportions, the expression of holy purpose which they embody, the feeling of harmony with God and man which they suggest? Does one get to love the very stones of which they are composed because they so completely belong to a building which looks and is the home of Christian worship and stands as the type of all that is firmest and deepest in our religious faith and affections?

Alas! we fear there are very few country churches in our land that exert this kind of spell, a spell which grows out of making stone, and brick, and timber obey the will of the living soul and express a religious sentiment. Most persons, most committees, selectmen, vestrymen, and congregations, who have to do with the building of churches, appear, indeed, wholly to ignore the fact that the form and feature of a building may be made to express religious, civil, domestic, or a dozen other feelings as distinctly as the form and features of the human face; and yet this is a fact as well known by all true architects as that joy and sorrow, pleasure and pain are capable of irradiating or darkening the countenance. Yes, and we do not say too much when we add that right expression in a building for religious purposes has as much to do with awakening devotional feelings and begetting an attachment in the heart as the unmistakable signs of virtue and benevolence in our fellow creatures have in awakening kindred feeling in our own breasts.

We do not, of course, mean to say that a beautiful rural church will make all the population about it devotional, anymore than that sunshine will banish all gloom; but it is one of the influences that prepare the way for religious feeling, and which we are as unwise to neglect as we should be to abjure the world and bury ourselves like the ancient troglodytes in caves and caverns.

To speak out the truth boldly would be to say that the ugliest church architecture in Christendom is at this moment to be found in the country towns and villages of the United States. Doubtless, the hatred which originally existed in the minds of our Puritan ancestors against everything that belonged to the Romish Church, including in one general sweep all beauty and all taste, along with all the superstitions and errors of what had become a corrupt system of religion, is a key to the bareness and baldness and absence of all that is lovely to the eye in the primitive churches of New England, which are for the most part the type-churches of all America.

But, little by little, this ultra-puritanical spirit is wearing off. Men are not now so blinded by personal feeling against great spiritual wrongs as to identify forever all that blessed boon of harmony, grace, proportion, symmetry, and expression which make what we call beauty with the vices, either real or supposed, of any particular creed. In short, as a people, our eyes are opening to the perception of influences that are good, healthful, and elevating to the soul in all ages and all countries — and we separate the vices of men from the laws of order and beauty by which the universe is governed.

The first step which we have taken to show our emancipation from puritanism in architecture is that of building our churches with porticoes, in a kind of shabby imitation of Greek temples. This has been the prevailing taste, if it is worthy of that name, of the Northern states, for the last fifteen or twenty years. The form of these churches is a parallelogram. A long row of windows, square or roundheaded, and cut in two by a gallery on the inside; a clumsy portico of Doric or Ionic columns in front, and a cupola upon the top (usually stuck in the only place where a cupola should never be, that is, directly over the pediment or portico) such are the *chef d'oeuvres* [masterpieces] of ecclesiastical architecture, standing, in nine cases out of ten, as the rural churches of the country at large.

Now, architecturally, we ought not to consider these churches at all. And by churches we mean no narrow sectarian phrase but a place where Christians worship God. Indeed, many of the congregations seem to have felt this and contented themselves with calling them "meeting-houses." If they would go a step farther and turn them into town meetinghouses, or at least would, in future, only build such edifices for town meetings or other civil purposes, then the building and its purpose would be in good keeping, one with the other.

Not to appear presumptive and partial in our criticism, let us glance for a moment at the opposite purposes of the Grecian or classical, and the Gothic or pointed styles of architecture, as to what they really mean; for our readers must not suppose that all architects are men who merely put together certain pretty lines and ornaments to produce an agreeable effect and please the popular eye.

In these two styles, which have so taken root that they are employed at the present moment all over Europe and America, there is something more than a mere conventional treatment of doors and windows; the application of columns in one case and the introduction of pointed arches in the other. In other words, there is an intrinsic meaning or expression involved in each, which, not to understand, or vaguely to understand, is to be working blindly or striving after something in the dark.

The leading idea of the Greek architecture, then, is in its horizontal lines, the unbroken level of its cornice, which is the "level line of rationality." In this line, in the regular division of spaces, both of columns and windows, we find the elements of order, law, and human reason, fully and completely expressed. Hence, the fitness of classical architecture for the service of the state, for the town hall, the legislative assembly, the lecture room, for intellectual or scientific debate, and, in short, for all civil purposes where the reason of man is supreme. So, on the other hand, the leading idea of Gothic architecture is found in its upward lines, its aspiring tendencies. No weight of long cornices or flat ceilings can keep it down; upward; higher and higher, it soars, lifting everything, even heavy, ponderous stones, poising them in the air in vaulted ceilings, or piling them upward toward heaven, in spires, and steeples, and towers, that, in the great cathedrals, almost seem to pierce the sky. It must be a dull soul that does not catch and feel something of this upward tendency in the vaulted aisles and high, open, pointed roofs of the interior of a fine Gothic church, as well as its subdued and mellow light, and its suggestive and beautiful forms; forms, too, that are rendered more touching by their associations with Christian worship in so many ages, not, like the Greek edifices, by associations with heathen devotees.

Granting that the Gothic cathedral expresses, in its lofty, aspiring lines, the spirit of that true faith and devotion which leads us to look upward, is it possible, in the narrow compass of a village church which costs but a few hundred or, at most, a few thousand dollars, to preserve this idea?

We answer, yes. A drop of water is not the ocean, but it is still a type of the infinite; and a few words of wisdom may not penetrate the understanding so deeply — as a great volume by a master of the human heart — but they may work miracles, if fitly spoken. For it is not the magnitude of things that is the measure of their excellence and power; and there is space enough for the architect to awaken devotional feelings and lead the soul upward, so far as material form can aid in doing this, though in a less degree, in the little chapel that is to hold a few hundred, as in the mighty minster where thousands may assemble.

And the cost, too, shall not be greater; that is, if a substantial building is to be erected, and not a flimsy frame of boards and plaster. Indeed, we could quote numberless instances where the sums expended in classical buildings of false proportions but costly execution,[1] which can never raise other than emotions of pride in the human heart, would have built beautiful rural churches, which every inhabitant of the town where they chanced to stand would remember with feelings of respect and affection to the end of all time.

And, in truth, we would not desire to make the country church other than simple, truthful, and harmonious. We would avoid all pretensions to elaborate architectural ornament; we would depend upon the right proportions, forms, outlines, and the true expression. Above all, we would have the country church rural and expressive by plac-

1. We have seen with pain, lately, one of those great temple churches erected in a country town on the Hudson at a cost of $20,000. It looks outside and inside no more like a church than does the Custom House. And yet this sum would have built the most perfect of devotional edifices for that congregation.

ing it in a spot of green lawn, surrounding it with our beautiful natural shade trees and decorating its walls (for no church built in any but the newest settlements where means are utterly wanting should be built of so perishable a material as wood) with climbing plants — the ivy or, where that would not thrive, the Virginia creeper. And so we would make the country church, in its forms and outlines, its walls and the vines that enwreath them, its shady green and the elms that overhang it, as well as in the lessons of goodness and piety that emanate from its pulpit, something to become a part of the affections, and touch and better the hearts of the whole country about it.

24.

HENRY DAVID THOREAU: Walking Westward

It was at the suggestion of Emerson that Thoreau began in 1834 to keep a journal of his activities and thoughts. Notes in his journal provided the material used by him for his lecture on "Walking," given in Worcester, Massachusetts, on May 31, 1851, and reproduced here in part. The selection reflects Thoreau's feeling that walking was much more than mere exercise; it is a spiritual walk that he describes, and its direction was always westerly, for to Thoreau the West was not only a geographic designation but also a symbol of the free, the uninhibited, the "wild." Thoreau's principal occupation was in fact walking — he was a surveyor during much of his life — but he reveals here the richness of the speculations that occupied him during his perambulations.

Source: *Excursions*, Boston, 1893, pp. 161-214.

WHAT IS IT THAT MAKES IT SO HARD sometimes to determine whither we will walk? I believe that there is a subtle magnetism in nature which, if we unconsciously yield to it, will direct us aright. It is not indifferent to us which way we walk. There is a right way; but we are very liable from heedlessness and stupidity to take the wrong one. We would fain take that walk never yet taken by us through this actual world, which is perfectly symbolical of the path which we love to travel in the interior and ideal world; and sometimes, no doubt, we find it difficult to choose our direction, because it does not yet exist distinctly in our idea.

When I go out of the house for a walk, uncertain as yet whither I will bend my steps, and submit myself to my instinct to decide for me, I find, strange and whimsical as it may seem, that I finally and inevitably settle southwest, toward some particular wood or meadow or deserted pasture or hill in that direction. My needle is slow to settle — varies a few degrees, and does not always point due southwest, it is true, and it has good authority for this variation, but it always settles between west and south-southwest. The future lies that way to me, and the earth seems more unexhausted and richer on that side. The outline which would bound my walks would be not a circle but a parabola, or rather like one of those cometary orbits which have been thought to be nonreturning curves, in this case opening westward, in which my house occupies the place of the sun.

I turn round and round, irresolute, sometimes for a quarter of an hour, until I decide, for a thousandth time, that I will walk into the southwest or west. Eastward I go only by force; but westward I go free. Thither no business leads me. It is hard for me to believe that I shall find fair landscapes or sufficient wildness and freedom behind the eastern horizon. I am not excited by the prospect of a walk thither; but I believe that the forest which I see in the western horizon stretches uninterruptedly toward the setting sun, and there are no towns nor cities in it of enough consequence to disturb me.

Let me live where I will, on this side is the city, on that the wilderness, and ever I am leaving the city more and more and withdrawing into the wilderness. I should not lay so much stress on this fact if I did not believe that something like this is the prevailing tendency of my countrymen. I must walk toward Oregon and not toward Europe. And that way the nation is moving, and I may say that mankind progress from east to west. Within a few years we have witnessed the phenomenon of a southeastward migration, in the settlement of Australia; but this affects us as a retrograde movement, and, judging from the moral and physical character of the first generation of Australians, has not yet proved a successful experiment. The Eastern Tartars think that there is nothing west beyond Tibet. "The world ends there," say they; "beyond there is nothing but a shoreless sea." It is unmitigated East where they live.

We go eastward to realize history and study the works of art and literature, retracing the steps of the race; we go westward as into the future, with a spirit of enterprise and adventure. The Atlantic is a Lethean stream, in our passage over which we have had an opportunity to forget the Old World and its institutions. If we do not succeed this time, there is perhaps one more chance for the race left before it arrives on the banks of the Styx; and that is in the Lethe of the Pacific, which is three times as wide.

I know not how significant it is, or how far it is an evidence of singularity that an individual should thus consent in his pettiest walk with the general movement of the race; but I know that something akin to the migratory instinct in birds and quadrupeds — which, in some instance, is known to have affected the squirrel tribe, impelling them to a general and mysterious movement, in which they were seen, say some, crossing the broadest rivers, each on its particular chip, with its tail raised for a sail, and bridging narrower streams with their dead — that something like the *furor* which affects the domestic cattle in the spring, and which is referred to a worm in their tails, affects both nations and individuals, either perennially or from time to time. Not a flock of wild geese cackles over our town but it to some extent unsettles the value of real estate here, and, if I were a broker, I should probably take that disturbance into account.

Than longen folk to goon on pilgrimages,
And palmers for to seken straunge
                strondes.

Every sunset which I witness inspires me with the desire to go to a West as distant and as fair as that into which the sun goes down. He appears to migrate westward daily and to tempt us to follow him. He is the Great Western Pioneer whom the nations follow. We dream all night of those mountain ridges in the horizon, though they may be of vapor only, which were last gilded by his rays. The island of Atlantis, and the islands and gardens of the Hesperides, a sort of terrestrial paradise, appear to have been the Great West of the ancients, enveloped in mystery and poetry. Who has not seen in imagination, when looking into the sunset sky, the gardens of the Hesperides and the foundation of all those fables?

Columbus felt the westward tendency

more strongly than any before. He obeyed it and found a New World for Castile and Leon. The herd of men in those days scented fresh pastures from afar.

> And now the sun had stretched out all
> the hills,
> And now was dropped into the western
> bay;
> At last *he* rose, and twitched his mantle
> blue;
> Tomorrow to fresh woods and pastures
> new.

Where on the globe can there be found an area of equal extent with that occupied by the bulk of our states, so fertile and so rich and varied in its productions, and at the same time so habitable by the European, as this is? Michaux, who knew but part of them, says that "the species of large trees are much more numerous in North America than in Europe; in the United States there are more than 140 species that exceed 30 feet in height; in France there are but 30 that attain this size." Later botanists more than confirm his observations. Humboldt came to America to realize his youthful dreams of a tropical vegetation, and he beheld it in its greatest perfection in the primitive forests of the Amazon, the most gigantic wilderness on the earth, which he has so eloquently described. The geographer Guyot, himself a European, goes farther — farther than I am ready to follow him; yet not when he says:

> As the plant is made for the animal, as the vegetable world is made for the animal world, America is made for the man of the Old World. . . . The man of the Old World sets out upon his way. Leaving the highlands of Asia, he descends from station to station toward Europe. Each of his steps is marked by a new civilization superior to the preceding by a greater power of development. Arrived at the Atlantic, he pauses on the shore of this unknown ocean, the bounds of which he knows not, and turns upon his footprints for an instant.

When he has exhausted the rich soil of Europe and reinvigorated himself, "then recommences his adventurous career westward as in the earliest ages." So far Guyot.

From this Western impulse coming in contact with the barrier of the Atlantic sprang the commerce and enterprise of modern times. The younger Michaux, in his *Travels West of the Alleghanies in 1802*, says that the common inquiry in the newly settled West was, " 'From what part of the world have you come?' As if these vast and fertile regions would naturally be the place of meeting and common country of all the inhabitants of the globe."

To use an obsolete Latin word, I might say, *ex Oriente lux; ex Occidente frux* — from the East light; from the West fruit.

Sir Francis Head, an English traveler and governor-general of Canada, tells us that

> in both the Northern and Southern hemispheres of the New World, nature has not only outlined her works on a larger scale but has painted the whole picture with brighter and more costly colors than she used in delineating and in beautifying the Old World. . . . The heavens of America appear infinitely higher, the sky is bluer, the air is fresher, the cold is intenser, the moon looks larger, the stars are brighter, the thunder is louder, the lightning is vivider, the wind is stronger, the rain is heavier, the mountains are higher, the rivers longer, the forests bigger, the plains broader.

This statement will do at least to set against Buffon's account of this part of the world and its productions. . . .

THE WEST OF WHICH I SPEAK is but another name for the wild; and what I have been preparing to say is that in wildness is the preservation of the world. Every tree sends its fibers forth in search of the wild. The cities import it at any price. Men plow and sail for it. From the forest and wilderness come the tonics and barks which brace mankind. Our ancestors were savages. The story of Romulus and Remus being suckled by a wolf is not a meaningless fable. The founders of every state which has risen to eminence have drawn their nourishment and vigor from a similar wild source. It was because the children of the empire were not suckled by the wolf that they were conquered and displaced by the children of the Northern forests who were. . . .

Life consists with wildness. The most alive is the wildest. Not yet subdued to man, its presence refreshes him. One who pressed forward incessantly and never rested from his labors, who grew fast and made infinite demands on life, would always find himself in a new country or wilderness, and surrounded by the raw material of life. He would be climbing over the prostrate stems of primitive forest trees.

25.

Nostalgic Songs of the Westward Movement

The men and women who traveled westward to seek their fortune in California, Oregon, and elsewhere, always experienced hardships, and sometimes met with disaster. As the wagon trains progressed slowly along rough roads, or the pioneers camped in the wilderness during long cold nights, they often sang to lift their spirits. The three songs reprinted below reflect a unique part of America's cultural heritage. Pike County, Missouri, was the point of origin for many gold-seeking adventurers as well as the fictitious characters of the first two songs, "Sweet Betsy From Pike" and "Joe Bowers." The third song, "Acres of Clams," describes the lot of the many "busted" prospectors who left California to settle farther north, in Washington.

🎵 SWEET BETSY FROM PIKE

Oh don't you remember sweet Betsy from Pike,
Who crossed the big mountains with her lover Ike,
With two yoke of oxen, a big yellow dog,
A tall Shanghai rooster, and one spotted hog?

Chorus:
Singing dang fol dee dido,
Singing dang fol dee day.

One evening quite early they camped on the Platte.
'Twas near by the road on a green shady flat,
Where Betsy, sore-footed, lay down to repose —
With wonder Ike gazed on that Pike County rose.

The Shanghai ran off, and their cattle all died;
That morning the last piece of bacon was fried;
Poor Ike was discouraged and Betsy got mad,
The dog drooped his tail and looked wondrously sad.

They stopped at Salt Lake to inquire of the way,
Where Brigham declared that sweet Betsy should stay;
But Betsy got frightened and ran like a deer,
While Brigham stood pawing the ground like a steer.

They soon reached the desert where Betsy gave out,
And down in the sand she lay rolling about;
While Ike, half distracted, looked on with surprise,
Saying, "Betsy, get up, you'll get sand in your eyes."

Sweet Betsy got up in a great deal of pain,
Declared she'd go back to Pike County again;
But Ike gave a sigh, and they fondly embraced,
And they traveled along with his arm round her waist.

The Injuns came down in a wild yelling horde,
And Betsy was scared they would scalp her adored;
Behind the front wagon wheel Betsy did crawl,
And there fought the Injuns with musket and ball.

They suddenly stopped on a very high hill,
With wonder looked down upon old Placerville;
Ike sighed when he said, and he cast his eyes down,
"Sweet Betsy, my darling, we've got to Hangtown."

Long Ike and sweet Betsy attended a dance;
Ike wore a pair of his Pike County pants;
Sweet Betsy was dressed up in ribbons and rings;
Says Ike, "You're an angel, but where are your wings?"

❦ JOE BOWERS

My name it is Joe Bowers, and I've got a brother Ike;
I'm just here from old Missouri, and all the way from Pike;
I tell you why I left there and why I began to roam,
And left my aged parents, so far away from home.

I used to court a girl there, her name was Sally Black,
I asked her if she'd marry me, she said it was a whack;
She says to me, "Joe Bowers, before we've hitched for life,
You ought to get a little home to keep your little wife."

Says I, "My dearest Sally, oh, Sally, for your sake,
I'll go to California and try to raise a stake."
Says she to me, "Joe Bowers, you're just the one to win."
She gave me a kiss to seal the bargain and throwed a dozen in.

I'll never forget my feelings when I bid adieu to all.
Sal she cotched me around the neck, and I began to bawl.
When I began they all commenced, you never heard the like,
How they took on and cried the day I left old Pike.

When I got to this country, I had nary a red;
I had such wolfish feelings, I wished myself most dead.
But the thoughts of my dear Sally soon made this feeling git,
And whispered hopes to Bowers, Lord, I wish I had 'em yet.

At last I went to mining, put in my biggest licks,
Came down upon the boulders just like a thousand bricks;
I worked both late and early, in rain, in sun and snow,
I was working for my Sally, 'twas all the same to Joe.

One day I got a letter from my dear brother Ike,
It came from old Missouri, all the way from Pike.
It brought me the darndest news that ever you did hear,
My heart it is a-breaking, so please excuse this tear.

It said my Sal was false to me, that her love for me had fled,
That she had got married to a butcher whose hair was red;
It told me more than that — it's enough to make me swear —
That Sal had had a baby and the baby had red hair.

ACRES OF CLAMS

I've wandered all over this country,
Prospecting and digging for gold;
I've tunneled, hydraulicked, and cradled,
And I have been frequently sold.

  And I have been frequently sold,
  And I have been frequently sold.
  I've tunneled, hydraulicked, and cradled,
  And I have been frequently sold!

For one who got rich by mining,
I saw there were hundreds grew poor;
I made up my mind to try farming,
The only pursuit that is sure.

I rolled up my grub in my blanket,
I left all my tools on the ground,
I started one morning to shank it
For the country they call Puget Sound

No longer the slave of ambition,
I laugh at the world and its shams,
And think of my happy condition,
Surrounded by acres of clams.

  Surrounded by acres of clams,
  Surrounded by acres of clams.
  And think of my happy condition,
  Surrounded by acres of clams!

26.

Adin Ballou: The Hopedale Community

The 1840s was a decade of social reform. In addition to the many associations devoted to temperance, women's rights, abolition, and peace, nearly fifty "utopian" communities were established around the country. Each of these, by avoiding the complexities of society at large, hoped to initiate the Kingdom of God or at least perfect the social structure. One of the early communities was Hopedale, founded in 1841 near Milford, Massachusetts, by Adin Ballou, a Universalist spiritualist. Ballou had been active in several reform movements, and he combined their tenets in the Hopedale Community. The enterprise lasted for fifteen years and was moderately successful until Ballou stepped down as its leader in 1852. Those who replaced him dissolved the community within a few years. The following tract was written by Ballou in 1851.

Source: John Humphrey Noyes, *History of American Socialisms*, Philadelphia, 1870, pp. 120-127.

THE HOPEDALE COMMUNITY, originally called Fraternal Community No. 1, was formed at Mendon, Massachusetts, January 28, 1841, by about thirty individuals from different parts of the state. In the course of that year they purchased what was called the "Jones Farm," alias "The Dale," in Milford. This estate they named Hopedale, joining the word "Hope" to its ancient designation, as significant of the great things they hoped for from a very humble and unpropitious beginning. About the 1st of April, 1842, a part of the members took possession of their farm and commenced operations under as many disadvantages as can well be imagined.

Their present domain (December 1, 1851), including all the lands purchased at different times, contains about 500 acres. Their village consists of about thirty new dwelling houses, three mechanic shops, with waterpower, carpentering and other machinery, a small chapel, used also for the purposes of education, and the old domicile, with the barns and outbuildings much improved. There are now at Hopedale some 36 families, besides single persons, youth and children, making in all a population of about 175 souls.

It is often asked, what are the peculiarities, and what the advantages of the Hopedale Community? Its leading peculiarities are the following:

1. It is a church of Christ (so far as any human organization of professed Christians, within a particular locality, have the right to claim that title), based on a simple declaration of faith in the religion of Jesus Christ as he taught and exemplified it, according to the Scriptures of the New Testament, and of acknowledged subjection to all the moral obligations of that religion. No person can be a member who does not cordially assent to this comprehensive declaration.

Having given sufficient evidence of truthfulness in making such a profession, each individual is left to judge for him or herself, with entire freedom, what abstract doctrines are taught and also what external religious rites are enjoined in the religion of Christ. No precise theological dogmas, ordinances, or ceremonies are prescribed or prohibited. In such matters all the members are free, with mutual love and toleration, to follow their own highest convictions of truth and religious duty, answerable only to the great Head of the true Church Universal.

But in practical Christianity this church is precise and strict. There its essentials are specific. It insists on supreme love to God and man — that love which "worketh no ill" to friend or foe. It enjoins total abstinence from all God-contemning words and deeds; all unchastity; all intoxicating beverages; all oath-taking; all slaveholding and pro-slavery compromises; all war and preparations for war; all capital and other vindictive punishments; all insurrectionary, seditious, mobocratic, and personal violence against any government, society, family, or individual; all voluntary participation in any antichristian government, under promise of unqualified support — whether by doing military service, commencing actions at law, holding office, voting, petitioning for penal laws, aiding a legal posse by injurious force, or asking public interference for protection which can be given only by such force; all resistance of evil with evil; in fine, from all things known to be sinful against God or human nature. This is its acknowledged obligatory righteousness. It does not expect immediate and exact perfection of its members but holds up this practical Christian standard that all may do their utmost to reach it, and at least be made sensible of their shortcomings. Such are the peculiarities of the Hopedale Community as a church.

2. It is a civil state, a miniature Christian republic, existing within, peaceably subject to, and tolerated by the governments of Massachusetts and the United States, but otherwise a commonwealth complete within itself. Those governments tax and control its property according to their own laws, returning less to it than they exact from it. It makes them no criminals to punish, no disorders to repress, no paupers to support, no burdens to bear. It asks of them no corporate powers, no military or penal protection. It has its own constitution, laws, regulations, and municipal police; its own legislative, judiciary, and executive authorities; its own educational system of operations; its own methods of aid and relief; its own moral and religious safeguards; its own fire insurance and savings institutions; its own internal arrangements for the holding of property, the management of industry, and the raising of revenue; in fact, all the elements and organic constituents of a Christian republic on a miniature scale. There is no red republicanism in it because it eschews blood; yet it is the seedling of a true democratic and social republic wherein neither caste, color, sex, nor age stands proscribed, but every human being shares justly in "liberty, equality, and fraternity." Such is the Hopedale Community as a civil state.

3. It is a universal religious, moral, philanthropic, and social reform association. It is a missionary society for the promulgation of New Testament Christianity, the reformation of the nominal church, and the conversion of the world. It is a moral suasion temperance society on the teetotal basis. It is a moral power antislavery society, radical and without compromise. It is a peace society on the only impregnable foundation of Christian nonresistance. It is a sound theoretical and practical woman's rights association. It is a charitable society for the relief of suffering humanity to the extent of its humble ability. It is an educational society preparing to act an important part in the training of the young. It is a socialistic community successfully actualizing as well as

promulgating practical Christian socialism — the only kind of socialism likely to establish a true social state on earth. The members of this community are not under the necessity of importing from abroad any of these valuable reforms or of keeping up a distinct organization for each of them, or of transporting themselves to other places in search of sympathizers. Their own Newcastle can furnish coal for home consumption and some to supply the wants of its neighbors. Such is the Hopedale Community as a universal reform association on Christian principles.

What are its advantages?

1. It affords a theoretical and practical illustration of the way whereby all human beings willing to adopt it may become individually and socially happy. It clearly sets forth the principles to be received, the righteousness to be exemplified, and the social arrangements to be entered into in order to this happiness. It is in itself a capital school for self-correction and improvement. Nowhere else on earth is there a more explicit, understandable, practicable system of ways and means for those who really desire to enter into usefulness, peace, and rational enjoyment. This will one day be seen and acknowledged by multitudes who now know nothing of it, or knowing, despise it, or conceding its excellence are unwilling to bow to its wholesome requisitions. "Yet the willing and the obedient shall eat the good of the land."

2. It guarantees to all its members and dependents employment, at least adequate to a comfortable subsistence; relief in want, sickness, or distress; decent opportunities for religious, moral, and intellectual culture; an orderly, well-regulated neighborhood; fraternal counsel, fellowship, and protection under all circumstances; and a suitable sphere of individual enterprise and responsibility in which each one may, by due self-exertion, elevate himself to the highest point of his capabilities.

3. It solves the problem which has so long puzzled socialists, the harmonization of just individual freedom with social cooperation. Here exists a system of arrangements, simple and effective, under which all capital, industry, trade, talent, skill, and peculiar gifts may freely operate and cooperate with no restrictions other than those which Christian morality everywhere rightfully imposes, constantly to the advantage of each and all. All may thrive together as individuals and as a community without degrading or impoverishing any. This excellent system of arrangements in its present completeness is the result of various and wisely improved experiences.

4. It affords a peaceful and congenial home for all conscientious persons of whatsoever religious sect, class, or description heretofore who now embrace practical Christianity substantially as this community holds it, and can no longer fellowship the popular religionists and politicians. Such need sympathy, cooperation, and fraternal association without undue interference in relation to nonessential peculiarities. Here they may find what they need. Here they may give and receive strength by rational, liberal Christian union.

5. It affords a most desirable opportunity for those who mean to be practical Christians in the use of property, talent, skill, or productive industry to invest them. Here those goods and gifts may all be so employed as to benefit their possessors to the full extent of justice, while at the same time they afford aid to the less favored; help build up a social state free from the evils of irreligion, ignorance, poverty, and vice; promote the regeneration of the race; and thus resolve themselves into treasure laid up where neither moth, nor rust, nor thieves can reach them. Here property is preeminently safe, useful, and beneficent. It is Christianized. So, in a good degree, are talent, skill, and productive industry.

6. It affords small scope, place, or en-

couragement for the unprincipled, corrupt, supremely selfish, proud, ambitious, miserly, sordid, quarrelsome, brutal, violent, lawless, fickle, high-flying, loaferish, idle, vicious, envious, and mischief-making. It is no paradise for such, unless they voluntarily make it first a moral penitentiary. Such will hasten to more congenial localities, thus making room for the upright, useful, and peaceable.

7. It affords a beginning, a specimen, and a presage of a new and glorious social Christendom, a grand confederation of similar communities, a world ultimately regenerated and Edenized. All this shall be in the forthcoming future.

The Hopedale Community was born in obscurity, cradled in poverty, trained in adversity, and has grown to a promising childhood under the Divine guardianship, in spite of numberless detriments. The bold predictions of many who despised its puny infancy have proved false. The fears of timid and compassionate friends that it would certainly fail have been put to rest. Even the repeated desertion of professed friends, disheartened by its imperfections or alienated by too heavy trials of their patience, has scarcely retarded its progress. God willed otherwise. It has still many defects to outgrow, much impurity to put away, and a great deal of improvement to make, moral, intellectual and physical. But it will prevail and triumph. The Most High will be glorified in making it the parent of a numerous progeny of practical Christian communities. Write, saith the Spirit, and let this prediction be registered against the time to come, for it shall be fulfilled.

27.

Levi Coffin: The Underground Railroad

The "underground railroad" was a vast interstate network established by Abolitionists to aid slaves in escaping to freedom. Focal points of the "road" were in such places as southern Indiana and Ohio, free states, yet close to slave states. The number of Negroes who actually gained their freedom by this means is uncertain, but Southern outrage over the system far exceeded its actual effectiveness. One of the leaders of the underground railroad was Levi Coffin, who worked both in Indiana and in Ohio to help slaves escape. The following selection from his Reminiscences *describes the operation of the road.*

Source: *Reminiscences*, 2nd edition, Cincinnati, 1880, pp. 298-311.

I was personally acquainted with all the active and reliable workers on the Underground Railroad in the city, both colored and white. There were a few wise and careful managers among the colored people, but it was not safe to trust all of them with the affairs of our work. Most of them were too careless, and a few were unworthy — they could be bribed by the slave hunters to betray the hiding places of the fugitives. We soon found it to be the best policy to confine our affairs to a few persons and to let the whereabouts of the slaves be known to as few people as possible.

When slave hunters were prowling around the city we found it necessary to use every precaution. We were soon fully initiated into the management of Underground Railroad matters in Cincinnati, and did not lack for work. Our willingness to aid the slaves was soon known, and hardly a fugitive came to the city without applying to us for assistance. There seemed to be a continual increase of runaways, and such was the vigilance of the pursuers that I was obliged to devote a large share of time from my business to making arrangements for their concealment and safe conveyance of the fugitives.

They sometimes came to our door frightened and panting and in a destitute condition, having fled in such haste and fear that they had no time to bring any clothing except what they had on, and that was often very scant. The expense of providing suitable clothing for them when it was necessary for them to go on immediately, or of feeding them when they were obliged to be concealed for days or weeks, was very heavy.

Added to this was the cost of hiring teams when a party of fugitives had to be conveyed out of the city by night to some Underground Railroad depot, from twenty to thirty miles distant. The price for a two-horse team on such occasions was generally ten dollars, and sometimes two or three teams were required. We generally hired these teams from a certain German livery stable, sending some irresponsible though honest colored man to procure them, and always sending the money to pay for them in advance. The people of the livery stable seemed to understand what the teams were wanted for, and asked no questions.

It was necessary to use every precaution, and I thought it wise to act, as the monkey did, take the cat's paw to draw the chestnut from the fire, and not burn my own fingers. I generally gave the money to a second person to hand to the colored man. We had several trusty colored men who owned no property and who could lose nothing in a prosecution, who understood Underground

Railroad matters; and we generally got them to act as drivers, but in some instances white men volunteered to drive — generally young and able-bodied. Sometimes the depot to which the fugitives were consigned was not reached until several hours after daylight, and it required a person of pluck and nerve to conduct them to their stopping place. If the party of fugitives were large they were soon scattered among the Abolitionists in the neighborhood, and remained in safe concealment until the next night. . . .

Our house was large and well adapted for secreting fugitives. Very often slaves would lie concealed in upper chambers for weeks without the boarders or frequent visitors at the house knowing anything about it. My wife had a quiet unconcerned way of going about her work as if nothing unusual was on hand, which was calculated to lull every suspicion of those who might be watching, and who would have been at once aroused by any sign of secrecy or mystery. Even the intimate friends of the family did not know when there were slaves hidden in the house, unless they were directly informed. . . .

The fugitives generally arrived in the night and were secreted among the friendly colored people or hidden in the upper room of our house. They came alone or in companies, and in a few instances had a white guide to direct them.

One company of twenty-eight that crossed the Ohio River at Lawrenceburg, Indiana — twenty miles below Cincinnati — had for conductor a white man whom they had employed to assist them. The character of this man was full of contradictions. He was a Virginian by birth and spent much of his time in the South, yet he hated slavery. He was devoid of moral principle, but was a true friend to the poor slave.

Sometimes slaves would manage to accumulate a little money by working at making baskets at night or on the Sabbath, and when they had saved a few dollars they

Society of Friends, Swarthmore College
Levi Coffin

were very willing to give it all to some white man in whom they had confidence, if he would help them across the river and direct them how to reach the Underground Railroad. Thus I have always contended that this road was a Southern institution, being conducted however on a different principle from what it was on this side Mason and Dixon's line.

The company of twenty-eight slaves referred to, all lived in the same neighborhood in Kentucky, and had been planning for some time how they could make their escape from slavery. This white man — John Fairfield — had been in the neighborhood for some weeks buying poultry, etc., for market, and though among the whites he assumed to be very pro-slavery, the Negroes soon found that he was their friend. He was engaged by the slaves to help them across the Ohio River and conduct them to Cincinnati. They paid him some money which they had managed to accumulate. The amount was small considering the risk the conductor assumed, but it was all they had.

Several of the men had their wives with them, and one woman a little child with her, a few months old. John Fairfield conducted the party to the Ohio River opposite the mouth of the Big Miami, where he knew there were several skiffs tied to the bank, near a woodyard. When I asked him afterward if he did not feel compunctions of conscience for breaking these skiffs loose and using them, he replied: "No; slaves are stolen property, and it is no harm to steal boats or anything else that will help them gain their liberty."

The entire party crowded into three large skiffs or yawls and made their way slowly across the river. The boats were overloaded and sank so deep that the passage was made in much peril. The boat John Fairfield was in was leaky and began to sink when a few rods from the Ohio bank, and he sprang out on the sandbar, where the water was two or three feet deep, and tried to drag the boat to the shore. He sank to his waist in mud and quicksands and had to be pulled out by some of the Negroes.

The entire party waded out through mud and water and reached the shore safely, though all were wet and several lost their shoes. They hastened along the bank toward Cincinnati, but it was now late in the night and daylight appeared before they reached the city. Their plight was a most pitiable one. They were cold, hungry and exhausted; those who had lost their shoes in the mud suffered from bruised and lacerated feet, while to add to their discomfort a drizzling rain fell during the latter part of the night. They could not enter the city for their appearance would at once proclaim them to be fugitives.

When they reached the outskirts of the city, below Mill Creek, John Fairfield hid them as well as he could in ravines that had been washed in the sides of the steep hills, and told them not to move until he returned. He then went directly to John Hatfield, a worthy colored man, a deacon in the Zion Baptist Church, and told his story. He had applied to Hatfield before and knew him to be a great friend to the fugitives — one who had often sheltered them under his roof and aided them in every way he could.

John Fairfield also knew me and knew that I was a friend to the slave. I had met him several times and was acquainted with the plan of his operations in the South, but I was opposed to the principles on which he worked. . . .

When he arrived, wet and muddy, at John Hatfield's house, he was scarcely recognized. He soon made himself and his errand known, and Hatfield at once sent a messenger to me, requesting me to come to his house without delay, as there were fugitives in danger. I went at once and met several prominent colored men who had also been summoned. While dry clothes and a warm breakfast were furnished to John Fairfield, we anxiously discussed the situation of the twenty-eight fugitives who were lying hungry and shivering in the hills in sight of the city.

Several plans were suggested, but none seemed practicable. At last I suggested that someone should go immediately to a certain German livery stable in the city and hire two coaches, and that several colored men should go out in buggies and take the women and children from their hiding places, then that the coaches and buggies should form a procession as if going to a funeral, and march solemnly along the road leading to Cumminsville, on the west side of Mill Creek.

In the western part of Cumminsville was the Methodist Episcopal burying ground, where a certain lot of ground had been set apart for the use of the colored people. They should pass this and continue on the Colerain pike till they reached a right-hand road leading to College Hill. At the latter place they would find a few colored families living in the outskirts of the village, and

could take refuge among them. Jonathan Cable, a Presbyterian minister, who lived near Farmer's College, on the west side of the village, was a prominent Abolitionist, and I knew that he would give prompt assistance to the fugitives.

I advised that one of the buggies should leave the procession at Cumminsville, after passing the burying ground, and hasten to College Hill to apprise friend Cable of the coming of the fugitives that he might make arrangements for their reception in suitable places. My suggestions and advice were agreed to and acted upon as quickly as possible, John Hatfield agreeing to apprise friend Cable of the coming of the fugitives. We knew that we must act quickly and with discretion, for the fugitives were in a very unsafe position, and in great danger of being discovered and captured by the police, who were always on the alert for runaway slaves.

While the carriages and buggies were being procured, John Hatfield's wife and daughter, and other colored women of the neighborhood, busied themselves in preparing provisions to be sent to the fugitives. A large stone jug was filled with hot coffee, and this, together with a supply of bread and other provisions, was placed in a buggy and sent on ahead of the carriages that the hungry fugitives might receive some nourishment before starting. The conductor of the party, accompanied by John Hatfield, went in the buggy, in order to apprise the fugitives of the arrangements that had been made, and have them in readiness to approach the road as soon as the carriages arrived.

Several blankets were provided to wrap around the women and children, whom we knew must be chilled by their exposure to the rain and cold. The fugitives were very glad to get the supply of food, the hot coffee especially being a great treat to them, and felt much revived. About the time they finished their breakfast the carriages and buggies drove up and halted in the road, and the fugitives were quickly conducted to them and placed inside. The women in the tight carriages wrapped themselves in the blankets, and the woman who had a young babe muffled it closely to keep it warm, and to prevent its cries from being heard. The little thing seemed to be suffering much pain, having been exposed so long to the rain and cold.

All the arrangements were carried out, and the party reached College Hill in safety, and were kindly received and cared for. But, sad to relate, it was a funeral procession not only in appearance but in reality, for when they arrived at College Hill, and the mother unwrapped her sick child, she found to her surprise and grief that its stillness, which she supposed to be that of sleep, was that of death. All necessary preparations were made by the kind people of the village, and the child was decently and quietly interred the next day in the burying ground on the hill.

When it was known by some of the prominent ladies of the village that a large company of fugitives were in the neighborhood, they met together to prepare some clothing for them. Jonathan Cable ascertained the number and size of the shoes needed, and the clothes required to fit the fugitives for traveling, and came down in his carriage to my house, knowing that the Antislavery Sewing Society had their depository there. I went with him to purchase the shoes that were needed, and my wife selected all the clothing we had that was suitable for the occasion; the rest was furnished by the noble women of College Hill.

I requested friend Cable to keep the fugitives as secluded as possible until a way could be provided for safely forwarding them on their way to Canada. Friend Cable was a stockholder in the Underground Railroad, and we consulted together about the best route, finally deciding on the line by way of Hamilton, West Elkton, Eaton, Paris and Newport, Indiana. West Elkton, twenty-five or thirty miles from College Hill, was the first Underground Railroad depot. That line always had plenty of locomotives and cars in readiness.

I agreed to send information to that point, and accordingly wrote to one of my particular friends at West Elkton, informing him that I had some valuable stock on hand which I wished to forward to Newport, and requested him to send three two-horse wagons — covered — to College Hill, where the stock was resting, in charge of Jonathan Cable. I said: "Please put straw in the wagons so that they may rest easy on the journey, for many of them have sore feet, having traveled hastily over rough ground. I wish you to get to College Hill tomorrow evening; come without fail."

The three wagons arrived promptly at the time mentioned, and a little after dark took in the party, together with another fugitive, who had arrived the night before, and whom we added to the company. They went through to West Elkton safely that night, and the next night reached Newport, Indiana. With little delay they were forwarded on from station to station through Indiana and Michigan to Detroit, having fresh teams and conductors each night and resting during the day. I had letters from different stations, as they progressed, giving accounts of the arrival and departure of the train, and I also heard of their safe arrival on the Canada shore.

Sold down the river.

Of slaves sold to plantations in the Deep South, *c.* 1850

28.

Anonymous: A Uniform System of Jurisprudence

The American legal system, faced with problems of social ordering in a society essentially unprecedented in history, strove to keep step with the expansion of the nation after 1800. By mid-century, the United States found itself with a great diversity of laws. Most states had adapted the English common law heritage to meet its own special needs. Reacting to this, the legal profession divided into two camps: those who supported the diversity of local laws as one of the necessary accompaniments of state sovereignty, and those who feared that it threatened political unification. The following article, reprinted from a leading law journal, exemplifies the views of the latter group. It was a forerunner of the movement to make civil and criminal laws uniform throughout the country.

Source: *United States Monthly Law Magazine*, January 1851: "National Jurisprudence."

OUR COUNTRY HAS no general and common system of national jurisprudence. That which is furnished by the legislation of Congress and the decisions of the Supreme Court of the United States is limited in its character and restricted in its application. On the other hand, no less than thirty-one distinct systems, founded upon the legislation and judicial decisions of as many different states, subject to continual change and contradiction, baffle all attempts to master their various details, harmonize and reconcile their multitudinous incongruities and contradictions, or trace the new forms and features which they assume in almost each successive year. Yet some degree of knowledge of all these systems is necessary for the advocate and jurist before he is master of his profession, and for the judge before he is fully competent to meet all the questions which may come before him for decision; for the tribunals of each state are liable to be called upon to consider the laws of every other; nor are the occasions of such liability by any means infrequent.

There may have been a reason for this want of uniformity, at the commencement, in the nature and origin of our political institutions, and an excuse for it in the comparatively slight inconvenience which it at first occasioned. But at the present time, when all our interests are so closely interwoven and united, the reason and the excuse can hardly exist, or at all events weigh against the more powerful considerations which seem to demand a uniform national jurisprudence, prevailing and administered alike in every state.

This subject has not hitherto been mentioned among the number of judicial reforms, but seems to have been wholly unheeded, perhaps unthought of, among all the projects for new codes and new systems which have sprung up with such unparalleled facility within the last few years. It is not, however, any the less worthy of consideration on account of its former neglect, and if the thoughts which are presented in the following pages should happen to excite favorable attention in the minds of those whose talents and position can give them influence, the labor which has been expended in giving them expression will not be wholly in vain.

"The Union" is a term which we most often use to designate our common country. This Union signifies something more than a mere political compact. In the first place, it represents unity of language. The citizen of one state needs no interpreter when he steps beyond its confines into another. Wherever he may go, he understands all whom he may meet and is understood by all. Strangers from remote parts meet almost as familiar acquaintances. Facility of intercourse wakens harmony of feeling, sows the seeds of friendship, and opens the way to the multiplied transactions of business. This bond of union is of mighty strength in our political relations. . . .

This *Union* also reminds us of an identity of race. In every state are the endearing monuments of our common origin, significant of indomitable energy, commanding talents, and unparalleled enterprise. Nor do the occasional intermingling and contact of other races in any respect destroy this identity. We invite among us the exiles of the world; they are received in our midst and become part and parcel of ourselves. Even the nation which we have so recently added to our own is already receiving the impress of our language, our manners, our laws, and our character, so that the recent Mexican will a few years hence be scarcely conscious that he was not always an American.

But there is yet a closer union than that of race. The ties of kindred and blood embrace the inhabitants of every state. Fathers, sons, and brothers are scattered from Maine to California, from Georgia to Oregon. He who sets out in search of fortune, fame, or adventures girds himself for no slight journey. He seeks the farthest wild, the outmost verge of civilization; neither desert nor mountain nor river stops his progress. Now his impatient step is on the shores of the Atlantic; next his restless tread is along the sands of the Pacific: but he ever has in remembrance the friends he has left behind;

and this remembrance is among the ties that bind states together.

From this identity of language and race, and from this scattering abroad of kindred and friends, springs a community of interest whose influence knows no limit either of extent or power. We are united for a common protection and defense — how effectually has been proved in many a well-fought field. We are united in all the interests of literature, science, and the arts. It is a national measure that secures to the author the profit of his works and to the inventor the benefit of his discoveries. Yet, in the end, the profit and the benefit, if any there be, are not confined to one but enjoyed by all. But more intimate still are the interests of trade, commerce, and business. These penetrate and pervade every state, county, and village. No inhabited spot, however remote, is exempt from their influence. Nor is this the less so because the inhabitants of some sections are engaged in pursuits of trade, those of others in agriculture, and those of others still in manufactures or mechanic arts.

These pursuits materially depend upon and support each other. The cotton, sugar, rice, and tobacco of the South, the products of the teeming fields of the West, and the various fabrics of the North and East meet daily upon some common ground. The princely merchant of the city and the smaller dealer of the country are daily brought into communion. The proud ship of the ocean receives its lading from the little bark or pygmy car of the distant interior, and freights the bark and car back again in return. All these interests grow and expand by each other's aid. They are the pride and power of our country, and more glorious than the imperial legions and subject provinces of ancient Rome. They are not confined to any one community or exclusive limits, and the facilities for their development and expansion are continually growing more perfect and extended.

Memory runs back but a brief space of

time when the slow-moving coach bore us in our painful and halting journey for days and weeks to another state — then to us as a distant and foreign country — or the lazy sloop, ever at the mercy of adverse winds, carried us on a lingering, seasick voyage from port to port; or we were, and indeed are sometimes now, compelled to wait for annual floods to bear ourselves and the products of our industry down rapid and dangerous rivers to seek a market. After weeks and months the slow mail brought replies to our letters from distant friends.

Now the swift car wheels the traveler over the iron track, and the distant city is reached in a day. Now the traveler puts himself, at night, upon some palace of the deep, and during the hours of repose a long voyage is accomplished. Now we seek converse with a friend a thousand miles remote; sooner than the words can be formed the message flies, and swift as thought the answer returns. The neighbor is no longer confined to the next door, the next street, or the next farm. What seemed great distance a few years since is but small now. Friends and kindred separate for distant places but the separations seem slight. The calls of business are heard from distant points, but they occasion no extraordinary stir; they are obeyed with the same facility as if made in the same town.

Intervening space seems scarcely longer to exist. The vast and complicated details of business every day make a wide circle. They constantly operate to diminish the distinctness of state lines and obliterate geographical divisions and distinctions. Despite the threatening portents which are sometimes seen in the political sky, our country is all the time becoming more as one, and the necessity of union is increasing in an equal ratio with the increase of facilities for travel, communication, and mutual intercourse.

But that which has been predicated of almost every other interest of our country cannot truly be said of our jurisprudence. In this respect, there seems to be no sympathy, intercourse, or communion between the different states. The jurisprudence of the country enters into, and indeed forms a part of, all its business relations. These business relations are everywhere extended, interwoven, and connected together; yet they are subject in each different state to the application of a different legal system. There is no man of considerable business but has experienced the inconvenience and evil of this state of things.

It is not necessary or desirable to interfere with the more local police regulations of the states or trample upon their sovereign rights. But there are certain general principles applicable to legislation and judicial systems which should prevail everywhere alike. Nor is it less necessary, so far as practical results are concerned, that the details of legal proceedings, through a country like ours, should be everywhere the same. The like may be said of many of those arbitrary regulations which have no inherent foundation in right or wrong, but which should, in some form or other, be adopted in every government.

Of this character is the rate of interest upon the loan or forbearance of money, which is universally fixed, and some restriction upon the taking of usury imposed by law. In the different states are no less than four different rates. In nineteen, the rate is 6 percent; in five, 7; in four, 8; and in one, 5. This difference is no slight embarrassment to our commercial intercourse. Besides the legal questions to which it gives occasion, it tends to direct capital from the states where the lower rates of interest prevail to those in which the rates are higher. The one state is deprived of its necessary and proper capital, and the other, by offering a bounty upon its importation in the higher rate of interest, stimulates enterprise and business to an unnatural degree.

The businessman who constantly pays high for the use of money sooner or later becomes bankrupt. It is so in general with states; and it will be found, upon comparison, that those localities which sustain high rates of interest enjoy far less commercial stability than those where the lower rates prevail. In the newly settled portions of the country which are difficult of access, capital is usually scarce, and the scarcity furnishes an excuse for a temporary disregard of the principle above stated. But, as a general thing, in respect to the country at large, its business is now so connected together, and the facilities for intercourse, communication, and the transmission of property are so great that there is, in reality, no longer any reason for a higher rate of interest in one state than another.

This diversity in the rate of interest has its effect upon the value of property, which must always maintain a relative position with the value of money. The higher the value of the one, the less is the relative value of the other. If, therefore, the value of money is fixed by law at a higher point in one state than another, the value of property must be relatively greater in the latter. The value of money is determined by the rate of interest.

There is also a want of uniformity in the tenure of lands and the rules which govern the descent, transmission, and distribution of property. There is a diversity even in the formalities of a conveyance, the mode of proof or acknowledgment, and the proper officer to take the same. This is not merely an inconvenience, it is a positive evil. It embarrasses the interchange of property, leads to defective titles, and in the end engenders expensive litigation. Citizens of one state become owners of land in another, but are never certain without much trouble and expense of the nature and conditions of the title they acquire; and if they seek to dispose of such land, they are subjected to the same or greater difficulties in making the proper conveyance with the proper formalities. Indeed, it often happens that they are only successful after repeated trials, and even then sometimes fail.

To comprehend the full force of these difficulties, it is only necessary to look at the various statutes of the several states regulating the acquisition and disposition of real estate, the variety of rules concerning the right of dower, the laws of descent, the mode of conveyance, the attestation, proof, or acknowledgment of the same, the disposition of property by will — all founded indeed upon the same general principles, yet so differing in the details as on that very account to occasion the greater perplexity and inconvenience.

This is not a necessary state of things. These differences and distinctions are not founded upon principle but are entirely arbitrary. They are not founded on difference of location, of population, or other circumstances; for of all the rules referred to, those which are found most suitable and convenient for one state must be equally suitable and convenient for another.

But there are still other vexations and difficulties to which the citizen of one state is subject who has business intercourse in another. He finds, in that intercourse, if it ever requires resort to legal proceedings, a different mode of administering justice from that to which he has been accustomed. The courts to which he is compelled to apply exercise a different jurisdiction and are governed by different rules of practice and procedure. He finds different laws relating to frauds, to the limitation of actions, to insolvency, and other matters relating to remedial justice — in all which, as in the commercial law of the country, there should be universal uniformity.

The various, multiplied, and often vast commercial dealings between the citizens of different states, the constantly increasing advantages for commercial intercourse, and the immense interests involved render it indispensable that the utmost facility should be afforded in the pursuit of remedies for every wrong or breach of good faith. This facility cannot exist unless he who has suffered injury shall be entitled to avail himself of the same exercise of jurisdiction and the same remedies in the courts of every part of the Union. But this is not, at present, the case. In some states, a summary process is allowed which at once affords a creditor security for his debt. In others, he is subjected to such delays that the debtor, if dishonestly disposed, conceals, disposes of, or squanders his property to the defeat of a just claim. In some, the creditor can compel a sale of property to the ruin of his debtor. In others, he can only get satisfaction out of the rents and profits of his debtor's estate. In some, the law secures to the debtor, from liability for debts, sufficient property for a competence. In others, it sacrifices almost everything to the claim of the creditor.

In addition to individual inconvenience, this state of things begets evils of a political character which seem never to have been contemplated by statesmen or politicians. It fixes upon the states subject to these differences different characters for credit, responsibility, morals, and security for property. Those states which afford the best facilities for enforcing the obligations of contracts, good faith, and the various duties owing from one man to another, ever enjoy a higher character in these particulars. In such states, property is more secure, and moral and business integrity stands higher.

On the other hand, in those states whose systems are lax in compelling those obligations and afford opportunity for evasion or delay, there is less confidence, credit is at a lower ebb and pays a higher premium. In the former states, those who are impatient of the restraints of good laws, thoroughly enforced, seek refuge in the latter; while, in the latter, those who are disposed to perform all their obligations are compelled to resort to the former. The laxity or stringency of laws to compel the duties of citizens has not a little to do with public and private morals. When these laws are stringent within the proper limits and rigidly enforced, good morals are more generally found. On the contrary, extreme laxity and leniency in such laws, either in their letter or enforcement, result in public degeneracy.

By the term "morals," regard is had not merely to those scandalous offenses against society which outrage sense and decency but that disregard of the duties which one man owes to another, of pecuniary obligations, that trifling with the promise to pay and to do, and the thousand frauds and devices which spring from the effort to avoid those obligations and are no less pestilential to society than open and acknowledged vices. It has already remarked that the variety of laws in these respects operates in favor of some states, at the expense of others. No man loans his money or sells his property on credit but looks to the security which he may have for its repayment. The means of coercing repayment in case of default is part of that security. If these means be prompt and efficient, it adds to the security. The terms of credit are favorable in proportion to the safety of the security. That state, therefore, which affords to the creditor the least efficient means for the recovery and satisfaction of his debt, and affixes the slightest penalties to the breach of contract and obligations, to that degree suffers in credit and character. Its citizens pay higher interest in proportion to the increased risks.

It is true that when one trusts to the word or obligation of another he does it in the hope and expectation that the word or obligation will be performed; yet he never loses sight of the fact that accident, misfortune, or fraud may interfere, and therefore looks to his ultimate means of security and satisfaction. It is not to be disguised that a strife is going on, if not between states at least between political parties, to see which shall afford laws most lenient to the debtor, in utter forgetfulness that the helpless orphan and unprotected widow, or even poor laborer, are as likely to suffer by a dishonest debtor as poverty from the exactions of a merciless creditor.

We advocate no unnecessary rigor, but a just medium between that excessive mildness and that unrelenting severity which equally tend to defeat the ends of justice. This just medium, when ascertained, as it doubtless may be, from the experience of the past, should be confined to no locality, but should be uniform and universal.

There is the same variety to be found in the criminal as in the civil codes of the several states, often giving rise to serious questions of jurisdiction, and involving the states themselves in bitter and recriminating controversies. It is therefore a reasonable subject of inquiry, whether, among states whose citizens are in habits of such common and familiar intercourse, they should not be subject to one common criminal code, at least, except so far as locality or circumstances may require a difference. There is and there can be no substantial reason why an act innocent in one state should be criminal in another, except it be in relation to some subject existing in the former and not in the latter; why an act constituting one degree of crime in one state should be of a different degree in another; why the same offense should be punished by death in one state and by a milder penalty in another; why one mode of trial and certain rules of evidence should prevail in one state and other modes of trial and different rules of evidence in another. . . .

Acts which are really offenses against society anywhere are equally so everywhere. If innocent and beneficial anywhere, they are equally so everywhere; and when they are allowed in one place and restricted in another, the former becomes the abode of all those in the latter who desire to practise them. The citizen of one state should not, when he steps into another, find himself subject to punishment for an act which in his own would be entirely innocent. There may be some regulations required by the peculiar situation or circumstances of a state to which these principles will not apply, but in regard to all acts which are really offenses against society at large, there can be no exception. Uniformity of criminal codes, however, although desirable, is not indispensable, and does not necessarily enter into the plan which it is the object of this article to suggest. It would certainly tend to render the system more harmonious and perfect, and render stronger and more entire that unity which is so essential to the perfection of every system.

The foregoing are a few of the legal topics out of which spring that variety, contrariety, and conflict of laws which tend to embarrass the business, restrict the intercourse, and obstruct the justice of the country. All, or nearly all, legal questions and titles are subject to the same difficulties as those which have been mentioned. To obviate these difficulties, to advance legal science and philosophy, and to promote universal justice, it is proposed to have in this country but one legal system in its principles or its details; or rather that all legal systems should be founded upon the same model and pursue the same plan, embracing every principle of universal application and every subject upon which a conflict of laws can arise. Thus may we hope to realize for the several states of our Union the mere enlarged aspirations of a writer deeply and ardently imbued with the sound and conservative spirit of legal philosophy, progress, and reform —

> such a similarity of laws and institutions as will favor intercommunion, diminish state jealousies, lessen the causes of discord, and prepare the American family, if not for one religious and political faith, at least for such an approximation as will greatly enlarge the sphere of reciprocal usefulness and of national and individual enjoyment.

— Hoffman's *Legal Studies*.

It is true that by the general maxims of jurisprudence, every state possesses exclusive sovereignty and jurisdiction within its own territory; that no state can by its laws directly affect or bind property out of its own territory, or bind persons not resident therein; and that whatever force and obligation the laws of one state have in another depend solely upon the laws and regulations of the latter. . . . Yet that comity which has become a part of every enlightened system of jurisprudence in many instances gives force and effect to the laws and judicial proceedings of other states. Still there are many instances in which this comity is not applicable and does not prevail. That such is the case is owing to the existing diversity of laws and legal systems. Do away with this diversity and adopt the principle of uniformity, and every state in the exercise of its proper jurisdiction will accord to the laws of every other the same respect that is conceded to its own. . . .

Suppose each of the thirty-one states to adopt the same legal and judicial system, subject to no change which shall not be adopted by all, or at least a majority, how will many of our doubts, difficulties, and uncertainties disappear! How much learning will be no longer necessary! What study and toil of the jurist, the judge, the legislator, and the student may be dispensed with! To what perfection may not American legal science, thus adopting some degree of unity and simplicity, be brought! The legal learning and talent of the thirty-one states, instead of being devoted to as many different systems will be concentrated on one, and it will ill accord with our character in other respects if they do not produce a body of jurisprudence as perfect as the world has ever seen. National, not sectional, in its character, and universal, if not in the obligations it shall impose, at least, in the respect it shall win from the civilized world.

It is true that there can be no appellate jurisdiction to control these systems and correct their errors, and that each must in general be supreme in its own state. Yet the defect will be in a measure supplied by the Supreme Court of the United States. That Court now administers and expounds the laws of the several states as it finds them, adopts the practice, and is governed by the decisions of the courts of the states in which the questions to be decided arise. The hitherto divided labors of that Court, therefore, will become more concentrated and consequently tend to greater certainty, uniformity, and perfection.

But it is not the desirableness and necessity of uniformity in our legal systems that require demonstration. The only question is as to its feasibility. We shall be met with the ever active jealousy of encroachment on state rights. We shall be told that there nowhere resides the power to effect the object. But it is not necessary to interfere with state sovereignty, nor is it desirable to exercise compulsion. The whole scheme can be accomplished by voluntary action.

Let a correspondence be opened by and with the proper authorities of the several states recommending the appointment of a commissioner, or commissioners, from each state, not exceeding three, whose duty it shall be to meet from time to time and frame a code of statute law, embracing only these provisions which shall be equally applicable in every state and shall not interfere with the constitutional provisions of any. This commission will, of course, examine and scrutinize carefully the statute codes of each state and inquire into the operations and defects of each particular law. Nor will the inquiry be confined to the codes of our own states but those of every civilized country may be brought into requisition, and the best features of all, so far as they may be in harmony with the genius of our government and institutions, contribute to the perfection of the plan to be adopted.

When any branch of the labors of this commission have been finished, let it be submitted to the legislatures of the several states for such corrections and improvements as they, in their wisdom, may deem it necessary to make; and let it then be again recommitted, for the final action of the commission, when they shall have completed their plan.

When all the heads and titles of statute law shall have been subjected to this process and framed into a complete body by the commission in that form, let it be adopted by the legislature of each state. In carrying out this plan, it is not necessary to overturn existing systems or make great and radical changes. The grand features and fundamental principles of each present system may be preserved and yet the whole be reduced to harmonious uniformity. It is not recommended to strike out new paths, to seek new inventions, or even disturb ancient prejudices. Neither is it expected that this is to be the work of a day or even a year. Such are the checks against sudden innovations that no change can be effected without the most thorough scrutiny and every needful preparation on the part of the public mind.

The system may require five or even ten years for its perfection. Nor is it proposed to stop when the system is once adopted. Like all human productions, it will be liable to imperfections, and the many changes and improvements which grow out of the progressive spirit of the age will call for corresponding change and adaptation in the laws. The commission should therefore be continued or reappointed from time to time for the purpose of remedying imperfections and recommending the necessary improvements and reforms.

The scheme of uniting every state in some uniform system of jurisprudence is herein shadowed forth, for it does not profess to be complete. But the task of its accomplishment will devolve upon those who see, in the science of law, something more than the daily routine of professional duty; something more than the mere means of acquiring a livelihood, or even wealth; who see in it a profound and sublime philosophy, teaching mankind the source of their rights and obligations and the means by which those rights and obligations are to be maintained. *Jurisprudentia est divinarum atque humanarum rerum notitia, justi atque injusti scientia* [Jurisprudence is the knowledge of human and divine affairs and an understanding of justice and injustice]. . . .

The success of the system which is here recommended has no less importance in a political view. How would it tend to connect the bonds of union? How would it operate to dissipate the enmities, the prejudices, and jealousies which so often threaten our national existence? Might we not reasonably hope for the day when one section, arrayed against the other, will no longer study and strive how to get and maintain a political supremacy over the other, but the sole study and the sole strife shall be in the spirit of comity to suggest and perfect measures for the universal and common good; when the states (while they remain in all that pertains to individual interests several) shall yet deem themselves in all that concerns national greatness, glory, and happiness, one.

Then, to borrow and apply to our country, the prediction of Cicero, which Story has so beautifully applied to his subject in his commentaries on the conflict of laws: *Non erit alia lex Romae, alia Athenis, alia nunc, alia posthuc; sed et omnis gentis, et omni tempore, una lex et sempiterna, et immortalis continebit* [There will not be one law for Rome, another for Athens, one now, another hereafter; but one eternal and imperishable law will encompass all people for all time].

Miners panning for gold in Spanish Flat, California, 1852

THE GOLD RUSH

The discovery of gold on the American River, California, in January of 1848 opened a new way of life for hundreds of thousands. The immigrant from Europe was often told the streets of American cities were paved with gold; Spanish explorers had spent their lives in fruitless search for Cibola or Eldorado. Now all the myths seemed to be verified by wild tales from California, improved by hundreds of retellings before they reached the East Coast or traveled overseas.

Easterners sailed around the Horn or crossed the Isthmus of Panama in the rush to San Francisco and the gold fields be-yond. Many made the long trek westward across the Great Plains, the Rockies, and the Sierras. This migration was unlike any other in American history. Few women took part, and nearly all were driven by a desire to get rich quickly, not to settle the land.

While many reputable people took part in the rush, those who had least to lose by pulling up stakes, those with few if any responsibilities, were the first to go. An immediate result was a reign of lawlessness and terrorism that spread from the mining camps to San Francisco. In response, Vigilance Committees were established and lynch law was invoked to restore order.

"The Way They Go To California"; lithograph by N. Currier, 1849

(Left) Crossing the Panama isthmus enroute to California; (right) Capt. Wakeman, who sailed to "Adelaide" between Panama and San Francisco; (below) Panama railroad terminus at Culebra, 1854

View of San Francisco in 1849

Daguerreotype view
of hotel construc-
tion in San Fran-
cisco, 1850

Montgomery Street
in San Francisco,
1850; daguerreo-
type by Fred Coombs

San Francisco, 1852. The harbor is jammed with ships abandoned by crews gone to the gold fields

(Right) Exchange Bank on Montgomery Street in San Francisco, 1856; (below) procession in plaza in San Francisco celebrating admission to the Union in 1850

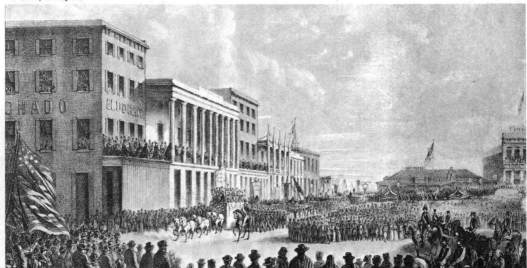

(Above) Infantry regiment on patrol in San Francisco, 1856; (below) warehouse converted into Fort Vigilance during 1856-1857 by the San Francisco Vigilance Committee

(Above) Miners in Auburn Ravine, 1852; (below) Maine Bar claim, California, 1859

(Left) Daguerreotype of miners panning for gold; (below) mining camp at Forrest Tunnel, California

Sacramento City, Cal., from the foot of "J" Street; drawn in 1849 by G. V. Cooper

(Right) Placerville, formerly Hangtown, Cal.; (below) view from the east of the mining camp at Poverty Bar, 1859

Sketch of Los Angeles prepared for the Pacific Railroad survey report in 1853

(Left) Two sketches from "Gleason's Pictorial" of a native Californian and a California miner; (below) Mission Dolores, founded in 1776. Photograph from "San Francisco Album," 1856-1857

Coeur-d'Alene Mission, established by the Jesuit fathers in the Rocky Mountains, 1842; drawing by Sohon

Jason Lee, Methodist missionary

When the United States gained undisputed possession of the Oregon Territory by treaty in 1846, several thousand American settlers had already established themselves. American communities had grown up in the Willamette Valley and elsewhere around missionary outposts founded by Rev. Jason Lee and Dr. Marcus Whitman in the 1830s. By 1846 these farmers far outnumbered the fur-traders, like Peter Ogden, who were the first settlers.

(Above) Front Street, Portland, Ore., in 1852; (below) parade celebrating admission to the Union, 1859

Peter Skeur Ogden

29.

JONATHAN BALDWIN TURNER: An Industrial University for Illinois

Until the 1850s, most schools of higher education were devoted to the study of the classics, general science, political economy, and moral philosophy, and few excelled even in this "liberal arts" curriculum. The increased industrialism and the application of scientific techniques to agriculture brought forth demands for education that would benefit more than the few who received the "professional" schooling that was available. One of the earliest plans for an industrial educational institution was proposed by J. B. Turner, a graduate of Yale and an important figure in the development of education in Illinois. The following selection, incorporating his ideas for a university for the industrial classes, was presented by Turner to a farmers' convention at Granville, Illinois, on November 18, 1851. The University of Illinois, which was founded in 1867 as the Illinois Industrial University, owed much to Turner's work in the Industrial League, organized to promote industrial education, and to his agitation in the state legislature after the Morrill Act passed in 1862.

Source: *A Plan for an Industrial University for the State of Illinois*, n.p., 1851.

ALL CIVILIZED SOCIETY is, necessarily, divided into two distinct cooperative, not antagonistic, classes: a small class whose proper business it is to teach the true principles of religion, law, medicine, science, art, and literature; and a much larger class who are engaged in some form of labor in agriculture, commerce, and the arts. For the sake of convenience, we will designate the former the professional and the latter the industrial class; not implying that each may not be equally industrious: the one in their intellectual, the other in their industrial, pursuits. Probably in no case would society ever need more than 5 men out of 100 in the professional class, leaving 95 in every 100 in the industrial; and so long as so many of our ordinary teachers and public men are taken from the industrial class as there are at present, and probably will be for generations to come, we do not really need over 1 professional man for every 100, leaving 99 in the industrial class.

The vast difference, in the practical means, of an *appropriate liberal education*, suited to their wants and their destiny, which these two classes enjoy and ever have enjoyed the world over, must have arrested the attention of every thinking man. True, the same general abstract science exists in the world for both classes alike, but the means of bringing this abstract truth into effectual contact with the daily business and pursuits of the one class does exist, while in the other case it does not exist, and never can, till it is new created.

The one class has schools, seminaries, colleges, universities, apparatus, professors, and multitudinous appliances for educating and training them for months and years for the peculiar profession which is to be the business of their life. And they have already created, each class for its own use, a vast and voluminous literature that would well-nigh sink a whole navy of ships.

But where are the universities, the apparatus, the professors, and the literature specifically adapted to any one of the industrial classes? Echo answers, where? In other words, society has become, long since, wise enough to know that its *teachers* need to be educated; but it has not yet become wise enough to know that its *workers* need education just as much.

In these remarks I have not forgotten that our common schools are equally adapted and applied to all classes; but reading, writing, etc., are, properly, no more education than gathering seed is agriculture, or cutting ship timber, navigation. They are the mere rudiments, as they are called, or means, the mere instrument of an after education; and, if not so used, they are, and can be, of little more use to the possessor than an axe in the garret or a ship rotting upon the stocks. . . .

But an answer to two simple questions will perhaps sufficiently indicate our ideas of the whole subject, though that answer, on the present occasion, must necessarily be confined to a bare outline.

The first question, then, is this: *What do the industrial classes want?*

[This] may be answered in few words. They want, and they ought to have, the same facilities for understanding the true philosophy, the science and the art of their several pursuits (their life business), and of efficiently applying existing knowledge thereto and widening its domain, which the professional classes have long enjoyed in their pursuits. Their first labor is, therefore, to supply a vacuum from fountains already full and bring the living waters of knowledge within their own reach. Their second is to help fill the fountains with still greater supplies. They desire to depress no institution, no class whatever; they only wish to elevate themselves and their pursuits to a position in society to which all men acknowledge they are justly entitled, and to which they also desire to see them aspire.

2. *How, then, can that want be supplied?* In answering this question, I shall endeavor

to present, with all possible frankness and clearness, the outline of impressions and convictions that have been gradually deepening in my own mind for the past twenty years, and let them pass for whatever the true friends of the cause may think them worth.

And I answer, first, negatively, that this want cannot be supplied by any of the existing institutions for the professional classes, nor by any incidental appendage attached to them as a mere secondary department.

These institutions were designed and adapted to meet the wants of the professional classes, as such, especially the clerical order; and they are no more suited to the real wants of the industrial class than the institution we propose for them would be suited to the professional class.

Their whole spirit and aim is, or should be, literary and intellectual, not practical and industrial; to make men of books and ready speech, not men of work and industrial, silent thought. But the very best classical scholars are often the very worst practical reasoners; and that they should be made workers is contrary to the nature of things, the fixed laws of God. The whole interest, business, and destiny for life of the two classes run in opposite lines; and that the same course of study should be equally well adapted to both is as utterly impossible as that the same pursuits and habits should equally concern and befit both classes.

The industrial classes know and feel this, and therefore they do not, and will not, patronize these institutions, only so far forth as they desire to make professional men for public use. As a general fact, their own multitudes do, and *will forever,* stand aloof from them; and, while they desire to foster and cherish them for their own appropriate uses, they know that they do not, and cannot, fill the sphere of their own urgent industrial wants. They need a similar system of *liberal education* for their own class and adapted to their own pursuits; to create for them an *industrial literature* adapted to their professional wants, to raise up for them *teachers* and *lecturers* for subordinate institutes, and to elevate them, their pursuits, and their posterity to that relative position in human society for which God designed them.

The whole history of education, both in Protestant and Catholic countries, shows that we must begin with the higher institutions, or we can never succeed with the lower; for the plain reason that neither knowledge nor water will run uphill. No people ever had, or ever can have, any system of common schools and lower seminaries worth anything until they first founded their higher institutions and fountains of knowledge from which they could draw supplies of teachers, etc., for the lower. We would begin, therefore, where all experience and common sense show that we must begin if we would effect anything worthy of an effort.

In this view of the case, the first thing wanted in this process is a *national institute of science* to operate as the great central luminary of the national mind, from which all minor institutions should derive light and heat, and toward which they should also reflect back their own. This primary want is already, I trust, supplied by the Smithsonian [Institution], endowed by James Smithson and incorporated by the U.S. Congress at Washington, D.C.

To cooperate with this noble institute and enable the industrial classes to realize its benefits in practical life, we need a *university for the industrial classes* in each of the states, with their consequent subordinate institutes, lyceums, and high schools, in each of the counties and towns. . . .

PLAN FOR THE STATE UNIVERSITY

THERE SHOULD BE CONNECTED with such an institution, in this state, a sufficient quantity of land of variable soil and aspect for all its needful annual experiments and processes in the great interests of agriculture and horticulture.

Buildings of appropriate size and construction for all its ordinary and special uses; a complete philosophical, chemical, anatomical, and industrial apparatus; a general cabinet embracing everything that relates to, illustrates, or facilitates any one of the industrial arts; especially all sorts of animals, birds, reptiles, insects, trees, shrubs, and plants found in this state and adjacent states.

Instruction should be constantly given in the anatomy and physiology, the nature, instincts, and habits of animals, insects, trees, and plants; their laws of propagation, primogeniture, growth and decay, disease and health, life and death; on the nature, composition, adaptation, and regeneration of soils; on the nature, strength, durability, preservation, perfection, composition, cost, use, and manufacture of all materials of art and trade; on political, financial, domestic, and manual economy (or the saving of labor of the hand) in all industrial processes; on the true principles of national, constitutional, and civil law; and the true theory and art of governing and controlling, or directing, the labor of men in the state, the family, shop, and farm; on the laws of vicinage, or the laws of courtesy and comity between neighbors, as such, and on the principles of health and disease in the human subject, so far, at least, as is needful for household safety; on the laws of trade and commerce, ethical, conventional, and practical; on bookkeeping and accounts; and, in short, in all those studies and sciences, of whatever sort, which tend to throw light upon any art or employment which any student may desire to master, or upon any duty he may be called to perform, or which may tend to secure his moral, civil, social, and industrial perfection as a man.

No species of knowledge should be excluded, practical or theoretical; unless, indeed, those specimens of "organized ignorance" found in the creeds of party politicians and sectarian ecclesiastics should be mistaken by some for a species of knowledge.

Whether a distinct classical department should be added or not would depend on expediency. It might be deemed best to leave that department to existing colleges as their more appropriate work, and to form some practical and economical connection with them for that purpose; or it might be best to attach a classical department in due time to the institution itself.

To facilitate the increase and practical application and diffusion of knowledge, the professors should conduct, each in his own department, a continued series of *annual experiments*.

For example, let twenty or more acres of each variety of grain (each acre accurately measured) be annually sown, with some practical variation on each acre as regards the quality and preparation of the soil; the kind and quantity of seed; the time and mode of sowing or planting; the time, and modes, and processes of cultivation and harvesting; and an accurate account kept of all costs, labor, etc., and of the final results.

Let analogous experiments be tried on all the varied products of the farm, the fruit yard, the nursery, and the garden; on all modes of crossing, rearing, and fattening domestic animals, under various degrees of warmth and of light, with and without shelter; on green, dry, raw, ground, and cooked food, cold and warm; on the nature, causes, and cure of their various diseases, both of those on the premises and of those brought in from abroad; and advice given and annual reports made on those and all similar topics.

Let the professors of physiology and entomology be ever abroad at the proper seasons, with the needful apparatus for seeing all things visible and invisible, and scrutinizing the latent causes of all those blights, blasts, rots, rusts, and mildews which so often destroy the choicest products of industry, and thereby impair the health, wealth, and comfort of millions of our fellowmen. Let the professor of chemistry carefully analyze the various soils and products of the state, retain specimens, give instruction, and report on their various qualities, adaptations, and deficiencies.

Let similar experiments be made in all other interests of agriculture and mechanic or chemical art, mining, merchandise and transportation by water and by land, and daily practical and experimental instruction given to each student in attendance in his own chosen sphere of research or labor in life. Especially let the comparative merits of all laborsaving tools, instruments, machines, engines, and processes be thoroughly and practically tested and explained, so that their benefits might be at once enjoyed or the expense of their cost avoided by the unskillful and unwary.

It is believed by many intelligent men that from one-third to one-half the annual products of this state are annually lost from ignorance on the above topics. And it can scarcely be doubted that in a few years the entire cost of the whole institution would be annually saved to the state in the above interests alone, aside from all its other benefits intellectual, moral, social, and pecuniary.

The *apparatus* required for such a work is obvious. There should be grounds devoted to a botanical and common garden; to orchards and fruit yards; to appropriate lawns and promenades in which the beautiful art of landscape gardening could be appropriately applied and illustrated; to all varieties of pasture, meadow, and tillage needful for the successful prosecution of the needful annual experiments. And on these grounds should be collected and exhibited a sample of every variety of domestic animal and of every tree, plant, and vegetable that can minister to the health, wealth, or taste and comfort of the people of the state; their nature, habits, merits, production, improvement, culture, diseases, and accidents thoroughly scrutinized, tested, and made known to the students and to the people of the state.

There should also be erected a sufficient number of buildings and outbuildings for all the purposes above indicated, and a repository in which all the ordinary tools and implements of the institution should be kept, and models of all other useful implements and machines from time to time collected and tested as they are proffered to public use. At first it would be for the interest of inventors and vendors to make such deposits. But, should similar institutions be adopted in other states, the general government ought to create in each state a general patent office, attached to the universities, similar to the existing deposits at Washington, thus rendering this department of mechanical art and skill more accessible to the great mass of the people of the Union.

I should have said, also, that a suitable industrial library should be at once procured, did not all the world know such a thing to be impossible, and that one of the first and most important duties of the professors of such institutions will be to begin to create, at this late hour, a proper practical literature and series of textbooks for the industrial classes.

As regards the professors, they should, of course, not only be men of the most eminent practical ability in their several departments but their connection with the institution should be rendered so fixed and stable as to enable them to carry through such designs as they may form, or all the peculiar benefits of the system would be lost.

Instruction, by lectures or otherwise, should be given mostly in the colder months of the year, leaving the professors to prosecute their investigations and the students, their necessary labor, either at home or on the premises, during the warmer months.

The institution should be open to all classes of students above a fixed age, and for any length of time, whether three months or seven years, and each taught in those particular branches of art which he wishes to pursue, and to any extent, more or less. And all should pay their tuition and board bills in whole or in part, either in money or necessary work on the premises, regard being had to the ability of each.

Among those who labor, medals and testimonials of merit should be given to those who perform their task with most promptitude, energy, care, and skill; and all who prove indolent or ungovernable, excluded at first from all part in labor, and speedily, if not thoroughly, reformed, from the institution itself. And here again let the law of nature instead of the law of rakes and dandies be regarded, and the true impression ever made on the mind of all around that *work alone is honorable,* and indolence, certain disgrace, if not ruin.

At some convenient season of the year, the commencement, or *annual fair,* of the university should be held through a succession of days. On this occasion the doors of the institution, with all its treasures of art and resources of knowledge, should be thrown open to all classes, and as many other objects of agricultural or mechanical skill, gathered from the whole state, as possible, and presented by the people for inspection and premium on the best of each kind; judgment being rendered, in all cases, by a committee wholly disconnected with the institution. On this occasion, all the professors and as many of the pupils as are sufficiently advanced should be constantly engaged in lecturing and explaining the diverse objects and interests of their departments. In short, this occasion should be made the great annual Gala Day of the institution, and of all the industrial classes and all other classes in the state for the exhibition of their products and their skill, and for the vigorous and powerful diffusion of practical knowledge in their ranks, and a more intense enthusiasm in its extension and pursuit.

As matters now are, the world has never adopted any efficient means for the application and diffusion of even the practical knowledge which does exist. True, we have fairly got the primer, the spelling book, and the newspaper abroad in the world, and we think that we have done wonders; and so, comparatively, we have. But if this is a wonder, there are still not only wonders but, to most minds, inconceivable miracles, from new and unknown worlds of light, soon to break forth upon the industrial mind of the world.

Here, then, is a general, though very incomplete, outline of what such an institution should endeavor to become. Let the reader contemplate it as it will appear when generations have perfected it, in all its magnificence and glory; in its means of good to man, to *all men* of *all classes*; in its power to evolve and diffuse practical knowledge and skill, true taste, love of industry, and sound morality, not only through its apparatus, experiments, instructions, and annual lectures and reports but through its thousands of graduates, in every pursuit in life, teaching and lecturing in all our towns and villages; and then let him seriously ask himself — Is not such an object worthy of at least an effort and worthy of a state which God Himself, in the very act of creation, designed to be the first agricultural and commercial state on the face of the globe?

Who should set the world so glorious an example of educating their sons worthily of their heritage, their duty, and their destiny if not the people of such a state? In our country we have no aristocracy, with the inalienable wealth of ages and constant leisure and means to perform all manner of useful experiments for their own amusement; but we must create our nobility for this purpose, as we elect our rulers, from our own ranks, to aid and serve, not to domineer over and control us. And this done, we will not only beat England and beat the world in yachts, and locks, and reapers, but in all else that contributes to the well-being and true glory of man.

I maintain that, if every farmer's and me-

chanic's son in this state could now visit such an institution but for a single day in the year, it would do him more good in arousing and directing the dormant energies of mind than all the cost incurred, and far more good than many a six months of professed study of things he will never need and never want to know.

As things now are, our best farmers and mechanics, by their own native force of mind, by the slow process of individual experience, come to know at forty what they might have been taught in six months at twenty; while a still greater number of the less fortunate or less gifted stumble on through life almost as ignorant of every true principle of their art as when they began. A man of real skill is amazed at the slovenly ignorance and waste he everywhere discovers on all parts of their premises, and still more to hear them boast of their ignorance of all "book farming," and maintain that "their children can do as well as they have done"; and it certainly would be a great pity if they could not.

The patrons of our university would be found in the former, not in the latter, class. The man whose highest conception of earthly bliss is a log hut, in an unenclosed yard, where pigs of two species are allowed equal rights, unless the four-legged tribe chance to get the upper hand, will be found no patron of industrial universities. Why should he be? He knows it already.

There is another class of untaught farmers who devote all their capital and hired labor to the culture, on a large scale, of some single product, which always pays well when so produced on a fresh soil, even in the most unskillful hands. Now, such men often increase rapidly in wealth, but it is not by their skill in agriculture, for they have none; their skill consists in the management of capital and labor, and, deprive them of these and confine them to the varied culture of a small farm and they would starve in five years, where a true farmer would amass a small fortune. This class are, however, generally the fast friends of education, though many a looker-on will cite them as instances of the uselessness of acquired skill in farming, whereas they should cite them only as a sample of the resistless power of capital, even in comparatively unskillful hands.

Such institutions are the only possible remedy for a caste education, legislation, and literature. If any one class provide for their own liberal education in the state, as they should do, while another class neglect this, it is as inevitable as the law of gravitation that they should form a ruling caste or class by themselves and wield their power more or less for their own exclusive interests and the interests of their friends.

If the industrial were the only educated class in the state, the caste power in their hands would be as much stronger than it now is, as their numbers are greater. But now industrial education has been wholly neglected and the various industrial classes left still ignorant of matters of the greatest moment pertaining to their vital interests, while the professions have been studied till trifles and fooleries have been magnified into matters of immense importance and tornadoes of windy words and barrels of innocent ink shed over them in vain.

This, too, is the inevitable result of trying to crowd all liberal, practical education into one narrow sphere of human life. It crowds their ranks with men totally unfit by nature for professional service. Many of these, under a more congenial culture, might have become, instead of the starving scavengers of a learned profession, the honored members of an industrial one. Their love of knowledge was indeed amiable and highly commendable; but the necessity which drove them from their natural sphere in life in order to obtain it is truly deplorable.

But such a system of general education as we now propose would (in ways too numerous now to mention) tend to increase the respectability, power, numbers, and resources of the true professional class.

Nor are the advantages of the mental and moral discipline of the student to be overlooked; indeed, I should have set them down as most important of all had I not been distinctly aware that such an opinion is a most deadly heresy; and I tremble at the thought of being arraigned before the tribunal of all the monks and ecclesiastics of the Old World and no small number of their progeny in the New.

It is deemed highly important that all in the professional classes should become writers and talkers; hence they are so incessantly drilled in all the forms of language, dead and living, though it has become quite doubtful whether, even in their case, such a course is most beneficial, except in the single case of the professors of literature and theology, with whom these languages form the foundation of their professions and the indispensable instruments of their future art in life.

No inconsiderable share, however, of the mental discipline that is attributed to this peculiar course of study arises from daily intercourse, for years, with minds of the first order in their teachers and comrades, and would be produced under any other course if the parties had remained harmoniously together. On the other hand, a classical teacher who has no original, spontaneous power of thought, and knows nothing but Latin and Greek, however perfectly, is enough to stultify a whole generation of boys and make them all pedantic fools like himself. The idea of infusing mind, or creating, or even materially increasing it by the mere daily inculcation of unintelligible words — all this awful wringing to get blood out of a turnip — will, at any rate, never succeed except in the hands of the eminently wise and prudent, who have had long experience in the process; the plain, blunt sense of the unsophisticated will never realize cost in the operation.

There are, moreover, probably few men who do not already talk more, in proportion to what they really know, than they ought to. This chronic diarrhea of exhortation, which the social atmosphere of the age tends to engender, tends far less to public health than many suppose. The history of the Quakers shows that more sound sense, a purer morality, and a more elevated, practical piety can exist, and does exist, entirely without it than is commonly found with it.

Still, some should, doubtless, be so educated as readily to discharge all the uncomfortable popular wind they may chance, at any time, to have on their stomachs; but the industrial classes, for most part, had better work theirs off in some other way. And, if they cannot find words to express their ideas, let them teach others, in the most effective of all ways, by action and example.

At all events we find, as society becomes less conservative and pedantic, and more truly and practically enlightened, a growing tendency of all other classes, except the literary and clerical, to omit this supposed linguistic discipline and apply themselves directly to the more immediate duties of their calling; and, aside from some little inconvenience at first in being outside of caste, that they do not succeed quite as well in advancing their own interests in life and the true interests of society, there is no sufficient proof. . . .

The most natural and effectual mental discipline possible for any man arises from setting him to earnest and constant thought about the things he daily does, sees, and handles, and all their connected relations and interests. The final object to be attained with the industrial class is to make them *thinking laborers;* while of the professional class we should desire to make *laborious thinkers:* the production of goods to feed and adorn the body being the final end of one class of pursuits; and the production of thought to do the same for the mind, the end of the other. But neither mind nor body can feed on the offals of preceding generations. And this constantly recurring necessity of reproduction leaves an equally honorable, though somewhat different, ca-

reer of labor and duty open to both, and, it is readily admitted, should and must vary their modes of education and preparation accordingly.

It may do for the man of books to plunge at once amid the catacombs of buried nations and languages, to soar away to Greece, or Rome, or Nova Zembla, Kamchatka, and the fixed stars before he knows how to plant his own beans, or harness his own horse, or can tell whether the functions of his own body are performed by a heart, stomach, and lungs, or with a gizzard and gills. But for the man of work thus to bolt away at once from himself and all his pursuits in afterlife contravenes the plainest principles of nature and common sense.

No wonder such educators have ever deemed the liberal culture of the industrial classes an impossibility; for they have never tried nor even conceived of any other way of educating them, except that by which they are rendered totally unfit for their several callings in afterlife. How absurd would it seem to set a clergyman to plowing and studying the depredations of blights, insects, the growing of crops, etc., etc., in order to give him habits of thought and mental discipline for the pulpit; yet this is not half as ridiculous, in reality, as the reverse absurdity of attempting to educate the man of work in unknown tongues, abstract problems and theories, and metaphysical figments and quibbles.

Some, doubtless, will regard the themes of such a course of education as too sensuous and gross to be at the basis of a pure and elevated mental culture. But the themes themselves cover all possible knowledge of all modes and phases of science, abstract, mixed, and practical. In short, the field embraces all that God has made and all that human art has done; and if the created universe of God and the highest art of man are too gross for our refined uses, it is a pity the "morning stars and the sons of God" did not find it out as soon as the blunder was made. But, in my opinion, these topics are of quite as much consequence to the well-being of man and the healthful development of mind as the concoction of the final nostrum in medicine, or the ultimate figment in theology and law, or conjectures about the galaxy or the Greek accent; unless, indeed, the pedantic professional trifles of one man in a thousand are of more consequence than the daily vital interests of all the rest of mankind.

But can such an institution be created and endowed? Doubtless it can be done, and done at once, if the industrial classes so decide. The fund given to this state by the general government expressly for this purpose is amply sufficient, without a dollar from any other source; and it is a mean, if not an illegal, perversion of this fund to use it for any other purpose. It was given to the people, the whole people, of this state; not for a class, a party, or sect, or conglomeration of sects; not for common schools, or family schools, or classical schools; but for "a university," or seminary of a high order, in which should of course be taught all those things which every class of the citizens most desire to learn — their own duty and business for life. This, and this alone, is a university in the true, original sense of the term. And if an institution which teaches all that is needful only for the three professions of law, divinity, and medicine is, therefore, a university, surely one which teaches all that is needful for all the varied professions of human life is far more deserving of the name and the endowments of a university.

But in whose hands shall the guardianship and oversight of this fund be placed in order to make it of any real use for such a purpose? I answer, without hesitation and without fear, that this whole interest should, from the first, be placed directly in the hands of the people, and the whole people, without any mediators or advisers, legislative or ecclesiastical, save only their own appointed agents, and their own jurors and courts of justice, to which, of course, all alike must submit. It was given to the people and is the property of the people, not of legislators, parties, or sects, and they ought to have the whole control of it, so far as is possible, consistently with a due security of the funds and needful stability of plans of action and instruction. This control, I believe, they will be found abundantly able to exercise; and more than this no well-informed man would desire.

The reasons for placing it at once and forever beyond all legislative and ecclesiastical control are obvious to all; for, if under the former, it will continually exist as the mere tool of the dominant party and the object of jealous fear and hatred of their opponents, or else it will become the mere football of all parties, to be kicked hither and thither as the party interests and passion of the hour may dictate. We well know how many millions of money have been worse than thrown away by placing professed seminaries of learning under the influence of party passion through legislative control. And it is surely a matter of devout gratitude that our legislators have had wisdom enough to see and feel this difficulty, and that they have been led, from various causes, to hold this fund free from all commitment, to the present hour, when the people begin to be convinced that they need it and can safely control it; and no legislator but an aristocrat or a demagogue would desire to see it in other hands.

The same difficulty occurs as regards sects. Let the institution be managed ever so well by any one party or sect, it is still certain their opponents will stand aloof from it, if not oppose and malign it for that very reason. Hence, all will see at once that the greatest possible care should be taken to free it from not only the reality but even from the *suspicion* of any such influence. Should the party in power when the charter may be granted appoint a majority of the board of trustees from the parties in the minority, it would show a proper spirit and be, in all coming time, an example of true magnanimity, which their opponents could not fail to respect and to imitate, and which the people at large would highly approve.

Let the governor of the state nominate a board of trust for the funds of the institution. Let this board consist of five of the most able and discreet men in the state, and let at least four of them be taken from each of the extreme corners of the state, so remote from all proximity to the possible location of the institution, both in person and in property, as to be free from all suspicion of partiality. Let the Senate confirm such nomination. Let this board be sworn to locate the institution from a regard to the interests and convenience of the people of the whole state; and when they have so done, let them be empowered to elect twelve new members of their own body, with perpetual power of filling their own vacancies, each choice requiring a vote of two-thirds of the whole body, and upon any failure to elect at the appointed annual meeting, the governor of the state to fill the vacancy for one year, if requested by any member of the board so to do.

Let any member of the board who shall be absent from any part of its annual meetings thereby forfeit his seat, unless detained by sickness, certified at the time, and the board on that occasion fill the vacancy either by his reelection or by the choice of some other man. Let the funds, then, by the same act, pass into the hands of the trustees so organized as a perpetual trust, they giving proper bonds for the same, to be used for the endowment and erection of an industrial university for the state of Illinois.

This board, so constituted, would be, and ought to be, responsible to no legislature, sect, or party, but directly to the people themselves, to each and every citizen, in the courts of law and justice; so that, should any trustee of the institution neglect, abuse, or pervert his trust to any selfish, local, po-litical, or sectarian end, or show himself incompetent for its exercise, every other member of the board, and every citizen at large, should have the right of impeaching him before the court, and, if guilty, the court should discharge him and order his place to be filled by a more suitable man. Due care should be taken, of course, to guard against malicious prosecutions.

Doubtless, objections can be urged against this plan and all others that can be proposed. Most of them may be at once anticipated, but there is not space enough to notice them here. Some, for example, cherish an ardent and praiseworthy desire for the perfection of our common schools, and desire still longer to use that fund for that purpose. But no one imagines that it can long be kept for that use; and if it could, I think it plain that the lower schools of all sorts would be far more benefited by it here than in any other place it could be put.

Others may feel a little alarm, when, for the first time in the history of the world, they see the millions throwing themselves aloof from all political and ecclesiastical control, and attempting to devise a system of liberal education for themselves. But on mature reflection, we trust they will approve the plan; or, if they are too old to change, their children will.

I shall enter upon no special pleas in favor of this plan of disposing of our state fund. I am so situated in life that it cannot possibly do me any personal good, save only in the just pride of seeing the interests of my brethren of the industrial class cared for and promoted, as in such an age and such a state they ought to be. If they want the benefit of such an institution, they can have it. If they do not want it, I have not another word to say. In their own will alone lies their own destiny and that of their children.

1852

30.

The Suitability of Moral Declarations in Foreign Policy

American sympathy for the revolution in Hungary in 1849, and the subsequent visit to America of its revolutionary leader Lajos Kossuth in 1851, precipitated a flurry of journalistic debate over U.S. foreign policy. While few Americans called for material support of the revolution, demands for proclamation of sympathy were numerous enough to bring the matter before the Senate. Opinion was about evenly divided between those who thought an official statement of moral support could be made without "intervening" in the affairs of a foreign nation, and those who did not. The following selections, representative of these opposing views, are taken from speeches by Senators Lewis Cass of Michigan and James C. Jones of Tennessee, delivered on February 10 and March 18, 1852.

Source: *Globe, App.*, 32 Cong., 1 Sess., pp. 158-165, 303-311.

I.

LEWIS CASS: In Defense of Such Declarations

UNLESS THE MANY WERE MADE for the few, the governed for the governors, our sympathies should be excited, as were those of Washington, *for every people unfurling the banner of freedom,* and a Godspeed them be uttered, not only in the effort to improve their political system but in the greater effort to maintain it, by improving the condi-

tion of the great body of those for whom governments are instituted. . . .

If one nation issue a manifesto announcing what its coequals believe to be a dangerous innovation in the principles of public law, and support its declaration by its acts, or endeavor by the acts themselves to give authority to its own assumptions, is the world to look on, indignantly but silently, until precedent usurp the place of principle and acquiescence is appealed to in support of the new pretension? There is not a civilized nation on the face of the earth which has not, time and again, given its opinion upon questions of public law in some form, more or less imposing — in correspondence, in protocols, in declarations, in manifestos, in protests, and in whatever mode national representations are made and received. . . .

The particular form in which a nation makes known its views, from the most common diplomatic note to the most solemn protest, neither adds to nor takes from its responsibility or obligation. It appears to be assumed that there is some peculiar pugnacious quality attached to a protest which necessarily leads to armed action. This is not so. A public declaration in that form no more imposes on the nation making it the duty of vindicating it by arms than the everyday representations which the usual diplomatic intercourse renders necessary. To be sure, the proceeding is more solemn, as the subjects generally are more grave; and it goes forth to the world under circumstances of deliberation which give to such declarations more than usual importance. But that they are necessarily followed by war, whenever they fail in the result, is contradicted by all the diplomatic experience of modern times. . . .

Our own history presents a memorable example of the exercise of this right to declare a principle of national law. Mr. Monroe's views on a similar question, solemnly announced to Congress and the world, form a well-known part of our political history. He denied to the European powers the right to intermeddle with the new governments of this hemisphere, and also the right to establish new colonies in any part of America. He did not, he could not pledge his country to go to war to maintain this position. He wisely said nothing upon that subject, leaving to the future the duties it might bring with it. His declaration is yet upon record, neither repealed nor disavowed, but remains as the expression of the sentiments of the United States upon this subject. And though it has not been wholly efficacious, it has no doubt contributed, with other causes, to the stability of the independence of the American states, and to check the spirit of colonization. . . .

Certainly solemn public declarations of this nature should not, would not, indeed, often be made, for their frequent occurrence would impair, if not destroy, their moral effect. They should be reserved for those extraordinary events, affecting the honor and stability of all nations, which stand prominently forward in the history of the world; characteristics, indeed, of the age in which they occur. Let no man, therefore, object that such a *conservative* remedy, for once the epithet is a just one, will lead to abuse or will destroy itself by too frequent application.

We ought neither to mistake our position, nor neglect the obligations it brings with it. We have at length reached the condition of one of the great powers of the earth, and yet we are but in the infancy of our career. The man yet lives who was living when a primitive forest extended from the Allegheny to the Rocky mountains, trodden only by the Indian, and by the animals, his co-tenants of a world of vegetation, whom God had given to him for his support. Then a narrow strip upon the seacoast, thirteen remote and dependent colonies, and less than 3 million people, constituted what is now this vast republic, stretching across the continent and extending almost from the Northern Tropic to the Arctic Circle. And the man is now living who will live to see 150 million people, free, prosperous, and intelligent, swaying the destinies of this country, and exerting a mighty influence upon those of the world. And why not, Mr. President? Is it not likely to be more beneficially exerted than the influence now exercised by the despotic powers of the earth? No one can doubt this. . . .

It has been said, in condemnation, or in

reproach, of this effort, that there are many other suffering people and violated principles calling equally for the assertion of this right; and why, it is asked sneeringly, if not triumphantly, why do you not extend your regards and your action to all such cases? And as that is impossible with any useful result, as everyone knows, we are, therefore, to sit still and do nothing, because we cannot do everything. Such is no dictate of wisdom or duty, either in political or ethical philosophy. The prudent statesman looks to what is practicable as well as what is right.

The principle embodied in the substitute is general and applies to all cases of armed intervention in the internal affairs of other countries; and if our discussion and our immediate action have reference to the attack upon Hungary, the reason is obvious and justifiable. There are conditions of the public mind arising out of passing events favorable to the consideration of particular questions, while others are cast into the shade and command no attention. The former is the state of things in relation to Hungary; to her rights and her wrongs. And the principles thus brought up are attracting the attention of the world, and are discussed in conversation, in legislative assemblies, in the public journals, and in diplomatic correspondence; and they thus commend themselves to general consideration. And the facts have been of a nature to impart deep interest to the whole subject, and without some degree of interest it were vain to endeavor to engage the public attention.

Mr. President, what earthly tribunal has a better right than the Congress of the American people to pronounce the opinion of that people upon such subjects? I do not speak, lest I should be accused of patriotic exaggeration, of those qualities, intellectual and moral, which are found here, and which are essential to a sound decision; but I speak of its representative capacity as the depository of much of the power of a people whose interest and feelings are intimately connected with the broadest principles of freedom and independence. . . .

Many objections, more or less plausible, have been presented to deter us from any action in this matter, but not one of them with more confidence or pertinacity, nor with less regard to the true circumstances of our position, than that which warns us that by such a proceeding we should violate alike the traditions of our policy and the advice of our wisest statesmen, and especially the injunctions of Washington and Jefferson. Never were just recommendations more inappropriately applied than in this attempt to apply the views of those great men to the circumstances in which we are placed.

Nonintervention, it is said, was the policy they maintained and the legacy they bequeathed to us; but is it possible that a single American can be found who believes that either of those patriots would condemn the declaration of his country's opinion upon a great question of public law because they condemned its interference with the affairs of other nations? Why, this is our affair, sir; an affair as interesting to us as to any other community on the face of the globe; one which involves the safety of independent states, and the true intent and obligation of the code that regulates their intercourse. . . .

Mr. President, it has often been said that we have a mission to fulfill, and so, indeed, has every nation; and the first mission of each is to conduct its own affairs honestly and fairly for its own benefit; but after that, its position and institutions may give to it peculiar influence in the prevailing moral and political controversies of the world, which it is bound to exert for the welfare of all. While we disclaim any crusading spirit against the political institutions of other countries, we may well regard with deep interest the struggling efforts of the oppressed through the world, and deplore their defeat and rejoice in their success. And can anyone

Lewis Cass, engraving from a Brady photograph, 1850

doubt that the evidences of sympathy which are borne to Europe from this great republic will cheer the hearts, even when they do not aid the purposes, of the downtrodden masses to raise themselves, if not to power at least to protection?

Whatever duties may be ultimately imposed on us by that dark future which overshadows Europe, and which we cannot foresee and ought not to undertake to define, circumstances point out our present policy, while, at the same time, they call upon us to exert our moral influence in support of the existing principles of public law, placed in danger not merely by the ambition but still more by the fear of powerful monarchs — the fear lest the contagion of liberty should spread over their dominions, carrying destruction to the established systems of oppression. But I repeat emphatically what I said upon a former occasion when this subject was before us, and what upon no occasion have I since contradicted or unsaid, and I may add, what I distinctly stated to the martyr of the struggles of his own country, now the honored guest of ours, in the first conversation I had with him upon this subject — that the people of the United States were not prepared to maintain the rights of Hungary by war; that the only influence we could exert was a moral and not a physical one.

II.

James C. Jones: In Opposition to Such Declarations

The senator from Michigan, in his able and learned speech which was filled with beauty, made a declaration to which I freely assent. It is this, in substance: That every nation has a right to determine for itself when its safety demands that it shall interpose. Now, if that be true (and I am not disposed to controvert it), I ask, upon what pretext is Russia arraigned at the bar of the enlightened judgment of the world? I am no eulogist of Russia. I am not her advocate. I despise her cruelty; I scorn and condemn her wrongs and outrages. But if that principle which is asserted by the senator from Michigan be true, then Russia had a right to intervene. If that is the law of nations, and if each nation has a right to judge for itself, then Russia had that right; and judging for herself, and acting upon that judgment, I want to know how the honorable senator can get up here and arraign her. I believe there was no necessity for the interposition of Russia, but, according to the principles laid down by the senator from Michigan, she must be the judge of that. She put it upon that express ground, and used the express words that her safety depended upon it.

But have we a right to interfere at all, and is it proper and expedient that we should interfere? My doctrine is that our best interests would be subserved by having nothing to do with this matter. If we have a right to speak out at all, we have a right to speak boldly, to speak freely, and to speak authoritatively. If it is the policy of this government to interfere in the affairs of foreign countries, though I shall oppose it at every step, I want to see gentlemen come up and speak boldly, fearlessly, frankly, independently, and authoritatively; and when we have spoken, then, to borrow the language of a distinguished gentleman of your party, let us maintain it "at all hazards, and to the last extremity."

Suppose you make this protest and it goes to Russia, and Russia receives it and treats it with scorn and contempt, tramples it underfoot, sends back an indignity and an insult, what do you propose to do then? The senator from Michigan says that the man who is in favor of an armed intervention is a madman. The senator from New York says we must not go to war except in self-defense. Then your protest is received with scorn and contempt, and a re-protest is sent back here, full of insolence. How will you receive it? I can speak for you, Mr. President. You would not pocket the insult, you would not submit to the indignity. Now, if we take this step at all, I want to know from the learned senators from Michigan and from New York whether they are ready to take the next step? If Russia treat us with scorn and contempt, and heap odium upon our government and nation, are we ready to vindicate it? Are we ready to stand up to it, and to vote the men and the money necessary to vindicate the honor of the government? If they are not ready to do this, in the name of God, in the name of liberty, in the name of the honor of this country, let us stop before we take another step. They have no right to involve the pride and the honor of this country, unless they are willing also to take the necessary steps to vindicate and maintain them.

My policy is to let them alone; to let them manage their own affairs in their own way. But if we speak at all, speak like men; speak like Americans; speak as senators ought to speak. Let us say to Russia, "Hands off; a clear field and a fair fight"; and if she disregards it and treats it with contempt, we know where duty points the way. I shall oppose it; but if this government takes the step, if she madly forgets her best interests, for one — though I shall have no agency in it, it may be carried by a majority of the Senate and House — "I am for my country, right or wrong." And if it should take the last ship that floats upon our seas, the last American ship upon all seas, and every American soldier that wears the insignia of his country's arms, and every dollar in the American Treasury, I would bring them all and lay them down at the footstool of my country to vindicate the honor of the nation.

But the gentlemen say they will not fight over this. Well, if you do not mean to fight about it, just let it alone. [*Laughter.*] I am opposed to fighting as much as you are; but if you mean to get us into a quarrel in which our honor will be at stake, in which our pride will be involved, I want you to stand up and fight it out, and have no dodging.

But I would like to know why we should go out upon this crusade? This is a wonderful age, Mr. President. Oh! it is a stupendous age! We are to go out upon a crusade for the liberties of the whole world? There is not enough in this broad Union of ours — "oceanbound" I believe my friend from Illinois calls it — to engage the time and the intellect of senators; but the redemption, the political redemption, of the whole world is brought up, and we are to march out upon that grand crusade. I should like to see the world redeemed; but I am no propagandist, and while I feel a devotion amounting to idolatry for my country and her institutions, and her peculiar form of government, deeply as I am devoted to it, high and holy as I conceive it to be, I would not impose it upon one single, solitary being upon earth. If a man chooses to be a slave, let him be so. I would not force him from any position he might occupy. Let every people choose their own government; and let us choose ours, and take care of it, and guard it, and protect it, and defend it.

But the very distinguished senator from Michigan claims that the chief virtue which is to be found in his resolution — his protest, I believe, it is called, though I do not know what notary public has signed it; I suppose when you sign it, Mr. President, it will be — is the moral influence it is to exert upon Russia and the world. Do you remember, Mr. President and senators, the speech of that learned gentleman in which he inveighed with such touching and powerful eloquence against the cruelties, the enormities, and the outrages of the czar of Russia? Why, sir, the veriest monster that ever disgraced the image of his God is an angel transformed into the brightness of light compared with that miserable wretch, and yet the senator from Michigan thinks there is virtue enough, in this protest to rouse the moral sensibilities of such a devil. It may be so. I cannot tell, but it does seem to me that there is some mistake about the moral influence of such a protest. What amount of moral power and influence is to attach to it? How is it to arise? It must arise either from the inherent virtue and justice of the thing said, the manner of saying it, or the source from which it comes.

Now, if that be so, let us see how it would work. The distinguished senator has said it as strongly as it can be said; but would that give it weight and influence with His Royal Highness, the emperor of Russia? If there is virtue in the thing said, and that is the moral influence which it is to exert, why, sir, coming from the distinguished senator, and said in terms so beautiful and classical, and coming from so high a source, it would be entitled to all the moral influence which could attach to it. Yet, with the profoundest respect for that

senator, how do you suppose such a protest going to the czar of Russia would be received? The distinguished senator from Michigan protests, in the presence of His Majesty, against this outrage upon the rights of humanity and justice. But, going a little further, suppose the little republic of San Marino should publish just such a protest as this and send it to the Russian court, what moral influence would it possess? I do not suppose it would disturb the quietude of the emperor for a single moment.

Then, I apprehend, the moral influence of a legislative declaration or governmental edict is to be found in the virtue and merit of the thing said, and the physical power and force possessed to constrain obedience to it. I would not give a straw for all the moral influences of your declarations unless there be a power behind the throne greater than the throne. There must be physical power, and force, and will, to execute and require obedience to the protest. If that be so, I would like to see in what position we stand. A protest is to go out from the United States, passed by the Senate, passed by the House of Representatives, receiving the signature of the President of the United States. It goes to the court of His Imperial Majesty. It is there read — a solemn protest that we cannot behold these things without deep concern — and accompanying it is the speech of the senator from Michigan saying that he who talks about enforcing this protest with armed intervention is a madman. How much virtue do you suppose would emanate from the protest? Just none at all, as it seems to me. . . .

Are all our sympathies to be exhausted on Hungary? Weep over her wrongs to your heart's content; I will join you in the holy office; but I ask you to come back in the hours of quietude and look to your own country. Have you not enough here to engage your time, to enlist your talents, to enlist the talents of the loftiest intellect of the age? See your country, with 25 million population, extending from ocean to ocean; a territory of empires in extent, and yet not enough for the enlarged capacity of some gentlemen. The world itself seems scarcely large enough to contain their boundless sympathies. It is enough for me to know that there are interests here that command and demand my attention.

Look at the interests of this country! You have a territory almost boundless; unnumbered millions and hundreds of millions of public domain that might be made the basis upon which the hopes, the prosperity, the happiness, the grandeur, and the glory of the mightiest nation upon earth might be established. And yet, sir, that is a small matter that concerns nobody. We must go and weep over Hungary. If your sympathies are so large, go into the valley of the Mississippi, that I have the honor in part to represent. I see the honored representative of my district here now. Go there and see the unnumbered and numberless lives that are constantly sacrificed to the imbecility and weakness of this government of ours.

There is a hecatomb of living spirits carried down into the deep and angry waters of the Mississippi and its tributaries. There is no sympathy for them. We must go abroad and shed tears of blood and compassion for the sufferings of Hungary. Better come home and weep over widows and orphans left husbandless and fatherless by the neglect of the government to give protection, and to improve her inland and her external commerce. That is enough to engage the time and the talents of the whole Senate — of the loftiest genius that ever lived. Yet these are very small matters — we may forget them all!

We have a seacoast almost boundless, with harbors to improve, interests to protect, thousands and tens of thousands of American citizens languishing for the want of that paternal regard which the government ought to extend them, in giving protection to the honest labor of the country. All that moves no sympathetic cord in those hearts that sympathize with the oppressed of all nations.

Come home, gentlemen, come home, and let us see if we cannot do something here. When we shall have made our own people happy and prosperous, when the Treasury shall be overflown, when the Navy shall find nothing to do, when the Army shall be a burden upon our hands, then you may go out and fight the battles of other people. But first let us establish ourselves upon a basis, not only honorable but safe and perpetual.

31.

Charles Magill Conrad: Instructions for Commodore Perry

The opening of California ports paved the way for American merchants to establish trade routes to the Pacific islands and to the Orient. An American diplomatic mission to China in 1843 resulted in a treaty the following year, but Japan's military rulers, who wished to keep intact their ancient feudal system, rebuffed any attempt by Western powers to establish commercial relations. By 1852 Americans, interested in commerce with Japan and concerned for the welfare of sailors near Japanese coasts, were pressuring their government to secure more amicable relations with Japan. President Fillmore placed Commodore Matthew C. Perry in command of a fleet of warships and directed him to deliver a letter and gifts to the emperor in preparation for negotiations. The objectives of the mission were explained in a letter from Acting Secretary of State C. M. Conrad to John P. Kennedy, secretary of the navy. A portion of the instructions, dated November 5, 1852, is reprinted here. Perry concluded a treaty with Japan on March 31, 1854.

Source: 33 Congress, 2 Session, Senate Executive Document No. 34, pp. 4 9.

As the squadron destined for Japan will shortly be prepared to sail, I am directed by the President to explain the objects of the expedition, and to give some general directions as to the mode by which those objects are to be accomplished.

Since the islands of Japan were first visited by European nations, efforts have constantly been made by the various maritime powers to establish commercial intercourse with a country whose large population and reputed wealth hold out great temptations to mercantile enterprise. Portugal was the first to make the attempt, and her example was followed by Holland, England, Spain, and Russia, and finally by the United States. All these attempts, however, have thus far been unsuccessful; the permission enjoyed for a short period by the Portuguese to trade with the islands and that granted to Holland to send annually a single vessel to the port of Nagasaki hardly deserving to be considered exceptions to this remark.

China is the only country which carries on any considerable trade with these islands.

So rigorously is this system of exclusion carried out that foreign vessels are not permitted to enter their ports in distress, or even to do an act of kindness to their own people. In 1831, a Japanese junk was blown out to sea, and, after drifting about for several months, was cast ashore near the mouth of the Columbia River in Oregon. An American ship, the *Morrison*, undertook to carry the survivors of the crew back to their country, but, on reaching the bay of Yedo, she was fired into from the neighboring shore. She repaired to another part of the island and attempted to land, but, meeting with the same reception there, she returned to America with the Japanese on board.

When vessels are wrecked or driven ashore on the islands, their crews are subjected to the most cruel treatment. Two instances of this have recently occurred. In the year 1846, two American whaling ships, the *Lagoda* and the *Lawrence*, having been wrecked on the island of Niphon, their crews were captured and treated with great barbarity; and it is believed that their lives were spared only through the intercession of the Dutch governor of Nagasaki. . . .

Every nation has undoubtedly the right to determine for itself the extent to which it will hold intercourse with other nations. The same law of nations, however, which protects a nation in the exercise of this right imposes upon her certain duties which she cannot justly disregard. Among these duties none is more imperative than that which requires her to succor and relieve those persons who are cast by the perils of the ocean upon her shores. This duty is, it is true, among those that are denominated by writers on public law imperfect, and which confer no right on other nations to exact their performance; nevertheless, if a nation not only habitually and systematically disregards it but treats such unfortunate persons as if they were the most atrocious criminals, such nations may justly be considered as the most common enemy of mankind.

That the civilized nations of the world should for ages have submitted to such treatment by a weak and semi-barbarous people can only be accounted for on the supposition that, from the remoteness of the country, instances of such treatment were of rare occurrence and the difficulty of chastising it very great. It can hardly be doubted that if Japan were situated as near the continent of Europe or of America as it is to that of Asia, its government would long since have been either treated as barbarians or been compelled to respect those usages of civilized states of which it receives the protection.

This government has made two attempts to establish commercial intercourse with Japan. In the year 1832, a Mr. Roberts was appointed a special agent of the government with authority to negotiate treaties with sundry nations in the East, and among others with Japan, but he died before he arrived at the island.

In 1845, Commodore Biddle was sent with two vessels of war to visit Japan and ascertain whether its ports were accessible. He was cautioned, however, "not to excite a hostile feeling or a distrust of the government of the United States." He proceeded to Yedo, but was told that the Japanese could trade with no foreign nations except the Dutch and Chinese, and was peremptorily ordered to leave the island and never to return to it. . . .

Recent events — the navigation of the ocean by steam, the acquisition and rapid settlement by this country of a vast territory on the Pacific, the discovery of gold in that region, the rapid communication established across the isthmus which separates the two oceans — have practically brought the countries of the East in closer proximity to our own. Although the consequences of these events have scarcely begun to be felt, the intercourse between them has already greatly increased, and no limits can be assigned to its future extension.

The duty of protecting those American citizens who navigate those seas is one that can no longer be deferred. . . .

The objects sought by this government are:

1. To effect some permanent arrangement for the protection of American seamen and property wrecked on these islands or driven into their ports by stress of weather.

2. The permission to American vessels to enter one or more of their ports in order to obtain supplies of provisions, water, fuel, etc., or, in case of disasters, to refit so as to enable them to prosecute their voyage.

It is very desirable to have permission to establish a depot for coal, if not on one of the principal islands, at least on some small uninhabited one, of which, it is said, there are several in their vicinity.

3. The permission to our vessels to enter one or more of their ports for the purpose of disposing of their cargoes by sale or barter.

As this government has no right to make treaties for, or to redress the grievances of, other nations, whatever concessions may be obtained on either of the above points need not, of course, apply in terms to the inhabitants or vessels of any other nation. This government, however, does not seek by this expedition to obtain any exclusive commercial advantage for itself but, on the contrary, desires and expects that whatever benefits may result from it will ultimately be shared by the civilized world. . . .

The next question is — How are the above-mentioned objects to be attained?

It is manifest from past experience that arguments or persuasion addressed to this people, unless they be seconded by some imposing manifestation of power, will be utterly unavailing. You will, therefore, be pleased to direct the commander of the squadron to proceed, with his whole force, to such point on the coast of Japan as he may deem most advisable, and there endeavor to open a communication with the government, and, if possible, to see the emperor in person, and deliver to him the letter of introduction from the President with which he is charged.

He will state that he has been sent across the ocean by the President to deliver that letter to the emperor and to communicate with his government on matters of importance to the two countries; that the President entertains the most friendly feeling toward Japan, but has been surprised and grieved to learn that, when any of the people of the United States go, of their own accord, or are thrown by the perils of the sea, within the dominions of the emperor, they are treated as if they were his worst enemies. . . .

He will inform him of the usages of this country and of all Christian countries in regard to shipwrecked persons and vessels, and will . . . make arrangements for a more extended commercial intercourse between the two countries. The establishment of this intercourse will be found a difficult but, perhaps, not an impossible task. . . . As the United States and Japan are becoming every day nearer and nearer to each other, the President desires to live in peace and friendship with the emperor; but . . . no friendship can long exist between them unless Japan should change her policy and cease to act toward the people of this country as if they were her enemies. . . . However wise this policy may originally have been, it is unwise and impracticable now that intercourse between the two countries is so much more easy and rapid than it formerly was.

If, after having exhausted every argument and every means of persuasion, the commodore should fail to obtain from the government any relaxation of their system of exclusion, or even any assurance of humane treatment of our shipwrecked seamen, he will then change his tone and inform them in the most unequivocal terms that it is the determination of this government to insist that hereafter all citizens or vessels of the United States that may be wrecked on their coasts or driven by stress of weather into their harbors shall, so long as they are compelled to remain there, be treated with humanity; and that if any acts of cruelty should hereafter be practised upon citizens of this country, whether by the government or by the inhabitants of Japan, they will be severely chastised.

In case he should succeed in obtaining concessions on any of the points above mentioned, it is desirable that they should be reduced into the form of a treaty, for negotiating which he will be furnished with the requisite powers. . . . He will bear in mind that, as the President has no power to declare war, his mission is necessarily of a pacific character, and will not resort to force unless in self-defense in the protection of the vessels and crews under his command, or to resent an act of personal violence offered to himself or to one of his officers.

In his intercourse with this people, who are said to be proud and vindictive in their character, he should be courteous and conciliatory, but, at the same time, firm and decided. He will, therefore, submit with patience and forbearance to acts of discourtesy to which he may be subjected by a people to whose usages it will not do to test by our standard of propriety; but, at the same time, will be careful to do nothing that may compromise, in their eyes, his own dignity or that of the country. He will, on the contrary, do everything to impress them with a just sense of the power and greatness of this country, and to satisfy them that its past forbearance has been the result, not of timidity but of a desire to be on friendly terms with them.

32.

Economic Effect of Railroads

By the 1850s a network of railroads had been built connecting the major agricultural and industrial regions east of the Mississippi River, and speculative interest in extending lines west to the Pacific was growing. Faster, more efficient, and in the long run cheaper than river and canal transportation, the railroads helped to increase the profits of both businessmen and farmers. In an 1852 report to Congress the economic influence of the railroads was assessed in relation to the geographical features of the country. Part of the report is reprinted here.

Source: 32 Congress, 1 Session, Senate Executive Document No. 112, pp. 379-384.

THE FIRST STEP toward a correct idea of our railroads, as far as their uses, objects, costs, and results are concerned, is a thorough understanding of the social and industrial character of our people, the geographical and topographical features of the country, the uniformity in the pursuits of the great mass of our people, and the great distance that separates the consuming from the producing regions.

Assuming the occupied area of that portion of our territory east of the Rocky Mountains to be 1,100,000 sq. mi., at least 1,050,000 are devoted to agriculture, while not more than 50,000 are occupied by the manufacturing and commercial classes. These compose a narrow belt of territory lying upon the seacoast, extending from Baltimore to the eastern part of Maine, and are more widely separated from the great producing regions than any other settled portion of the country. The great peculiarity that distinguishes our own from older countries is that we have no *interior* markets. The greater part of our territory has not been long enough settled for the development of a *variety* of industrial pursuits, which constitute them. So entirely are our people devoted to agriculture, and so uniformly distributed are they over the whole country, that some of our largest states, Tennessee and Indiana for instance, had no towns in 1850 containing a population of over 10,000.

This homogeneousness in the pursuits of the great mass of our people, and the wide space that separates the producing and consuming classes, as they are popularly termed, necessarily implies the exportation of the surplus products of each. The Western farmer has no home demand for the wheat he raises, as the surplus of all his neighbors is the same in kind. The aggregate surplus of the district in which he resides has to be exported to find a consumer; and the producer, for a similar reason, is obliged to import all the various articles that enter into consumption which his own industry does not immediately supply; and, further, as the markets for our agricultural products lie either upon the extreme verge of the country, or in Europe, the greater part of our domestic commerce involves a *through* movement of nearly all the articles of which it is composed. . . .

It is well known that upon the ordinary highways the economical limit to transportation is confined within a comparatively few miles, depending, of course, upon the *kind* of freight and character of the roads. Upon the average of such ways, the cost of transportation is not far from 15 cents per ton per mile, which may be considered as a sufficiently correct estimate for the whole country. Estimating, at the same time, the value of wheat at $1.50 per bushel and corn at 75 cents, and that 33 bushels of each are equal to a ton, the value of the former would be equal to its cost of transportation for 330 miles, and the latter, 165 miles. At these respective distances from market, neither of the above articles would have any commercial value, with only a common earth road as an avenue to market.

But we find that we can move property upon railroads at the rate of 1.5 cent per ton per mile, or for one-tenth the cost upon the ordinary road. These works, therefore, extend the economic limit of the cost of transportation of the above articles to 3,300 and 1,650 miles, respectively. At the limit of the economical movement of these articles upon the common highway, by the use of railroads, wheat would be worth $44.50

and corn $22.27 per ton, which sums, respectively, would represent the actual increase of value created by the interposition of such a work. . . .

The value of lands is affected by railroads in the same ratio as their products. For instance, lands lying upon a navigable watercourse or in the immediate vicinity of a market may be worth, for the culture of wheat, $100. Let the average crop be estimated at 22 bushels to the acre, valued at $33, and the cost of cultivation at $15; this would leave $18 per acre as the net profit. This quantity of wheat (two-thirds of a ton) could be transported 330 miles at a cost of 10 cents per mile, or $3.30, which would leave $14.70 as the net profit of land at that distance from a market when connected with it by a railroad. The value of the land, therefore, admitting the quality to be the same in both cases, would bear the same ratio to the assumed value of $100 as the value of its products, $14.70, does to $18, or $82 per acre; which is an actual creation of value to that amount, assuming the correctness of the premises.

The same calculation may, of course, be applied with equal force to any other kind and species of property. The illustration given establishes a principle entirely correct in itself, but of course liable to be modified to meet the facts of each case. Vast bodies of the finest land in the United States, and lying within 200 miles of navigable watercourses, are unsalable, and nearly, if not quite, valueless for the culture of wheat or corn for exportation, from the cost of transportation. . . . Under such circumstances, products are often fed out to livestock and converted into higher values, which will bear transportation when the former will not. In this manner, lands are turned into account, where their immediate products would otherwise be valueless. But in such cases the profit per acre is often very small; as, in the districts best adapted to the culture of corn, it is considered more profitable to sell it for 25 cents per bushel than to feed it out to animals. It will be seen that at this price thrice its value is eaten up by the cost of transportation of 165 miles.

In this manner, railroads in this country actually add to the immediate means of our people by the saving effected in the expenses of transportation, to a much greater extent than cost. We are, therefore, in no danger from embarrassment on account of the construction of lines called for by the business wants of the community, as these add much more to our active capital than they absorb. Only a very few years are required to enable a railroad to repay its cost of construction in the manner stated.

Railroads in the United States exert a much greater influence upon the value of property than in other countries. . . . The actual increase in the value of lands due to the construction of railroads is controlled by so many circumstances that an accurate estimate can only be approximated and must, in most cases, fall far short of the fact. Not only are cultivated lands and city and village lots lying immediately upon the route affected but the real estate in cities hundreds and thousands of miles distant. The railroads of Ohio exert as much influence in advancing the prices of real property in the city of New York as do the roads lying within that state. This fact will show how very imperfect every estimate must be. But taking only the farming lands of the particular district traversed by a railroad, where the influence of such a work can be more directly seen, there is no doubt that in such case the increased value is many times greater than the cost of the road.

It is estimated by the intelligent president of the Nashville and Chattanooga Railroad that the increased value of a belt of land ten miles wide, lying upon each side of its line, is equal to at least $7.50 per acre, or $96,000 for every mile of road, which will cost only about $20,000 per mile. That work has already created a value in its influence upon real property alone equal to about five times its cost. What is true of the

Nashville and Chattanooga Road is equally so, probably, of the average of roads throughout the country. It is believed that the construction of the 3,000 miles of railroad of Ohio will add to the value of the landed property in the state at least five times the cost of the roads, assuming this to be $60 million. In addition to the very rapid advance in the price of farming lands, the roads of Ohio are stimulating the growth of her cities with extraordinary rapidity, so that there is much greater probability that the above estimate will be exceeded, than not reached, by the actual fact.

We are not left to estimate in this matter. In the case of the state of Massachusetts, what is conjecture in regard to the new states has with her become a matter of history. The valuation of that state went up, from 1840 to 1850, from $290 million to $580 million — an immense increase, and by far the greater part of it due to the numerous railroads she has constructed. This increase is in a much greater ratio to the cost of her roads than has been estimated of those of Ohio.

We have considered the effect of railroads in increasing the value of property in reference only to lands devoted to agriculture; but such results do not by any means give the most forcible illustration of their use. An acre of farming land can at most be made to yield only a small annual income. An acre of coal or iron lands, on the other hand, may produce a thousandfold more in value than the former. These deposits may be entirely valueless without a railroad. With one, every ton of ore they contain is worth $1, $2, $3, or $4, as the case may be.

Take, for example, the coalfields of Pennsylvania. The value of the coal sent yearly from them, in all the agencies it is called upon to perform, is beyond all calculation. Upon this article are based our manufacturing establishments, and our government and merchant steamships, representing values, in their various relations and ramifications, equal to thousands of millions of dollars. Without coal it is impossible to conceive the spectacle that we should have presented as a people, so entirely different would it have been from our present condition. Neither our commercial nor our manufacturing, nor, consequently, our agricultural interests, could have borne any relation whatever to their present enormous magnitude. Yet all this result has been achieved by a few railroads and canals in Pennsylvania, which have not cost over $50 million. With these works, coal can be brought into the New York market for about $3.50 per ton; without them, it could not have been made available either for ordinary fuel or as a motive power. So small, comparatively, are the agencies by which such immense results

have been effected that the former are completely lost sight of in the magnitude of the latter.

What is true of the Pennsylvania coalfields is equally true of all others to a greater or lesser extent. The coalfields of Alabama may be made to bear the same relation to the Gulf of Mexico and to the manufactures of the Southern states as have those of Pennsylvania to the North. The Gulf of Mexico is to become the seat of a greater commerce than the world ever yet saw upon any sea; and this commerce, and all the vast interests with which it will be connected, will to a very great extent owe its development and magnitude to the coalfields that slope toward the Gulf.

33.

Josiah Sutherland: Free Land and the Supply of Labor

As working and living conditions worsened with the onset of industrialism, many laborers joined the already large contingent of adventurers who were pouring into the unsettled Western lands of the United States. The decrease in the supply of labor enabled workers to exact higher wages from their employers. During the late 1840s and early 1850s, agitation began for a free land policy that would encourage even more extensive settlement. The Homestead Bill that came before Congress in 1852 would have specifically favored the poorer classes, thereby making the price of labor even more dear in the industrial states. Representative Josiah Sutherland of New York summed up the arguments against the bill on April 22, 1852.

Source: *Globe, App.*, 32 Cong., 1 Sess., pp. 729-738.

ANY ACT OR MEASURE of the government which would increase the profit of the agriculturist, either by lessening the cost of production or by increasing the product with a given amount of labor and of land, would

be an encouragement to agriculture; but is it not strange that a bill which offers a *bonus* to the mechanic and manufacturer to quit his calling and engage in agriculture, and thus become a *producer* instead of a *consumer*, should be called a bill to *encourage* agriculture, especially when you take into view the fact that the market for nearly the whole of our agricultural products is a home market, and that it has been, and is yet thought to be, the policy of the government to create and increase that home market by protecting our manufactures against foreign competition? . . .

What is there on the face of this bill to show that it is intended to benefit "manufactures and all other branches of industry"? It brings no additional labor to the country, for foreigners are carefully excluded from the benefit of its operation. It creates no additional capital — it merely changes the owner. It takes the property of *all* of the citizens of the United States and gives it to a few of them exclusively. True, it does this on condition of settlement and cultivation; but those who are to settle on and cultivate the land, under the act, are to be full-grown men and women, "heads of families." They are not created by the act; they are not to come from the heads of the statesmen who originated this measure or of the legislators who may pass it, however wise, as Minerva is said to have come from the head of Jupiter "all armed and grown." Where, then, are these settlers to come from, unless they come from the workshops and manufactories of "other branches of industry," and from the farms of those now engaged in agriculture?

Now, Mr. Chairman, I will not say, if we had a *limited* territory with a *surplus* of population; if there was an abundance of labor instead of a scarcity; if labor was here, waiting, looking for employment, instead of *demanding* its own terms; if the price of labor was not increasing while the price of the products of labor are diminishing; if, in consequence of this high price of labor, "manufactures and other branches of industry" did not claim protection against foreign competition; and if it had not been the past policy of the government, and it was not

thought now to be the present and future policy of the government, to afford that protection, at least incidentally, by taxing, through a system of duties on foreign importations, the consumer for the benefit of the manufacturer, and thus indirectly compelling the consumer to pay a portion of the wages paid by the manufacturer — if these "manufactures and other branches of industry" thus protected had not been, were not now, and were not likely to be almost the only markets for the products of our agricultural labor; whatever might be thought or said of the *constitutionality* and *policy* of this bill, yet I would not say that its title was wholly inconsistent with its provisions.

But in the present condition of things, and in view of the immense number of acres of unimproved land comparatively near market, owned by *individuals*, companies, corporations, and states, now waiting for sale, settlement, and cultivation, and to bring about the sale, settlement, and cultivation of which an immense capital has been invested in railroads and other internal improvements; I do say that to call this bill (by which the government, for the supposed benefit of the laborer and the landless, does nothing more nor less than offer a *bonus* to the laborer and landless to leave the manufactories, workshops, and farms in the old states and settle on the public domain in the new states) "a bill to encourage agriculture, commerce, manufactures, and *all other* branches of industry" is a gross perversion of truth, that its title is wholly inconsistent with its real intent, object, and provisions. . . .

I ask, why are foreigners excluded from the benefit of the act? Anyone can see that every able-bodied foreigner that might be induced to come and make his home among us would be a clear gain to the wealth and power of the whole country: and whatever political reasons might be urged against such a policy, yet it must be admitted that any act which tended to induce such immigration would so far plausibly present itself as an act of public policy, as an act intended to promote the public welfare. If the *public welfare* is to be promoted by adding, in this sudden and extraordinary way, to the total number of acres of land now cultivated, and thus adding to the total of the agricultural products of the country, it should be done by adding to the labor of the whole country and not by taking the labor which we now have employed in agriculture, manufactures, and other branches of industry in the old states and transferring it, by an act of Congress, to the new lands of the West. . . .

What is this bill then, Mr. Chairman? What ought it to be called? What ought to be its title? It is in fact a bill to grant to every man or widow in the United States who is the head of a family and has no land, and is not worth $500, 160 acres of the public domain, on certain conditions, *for his or her benefit, and thus more nearly equalize the distribution of property*. It should be so entitled — it should be so called.

What is it called by the newspapers, by the whole country, by the members of this House, by senators in the other end of the Capitol, by everybody, everywhere, except by you, sir, when you take the chair? The Homestead Bill, the Free Farm Bill. Who thinks of calling it "a bill to encourage agriculture," etc., except you, sir, as chairman of this committee, when compelled by the rules of the House to call it by the name it in fact has upon the record. . . .

Who ask for it? Who demand it? Certain associations called "Industrial Congresses" — offsprings of the German school of socialism and of the American school of "higher law" transcendentalism — partly political, partly agrarian. Upon what ground do they ask for it? Upon what ground do they *demand* it? They ask for it as a gift, as a charity, to better their condition and to enable them to live without working, at least for others. And while they *ask* for it as a gift, as a charity, they at the same time *demand* it as a matter of right, for which, even if granted, they will owe no thanks to the government; for they place their right to it upon the *natural rights of man* and not upon the Constitution and laws of their country or the charity of Congress. They ask and demand it upon grounds and theories of the natural rights of man, as I understand them, utterly inconsistent with that great principle, the recognition and security of individual property, which lies at the foundation of all civilized government not only but of all civilized society. For upon the security of property hangs industry, the mother of all arts, of all science, of all wealth; the mother and supporter of all law, order, government; of the virtues and charities of individuals and of the wealth and power of nations, and without which the whole earth would be but one moral and physical waste. . . .

This whole question has been argued as if we had a *surplus population;* as if we had 50 million men ready and waiting to take immediate possession, not only of the lands to be disposed of by the Homestead Bill and of the lands to be granted for railroads, but also of the unimproved lands *heretofore* disposed of by the government; whereas the truth is the public lands have been heretofore thrown into market by the government vastly in advance of the requirement for settlement and cultivation from the increase of our population from all sources. What have been the consequences? Depreciated prices. The lands have passed into the hands of speculators and are held by them in large tracts, unimproved, to the great injury, no doubt, of the new states and to the ruin of thousands who have found themselves unable to hold on to their lands and pay the state taxes. . . .

This Homestead Bill is unjust and will be injurious to the old states, or states in which there are no public lands, and to the capital invested in unimproved land, railroads, agriculture, and manufactures in these states. . . . What is the wealth of a state but its productive labor? And what is this bill but a *bonus, a bounty offered by the government for labor to leave the old states and settle in the new states?* How can it benefit the land states unless it induces additional emigration from the old states to them — an emigration greater than would take place under the "preemption rights and minimum price" of the old land system?

Neither this Homestead Bill nor any other land measure of this session can benefit the land states as a whole by taking the population of one land state and transferring it to another; nor can they benefit any one land state by taking the population from one part of that state and transferring it to another part of the same state. The benefit which the land states expect to receive and which they claim from these measures is that they will cause persons, or a class of persons, to leave the old states and settle in the land states who would not otherwise do so. . . .

Mr. Chairman, I must not be misunderstood. As a resident of New York, I do not complain of or envy the prosperity of the West. I do not object to the people of the East going and settling there by thousands or hundreds of thousands at a time, if they choose. I am not the advocate of *low wages* or of a protective policy. I do not object to the wages of labor, however high, which may be the result of the general prosperity of the country, of general causes, of laws, or measures of the government, *general* or *equal* in their operation. . . . I object to the government *interfering* in this way; and by means of this *bounty of land* offered to the landless, inducing labor to leave the old states for the benefit of the new states, and to the injury of the old states. . . .

I am as much the friend of the laborer as the gentlemen on the other side of this question. We differ in the way of showing our friendship, in the way of benefiting him. I would do it by encouraging his industry, protecting his person and property, and by giving him all possible liberty, both of person and property, consistent with a well-organized, efficient civil government, and the rights of others. They (if I am correct in my view of this bill) would do it by taking the property of all and giving it to the few; they would do it by giving the same reward to the vicious and idle poor man as to the honest and industrious laborer, and thus put honest labor and vicious poverty on a par.

I think this bill is an attack on the rights of property, for I can see no difference in principle in taking the property of *AB* and giving it to *CD,* because he has none: and taking the property of all the people of the United States and giving it to those only who have no land. I look upon this bill as agrarian and, if it should become a law, as the *first* only of measures brought forward to more nearly equalize the distribution of property.

I say the honest and industrious laborer will be injured by any departure from that great principle, the *security* and *freedom* of the rights of property, and therefore I am his friend by defending it.

34.

Horace Greeley: Women's Rights

One of the relatively few influential males in the crusade for women's rights was Horace Greeley. His newspaper, the New York Tribune, *spoke out against the throngs of men who yelled insults and made jeering remarks at women speakers. Though not an advocate of woman suffrage, Greeley diligently tried to help women gain economic opportunities. The following letter of September 1, 1852, addressed to Paulina W. Davis, a leader of the women's rights movement in Massachusetts, expressed what he believed to be fundamental in the struggle for equality between the sexes.*

Source: *History of Woman Suffrage,* Elizabeth C. Stanton *et al.,* eds., New York, 1881, Vol. I, pp. 520-521.

I HAVE ONCE OR TWICE been urged to attend a convention of the advocates of woman's rights; and though compliance has never been within my power, I have a right to infer that some friends of the cause desire suggestions from me with regard to the best means of advancing it. I therefore venture to submit some thoughts on that subject. To my mind the *bread* problem lies at the base of all the desirable and practical reforms which our age meditates. Not that bread is intrinsically more important to man than temperance, intelligence, morality, and religion, but that it is essential to the just appreciation of all these. Vainly do we preach the blessings of temperance to human beings cradled in hunger and suffering at intervals the agonies of famine; idly do we commend intellectual culture to those whose minds are daily racked with the dark problem, "How shall we procure food for the morrow?" "Morality," "religion," are but words to him who fishes in the gutters for the means of sustaining life and crouches behind barrels in the street for shelter from the cutting blasts of a winter's night.

Before all questions of intellectual training or political franchises for women, not to speak of such a trifle as costume, do I place the question of enlarged opportunities for work, of a more extended and diversified field of employment. The silk culture and manufacture, firmly established and thriftily prosecuted to the extent of our home demand for silk, would be worth everything to American women. Our now feeble and infantile schools of design should be encouraged with the same view. A wider and more prosperous development of our manufacturing industry will increase the demand for female labor, thus enhancing its average reward and elevating the social position of woman. I trust the future has, therefore, much good in store for the less muscular half of the human race.

But the reform here anticipated should be inaugurated in our own households. I know how idle is the expectation of any general and permanent enhancement of the wages of any class or condition above the level of equation of supply and demand, yet it seems to me that the friends of woman's rights may wisely and worthily set the example of paying juster prices for female assistance in their households than those now current. If they would but resolve never to pay a capable, efficient woman less than two-thirds the wages paid to a vigorous, effective man employed in some corresponding vocation, they would very essentially aid the movement now in progress for the general recognition and conception of equal rights to woman.

Society is clearly unjust to woman in according her but $4 to $8 per month for labor equally repugnant with, and more protracted than, that of men of equal intelligence and relative efficiency, whose services command from $10 to $20 per month. If, then, the friends of woman's rights could set the world an example of paying for female service not the lowest pittance which stern necessity may compel the defenseless to accept but as approximately fair and liberal compensation for the work actually done, as determined by a careful comparison with the recompense of other labor. I believe they would give their cause an impulse which could not be permanently resisted.

35.

CHARLES SEARS: The North American Phalanx

The North American Phalanx at Red Bank, New Jersey, was founded by Albert Brisbane, a student of the social and economic ideas of the French socialist Charles Fourier. By the 1840s industrialism and commercial enterprise were bringing a greater portion of the nation's wealth into fewer hands, and many social reformers saw a practicable solution to the workingman's problems in the phalanx idea. Numerous phalanxes were organized, but the North American Phalanx was of the longest duration, lasting twelve years. It was, according to John H. Noyes, "the test-experiment on which Fourierism practically staked its all in this country." The following selection is taken from a December 1852 report by Charles Sears on the organization's first nine years.

Source: John Humphrey Noyes, *History of American Socialisms*, Philadelphia, 1870, pp. 450-466.

PRIOR TO THE SPRING OF 1843, Mr. Albert Brisbane had been publishing, principally in the New York *Tribune*, a series of articles on the subject of social science. He had also published his larger work on *Association*, which was followed by his pamphlet containing a summary of the doctrines of a new form of society and the outline of a project to found a practical association, to be called the North American Phalanx.

There was nominally a central organization in the city of New York, and affiliated societies were invited to cooperate by subscribing the means of endowing the proposed Phalanx and furnishing the persons to engage personally in the enterprise. It was proposed to raise about $400,000, thus making the attempt with adequate means to establish the conditions of attractive industry.

The essays and books above mentioned had a wide circulation, and many were captivated with the glowing pictures of a new life thus presented; others were attracted by the economies of the combined order which were demonstrated; still others were inspired by the hopes of personal distinction in the brilliant career thus opened to their ambition; others again were profoundly impressed by Fourier's sublime annunciation of the general destinies of globes and humanities — that progressive development through careers characterized all movement and all forms; that in all departments of creation, the law of the series was the method observed in distributing harmonies. Consequently, that human society and human activity, to be in harmony with the universe of relations, cannot be an exception to the great law of the series; consequently, that the existing order of civilization and the societies that preceded it are but phases in the growth of the race, and having subserved their more active uses, become bases of further development.

Among those who became interested in the idea of social progress were a few persons in Albany, New York, who from reading and interchange of views were induced to unite in an organization for the purpose of deliberately and methodically investigating the doctrines of a new social order as announced by Fourier, deeming these doctrines worthy of the most profound and serious consideration.

This body, after several preliminary meetings, formally adopted rules of organization on the 6th of April, 1843, and the declaration of their objects is in the following words:

We, the undersigned, for the purpose of investigating Fourier's theory of social reform as expounded by Albert Brisbane, and if deemed expedient, of cooperating with like organizations elsewhere, do associate, with the ulterior view of organizing and founding an industrial and commercial Phalanx.

Proceeding in this direction, the body assumed the name of "The Albany Branch of the North American Phalanx"; opened a correspondence with Messrs. Brisbane, Greeley, Godwin, Channing, Ripley, and others; and had lectures of criticism on existing institutions and in exposition of the doctrines of the proposed new order.

During the summer practical measures were so matured that a commission was appointed to explore the country, more particularly in the vicinity of New York and of Philadelphia, for a suitable domain upon which to commence the foundation of new social institutions. Mr. Brisbane was the delegate on the part of the New York friends and Mr. Allen Worden on the part of the Albany Branch. A site was selected in Monmouth County, New Jersey, about forty miles south of New York; and on the 12th day of August, 1843, pursuant to public notice, a convention was held in the Albany Exchange, at which the North American Phalanx was organized by adopting a constitution and subscribing to a covenant to invest in the capital stock.

At this convention were delegates from New York, Catskill, Troy, Brook Farm Association, and the Albany Branch; and when the real work of paying money and elevating life to the effort of social organization was to be done, about a dozen subscribers were found equal to the work, ten of whom finally cooperated personally in the new life, with an aggregate subscription of $8,000. This, by common consent, was the absolute minimum of men and means; and, contrasted with the large expectations and claims originally stated, was indeed a great falling-off; but the few who had committed themselves with entire faith to the movement went forward, determined to do what they could to make a worthy commencement, hoping that with their own families and such others as would from time to time be induced to cooperate, the germs of new institutions might fairly be planted.

Accordingly, in the month of September 1843, a few families took possession of the domain, occupying to overfullness the two farmhouses on the place, and commenced building a temporary house, 40 ft. by 80, of two stories, for the accommodation of those who were to come the following spring.

During the year 1844 the population numbered about ninety persons, including at one period nearly forty children under the age of sixteen years. Crops were planted, teams and implements purchased, the building of shops and mills was commenced, measures of business and organization were discussed, the construction of social doctrines debated, personal claims canvassed, and thus the business of life was going on at full tide, and now also commenced the real development of character.

Hitherto there had been no settled science of society. Fourier, the man of profound insight, announced the law of progress and indicated the new forms that society would take. People accepted the new ideas gladly and would as gladly institute new forms; but there was a lack of well-defined views on the precise work to be done. Besides, education tended strongly to confirm in most minds the force of existing institutions, and, after attaining to middle age, and even before this period, the character usually becomes quite fixed; so that to break up habitudes, relinquish prejudices, sunder ties, and to adopt new modes of action, accept of modified results, and readjust themselves to new relations was a difficult, and to the many, almost impossible work, as is proved by the fact that, of the thirty or forty similar attempts at associated life within the past ten years in this country, only the North American Phalanx now [1852] remains. Nor did this association escape the inevitable consequences of bringing together a body of grown-up people with their families, many of whom came reluctantly, and whose characters were formed under other influences.

Personal difficulties occurred as a matter of course, but these were commonly overruled by a healthy sentiment of self-respect. Parties also began to form, but they were not fully developed until the first annual settlement and distribution of profits was attempted. Then, however, they took a variety of forms according to the interest or ambition of the partisans; though two principal views characterized the more permanent and clearly defined party divisions: one party contending for authority, enforced with stringent rules and and final appeal to the dictation of the chief officer; the other party standing out for organization and distribution of authority. The former would centralize power and make administration despotic, claiming that thus only could order be maintained; the latter claimed that to do this would be merely to repeat the institutions of civilization, that association thus controlled would be devoid of corporate life, would be dependent upon individuals, and quite artificial; whereas what we wanted was a wholly different order, viz., the enfranchisement of the individual, order through the natural method of the series, institutions that would be instinct with the life that is organic, from the sum of the series down to the last subdivision of the group.

The strife to maintain these several views was long and vigorous, and it would scarcely be an exaggeration to say that our days were spent in labor and our nights in legislation for the first five years of our associative life. The question at issue was vital. It was whether the infant association should or should not have new institutions, whether it should be Civilizee or Phalansterian, whether it should be a mere joint-stock corporation such as had been before, or whether the new form of industrial organization indicated by Fourier should be initiated. In the contest between the two principles of civilized joint-stock association and of the Phalansterian or Serial organization, the latter ultimately prevailed; and in this triumph of the idea of the natural organic forms of society through the method of the series, we see distinctly the development of the germ of the Phalanx. For when we have a true principle evolved, however insignificant the development may be, the results, although limited by the smallness of the development, will nevertheless be right in kind. It is perhaps important, to the end that the results of our experience be rightly

The North American Phalanx in New Jersey, artist unknown, mid-19th century

comprehended, to indicate the essential features of the order of society that is to succeed present disorder, and wherein it differs from other social forms.

A fundamental feature is that we deny the bald atheism that asserts human nature to be a melancholy failure and unworthy of respect or trust, and therefore to be treated as an alien and convict. On the contrary, we hold that, instead of chains, man requires freedom; instead of checks, he requires development; instead of artificial order through coercion, he requires the divine harmony that comes through counterpoise. Hence society is bound by its own highest interests, by the obligation it owes to its every member, to make organic provision for the entire circle of human wants, for the entire range of human activity; so that the individual shall be emancipated from the servitude of nature, from personal domination, from social tyrannies; and that thus fully enfranchised and guaranteed by the whole force of society into all freedoms and the endowment of all rights pertaining to manhood, he may fulfill his own destiny in accordance with the laws written in his own organization.

In the Phalanx, then, we have, in the sphere of production, the relation of employer and employed stricken out of the category of relations, not merely as in the simple joint-stock corporations, by substituting for the individual employer the still more despotic and irresistible corporate employer, but by everyone becoming his own employer, doing that which he is best qualified by endowment to do, receiving for his labor precisely his share of the product, as nearly as it can be determined while there is no scientific unit of value.

In the sphere of circulation or currency, we have a representative of all the wealth produced, so that everyone shall have issued to him for all his production the abstract or protean form of value, which is convertible into every other form of value; in commerce or exchanges, reducing this from a speculation, as now, to a function, employing only the necessary force to make distributions and exchanging products or values on the basis of cost.

In the sphere of social relations, we have freedom to form ties according to affinities of character.

In the sphere of education, we establish

the natural method, not through the exaltation into professorships of this, that, or other notable persons but through a body of institutions reposing upon industry and having organic vitality. Commencing with the nursery, we make, through the living corporation, through adequately endowed institutions that fail not, provision for the entire life of the child from the cradle upward; initiating him step by step not into nominal, ostensible education apart from his life but into the real business of life, the actual production and distribution of wealth, the science of accounts and the administration of affairs; and providing that, through uses, the science that lies back of uses shall be acquired also theory and practice, the application of science to the pursuits of life shall, through daily use, become as familiar as the mother tongue; and thus place our children at maturity in the ranks of manhood and womanhood, competent to all the duties and activities of life that they may be qualified by endowment to perform.

In the sphere of administration, we have a graduated hierarchy or orders from the simple chief of a group, or supervisor of a single function, up to the unitary administration of the globe.

In the sphere of religion, we have religious life as contrasted with the profession of a religious faith. The intellect requires to be satisfied as well as the affections, and is so with the scientific and therefore universal formula, that the religious element in man is the passion of unity; that is, that all the powers of the soul shall attain to true equilibrium and act normally in accordance with divine law, so that human life in all its powers and activities shall be in harmonious relations with nature, with itself, and with the supreme center of life.

Of course we speak of the success of an idea, and only expect realization through gradual development. It is obvious, also, that such realization can be attained only through organization; because, unaided, the individual makes but scanty conquests over nature and but feeble opposition to social usurpations.

The principle, then, of the Serial organization being established, the whole future course of the association, in respect to its merely industrial institutions, was plain, viz.: to develop and mature the Serial form.

Not that the old questions did not arise subsequently. On the contrary, on the admission of new members, from time to time, they did arise and have discussion anew, but the contest had been virtually decided. The association had pronounced with such emphasis in favor of the organization of labor upon the basis of cooperative efforts, joint-stock property, and unity of interests, that those holding adverse views gradually withdrew, and the harmony of the association was never afterward in serious jeopardy.

During the later as well as earlier years of our associated life, the question of preference of modes of realization came under discussion in the Phalansterian school, one party advocating the measure of obtaining large means and so fully endowing the Phalanx with all the external conditions of attractive industry, and then introducing gradually a body of select associates. The North American Phalanx, as represented in the conventions of the school, held to the view that new social institutions, new forms into which the life of a people shall flow, cannot be determined by merely external conditions and the elaboration of a theory of life and organization but are matters of growth.

Our view is that the true divine growth of the social, as of the individual, man is the progressive development of a germ; and while we would not in the slightest degree oppose a scientific organization upon a large scale, it is our preference to pursue a more progressive mode, to make a more immediately practical and controllable attempt. . . .

The possibility of establishing true social relations, increased production, and the embodiment of the religious sentiment are, if we read the signs aright, the points upon which the question of association now hinges in the public mind. Because, first, man's capacity for these relations is doubted; because, second, production is an essential and permanent condition of life and means of progress; because, third, it is apprehended that the religious element is not sufficiently regarded and provided for in association.

Demonstrate that capacity, prove that men by their own efforts may command all the means of life, show in institutions the truly religious nature of the movement and the relations that are to obtain, and the public will be gained to the idea of association.

Another question still has been pressed upon us offensively by the advocates of existing institutions as though their life were pure and their institutions perfect, while no terms of opprobrium could sufficiently characterize the depravity of the Socialists, and this question is that of the marriage relation. Upon this question a form of society that is so notoriously rotten as existing civilization is, a society that has marriage and prostitution as complementary facts of its relations of the sexes, a society which establishes professorships of abortion, which methodizes infanticide, which outlaws woman, might at least assume the show of modesty, might treat with common candor any and all who are seeking the divine law of marriage. Instead, therefore, of recognizing its right to defame us, we put that society upon its defense and say to it, Come out of your infidelities and your crimes and your pretenses; seek out the law of righteousness, and deal justly with woman. Nevertheless, this is a question in which we, in common with others, have a profound interest; it is a question which has by no means escaped consideration among us, and we perhaps owe it to ourselves to state our position.

What the true law of relationship of the sexes is we as a body do not pretend to determine. Here, as elsewhere, individual opinion is free, but there are certain conditions, as we think, clearly indicated, which are necessary to the proper consideration of the question, and our view is that it is one that must be determined mainly by woman herself. When she shall be fully enfranchised, fully endowed with her rights, so that she shall no longer be dependent on marriage for position, no longer be regarded as a pensioner but as a constituent of the state; in a single phrase, when society shall, independently of other considerations than that of inherent right, assure to woman social position and pecuniary independence so that she can legislate on a footing of equality, then she may announce the law of the sexual relations. But this can only occur in organized society; society in which there is a complete circle of fraternal institutions that have public acceptance; this can only occur when science enters the domain of human society and determines relations as it now does in astronomy or physic.

We therefore say to civilization, You have no adequate solution of this problem that is convulsing you, and in which every form of private and public protest against the actual condition is expressing itself. Besides this we claim what cannot be claimed for any similar number of people in civilization, viz., that we have been here over nine years, with an average population of nearly 100 persons of both sexes and all ages, and, judged by the existing standard of morals, we are above reproach on this question.

Thus we have proceeded, disposing of our primary legislation, demonstrating to general acceptance the rectitude of our awards and distributions of profit, determining questions of social doctrine, perfecting methods of order, and developing our industry, with a fair measure of success.

36.

Anonymous: Arguments Against the Maine Liquor Law

*Many temperance crusaders and social reformers of the nineteenth century believed
that delinquency and poverty were frequently caused by the use of intoxicating
beverages. By mid-century the temperance organizations had gained enough strength
to seek legislation prohibiting the sale of liquor. One of the earliest laws was passed
in Maine on June 2, 1851, under the leadership of Neal Dow. The "Maine Law,"
defended as a measure to protect the public welfare, served as a model for legislation
in other states. "Nine-tenths of the alcoholic stimulus that is used is abused,"
claimed Theodore Parker. "The evil is so monstrous, so patent, so universal, that
it becomes the duty of the state to take care of its citizens; the whole of its parts."
However, many argued against the law on the ground that such legislation was an
infringement of personal rights. The following selection, taken from an article
in the* Democratic Review *for 1852, is representative of the opposition to
temperance laws.*

Source: *United States Magazine and Democratic Review*, May 1852.

It seems that the rights of man have again to be written out. Heaven forfend that there be no need of again fighting them out this side of the water: it would not tell prettily on the other side, just now.

Precisely the old pretexts for state churches, inquisitions, censorship and prohibition of the press, suppression of thought and discussion, and shooting down or imprisoning of murmurers against the government are relied on now to justify one of the grossest, yet cutest, attempts against the liberty of the person that ever entered into the heart of a Metternich to conceive of. . . .

That freedom of opinion and conscience, about which we know a little and talk much, has its origin in something deeper than the kind disposition which the rulers (whether republican or monarchical) are supposed to feel toward the governed; it rests upon a *principle*, which we recommend our Maine people and their upholders to find out and become acquainted with without delay, for in it lies their only safety

from other things we might name, which they could hardly bear the mention of.

In school it was taught us — in Fourth of July addresses we have heard it declared (and always in connection with Bunker Hill and Yorktown) — nay, in every newspaper of every shade of politics we daily read it — that man has some rights which are his own and not another's. And, if the point is anywhere found at which he may take his stand and draw around him a circle of enclosure, saying to his ruler, "Thus far shalt thou go, and no farther," it is at the verge of the sacred precincts of strictly personal liberty. Whether he is assailed by decrees which seek to fetter him for the benefit or aggrandizement of aristocrats and despots, or for the whimsical pleasure of new-lights in morals or dietetics, there is surely for him some city of safety where, surrounded and sheltered by the few rights that pertain to his privacy, his person, his conscience, his intellect, and his ailments, he may, with the light of his own conscience, deal with his own soul and mind and body as best he pleases himself, think his own thoughts, feel his own impulses, smoke his own pipe, mix his own mess, eat the fruit of his own fig tree, and drink the juice of his own vine, with *none* to molest him or make him afraid.

The sphere of individual liberty must be shrunken, indeed, if it cannot enclose all that lies within a man's skin, and the powers of the ruler, extensive indeed, if they can reach down the citizen's throat and explore his digestive organs. It is not mere bombast to declare that the esophagus, the duodenum, lacticals, and capillary ducts of freeborn Americans are, and of right should be, forever inviolable; and that if the Declaration of Independence does not avail to save the contents of our stomachs and bladders from chemical analysis and legislative discussion, it is full time to make another declaration that shall mean something.

Nature hates such espionage. Human instinct, which teaches the human animal whether rude or refined to revolt against any interference with his bodily matters, and, above all, with his mess, perfectly well understands the distinction I aim at, and may be trusted to remember it when rulers forget it.

Drinking! Why, does it not belong to the same category with eating, sleeping, walking, fashion of dress, cut of hair, choice of pursuit, amusements, and associates, laughing, crying, sneezing, sweating, and winking? Nearly all of which, though undoubtedly influencing the individual's actions and greatly tending to make him either a good or a bad citizen, and though most of them have at times been subjected to laws more or less stringent in proportion as they violated nature, even teetotalers will concede to be quite beyond the proper scope of civil government, and to pertain, under the ministration of moral influence of milder sway, to each one's most private judgment, notwithstanding that in the exercise of that judgment, as between himself and his conscience, his conscience and his God, he may commit as much wickedness as you please.

But there is another category of rights of a graver character to which the one under consideration belongs, and with which it must sink or swim. I mean that which includes freedom of opinion, of the press and of speech, freedom of conscience, creed, and worship; rights well known to us all, and which we are all accustomed to hold ourselves ready to defend with thrusting bayonets and gunpowder. And the wrong that has been perpetrated is identical in its nature with those we so often and freely berate with the epithets "censorship of the press," "religious tyranny," "Russian despotism," and "Spanish Inquisition."

The freedom of the gullet cannot be distinguished in any classification of rights from freedom of the windpipe, of the heart, and of the brain. To invade the citizen's larder and cellar is to invade his library and his sanctuary. To legislate for his palate is no better than to control his tongue, regulate his thoughts, and explore his conscience. All of these equally lie within the same degree of causation, impulse, life — all equally far beyond the safe limits of human government. And this I claim will abundantly appear when we consider the pretexts that are used to justify this new and strange enactment, and the arguments which naturally suggest themselves against it.

A fair statement of those pretexts I suppose to be found in the following extract of a speech made in the Maine legislature, while sitting in committee of the whole on the human stomach and human nature in general, by Brandy Smasher, Esq., of the town of Down East:

I don't p'tend to say, Mr. Chairman, that the simple act of swollerin a glass of licker is of itself a depredation on any buddy's parson *ur* property, nor agin the suvrinity of the state; but this I dew say; that it *tends* through its action on the membrane and nerve to create an intemprit thirst for more licker, which, agin, *tends* to indoose a pervarted moral condition, which again, *tends* to the commission of crime, and poverty. Therefore and bekase its ultimate and ulterior *tendencies* is bad, I go in for the peribition of its use throughout the length and breadth of all the diggins and choppins of this free and happy land. Intem'prance, sir, wastes the individooal's puss, stimulates his passions, spiles his digestion, beclouds his reason, debases his natur, and finally, brings him and his'n to the poorhouse or the jail, if not both. Some folks, with red noses, on 'tother side of the house, object that we carnt suppress sperrits without runnin' agin constitootions and rights, and sitch like abstractions, but, sir, I turn away from sitch nonsense, to contemplate the orful spectickle of besotted drunkards — weeping wives, starvin orphins, and poor rates. Then there's an old story about moral suasion. Why, sir, arter a quarter of a century of *pur*suasion, of *dis*uasion, and all sorts of suasion, a'most half this commoonity deny the great and glorious truth of tetotalism. Sayin' nothin' of nearly all the world who go on drinkin' just as they ollers did. Moral suasion! Sqinch the tarnal fires of Vesoovius with a pewter squirt — whistle the wild whirlwind to repose, or sit on the table rock, and coax Niagary to turn and run up hill by talking moral suasion to it! I go in for bringin' the strong arm of the law to bear upon them that's been laffin at us lect'rers, 'specially them stuck-up folks, what thought 'umselves better than us bekase they could have furrin wines on their table, so't in fewter they may grin on the *dry* side of their mouth!

The "rub" of this logic is that an act not of itself harmful to others, but which may in the opinion of the legislator, in a remote degree, *tend* to the commission of injurious acts, may be prohibited, even though personal liberty be thereby invaded. This logic is not new. It is as old as folly and as decrepit as despotism. . . .

And even in a case where the good of the people was really considered (which none will deny is true with the majority of the decrees of despotic governments), must not

the same chain of reasoning suffice to justify the establishment of a state church to the exclusion of all others, the censorship or complete suppression of the press, the destruction of all infidel, heretical, or democratic books, the inhibition of public assemblages, and even of private discussion, and the controlling of the schools and universities — in short, to justify every decree, however stringent, which might in the opinion of the rulers be requisite, in order to rear up a moral, religious, and orderly population; to kill wickedness in the germ of false opinions, to take in time the stitch that saves nine, to administer the ounce of prevention that is worth tons of cure, and keep the jails and poorhouses empty by keeping the heads of the subject so. . . .

All of these absurdities are equally founded on the plausible notion that the easiest and surest way to prevent crime is rightly to regulate the individual's conscience, opinions, passions, and temperament, in the midst of which wickedness has its earliest origin, and out of which, as effects from causes, flow those evil intentions and violations from which, again, all sin and crime result. And the notion would be indisputably sound were rulers only all wise, all good, and all powerful; were they equal to Deity itself, or even equal to a well-informed archangel; but here is the difficulty — they are neither the one nor the other. On the contrary, some of Brandy Smasher's colleagues are confoundedly stupid and others confoundedly wicked. Though personally unacquainted with them, I do not hesitate to accuse them of wickedness, folly, and weakness in good large proportions, for, if I am not mistaken, they are *men*.

Now I insist that while those operations are going on within the man, which precede the formation of intentions and volitions that are subsequently to develop into open actions, which may or may not be hurtful to society, *no* civil government can rightfully interfere in the process with its pains, penalties, or prohibitions; and the reasons for this are:

First, because to do so is to impose prohibitions and penalties upon probable or possible, instead of actual, offenses. The deprivation or the punishment are made certain or immediate, while the offense aimed at is distant, contingent, uncertain. While the operation of the moral forces remains unfolded within the breast or brain, it is beyond human ken to know what the result will be; but when the *overt* act is committed, then the arm of the law may fall without risk of injustice, and what punishment the open act receives, suffices — *must* suffice for whatever evil element entered into its composition, within the laboratory where it was compounded. . . .

It is by no means safe logic to argue that because large numbers of the criminal and vicious are free drinkers, therefore intemperance causes every other vice that happens to accompany it, for vices usually herd together. I know that the bold assertion is freely made that nine-tenths of our pauperism and crime spring from this cause, but this I deny in a specific manner. . . .

There are other causes of evil which answer the devil's turn where this one fails and by means of which he is able to scatter sin and misery most thickly over the *most* dry-mouthed countries of the globe. Who does not know that about half these expensive commodities — pauperism and crime — are imported here from foreign parts, where they have been manufactured by overpopulation, misgovernment, famine, pestilence, absenteeism, and so forth? Consider that, independent of rum drinking, we have improvidence, laziness, extravagance, self-indulgence of all kinds, cards, dice, roly-poly, fast horses, failure of crops, hard times, bad wives, sick families, lawsuits, war, oppression, priest-riding, and all the various causes of poverty; and that if you make crime the child of rum alone, you rob poverty of her firstborn darling. Consider bad education, immoral books, irreligion, a false religion, infidelity, naughty women such as overcame Sampson, the water drinker.

Then there is old-fashioned original sin, not such as is found only in a fluid state, but the Bible article, that abounds in every form of existence — the "birth sin," as it is called in certain institutions termed churches where wine is drunk as a cure for it — the *ineradicable taint* against which *religion* battled so long, and with such varied success, before temperance societies usurped its vocation, and which a whole worldhood of cold water administered on a celebrated occasion failed to wash away. O, it's a wicked world! And though we stop every drop of its liquor, I fear it will manage to commit crime enough and suffer poverty enough to render it little better than a sore spot on the face of creation.

But, to resume, the result of all those contingencies is that there is about one chance in some thousands that my friend's present modicum of white wine will, some day, bring him to the poorhouse or jail; and it is for subjecting himself to this one chance of being punished by public charity, or public justice, that he is to be punished now; it is for this that the citizen must, through life, be restricted in his personal liberty and a vital principle of republicanism be trampled on by a republican state.

It is to prevent this shadow of a chance of ultimate, possible, vague, indefinite, far-distant crime!

It is only a very small portion of a man's conduct that pertains to the province of the civil ruler. The church, the private conscience, the reason, public opinion, the social system, each in its own way, guiding and controlling the human impulses, prophecy claims the rest. Unlike the iron hand of municipal regulation, these press lightly, gently, yieldingly upon his moral nature without crushing out of it that free will in which alone lies his responsibility, his identity, allowing development and growth to go on, and the ways of Providence to work out their end. The legislator who enters on this realm will find its paths vague, uncertain, and leading to little good; for though it is a realm tempting to human tyranny and conceit to usurp, it is one that baffles human wisdom to find out. It is the grand *via* by which the creative sphere flows down into the actual; and whatever day-built erections the most enlightened science may strive to raise by which to explore that sphere, the builders are sure to be smitten with the curse of Babel, and babble in many and diverse tongues.

I fear, Brandy Smasher, representative of all the wisdoms of the enlightened town of Down East though you be, that you are in the wrong place, and that your long, prying nose is leading you farther than it can guide you. I humbly suggest that your capacity is hardly equal to the task of overhauling and "setting to rights" the interior moral arcana of man. Excuse me, but I dread lest you should break something valuable where you are now so bravely stamping about. . . .

But it is said that you have the majority of the voters with you? Alas! Friend Smasher, we may more than guess that you and your majority need instruction in the principles of free government, a trifle more than the emperor of Japan or a French republican. Be informed, I pray you, that although the minority may not count quite as many votes as the majority, they may, nevertheless, number considerably more than naught, and that to split the few in the back and broil them for the breakfast of the many is justifiable solely by the very old and bad rule:

The simple plan,
That they may *take* who have the *power*,
And they may *keep* who *can;*

and that, though eleven be fully agreed and only one dissent, there may be folly as well as wickedness in selling him to the Ishmaelites.

I beseech you not to hold yourself responsible for every moral transgression of your fellow citizen, though sinner he may be, but to let him now and then exercise a little moral responsibility on his own account. Leave to him a few rights of the inviolate sort; it may be good for him and you too. As a creature born into original sin with a chance of salvation, he should be allowed a portion at least of that free will which we read of in catechisms, and on the use of which his future and eternal condition depends, and suffer him to account for some few matters and things done in the flesh to his God above. Even an act of the Maine legislature may fail to effect the process of regeneration for him. He is the creature of God, I assure you; and it is not possible to make him wholly the creature of law without danger of putting out his life. A straitjacket is well enough for a maniac, but it is far from being a healthy garment for a growing child. Fastening one by mistake on a sane person has been known to drive him raving crazy; and the citizen restricted in his elbowroom by the straitjacket of strict law and fed with the long iron spoon of dietetic legislation can do but little good to the state, and is in danger of becoming neither useful nor safe.

In no commonwealth can it be salutary for a large class, though less numerous than the majority by a casting vote, to be driven to regard the government as its oppressors; nor does it help the matter for that government to put on the self-righteous and self-conceited garb of priest, pedagogue, and physician for the purpose of snatching away, and with pretended or real solicitude for the health, wealth, and salvation of the disciple, pupil, and patient, stand at his table to order the arrangement of the courses and the quality of the beverages.

Second, like bad paymasters of one sort, such laws as these of Bloody Mary, Louis Napoleon, and Brandy Smasher inflict the penalty considerably too far in advance; and like the good woman who whipped her children "all around" every Monday morning, furnishes us *de bene esse* (for the good that may come of it), a plan from which little good can ever come whether false religion, bad opinions, or bad liquor be aimed at. It is beginning rather early in the day to punish wicked thoughts while brewing in the brain, or wicked beer while brewing in the barrel. . . .

Third, such laws, and especially this liquor law, commit the gross and patent injustice of punishing the many for the faults of the few. . . . Really we are in danger of coming to the pass of holding all our sins and crimes in common, just as the communists would have us hold our goods, so that no one will be able to know which are his own and which are his neighbor's transgressions.

We are approaching guaranteeism in morals, a sort of system of soul insurance, which, like fire and marine insurance, though like them it would encourage carelessness, may be well enough where it remains, a voluntary arrangement, is, nevertheless, not quite the thing to be effected by force of law. I think few, except the ultracareless, would relish a statute which should tax the citizens at large to compensate for every loss sustained by fire and tempest. Virtues, like all faculties of the soul or body, grow by *exercise;* and as the virtue of temperance, above all others, is strengthened by use, so laws that supersede the need of calling it into play — which swaddle up the moral responsibility with parchment and tape, and make a baby of the full-grown man, are antitemperance — and that's the short of it.

However it may appear to a teetotal exhorter who has pursued his fraction of the idea until he has become monomaniac with water on the brain, to the sane mind it would seem much more just to separate the drunken from the sober, and confine them within certain established districts, where the prohibition of those drinks which they shall have demonstrated themselves unfit to enjoy might be imposed without harming innocent persons — or to inflict a tenfold

penalty on every offense the drunkard might commit — or to divorce his wife and children and sequester his services in some public workhouse for their support. This would at least be placing the burden on the proper shoulders, and stand on its own proper and peculiar bottom. It would be equal and it would be exact.

It is true that Paul once enjoyed the religious duty of abstaining from meats offered to idols lest weaker brothers might be caused to offend, but then there was a plenty of Christian beef to be had, and he only *preached.* And it is preaching and not lawmaking that I consider Brandy Smasher's best vogue.

These are some of the principal objections to laws which prohibit acts, whose only harmless quality consists in their possible *tendency* to induce the one who commits them to do other acts of a nature directly injurious to society. These are some of the considerations which prove the right of drinking to lie within the strict limits of intimate personal liberty, where also lie, inseparable from it, the rights of free thought, free speech, free conscience, free worship — to prove that they are all included in the same definition and protected by the same panoply; that of free alimentation being in a special and intimate manner connected with "life, liberty, and the pursuit of happiness." The circle of enclosure around all these cannot be broken down in one place without laying the whole bare and defenseless to the meddling, the bungling, and the crushing of oppression of the lawmaker. The freedom of the wine press and cider press and the freedom of the printing press are one and the same. The instinct of self-defense and of self-preservation it is which guards them all or guards none. All of them, or more, take their place in schedule A.1, of the unprescriptible rights of man, and all or none are, by the organic law of every free commonwealth, sacred from scrutiny, as they also are by virtue of those higher and more abstract, yet simple and easily known principles, superior and anterior to all human institutions, which lie in the nature and fitness of things.

Yet, if this right to drink stood by itself and alone, and involved in its fall no other principle of civil liberty, we could gain nothing by saving all the crime and misery, and consequent taxation, attributable to intemperance, at the expense of this one item of human freedom.

37.

A Public Library for Boston

A few public libraries had existed in America since the early years of the republic, but the public library movement, properly so-called, did not get under way until the middle of the nineteenth century. Massachusetts, always a leader in educational matters, was the first to take steps to provide the general public with free reading material on a large scale. The proposed Boston Public Library was discussed by its trustees in a report issued in 1852, from which the following selection is taken. The library building was dedicated and opened to the public in 1854.

Source: *Bulletin of the Public Library of the City of Boston,* April 1893:
"Report of the Trustees of the Public Library, July 1852."

WITHOUT ASSERTING that the [Boston] schools are perfect, it may truly be said that the general principle and plan on which they are founded are as nearly so as the nature of the case admits. They compose a great system of instruction, administered in schools rising in gradation from the most elementary to those of a highly advanced character, open to the whole population, and supported by a most liberal public expenditure. The schools themselves may admit improvement, and the utmost care should be taken that they keep pace with the progress of improvement in other things; but the system itself, in the great features just indicated, seems perfect; that is, in a word, to give a first-rate school education, at the public expense, to the entire rising generation.

But when this object is attained, and it is certainly one of the highest importance, our system of public instruction stops. Although the school and even the college and university are, as all thoughtful persons are well aware, but the first stages in education, the public makes no provision for carrying on the great work. It imparts, with a noble equality of privilege, a knowledge of the elements of learning to all its children, but it affords them no aid in going beyond the elements. It awakens a taste for reading, but it furnishes to the public nothing to be read. It conducts our young men and women to that point where they are qualified to acquire from books the various knowledge in the arts and sciences which books contain, but it does nothing to put those books within their reach. As matters now stand, and speaking with general reference to the mass of the community, the public makes no provision whatever by which the hundreds of young persons annually educated, as far as the elements of learning are concerned, at the public expense, can carry on their education and bring it to practical results by private study.

We do not wish to exaggerate in either part of this statement, although we wish to call attention to the point as one of great importance and not yet, as we think, enough considered. We are far from intimating that school education is not important because it is elementary; it is, on the contrary, of the utmost value. Neither do we say, on the other hand, because there are no libraries which in the strict sense of the word are public, that, therefore, there is absolutely no way by which persons of limited means can get access to books. There are several libraries of the kind usually called public, belonging, however, to private corporations; and there are numerous private libraries from which books are liberally loaned to those wishing to borrow them.

It will, however, be readily conceded that this falls far short of the aid and encouragement which would be afforded to the reading community (in which we include all persons desirous of obtaining knowledge or an agreeable employment of their time from the perusal of books) by a well-supplied public library.

If we had no free schools, we should not be a community without education. Large numbers of children would be educated at private schools at the expense of parents able to afford it, and considerable numbers in narrow circumstances would, by the aid of the affluent and liberal, obtain the same advantages. We all feel, however, that such a state of things would be a poor substitute for our system of public schools, of which it is the best feature that it is a public provision for all; affording equal advantages to poor and rich; furnishing at the public expense an education so good as to make it an object with all classes to send their children to the public schools.

It needs no argument to prove that, in a republican government, these are features of the system, quite as valuable as the direct benefit of the instruction which it imparts. But it is plain that the same principles apply to the further progress of education in which each one must be mainly his own teacher. Why should not this prosperous and liberal city extend some reasonable amount of aid to the foundation and support of a noble public library to which the young people of both sexes, when they leave the schools, can resort for those works which pertain to general culture, or which are needful for research into any branch of useful knowledge?

At present, if the young machinist, engineer, architect, chemist, engraver, painter, instrument maker, musician (or student of any branch of science or literature) wishes to consult a valuable and, especially, a rare and costly work, he must buy it, often import it at an expense he can ill afford, or he must be indebted for its use to the liberality of private corporations or individuals. The trustees submit that all the reasons which exist for furnishing the means of elementary education at the public expense apply, in an equal degree, to a reasonable provision to aid and encourage the acquisition of the knowledge required to complete a preparation for active life or to perform its duties.

We are aware that it may be said, and truly, that knowledge acquired under hardships is often more thorough than that to which the learner is invited without effort on his part; that the studious young man who makes sacrifices and resorts to expedients to get books values them the more and reads them to greater profit. This, however, is equally true of school education and of every other privilege in life. But the city of Boston has never deemed this a reason for withholding the most munificent appropriations for the public education. It has not forborne to support an expensive system of free schools because without such a system a few individuals would have acquired an education for themselves, under every possible discouragement and disadvantage, and because knowledge so acquired is usually thorough, well-digested, and available beyond what is got in an easier way.

The question is not what will be brought

about by a few individuals of indomitable will and an ardent thirst for improvement but what is most for the advantage of the mass of the community. In this point of view we consider that a large public library is of the utmost importance as the means of completing our system of public education. . . .

Libraries were originally intended for only a very small proportion of the community in which they were established, because few persons could read and fewer still desired to make inquiries that involved the consultation of many books. Even for a long time after the invention of printing, they were anxiously shut up from general use; and, down to the present day, a large proportion of the best libraries in the world forbid anything like a free circulation of their books — many of them forbidding any circulation at all. . . .

Strong intimations, therefore, are already given that ampler means, and means better adapted to our peculiar condition and wants, are demanded in order to diffuse through our society that knowledge without which we have no right to hope that the condition of those who are to come after us will be as happy and prosperous as our own. The old roads, so to speak, are admitted to be no longer sufficient. Even the more modern turnpikes do not safisfy our wants. We ask for railcars and steamboats, in which many more persons — even multitudes — may advance together to the great end of life, and go faster, farther, and better, by the means thus furnished to them, than they have ever been able to do before.

Nowhere are the intimations of this demand more decisive than in our own city; nor, it is believed, is there any city of equal size in the world where added means for general popular instruction and self-culture — if wisely adapted to their great ends — will be so promptly seized upon or so effectually used as they will be here. One plain proof of this is the large number of good libraries we already possess which are constantly resorted to by those who have the right, and which yet — it is well-known — fail to supply the demand for popular reading. For we have respectable libraries of almost every class, beginning with those of the Athenaeum, of the American Academy, of the Historical Society, and of the General Court, the Social Library of 1792, the Mercantile Library, the Mechanics Apprentices' Library, the libraries of the Natural History Society, of the Bar, of the Statistical Association, of the Genealogical Society, of the Medical Society, and of other collective and corporate bodies; and coming down to the "circulating libraries" strictly so-called; the Sunday school libraries, and the collections of children's books found occasionally in our primary schools.

Now, all these are important and excellent means for the diffusion of knowledge. They are felt to be such, and they are used as such, and the trustees would be especially careful not to diminish the resources or the influence of any one of them. They are sure that no public library can do it. But it is admitted — or else another and more general library would not now be urged — that these valuable libraries do not, either individually or in the aggregate, reach the great want of this city, considered as a body politic bound to train up its members in the knowledge which will best fit them for the positions in life to which they may have been born, or any others to which they may justly aspire through increased intelligence and personal worthiness. For multitudes among us have no right of access to any one of the more considerable and important of these libraries; and, except in rare instances, no library among us seeks to keep more than a single copy of any book on its shelves so that no one of them, nor, indeed, all of them taken together, can do even a tolerable amount of what ought to be done toward satisfying the demands for healthy, nourishing reading made by the great masses of our people who cannot be expected to purchase such reading for themselves.

And yet there can be no doubt that such reading ought to be furnished to all as a matter of public policy and duty, on the same principle that we furnish free education, and, in fact, as a part, and a most important part, of the education of all. For it has been rightly judged that, under political, social, and religious institutions like ours, it is of paramount importance that the means of general information should be so diffused that the largest possible number of persons should be induced to read and understand questions going down to the very foundations of social order, which are constantly presenting themselves and which we, as a

people, are constantly required to decide, and to decide either ignorantly or wisely.

That this *can* be done — that is, that such libraries *can* be collected and that they will be used to a much wider extent than libraries have ever been used before, and with much more important results — there can be no doubt; and if it can be done *anywhere*, it can be done *here*, in Boston; for no population of 150,000 souls, lying so compactly together as to be able, with tolerable convenience, to resort to one library, was ever before so well fitted to become a reading, self-cultivating population as the population of our own city is at this moment.

38.

Harriet Beecher Stowe: Uncle Tom Defies Simon Legree

Few attacks upon slavery were as effective as Harriet Beecher Stowe's Uncle Tom's Cabin. *First written as a serial for the Abolitionist journal,* National Era, *beginning in 1851, it appeared in book form in 1852. It was an immediate and enduring success, selling 300,000 copies during the first year and nearly 3,000,000 since. The portrayal of Uncle Tom, the first Negro fictional hero created by an American author, elicited much sympathy for the plight of the slave. Southerners, challenging the book's authenticity, wrote seething denunciations; it was a "criminal prostitution," according to a critic in the* Southern Literary Messenger, *"of the high functions of the imagination." Mrs. Stowe attempted to silence this criticism with a sequel,* A Key to Uncle Tom's Cabin *(1853), documenting the characters and events.*

Source: *Uncle Tom's Cabin,* Boston, 1883, pp. 419-423.

Long after dusk, the whole weary train, with their baskets on their heads, defiled up to the building appropriated to the storing and weighing the cotton. Legree was there, busily conversing with the two drivers.

"Dat ar Tom's gwine to make a powerful deal o' trouble; kept a puttin' into Lucy's basket. One o' these yer dat will get all der

niggers to feelin' 'bused if Mas'r don't watch him!" said Sambo.

"Hey-dey! The black cuss!" said Legree. "He'll have to get a breakin' in, won't he, boys?"

Both Negroes grinned a horrid grin at this intimation.

"Ay, ay! let Mas'r Legree alone, for

breakin' in! De debil heself couldn't beat Mas'r at dat!" said Quimbo.

"Wal, boys, the best way is to give him the flogging to do, till he gets over his notions. Break him in!"

"Lord, Mas'r'll have hard work to get dat out o' him!"

"It'll have to come out of him, though!" said Legree, as he rolled his tobacco in his mouth.

"Now, dar's Lucy — de aggravatinest, ugliest wench on de place!" pursued Sambo.

"Take care, Sam; I shall begin to think what's the reason for your spite agin Lucy."

"Well, Mas'r knows she sot herself up agin Mas'r, and wouldn't have me, when he telled her to."

"I'd a flogged her into 't," said Legree, spitting, "only there's such a press o' work, it don't seem wuth a while to upset her jist now. She's slender; but these yer slender gals will bear half killin' to get their own way!"

"Wal, Lucy was real aggravatin' and lazy, sulkin' round; wouldn't do nothin' — and Tom he tuck up for her."

"He did, eh! Wal, then, Tom shall have the pleasure of flogging her. It'll be a good practice for him, and he won't put it on to the gal like you devils, neither."

"Ho, ho! haw! haw! haw!" laughed both the sooty wretches; and the diabolical sounds seemed, in truth, a not unapt expression of the fiendish character which Legree gave them.

"Wal, but, Mas'r, Tom and Misse Cassy, and dey among 'em, filled Lucy's basket. I ruther guess der weight's in it, Mas'r!"

"*I do the weighing!*" said Legree, emphatically.

Both the drivers laughed again their diabolical laugh.

"So!" he added, "Misse Cassy did her day's work."

"She picks like de debil and all his angels!"

"She's got 'em all in her, I believe!" said Legree; and growling a brutal oath, he proceeded to the weighing room. . . .

Slowly, the weary, dispirited creatures wound their way into the room, and, with crouching reluctance, presented their baskets to be weighed.

Legree noted on a slate, on the side of which was pasted a list of names, the amount.

Tom's basket was weighed and approved; and he looked, with an anxious glance, for the success of the woman he had befriended.

Tottering with weakness, she came forward and delivered her basket. It was of full weight, as Legree well perceived; but, affecting anger, he said,

"What, you lazy beast! Short again! Stand aside, you'll catch it, pretty soon!"

The woman gave a groan of utter despair and sat down on a board.

The person who had been called Misse Cassy now came forward and, with a haughty, negligent air, delivered her basket. As she delivered it, Legree looked in her eyes with a sneering yet inquiring glance.

She fixed her black eyes steadily on him, her lips moved slightly, and she said something in French. What it was, no one knew, but Legree's face became perfectly demoniacal in its expression as she spoke; he half raised his hand as if to strike — a gesture which she regarded with fierce disdain as she turned and walked away.

"And now," said Legree, "come here, you Tom. You see I telled ye I didn't buy ye jest for the common work; I mean to promote ye and make a driver of ye; and tonight ye may jest as well begin to get yer hand in. Now, ye jest take this yer gal and flog her; ye've seen enough on't to know how."

"I beg Mas'r's pardon," said Tom, "hopes Mas'r won't set me at that. It's what I an't used to — never did — and can't do, no way possible."

"Ye'll larn a pretty smart chance of things ye never did know before I've done with ye!" said Legree, taking up a cowhide and striking Tom a heavy blow across the cheek, and following up the infliction by a shower of blows.

"There!" he said, as he stopped to rest, "now will ye tell me ye can't do it?"

"Yes, Mas'r," said Tom, putting up his hand to wipe the blood that trickled down his face. "I'm willin' to work night and day, and work while there's life and breath in me; but this yer thing I can't feel it right to do; and, Mas'r, I *never* shall do it — *never!*"

Tom had a remarkably smooth, soft voice, and a habitually respectful manner that had given Legree an idea that he would be cowardly and easily subdued. When he spoke these last words, a thrill of amazement went through everyone; the poor woman clasped her hands and said, "O Lord!" and everyone involuntarily looked at each other and drew in their breath, as if to prepare for the storm that was about to burst.

Legree looked stupefied and confounded; but at last burst forth —

"What! ye blasted black beast! tell *me* ye don't think it *right* to do what I tell ye! What have any of you cussed cattle to do with thinking what's right? I'll put a stop to it! Why, what do ye think ye are? May be ye think ye're a gentleman, master Tom, to be a telling your master what's right and what an't! So you pretend it's wrong to flog the gal!"

"I think so, Mas'r," said Tom, "the poor crittur's sick and feeble; 't would be downright cruel, and it's what I never will do, not begin to. Mas'r, if you mean to kill me, kill me; but as to my raising my hand agin anyone here, I never shall — I'll die first!"

Tom spoke in a mild voice but with a decision that could not be mistaken. Legree shook with anger; his greenish eyes glared fiercely and his very whiskers seemed to curl with passion; but, like some ferocious beast that plays with its victim before he devours it, he kept back his strong impulse to proceed to immediate violence and broke out into bitter raillery.

"Well, here's a pious dog, at last, let down among us sinners! — a saint, a gentleman, and no less, to talk to us sinners about our sins! Powerful, holy crittur, he must be! Here, you rascal, you make believe to be so pious — didn't you never hear out of yer Bible, 'Servants, obey yer masters'? An't I yer master? Didn't I pay down $1,200 cash for all there is inside yer old cussed black shell? An't yer mine, now, body and soul?" he said, giving Tom a violent kick with his heavy boot. "Tell me!"

In the very depth of physical suffering, bowed by brutal oppression, this question shot a gleam of joy and triumph through Tom's soul. He suddenly stretched himself up, and, looking earnestly to heaven, while the tears and blood that flowed down his face mingled, he exclaimed —

"No! no! no! my soul an't yours, Mas'r! You haven't bought it — ye can't buy it! It's been bought and paid for by one that is able to keep it — no matter, no matter, you can't harm me!"

"I can't!" said Legree, with a sneer, "we'll see — we'll see! Here, Sambo, Quimbo, give this dog such a breakin' in as he won't get over this month!"

The two gigantic Negroes that now laid hold of Tom, with fiendish exultation in their faces, might have formed no unapt personification of the powers of darkness. The poor woman screamed with apprehension and all arose as by a general impulse while they dragged him unresisting from the place.

39.

Songs of Slaves and Their Masters

While the future and the moral status of slavery were debated by statesmen, little was heard from the slaves themselves. However, an indication of their attitude may be seen in the songs they sang as they worked the fields and carried out their domestic tasks. "Blue Tail Fly," also known as "Jimmy Crack Corn," probably originated with the blackface minstrels, but it was taken up by slaves and became widely popular among them. It tells of the delight, only half hidden, with which a slave might view the untimely death of his master. "All the Pretty Little Horses" is an authentic slave lullaby; it reveals the bitter feelings of Negro mothers who had to watch over their white charges while neglecting their own children.

Source: *Minstrel Songs, Old and New*, Boston, 1882, p. 211.

BLUE TAIL FLY

When I was young I use to wait
On Master and give him his plate,
And pass the bottle when he got dry,
And brush away the blue tail fly.

Chorus:
 Jimmy crack corn and I don't care,
 Jimmy crack corn and I don't care,
 Jimmy crack corn and I don't care,
  My master's gone away.

When he ride in the afternoon,
I follow him with a hickory broom;
The pony being rather shy
When bitten by a blue tail fly.

One day he ride around the farm,
The flies so numerous they did swarm;
One chanced to bite him on the thigh —
The devil take the blue tail fly.

The pony run, he jump, he pitch;
He tumble Master in the ditch.
He died and the jury wondered why —
The verdict was the blue tail fly.

They laid him under a 'simmon tree;
His epitaph is there to see:
"Beneath this stone I'm forced to lie,
A victim of the blue tail fly."

Old Master's gone, now let him rest,
They say all things are for the best;
I'll never forget, till the day I die,
Old Master and that blue tail fly.

ALL THE PRETTY LITTLE HORSES

Hushaby, don't you cry,
Go to sleepy, little baby.
When you wake, you shall have cake,
And all the pretty little horses.
Blacks and bays, dapples and grays,
Coach and six-a little horses.

 Way down yonder in the meadow,
 There's a poor little lambie;
 The bees and the butterflies pickin' out
  his eyes,
 The poor little thing cries, "Mammy."

Hushaby, don't you cry,
Go to sleepy, little baby.

1853

40.

Plan for a Negro School

While Abolitionists were agitating for the freedom of slaves in the South, the free Negroes of the North were fighting another battle against civil and economic inequities. Several national Negro conventions were held prior to the Civil War. At a convention in Rochester, New York, July 6-8, 1853, a National Council of Colored People was formed as a permanent body to pursue equal rights for Negroes. The following report, emphasizing the Negro's need for training in manual labor, was submitted on July 8.

Source: *Proceedings of the National Colored Convention held in Rochester, July 6th, 7th and 8th, 1853*, Rochester, 1853, pp. 30-33.

THE AIM AND THE END of a right culture is primarily to develop power and to turn that power into a proper channel. Educational institutions ought therefore to be so modeled and so conducted as to draw out thought, incite useful inquiry, and give such aid and strength to the individual as will enable him to be something in the world, in addition to the mere scholar. Every person is here not merely to enjoy but to work; and schools are only valuable in their teachings as they assist in making both thinker and worker. They may saturate men with the learning of every age, yet, except they strive to make them something more than literary flowers, they sin greatly against the individual and humanity also. The hungry world asks for grain and those growths that give nutriment. Not by floral beauty is the physical being built up. Not by mere word study do the races grow intellectually strong. Not by eloquent, abstract preaching

do the nations prove Christianity. The elements of truth, the principles of industrial advancement, of national greatness, that lie in questionable shapes amid the knowledge of the schools must be separated from the useless materials that surround them, and made as chyle to the human body, the givers of nutriment, the restorers of expended energy.

And as in the human body the richness of the digested food goes to make up bone, and muscle, and flesh, and the various tissues of vessels of the system, in like manner schools ought so to be fashioned as to deposit here and there, on the surface of society, artisan and merchant, mechanic and farmer, linguist and mathematician: mental power in every phase and practical science in as many as may be. The truth of this view is virtually acknowledged in part already. Where men know beforehand what kind of knowledge their duties in life will require, they avail themselves of institutions whose course of study is specific and well-digested. Hence exist our law schools, and military academies, and medical colleges. And these are necessary, even amid a class of people whose position enables them to make the most of a *general* course of study, by the application of some of the specialties of such course, to any avocation that in afterlife they may choose to pursue.

When *we* are called upon to consider the subject of education with reference to ourselves, and to ask what kind of an institution would best befit *us*, the answer comes in the light of the announced doctrine, namely, one that would develop *power;* and that kind of power most essential to our elevation. If after submitting to a general system of instruction, according to the provisions of the colleges of the land, *we* can add the store of knowledge gained to any pursuit in life *we* please, as so much starting capital, then we might not need to ask the establishing of institutions different from those already erected. But this is not the case. We have, indeed, a few literary colleges accessible to those of us who can pay; two manual labor colleges with the system partially carried out; besides an academy of the same kind established in southern Ohio.

Between these two varieties of schools, there need be no hesitation in deciding as to which is best adapted to our special wants. Under any circumstance, manual labor establishments commend themselves to the patronage of all classes. The long-entertained beliefs that mental effort may be made and continued without any reference to physical exercise are rapidly passing away. And with them, also, those more injurious and unfriendly views of true gentility and scholarship that hitherto have held labor in contempt. Literature has too long kept itself aloof from the furrowed field, and from the dust and bustle of the workshop. The pale, sickly brow and emaciated form have been falsely shown to the world as the ripeness of mental discipline; and

sunburnt and brawny muscular arms have been among the majority of students synonymous with dullness of parts and ignorant vulgarity. Thanks, however, to true views of the dignity of human nature and an appreciation of the correct laws of physical development, labor has received the anointing of the highest refinement, and healthy frames are proven to be the best accompaniment to high intellectual power.

Moreover, with regard to ourselves, a consideration of our position in this country teaches us that our inheritance is one that can only be ameliorated by the combination of practical art with literary preparation. Hitherto our educated youth have found no corresponding channel to their academic equipment, and so they have failed to make their mark on society and the age. The workshops, as a general thing, are closed to them, while at the same time they are reproached for lack of inventive or industrial talent. We know that we cannot form an equally useful part of any people without the ability to contribute our full share to the wealth, activity, social comforts, and progress of such people. If, then, the necessary education to fit us to share in these responsibilities cannot be generally had, by reason of the prejudices of the country, where best they can be taught, namely in the workshops and countinghouses, and the other varied establishments of the land that have to do with the machinery of activities carried on around us; we must needs consider the importance of making our literary institutions contribute by a change of form to filling up this want in our midst.

The agricultural life, standing preeminent and looming in importance above all others, would demand a prominent place among the internal arrangements of such a school. Farming, as a scientific system, ought to be a part of the course of every scholar, and especially of that class of students whose highest interests would be benefited by leaving the cities for the freer and no less noble life in the country. No professorship in any college can claim more on the score of usefulness than that of agriculture. In none of the institutions thus far open to us has labor in this department been at all regulated on scientific principles.

Literary preparation has absorbed most of the attention of students because of the order and beauty infused into that phase of college life. The department of labor has ever remained crude and unseemly — subordinate in position and outline to the other, and therefore unable to provide that extensive field for industry as to warrant the title assumed by them of manual labor institutions. We make no complaint against the incompleteness of any of the existing schools in order to detract from their usefulness in other ways. We only believe it desirable that a more thorough plan be established that will combine the literary course of the schools, scientific agricultural knowledge, theoretic mechanics and engineering, and, what is a feature we hope to see engrafted on the plan, a series of workshops under systematic and skillful instruction; not simply as a means of furnishing poor students with the facilities of continuing under instruction but to remedy also as far as may be the disadvantages under which we labor in acquiring a knowledge of the mechanical arts.

To this end we advise the maturing of a plan by some other suitable committee for erecting in some locality, central as to population, a school of a high intellectual grade, having incorporated an agricultural professorship, or an equivalent thereto, a professorship to superintend the practical application of mathematics and natural philosophy to surveying, mechanics, and engineering, the following branches of industry: general smithing, turning, wheelwrighting, and cabinetmaking; and a general workshop in which may be combined such application of skill in wood, iron, and other material as to produce a variety of salable articles, with suitable buildings and machinery for producing the same. These superintended by

competent workmen, under pay precisely as other teachers, would give students a foundation for after self-support in life, and break down the distinctions that never ought to exist between the study and the workshop.

The above industrial pursuits are named, not because others more desirable, perhaps, or more difficult to secure, might not have had a place given them in this imperfect report but because it seemed wise to choose some which are primary to most others in general usefulness and, at the same time, such as whose products have an extensive marketable demand. In establishing workshops, it must be remembered that the introducing of any large part of the very useful or lucrative branches is an utter impossibility. All that can be aimed at in the beginning is to elevate labor to its own true standard — vindicate the laws of physical health, and, at the same time, as a repaying benefit, make the work done as intrinsic and *profitable*, a part of education as a proficiency in Latin, mathematics, or medicine.

As to the *means* by which such an institution may be erected and carried on, we advise the issuing of joint stock under proper directors, to the amount of $50,000 in shares of $10 each, or a less number of a larger amount, if considered advisable. The committee are of opinion that $50,000 used in the purchase of land and the erecting and fitting up of buildings will be fully enough to warrant the beginning of a thorough manual labor school on the plan suggested.

The sale of scholarships at judicious rates and the contributions of the liberal and the philanthropic ought to give an additional $100,000 as an endowment, which sum properly invested would be a guarantee that the liabilities and expense of the institution would be faithfully met.

The department of industry for females, the committee cannot, in the short time given them, intelligently settle upon, except in outline. We are of opinion that looms could be erected for the weaving of carriage and other trimmings; for bindings of various kinds; that the straw hat business in some of its branches, paper box making, and similar occupations, might from time to time be connected.

The shareholders, if such a plan be approved, would compose the college association; and would have a right to appoint the trustees of the school, said trustees being citizens of the state wherein such institution shall be located.

Such is the rough outline of a plan which we think would be, in judicious hands, and so modified as to conform to the proper school laws, feasible and fraught with unbounded good.

In the past, the misfortune has been that our knowledge has been much distributed. We have had educated *heads* in one large division among us and educated *hands* in another. We do not concede in this remark that the mind worker is not a benefactor and a creator. The inventing, the directing intellect produces the demand for mechanical labor; but we believe that the instances of the marriage, so to speak, of thoroughly educated mind with manual labor are lamentably rare among us. All over the land, our earnest youth have gone asking to be cared for by the workshops of the country, but no acknowledgment has been made of their human relationships; their mental and bodily fitness have had the same contumely heaped upon them as is received by those unfortunate beings who in social life bear upon their persons the brand of illegitimacy.

As a consequence, we have grown up to too large an extent — mere scholars on one side and muscular giants on the other. We would equalize those discrepancies. We would produce a harmonious development of character. In the sweat of their brows, we would have our scholars grow powerful, and their sympathies run out for humanity everywhere. On the altar of labor, we would have every mother dedicate her child to the cause of freedom; and then, in the breeze wafted over the newly plowed field, there will come encouragement and hope; and the ringing blows of the anvil and the axe, and the keen cutting edge of the chisel and the plane will symbolize, on the one hand, human excellence is rough hewn by self-exertion, and, on the other, fashioned into models of beauty by reflection and discipline.

Let us educate our youth in suchwise as shall give them means of success adapted to their struggling condition; and ere long, following the enterprise of the age, we may hope to see them filling everywhere positions of responsibility and trust, and, gliding on the triple tide of wealth, intelligence, and virtue, reach eventually to a sure resting place of distinction and happiness.

41.

CHARLES LORING BRACE: The Children's Aid Society

One of the earliest organizations designed to help the homeless and poor children of New York was the Children's Aid Society, established in 1853 under the leadership of Charles Loring Brace. The Society set up industrial schools, inexpensive living quarters, summer camps, and evening schools for those children who had previously had no direction or opportunity to improve themselves. During Brace's lifetime, thousands of immigrant children and city waifs benefited from the Society's work. In March 1853, Brace distributed the following circular explaining the Society's purpose and asking for the public support.

Source: *The Life of Charles Loring Brace*, Emma Brace, ed., London, 1894, pp. 489-492.

To the public:

This Society has taken its origin in the deeply settled feeling of our citizens that something must be done to meet the increasing crime and poverty among the destitute children of New York. Its objects are to help this class by opening Sunday meetings and industrial schools, and gradually, as means shall be furnished, by forming lodging houses and reading rooms for children, and by employing paid agents, whose sole business shall be to care for them.

As Christian men, we cannot look upon this great multitude of unhappy, deserted, and degraded boys and girls without feeling our responsibility to God for them. We remember that they have the same capacities, the same need of kind and good influences, and the same immortality as the little ones in our own homes. We bear in mind that One died for them, even as for the children of the rich and the happy. Thus far, almshouses and prisons have done little to affect the evil. But a small part of the vagrant population can be shut up in our asylums; and judges and magistrates are reluctant to convict children, so young and ignorant,

that they hardly seem able to distinguish good and evil.

The class increases. Immigration is pouring in its multitudes of poor foreigners, who leave these young outcasts everywhere abandoned in our midst. For the most part, the boys grow up utterly by themselves. No one cares for them, and they care for no one. Some live by begging, by petty pilferings, by bold robbery. Some earn an honest support by peddling matches, or apples, or newspapers. Others gather bones and rags in the street to sell. They sleep on steps, in cellars, in old barns, and in markets; or they hire a bed in filthy and low lodging houses. They cannot read. They do not go to school or attend a church. Many of them have never seen the Bible. Every cunning faculty is intensely stimulated. They are shrewd and old in vice when other children are in leading strings. Few influences which are kind and good ever reach the vagrant boy. And yet, among themselves, they show generous and honest traits. Kindness can always touch them.

The girls too often grow up even more pitiable and deserted. Till of late, no one has ever cared for them. They are the cross-walk sweepers, the little apple peddlers and candy sellers of our city; or, by more questionable means, they earn their scanty bread. They traverse the low, vile streets alone, and live without mother or friends, or any share in what we should call *home*. They, also, know little of God or Christ, except by name. They grow up passionate, ungoverned; with no love or kindness ever to soften the heart. We all know their short, wild life, and the sad end.

These boys and girls, it should be remembered, will soon form the great lower class of our city. They will influence elections; they may shape the policy of the city; they will, assuredly, if unreclaimed, poison society all around them. They will help to form the great multitude of robbers, thieves, and vagrants who are now such a burden upon the law-respecting community. In one ward alone of the city, the Eleventh, there was in 1852, out of 12,000 children between the ages of five and sixteen, only 7,000 who attended school, and only 2,500 who went to Sabbath school, leaving 5,000 without the common privileges of education, and about 9,000 destitute of public religious influence.

In view of these evils, we have formed an association which shall devote itself entirely to this class of vagrant children. We do not propose in any way to conflict with existing asylums and institutions but to render them a hearty cooperation, and at the same time to fill a gap which, of necessity, they have all left. A large multitude of children live in the city who cannot be placed in asylums and yet who are uncared for and ignorant and vagrant. We propose to give to these work and to bring them under religious influences. A central office has been taken and an agent, Charles L. Brace, has been engaged to give his whole time to efforts for relieving the wants of this class. As means shall come in, it is designed to district the

city, so that hereafter every ward may have its agent, who shall be a friend to the vagrant child. "Boys' Sunday Meetings" have already been formed, which we hope to see extended, until every quarter has its place of preaching to boys.

With these, we intend to connect "Industrial Schools," where the great temptations to this class, arising from *want of work,* may be removed and where they can learn an honest trade. Arrangements have been made with manufacturers by which, if we have the requisite funds to begin, 500 boys in different localities can be supplied with paying work. We hope, too, especially to be the means of draining the city of these children by communicating with farmers, manufacturers, or families in the country who may have need of such for employment. When homeless boys are found by our agents, we mean to get them homes in the families of respectable persons in the city, and to put them in the way of an honest living. We design, in a word, to bring humane and kindly influences to bear on this forsaken class — to preach in various modes the Gospel of Christ to the vagrant children of New York.

Numbers of our citizens have long felt the evils we would remedy, but few have the leisure or the means to devote themselves personally to this work with the thoroughness which it requires. This society, as we propose, shall be a medium through which all can, in their measure, practically help the poor children of the city. We call upon all who recognize that these are the little ones of Christ; all who believe that crime is best averted by sowing good influences in childhood; all who are the friends of the helpless, to aid us in our enterprise. We confidently hope this wide and practical movement will have its share of Christian liberality. And we earnestly ask the contributions of those able to give, to help us in carrying forward the work.

42.

Appeal by the Women of Massachusetts for Civil Rights

Most men opposed and ridiculed the idea of woman suffrage, and many women regarded politics as outside their proper sphere. Nevertheless, organized efforts continued to be made to persuade state legislatures to give voting rights to women. In April 1853 the following petition was prepared for presentation to the Massachusetts legislature. It was drawn up by a group that included such widely known reformers as Wendell Phillips, Thomas W. Higginson, Theodore Parker, William Lloyd Garrison, and Bronson Alcott, as well as several of the women active in the suffrage movement.

Source: *The Una*, April 1853 [*History of Woman Suffrage*, Elizabeth C. Stanton *et al.*, eds., New York, 1881, Vol. I, pp. 247-248].

WE DEEM THE EXTENSION to woman of all civil rights a measure of vital importance to the welfare and progress of the state. On every principle of natural justice, as well as by the nature of our institutions, she is as fully entitled as man to vote and to be eligible to office. In governments based on force, it might be pretended with some plausibility that woman being supposed physically weaker than man should be excluded from the state. But ours is a government professedly resting on the consent of the governed. Woman is surely as competent to give that consent as man. Our Revolution claimed that taxation and representation should be coextensive. While the property and labor of women are subject to taxation, she is entitled to a voice in fixing the amount of taxes and the use of them when collected, and is entitled to a voice in the laws that regulate punishments. It would be a disgrace to our schools and civil institutions for anyone to argue that a Massachusetts woman who has enjoyed the full advantage of all their culture is not as competent to form an opinion on civil matters as the illiterate foreigner landed but a few years before upon our shores, unable to read or write, by no means free from early prejudices, and little acquainted with our institutions. Yet such men are allowed to vote.

Woman as wife, mother, daughter, and owner of property has important rights to be protected. The whole history of legislation so unequal between the sexes shows that she can not safely trust these to the other sex. Neither have her rights as mother, wife, daughter, laborer ever received full legislative protection. Besides, our institutions are not based on the idea of one class receiving protection from another but on the well-recognized rule that each class, or sex, is entitled to such civil rights as will enable it to protect itself. The exercise of civil rights is one of the best means of education. Interest in great questions and the discussion of them under momentous responsibility call forth all the faculties and nerve them to their fullest strength. The grant of these rights on the part of society would quickly lead to the enjoyment by woman of a share in the higher grades of professional employment.

Indeed, without these, mere book study is often but a waste of time. The learning for which no use is found or anticipated is too frequently forgotten, almost as soon as acquired. The influence of such a share on the moral condition of society is still more important. Crowded now into few employments, women starve each other by close competition; and too often vice borrows overwhelming power of temptation from poverty. Open to women a great variety of employments and her wages in each will rise; the energy and enterprise of the more highly endowed will find full scope in honest effort; and the frightful vice of our cities will be stopped at its fountainhead. . . .

Some may think it too soon to expect any action from the convention. Many facts lead us to think that public opinion is more advanced on this question than is generally supposed. Besides, there can be no time so proper to call public attention to a radical change in our civil polity as now, when the whole framework of our government is to be subjected to examination and discussion. It is never too early to begin the discussion of any desired change. To urge our claim on the convention is to bring our question before the proper tribunal and secure at the same time the immediate attention of the general public. Massachusetts, though she has led the way in most other reforms, has in this fallen behind her rivals, consenting to learn, as to the protection of the property of married women of many younger states. Let us redeem for her the old preeminence, and urge her to set a noble example in this, the most important of all civil reforms.

43.

JESUP W. SCOTT: The Promise of the Great Plains

The first white settlers of the central plains of North America were farmers, and it was generally assumed that the American Midwest would retain its rural characteristics even after the tremendous growth of the railroads in the 1850s. As early as 1830, however, Jesup Scott, whose work was often quoted by promoters but has been largely neglected since, insisted that the great cities of America would eventually be located in the Midwest, especially in the Great Lakes region. He based his predictions, reasonably enough, on the effects of an expansion of commerce facilitated by technological advances and a keen analysis of population trends. Although he was wrong about the site of the giant new metropolis (he picked Toledo as the "future great city of the world"), he correctly anticipated the urban growth of the Midwest. One of Scott's many articles on the future of Western cities is reprinted below.

Source: *De Bow's Review*, July 1853: "The Great West."

THE WEST IS NO LONGER THE WEST; nor even the *great* West. It is the great center. It is the body of the American eagle whose wings are on the two oceans. The center of population seeking the center of territorial productiveness, long since, in its movement westward, passed the Alleghenies and is now making its way in a northwesterly direction through Ohio. Our people, after nearly two centuries, spent in multiplying their numbers and gathering their strength on the Atlantic border, broke over the mountain barriers and spread themselves, scatteringly, over the vast interior plain. Persons are living who saw this plain one vast desert of forest and prairie; it now contains, within our national boundary, 14 million people; including the Canadas, it numbers 16 million.

Every year is adding, by natural increase and immigration, materially to this number. From the old states and from Europe, an annual tide pours into it, rich with the youth and vigor inherited from generations inured to think and to labor. This tide, increasing from year to year, promises to swell from hundreds of thousands to millions; and, so far is this influx from lessening the inducements to future immigration that every million newcomers creates new comforts for the common use of the millions who follow.

The central plain, including Texas and Canada, contains not less than 1,600,000 sq.mi., equal to 1 billion acres of land, fit for cultivation. Divided equally among the 16 million now living on it, every man, woman, and child would have 64 acres, and the population average 10 to the square mile; with 50 to the square mile, like Ohio, it would contain 80 million; or, like Massachusetts, 132 to the square mile, it would number 212 million; or if, like England, it had 327 to the square mile, it would have 523 million. All these millions and more will one day find here an ample and happy home. They will have descended from an ancestry formed of the strongest spirits of the Old World and the New; men seeking difficulties for the enjoyment of overcoming them. It may require a period of 200 years fully to people the North American plain; but, within the present century, before the year 1900, within the lifetime of persons now living, it will contain 75 million, being nearly three times the present number of the whole nation.

In its vast extent it has a marked unity of character. From the Gulf of Mexico to Hudson Bay and the Polar Sea, from the Appalachian Mountains on the east to the Rocky Mountains bounding it on the west, its surface is nearly unbroken. The lakes of the north spread out their wide waters almost on the general level of the plain, while the rivers, which pour their accumulated waters into the Gulf, have excavated their own channels, deep but narrow, toward their sources, gradually approximating their waters to the general surface, until they elevate their beds above the general plain at their mouths. For commercial and social purposes, it is the more one whole because of its lakes and rivers. By these channels are its people bound together. Even if steam had not begun its race on the land, its triumph on our interior waters, in cementing the bonds of union among its various parts, would have been complete. From the remotest regions, men and the products of their labor are transported by steam to the central marts of trade. In short, steam, working on our waters, has made our commerce one and our people a brotherhood.

Diversity of climate, employment, and mineral products tend only to strengthen this unity. Steam, working on railroads, will soon give great intensity to the forces now operating to bring the remotest parts of the Plain into intimate relations of friendship and trade. The change is coming upon us so rapidly that only the young can fully comprehend it. Like a splendid dream will it appear to people of mature age. Before the census of 1860 shall be printed, the whistle of the locomotive and the roar of the rolling train will be heard at nearly every house and hamlet of the wide Central Plain; and no one but a hermit will be willing to live beyond the cheering sound these will give forth.

All the changes in business and social relations which will grow directly out of the general extension of railroads it is not given to anyone to foresee. That it will promote the growth of leading centers of commerce and manufacture is already made manifest by the experience of the old states and England. Indeed, no one could, with reason, expect any other result. Whether this will be permanent or not may admit of a doubt. The railroad has the power to spread out the city as well as to bring within its borders, the various people needful to furnish it with the many wants of a high civilization. Our leading cities will be very populous and spread over a wide surface. In our Central Plain will probably grow up the hugest aggregations of people in the world. Before it reaches the density of England, it will contain one or more cities numbering 10 million. Long before that period elapses, improvements in cultivation will so reduce the number needed to grow the food and raw materials of manufacture that one-fourth of the population will be ample to effect that result; leaving three-fourths to be engaged in pursuits more profitably carried on in cities, where the greatest variety of employments furnishes the needed materials for the most effective cooperative industry.

The most fertile imagination, furnished with all the facts, would be at fault in predicting the condition of the community who will dwell on the Central Plain twenty years in the future. What development of commercial intercourse; what diversification of agricultural and mechanical operations, invited and rewarded by quick and cheap channels of transport; what development of architectural beauty in railroad stations, private residences, villages and cities; what public adornment of grounds, where learning, religion, and gratitude erect their spacious halls, beautiful temples, and lofty monuments! The earth has no other such theater for the growth of a rich and virtuous community. Nowhere else can so great a plain, of such fertility, in a climate so temperate, provided with so many natural channels of intercourse, and inviting so strongly such as man can make, inhabited by so energetic and intelligent a people, be pointed out on the face of our globe. Hither are hastening, as if conscious that a new Eden of happiness is about to be opened, hopeful and strong men, from all the nations and regions which breed reading, thinking, and promptly acting people.

The history of mankind furnishes no parallel to the rapid colonization in progress here. From all the enlightened nations of the Old World and from all the old states of our Union multitudes are pouring in, which swell in magnitude with every revolving year. The imagination can conceive nothing more imposingly grand than this march of humanity westward, to enter into possession of "time's noblest empire." No logical induction, no mathematical demonstration can be clearer to our mind than that here will come together the greatest aggregations of men in cities — outrivaling in splendor as in magnitude all which past ages have produced.

In commencing this article, it was intended to lay before our readers such facts in relation to the navigable waters (lakes, rivers, and canals), and the railroads of the Great Plain, as would show the present and prospective rapid growth of the internal commerce of this new empire. The foregoing is scarcely more than a prelude to the execution of this purpose.

44.

"Canaday-I-O"

Few Americans knew the harshness of the Northern winters better than the Maine lumberjacks who worked in both Canadian and American lumber camps along the St. Lawrence River. The hardships endured by these men, caused on the one hand by bad weather and on the other hand by tough bosses, were reflected in the rough songs they sang, one of which was "Canaday-I-O." The verses are said to have been derived from an old English sea song, "Canada-I-O," which in turn was adapted from a Scotch love song, "Caledonia."

CANADAY-I-O

"Come all ye jolly fellows, how would you like to go
And spend one winter in the woods of Canaday-I-O?"
"We're going up to Canaday," is what we young men say,
"And going up to Canaday depends upon the pay."

"It's sure we'll pay good wages; we'll pay your passage out,
But you must sign the papers that you will stay the route,
For if you should get homesick, and say back home you'll go,
We will not pay your passage from Canaday-I-O."

We had a pleasant journey on the route we had to go,
And landed in Three Rivers in Canaday-I-O.
Oh, then the Norcross agent, he came a-prowling round
And said, "My jolly fellows, why don't you all lie down?"

Our hearts were made of iron; our souls were cased with steel;
The hardships of that winter could never make us yield.
Our food the dogs would bark at; our beds were on the snow —
We suffered worse than poison in Canaday-I-O.

And now the winter's over, it's homeward we are bound,
And in this cursed country we'll never more be found.
Go back to your wives and sweethearts, tell others not to go
To that God-forsaken country called Canaday-I-O.

45.

FRANCIS AND THERESA PULSZKY: Observations of Some Hungarian Visitors

Francis and Theresa Pulszky, associates of the exiled leader of the Hungarian revolution, Lajos Kossuth, traveled with him through the United States in 1852. Having fought for democratic principles in their native land, they were particularly interested in the governmental processes, social customs, and intellectual life that contributed to the American national character. The Pulszkys' observations of the United States, recorded in English in a book, White, Red, Black, *reflect an acute awareness of the practical aspects of democratic politics. A portion of this work, published in 1853, is reprinted below.*

Source: *White, Red, Black: Sketches of American Society in the United States,* Redfield, N.Y., 1853, Vol. I, pp. 183-193.

WASHINGTON IS AN ARTIFICIAL CITY without any other importance than that it is the seat of the government and of the legislature of the United States. Like Munich, Stuttgart, or Karlsruhe, expansions of the court of the princes, built only by their command and encouragement, and therefore without importance for commercial intercourse, Washington, too, has its origin, not in the natural requirements of the country but in the decision of Congress, which placed the seat of the government on the banks of the Potomac. The riots in Philadelphia, when the mutinous soldiers had threatened the Continental Congress in Independence Hall, were a warning to the statesmen of America not to put their government within the reach of the excitable population of large cities.

In order to prevent a pressure from without as dangerous for the dignity of the government as to the liberty of the people, it has become a political maxim in every state to fix the Capitol[1] in some central place, but not in the commercial metropolis. Boston is the only exception to this rule, but the natural coolness of the New Englanders divests the experiment of connecting the center of commerce with the seat of government, of the danger which would encompass it in the excitable Middle states or the South.

Though Washington was intended to be only a city of the government and of the Congress, yet there was a secret hope that the vitality of the United States might give an independent and growing life even to this artificial offspring. And, why not? The Potomac is a noble stream, which can carry steamers and merchant vessels as well as shads, and Chesapeake Bay, into which it discharges its waters, has raised Baltimore to prosperity. The city, therefore, was laid out on a wide plan, but the great extension

1. The statehouses of the states and the palace of the Congress in Washington bear all this name.

is not yet filled up; the resources of the back country of Washington remain undeveloped, and, therefore, commerce does not impart life to the city; it has remained what it was in the beginning, the seat of the departments and officials. It spreads only in proportion as the extension of the territory of the United States leads to a natural increase of the members of Congress, of the government officers, and government expenditure.

Washington is the best evidence that no city can grow up artificially where a government has no revenues to squander. Everything has here turned out differently from what had been intended. It strips bare the fact that, when a great city seems to be enriched at the will of a despot, this is only because the public revenues are artificially squandered on it, but no new wealth is created.

When the Capitol was laid out on the hill, the city was to grow up in front of the building, in the shape of a fan, and the White House, the residence of the President, to remain a country seat, at a distance of two or three miles from the city, that the President might not be importuned by frequent visitors. The grounds in front of the Capitol naturally rose in price, while the lots in the valley, sloping toward the White House, had no pretension of becoming the American metropolis and remained cheap. But precisely because they were cheap, they were taken up; buildings rose here and there very irregularly; and when the central building was finished, it had nothing but the fields in front, and it turned its back to the city, of which the White House and the Capitol became the two extremities.

A dozen of columns were thereupon patched to the back of the Congress hall that it might become the front. Staircases were made and gardens laid out to ornament the hill on which it is raised; but all these changes have not improved its style. From afar it looks commanding, but as you approach and can distinguish the decorations, you see the meagerness of the design and the meanness of the execution. In the old front it looks better.

The general aspect of the city is very strange. The Capitol, the Post Office, the Treasury, the Home Office, the Smithsonian Institution, and the White House, decorated with a profusion of white marble, of dark granite, and architectural ornaments, form a remarkable contrast to the unconnected patches of low brick houses which line the streets. These also are broad enough for the traffic of a ten times larger population than it is now. The American applies proudly to his Capitol the lines of Horace: *Privatus illis census erat brevis, commune magnum* [Private property was scarce to them, but that commonly held was great]; but to a foreigner it makes the impression of an Eastern metropolis of a half-nomad nation, where the palaces of the king are surrounded by the temporary buildings of a people, held together only by the presence of the court.

And this is really the character of the population of Washington. Society is formed here by two distinct classes of inhabitants — one temporary, the other permanent. For the President, the heads of department, the senators, and members of the House, it is but a temporary abode, it is not their home; they live almost all in hotels and lodgings, not in their own house. They do not care for domestic comforts, and therefore they do not ornament their abodes; they look on them as the banker does on his dark and dreary countinghouse. They remain strangers in Washington. Even those who live here for ten years and longer do not feel at home. Henry Clay lived and died in a hotel, and during his long career connected with Washington city, Mrs. Clay never visited him, though their marriage was always a happy one.

The permanent population in the city are the clerks in the departments, the judges of the Supreme Court, the editors of the papers, a few merchants and bankers, and the foreign ambassadors, who keep house here, and in social respect have an importance far superior to any that they could occupy in Philadelphia or New York. They are the hosts who give elegant dinners, and balls, and evening parties. The members of Congress, and their wives and daughters, are the guests, unable to return at Washington the hospitality they receive — a position which, for a clever diplomatist, is of no small avail. To the floating population belong also the agents for elections, for private claims, and for government grants; "the lobby members," as they are called, who, like the sharks around vessels, ply around the senators, rushing at every job and government contract. For political intriguers, there is no richer goldfield in the United States than Washington — an arena not only of political contests but also of "logrolling," "pipe-laying," and "wire-pulling."

As to the wire-pullers, they are known all over the political world; and the philosopher, studying history, is astonished how men often act the part of puppets without their own knowledge. The greatest wire-puller is, of course, Russian diplomacy; and the words "legitimacy," "demagogy," "democracy," "socialism," and "family" are those by which European nations and statesmen are moved to dance as St. Petersburg fiddles. In America, the magic word is different; it is called "peculiar institution" and "abolitionism."

Whenever an opportunity is wanted to disturb men's minds, to raise politicians to greatness, or to bury others, the stage is always ready, and the play always successful. The plot is "secession from the Union," and the finale, "the country saved," with triumphal arches, and nosegays, and garlands for the saviors of the country. Minor plays are daily enacted by the wire-pullers, who have a continual practice in the elections; where it is not only important to

canvass for the friend but also to weaken the enemy by drawing off his votes for a third person.

"Logrolling" is a more simple affair. It is the combination of different interests on the principle, "daub me and I daub thee." Whoever is too feeble to carry his own project combines with others in the same position in order to get influence. Local affairs and grants are often brought to notice and pass the Congress in this way.

Of "pipe-laying," I got two different definitions. According to one, the origin of this expression is traced to an election job, where an undertaker sold some Irish and German votes by a written agreement, in which, of course, the ware could not be named; it was therefore styled "pipes"; pipe-laying would therefore mean "corruption." But it also applied to political maneuvers for an aim entirely different from what it seems to be. For instance, wishing to defeat the grant of land for a special railway or canal, which has every chance to pass, you vote for it, but in your speech you describe in glowing colors the advantages of railroads in general, and wind up by presenting an amendment for the extension of the grant to all the other railroads in construction, on the principle of equality; and thus you make the grant impossible.

In a democratic country, where freedom of speech is not limited and the press is unfettered even by fiscal laws, every movement of government is exposed, judged, and condemned in the most unmeasured words. One party denounces the other, and corruption is mentioned so often that it would be very easy for a malicious tourist to write a book on the decline of the United States, composed exclusively from extracts from public speeches and party papers. But every impartial observer will find that government is carried on in America with remarkable integrity and economy.

Large as the Union is, the expenditure of the federal government, including the interest of the United States debt and the annual payment toward its extinction, is met by the income from the duties on importation and the sales of land. No direct taxes are levied for federal purposes. If we compare the estimates of the United States with the European budgets, we find that the sums expended without necessity are much smaller than anywhere else, though the party criminations and recriminations are so loud that a foreigner is tempted to believe the government to be a compound of corruption and dishonesty.

The Galphin and Gardiner claims were often mentioned by the opposition as evidences of mismanagement. But they have been thoroughly investigated, and no blame could be attached to the departments. The Galphin claim arose out of old English pretensions from the Cherokee war. After many years' solicitation, it was fully established by Congress, and the attorney general had no objection to it; but when it was paid, it appeared that the acting secretary at war had formerly been the legal counsel of the claimant, and was entitled, in case of success, to a considerable share of the amount received. Though the justice of the claim was not disputed, the House blamed the President for not immediately dismissing the secretary at war; and a law was passed prohibiting any senator, member of the House, head of department, or any public officer whosoever to participate in any emolument proceeding out of claims before Congress.

The Gardiner claim was paid under the treaty with Mexico at Guadalupe Hidalgo, where $2 million had been set aside for the discharge of all claims of American citizens against the Mexican government. This claim, too, was acknowledged by Congress and paid by the Treasury; yet it turned out to be altogether a forgery. A committee was appointed to inquire into the facts of the case, but until now it has not found any

connection of the claimant with the departments of state. The secretary of the treasury had been originally the counsel of the claimant, but had given up his interest in the cause as soon as promoted to office.

The Senate of the United States, as a body, contains more practical statesmanship and administrative experience than any other legislative assembly. All its members have been trained in the legislative assemblies and Senates of the individual states. Many of them have passed several years in the House at Washington, or have been at the head of their state as governors, or have transacted the business of the Union as heads of the departments of state. But Southern rashness sometimes deprives the Senate of the gravity and dignity which behooves the fathers of the great republic.

During the session of 1852, Mr. Rhett of South Carolina having, in a speech, violently and personally attacked Mr. Clemens of Alabama, was openly challenged by his opponent in a reply more violent than the attack. The senator of South Carolina, however, is not only chivalrous but also pious; he declared to the Senate that he is a member of the church, and that religion forbade him to fight, though, as it seems, it had not restrained him from an abusive attack.

But Solon Borland, the senator of Arkansas, went much further and rehearsed, with modern improvements, the scene of the Spartan chief, who, in the council of war before the battle of Salamis, impatiently raised his cane when he saw that Themistocles was about to speak. "Strike, but listen!" was the celebrated answer of the great Athenian, which disarmed the angry Spartan.

At the Capitol, a similar scene terminated differently. The estimates for printing the last census seemed extravagant to the economical senator from the Red River; he could not conceive how the publication of the statistical details could be of a use commensurate to the costs of printing; and when Mr. Kennedy, the chief of the Census Office, in order to explain the importance of the documents, came to the seat of the Senator and requested him to listen to his explanation, the modern Solon of Arkansas improved the part of the Spartan chief; he raised his fist, knocked down Mr. Kennedy with a powerful blow, and did *not* listen.

The House of Representatives, renewed every two years by general election, has here a more subordinate position than in any other constitutional realm. The great parliamentary battles are all fought in the Senate. The speeches of the great American orators, Clay, Webster, Calhoun, and Cass, have resounded within its walls; and the eloquence of Soulé, Seward, and Sumner is equal to that of their illustrious predecessors. Personal collisions, rare in the Senate, are frequent in the House. During the last session, Messrs. Wilcox and Brown, both from Mississippi, boxed one another's ears in open session. The Tennesseean representative gave the lie to his colleague from Kentucky, and abusive language was often heard, though it was not a time of great political excitement and no important question stirred up the passions.

The powers of Congress are very different from those of the legislative assemblies in other countries. Congress does not govern nor control the government of the states; nor has it anything to do with the church, the education, the prisons, the civil or criminal law, or with private bills. The chief objects of the English Parliament are therefore removed from its sphere. Congress has only the power to decide upon the commercial policy of the United States and to provide for their defense and for certain matters of general interest. It makes the tariff, regulates commerce with foreign nations, coins money, regulates its value, and provides for the punishment of forgery. It fixes the standard of weights and measures, establishes post offices and post roads, defines

and punishes piracy and offenses against the law of nations.

It declares war, raises and supports armies, provides and maintains a navy, calls forth the militia to execute the laws of the Union, and makes rules for the regulation and government of the land and naval forces. It borrows money on the credit of the United States, votes the budget, and settles claims against the federal government; it admits new states; it exercises exclusive legislation in the District of Columbia, and makes all needful regulations respecting any "territory" or other property belonging to the United States. It has, moreover, to establish a uniform rule of naturalization, and uniform laws on the subject of bankruptcies throughout the United States. The Senate has to discuss the treaties and nominations of ambassadors and of the judges of the Supreme Court made by the President, and to try all impeachments of public officers.

The ministers, or, as they are called, the heads of the executive departments, are not members of Congress; they are only the advisers of the President, and it is not necessary that they should have a parliamentary majority. The chief function of European parliaments, the defeat or support of the Ministry, is, therefore, not to be found at the Capitol. A Frenchman would find the Congress very dull, but, as a President is elected every fourth year by universal suffrage, the American can easily spare the excitement of a ministerial crisis, though this is the necessary safety valve to constitutional Europe.

With such restrictive powers — all those not mentioned in the Constitution as belonging to Congress being reserved to the individual states — the members of Congress and the senators are not overwhelmed by business. Unless, therefore, the Union needs again to be saved from secession, or the tariff is discussed, or the admission of a new state, connected with the question of slavery, to be decided, the spare time of Congress is employed for personal explanations and political speeches, as they are called, or "speeches for Buncombe," as they are nicknamed.

In fact, they are lectures on every topic which has political interest, on slavery or abolition, on the land system, the Maine liquor law, on the merits or demerits of the parties, or on any other abstract political principle intended for the constituents of the representative or senator, not for the House or the Senate. This is so well understood that members often are considerate enough to announce that they will send their speeches straight to the congressional newspaper without robbing the House or Senate of its time by delivering them.

But the great object of Congress, every fourth year, is the making of a President. The election belongs, of course, to the people, but the masses are influenced from Washington; and therefore speeches on the merits of the party nominees, and the defense of them against party attacks, are great themes in the halls of the Capitol. The session preceding the presidential election always lasts long, from the first Monday of December often till the end of July. Then follows a short one, closed after the inauguration of the new President, which takes place on the 4th of March. The ensuing session is again long and important, succeeded by a short one; thus their duration alternates from four to seven months.

46.

Fredrika Bremer: The American Proclivity for Association

Fredrika Bremer had already achieved wide recognition as a novelist in both Europe and the United States when she came to America in 1849. The well-educated daughter of a wealthy Swedish merchant, she received a warm welcome in the important intellectual circles of the day. Her observations on the United States, recorded in Hemmen i den nya Verlden (1853), reflect her interest in the common people and their national characteristics. The following selection from Miss Bremer's book comments on the American tendency to form associations, a proclivity that caught the eye of numerous foreign visitors.

Source: TWA, pp. 230-231.

THERE IS ONE PRINCIPLE of movement in the United States which seems to me creative, or, at all events, a power of organization. This is the movement of association. The association, founded already in the federal government — an association of states, governed by a general law, or Constitution — exists as a fundamental feature of popular life. These people associate as easily as they breathe.

Whenever any subject or question of interest arises in society which demands public sympathy or cooperation, a "convention" is immediately called to take it into consideration; and immediately, from all ends of the city or the state, or from every state in the Union, all who feel an interest in the subject fly upon wings of steam to the appointed place of meeting. The hotels and boardinghouses of the city are rapidly filled; people come together in the great hall of assembly, they shake hands, they become acquainted with one another, they make speeches, they vote, they carry their resolutions. And forth upon the wings of a thousand daily papers flies that which the meeting or convention has resolved. These resolutions may sometimes be merely the expression of opinion; they hold, for example, "indignation meetings" when they wish to express disapprobation either of public men or of measures. The *savoir-faire* with which these people act in self-government, the rapidity with which they proceed from "proposed" to "resolved" is always admirable.

In the populous free states, meetings of the members of different trades and professions, as well as of agriculture, are ordinary occurrences. Thus one hears now of industrial congresses in New York, where the trades brethren of certain kindred occupations meet every month; and agricultural fairs are already held in the young states of Michigan and Illinois.

The great trading towns have mechanical and mercantile associations, meetinghouses, libraries, assembly rooms, and guilds on a large scale. And these related associations are all connected with each other. An artisan who cannot get work in the Eastern states is, for instance, passed on by means of these associations to the West, where there is abundance of work for all hands.

Life in this country need never stand still or stagnate. The dangers lie in another direction. But this free association is evidently an organizing and conservative principle of life, called forth to give law and centralization to the floating atoms, to the disintegrated elements. The United States thus provides at the same time for the highest development of the individual and of the community at large.

This internal social movement of humanity is assisted from without by the free circulation and communication which is afforded by the numerous navigable rivers of North America, upon which thousands of steamboats go and come; and in still later years by the railroads and telegraphic lines which extend over all parts of America. The great diffusion of newspapers within the country, of every book which wins the love of the popular heart, of that religious popular literature which in millions of small tracts is poured forth over the nation, these all belong essentially to this life-giving circulation.

Wherever the sons and daughters of the Pilgrims find their way there are established homes, schools, and churches, shops, and legislative assemblies, the free press, hotels for strangers, and asylums for the unfortunate or the orphaned. There the prison is converted into the reformatory, a new school for the ignorant and depraved children of the earth. Wherever the Anglo-American advances, the same cultivation, the same vitality arises. He accomplishes with astonishing certainty his mission as cultivator of the New World and framer of free, self-governing communities. Not even the institution of slavery is able to withstand the power of cultivation which advances with him over the earth.

———◆———

No man is good enough to govern another man without that other's consent.
ABRAHAM LINCOLN, speech, Peoria, Oct. 16, 1854

47.

WILBUR F. STOREY: Against the Imitation of European Universities

The low standards and the emphasis on traditional studies evident in many American institutions of higher learning led some educators to travel abroad to observe European university systems. Inspired particularly by the German universities, educational innovators such as Henry Philip Tappan, president of the University of Michigan, sought to emulate the German model of professional and vocational training. Public opposition to such changes was aroused by Wilbur Storey, editor of the Detroit Free Press, *in the following attack on Tappan that appeared in his paper on December 28, 1853.*

Source: *Detroit Free Press*, December 28, 1853 [*The Colleges and The Public, 1787-1862*, Theodore R. Crane, ed., New York, 1963].

PRESIDENT TAPPAN'S IDEA of a university is grand — imposing! The German university at Berlin is his model, and he would bring the Wolverine institution up to the Berlin standard with all possible haste. He has a similar idea of cities and towns, though he don't say so in this report. He thinks no city should be without its heaven-pointing monuments and great public works. He conceives that it is a mistake of the Americans that they build warehouses and neglect monuments. He wants to know what will be thought of our country by future generations, when our structure shall have crumbled, if there shall be no silent, gloomy monuments found overlooking the general wreck of matter? With a far-stretching vision, he sees America reduced to Egyptian decay, and he is of opinion that we ought to write the history of our rise and progress upon tall monuments for the special edification of generations that will be yet unborn half a dozen centuries hence! Something akin to this is his notion of institutions of learning:

One thing is certain, that whether we consider the resources of the state of Michigan and its rapidly advancing greatness, or its position in reference to surrounding states, we shall neither be true to our own trust, nor shall we pursue a wise policy, if we make our calculations upon a diminutive scale. Divine Providence has afforded us a great opportunity and given us indications *which seem almost like a positive command.* To embrace the opportunity, to obey the indications is the true way of success.

This looks very well on paper to one who has little sense of the ludicrous and the bombastic. With proper management and steady perseverance — such perseverance as has, after the lapse of a century and a half, made Yale what it is — the University of Michigan can be made one of the first institutions of learning in the country. There is such a thing, especially in educational matters, as going too fast as well as too slow; and often the one is more fatal than the other. A wise statesman makes haste slowly. . . .

At this stage of the report President Tappan starts for Berlin:

In speaking of the condition of our university and of what is required for its proper and full development, you will naturally inquire what light I have gained on the subject of education from my visit abroad. This visit, as you are aware, was arranged before I had been called to take charge of the university. It was a fortunate concurrence by which a visit to Europe necessary to be undertaken by someone in respect to the observatory, and important in respect to the purchase of books and the general interests of our educational system, was accomplished without imposing any expense upon the university. Besides revisiting England, France, Switzerland, and the Rhine country, I have traveled through Italy and spent some time in the northern part of Germany, more than two weeks of which was devoted entirely to the examination of the Prussian system of education in the city of Berlin.

We do not understand what President Tappan means when he says "besides revisiting England," etc., unless he desires to tell us that this was not the first time he had been to Europe.

A practical man, situated as President Tappan was, may unquestionably learn much by an examination of the "Prussian system" which he can make available in the administration of a collegiate institution in this country; but the belief that we want *the* "Prussian system" is preposterous. We want just so much of it as can be profitably adapted to our altered system of government, of trade, of commerce, and so forth. To make this adaptation requires great judgment and caution — a thorough understanding of the genius of our institutions and of the educational necessities of our people. Our schools, and academies, and universities need to be *American* rather than Prussian — that is, instead of treading in a mere beaten track, we want institutions that shall fit men for all the practical duties of American life; that shall strike out in the wilderness of progress, availing themselves of the new philosophy and rejecting all of the old that is not instinct with life and spirit.

Our faith is not the strongest, after reading this report, that President Tappan is quite likely to accommodate himself to things as they exist here, and proceed cautiously in gradually enlarging the capacity and power of our university. With the University of Berlin for his idol, he seems in danger of forgetting that Michigan is not Prussia, and Ann Arbor not Berlin. He anticipates a scale of operations that the present resources of the university will not justify, and calculates upon direct aid regularly hereafter from the state treasury that the sequel will not realize. With many just and enlightened views he combines projects that are at once impracticable and visionary.

The first interrogatory, viz., "What is yet to be done?" is answered, then, mainly by a recommendation to adopt the Prussian system, including the high university and gymnasium, and "special schools for the useful and fine arts" — a system of such huge proportions that it must indeed become a government institution — a central power greater than the state itself, and involving an annual outlay from the treasury larger than the gross expenditures for the support of the state government!

The answer to the other interrogatory, "How shall we do it?" is already anticipated. But President Tappan does not mince the matter; he declares:

The sale of our lands from year to year will continue to add to our income, until we have realized all which this source of income can afford us. *Beyond this we must look mainly to the state.*

To what extent the people of Michigan will feel inclined to maintain a grand Prussian university at Ann Arbor by direct appropriations from the public treasury is a pretty grave question. We have no hesitation in saying, in the outset, as one of the people, that we are hostile to any such use of money that is drawn from the pockets of the whole people. If the permanent endowment of the university is not sufficient to support it, it must tax the recipients of its benefits to make up the deficiency.

1854

48.

RICHARD BAKER: The Crime of Mrs. Douglass in Teaching Colored Children to Read

Except for the most elementary religious instruction, all education in the Southern states was forbidden to slaves. In Virginia it was also unlawful for any white person to assemble even free Negroes for educational purposes. In 1853 Mrs. Margaret Douglass was arrested for teaching free Negro children to read and write in Norfolk. She was tried and convicted of the offense before the Circuit Court of Norfolk in November 1853. Although the jury fixed a nominal fine of one dollar, this was overruled by Judge Richard Baker on January 10, 1854. Mrs. Douglass spent one month in prison.

Source: *American State Trials*, John D. Lawson, ed., Vol. VII, St. Louis, 1917, pp. 56-60.

UPON AN INDICTMENT found against you for assembling with Negroes to instruct them to read and write, and for associating with them in an unlawful assembly, you were found guilty, and a mere nominal fine imposed, on the last day of this court held in the month of November.

At the time the jury came in and rendered their verdict, you were not in court, and the court, being about to adjourn for the purpose of attending to other official duties in a distant part of the state, it was necessary and proper, under the law, to award a *capias* against you, returnable to the present adjourned term, so that the judgment and sentence of the law may be ful-

filled. The court is not called on to vindicate the policy of the law in question, for so long as it remains upon the statute book, and unrepealed, public and private justice and morality require that it should be respected and sustained.

There are persons, I believe, in our community opposed to the policy of the law in question. They profess to believe that universal intellectual culture is necessary to religious instruction and education, and that such culture is suitable to a state of slavery, and there can be no misapprehension as to your opinions on this subject, judging from the indiscreet freedom with which you spoke of your regard for the colored race in general. Such opinions in the present state of our society I regard as manifestly mischievous.

It is not true that our slaves cannot be taught religious and moral duty without being able to read the Bible and use the pen. Intellectual and religious instruction often go hand in hand, but the latter may well exist without the former; and the truth of this is abundantly vindicated by the well-known fact that in many parts of our own commonwealth, as in other parts of the country in which among the whites one-fourth or more are entirely without a knowledge of letters, respect for the law, and for moral and religious conduct and behavior, are justly and properly appreciated and practised.

A valuable report, or document, recently published in the city of New York by the Southern Aid Society sets forth many valuable and important truths upon the condition of the Southern slaves, and the utility of moral and religious instruction, apart from a knowledge of books. I recommend the careful perusal of it to all whose opinions concur with your own. It shows that a system of catechetical instruction, with a clear and simple exposition of Scripture, has been employed with gratifying success; that the slave population of the South are peculiarly susceptible of good religious influences. Their mere residence among a Christian people has wrought a great and happy change in their condition: they have been raised from the night of heathenism to the light of Christianity, and thousands of them have been brought to a saving knowledge of the Gospel.

Of the 100 million of the Negro race, there cannot be found another so large a body as the 3 million slaves in the United States, at once so intelligent, so inclined to the Gospel, and so blessed by the elevating influence of civilization and Christianity. Occasional instances of cruelty and oppression, it is true, may sometimes occur, and probably will ever continue to take place under any system of laws; but this is not confined to wrongs committed upon the Negro. Wrongs are committed and cruelly practised in a like degree by the lawless white man upon his own color; and while the Negroes of our town and state are known to be surrounded by most of the substantial comforts of life, and invited both by precept and example to participate in proper moral and religious duties, it argues, it seems to me, a sickly sensibility toward them to say their persons, and feelings, and interests are not sufficiently respected by our laws, which, in effect, tend to nullify the act of our legislature passed for the security and protection of their masters.

The law under which you have been tried and found guilty is not to be found among the original enactments of our legislature. The first legislative provision upon this subject was introduced in the year 1831, immediately succeeding the bloody scenes of the memorable Southampton insurrection; and that law, being found not sufficiently penal to check the wrongs complained of, was reenacted with additional penalties in the year 1848, which last mentioned act, after several years' trial and experience, has been reaffirmed by adoption and incorporated into our present code.

After these several and repeated recognitions of the wisdom and propriety of the said act, it may well be said that bold and open opposition to it is a matter not to be slightly regarded, especially as we have reason to believe that every Southern slave state in our country, as a measure of self-preservation and protection, has deemed it wise and just to adopt laws with similar provisions. There might have been no occasion for such enactments in Virginia, or elsewhere, on the subject of Negro education but as a matter of self-defense against the schemes of Northern incendiaries and the outcry against holding our slaves in bondage.

Many now living well remember how and when and why the antislavery fury began, and by what means its manifestations were made public. Our mails were clogged with Abolition pamphlets and inflammatory documents, to be distributed among our Southern Negroes to induce them to cut our throats. Sometimes, it may be, these libelous documents were distributed by Northern citizens professing Southern feelings, and at other times by Southern people professing Northern feelings. These, however, were not the only means resorted to by the Northern fanatics to stir up insubordination among our slaves. They scattered, far and near, pocket handkerchiefs and other similar articles, with frightful engravings and printed over with antislavery nonsense, with the view to work upon the feeling and ignorance of our Negroes, who otherwise would have remained comfortable and happy. Under such circumstances there was but one measure of protection for the South, and that was adopted.

Teaching the Negroes to read and write is made penal by the laws of our state. The act imposes a fine not exceeding $100, to be ascertained by the jury, and imprisonment not exceeding six months, to be fixed and ascertained by the court. And, now, since the jury in your case has in my opinion properly settled the question of guilt, it devolves on me, under the law, to ascertain and decide upon the quantum of imprisonment under the circumstances of your trial; and I exceedingly regret that, in being called on for the first time to act under the law in question, it becomes my duty to impose the required punishment upon a female, apparently of fair and respectable standing in the community. The only mitigating circumstance in your case, if in truth there be any, according to my best reason and understanding of it, is that to which I have just referred, namely, you being a female.

Under the circumstances of this case, if you were of a different sex, I should regard the full punishment of six months' imprisonment as eminently just and proper. Had you taken the advice of your friends and of the court and had employed counsel to defend you, your case, no doubt, would have been presented in a far more favorable light, both to the court and to the jury. The opinions you advanced, and the pertinacity and zeal you manifested in behalf of the Negroes, while they indicated perfect candor and sincerity on your part, satisfied the court, and must have satisfied all who heard you, that the act complained of was the settled and deliberate purpose of your mind, regardless of consequences, however dangerous to your peace.

In conformity with these views, I am impelled by a feeling of common honesty to say that this is not a case in which a mere formal judgment should be announced as the opinion of the court. Something more substantial under the circumstances of this case, I think, is demanded and required. The discretionary power to imprison for the term of six months or less, in good sense and sound morality, does not authorize a mere minimum punishment, such as imprisonment for a day or week, in a case in which the question of guilt is free from doubt, and there are many facts and circumstances of aggravation. A judgment of that sort, therefore, in this case, would doubtless be regarded by all true advocates of justice and law as mere mockery. It would be no terror to those who acknowledge no rule of action but their own evil will and pleasure, but would rather invite to still bolder incendiary movements.

For these reasons, as an example to all others in like cases disposed to offend, and in vindication of the policy and justness of our laws, which every individual should be taught to respect, the judgment of the court is, in addition to the proper fine and costs, that you be imprisoned for the period of one month in the jail of this city.

P. T. Barnum and Commodore Nutt, a dwarf in one of Barnum's shows

BARNUM TO THOREAU

Four of the enduring classics of American literature were published between 1850 and 1855: "The Scarlet Letter," "Moby Dick," "Walden," and "Leaves of Grass." This was a period of major accomplishment in the theater, in historical scholarship, and in science, but the self-confidence of the times is best represented in the person of Phineas T. Barnum, America's first great showman and theatrical entrepreneur. Barnum began his career in 1835, exhibiting a woman supposedly 160 years old and said to have been Washington's nurse. He opened his American Museum in New York in 1842, attracting visitors with a mixture of legitimate curiosities, such as Tom Thumb, and outright hoaxes, like the Japanese Mermaids. He gave New Yorkers their first look at a white whale (Moby Dick, of course), as well as numerous freaks, albinos, wild animals, and circus acts. The exhibitions were wrapped in layers of colorful showmanship that made the public a party to a harmless, entertaining joke on themselves.

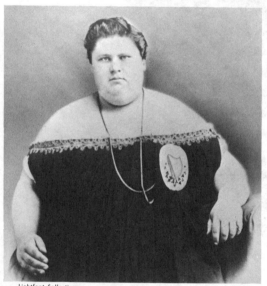

Barnum also promoted an array of novelty acts, comedies, and featured performances, including the immensely popular national tour of Jenny Lind. By the 1850s a variety of entertainments were touring the country. Acrobats, gymnasts, pantomimes, and minstrel shows were popular, as well as entertainers like Lola Montez. The public's interest in novelties compounded the financial problems of the legitimate theaters and led to the introduction of a highly competitive "star system."

(Top) Barnum's "American Museum" on Broadway; (center) the "Fat Lady," one of Barnum's curiosities; (bottom) Barnum's mammoth tent housing his menagerie and exhibits

An Indian group, a traveling show of the 1850s

An acrobatic team in costume for their circus sideshow act

Valentine Denzer, acrobat

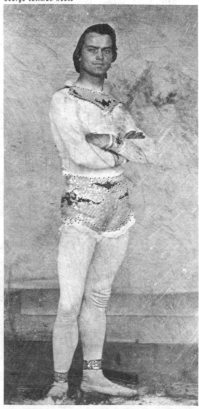

Jenny Lind, a Swedish operatic singer who toured the U.S. in the early 1850s

Lola Montez, entertainer who toured from New York to the California gold camps

A daguerreotype of Charlotte Cushman as Meg Merrilies in the operatic play "Guy Mannering"

D. W. O'Brien, the minstrel "Dan Bryant"

(Left) Laura Keene, a versatile actress and manager of her own popular theater (above)

One benefit of the competition for audiences in the legitimate theater was a number of memorable performances. The railroad was turning the country into one large circuit and good companies with stars like Edwin Forrest, Charlotte Cushman, the Booths, and Mary Gannon appeared all across the country. In New York an intense rivalry developed among the theaters managed by the stars themselves: Burton's, Wallack's and Laura Keene's. Shakespeare was the basic fare, along with tragic romances and opera.

(Right) Edwin Forrest in "Metamora," (below) interior of Niblo's Garden, a successful opera house in New York

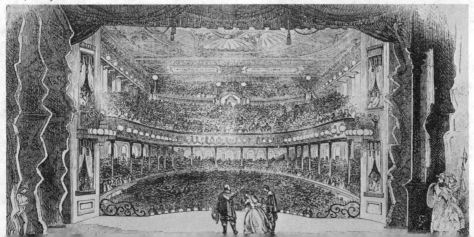

(Top left) Daguerreotype of Walt Whitman made in 1854; (top right) John Howard Payne, actor and dramatist, chiefly known for composing "Home, Sweet Home"; (bottom left) George Bancroft, historian; (bottom right) William H. Prescott

The literary maturity represented by the work of Melville, Hawthorne, and Walt Whitman found parallels in historical scholarship. Popular interest in history was growing; George Bancroft's "History of the United States" and William H. Prescott's histories of Mexico and Peru contributed to general interest by combining careful scholarship with a romantic, narrative style.

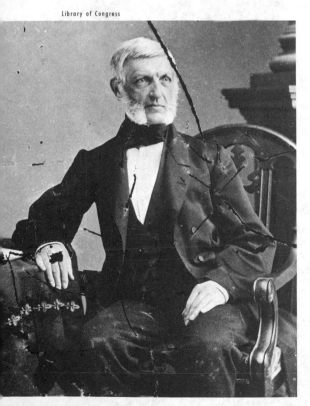

Outside established political or academic circles other independent minds were at work. Alexander Bryan Johnson was a banker and developer in Utica, N.Y. His thoughts on government involvement in the national economy, on the psychology of the Negro in slavery, and on the nature of language were remarkably visionary. Elihu Burritt championed the cause of peace and the idea of an international court, while Thoreau developed Emerson's moral self-reliance into a philosophy of radical individualism.

(Above left) Alexander Bryan Johnson; (above) Elihu Burritt, who promoted the Brussels Peace Conference of 1848; (below) Henry David Thoreau and his survey sketch of Walden Pond

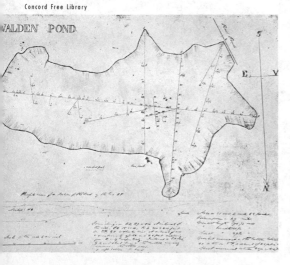

Concord Free Library

(Above) A. Bronson Alcott; (below) Harriet Beecher Stowe; (right) Uncle Tom and Little Eva in a popular print based on the book

Metropolitan Museum of Art, Stokes-Hawes Collection

In the rigorous moral climate of New England, slavery was anathema and much of the fire and righteousness of the Abolitionist movement originated in New England literary circles. Emerson's sentiments flowed directly from his moral philosophy; Thoreau's interpretation of the individual's responsibility to resist immoral authority was in reaction to the Mexican War, "slavery's war"; Bronson Alcott's activities were one aspect of a life of experiment and controversy, as a teacher, Utopian, temperance crusader and writer; Garrison's "Liberator" was the leading radical Abolitionist paper; and "Uncle Tom's Cabin" was singularly effective in fixing an image of slavery in the public consciousness.

Museum of the City of New York, Peters Collection

Francis Jackson, an early Abolitionist and president of the Boston Antislavery Society

William Lloyd Garrison

Wendell Phillips speaking against the fugitive slave act at an antislavery meeting in Boston

The Smithsonian Institution as it looked in 1849, three years after it was founded

The Smithsonian Institution was established in 1846 on an endowment from the estate of a British scientist, James Smithson, who had never been to America. The gift specified only that the money be used to set up an "establishment for the . . . diffusion of knowledge among men" in Washington. After much discussion and delay, Congress appropriated money for a building and outlined the Institution's relationship to the government. Joseph Henry, the first director, rejected pressure to organize a museum for the general public and sought to make the Institution a clearing house for scientific information and a stimulus both to pure and practical science.

Benjamin Silliman, a prominent scientist

Joseph Henry, first director of the Smithsonian

49.

Frederick Law Olmsted: King Cotton and His Subjects

*Landscape artist and city planner Frederick Law Olmsted was first encouraged to
tour the slave states by a conversation with William Lloyd Garrison. In 1852 he
began what was to be the first of three journeys through the South. His letters were
printed serially in the* New-York Daily Times, *whose editor, Henry J. Raymond,
had commissioned the trip. The reports of the three tours, later condensed and
published as* The Cotton Kingdom *(1861), have been acclaimed as the most accurate
and unprejudiced account of the region before the Civil War. The following article
of January 12, 1854, was one of the last written by Olmsted during his first trip.
It was titled "Slavery in its Effects on Character, and the Social Relations of the
Master Class," and was not included in his book.*

Source: *New-York Daily Times*, January 12, 1854.

The wealthy and educated, and especially the fashionable people of all civilized countries, are now so nearly alike in their ordinary manners and customs that the observations of a passing traveler upon them must commonly be of much too superficial a character to warrant him in deducing from them, with confidence, any important conclusions. I have spent an evening at the plantation residence of a gentleman in Louisiana, in which there was very little in the conversation or customs and manners of the family to distinguish them from others whom I have visited in Massachusetts, England, and Germany. I shall, therefore, undertake with diffidence to describe certain apparently general and fundamental peculiarities of character in the people, which it is a part of my duty to notice, from their importance with reference to the condition and prospects of the slave states and their institution.

Slavery exerts an immense quiet influence upon the character of the master, and the condition of the slave is greatly affected by the modifications of character thus effected. I do not believe there are any other people in the world with whom the Negro would be as contented and, if contentment is happiness, so happy as with those who are now his masters. The hopeless perpetuation of such an intolerable nuisance as this labor system, it is, however, also apparent, depends mainly upon the careless, temporizing, shiftless disposition to which the Negro is indebted for this mitigation of the natural wretchedness of slavery.

The calculating, indefatigable New Englander, the go-ahead Western man, the exact and stern Englishman, the active Frenchman, the studious, observing, economical German would all and each lose patience with the frequent disobedience and the constant indolence, forgetfulness, and carelessness, and the blundering, awkward, brutelike manner of work of the plantation slave.

The Southerner, if he sees anything of it, generally disregards it and neglects to punish it. Although he is naturally excitable and passionate, he is less subject to impatience and passionate anger with the slave than is, I believe, generally supposed, because he is habituated to regard him so completely as his inferior dependent and subject. For the same reason, his anger, when aroused, is usually easily and quickly appeased, and he forgives him readily and entirely, as we do a child or a dog who has annoyed us. And, in general, the relation of master and slave on small farms, and the relations of the family and its household servants everywhere, may be considered a happy one, developing, at the expense of decision, energy, self-reliance, and self-control, some of the most beautiful traits of human nature. But it is a great error — although one nearly universal with Southerners themselves — to judge of slavery by the light alone of the master's fireside.

The direct influence of slavery is, I think, to make the Southerner indifferent to small things; in some relations, we should say rightly, superior to small things; prodigal, improvident, and ostentatiously generous. His ordinarily uncontrolled authority (and from infancy the Southerner is more free from control, in all respects, I should judge, than any other person in the world) leads him to be habitually impulsive, impetuous, and enthusiastic; gives him self-respect and dignity of character; and makes him bold, confident, and true. Yet it has not appeared to me that the Southerner was frank as he is, I believe, commonly thought to be. He seems to me to be very secretive, or at least reserved, on topics which most nearly concern himself. He minds his own business and lets alone that of others, not in the English way but in a way peculiarly his own;

resulting partly, perhaps, from want of curiosity, in part from habits formed by such constant intercourse as he has with his inferiors (Negroes), and partly from the caution in conversation which the "rules of honor" are calculated to give.

Not, I said, in the English way, because he meets a stranger easily and without timidity or thought of how he is himself appearing, and is ready and usually accomplished in conversation. He is much given to vague and careless generalization, and greatly disinclined to exact and careful reasoning. He follows his natural impulses nobly, has nothing to be ashamed of, and is, therefore, habitually truthful; but his carelessness, impulsiveness, vagueness, and want of exactness in everything make him speak from his mouth that which is in point of fact untrue, rather more often than anyone else.

From early intimacy with the Negro (an association fruitful in other respects of evil) he has acquired much of his ready, artless, and superficial benevolence, good nature, and geniality. The comparatively solitary nature and somewhat monotonous duties of plantation life make guests usually exceedingly welcome, while the abundance of servants at command and other circumstances make the ordinary duties of hospitality very light. The Southerner, however, is greatly wanting in hospitality of mind, closing his doors to all opinions and schemes to which he has been bred a stranger, with a contempt and bigotry which sometimes seem incompatible with his character as a gentleman. He has a large but unexpansive mind.

The Southerner has no pleasure in labor except with reference to a result. He enjoys life itself. He is content with being. Here is the grand distinction between him and the Northerner; for the Northerner enjoys progress in itself. He finds his happiness in doing. Rest, in itself, is irksome and offensive to him, and however graceful or beatific that rest may be, he values it only with reference to the power of future progress it will bring him. Heaven itself will be dull and stupid to him if there is no work to be done in it — nothing to struggle for — if he reaches perfection at a jump and has no chance to make an improvement.

The Southerner cares for the end only; he is impatient of the means. He is passionate and labors passionately, fitfully, with the energy and strength of anger rather than of resolute will. He fights rather than works to carry his purpose. He has the intensity of character which belongs to Americans in general, and therefore enjoys excitement and is fond of novelty. But he has much less curiosity than the Northerner; less originating genius, less inventive talent, less patient and persevering energy. And I think this all comes from his want of aptitude for close observation and his dislike for application to small details. And this, I think, may be reasonably supposed to be mainly the result of habitually leaving all matters not either of grand and exciting importance, or of immediate consequence to his comfort, to his slaves, and of being accustomed to see them slighted or neglected as much as he will, in his indolence, allow them to be by them.

Of course, I have been speaking of the general tendencies only of character in the North and the South. There are individuals in both communities in whom these extreme characteristics are reversed, as there are graceful Englishmen and awkward Frenchmen. There are, also, in each, those in whom they are more or less harmoniously blended. Those in whom they are the most enviably so — the happiest and the most useful in the social sphere — are equally common, so far as I know, in both; and the grand distinction remains in the mass — manifesting itself, by strikingly contrasting symptoms, in our religion, politics, and social life.

In no way more than this: The South endeavors to close its eyes to every evil the removal of which will require self-denial, labor, and skill. If, however, an evil is too glaring to be passed by unnoticed, it is immediately declared to be constitutional, or providential, and its removal is declared to be either treasonable or impious — usually both; and, what is worse, it is improper, impolite, ungentlemanly, unmanlike. And so it is ended at the South. But at the North this sort of opposition only serves to develop the reform by ridding it of useless weight and drapery.

Northern social life usually leaves a rather melancholy and disagreeable feeling upon the minds of our Southern friends, as many have confessed to me. I think the different tendency of life at the North from that of existence at the South, which I have asserted, will give a key to this unfavorable impression which the Southerner obtains of our social character.

The people of the North are generally well aware of their social deficiencies, and of the unfitness of many of the customs and mannerisms, required by conventional politeness, to their character and duties. A man comes to our house, and custom requires that our countenance should brighten and that we should say we are glad to see him. This custom makes it unkind in us toward him not to do so. We have no unkindness in our hearts to the man, but entirely the contrary; yet it happens that we are not glad to see him, and such is our constitution that we have no impulsive and natural brightening up under hardly any circumstances. Now we have to choose between a forced, artificial, formal, and false expression of a true kindness and truth and simplicity. Amiable people take sides with kindness; the silent and reliable sort, with truth. Each are constantly aware, to a greater or less degree, of the difficulty they are engaged with. Some attach an absurd importance to the value of expression and become "affected"; others rebel against the falseness of the conventional forms of expression and become supercilious or sour and forbidding. Both classes are constantly led to make awkward attempts to compromise their quarrel with themselves.

The Southerner can understand nothing of all this. He naturally accepts the institutions, manners, and customs in which he is educated as necessities imposed upon him by Providence. He is loyal to "society," and it is opposed to his fundamental idea of a gentleman to essentially deduct from them or add to them. This "clothes philosophy" of the North he does not in the least comprehend, or, if he does, he sees nothing in it but impudent and vulgar quackery. And yet I think there is, perhaps, good to come out of it. We believe not, in our day, in good William of Wickham's maxim. This new democratic man is not "made of manners"; it may be best he should make manners to suit himself. Between this slavish conformity and anarchical nonconformity, it is to be hoped that the good sense of our society is drifting toward both a nobler and a happier social life.

But, at the present, the social intercourse of the wealthy people of the South is certainly more agreeable, rational, and to be respected than that of the nearest corresponding class at the North. I should be sorry to think this the highest compliment it deserved.

The wealthy class is the commanding class in most districts of the South and gives character to all the slaveholding class. Wealth is less distributed and is more retained in families at the South than the North. With the slaveholding class there is a pride of birth and social position, much more than in any class at the North. This affects the character and conduct of individuals, and reacts on their associates and on the whole community — in some respects perniciously, but in many respects favorably.

The "high-toned gentleman" (a Southern expression) of the South is rare at the North. He is not an article of city manufacture, as the most cultivated people of the North are. He has a peculiar character and peculiar habits — more like those of the "old English gentleman" than any class to be found now, perhaps, even in England itself. He rides much, and hunts, and is given to field sports, and never knows the want of oxygen; for, even in winter, his windows and doors are always forgotten to be closed. Accordingly, though his diet is detestable, he is generally well physically developed — lighter and more delicate of frame than the English squires, but tall and sinewy. His face would commonly be handsome but that his mouth is made gross, lifeless, and inexpressive by his habit of using tobacco excessively. He has a peculiar pride and romance, and, though he often appears laughably quixotic, he is, in the best sense of the word, also chivalrous. He is brave and magnanimous, courteous and polite to all white people.

If he often values his comfort, or the success of his designs, or the gratification of his passions more than he does a strict adherence to the received rules of Christian morality, he never values life or aught else more than he does his honor. This "honor" — though if you analyze it, it comes to be little else than a conventional standard of feelings and actions, which must be habitual to entitle a man to consider himself a gentleman — is often really far nobler, and makes a nobler man than what often passes for religion at the North, at least in this world.

There is, however, a quality, or perhaps it is a faculty of the soul, which is distinct, though seldom separate, from love to the person of God and love to man, or in our time from the Christian faith, which is most nearly defined by the term "an enlightened conscience" — a spontaneous requisite perception and loyal love of the fundamental laws of right — the laws that God himself is subject to. This quality or faculty is the noblest endowment of man and is essential to the noblest character. I think it is strongly developed in more individuals at the North than at the South, and I think there are obvious causes for its absence at the South. The habitual reference of the Southerner in his judgment of conduct, whether of himself or another, whether past or contemplated, to the conventional standard of honor prevents the ascendancy of a higher standard. This habitual contemplation of a relation so essentially wrong as that of slavery, as a permanent and necessary one not reformable, not in progress of removal and abolition, destroys or prevents the development of his sense of any standard of right and wrong above a mere code of laws or conventional rules.

But to the Southern gentleman (by distinction), as I have often met him, I wish to pay great respect. The honest and unstudied dignity of character, the generosity and the real nobleness of habitual impulses, and the well-bred, manly courtesy which distinguish him in all the relations and occupations of life, equally in his business, in his family, and in general society, are sadly rare at the North — much more rare at the North than at the South. I acknowledge it freely but with deep regret and melancholy. There are qualities of character (not of deportment, merely) which are common among the planters of many parts of the South, as they are among the aristocratic classes of Europe, which are incompatible with the possession of nothing else that a man should glory in, which the mass of the people of the North have nearly lost or have failed to gain.

This has been often observed by intelligent travelers visiting us, and is sometimes thought sufficient to condemn our democratic form of government and our approximately democratic state of society. This is the judgment of many Southerners (for the government and society of the South is the most essentially aristocratic in the world), and I have reason to believe that there are many whose confidence in the democracy of the North is so small that they anticipate, and are acting politically with reference to, a division of the present Union and the formation of another great Southern republic — that is, a republic of white capitalists, in which the slavery of the working classes shall be provided for and every means taken to make it complete and permanent.

But acknowledging the rarity of the thoroughbred gentleman at the North: Is an inference to be drawn from it unfavorable to democratic institutions? I think not. Without regard to the future and to what we may yet become under democracy, the condition and character of our people as a whole, to the best of my judgment, is better, more gentlemanly even, far more entitled to respect than that of the people, including all classes, of any other nation. Very much more so than of those of the South. I do not say more happy. The people of the Northern states, as a whole, probably enjoy life less than any other civilized people. Perhaps it would be equally true to add — or than any uncivilized people. Those who consider that, if so, the uncivilized people (perchance slaves) are to be envied will do right to condemn democracy.

But the only conclusion which the fact seems to me to suggest, with regard to our democratic government, is perhaps this: that simple protection to capital and letting alone to native genius and talent is not the whole duty of government; possibly that patent laws and the common schools, with their common teachers and common instruction (not education) such as our institutions as yet give to the people, are not enough. That the esthetic faculties need to be educated — drawn out; that taste and refinement need to be encouraged as well as the useful arts. That there need to be places and time for reunions, which shall be so attractive to the nature of all but the most depraved men, that the rich and the poor, the cultivated and well-bred, and the sturdy and self-made people shall be attached together and encouraged to assimilate.

I think there is no sufficient reason why the aid of the state should not be given to assist corporations and voluntary associations for such purposes, on the same principle and with the same restrictions that it is in New York to schools, to colleges, and to agricultural societies. Thus, I think, with a necessity for scarcely any additional governmental offices, or increase of the friction of governmental machinery, might be encouraged and sustained, at points so frequent and convenient that they would exert an elevating influence upon all the people, public parks and gardens, galleries of art and instruction in art, music, athletic sports, and healthful recreations, and other means of cultivating taste and lessening the excessive materialism of purpose in which we are, as a people, so cursedly absorbed that even the natural capacity for domestic happiness and, more obviously, for the enjoyment of simple and sensible social life in our community seems likely to be entirely destroyed. The enemies of democracy could bring no charge more severe against it than that such is its tendency, and that it has no means of counteracting it.

Slavery is claimed at the South to be the remedy for this evil. In some respects it is a remedy. But (disregarding the slaves and the poor whites) where there is one true gentleman, and to be respected, at the South, there are two whose whole life seems to be absorbed in sensualism and sickly excitements. Everywhere you meet them, well dressed and spending money freely, constantly drinking, smoking, and chewing; cardplaying and betting; and unable to converse upon anything that is not either grossly sensual or exciting, such as street rencounters, filibustering schemes, or projects of disunion or war. These persons are, however, gentlemen in the sense that they are familiar with the forms and usages of the best society, that they are deferential to women, and that (except in money matters) their word is to be implicitly relied upon. They far exceed in numbers any class of at all similar habits that we yet have at the North.

They are invariably politicians, and they generally rule in all political conventions and caucuses. They are brave in the sense that they are reckless of life, and they are exceedingly fond of the excitement of the hazard of life. They are as careless of the life of others as of themselves. They are especially ambitious of military renown, and in the Mexican War they volunteered almost to a man, many of those who went as privates taking with them several Negro servants. If they were not dependent on the price of cotton for the means of their idleness, they would keep the country incessantly at war. Being so, however, they are as conservative in the policy they favor toward any powerful nation as the cotton lords of England or the landlords of Austria. They hate and despise the democrats of Europe as much as Francis Joseph himself. They glorify Napoleon, and they boast of the contempt with which they were able to treat the humbug Kossuth.

They call themselves Democrats, and sometimes Democratic Whigs. Call them what you will, they are a mischievous class — the dangerous class at present of the United States. They are not the legitimate offspring of democracy; thanks to God, but of slavery under a democracy.

50.

George Fitzhugh: The Failure of Free Society

George Fitzhugh, Southern sociologist, lawyer, and apologist for the slave system, differed from most Southerners in his approach to the slavery issue. Whereas most Southerners were continually on the defensive against Abolitionist attacks on their "peculiar institution," Fitzhugh took the offensive and attacked the Northern economic system as a failure. In his view, the Southern patriarchal system was not only morally superior but he was also certain that it would eventually dominate all of the United States. His first major work was Sociology for the South, *published in 1854, from which the following selections are printed.*

Source: *Sociology for the South, or the Failure of Free Society*, Richmond, Va., 1854, pp. iii, 7-12, 34-48, 83-95, 161-163, 177-186.

To the People of the South:

We dedicate this little work to you, because it is a zealous and honest effort to promote your peculiar interests. Society has been so quiet and contented in the South — it has suffered so little from crime or extreme poverty, that its attention has not been awakened to the revolutionary tumults, uproar, mendicity and crime of free society. Few are aware of the blessings they enjoy, or of the evils from which they are exempt.

From some peculiarity of taste, we have for many years been watching closely the perturbed workings of free society. Its crimes, its revolutions, its sufferings and its beggary, have led us to investigate its past history, as well as to speculate on its future destiny. This pamphlet has been hastily written, but is the result of long observation, some research, and much reflection. Should it contain suggestions that will enlist abler pens to show that free society is a failure and its philosophy false, our highest ambition will be gratified. Believing our positions on these subjects to be true, we feel sanguine they are destined to final vindication and triumph. . . .

FREE TRADE

Political economy is the science of free society. Its theory and its history alike establish this position. Its fundamental maxims, *laissez faire* and *pas trop gouverner* [minimum government], are at war with all kinds of slavery, for they in fact assert that individuals and peoples prosper most when governed least. It is not, therefore, wonderful that such a science should not have been believed or inculcated while slavery was universal. . . .

Until now, industry had been controlled and directed by a few minds. Monopoly in its every form had been rife. Men were suddenly called on to walk alone, to act and work for themselves without guide, advice, or control from superior authority. In the past, nothing like it had occurred; hence no assistance could be derived from books. The prophets themselves had overlooked or omitted to tell of the advent of this golden era and were no better guides than the historians and philosophers.

A philosophy that should guide and direct industry was equally needed with a philosophy of morals. The occasion found and made the man. For writing a one-sided philosophy, no man was better fitted than Adam Smith. He possessed extraordinary powers of abstraction, analysis, and generalization. He was absent, secluded, and unobservant. He saw only that prosperous and progressive portion of society whom liberty or free competition benefited and mistook its effects on them for its effects on the world. He had probably never heard the old English adage, "Every man for himself, and devil take the hindmost." This saying comprehends the whole philosophy, moral and economical, of the *Wealth of Nations.* But he and the political economists who have succeeded him seem never to have dreamed that there would have been any "hindmost."

There can never be a wise moral philosopher, or a sound philosophy, till someone arises who sees and comprehends all the "things in heaven and earth." Philosophers are the most abstracted, secluded, and least observant of men. Their premises are always false, because they see but few facts; and hence their conclusions must also be false. Plato and Aristotle have today as many believers as Smith, Paley, or Locke, and between their times a hundred systems have arisen, flourished for a time, and been rejected. There is not a true moral philosophy, and from the nature of things there never can be. Such a philosophy has to discover first causes and ultimate effects, to grasp infinite, to deal with eternity at both ends. Human presumption will often attempt this, but human intellect can never achieve it. We shall build up no system, attempt to account for nothing, but simply point out what is natural and universal and humbly try to justify the ways of God to man.

Adam Smith's philosophy is simple and comprehensive (*teres et rotundus* [elegant and polished]). Its leading and almost its only doctrine is that individual well-being and social and national wealth and prosperity will be best promoted by each man eagerly pursuing his own selfish welfare unfettered and unrestricted by legal regulations, or governmental prohibitions, farther than such regulations may be necessary to prevent positive crime. That some qualifications of this doctrine will not be found in his book we shall not deny; but this is his system. It is obvious enough that such a governmental policy as this doctrine would result in would stimulate energy, excite invention and industry, and bring into livelier action, genius, skill, and talent. It had done so before Smith wrote, and it was no doubt the observation of those effects that suggested the theory. His friends and acquaintances were of that class who, in the war of the wits to which free competition invited, were sure to come off victors. His country, too, England and Scotland, in the arts of trade and in manufacturing skill, was an overmatch for the rest of the world. International free trade would benefit his country as much as social free trade would benefit his friends. This was his world, and had it been the only world his philosophy would have been true. . . .

FAILURE OF FREE SOCIETY AND RISE OF SOCIALISM

THE ADVOCATES OF UNIVERSAL liberty concede that the laboring class enjoy more material comfort, are better fed, clothed, and housed as slaves than as freemen. The statistics of crime demonstrate that the moral superiority of the slave over the free laborer is still greater than his superiority in animal well-being. There never can be among slaves a class so degraded as is found about the wharves and suburbs of cities. The master requires and enforces ordinary morality and industry. We very much fear, if it were possible to indite a faithful comparison of the conduct and comfort of our free Negroes with that of the runaway Anglo-Saxon serfs, that it would be found that the Negroes have fared better and committed much less crime than the whites. . . .

How slavery could degrade men lower than universal liberty has done, it is hard to conceive; how it did and would again preserve them from such degradation is well explained by those who are loudest in its abuse. A consciousness of security, a full comprehension of his position, and a confidence in that position, and the absence of all corroding cares and anxieties, make the slave easy and self-assured in his address, cheerful, happy, and contented, free from jealousy, malignity, and envy, and at peace with all around him. His attachment to his master begets the sentiment of loyalty than which none more purifies and elevates human nature. . . .

The free laborer rarely has a house and home of his own; he is insecure of employment; sickness may overtake him at any time and deprive him of the means of support; old age is certain to overtake him, if he lives, and generally finds him without the means of subsistence; his family is probably increasing in numbers and is helpless and burdensome to him. In all this there is little to incite to virtue, much to tempt to crime, nothing to afford happiness, but quite enough to inflict misery. Man must be more than human to acquire a pure and a high morality under such circumstances.

In free society the sentiments, principles, feelings and affections of high and low, rich and poor, are equally blunted and debased by the continual war of competition. It begets rivalries, jealousies, and hatred on all hands. The poor can neither love nor respect the rich, who, instead of aiding and protecting them, are endeavoring to cheapen their labor and take away their means of subsistence. The rich can hardly respect themselves, when they reflect that wealth is the result of avarice, caution, circumspection, and hard dealing. These are the virtues which free society in its regular operation brings forth. Its moral influence is therefore no better on the rich than on the poor. The number of laborers being excessive in all old countries, they are continually struggling with, scandalizing, and underbidding each other to get places and employment.

Every circumstance in the poor man's situation in free society is one of harassing care, of grievous temptation, and of excitement to anger, envy, jealousy, and malignity. That so many of the poor should nevertheless be good and pure, kind, happy, and high-minded is proof enough that the poor class is not the worst class in society. But the rich have their temptations, too. Capital gives them the power to oppress, selfishness offers the inducement, and political economy, the moral guide of the day, would justify the oppression. Yet there are thousands of noble and generous and disinterested men in free society who employ their wealth to relieve and not to oppress the poor. Still, these are exceptions to the general rule. The effect of such society is to encourage the oppression of the poor. . . .

Liberty places those classes in positions of antagonism and war. Slavery identifies the interests of rich and poor, master and slave, and begets domestic affection on the one side and loyalty and respect on the other. Young England sees clearly enough the character of the disease but is not bold enough to propose an adequate remedy.

The poor themselves are all practical Socialists and in some degree pro-slavery men. They unite in strikes and trade unions and thus exchange a part of their liberties in order to secure high and uniform wages. The exchange is a prudent and sensible one; but they who have bartered off liberty are fast verging toward slavery. Slavery to an association is not always better than slavery to a single master. The professed object is to avoid ruinous underbidding and competition with one another; but this competition can never cease while liberty lasts. Those who wish to be free must take liberty with this inseparable burden.

Odd Fellows' societies, temperance societies, and all other societies that provide for sick and unfortunate members are instances of socialism. The muse in England for many years has been busy in composing dissonant laborer songs, bewailing the hardships, penury, and sufferings of the poor, and indignantly rebuking the cruelty and injustice of their hardhearted and closefisted employers. . . .

A well-conducted farm in the South is a model of associated labor that Fourier might envy. One old woman nurses all the children while the mothers are at work; another waits on the sick, in a house set aside for them; another washes and cooks; and a fourth makes and mends the clothing. It is a great economy of labor and is a good idea of the Socialists.

Slavery protects the infants, the aged, and the sick; nay, takes far better care of them than of the healthy, the middle-aged, and the strong. They are part of the family, and self-interest and domestic affection combine to shelter, shield, and foster them. A man loves not only his horses and his cattle, which are useful to him, but he loves his dog, which is of no use. He loves them because they are his. What a wise and beneficent provision of Heaven that makes the selfishness of man's nature a protecting aegis to shield and defend wife and children, slaves, and even dumb animals. The Socialists propose to reach this result too, but they never can if they refuse to march in the only road Providence has pointed out. Who will check, govern, and control their superintending authority? Who prevent his abuse of power? Who can make him kind, tender, and affectionate to the poor, aged, helpless, sick, and unfortunate? *Qui custodiat* [*ipsos*] *custodes?* [Who is to guard the guards?]

Nature establishes the only safe and reliable checks and balances in government. . . .

Socialism proposes to do away with free competition; to afford protection and support at all times to the laboring class; to bring about, at least, a qualified community of property and to associate labor. All these purposes slavery fully and perfectly attains. . . .

NEGRO SLAVERY

IT IS CLEAR the Athenian Democracy would not suit a Negro nation, nor will the government of mere law suffice for the individual Negro. He is but a grown-up child, and must be governed as a child, not as a lunatic or criminal. The master occupies towards him the place of parent or guardian. We shall not dwell on this view, for no one will differ with us who thinks as we do of the Negro's capacity, and we might argue till doomsday, in vain, with those who have a high opinion of the Negro's moral and intellectual capacity.

Second, the Negro is improvident; will not lay up in summer for the wants of winter; will not accumulate in youth for the exigencies of age. He would become an insufferable burden to society. Society has the right to prevent this, and can only do so by subjecting him to domestic slavery.

In the last place, the Negro race is inferior to the white race, and living in their midst, they would be far outstripped or outwitted in the chase of free competition. Gradual but certain extermination would be their fate. We presume the maddest abolitionist does not think the Negro's providence of habits and moneymaking capacity at all to compare to those of the whites. This defect of character would alone justify enslaving him, if he is to remain here. In Africa or the West Indies, he would become idolatrous, savage and cannibal, or be devoured by savages and cannibals. At the North he would freeze or starve.

We would remind those who deprecate and sympathize with Negro slavery, that his slavery here relieves him from a far more cruel slavery in Africa, or from idolatry and cannibalism, and every brutal vice and crime that can disgrace humanity; and that it Christianizes, protects, supports, and civilizes him; that it governs him far better than free laborers at the North are governed. There, wife-murder has become a mere holiday pastime; and where so many wives are murdered, almost all must be brutally treated. Nay, more, men who kill their wives or treat them brutally must be ready for all kinds of crime, and the calendar of crime at the North proves the inference to be correct. Negroes never kill their wives. If it be objected that legally they have no wives, then we reply that in an experience of more than forty years, we have never yet heard of a Negro man killing a Negro woman. Our Negroes are not only better off as to physical comfort than free laborers, but their moral condition is better. . . .

Negro slavery would be changed immediately to some form of peonage, serfdom, or villeinage, if the Negroes were sufficiently intelligent and provident to manage a farm. No one would have the labor and trouble of management, if his Negroes would pay in hires and rents one-half what free tenants pay in rent in Europe. Every Negro in the South would be soon liberated, if he would take liberty on the terms that white tenants hold it. The fact that he cannot enjoy liberty on such terms seems conclusive that he is only fit to be a slave.

But for the assaults of the Abolitionists, much would have been done ere this to regulate and improve Southern slavery. Our Negro mechanics do not work so hard, have many more privileges and holidays, and are better fed and clothed than field hands, and are yet more valuable to their masters. The slaves of the South are cheated of their rights by the purchase of Northern manufactures which they could produce. Besides, if we would employ our slaves in the coarser processes of the mechanic arts and manufactures, such as brick making, getting and hewing timber for ships and houses, iron mining and smelting, coal mining, grading railroads and plank roads, in the manufacture of cotton, tobacco, etc., we would find a vent in new employments for their increase, more humane and more profitable than the vent afforded by new states and territories. The nice and finishing processes of manufactures and mechanics should be reserved for the whites, who only are fitted for them, and thus, by diversifying pursuits and cutting off dependence on the North, we might benefit and advance the interests of our whole population. Exclusive agriculture has depressed and impoverished the South. We will not here dilate on this topic, because we intend to make it the subject of a separate essay. Free trade doctrines, not slavery, have made the South agricultural and dependent, given her a sparse and ignorant population, ruined her cities, and expelled her people.

Would the Abolitionists approve of a system of society that set white children free, and remitted them at the age of fourteen, males and females, to all the rights, both as to person and property, which belong to adults? Would it be criminal or praiseworthy to do so? Criminal, of course. Now, are the average of Negroes equal in information, in native intelligence, in prudence or providence, to well-informed white children of fourteen? We who have lived with them for forty years think not. The competition of the world would be too much for the children. They would be cheated out of their property and debased in their morals. Yet they would meet everywhere with sympathizing friends of their own color, ready to aid, advise, and assist them. The Negro would be exposed to the same competition and greater temptations, with no greater ability to contend with them, with these additional difficulties. He would be welcome nowhere; meet with thousands of enemies and no friends. If he went North, the white laborers would kick him and cuff him, and drive him out of employment; if he went to Africa, the savages would cook him and eat him. If he went to the West Indies, they would not let him in, or if they did, they would soon make of him a savage and idolator.

We have a further question to ask. If it be right and incumbent to subject children to the authority of parents and guardians, and idiots and lunatics to committees, would it not be equally right and incumbent to give the free Negroes masters, until at least they arrive at years of discretion, which very few ever did or will attain? What is the difference between the authority of a parent and of a master? Neither pay wages, and each is entitled to the services of those subject to him. The father may not sell his child forever, but may hire him out till he is twenty-one. The free Negro's master may also be restrained from selling. Let him stand in *loco parentis,* and call him papa instead of master. Look closely into slavery, and you will see nothing so hideous in it, or if you do, you will find plenty of it at home in its most hideous form. . . .

But far the worst feature of modern civilization, which is the civilization of free society, remains to be exposed. While labor-saving processes have probably lessened by one half, in the last century, the amount of work needed for comfortable support, the free laborer is compelled by capital and competition to work more than he ever did before, and is less comfortable. The organization of society cheats him of his earnings, and those earnings go to swell the vulgar pomp and pageantry of the ignorant millionaires, who are the only great of the present day. These reflections might seem, at first view, to have little connection with Negro slavery; but it is well for us of the South not to be deceived by the tinsel glare and glitter of free society, and to employ ourselves in doing our duty at home, and studying the past, rather than in insidious rivalry of the expensive pleasures and pursuits of men whose sentiments and whose aims are low, sensual, and groveling.

Human progress consisting in moral and intellectual improvement, and there being no agreed and conventional standard weights or measures of moral and intellectual qualities and quantities, the question of progress can never be accurately decided. We maintain that man has not improved, because in all save the mechanic arts he reverts to the distant past for models to imitate, and he never imitates what he can excel. . . .

We abhor the doctrine of the *Types of Mankind;* first, because it is at war with Scripture, which teaches us that the whole human race is descended from a common parentage; and, second, because it encourages and incites brutal masters to treat Negroes, not as weak, ignorant, and dependent brethren, but as wicked beasts, without the pale of humanity. The Southerner is the Negro's friend, his only friend. Let no intermeddling Abolitionist, no refined philosophy, dissolve this friendship.

THE ASSOCIATION OF LABOR

If THE SOCIALISTS had done no other good, they would be entitled to the gratitude of mankind for displaying in a strong light the advantages of the association of labor. Adam Smith, in his elaborate treatise on the "Division of Labor," nearly stumbled on the same truth. But the division of labor is a curse to the laborer, without the association of labor. Division makes labor ten times more efficient, but, by confining each workman to some simple, monotonous employment, it makes him a mere automaton and an easy prey to the capitalist. The association of labor, like all association, requires a head or ruler, and that head or ruler will become a cheat and a tyrant unless his interests are identified with the interests of the laborer. In a large factory, in free society, there is division of labor, and association too, but association and division for the benefit of the employer and to the detriment of the laborer.

On a large farm whatever advances the health, happiness, and morals of the Negroes renders them more prolific and valuable to their master. It is his interest to pay them high wages in way of support, and he can afford to do so, because association renders the labor of each slave five times as productive and efficient as it would be, were the slaves working separately. One man could not enclose an acre of land, cultivate it, send his crops to market, do his own cooking, washing, and mending. One man may live as a prowling beast of prey but not as a civilized being. One hundred human beings, men, women, and children, associated, will cultivate ten acres of land each, enclose it, and carry on every other operation of civilized life. Labor becomes at least twenty times as productive when a hundred associate as when one acts alone. The same is as true in other pursuits as in farming. But in free society the employer robs the laborer, and he is no better off than the prowling savage, although he might live in splendor if he got a fair proportion of the proceeds of his own labor.

We have endeavored to show, heretofore, that the Negro slave, considering his indolence and unskillfulness, often gets his fair share, and sometimes more than his share of the profits of the farm and is exempted, besides, from the harassing cares and anxieties of the free laborer. Grant, however, that the Negro does not receive adequate wages from his master, yet all admit that in the aggregate the Negroes get better wages than free laborers; therefore, it follows that, with all its imperfections, slave society is the best form of society yet devised for the masses. When Socialists and Abolitionists, by full and fair experiments, exhibit a better, it will be time to agitate the subject of abolition.

The industrial products of black slave labor have been far greater and more useful to mankind than those of the same amount of any other labor. In a very short period the South and Southwest have been settled, cleared, fenced in, and put in cultivation by what were, a century ago, a handful of masters and slaves. This region now feeds and clothes a great part of mankind; but free trade cheats them of the profits of their labor. In the vast amount of our industrial products, we see the advantages of association; in our comparative poverty, the evils of free trade.

DECLARATION OF INDEPENDENCE AND VIRGINIA BILL OF RIGHTS

IT IS, WE BELIEVE, conceded on all hands that men are not born physically, morally, or intellectually equal; some are males, some females, some from birth, large, strong, and healthy, others weak, small, and sickly; some are naturally amiable, others prone to all kinds of wickedness; some brave, others timid. Their natural inequalities beget inequalities of rights. The weak in mind or body require guidance, support, and protection; they must obey and work for those who protect and guide them; they have a natural right to guardians, committees, teachers, or masters. Nature has made them slaves; all that law and government can do is to regulate, modify, and mitigate their slavery. In the absence of legally instituted slavery, their condition would be worse under that natural slavery of the weak to the strong, the foolish to the wise and cunning.

The wise and virtuous, the brave, the strong in mind and body, are by nature born to command and protect, and law but follows nature in making them rulers, legislators, judges, captains, husbands, guardians, committees, and masters. The naturally depraved class, those born prone to crime, are our brethren too; they are entitled to education, to religious instruction, to all the means and appliances proper to correct their evil propensities, and all their failings; they have a right to be sent to the penitentiary, for there, if they do not reform, they cannot at least disturb society. Our feelings and our consciences teach us that nothing but necessity can justify taking human life.

We are but stringing together truisms which everybody knows as well as ourselves, and yet, if men are created unequal in all these respects, what truth or what meaning is there in the passage under consideration? Men are not created or born equal, and circumstances and education and association tend to increase and aggravate inequalities among them from generation to generation. Generally, the rich associate and intermarry with each other, the poor do the same; the ignorant rarely associate with or intermarry with the learned; and all society

shuns contact with the criminal, even to the third and fourth generations.

Men are not "born entitled to equal rights!" It would be far nearer the truth to say that "some were born with saddles on their backs, and others booted and spurred to ride them" — and the riding does them good. They need the reins, the bit, and the spur. No two men by nature are exactly equal or exactly alike. No institutions can prevent the few from acquiring rule and ascendancy over the many. Liberty and free competition invite and encourage the attempt of the strong to master the weak and insure their success. . . .

Property is not a natural and divine but conventional right; it is the mere creature of society and law. In this all lawyers and publicists agree. In this country the history of property is of such recent date that the simplest and most ignorant man must know that it commenced in wrong, injustice, and violence a few generations ago and derives its only title now from the will of society through the sanction of law. Society has no right, because it is not expedient, to resume any one man's property because he abuses its possession and does not so employ it as to redound to public advantage; but if all private property, or if private property generally were so used as to injure, instead of promote public good, then society might and ought to destroy the whole institution.

From these premises it follows that government, in taxing private property, should only be limited by the public good. If the tax be so heavy as to deter the owner from improving the property, then, in general, will the whole public be injured.

False notions of the right of property and of the duties and liabilities of property-holders, destroy all public spirit and patriotism, cripple and injure, and prevent the growth and development of the South.

51.

Opposition to the Kansas-Nebraska Bill

The Compromise of 1850 initiated a period of uneasy truce between North and South on the question of extending slavery into the territories; but even before the Compromise became law political forces were at work to undermine it. As early as 1848 the Democrats had taken the position that each territory had the right to make its own decision about slavery. Democratic Senator Stephen A. Douglas adopted this principle of "popular sovereignty" in an 1854 plan for the organization of the Kansas and Nebraska territories, despite the fact both were north of the Missouri Compromise line of 1820 and under that agreement should have excluded slavery. Senator Salmon P. Chase, in an attempt to rally the antislavery Democrats, drew up (with the help of Joshua Giddings) the "Appeal of the Independent Democrats" in January 1854, hoping to prevent passage of the bill. Part of the Appeal is reprinted below.

Source: *Globe,* 33 Cong., 1 Sess., pp. 281-282.

AS SENATORS AND REPRESENTATIVES in the Congress of the United States, it is our duty to warn our constituents whenever imminent danger menaces the freedom of our institutions or the permanency of the Union. Such danger, as we firmly believe, now impends, and we earnestly solicit your prompt attention to it.

At the last session of Congress, a bill for the organization of the Territory of Nebraska passed the House of Representatives with an overwhelming majority. That bill was based on the principle of excluding slavery from the new territory. It was not taken up for consideration in the Senate and consequently failed to become a law.

At the present session, a new Nebraska bill has been reported by the Senate Committee on Territories, which, should it unhappily receive the sanction of Congress, will open all the unorganized territories of the Union to the ingress of slavery.

We arraign this bill as a gross violation of a sacred pledge; as a criminal betrayal of precious rights; as part and parcel of an atrocious plot to exclude from a vast, unoccupied region immigrants from the Old World and free laborers from our own states, and convert it into a dreary region of despotism, inhabited by masters and slaves. . . .

We beg your attention, fellow citizens, to a few historical facts:

The original settled policy of the United States, clearly indicated by the Jefferson proviso of 1784 and the Ordinance of 1787, was nonextension of slavery.

In 1803 Louisiana was acquired by purchase from France. At that time there were some 25,000 or 30,000 slaves in this territory, most of them within what is now the state of Louisiana; a few only, farther north, on the west bank of the Mississippi. Congress, instead of providing for the abolition of slavery in this new territory, permitted its continuance. In 1812 the state of Louisiana was organized and admitted into the Union with slavery.

In 1818, six years later, the inhabitants of the Territory of Missouri applied to Congress for authority to form a state constitution and for admission into the Union. There were, at that time, in the whole territory acquired from France, outside of the state of Louisiana, not 3,000 slaves.

There was no apology, in the circumstances of the country, for the continuance of slavery. The original national policy was against it, and, not less, the plain language of the treaty under which the territory had been acquired from France.

It was proposed, therefore, to incorporate in the bill authorizing the formation of a state government a provision requiring that the constitution of the new state should contain an article providing for the abolition of existing slavery and prohibiting the further introduction of slaves.

This provision was vehemently and pertinaciously opposed, but finally prevailed in the House of Representatives by a decided vote. In the Senate it was rejected, and, in consequence of the disagreement between the two houses, the bill was lost.

At the next session of Congress, the controversy was renewed with increased violence. It was terminated at length by a compromise. Missouri was allowed to come into the Union with slavery; but a section was inserted in the act authorizing her admission, excluding slavery forever from all the territory acquired from France, not included in the new state, lying north of 36°30′. We quote the prohibitory section:

Section 8. *Be it further enacted,* that in all that territory ceded by France to the United States, under the name of Louisiana, which lies north of 36°30′ of north latitude, not included within the limits of the state contemplated by this act, slavery and involuntary servitude, otherwise than as the punishment of crimes, shall be and is hereby forever prohibited.

The question of the constitutionality of this prohibition was submitted by President Monroe to his cabinet. John Quincy Adams was then secretary of state; John C. Cal-

houn was secretary of war; William H. Crawford was secretary of the treasury; and William Wirt was attorney general. Each of these eminent men, three of them being from slave states, gave a written opinion affirming its constitutionality, and thereupon the act received the sanction of the President himself, also from a slave state.

Nothing is more certain in history than the fact that Missouri could not have been admitted as a slave state had not certain members from the free states been reconciled to the measure by the incorporation of this prohibition into the act of admission. Nothing is more certain than that this prohibition has been regarded and accepted by the whole country as a solemn compact against the extension of slavery into any part of the territory acquired from France lying north of 36°30′ and not included in the new state of Missouri. The same act — let it be ever remembered — which authorized the formation of a constitution for the state, without a clause forbidding slavery, consecrated, beyond question and beyond honest recall, the whole remainder of the territory to freedom and free institutions forever. For more than thirty years — during more than half the period of our national existence under our present Constitution — this compact has been universally regarded and acted upon as inviolable American law. In conformity with it, Iowa was admitted as a free state and Minnesota has been organized as a free territory.

It is a strange and ominous fact, well calculated to awaken the worst apprehensions and the most fearful forebodings of future calamities, that it is now deliberately purposed to repeal this prohibition, by implication or directly — the latter certainly the manlier way — and thus to subvert this compact and allow slavery in all the yet unorganized territory.

We cannot, in this address, review the various pretenses under which it is attempted to cloak this monstrous wrong, but we must not altogether omit to notice one.

It is said that the Territory of Nebraska sustains the same relations to slavery as did the territory acquired from Mexico prior to 1850, and that the pro-slavery clauses of the bill are necessary to carry into effect the compromises of that year. No assertion could be more groundless. . . .

In 1820 the slave states said to the free states: "Admit Missouri with slavery and refrain from positive exclusion south of 36°30' and we will join you in perpetual prohibition north of that line." The free states consented. In 1854 the slave states say to the free states: "Missouri is admitted; no prohibition of slavery south of 36°30' has been attempted. We have received the full consideration of our agreement; no more is to be gained by adherence to it on our part; we therefore propose to cancel the compact." If this be not Punic faith, what is it? Not without the deepest dishonor and crime can the free states acquiesce in this demand. . . .

From the rich lands of this large territory, also, patriotic statesmen have anticipated that a free, industrious, and enlightened population will extract abundant treasures of individual and public wealth. There, it has been expected, freedom-loving emigrants from Europe, and energetic and intelligent laborers from our own land, will find homes of comfort and fields of useful enterprise. If this bill shall become a law, all such expectation will turn to grievous disappointment. The blight of slavery will cover the land. The Homestead Law, should Congress enact one, will be worthless there. Freemen, unless pressed by a hard and cruel necessity, will not, and should not, work beside slaves. Labor cannot be respected where any class of laborers is held in abject bondage. . . .

We appeal to the people. We warn you that the dearest interests of freedom and the Union are in imminent peril. Demagogues may tell you that the Union can be maintained only by submitting to the demands of slavery. We tell you that the safety of the Union can only be insured by the full recognition of the just claims of freedom and man. The Union was formed to establish justice and secure the blessings of liberty. When it fails to accomplish these ends, it will be worthless; and when it becomes worthless, it cannot long endure.

We entreat you to be mindful of that fundamental maxim of democracy — *equal rights and exact justice for all men.* Do not submit to become agents in extending legalized oppression and systematized injustice over a vast territory yet exempt from these terrible evils.

We implore Christians and Christian ministers to interpose. Their divine religion requires them to behold in every man a brother and to labor for the advancement and regeneration of the human race.

Whatever apologies may be offered for the toleration of slavery in the states, none can be urged for its extension into territories where it does not exist and where that extension involves the repeal of ancient law and the violation of solemn compact. Let all protest, earnestly and emphatically, by correspondence, through the press, by memorials, by resolutions of public meetings and legislative bodies, and in whatever other mode may seem expedient, against this enormous crime.

For ourselves, we shall resist it by speech and vote, and with all the abilities which God has given us. Even if overcome in the impending struggle, we shall not submit. We shall go home to our constituents, erect anew the standard of freedom, and call on the people to come to the rescue of the country from the domination of slavery. We will not despair; for the cause of human freedom is the cause of God.

52.

Stephen A. Douglas: Defense of the Kansas-Nebraska Bill

Stephen Douglas' Kansas-Nebraska Bill of 1854 was designed to allow the legislatures of Kansas and Nebraska to determine whether those territories should be slave or free. This plan, which in effect repealed the provisions of the Missouri Compromise, was attacked by Douglas' fellow Democrats under the leadership of Senator Salmon P. Chase. Douglas himself was so widely criticized that one Washington newspaper declared: "Never before has a public man been so hunted and hounded." In a speech of January 30, 1854, Douglas defended the constitutionality of his bill and denounced Senator Chase and the antislavery faction for refusing to compromise on an issue that threatened to disrupt the Union. Portions of the speech are reprinted below.

Source: *Globe*, 33 Cong., 1 Sess., pp. 275-280.

Mr. President, when I proposed on Tuesday last that the Senate should proceed to the consideration of the bill to organize the territories of Nebraska and Kansas . . . I desired to refer to two points: first, as to those provisions relating to the Indians; and second, to those which might be supposed to bear upon the question of slavery. . . .

Sir, this is all that I intended to say if the question had been taken up for consideration on Tuesday last; but since that time occurrences have transpired which compel me to go more fully into the discussion. It will be borne in mind that the senator from Ohio [Mr. Chase] then objected to the consideration of the bill and asked for its postponement until this day, on the ground that there had not been time to understand and consider its provisions; and the senator from Massachusetts [Mr. Sumner] suggested that the postponement should be for one week, for that purpose. These suggestions seeming to be reasonable to senators around me, I

yielded to their request and consented to the postponement of the bill until this day.

Sir, little did I suppose at the time that I granted that act of courtesy to those two senators that they had drafted and published to the world a document, over their own signatures, in which they arraigned me as having been guilty of a criminal betrayal of my trust, as having been guilty of an act of bad faith, and been engaged in an atrocious plot against the cause of free government. Little did I suppose that those two senators had been guilty of such conduct when they called upon me to grant that courtesy, to give them an opportunity of investigating the substitute reported from the committee.

I have since discovered that on that very morning the *National Era*, the Abolition organ in this city, contained an address, signed by certain Abolition confederates, to the people, in which the bill is grossly misrepresented, in which the action of the members of the committee is grossly falsified, in which our motives are arraigned and our characters calumniated. . . .

The argument of this manifesto is predicated upon the assumption that the policy of the fathers of the republic was to prohibit slavery in all the territory ceded by the old states to the Union and made United States territory for the purpose of being organized into new states. I take issue upon that statement. Such was not the practice in the early history of the government. It is true that in the territory northwest of the Ohio River slavery was prohibited by the Ordinance of 1787; but it is also true that in the territory south of the Ohio River, to wit, the territory of Tennessee, slavery was permitted and protected; and it is also true that in the organization of the territory of Mississippi, in 1798, the provisions of the Ordinance of 1787 were applied to it, with the exception of Article 6, which prohibited slavery.

Then, sir, you find upon the statute books under Washington and the early Presidents provisions of law showing that in the southwestern territories the right to hold slaves was clearly implied or recognized, while in the northwest territories it was prohibited. The only conclusion that can be fairly and honestly drawn from that legislation is that it was the policy of the fathers of the republic to prescribe a line of demarcation between free territories and slaveholding territories by a natural or a geographical line, being sure to make that line correspond, as near as might be, to the laws of climate, of production, and probably of all those other causes that would control the institution and make it either desirable or undesirable to the people inhabiting the respective territories. . . .

A senator from my state, Mr. Jesse B. Thomas, introduced an amendment, known as Section 8 of the bill, in which it was provided that slavery should be prohibited north of 36°30′ north latitude, in all that country which we had acquired from France. What was the object of the enactment of Section 8? Was it not to go back to the original policy of prescribing boundaries to the limitation of free institutions and of slave institutions by a geographical line, in order to avoid all controversy in Congress upon the subject? Hence they extended that geographical line through all the territory purchased from France, which was as far as our possessions then reached. It was not simply to settle the question on that piece of country but it was to carry out a great principle, by extending that dividing line as far west as our territory went, and running it onward on each new acquisition of territory. True, the express enactment of Section 8 of the Missouri Act, now called the Missouri Compromise act, only covered the territory acquired from France; but the principles of the act, the objects of its adoption, the reasons in its support required that it should be extended indefinitely westward, so far as our territory might go, whenever new purchases should be made. . . .

Then, sir, in 1848, we acquired from Mexico the country between the Rio Del Norte and the Pacific Ocean. Immediately after that acquisition, the Senate, on my own motion, voted into a bill a provision to extend the Missouri Compromise indefinitely westward to the Pacific Ocean, in the same sense and with the same understanding with which it was originally adopted. That provision passed this body by a decided majority — I think by ten at least — and went to the House of Representatives, and was there defeated by Northern votes.

Now, sir, let us pause and consider for a moment. The first time that the principles of the Missouri Compromise were ever abandoned, the first time they were ever rejected by Congress, was by the defeat of that provision in the House of Representatives in 1848. By whom was that defeat effected? By Northern votes, with Free-Soil proclivities. It was the defeat of that Missouri Compromise that reopened the slavery agitation with all its fury. It was the defeat of that Missouri Compromise that created the tremendous struggle of 1850. It was the defeat of that Missouri Compromise that created the necessity for making a new compromise in 1850. Had we been faithful to the principles of the Missouri Compromise in 1848, this question would not have arisen.

Who was it that was faithless? I undertake to say it was the very men who now insist that the Missouri Compromise was a solemn compact and should never be violated or departed from. Every man who is now assailing the principle of the bill under consideration, so far as I am advised, was opposed to the Missouri Compromise in 1848. The very men who now arraign me for a departure from the Missouri Compromise are the men who successfully violated it, repudiated it, and caused it to be superseded by the compromise measures of 1850. Sir, it is with rather bad grace that the men who proved false themselves should charge upon me and others who were ever faithful the responsibilities and consequences of their own treachery.

Then, sir, as I before remarked, the defeat of the Missouri Compromise in 1848 having created the necessity for the establishment of a new one in 1850, let us see what that compromise was.

The leading feature of the compromise of 1850 was congressional nonintervention as to slavery in the territories; that the people of the territories, and of all the states, were to be allowed to do as they pleased upon the subject of slavery, subject only to the provisions of the Constitution of the United States. That, sir, was the leading feature of the compromise measures of 1850.

Those measures, therefore, abandoned the idea of a geographical line as the boundary between free states and slave states; abandoned it because compelled to do it from an inability to maintain it; and, in lieu of that, substituted a great principle of self-government which would allow the people to do as they thought proper. Now, the question is, when that new compromise, resting upon that great fundamental principle of freedom, was established, was it not an abandonment of the old one — the geographical line? Was it not a supersedure of the old one within the very language of the substitute for the bill which is now under consideration? I say it did supersede it, because it applied its provisions as well to the north as to the south of 36°30′. It established a principle which was equally applicable to the country north as well as south of the parallel of 36°30′ — a principle of universal application. . . .

I am now dealing with the truth and veracity of a combination of men who have assembled in secret caucus upon the Sabbath Day to arraign my conduct and belie my character. I say, therefore, that their manifesto is a slander . . . for it says that the Missouri Compromise was not superseded by the measures of 1850, and then it says that the same words in my bill do repeal and annul it. They must be adjudged guilty of one falsehood in order to sustain the other assertion. . . .

Sir, this misrepresentation and falsification does not stop here. In order to give greater plausibility to their statement, they go further and state that:

> it is solemnly declared, in the very compromise acts, "that *nothing herein contained shall be construed to impair or qualify*" the prohibition of slavery north of 36°30′; and yet, in the face of this declaration, that sacred prohibition is said to be overthrown. Can presumption go further?

In the very teeth of the statute, saying that they should come in with or without slavery as they pleased, these men declare that it is stated that it should be forever prohibited. I repeat to them, "Could presumption go further?" Not only presumption in making these statements but the presumption that they could avoid the exposure of their conduct.

In order to give greater plausibility to this falsification of the terms of the compromise measures of 1850, the confederates also declare in their manifesto that they (the territorial bills for the organization of Utah and New Mexico) "applied to the territory acquired from Mexico, and to that only. They were intended as a settlement of the controversy growing out of that acquisition, and of that controversy only. They must stand or fall by their own merits."

I submit to the Senate if there is an intelligent man in America who does not know that that declaration is falsified by the statute from which they quoted? They say that the provisions of that bill were confined to the territory acquired from Mexico, when the very section of the law from which they quoted that proviso did purchase a part of that very territory from the state of Texas. And the next section of the law included that territory in the new territory of Mexico. It took a small portion, also, of the old Louisiana Purchase, and added that to the new territory of Mexico, and made up the rest out of the Mexican acquisitions.

Then, sir, your statutes show, when applied to the map of the country, that the territory of New Mexico was composed of territory acquired from Mexico . . . also of territory acquired from Texas, and of territory acquired from France; and yet, in defiance of that statute and in falsification of its terms, we are told, in order to deceive the people, that the bills were confined to the purchase made from Mexico alone; and in order to give it greater solemnity, as was necessary while uttering a falsehood, they repeat it twice, fearing that it would not be believed the first time. What is more, the territory of Utah was not confined to the country acquired from Mexico. That territory, as is well known to every man who un-

derstands the geography of the country, includes a large tract of rich and fertile country acquired from France in 1803, and to which Section 8 of the Missouri Act applied in 1820. If these confederates do not know to what country I allude, I only reply that they should have known before they uttered a falsehood and imputed a crime to me.

But I will tell you to what country I allude. By the treaty of 1819, by which we acquired Florida, and fixed a boundary between the United States and Mexico, the boundary was made of the Arkansas River to its source, and then the line ran due north of the source of the Arkansas to the 42nd parallel, then along on the 42nd parallel to the Pacific Ocean. That line, due north from the head of the Arkansas, leaves the whole Middle Park, described in such glowing terms by Colonel Frémont, to the east of the line, and hence a part of the Louisiana Purchase. Yet, inasmuch as that Middle Park is watered and drained by the waters flowing into the Colorado, when we formed the territorial limits of Utah, instead of running that air line, we ran along the ridge of the mountains and cut off that part from Nebraska, or from the Louisiana Purchase, and included it within the limits of the territory of Utah.

Why did we do it? Because we sought for a national boundary; and it was more natural to take the mountains as a boundary than by an air line to cut the valleys on one side of the mountains, and annex them to the country on the other side. And why did we take these natural boundaries, setting at defiance the old boundaries? The simple reason was that so long as we acted upon the principle of settling the slave question by a geographical line, so long we observed those boundaries strictly and rigidly; but when that was abandoned, in consequence of the action of Free-Soilers and Abolitionists — when it was superseded by the compromise measures of 1850, which rested upon a great universal principle — there was no necessity for keeping in view the old and unnatural boundary. For that reason, in making the new territories, we formed natural boundaries, irrespective of the source whence our title was derived. In writing these bills I paid no attention to the fact whether the title was acquired from Louisiana, from France, or from Mexico; for what difference did it make? The principle which we had established in the bill would apply equally well to either. . . .

Mr. President . . . so far as the question of slavery is concerned, there is nothing in the bill under consideration which does not carry out the principle of the compromise measures of 1850, by leaving the people to do as they please, subject only to the provisions of the Constitution of the United States. If that principle is wrong, the bill is wrong. If that principle is right, the bill is right. It is unnecessary to quibble about phraseology or words; it is not the mere words, the mere phraseology, that our constituents wish to judge by. They wish to know the legal effect of our legislation.

The legal effect of this bill, if it be passed as reported by the Committee on Territories, is neither to legislate slavery into these territories nor out of them, but to leave the people do as they please, under the provisions and subject to the limitations of the Constitution of the United States. Why should not this principle prevail? Why should any man, North or South, object to it? I will especially address the argument to my own section of country, and ask why should any Northern man object to this principle? If you will review the history of the slavery question in the United States, you will see that all the great results in behalf of free institutions which have been worked out have been accomplished by the operation of this principle, and by it alone. . . .

Under the operation of this principle, New Hampshire became free, while South Carolina continued to hold slaves; Connecticut abolished slavery, while Georgia held on to it; Rhode Island abandoned the institution, while Maryland preserved it; New York, New Jersey, and Pennsylvania abolished slavery, while Virginia, North Carolina, and Kentucky retained it. Did they do it at your bidding? Did they do it at the dictation of the federal government? Did they do it in obedience to any of your Wilmot Proviso or Ordinances of 1787? Not at all; they did it by virtue of their right as freemen under the Constitution of the United States, to establish and abolish such institutions as they thought their own good required.

Let me ask you where have you succeeded in excluding slavery by an act of Congress from one inch of the American soil? You may tell me that you did it in the Northwest Territory by the Ordinance of 1787. I will show you by the history of the country that you did not accomplish any such thing. You prohibited slavery there by law, but you did not exclude it in fact. Illinois was a part of the Northwest Territory. With the exception of a few French and white settlements, it was a vast wilderness, filled with hostile savages when the Ordinance of 1787 was adopted. Yet, sir, when Illinois was organized into a territorial government, it established and protected slavery, and maintained it in spite of your ordinance and in defiance of its express prohibition. It is a curious fact that so long as Congress said the territory of Illinois should not have slavery, she actually had it; and on the very day when you withdrew your congressional prohibition, the people of Illinois, of their own free will and accord, provided for a system of emancipation. . . .

How was it in regard to California? Every one of these Abolition confederates who have thus arraigned me and the Committee on Territories before the country, who have misrepresented our position, and misquoted the law and the fact, predicted that unless Congress interposed by law and prohibited slavery in California, it would inevitably become a slaveholding state. Congress did not interfere; Congress did not prohibit slavery. There was no enactment upon the subject; but the people formed a state constitution and then prohibited slavery. . . .

I know of but one territory of the United States where slavery does exist, and that one is where you have prohibited it by law, and it is this very Nebraska Territory. In defiance of Section 8 of the act of 1820, in defiance of congressional dictation, there have been, not many, but a few slaves introduced. . . .

I do not like, I never did like, the system of legislation on our part by which a geographical line, in violation of the laws of nature, and climate, and soil, and of the laws of God, should be run to establish institutions for a people; yet, out of a regard for the peace and quiet of the country, out of respect for past pledges, and out of a desire to adhere faithfully to all compromises, I sustained the Missouri Compromise so long as it was in force and advocated its extension to the Pacific. Now, when that has been abandoned, when it has been superseded, when a great principle of self-government has been substituted for it, I choose to cling to that principle and abide in good faith, not only by the letter but by the spirit of the last compromise.

Sir, I do not recognize the right of the Abolitionists of this country to arraign me for being false to sacred pledges, as they have done in their proclamation. Let them show when and where I have ever proposed to violate a compact. I have proved that I stood by the compact of 1820 and 1845, and proposed its continuance and observance in 1848. I have proved that the Free-Soilers and Abolitionists were the guilty parties who violated that compromise then.

I should like to compare notes with these Abolition confederates about adherence to compromises. When did they stand by or approve of any one that was ever made?

Did not every Abolitionist and Free-Soiler in America denounce the Missouri Compromise in 1820? Did they not for years hunt down ravenously for his blood every man who assisted in making that compromise? Did they not in 1845, when Texas was annexed, denounce all of us who went for the annexation of Texas, and for the continuation of the Missouri Compromise line through it? Did they not in 1848 denounce me as a slavery propagandist for standing by the principles of the Missouri Compromise, and proposing to continue the Missouri compromise line to the Pacific Ocean? Did they not themselves violate and repudiate it then? Is not the charge of bad faith true as to every Abolitionist in America, instead of being true as to me and . . . those who advocate this bill?

They talk about the bill being a violation of the compromise measures of 1850. Who can show me a man in either house of Congress who was in favor of the compromise measures of 1850, and who is not now in favor of leaving the people of Nebraska and Kansas to do as they please upon the subject of slavery according to the provisions of my bill? Is there one? If so, I have not heard of him. This tornado has been raised by Abolitionists, and Abolitionists alone. They have made an impression upon the public mind in the way in which I have mentioned, by a falsification of the law and the facts; and this whole organization against the compromise measures of 1850 is an Abolition movement. I presume they had some hope of getting a few tenderfooted Democrats into their plot; and, acting on what they supposed they might do, they sent forth publicly to the world the falsehood that their address was signed by the senators and a majority of the representatives from the state of Ohio; but when we come to examine signatures, we find no one Whig there, no one Democrat there; none but pure, unmitigated, unadulterated Abolitionists. . . . Now I ask the friends and the opponents of this measure to look at it as it is. Is not the question involved the simple one, whether the people of the territories shall be allowed to do as they please upon the question of slavery, subject only to the limitations of the Constitution? That is all the bill provides; and it does so in clear, explicit, and unequivocal terms. I know there are some men, Whigs and Democrats, who, not willing to repudiate the Baltimore platform of their own party, would be willing to vote for this principle, provided they could do so in such equivocal terms that they could deny that it means what it was intended to mean in certain localities. I do not wish to deal in any equivocal language.

If the principle is right, let it be avowed and maintained. If it is wrong, let it be repudiated. Let all this quibbling about the Missouri Compromise, about the territory acquired from France, about the act of 1820, be cast behind you; for the simple question is — Will you allow the people to legislate for themselves upon the subject of slavery? Why should you not? . . .

We intend to stand by the principle of the compromise measures of 1850 . . . that principle to which the Democracy are pledged, not merely by the Baltimore platform but by a higher and a more solemn obligation, to which they are pledged by the love and affection which they have for that great fundamental principle of democracy and free institutions which lies at the basis of our creed, and gives every political community the right to govern itself in obedience to the Constitution of the country.

53.

John Greenleaf Whittier: "The Kansas Emigrants"

Whittier's poem, "The Kansas Emigrants," celebrates the movement of Northern settlers into the territory of Kansas, where they hoped to attain sufficient numbers to defeat a territorial referendum on slavery. The referendum was a provision of the Kansas-Nebraska Act, which permitted those two territories to decide for themselves whether to be slave or free.

Source: *Complete Poetical Works*, Household Edition, Boston, 1894.

THE KANSAS EMIGRANTS

We cross the prairie as of old
  The Pilgrims crossed the sea,
To make the West, as they the East,
  The homestead of the free!

We go to rear a wall of men
  On freedom's southern line,
And plant beside the cotton tree
  The rugged Northern pine!

We're flowing from our native hills
  As our free rivers flow;
The blessing of our motherland
  Is on us as we go.

We go to plant her common schools
  On distant prairie swells,
And give the Sabbaths of the wild
  The music of her bells.

Upbearing, like the Ark of old,
  The Bible in our van,
We go to test the truth of God
  Against the fraud of man.

No pause, nor rest, save where the streams
  That feed the Kansas run,
Save where our Pilgrim gonfalon
  Shall flout the setting sun!

We'll tread the prairie as of old
  Our fathers sailed the sea,
And make the West, as they the East,
  The homestead of the free!

54.

RALPH WALDO EMERSON: On the Fugitive Slave Law

Emerson remained aloof from the Abolition movement through the 1830s and 1840s; as a descendant of nine generations of ministers he had "other slaves to free than those Negroes, to wit, imprisoned spirits, imprisoned thoughts." However, events ultimately drew him into the controversy, especially the enactment of the stronger fugitive slave law that was part of the Compromise of 1850. "This filthy enactment," he wrote in his journal, "was made in the nineteenth century, by people who could read and write. I will not obey it, by God!" He summarized his opposition to the law and to the slave system in an address delivered in New York on March 4, 1854, and reprinted here in part.

Source: *Miscellanies*, Boston, 1886, pp. 205-230.

I HAVE LIVED ALL MY LIFE without suffering any known inconvenience from American slavery. I never saw it; I never heard the whip; I never felt the check on my free speech and action until the other day, when Mr. Webster, by his personal influence, brought the Fugitive Slave Law on the country. I say Mr. Webster, for though the bill was not his, it is yet notorious that he was the life and soul of it, that he gave it all he had. It cost him his life, and under the shadow of his great name inferior men sheltered themselves, threw their ballots for it and made the law. I say inferior men. There were all sorts of what are called brilliant men, accomplished men, men of high station, a President of the United States, senators, men of eloquent speech, but men without self-respect, without character; and it was strange to see that office, age, fame, talent, even a repute for honesty all count for nothing.

They had no opinions, they had no memory for what they had been saying like the Lord's Prayer all their lifetime: they were only looking to what their great Captain did. If he jumped, they jumped; if he stood on his head, they did. In ordinary, the supposed sense of their district and state is their guide, and that holds them to the part of liberty and justice. But it is always a little difficult to decipher what this public sense is; and when a great man comes who knots up into himself the opinions and wishes of the people, it is so much easier to follow him as an exponent of this. He too is responsible; they will not be. It will always suffice to say, "I followed him." . . .

I said I had never in my life up to this time suffered from the slave institution. Slavery in Virginia or Carolina was like slavery in Africa or the Fijis for me. There was an old Fugitive Law, but it had become, or was fast becoming, a dead letter, and, by the genius and laws of Massachusetts, inoperative. The new bill made it operative, required me to hunt slaves, and it found citizens in Massachusetts willing to act as judges and captors. Moreover, it discloses the secret of the new times, that slavery was no longer mendicant but was become aggressive and dangerous.

The way in which the country was dragged to consent to this, and the disastrous defection (on the miserable cry of Union) of the men of letters, of the colleges, of educated men, nay, of some preachers of religion, was the darkest passage in the history. It showed that our prosperity had hurt us and that we could not be shocked by crime. It showed that the old religion and the sense of the right had faded and gone out; that while we reckoned ourselves a highly cultivated nation, our bellies had run away with our brains, and the principles of culture and progress did not exist.

For I suppose that liberty is an accurate index, in men and nations, of general prog-

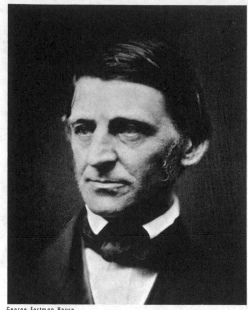

George Eastman House

Ralph Waldo Emerson, daguerreotype by Southworth and Hawes, c. 1850

ress. The theory of personal liberty must always appeal to the most refined communities and to the men of the rarest perception and of delicate moral sense. For there are rights which rest on the finest sense of justice, and, with every degree of civility, it will be more truly felt and defined. A barbarous tribe of good stock will, by means of their best heads, secure substantial liberty. But where there is any weakness in a race, and it becomes in a degree matter of concession and protection from their stronger neighbors, the incompatibility and offensiveness of the wrong will of course be most evident to the most cultivated. For it is — is it not? — the essence of courtesy, of politeness, of religion, of love, to prefer another, to postpone oneself, to protect another from oneself. That is the distinction of the gentleman, to defend the weak and redress the injured, as it is of the savage and the brutal to usurp and use others. . . .

Now, gentlemen, I think we have in this hour instruction again in the simplest lesson. Events roll, millions of men are engaged, and the result is the enforcing of some of those first commandments which we heard in the nursery. We never get beyond our first lesson, for, really, the world exists, as I understand it, to teach the science of liberty, which begins with liberty from fear.

The events of this month are teaching one thing plain and clear, the worthlessness of good tools to bad workmen; that official papers are of no use; resolutions of public meetings, platforms of conventions, no, nor laws, nor constitutions, anymore. These are all declaratory of the will of the moment, and are passed with more levity and on grounds far less honorable than ordinary business transactions of the street.

You relied on the Constitution. It has not the word "slave" in it; and very good argument has shown that it would not warrant the crimes that are done under it; that, with provisions so vague for an object not named, and which could not be availed of to claim a barrel of sugar or a barrel of corn, the robbing of a man and of all his posterity is effected. You relied on the Supreme Court. The law was right, excellent law for the lambs. But what if unhappily the judges were chosen from the wolves, and give to all the law a wolfish interpretation? You relied on the Missouri Compromise. That is ridden over. You relied on state sovereignty in the free states to protect their citizens. They are driven with contempt out of the courts and out of the territory of the slave states — if they are so happy as to get out with their lives — and now you relied on these dismal guarantees infamously made in 1850; and, before the body of Webster is yet crumbled, it is found that they have crumbled. This eternal monument of his fame and of the Union is rotten in four years. They are no guarantee to the free states. They are a guarantee to the slave states that, as they have hitherto met with no repulse, they shall meet with none.

I fear there is no reliance to be put on any kind or form of covenant, no, not on sacred forms, none on churches, none on Bibles. For one would have said that a Christian would not keep slaves; but the Christians keep slaves. Of course they will not dare to read the Bible. Won't they? They quote the Bible, quote Paul, quote Christ to justify slavery. If slavery is good, then is lying, theft, arson, homicide, each and all good, and to be maintained by Union societies.

These things show that no forms, neither constitutions, nor laws, nor covenants, nor churches, nor Bibles, are of any use in themselves. The devil nestles comfortably into them all. There is no help but in the head and heart and hamstrings of a man. Covenants are of no use without honest men to keep them; laws of none but with loyal citizens to obey them. To interpret Christ it needs Christ in the heart. The teachings of the Spirit can be apprehended only by the same spirit that gave them forth. To make good the cause of freedom, you must draw off from all foolish trust in others. You must be citadels and warriors yourselves, declarations of independence, the charter, the battle, and the victory. Cromwell said, "We can only resist the superior training of the king's soldiers by enlisting godly men." And no man has a right to hope that the laws of New York will defend him from the contamination of slaves another day until he has made up his mind that he will not owe his protection to the laws of New York, but to his own sense and spirit. Then he protects New York.

He only who is able to stand alone is qualified for society. And that I understand to be the end for which a soul exists in this world — to be himself the counterbalance of all falsehood and all wrong. "The army of unright is encamped from pole to pole, but the road of victory is known to the just." Everything may be taken away; he may be poor, he may be houseless, yet he will know out of his arms to make a pillow, and out of his breast a bolster. Why have the minority no influence? Because they have not a real minority of one. . . .

No excess of good nature or of tenderness in individuals has been able to give a new character to the system, to tear down the whipping house. The plea in the mouth of a slaveholder that the Negro is an inferior race sounds very oddly in my ear. "The masters of slaves seem generally anxious to prove that they are not of a race superior in any noble quality to the meanest of their bondmen." And, indeed, when the Southerner points to the anatomy of the Negro and talks of chimpanzee, I recall Montesquieu's remark, "It will not do to say that Negroes are men, lest it should turn out that whites are not."

Slavery is disheartening; but nature is not so helpless but it can rid itself at last of every wrong. But the spasms of nature are centuries and ages, and will tax the faith of short-lived men. Slowly, slowly the Avenger comes, but comes surely. The proverbs of the nations affirm these delays, but affirm the arrival. They say, "God may consent, but not forever." The delay of the divine justice — this was the meaning and soul of the Greek tragedy; this the soul of their religion. "There has come, too, one to whom lurking warfare is dear, Retribution, with a soul full of wiles; a violator of hospitality; guileful without the guilt of guile; limping, late in her arrival." They said of the happiness of the unjust that "at its close it begets itself an offspring and does not die childless, and instead of good fortune, there sprouts forth for posterity ever-ravening calamity"

For evil word shall evil word be said,
For murder-stroke a murder-stroke be paid.
Who smites must smart.

These delays, you see them now in the temper of the times. The national spirit in this country is so drowsy, preoccupied with interest, deaf to principle. The Anglo-Saxon race is proud and strong and selfish. They believe only in Anglo-Saxons. In 1825 Greece found America deaf, Poland found America deaf, Italy and Hungary found her deaf. England maintains trade, not liberty; stands against Greece; against Hungary; against Schleswig-Holstein; against the French Republic while it was a republic.

To faint hearts the times offer no invitation, and torpor exists here throughout the active classes on the subject of domestic slavery and its appalling aggressions. Yes, that is the stern edict of Providence, that liberty shall be no hasty fruit, but that event on event, population on population, age on age, shall cast itself into the opposite scale; and not until liberty has slowly accumulated weight enough to countervail and preponderate against all this can the sufficient recoil come. . . .

While the inconsistency of slavery with the principles on which the world is built guarantees its downfall, I own that the patience it requires is almost too sublime for mortals and seems to demand of us more than mere hoping. And when one sees how fast the rot spreads — it is growing serious — I think we demand of superior men that they be superior in this, that the mind and the virtue shall give their verdict in their day, and accelerate so far the progress of civilization. Possession is sure to throw its stupid strength for existing power, and appetite and ambition will go for that. Let the aid of virtue, intelligence, and education be cast where they rightfully belong. They are organically ours. Let them be loyal to their own. I wish to see the instructed class here know their own flag and not fire on their comrades. We should not forgive the clergy for taking on every issue the immoral side; nor the bench, if it put itself on the side of the culprit; nor the government, if it sustain the mob against the laws.

It is a potent support and ally to a brave man standing single, or with a few, for the right, and outvoted and ostracized, to know that better men in other parts of the country appreciate the service and will rightly report him to his own and the next age. Without this assurance, he will sooner sink. He may well say, "If my countrymen do not care to be defended, I too will decline the controversy, from which I only reap invectives and hatred."

Yet the lovers of liberty may with reason tax the coldness and indifferentism of scholars and literary men. They are lovers of liberty in Greece and Rome and in the English Commonwealth, but they are lukewarm lovers of the liberty of America in 1854. The universities are not, as in Hobbes's time, "the core of rebellion," no, but the seat of inertness. They have forgotten their allegiance to the Muse, and grown worldly and political. . . .

Now at last we are disenchanted and shall have no more false hopes. I respect the Anti-Slavery Society. It is the Cassandra that has foretold all that has befallen, fact for fact, years ago; foretold all, and no man laid it to heart. It seemed, as the Turks say, "Fate makes that a man should not believe his own eyes." But the Fugitive Law did much to unglue the eyes of men, and now the Nebraska Bill leaves us staring. The Anti-Slavery Society will add many members this year. The Whig Party will join it; the Democrats will join it. The population of the free states will join it. I doubt not, at last, the slave states will join it. But be that sooner or later, and whoever comes or stays away, I hope we have reached the end of our unbelief, have come to a belief that there is a divine Providence in the world which will not save us but through our own cooperation.

55.

"The Abolitionist Hymn"

In the years of rising tension before the Civil War, the Abolitionists of the North, like the slaves of the South, sang about their hopes for the end of slavery and for the future of the Negro people. Abolitionist societies sponsored antislavery sings, and provided the singers with music written for the occasion. Probably the most popular song of this kind was "The Abolitionist Hymn," set to the famous old tune of the doxology, or "Old Hundred."

THE ABOLITIONIST HYMN

We ask not that the slave should lie
As lies his master, at his ease,
Beneath a silken canopy,
Or in the shade of blooming trees.
We ask not "eye for eye," that all
Who forge the chain and ply the whip
Should feel their torture, while the thrall
Should wield the scourge of mastership.
We mourn not that the man should toil;
'Tis nature's need, 'tis God's decree;
But let the hand that tills the soil
Be, like the wind that fans it, free.

56.

WILLIAM J. GRAYSON: The Hireling and the Slave

The enormous success of Uncle Tom's Cabin, *both as a novel and a play, infuriated Southerners, who condemned the work as unrealistic, exaggerated, and oversentimental. In 1854 William Grayson, South Carolina lawyer and politician, attempted to counter the effectiveness of Mrs. Stowe's story in his long, didactic poem,* The Hireling and the Slave. *Like George Fitzhugh, he attacked the economic system of the industrial North as producing wage-slaves who, he contended, were much worse off than the average Negro slave in the South. A portion of Grayson's poem is reprinted below.*

Source: *The Hireling and the Slave, Chicora, and Other Poems,* Charleston, S.C., 1856.

Fallen from primeval innocence and ease,
When thornless fields employed him but to please,
The laborer toils; and from his dripping brow
Moistens the length'ning furrows of the plow;
In vain he scorns or spurns his altered state,
Tries each poor shift, and strives to cheat his fate;
In vain new shapes his name to shun the ill —
Slave, hireling, help — the curse pursues him still;
Changeless the doom remains, the mincing phrase
May mock high heaven, but not reverse its ways.
How small the choice, from cradle to the grave,
Between the lot of hireling, help, or slave!
To each alike applies the stern decree,
That man shall labor; whether bond or free,
For all that toil, the recompense we claim —
Food, fire, a home, and clothing — is the same.
　The manumitted serfs of Europe find
Unchanged this sad estate of all mankind;
What blessing to the churl has freedom proved,
What want supplied, what task or toil removed?
Hard work and scanty wages still their lot,
In youth o'erlabored, and in age forgot,
The mocking boon of freedom they deplore,
In wants, and labors never known before.
　Free but in name — the slaves of endless toil,
In Britain still they turn the stubborn soil,
Spread on each sea her sails for every mart,
Ply in her cities every useful art;

But vainly may the peasant toil and groan
To speed the plow in furrows not his own;
In vain the art is plied, the sail is spread,
The day's work offered for the daily bread;
With hopeless eye, the pauper hireling sees
The homeward sail swell proudly to the breeze,
Rich fabrics wrought by his unequaled hand,
Borne by each breeze to every distant land;
For him, no boon successful commerce yields,
For him, no harvest crowns the joyous fields;
The streams of wealth that foster pomp and pride,
No food nor shelter for his wants provide;
He fails to win, by toil intensely hard,
The bare subsistence — labor's least reward.

In squalid hut — a kennel for the poor,
Or noisome cellar, stretched upon the floor,
His clothing rags, of filthy straw his bed,
With offal from the gutter daily fed,
Thrust out from nature's board, the hireling lies —
No place for him that common board supplies,
No neighbor helps, no charity attends,
No philanthropic sympathy befriends;
None heed the needy wretch's dying groan,
He starves unsuccored, perishes unknown.

These are the miseries, such the wants, the cares,
The bliss that freedom for the serf prepares;
Vain is his skill in each familiar task,
Capricious fashion shifts her Protean mask,
His ancient craft gives work and bread no more,
And want and death sit scowling at his door.

. . . . .

Hesperian lands, beyond the Atlantic wave,
Home of the poor and refuge of the brave,
Who, vainly striving with oppression, fly
To find new homes beneath a happier sky;
Hither, to quiet vale or mountainside,
Where peace and nature undisturbed abide,
In humble scenes unwonted lore to learn,
Patriot and prince their banished footsteps turn.

. . . . .

Here, with determined will and patient toil,
From wood and swamp he wins the fertile soil;
To every hardship stern endurance brings,
And builds a fortune undisturbed by kings;
Fair fields of wealth and ease his children find,
Nor heed the homes their fathers left behind.
Companions of his toil, the axe to wield,

To guide the plow and reap the teeming field,
A sable multitude unceasing pour
From Niger's banks and Congo's deadly shore;
No willing travelers they, that widely roam,
Allured by hope to seek a happier home,
But victims to the trader's thirst for gold,
Kidnapped by brothers, and by fathers sold,
The bondsman born, by native masters reared,
The captive band in recent battle spared;
For English merchants bought; across the main,
In British ships, they go for Britain's gain;
Forced on her subjects in dependent lands,
By cruel hearts and avaricious hands,
New tasks they learn, new masters they obey,
And bow submissive to the white man's sway.
  But Providence, by his o'erruling will,
Transmutes to lasting good the transient ill,
Makes crime itself the means of mercy prove,
And avarice minister to works of love.
In this new home, whate'er the Negro's fate —
More bless'd his life than in his native state!

   . . . . .

  And now, with sturdy hand and cheerful heart,
He learns to master every useful art,
To forge the axe, to mold the rugged share,
The ship's brave keel for angry waves prepare:
The rising wall obeys his plastic will,
And the loom's fabric owns his ready skill.

   . . . . .

  In broader limits, by the loftier maize,
The silklike cotton all its wealth displays:
Through forked leaves, in endless rows unfold
Gay blossoms tinged with purple dyes and gold;
To suns autumnal bursting pods disclose
Their fleeces, spotless as descending snows;
These, a rich freight, a thousand ships receive,
A thousand looms with fairy fingers weave;
And hireling multitudes in other lands
Are blessed with raiment from the Negro's hands.

   . . . . .

New life he gives to Europe's busy marts,
To all the world new comforts and new arts;
Loom, spinner, merchant, from his hands derive
Their wealth, and myriads by his labor thrive;
While slothful millions, hopeless of relief,

The slaves of pagan priest and brutal chief,
Harassed by wars upon their native shore,
Still lead the savage life they led before.

   Instructed thus, and in the only school
Barbarians ever know — a master's rule,
The Negro learns each civilizing art
That softens and subdues the savage heart,
Assumes the tone of those with whom he lives,
Acquires the habit that refinement gives,
And slowly learns, but surely, while a slave,
The lessons that his country never gave.

. . . . .

   Hence is the Negro come, by God's command,
For wiser teaching to a foreign land;
If they who brought him were by Mammon driven,
Still have they served, blind instruments of Heaven;
And though the way be rough, the agent stern,
No better mode can human wits discern,
No happier system wealth or virtue find,
To tame and elevate the Negro mind:
Thus mortal purposes, whate'er their mood,
Are only means with Heaven for working good;
And wisest they who labor to fulfill,
With zeal and hope, the all-directing will,
And in each change that marks the fleeting year,
Submissive see God's guiding hand appear.

. . . . .

   But if, though wise and good the purposed end,
Reproach and scorn the instrument attend;
If, when the final blessing is confessed,
Still the vile slaver all the world detest.

. . . . .

But modern slavers, more sagacious grown,
In all the wrong, can see no part their own;
They drag the Negro from his native shore,
Make him a slave, and then his fate deplore;
Sell him in distant countries, and when sold,
Revile the buyers, but retain the gold.

. . . . .

   Such now the maxims of the purer school
Of ethic lore, where sons of slavers rule;
No more allowed the Negro to enslave,
They damn the master and for freedom rave,
Strange modes of morals and of faith unfold,

Make newer gospels supersede the old,
Prove that ungodly Paul connived at sin,
And holier rites, like Mormon's priest, begin;
There, chief and teacher, Gerrit Smith appears,
There Tappan mourns, like Niobe, all tears,
Carnage and fire, mad Garrison invokes,
And Hale, with better temper, smirks and jokes.

. . . . .

There supple Sumner, with the Negro cause,
Plays the sly game for office and applause;
What boots it if the Negro sink or swim?
He wins the Senate — 'tis enough for him.

. . . . .

There Greeley, grieving at a brother's woe,
Spits with impartial spite on friend and foe;
His Negro griefs and sympathies produce
No nobler fruits than malice and abuse;
To each fanatical delusion prone,
He damns all creeds and parties but his own.

. . . . .

There Seward smiles the sweet perennial smile,
Skilled in the tricks of subtlety and guile;
The sliest schemer that the world e'er saw;
Peddler of sentiment and patent law;
Ready for fee or faction to display
His skill in either, if the practice pay,
But void of all that makes the frank and brave,
And smooth, and soft, and crafty like the slave.

. . . . .

There Stowe, with prostituted pen, assails
One-half her country in malignant tales;
Careless, like Trollope, whether truth she tells,
And anxious only how the libel sells,
To slander's mart she furnishes supplies,
And feeds its morbid appetite for lies
On fictions fashioned with malicious art,
The venal pencil and malignant heart,
With fact distorted, inference unsound,
Creatures in fancy, not in nature found.

. . . . .

These use the Negro, a convenient tool,
That yields substantial gain or party rule,
Gives what without it they could never know,

To Chase, distinction, courtly friends to Stowe,
To Parker, themes for miracles of rant,
And Beecher blesses with new gifts of cant.
The master's task has been the black to train,
To form his mind, his passions to restrain;
With anxious care and patience to impart
The knowledge that subdues the savage heart,
To give the Gospel lessons that control
The rudest breast and renovate the soul —
Who does, or gives as much, of all who raise
Their sland'rous cry for foreign pence or praise,
Of all the knaves who clamor and declaim
For party power or philanthropic fame,
Or use the Negro's fancied wrongs and woes
As pretty themes for maudlin verse or prose?

  Taught by the master's efforts, by his care,
Fed, clothed, protected many a patient year,
From trivial numbers now to millions grown,
With all the white man's useful arts their own,
Industrious, docile, skilled in wood and field,
To guide the plow, the sturdy axe to wield,
The Negroes schooled by slavery embrace
The highest portion of the Negro race;
And none the savage native will compare,
Of barbarous Guinea, with its offspring here.
  If bound to daily labor while he lives,
His is the daily bread that labor gives;
Guarded from want, from beggary secure,
He never feels what hireling crowds endure,
Nor knows, like them, in hopeless want to crave,
For wife and child, the comforts of the slave,
Or the sad thought that, when about to die,
He leaves them to the cold world's charity,
And sees them slowly seek the poorhouse door —
The last, vile, hated refuge of the poor.

            . . . . .

No mobs of factious workmen gather here,
No strikes we dread, no lawless riots fear;
Nuns, from their convent driven, at midnight fly,
Churches, in flames, ask vengeance from the sky,
Seditious schemes in bloody tumults end,
Parsons incite, and senators defend,
But not where slaves their easy labors ply,
Safe from the snare, beneath a master's eye;
In useful tasks engaged, employed their time,
Untempted by the demagogue to crime,
Secure they toil, uncursed their peaceful life,

With labor's hungry broils and wasteful strife.
No want to goad, no faction to deplore,
The slave escapes the perils of the poor.

. . . . .

   Why peril, then, the Negro's humble joys,
Why make him free, if freedom but destroys?
Why take him from that lot that now bestows
More than the Negro elsewhere ever knows —
Home, clothing, food, light labor, and content,
Childhood in play, and age in quiet spent,
To vex his life with factious strife and broil,
To crush his nature with unwonted toil,
To see him, like the Indian tribes, a prey
To war or peace, destruction or decay?

. . . . .

   Let, then, the master still his course pursue,
"With heart and hope" perform his mission too;
Heaven's ruling power confessed, with patient care
The end subserve, the fitting means prepare,
In faith unshaken guide, restrain, command,
With strong and steady, yet indulgent hand,
Justly, "as in the great Taskmaster's eye,"
His task perform — the Negro's wants supply,
The Negro's hand to useful arts incline,
His mind enlarge, his moral sense refine,
With Gospel truth his simple heart engage,
To his dull eyes unseal its sacred page,
By gradual steps his feebler nature raise,
Deserve, if not receive, the good man's praise;
The factious knave defy, and meddling fool,
The pulpit brawler and his lawless tool,
Scorn the grave cant, the supercilious sneer,
The mawkish sentiment and maudlin tear,
Assured that God all human power bestows,
Controls its uses, and its purpose knows,
And that each lot on earth to mortals given,
Its duties duly done, is blessed of Heaven.

57.

Charlotte L. Forten: The Difficulty of Being a Negro Christian

Charlotte Forten was the child of a distinguished Negro family that had long worked toward the abolition of slavery. Her father, a wealthy Philadelphia merchant, sent Charlotte to school in Salem, Massachusetts, where she lived with a Negro Abolitionist family. It was there that she witnessed the capture of the fugitive slave Anthony Burns. She became a teacher and after the Civil War participated in the federal government's Sea Island program designed to instruct 10,000 former slaves in the rudiments of citizenship. The following selection from Miss Forten's Journal, *which was first published in 1953, is a vivid account of her daily struggle to live by Christian principles of love and tolerance in the face of overwhelming prejudice exhibited by whites toward her race.*

Source: *Journal of Charlotte L. Forten*, Ray A. Billington, ed., New York, 1953.

May 26, 1854. Had a conversation with Miss Shepard [grammar school principal in Salem] about slavery; she is, as I thought, thoroughly opposed to it, but does not agree with me in thinking that the churches and ministers are generally supporters of the infamous system; I believe it firmly.

Mr. Barnes, one of the most prominent of the Philadelphia clergy, who does not profess to be an Abolitionist, has declared his belief that "the American church is a bulwark of slavery."

Words cannot express all that I feel; all that is felt by the friends of freedom, when thinking of this great obstacle to the removal of slavery from our land. Alas! that it should be so.

June 2. Our worst fears are realized. The decision was against poor Burns [Anthony Burns, arrested in Boston under the Fugitive Slave Act], and he has been sent back to a bondage worse, a thousand times worse, than death.

With what scorn must that government be regarded which cowardly assembles thousands of soldiers to satisfy the demands of slaveholders; to deprive of his freedom a man, created in God's own image, whose sole offense is the color of his skin! And if resistance is offered to this outrage, these soldiers are to shoot down American citizens without mercy; and this by the express orders of a government which proudly boasts of being the freest in the world; this on the very soil where the Revolution of 1776 began.

I can write no more. A cloud seems hanging over me, over all our persecuted race, which nothing can dispel.

June 4. Tomorrow school commences, and although the pleasure I shall feel in again seeing my beloved teacher, and in resuming my studies, will be much saddened by recent events, yet they shall be a fresh incentive to more earnest study, to aid me in fitting myself for laboring in a holy cause, for enabling me to do much toward changing the condition of my oppressed and suffering people.

Would that those with whom I shall recite tomorrow could sympathize with me in this; would that they could look upon all

God's creatures without respect to color, feeling that it is character alone which makes the true man or woman!

June 5. Miss Church [a student from Nova Scotia] and I counted the merits of the first and second classes for Miss Shepard; after school, had an hour's conversation with her about slavery and prejudice.

I fully appreciate her kindness and sympathy with me; she wishes me to cultivate a Christian spirit in thinking of my enemies; I know it is right, and will endeavor to do so, but it does seem very difficult. . . .

June 25. This afternoon went to an antislavery meeting in Danvers, from which I have just returned. Mr. Foss spoke eloquently, and with that warmth and sincerity which evidently comes from the heart.

He said he was rejoiced that the people at the North were beginning to feel that slavery is no longer confined to the black man alone but that they too must wear the yoke; and they are becoming roused on the subject at last.

He spoke of the objections made by many to the Abolitionists, on the plea of their using too violent language; they say that the slaveholders are driven by it to worse measures; what they need is mild entreaty, etc. But the petition against the Nebraska Bill, couched in the very mildest terms by the clergymen of the North, was received even less favorably by the South than the hardest sayings of the Abolitionists; and they were abused and denounced more severely than the latter have ever been.

July 17. I have seen today a picture of a dear old English church. Oh, England, my heart yearns toward thee as to a loved and loving friend! I long to behold thee, to dwell in one of thy quiet homes, far from the scenes of my early childhood; far from the land, my native land, where I am hated and oppressed because God has given me a dark skin. How did this cruel, this absurd prejudice ever exist? How can it exist?

August 11. I have been thinking lately very much about death, that strange, mysterious, awful reality that is constantly around and among us, that power which takes away from us so many of those whom we love and honor, or those who have persecuted and oppressed us, our bitter enemies whom we vainly endeavor not to hate.

Oh! I long to be good, to be able to meet death calmly and fearlessly, strong in faith and holiness. But this I know can only be through One who died for us, through the pure and perfect love of Him who was all holiness and love.

But how can I hope to be worthy of His love while I still cherish this feeling toward my enemies, this unforgiving spirit? This is a question which I ask myself very often. Other things in comparison with this seem easy to overcome. But hatred of oppression seems to me so blended with hatred of the oppressor I cannot separate them. I feel that no other injury could be so hard to bear, so very hard to forgive, as that inflicted by cruel prejudice. How can I be a Christian when so many in common with myself, for no crime, suffer so cruelly, so unjustly?

September 5. I have suffered much today. My friends Mrs. Putnam [Negro wife of a Salem grocer] and her daughters were refused admission to the Museum, after having tickets given them, solely on account of their complexion. Insulting language was used to them. Of course they felt and exhibited deep, bitter indignation; but of what avail was it? None but to excite the ridicule of those contemptible creatures, miserable doughfaces who do not deserve the name of men. I will not attempt to write more. No words can express my feelings. But these cruel wrongs cannot be much longer endured. A day of retribution must come. God grant that it may come very soon!

September 12. I wonder that every colored person is not a misanthrope. Surely we have everything to make us hate mankind. I have met girls in the schoolroom — they have been thoroughly kind and cordial to me; perhaps the next day met them in the street — they feared to recognize me; these I can but regard now with scorn and contempt; once I liked them, believing them incapable of such meanness. Others gave the most distant recognition possible. I, of course, acknowledge no such recognitions, and they soon cease entirely.

These are but trifles, certainly, to the great public wrongs which we as a people are obliged to endure. But to those who experience them, these apparent trifles are most wearing and discouraging; even to the child's mind they reveal volumes of deceit and heartlessness, and early teach a lesson of suspicion and distrust.

O! it is hard to go through life meeting contempt with contempt, hatred with hatred, fearing, with too good reason, to love and trust hardly anyone whose skin is white, however lovable, attractive, and congenial in seeming.

In the bitter, passionate feelings of my soul, again and again there rises the questions — "When, oh! when shall this cease?" "Is there no help?" "How long, oh! How long must we continue to suffer, to endure?" Conscience answers it is wrong, it is ignoble to despair; let us labor earnestly and faithfully to acquire knowledge, to break down the barriers of prejudice and oppression. Let us take courage; never ceasing to work, hoping and believing that if not for us, for another generation there is a better, brighter day in store, when slavery and prejudice shall vanish before the glorious light of liberty and truth; when the rights of every colored man shall everywhere be acknowledged and respected, and he shall be treated as a *man* and a *brother!*

58.

ABRAHAM LINCOLN: Fragments on Government and Slavery

During his years as a state and national legislator and a lawyer in Illinois, Lincoln formulated a political philosophy that closely resembled the democratic liberalism of Thomas Jefferson. Although he took a moderate position on the slavery question (he did not want to interfere with the institution in the South), Lincoln's reverence for the principles of the Declaration of Independence rendered him morally opposed to any system that perpetuated enforced inequality. When he reentered political life in the turbulent year of the Kansas-Nebraska Act, he had learned to express his political ideas with wit and precise logic, as revealed in the following fragments on government and slavery, probably written on July 1, 1854.

Source: Nicolay-Hay, II, pp. 186-187.

THE LEGITIMATE OBJECT of government is to do for a community of people whatever they need to have done, but cannot do at all, or cannot so well do for themselves in their separate and individual capacities. In all that the people can individually do as well for themselves, government ought not to interfere.

The desirable things which the individuals of a people cannot do, or cannot well do, for themselves fall into two classes: those which have relation to wrongs, and those which have not. Each of these branch off into an infinite variety of subdivisions.

The first — that in relation to wrongs — embraces all crimes, misdemeanors, and non-performance of contracts. The other embraces all which, in its nature and without wrong, requires combined action, as public roads and highways, public schools, charities, pauperism, orphanage, estates of the deceased, and the machinery of government itself.

From this it appears that if all men were just, there still would be some, though not so much, need of government.

IF A CAN PROVE, however conclusively, that he may of right enslave B, why may not B snatch the same argument and prove equally that he may enslave A?

You say A is white, and B is black. It is color, then; the lighter having the right to enslave the darker? Take care. By this rule, you are to be slave to the first man you meet with a fairer skin than your own.

You do not mean color exactly? You mean the whites are intellectually the superiors of the blacks, and therefore have the right to enslave them? Take care again. By this rule, you are to be slave to the first man you meet with an intellect superior to your own.

But, say you, it is a question of interest; and if you can make it your interest, you have the right to enslave another. Very well. And if he can make it his interest, he has the right to enslave you.

59.

Abraham Lincoln: Against the Extension of Slavery

On May 30, 1854, Congress passed the Kansas-Nebraska Act, which repealed the Missouri Compromise and made slavery theoretically possible in all territories. Reaction in the North was immediate and vehement, and Senator Stephen A. Douglas, who was responsible for the bill, returned to his home state of Illinois to get away from the clamor against him and to defend the new law. Beginning at Springfield he made a series of speeches throughout the state. Abraham Lincoln, who had been out of the public eye since his term in Congress in 1847-1849, replied to Douglas on the issues that were disturbing the North. He gave the speech that is reprinted in part below at Peoria on October 16.

Source: Nicolay-Hay, II, pp. 190-262.

THE REPEAL OF THE MISSOURI COMPROMISE, and the propriety of its restoration, constitute the subject of what I am about to say. . . . And, as this subject is no other than part and parcel of the larger general question of domestic slavery, I wish to make and to keep the distinction between the existing institution and the extension of it so broad and so clear that no honest man can misunderstand me, and no dishonest one successfully misrepresent me. . . .

This declared indifference, but, as I must think, covert real zeal for the spread of slavery, I cannot but hate. I hate it because of the monstrous injustice of slavery itself. I hate it because it deprives our republican example of its just influence in the world; enables the enemies of free institutions with plausibility to taunt us as hypocrites; causes the real friends of freedom to doubt our sincerity; and especially because it forces so many good men among ourselves into an open war with the very fundamental principles of civil liberty, criticizing the Declaration of Independence, and insisting that there is no right principle of action but self-interest.

Before proceeding, let me say that I think I have no prejudice against the Southern people. They are just what we would be in their situation. If slavery did not now exist among them, they would not introduce it. If it did now exist among us, we should not instantly give it up. This I believe of the masses, North and South. Doubtless there are individuals on both sides who would not hold slaves under any circumstances, and others who would gladly introduce slavery anew if it were out of existence. We know that some Southern men do free their slaves, go North and become tip-top Abolitionists, while some Northern ones go South and become most cruel slave masters.

When Southern people tell us they are no more responsible for the origin of slavery than we are, I acknowledge the fact. When it is said that the institution exists and that it is very difficult to get rid of it in any satisfactory way, I can understand and appreciate the saying. I surely will not blame them for not doing what I should not know how to do myself. If all earthly power were given me, I should not know what to do as to the existing institution. My first impulse would be to free all the slaves and send them to Liberia, to their own native land. But a moment's reflection would convince me that whatever of high hope (as I think there is) there may be in this in the long run, its sudden execution is impossible. If they were all landed there in

a day, they would all perish in the next ten days, and there are not surplus shipping and surplus money enough to carry them there in many times ten days. What then? Free them all and keep them among us as underlings? Is it quite certain that this betters their condition? I think I would not hold one in slavery, at any rate; yet the point is not clear enough for me to denounce people upon.

What next? Free them and make them politically and socially our equals? My own feelings will not admit of this, and if mine would, we well know that those of the great mass of white peoples will not. Whether this feeling accords with justice and sound judgment is not the sole question, if, indeed, it is any part of it. A universal feeling, whether well- or ill-founded, cannot be safely disregarded. We cannot, then, make them equals. It does seem to me that systems of gradual emancipation might be adopted; but for their tardiness in this, I will not undertake to judge our brethren of the South.

When they remind us of their constitutional rights, I acknowledge them not grudgingly but fully and fairly; and I would give them any legislation for the reclaiming of their fugitives which should not, in its stringency, be more likely to carry a free man into slavery than our ordinary criminal laws are to hang an innocent one.

But all this, to my judgment, furnishes no more excuse for permitting slavery to go into our own free territory than it would for reviving the African slave trade by law. The law which forbids the bringing of slaves from Africa, and that which has so long forbidden the taking of them into Nebraska, can hardly be distinguished on any moral principle, and the repeal of the former could find quite as plausible excuses as that of the latter. . . .

Equal justice to the South, it is said, requires us to consent to the extension of slavery to new countries. That is to say, inasmuch as you do not object to my taking my hog to Nebraska, therefore I must not object to you taking your slave. Now I admit that this is perfectly logical, if there is no difference between hogs and Negroes. But while you thus require me to deny the humanity of the Negro, I wish to ask whether you of the South, yourselves, have ever been willing to do as much? It is kindly provided that of all those who come into the world, only a small percentage are natural tyrants. That percentage is no larger in the slave states than in the free. The great majority, South as well as North, have human sympathies of which they can no more divest themselves than they can of their sensibility to physical pain.

These sympathies in the bosoms of the Southern people manifest in many ways their sense of the wrong of slavery, and their consciousness that, after all, there is humanity in the Negro. If they deny this, let me address them a few plain questions. In 1820 you joined the North almost unanimously in declaring the African slave trade piracy and in annexing to it the punishment of death. Why did you do this? If you did not feel that it was wrong, why did you join in providing that men should be hung for it? The practice was no more than bringing wild Negroes from Africa to such as would buy them. But you never thought of hanging men for catching and selling wild horses, wild buffaloes, or wild bears.

Again, you have among you a sneaking individual of the class of native tyrants known as the "slave dealer." He watches your necessities and crawls up to buy your slave at a speculating price. If you cannot help it, you sell to him; but if you can help it, you drive him from your door. You despise him utterly. You do not recognize him as a friend, or even as an honest man. Your children must not play with his; they may rollick freely with the little Negroes, but not with the slave dealer's children. If you are obliged to deal with him, you try to get through the job without so much as touching him. It is common with you to join hands with the men you meet; but with the slave dealer you avoid the ceremony — instinctively shrinking from the snaky contact. If he grows rich and retires from business, you still remember him and still keep up the ban of nonintercourse upon him and his family. Now, why is this? You do not so treat the man who deals in corn, cotton, or tobacco.

And yet, again, there are in the United States and territories, including the District of Columbia, 433,643 free blacks. At $500 per head they are worth over $200 million. How comes this vast amount of property to be running about without owners? We do not see free horses or free cattle running at large. How is this? All these free blacks are the descendants of slaves or have been slaves themselves, and they would be slaves now but for something which has operated on their white owners, inducing them at vast pecuniary sacrifice to liberate them. What is that something? Is there any mistaking it? In all these cases it is your sense of justice and human sympathy continually telling you that the poor Negro has some natural right to himself; that those who deny it and make mere merchandise of him deserve kickings, contempt, and death.

And, now, why will you ask us to deny the humanity of the slave and estimate him as only the equal of the hog? Why ask us to do what you will not do yourselves? Why ask us to do for nothing what $200 million could not induce you to do?

But one great argument in the support of the repeal of the Missouri Compromise is still to come. That argument is "the sacred right of self-government." It seems our distinguished senator has found great difficulty in getting his antagonists, even in the Senate, to meet him fairly on this argument. Some poet has said: "Fools rush in where angels fear to tread." At the hazard of being thought one of the fools of this quotation, I meet that argument; I rush in, I take that bull by the horns.

I trust I understand and truly estimate the right of self-government. My faith in the proposition that each man should do precisely as he pleases with all which is exclusively his own lies at the foundation of the sense of justice there is in me. I extend the principles to communities of men as well as to individuals. I so extend it because it is politically wise as well as naturally just; politically wise in saving us from broils about matters which do not concern us. Here or at Washington, I would not trouble myself with the oyster laws of Virginia, or the cranberry laws of Indiana.

The doctrine of self-government is right — absolutely and eternally right — but it has no just application as here attempted. Or perhaps I should rather say that whether it has such application depends upon whether a Negro is not or is a man. If he is not a man, in that case he who is a man may, as a matter of self-government, do just what he pleases with him. But if the Negro is a man, is it not to that extent a total destruction of self-government to say that he too shall not govern himself? When the white man governs himself, that is self-government; but when he governs himself and also governs another man, that is more than self-government — that is despotism. If the Negro is a man, why then my ancient faith teaches me that "all men are created equal"; and that there can be no moral right in connection with one man's making a slave of another.

Judge Douglas frequently, with bitter irony and sarcasm, paraphrases our argument by saying: "The white people of Nebraska are good enough to govern themselves, but they are not good enough to govern a few miserable Negroes!" Well I doubt not that the people of Nebraska are, and will continue to be, as good as the average of people elsewhere. I do not say the contrary. What I do say is that no man is good enough to govern another man without that other's consent. I say this is the leading principle — the sheet anchor of American republicanism.

Our Declaration of Independence says:

> We hold these truths to be self-evident that all men are created equal, that they are endowed by their Creator with certain unalienable rights, that among these are life, liberty, and the pursuit of happiness. That, to secure these rights, governments are instituted among men, deriving their just powers from the consent of the governed.

I have quoted so much at this time merely to show that according to our ancient faith the just powers of governments are derived from the consent of the governed. Now the relation of master and slave is *pro tanto* [to that extent] a total violation of this principle. The master not only governs the slave without his consent but he governs him by a set of rules altogether different from those which he prescribes for himself. Allow all the governed an equal voice in the government, and that, and that only, is self-government. . . .

But Nebraska is urged as a great Union-saving measure. Well, I, too, go for saving the Union. Much as I hate slavery, I would consent to the extension of it rather than see the Union dissolved, just as I would consent to any great evil to avoid a greater one. But when I go to Union-saving, I must believe, at least, that the means I employ have some adaptation to the end. To my mind, Nebraska has no such adaptation. "It hath no relish of salvation in it." It is an aggravation, rather, of the only one thing which ever endangers the Union.

When it came upon us, all was peace and quiet. The nation was looking to the forming of new bonds of union, and a long course of peace and prosperity seemed to lie before us. In the whole range of possibility, there scarcely appears to me to have been anything out of which the slavery agitation could have been revived except the very project of repealing the Missouri Compromise. Every inch of territory we owned already had a definite settlement of the slavery question by which all parties were pledged to abide. Indeed, there was no uninhabited country on the continent which we could acquire, if we except some extreme northern regions which are wholly out of the question.

In this state of affairs, the genius of discord himself could scarcely have invented a way of again setting us by the ears but by turning back and destroying the peace measures of the past. The counsels of that genius seem to have prevailed; the Missouri Compromise was repealed, and here we are, in the midst of a new slavery agitation such, I think, as we have never seen before. Who is responsible for this? Is it those who resist the measure, or those who causelessly brought it forward and pressed it through, having reason to know, and in fact knowing, it must and would be so resisted? It could not but be expected by its author that it would be looked upon as a measure for the extension of slavery, aggravated by a gross breach of faith. Argue as you will, and long as you will, this is the naked front and aspect of the measure. And in this aspect it could not but produce agitation.

Slavery is founded in the selfishness of man's nature — opposition to it in his love of justice. These principles are an eternal antagonism; and when brought into collision so fiercely as slavery extension brings them, shocks and throes and convulsions must ceaselessly follow. Repeal the Missouri Compromise, repeal all compromises, repeal the Declaration of Independence, repeal all past history; you still cannot repeal human nature. It still will be the abundance of man's heart that slavery extension is wrong, and out of the abundance of his heart, his mouth will continue to speak. . . .

The Missouri Compromise ought to be restored. For the sake of the Union, it ought to be restored. We ought to elect a House of Representatives which will vote its restoration. If by any means we omit to do this, what follows? Slavery may or may not be established in Nebraska. But whether it be or not, we shall have repudiated — discarded from the councils of the nation — the spirit of compromise; for who, after this, will ever trust in a national compromise? The spirit of mutual concession — that spirit which first gave us the Constitution and which has thrice saved the Union — we shall have strangled and cast from us forever. And what shall we have in lieu of it? The South flushed with triumph and tempted to excess; the North betrayed, as they believe, brooding on wrong and burning for revenge. One side will provoke, the other resent. The one will taunt, the other defy; one aggresses, the other retaliates. Already a few in the North defy all constitutional restraints, resist the execution of the Fugitive Slave Law, and even menace the institution of slavery in the states where it exists.

Already a few in the South claim the constitutional right to take and to hold slaves in the free states, demand the revival of the slave trade, and demand a treaty with Great Britain by which fugitive slaves may be reclaimed from Canada. As yet they are but few on either side. It is a grave question for lovers of the Union, whether the final destruction of the Missouri Compromise, and with it the spirit of all compromise, will or will not embolden and embitter each of these and fatally increase the number of both.

But restore the Compromise, and what then? We thereby restore the national faith, the national confidence, the national feeling of brotherhood. We thereby reinstate the spirit of concession and compromise — that spirit which has never failed us in past perils and which may be safely trusted for all the future. The South ought to join in doing this. The peace of the nation is as dear to them as to us. In memories of the past and hopes of the future, they share as largely as we. It would be on their part a great act — great in its spirit and great in its effect. It would be worth to the nation a hundred years' purchase of peace and prosperity. . . .

I particularly object to the new position which the avowed principle of this Nebraska law gives to slavery in the body politic. I object to it because it. assumes that there can be moral right in the enslaving of one man by another. I object to it as a dangerous dalliance for a few people; a sad evidence that, feeling prosperity, we forget right; that liberty, as a principle, we have ceased to revere. I object to it because the fathers of the republic eschewed and rejected it. The argument of "necessity" was the only argument they ever admitted in favor of slavery, and so far, and so far only as it carried them, did they ever go. They found the institution existing among us, which they could not help; and they cast blame upon the British king for having permitted its introduction. Before the Constitution, they prohibited its introduction into the Northwestern Territory — the only country we owned then free from it. At the framing and adoption of the Constitution, they forbore to so much as mention the word "slave" or "slavery" in the whole instrument.

In the provision for the recovery of fugitives, the slave is spoken of as a "person held to service or labor." In that prohibiting the abolition of the African slave trade for twenty years, that trade is spoken of as "the migration or importation of such persons as any of the states now existing shall think proper to admit," etc. These are the only provisions alluding to slavery. Thus the thing is hid away in the Constitution, just as an afflicted man hides away a wen or a cancer which he dares not cut out at once lest he bleed to death; with the promise, nevertheless, that the cutting may begin at a certain time. Less than this our fathers could not do; and more they would not do. Necessity drove them so far, and further they would not go. But this is not all. The earliest Congress under the Constitution took the same view of slavery. They hedged and hemmed it in to the narrowest limits of necessity.

In 1794 they prohibited an outgoing slave trade; that is, the taking of slaves from the United States to sell.

In 1798 they prohibited the bringing of slaves from Africa into the Mississippi Territory, this territory then comprising what are now the states of Mississippi and Alabama. This was ten years before they had the authority to do the same thing as to the states existing at the adoption of the Constitution.

In 1800 they prohibited American citizens from trading in slaves between foreign countries — as, for instance, from Africa to Brazil.

In 1803 they passed a law in aid of one or two slave-state laws, in restraint of the internal slave trade.

In 1807, in apparent hot haste, they passed the law, nearly a year in advance, to take effect the first day of 1808 — the very first day the Constitution would permit — prohibiting the African slave trade by heavy pecuniary and corporal penalties.

In 1820, finding these provisions ineffectual, they declared the slave-trade piracy and annexed to it the extreme penalty of death. While all this was passing in the general government, five or six of the original slave states had adopted systems of gradual emancipation by which the institution was rapidly becoming extinct within these limits.

Thus we see that the plain, unmistakable spirit of that age toward slavery was hostility to the principle, and toleration only by necessity.

But now it is to be transformed into a

"sacred right." Nebraska brings it forth, places it on the highroad to extension and perpetuity; and, with a pat on its back, says to it, "Go, and Godspeed you." Henceforth it is to be the chief jewel of the nation — the very figurehead of the ship of state. Little by little, but steadily as man's march to the grave, we have been giving up the old for the new faith. Near eighty years ago we began by declaring that all men are created equal; but now from that beginning we have run down to the other declaration, that for some men to enslave others is a "sacred right of self-government." These principles cannot stand together. They are as opposite as God and Mammon, and whoever holds to the one must despise the other.

When Pettit, in connection with his support of the Nebraska bill, called the Declaration of Independence "a self-evident lie," he only did what consistency and candor require all other Nebraska men to do. Of the forty-odd Nebraska senators who sat present and heard him, no one rebuked him. Nor am I apprised that any Nebraska newspaper, or any Nebraska orator in the whole nation, has ever yet rebuked him. If this had been said among Marion's men, Southerners though they were, what would have become of the man who said it? If this had been said to the men who captured André, the man who said it would probably have been hung sooner than André was. If it had been said in old Independence Hall seventy-eight years ago, the very doorkeeper would have throttled the man and thrust him into the street.

Let no one be deceived. The spirit of '76 and the spirit of Nebraska are utter antagonisms, and the former is being rapidly displaced by the latter.

Fellow countrymen, Americans — South as well as North — shall we make no effort to arrest this? Already the liberal party throughout the world express the apprehension "that the one retrograde institution in America is undermining the principles of progress and fatally violating the noblest political system the world ever saw." This is not the taunt of enemies but the warning of friends. Is it quite safe to disregard it, to despise it? Is there no danger to liberty itself in discarding the earliest practice and first precept of our ancient faith? In our greedy chase to make profit of the Negro, let us beware lest we "cancel and tear in pieces" even the white man's charter of freedom.

Our republican robe is soiled and trailed in the dust. Let us repurify it. Let us turn and wash it white in the spirit, if not the blood, of the Revolution. Let us turn slavery from its claims of "moral right" back upon its existing legal rights and its arguments of "necessity." Let us return it to the position our fathers gave it, and there let it rest in peace. Let us readopt the Declaration of Independence and with it the practices and policy which harmonize with it. Let North and South, let all Americans, let all lovers of liberty everywhere join in the great and good work. If we do this, we shall not only have saved the Union but we shall have so saved it as to make and to keep it forever worthy of the saving. We shall have so saved it that the succeeding millions of free, happy people, the world over, shall rise up and call us blessed to the latest generations.

A peculiar institution.

Phrase describing slavery in the South, the origin of which is mysterious. One of the earliest known uses is in an article in the *New York Tribune*, Oct. 19, 1854.

60.

William H. Seward: Providing for the Indigent Insane

*Among the several reform interests William H. Seward sought to advance in his work
as an attorney, as governor of New York, and as a U.S. senator, was improved
treatment of the mentally ill. His interest in the problem was evident as early as
1846, when he defended William Freeman, a poor insane Negro, in a murder case.
In that case, which he accepted at the risk of his career, Seward made one of his most
eloquent addresses in behalf of considerate treatment for the insane. Eight years
later he supported a Senate bill to provide public land for institutions to care for the
indigent insane. In response to President Pierce's veto of the bill, Seward made a
speech on June 19, 1854, from which the following selection is taken.*

Source: *Globe, App.,* 33 Cong., 1 Sess., pp. 959-961.

CONGRESS HAS PASSED A BILL by which 10 million acres of the public domain are granted to the several states, with unquestioned equality, on condition that they shall accept the same and sell the lands at not less than $1 per acre, and safely invest the gross proceeds and forever apply the interest thereon to the maintenance of their indigent insane inhabitants. This bill is a contribution to the states, made from a peculiar national resource, at a time when the Treasury is overflowing. It is made at the suggestion, and it is not stating the case too strongly to say, through the unaided, unpaid, and purely disinterested influence of an American woman [Miss Dix] who, while all other members of society have been seeking how to advance their own fortunes and happiness, or the prosperity and greatness of their country, has consecrated her life to the relief of the most pitiable form in which the Divine Ruler afflicts our common humanity.

The purpose of the bill has commended it to our warmest and most active sympathies. Not a voice has censured it in either house of Congress. It is the one only purpose of legislation, sufficiently great to arrest attention, that has met with universal approbation throughout the country during the present session. It seems as if some sad fatality attends our public action, when this measure is singled out from among all others, to be baffled and defeated by an executive veto. Such, however, is the fact. The bill has been returned by the President with objections which it is now our constitutional duty to consider. . . .

In considering the President's message, we are struck with the fact that it is desultory, illogical, and confused. While commending the purpose of the bill, the President denies the expediency of the measure, and denies also the power of Congress to adopt it. It is impossible, however, to separate the argument directed against the expediency of the measure from the argument directed against the power. So the argument against the expediency rests chiefly on an assumption that the measure is a usurpation of power, while the argument against the power reposes chiefly on the inexpediency of its exercise.

This criticism is important, because the

confusion I have described impairs the force of the argument, and because, moreover, Congress may well confide in their own conclusions as to the expediency of a measure, while they are bound to pay extraordinary respect to executive suggestions impugning its constitutionality. I do not stop to demonstrate the correctness of this criticism. Every senator who has discussed the message, on either side, has betrayed, I think, an embarrassment resulting from it.

In the second place, the message seems to me, I do not say disingenuous, but singularly unfair and unjust in the statement of the question.

The bill confines itself to a single purpose, viz.: that of aiding the states in enabling them to maintain one peculiar class of destitute persons, by an appropriation of equal and just parts of the public domain, leaving all other objects and all other sources of public wealth out of view, and abstaining altogether from interference with the states in the performance of even that one duty.

But the President is not content to state the question thus. He approaches it by an induction. He says:

It cannot be questioned that if Congress have power to make provision for the indigent insane without the limits of this district, it has the same power to provide for the indigent who are not insane, and thus to transfer to the federal government the charge of all the poor in all the states.

After amplification of this proposition, without argument, the President arrives at the statement of the question before him, and announces it in these words:

The question presented, therefore, clearly is upon the constitutionality and propriety of the federal government assuming to enter into a novel and vast field of legislation, namely, that of providing for the care and support of all those among the people of the United States who by any form of calamity become fit objects of public philanthropy.

The Granger Collection

William H. Seward, engraving after a painting by Inman

You need only place this statement of the case by the side of the President's own statement of the provisions of the bill to enable you to see that it is flagrantly erroneous and unjust. But I will illustrate it directly. Congress does, in unquestioned conformity with the Constitution, exercise some powers in the states which are concurrent with similar powers enjoyed by the states themselves.

Thus Congress establishes here and there, throughout the states, hospitals for sick and disabled seamen. Is that equivalent to assuming the support and care of all the poor, on land as well as sea, belonging to the states? Congress establishes lighthouses and constructs harbors of refuge within the states, and provides regulation for the construction and management of steamboats and ships on navigable waters within the states. Is that equivalent to usurpation of the entire control over commerce and navigation within the states? Congress distributes seeds and treatises on agriculture. Is that equivalent to usurpation of jurisdiction over agriculture throughout the states? Congress discriminates by bounties, drawbacks, and duties, so as to favor agriculture, the fisheries, and manufactures. Is that equivalent to assumption of supreme and exclusive power over all those great national interests? Congress prescribes regulations of the militia, and furnishes to the states arms, ammunition, and ordnance for the equipment and exercise of the militia. Is that equivalent to usurpation of the entire support, control, and direction of the armed police of the states?

I call your attention, next, sir, to the fact that this message presents unfairly the relative structures and characters of the federal Union and of the states. The President says:

> Are we not too prone to forget that the federal Union is the creature of the states, and not they of the federal Union?

And again he says that

> The independent and sovereign states united themselves for certain specified objects and purposes, and for those only.

thereby implying that the states are still entirely sovereign, while the federal government is a mere confederation, and not equally sovereign within its sphere. Now, no one ever thought that the states were creatures of the federal Union; but it is equally true, in my judgment, that the federal Union is not the creature of the states. Both are states connected with and yet independent of each other. Each of them was established directly by the people: the several state governments by the people of the states, respectively, and the federal Union by the people of all the states. Each is shorn of some attributes of sovereignty, and each is supreme within its sphere.

Once more: the message is unfair in drawing into the discussion and discussing a question whether a power to pass the bill can be derived from the 8th Section of the Constitution, which gives Congress the authority "to lay and collect taxes, duties, imposts, and excises, to pay the debts and provide for the common defense and general welfare of the United States." No member of Congress has advocated that principle since this bill was inaugurated half a dozen years ago. The principle is obsolete, if it ever had advocates. No statesman has advocated it in or out of Congress for a period of forty years.

While, therefore, the President's expositions of that subject may serve to raise prejudices against the bill, it is quite certain that they are altogether foreign from a consideration of its merits.

If it shall seem to you, Mr. President, that the criticisms I have offered might have been spared, I hope it will be a sufficient defense to say that those criticisms dispose of two-thirds of the entire message of the President, and leave only two or three points in the whole case to be examined. In the manner I have described, the President reaches at last the principal question, viz.: whether Congress has power to pass this bill by virtue of the 3rd Section of the 4th Article of the Constitution, which is as follows:

> The Congress shall have power to dispose of and make all needful rules and regulations respecting the territory or other property belonging to the United States; and nothing in this Constitution shall be so construed as to prejudice any claims of the United States, or of any particular state.

The President denies that this section contains the power claimed by Congress. Now, it is apparent, first, that the land appropriated by the bill is a part of "the territory or other property of the United States"; and, second, that the term "to dispose of" includes any way and every way by which Congress can divest the United States of those lands, whether by sales to states or individuals, or by gifts to states or individuals.

The bill apportions and bestows the lands among and upon the states and is therefore constitutional, unless it can be shown that the absolute power contained in that section is limited by some other provision of the Constitution which inhibits the proposed disposal of them. The President says that there is such an inhibition, and he finds it in the last clause of the section collated with the 6th Article, which is as follows, to wit:

> All debts contracted and engagements entered into, before the adoption of this Constitution, shall be as valid against the United States under this Constitution as under the Confederation.

The President brings into this connection also a provision contained in the deed by which Virginia ceded her share of the public domain of the United States, to wit:

> All the lands within the territory so ceded to the United States, and not reserved for, or appropriated to, any of the beforementioned purposes, or disposed of in bounties to the officers and soldiers of the American Army, shall be considered a common fund for the use and benefit of such of the United States as have become or shall become members of the confederation or federal alliance of the said states, Virginia included, according to their usual respective proportions in the general charge and expenditure, and shall be faithfully and *bona fide* disposed of for that purpose, and for no other purpose whatever.

The President adds:

> Here the object for which these lands are to be disposed of are clearly set forth.

And he adds that

> The provisions recited not only contain no implication in favor of the contemplated grant but furnish the strongest authority against it.

I proceed to examine this argument, and remark, first, that the words quoted from the 3rd Section of the 4th Article of the Constitution, viz.: "And nothing in this Constitution shall be so construed as to prejudice any claims of the United States, or of any particular state," have no application here.

We know historically, and from the commentators in *The Federalist*, that there was, at the time of the adoption of the Constitution, much uncertainty about the boundary lines between the states and, of course, about their respective titles to, or interest in, the unoccupied domain which was ceded by the several states to the United States, and also that all of the states interested in the said domain had not executed deeds of cession at the time the Constitution was framed by the Convention. And we know, from the same evidence, that the clause relied upon by the President was designed merely to save any rights or titles which had not been and should not be ceded to the United States, and also at the same time to save just claims which the United States had, by or independent of such deeds of cession. Now, it is absurd to say that the bill before us prejudices any claim of the United States; for it assumes that the property disposed of is exclusively the property of the United States. It is equally absurd to say that it prejudices the claim of any particular state; for no state has laid any claim, or can lay claim, to the lands in question. This disposes of the supposed limitation in the 3rd Section of the 4th Article.

The 6th Article manifestly has no relation to the public domain. It is in these words:

> All debts contracted and engagements entered into, before the adoption of this Constitution, shall be as valid against the United States under this Constitution as under the Confederation.

It is satisfied by applying it to the then existing public debt, and to then existing treaties. We learn from *The Federalist* that it was so understood by the framers of the Constitution.

Mr. Madison recites it in the forty-third number of *The Federalist*, with this remark:

> This can only be considered as a declaratory proposition, and may have been inserted, among other reasons, for the satisfaction of the foreign creditors of the United States, who cannot be strangers

to the pretended doctrine that a change in the political form of society has the magical effect of dissolving its moral obligations.

There is, then, no limitation or qualification of the absolute power of Congress to dispose of the domain contained in the Constitution itself. Nor does the provision contained in the deed of cession from Virginia affect it.

Let us now concede that the constitutional power to dispose of the public domain is affected, and even controlled, by the deed of cession from Virginia. There is nothing in the bill which conflicts with that provision. The provision is only this: that the lands ceded by Virginia shall be considered a *common fund,* for the use and benefit of all the states, and be faithfully and *bona fide* disposed of for that purpose. The bill under consideration does consider the 10 million acres a common fund for the use and benefit of all the states, and does faithfully and *bona fide* dispose of it for their common and equal use and benefit.

But the President argues that the public domain, or the proceeds resulting from sales of it, and not expended, cannot be apportioned among the states, but must remain a common fund, which, as it has been pledged heretofore, and is now pledged, so hereafter it may again be pledged for public debts. But this argument proves too much. It would invalidate all grants of bounty lands in consideration of past services in the Army and Navy of the United States. And it would equally invalidate all grants for the construction of canals and railroads, neither of which modes of disposing of the public lands has the President condemned.

The President seeks to extricate himself from this dilemma by raising a theory which has no foundation in the Constitution, or in any contemporaneous exposition of it, and justifies the grants which have been made for the construction of railroads and canals upon the principle that the United States, being a landholder within

the states, may lawfully give away one portion of its lands, without consideration, for the purpose of thereby enhancing the value of what remains. But it is apparent that the constitutionality of a grant is thus made to depend upon the fact that the value of the land given away is not more than the increase of the value of what remains; and so that government must necessarily raise the price of the lands retained to the utmost of their increased value.

Such a course is never pursued. The government which should pursue it might act as a prudent landholder, but would, at the same time, act as an oppressive and tyrannical ruler. This theory, that the government must act as a prudent landholder, seems to me altogether fanciful. It is not capable of universal application at all places and under all circumstances. A prudent landholder might give away one-fourth of his land, in some places, to enhance the value of the rest; and at other times half, and at other times three-fourths, but not everywhere and always the same proportion.

But there is another consideration which is fatal to the theory.

The policy which a prudent landholder might pursue, merely as a landholder, to increase the value of his estate might be altogether inconsistent with the policy which a great, rich, and beneficent government ought to pursue to increase the wealth, the greatness, and the strength of a nation. Many a prudent proprietor has changed his allegiance to save his domain; and many a brave people have sacrificed their domain to save their liberties. The United States are not a mere landowner. They are a state — a political state. They are, indeed, a landowner; and they ought to be a prudent one. But landownership is the lowest of their functions, and land speculation ought to be the last which they should assume.

Without tracing further this new and idle theory of prudent proprietorship, it may be dismissed with two remarks. First, that it rests altogether upon the restraining provision contained in the deed of cession from Virginia, which applied only to the original domain of the United States and not to those portions since acquired; second, that the 10 million acres apportioned by this bill are virtually to be selected in regions subsequently acquired and entirely distinct from that original domain.

The President's next objection is that there is an act of Jan. 28, 1847, which pledges the sales of the public lands for the payment of the debt contracted in the Mexican War. I reply, first, that that debt is virtually paid, insomuch as we have a surplus revenue, constantly accumulating, and are buying up the stock in advance of its maturity, at enormous premiums, and the creditor who complains of this bill may at once receive payment in full; second, that pledge was never understood to prohibit judicious appropriations of the public domain, and the objection, if good against this bill, annuls all the laws by which we have given homesteads to the survivors of all our wars, as well as those by means of which we have procured capitalists to cover with a network of railroads the broad region which stretches away from the base of the Allegheny Mountains to the Mississippi River.

The President expresses deep concern lest this contribution by the federal government to the states should impair their vigor and independence. But it is not easy to see how a contribution which they are at liberty to reject, and which they are to apply to a necessary and to a proper purpose of government, in entire independence of the federal government, can wound their self-respect or deprive them of any of their attributes of sovereignty.

The President is, moreover, deeply disturbed by an apprehension that if the policy of this bill should be pursued, its noble purposes would be defeated and the fountains of charity within the states would be dried up. The President must not needlessly afflict himself in this wise on the score of humanity. Experience is against his fears. Congress has never manifested a disposition of profuse liberality toward the states. Every community that has received from the federal territory or property military bounties or pensions is at least as brave and patriotic as it was before. Every community that has received from the same sources contributions for the purposes of internal improvement is more enterprising than before. Every community that has received aid for its schools of learning has been rendered more zealous and more munificent in the cause of education.

Thus, sir, I have reviewed the President's objections. In conclusion, it remains for me to express the opinion that, as in the early days of the republic, there was a school of latitudinarian construction of the Constitution, which school was quite erroneous, so, also, there was a school whose maxim was strict construction of the Constitution, and this school has accumulated precedents and traditions equally calculated to extinguish the spirit of the Constitution. Circumstances have together changed since that school was founded. The states were then rich and strong; the Union was poor and powerless. Virginia lent to the United States $100,000 to build their Capitol.

But the states could not enlarge themselves. They possessed respectively either no public lands at all or very small domains, and to such domains they have added nothing by purchase or conquest. Charged with all the expenses of municipal administration, including the relief of the indigent, the cure of the diseased, the education of the people, and the removal of natural obstructions to trade and intercourse, they reserved, nevertheless, only the power to raise revenues by direct taxation, one which always was, and always will be, regarded with jealousy and dislike, and is therefore never one that can be freely exercised.

The Union, on the contrary, by conquest and purchase, has quadrupled its domain, and is in possession of superabundant revenues derived from that domain and from imposts upon foreign commerce, while it also enjoys the power of direct taxation. Contrast the meager salaries of the officers of the states with the liberal ones enjoyed by the agents of the Union. Contrast the ancient, narrow, and cheerless Capitols of Annapolis, Harrisburg, and Albany with this magnificent edifice, amplifying itself to the north and the south, while it is surrounded by gardens traversed by spacious avenues and embellished with fountains and statuary, and you see at once that the order of things has been reversed, and that it tends now not merely to concentration but to consolidation. I know not how others may be affected by this tendency, but I confess that it moves me to do all that I can, by a fair construction of the Constitution, not to abate the federal strength and diminish the majesty of the Union but to invigorate and aggrandize the states, and to enable them to maintain their just equilibrium in our grand but exquisitely contrived political system.

61.

The Ostend Manifesto

In the four years between the Compromise of 1850 and the passage of the Kansas-Nebraska Act, during which the South was prevented from acquiring any new slave areas within the territorial limits of the United States, slaveholders prevailed upon President Franklin Pierce to secure suitable lands outside the country. In August 1854, Secretary of State William Marcy instructed the American ministers to France, Spain, and Great Britain to investigate the feasibility of obtaining Cuba from Spain. The following report of Ministers John Mason, Pierre Soulé, and James Buchanan, drafted at Ostend, Belgium, on October 18, 1854, encouraged such a venture, but the manifesto aroused so much Northern protest that the plan was abandoned. Marcy later repudiated the report and Soulé resigned his mission, but Buchanan was rewarded with Southern support in his bid for the presidency in 1856.

Source: 33 Congress, 2 Session, House Executive Document No. 93.

THE UNDERSIGNED, in compliance with the wish expressed by the President in the several confidential dispatches you have addressed to us, respectively, to that effect, have met in conference, first at Ostend, in Belgium, on the 9th, 10th, and 11th instant, and then at Aix-la-Chapelle, in Prussia, on the days next following, up to the date hereof. There has been a full and unreserved interchange of views and sentiments between us, which we are most happy to inform you has resulted in a cordial coincidence of opinion on the grave and important subjects submitted to our consideration.

We have arrived at the conclusion, and are thoroughly convinced, that an immedi-

New York Historical Society

Cartoon criticizing Buchanan for his statement that the United States was justified in using force to obtain Cuba from Spain

ate and earnest effort ought to be made by the government of the United States to purchase Cuba from Spain at any price for which it can be obtained, not exceeding the sum of $—.

The proposal should, in our opinion, be made in such a manner as to be presented through the necessary diplomatic forms to the Supreme Constituent Cortes about to assemble. On this momentous question, in which the people both of Spain and the United States are so deeply interested, all our proceedings ought to be open, frank, and public. They should be of such a character as to challenge the approbation of the world.

We firmly believe that, in the progress of human events, the time has arrived when the vital interests of Spain are as seriously involved in the sale as those of the United States in the purchase of the island, and that the transaction will prove equally honorable to both nations.

Under these circumstances we cannot anticipate a failure, unless possibly through the malign influence of foreign powers who possess no right whatever to interfere in the matter.

We proceed to state some of the reasons which have brought us to this conclusion, and, for the sake of clearness, we shall specify them under two distinct heads:

1. The United States ought, if practicable, to purchase Cuba with as little delay as possible.

2. The probability is great that the government and Cortes of Spain will prove willing to sell it, because this would essentially promote the highest and best interests of the Spanish people.

[First] then, it must be clear to every reflecting mind that, from the peculiarity of its geographical position and the considerations attendant on it, Cuba is as necessary to the North American republic as any of its present members, and that it belongs naturally to that great family of states of which the Union is the providential nursery.

From its locality it commands the mouth of the Mississippi and the immense and annually increasing trade which must seek this avenue to the ocean. On the numerous navigable streams, measuring an aggregate course of some 30,000 miles, which disembogue themselves through this magnificent river into the Gulf of Mexico, the increase of the population within the last ten years amounts to more than that of the entire Union at the time Louisiana was annexed to it.

The natural and main outlet to the products of this entire population, the highway of their direct intercourse with the Atlantic and the Pacific states, can never be secure, but must ever be endangered while Cuba is a dependency of a distant power, in whose possession it has proved to be a source of constant annoyance and embarrassment to their interests. Indeed, the Union can never enjoy repose nor possess reliable security as long as Cuba is not embraced within its boundaries.

Its immediate acquisition by our government is of paramount importance, and we cannot doubt but that it is a consummation devoutly wished for by its inhabitants.

The intercourse which its proximity to our coasts begets and encourages between them and the citizens of the United States has, in the progress of time, so united their interests and blended their fortunes that they now look upon each other as if they were one people and had but one destiny.

Considerations exist which render delay in the acquisition of this island exceedingly dangerous to the United States. The system of immigration and labor lately organized within its limits, and the tyranny and oppression which characterize its immediate rulers, threaten an insurrection at every moment which may result in direful consequences to the American people. Cuba has thus become to us an unceasing danger and a permanent cause of anxiety and alarm.

But we need not enlarge on these topics. It can scarcely be apprehended that foreign powers, in violation of international law, would interpose their influence with Spain to prevent our acquisition of the island. Its inhabitants are now suffering under the worst of all possible governments, that of absolute despotism, delegated by a distant power to irresponsible agents, who are changed at short intervals and who are tempted to improve the brief opportunity thus afforded to accumulate fortunes by the basest means.

As long as this system shall endure, humanity may in vain demand the suppression of the African slave trade in the island. This is rendered impossible while that infamous traffic remains an irresistible temptation and a source of immense profit to needy and avaricious officials, who, to attain their ends, scruple not to trample the most sacred principles underfoot.

The Spanish government at home may be well-disposed, but experience has proved that it cannot control these remote depositaries of its power.

Besides, the commercial nations of the world cannot fail to perceive and appreciate the great advantages which would result to their people from a dissolution of the forced and unnatural connection between Spain and Cuba, and the annexation of the latter to the United States. The trade of England and France with Cuba would, in that event, assume at once an important and profitable character, and rapidly extend with the increasing population and prosperity of the island.

[Second,] if the United States and every commercial nation would be benefited by this transfer, the interests of Spain would also be greatly and essentially promoted.

She cannot but see what such a sum of money as we are willing to pay for the island would effect in the development of her vast natural resources.

Two-thirds of this sum, if employed in the construction of a system of railroads, would ultimately prove a source of greater wealth to the Spanish people than that opened to their vision by Cortés. Their prosperity would date from the ratification of the treaty of cession. . . . While two-thirds of the price of the island would be ample for the completion of her most important public improvements, she might, with the remaining $40 million, satisfy the demands now pressing so heavily upon her credit, and create a sinking fund which would gradually relieve her from the overwhelming debt now paralyzing her energies. . . .

Should Spain reject the present golden opportunity for developing her resources and removing her financial embarrassments, it may never again return.

Cuba, in its palmiest days, never yielded her exchequer, after deducting the expenses of its government, a clear annual income of more than $1,500,000. These expenses have increased to such a degree as to leave a deficit chargeable on the treasury of Spain to the amount of $600,000. In a pecuniary point of view, therefore, the island is an encumbrance instead of a source of profit to the mother country. Under no probable circumstances can Cuba ever yield to Spain 1 percent on the large amount which the United States are willing to pay for its acquisition.

But Spain is in imminent danger of losing Cuba without remuneration. Extreme oppression, it is now universally admitted, justifies any people in endeavoring to relieve themselves from the yoke of their oppressors. The sufferings which the corrupt, arbitrary, and unrelenting local administration necessarily entails upon the inhabitants of Cuba cannot fail to stimulate and keep alive that spirit of resistance and revolution against Spain which has, of late years, been so often manifested. In this condition of affairs, it is vain to expect that the sympathies of the people of the United States will not be warmly enlisted in favor of their oppressed neighbors.

We know that the President is justly inflexible in his determination to execute the neutrality laws; but should the Cubans themselves rise in revolt against the oppression which they suffer, no human power could prevent citizens of the United States and liberal-minded men of other countries from rushing to their assistance. Besides, the present is an age of adventure, in which restless and daring spirits abound in every portion of the world.

It is not improbable, therefore, that Cuba may be wrested from Spain by a successful revolution; and in that event she will lose both the island and the price which we are now willing to pay for it: a price far beyond what was ever paid by one people to another for any province.

It may also be remarked that the settlement of this vexed question, by the cession of Cuba to the United States, would forever prevent the dangerous complications between nations to which it may otherwise give birth.

It is certain that, should the Cubans themselves organize an insurrection against the Spanish government, and should other independent nations come to the aid of Spain in the contest, no human power could, in our opinion, prevent the people and government of the United States from taking part in such a civil war in support of their neighbors and friends.

But if Spain, dead to the voice of her own interest and actuated by stubborn pride and a false sense of honor, should refuse to sell Cuba to the United States, then the question will arise: What ought to be the course of the American government under such circumstances? Self-preservation is the first law of nature with states as well as with individuals. All nations have, at different periods, acted upon this maxim. Although it has been made the pretext for committing flagrant injustice, as in the partition of Poland and other similar cases which history records, yet the principle itself, though often abused, has always been recognized.

The United States have never acquired a

foot of territory except by fair purchase, or, as in the case of Texas, upon the free and voluntary application of the people of that independent state who desired to blend their destinies with our own. Even our acquisitions from Mexico are no exception to this rule, because, although we might have claimed them by the right of conquest in a just war, yet we purchased them for what was then considered by both parties a full and ample equivalent.

Our past history forbids that we should acquire the island of Cuba without the consent of Spain, unless justified by the great law of self-preservation. We must, in any event, preserve our own conscious rectitude and our own self-respect. While pursuing this course, we can afford to disregard the censures of the world to which we have been so often and so unjustly exposed.

After we shall have offered Spain a price for Cuba, far beyond its present value, and this shall have been refused, it will then be time to consider the question — Does Cuba, in the possession of Spain, seriously endanger our internal peace and existence of our cherished Union?

Should this question be answered in the affirmative, then, by every law, human and divine, we shall be justified in wresting it from Spain if we possess the power; and this upon the very same principle that would justify an individual in tearing down the burning house of his neighbor if there were no other means of preventing the flames from destroying his own home.

Under such circumstances we ought neither to count the cost nor regard the odds which Spain might enlist against us. We forbear to enter into the question whether the present condition of the island would justify such a measure. We should, however, be recreant to our duty, be unworthy of our gallant forefathers, and commit base treason against our posterity should we permit Cuba to be Africanized and become a second Santo Domingo, with all its attendant horrors to the white race, and suffer the flames to extend to our own neighboring shores, seriously to endanger or actually to consume the fair fabric of our Union.

We fear that the course and current of events are rapidly tending toward such a catastrophe. We, however, hope for the best, though we ought certainly to be prepared for the worst.

We also forbear to investigate the present condition of the questions at issue between the United States and Spain. A long series of injuries to our people have been committed in Cuba by Spanish officials and are unredressed. But recently a most flagrant outrage on the rights of American citizens and on the flag of the United States was perpetrated in the harbor of Havana, under circumstances which, without immediate redress, would have justified a resort to measures of war in vindication of national honor. That outrage is not only unatoned but the Spanish government has deliberately sanctioned the acts of its subordinates and assumed the responsibility attaching to them.

Nothing could more impressively teach us the danger to which those peaceful relations, it has ever been the policy of the United States to cherish with foreign nations, are constantly exposed than the circumstances of that case. Situated as Spain and the United States are, the latter have forborne to resort to extreme measures.

But this course cannot, with due regard to their own dignity as an independent nation, continue; and our recommendations, now submitted, are dictated by the firm belief that the cession of Cuba to the United States, with stipulations as beneficial to Spain as those suggested, is the only effective mode of settling all past differences and of securing the two countries against future collisions.

We have already witnessed the happy results for both countries which followed a similar arrangement in regard to Florida.

62.

James B. Finley: Life in the Backwoods

Of the numerous educational and reform societies that flourished in the first half of the nineteenth century, none worked so effectively as the churches that were intent on the spread of religion through revivalism. In the Eastern states revival meetings were so common that one area of New York State became known as the "burned-over district" — owing to the great number of revival fires that had burned back and forth across it. Not content with this, many hardy evangelists like the Reverend James B. Finley traveled into the West to bring religion to the frontier. In the following selection from his autobiography Finley describes the life of the backwoods as he knew it during his career as an evangelist.

Source: *Autobiography of Rev. James B. Finley; or, Pioneer Life in the West,*
W. P. Strickland, ed., Cincinnati, 1854, pp. 69–98.

THE FIRST SETTLERS could not have sustained themselves had it not been for the wild game that was in the country. This was their principal subsistence; and this they took at the peril of their lives, and often many of them came near starving to death. Wild meat, without bread or salt, was often their food for weeks together. If they obtained bread, the meal was pounded in a mortar or ground on a hand mill. Hominy was a good substitute for bread; or parched corn, pounded and sifted, then mixed with a little sugar and eaten dry or mixed with water was a good beverage. On this coarse fare the people were remarkably healthy and cheerful. No complaints were heard of dyspepsia. I never heard of this fashionable complaint till I was more than thirty years old; and if the emigrants had come to these backwoods with dyspepsia, they would not have been troubled long with it; for a few months' living on buffalo, venison, and good, fat bear meat, with the oil of the raccoon and opossum mixed up with plenty of hominy, would soon have effected a cure.

Their children were fat and hearty, not having been fed with plum pudding, sweetmeats, and pound cake. A more hardy race of men and women grew up in this wilderness than has ever been produced since, with more common sense and enterprise than is common to those who sleep on beds of down and feast on jellies and preserves; and although they had not the same advantages of obtaining learning that the present generation have, yet they had this advantage: they were sooner thrown upon the world, became acquainted with men and things, and entirely dependent on their own resources for a living. A boy at the age of sixteen was counted a man in labor and hunting and was ready to go to war; and, now, one of that age hardly knows the road to mill or market.

Their attire was in perfect keeping with their fare. The men's apparel was mostly made of the deer's skin. This, well-dressed, was made into hunting shirts, pantaloons, coats, waistcoats, leggins, and moccasins. The women sometimes wore petticoats made of this most common and useful article; and it supplied, almost universally, the place of shoes and boots. If a man was blessed with a linsey hunting shirt, and the ladies with linsey dresses, and the children with the same, it was counted of the first order, even if the linsey was made of the wool of the buffalo. On some occasions, the men could purchase a calico shirt — this was thought to be extra — for which they paid $1.50 or $2 in skins or furs. And if a woman had one calico dress to go abroad in, she was considered a finely dressed lady. Deer's hair or oak leaves was generally put into the moccasin and worn in place of stockings or socks.

The household furniture consisted of stools and bedsteads made with forks driven into the ground and poles laid on these, with the bark of the trees, and, on this, beds made of oak leaves or cattail stripped off and dried in the sun. They rocked their children in a sugar trough or packsaddle. The cooking utensils consisted of a pot, Dutch oven, skillet, frying pan, wooden trays and trenchers, and boards made smooth and clean. The table was made of a broad slab. And with these fixtures, there never was a heartier, happier, more hospitable or cheerful people. Their interests were one, and their dependence on each other was indispensable, and all things were common. Thus united, they lived as one family.

They generally married early in life — the men from eighteen to twenty-one, and the girls from sixteen to twenty. The difficulties of commencing the world were not so great; and, as both parties were contented to begin with nothing, there was no looking out for fortunes or the expectation of living without labor. Their affections were personal and sincere, which constituted a chief part of their domestic happiness and endeared them to home. The sparkling log fire in the backwoods cabin, the gambols of half a dozen cheerful, healthy children, and the smiles of the happy wife and mother made an earthly paradise.

Nothing could excite more hilarity than a backwoods wedding. Most generally, all the neighborhood, for miles around, were invited; and if it was in the winter, there would be a log heap or two somewhere near the cabin. Around these fires the men assembled with their rifles; the women in the cabin; and if there was a fiddler in the neighborhood, he must be present at an hour stated. The parson, if one could be had, if not, the justice of the peace, called the assembly together, then the couple to be married. After the ceremony was over and all had wished the happy pair much joy, then, if it could be had, the bottle passed round; the men then went some to shooting at a mark, some to throwing the tomahawk, others to hopping and jumping, throwing the rail or shoulder stone, others to running footraces; the women were employed in cooking.

When dinner was ready, the guests all partook of the very best venison, bear meat, roast turkeys, etc. This being over, the dance commences, and, if there is no room in the cabin, the company repair to or near one of the log fires; there they dance till night, and then they mostly return home; yet many of the young people stay, and perhaps dance all night on a rough puncheon floor, till the moccasins are worn through. The next day is the infair [housewarming]. The same scenes are again enacted, when the newly married pair single off to a cabin built for themselves, without $20 worth of property to begin the world with, and live more happily than those who roll in wealth and fortune.

I recollect, when a boy, to have seen a pair of those backwoods folks come to my father's to get married. The groom and bride had a bell on each of their horse's necks, and a horse collar made of corn husks on each horse, to pay the marriage fee. The groomsman had a bottle of whiskey in his huntingshirt bosom. When they had entered the house, the groom asked if the parson was at home. My father replied that he was the parson. Then said the groom, "May it please you, Mary M'Lain and I have come to get married. Will you do it for us?" "Yes," replied my father. "Well, then," said the groom, "we are in a hurry." So the knot was tied, and the groomsman pulled out his bottle of whiskey to treat the company. He then went out and took the collars off the horses of the bride and groom and brought them in as the marriage fee; and soon after they started for home, in Indian file, with the bells on their horses open, to keep the younger colts, which had followed them, together.

The manner in which the cabins were built, I have described elsewhere. The chimneys were built on the inside of the house by throwing on an extra log, three feet and a half from the wall, on which to build the chimney: from this it was carried up with sticks and clay to the roof of the house, and some two feet above it. The whole width of the house was occupied for a fireplace, and wood ten or twelve feet long could be laid on; when burned in two in the middle, the ends could be pushed up so as to keep a good fire through a long winter's night. When there was but one bed in the cabin, it was no sign that you would not have a good night's rest; for, after supper was over, and the feats of the day about hunting were all talked over, the skins were brought forth — bear, buffalo, or deer — and spread down before a sparkling fire, and a blanket or buffalo robe to cover with; and you could sleep sweetly as the visions of the night roll over the senses, till the morning dawn announced the approach of day.

There were no windows and but one opening for a door; this was generally narrow and the shutter made of two slabs, or a tree split in two, then hewed off to the thickness say of six or eight inches, then set up endwise, and made with a bevel to lap over. The fastenings consisted of three large bars, fastened to staples in the walls. The floor, if not of the earth, was of hewn slabs and covered with clapboards. These cabins, if there was some care taken in putting down the logs close together, and they were scutched down, would make the sweetest and healthiest habitations that man can live in. They are much healthier than either stone or brick houses; and I have no doubt but that there is a greater amount of health and happiness enjoyed by the inmates of the former than the latter.

All the mills that the early settlers had were the hominy block or a hand mill. The water mills or horse mills were so far off that it was like going on a pilgrimage to get a grist; and besides the toll was so enormously high — one-half being required for grinding the other half — that they preferred doing their own milling.

Almost every man and boy were hunters, and some of the women of those times were expert in the chase. The game which was considered the most profitable and useful was the buffalo, the elk, the bear, and the deer. The smaller game consisted of raccoon, turkey, opossum, and groundhog. The panther was sometimes used for food, and considered by some as good. The flesh of the wolf and wildcat was only used when nothing else could be obtained.

The buffalo is of the kine species, with a large hump on its shoulders, generally of a dun color, with short, thick horns. The male buffalo is distinguished from the female by having a short mane. They go usually in large droves or herds, feeding on cane in the winter. They frequent salt licks; and in going to and from these places they beat large roads.

Buffaloes were abundant in Kentucky and were used by the first settlers as their most common food. They have a very shaggy or woolly skin. The wool was often spun and woven into cloth by the women; and sometimes it was mixed with raccoon fur and knit into stockings, which were very warm and serviceable. The fashionable clothes cut out of the finest French and English broad-

cloths, and made in such a style as to provoke the idea that they were designed to
invite instead of protect us from the chilling
blasts of winter, would be no comparison
with the warm and comfortable clothing
which was worn at that day.

After the wool was taken off, the hide
answered a valuable purpose. Being cut into
strips and twisted, it made strong tugs,
which were used for plowing. It was also
made into plowlines, bedcords, etc. When
dressed it was made into shoepacks, or a
kind of half shoe and half moccasin.

The way of hunting the buffalo was in
the following manner: A company was
formed, well supplied with dogs and guns.
Being mounted on horses, they started for
the woods. When a herd was found, one of
the company would creep up softly and fire
into their midst; then the whole company
would rush in upon them with their dogs,
which would throw them into confusion.
After all had discharged their pieces, the
dogs would attack them; and while they
were engaged in fighting with the dogs, the
hunters would have time to reload and pursue the chase. After the conflict was over,
they would return and collect the spoil. To
enable the horses to carry them, they would
take out the entrails and split them in two,
and then throw them over the packsaddles
and carry them home. . . .

The hunter, or backwoodsman — for all
backwoodsmen were hunters — made his
summer bacon out of bear meat. He would
take out the fat and salt it, if he had salt,
and then hang it up to smoke. The fat was
rendered into oil, which was put away in
deerskins, neatly and cleanly dressed for the
purpose. This oil served many valuable purposes to the hunter, supplying the place of
butter and hog's lard. He could fry his venison and turkey in it; and if he had neither
of these, it was admirable sop for his corn
dodger; and when mixed with his jerky and
parched corn was regarded as one of the
greatest delicacies of a hunter's larder.

The bear is hunted with dogs, and if they
are well trained but few will escape. They
are remarkably afraid of the dogs; and as
they will attack them nowhere else than at
their hind legs, which are very tender, they
tree as soon as possible, and generally remain till the hunter can come up and shoot
them. Sometimes, however, they will let go
and fall fifty or sixty feet without doing
themselves the slightest injury. Often, when
fat, they go to a hole in a tree and must be
sought for. A well-trained hunter can tell by
the marks of the claws in the bark of the
tree whether the bear is holed or not. A
tree or sapling is felled and lodged against
the one in which is the bear. If a tree
should be near, the hunter takes a long,
slim pole, attaches some spunk or rotten
wood to it, climbs up as far as the hole,
and, igniting the end, sets fire to the hole,
which is filled with rotten wood. He then
descends and gets his gun, and awaits the
appearance of bruin, who, being unable to
stand the fire, rushes out in great rage and
meets his fate.

If he has made his den in the rocks,
greater caution is necessary; for if he should
only be wounded, the hunter must be prepared for a swift retreat or a single combat
with spear or tomahawk. These animals, in
the fall, before the time of mast, climb up
trees, pull in the limbs, and gather the fruit,
which is called lopping. Often the hunter
steals up and kills them; but if they should
happen to see him before he fires, they let
all go and fall down. . . .

The deer is the most beautiful wild animal that roams in American forests. They
change their color three times a year, and
every winter they cast their horns. The col-
or they assume in the spring is red, in the
fall it is blue, and in the winter it is gray.
Their skins are the most valuable when in
the red or blue. . . .

The dressing of deerskins did not require
a long process. As soon as the skin was off
the deer's back, while yet warm and green,

was the best time to begin the graining process, which was as follows: The brains of the animal were dried on a board before the fire, then they were put into a cloth and washed out in warm water, which made a kind of suds, into which the skin was put; and, after being well rubbed, was taken out and wrung as dry as possible. Then it was pulled and worked over a board made for the purpose till it was dry. It was then taken again through the same process, with the exception that the brain water was stronger, and worked till it became soft, when it was hung up and smoked with rotten hickory wood for a short time, and was then ready for use.

The ladies had but little time to devote to making clothes for the gentlemen, and but little was required, as the fashions were then as simple as the material out of which the clothes were made. They generally cut out the garment with a butcher knife and used an awl in the place of a needle, and the sinews of the deer instead of thread. With this article the moccasins are always made, when they are made neatly, though sometimes they were made with a whang cut from the skin. A hunting shirt made of this article will wear a long time. The hunting shirt is a very comfortable garment in cold weather, and when worn awhile and well saturated with deer's tallow or bear's oil, will turn the rain like a goose's back; and for the brush and greenbrier there is nothing so good. . . .

Many were the sports, in an early day, connected with coon hunting. They are a nocturnal animal, and hence they are hunted in the night. Dogs, well trained to the business, will find them and tree them. When this is accomplished, the next thing is to cut down the tree or send up someone to shake them off.

Many are the anecdotes that are told of coon hunters. A laughable one is related of a clerical friend of mine during his younger days. He was out with a party one night coon hunting, and the dogs, having treed an old coon, it was determined by the party that our friend should climb the tree and shake him off so that the dogs might catch him. Accordingly, he ascended, and, stealing softly from branch to branch in search of the coon, he finally espied him snugly ensconced on one of the topmost branches, a somewhat interested spectator of the scene which was transacting below. Proceeding cautiously, he reached the limb below that on which was the coon. Raising himself up for the purpose of reaching the limb which he intended to shake, the one on which he stood was heard to crack and began to give way. He was now thirty feet from the ground.

Aware of his perilous condition, he cried out to his companions below, "I'm falling." Seeing his danger, and that nothing scarcely less than a miracle could save him from death, they besought him to pray. "Pray," said he, "I haven't time, I can't pray." "But you must pray. If you fall, you will be killed." He then commenced repeating the only prayer he knew: "Now I lay me down to sleep"; but he could proceed no further, as the cracking of the limb indicated its speedy severance from the trunk; and he cried out at the top of his voice, "Hold the dogs; I'm coming." And sure enough, down he came with a crash; and the dogs, thinking it to be the coon, were with difficulty restrained from attacking the coon hunter, who was considerably stunned by the fall. . . .

A hunter's life is one of constant excitement. He is always on the lookout and filled with constant expectation. His narratives always possess a thrilling interest and are listened to with the greatest attention. His wants are but few, and he is not disturbed with cankering care about the future. His employment does not lead him to covetousness, and he is always characterized by a generous hospitality. His hut or cabin is always a sure asylum for the hungry and destitute. Whoever crossed its threshold and was turned away unfed and uncared for? The poor and the stranger will feel much better in the log cabin, partaking of its hospitalities by a cheerful fire, than when surrounded by the cold constraint of a nabob's table. With these sons and daughters of nature will be found the genuine hospitalities of nature's noblemen. . . .

The backwoodsman usually wore a hunting shirt and trousers made of buckskin, and moccasins of the same material. His cap was made of coonskin, and sometimes ornamented with a fox's tail. The ladies dressed in linsey-woolsey, and sometimes buckskin. A gradual improvement, however, took place in the manners and customs of the people.

About the period in which the British forces at Yorktown surrendered, the colonists were in a complete state of transition. Commerce began to revive. Many small prizes were taken by the American cruisers, brought in, condemned, and sold. Many merchant vessels, richly laden, sailing under the protection of the French flag, reached in safety their ports of destination; and the merchandise thus brought in soon found its way into the interior, and was exchanged for skins, furs, ginseng, black and Seneca snakeroots, sarsaparilla, etc. In search of those roots the mountains were traversed, and employment given to vast numbers of persons.

The effects from thence resulting soon manifested themselves in the improved dress of the females, as well as in the furniture of each household and in many other particulars. Singing and common reading schools began to be encouraged, and males and females vied with each other in the culture of their intellects, conversational powers, and address. There were several ancient families in Oldtown and its vicinity, who, in early life, had been well educated, whose wealth enabled them to procure the richest articles of dress and furniture to be had in the cities. By them the ancient customs and fashions of the English were kept up, till modified or changed by the introduction of French customs and manners.

Prior to the commencement of the transition indicated, the dress of females, as at present, greatly differed. Among the laboring classes, the usual summer dress consisted of a tow or linen chemise, short gown, and petticoat, which extended down a little below the calf of the leg, without stockings or shoes. The hair was either tied in a hard knot on the nape of the neck, or plaited and confined on the top of the head; and their toilet was completed either with or without a coarse neckerchief. The dress on gala days of those who moved in the higher circles of society also varied. Their shoes differed from those worn by ladies of the present day in this: they had high heels. Those heels were made of wood, beautifully tapered, neatly covered with leather, and varied in height from one to two inches.

The underclothing was confined by stays, tightly laced, The outer covering was composed of the richest brocade, or other silks and satins, and stomacher, neckerchief, gloves, rings, and ruffles in profusion. The hair was combed forward, and a cushion, suited to the form of the head, varying from three to six inches in height, was placed upon the top of the head, over which the hair was neatly spread and fastened behind with a comb and ribbons, by which a rich, towering plume of feathers was also fastened. A lady in full dress, entering a drawing room, would appear to be as tall as a Maypole, if not as cadaverous as a death's-head. The bonnet was of enormous size, and usually measured from three to three and a half feet in circumference.

Hence, against the form of dressing here indicated, the rule in the Methodist Discipline was framed: "Give no tickets to any who wear high heads, enormous bonnets, ruffles, or rings." The rule has become a dead letter among preachers and people.

63.

James G. Bell: Riding Herd to California

Texans, in fact as well as in story, were the first to bring cattle-raising on a large scale to the Great Plains, and to make it profitable by developing markets for the beef. Before the "Long Drives" of the 1860s, in which they drove steers to the Northern and Eastern markets via Kansas and Missouri, Texas cattlemen found a lucrative market in the gold fields of Colorado, Arizona, and California, where beef sold for $6 or $7 a head on the hoof. On a drive to California in 1854, the noted Texas rancher John James supplemented his regular crew with a group of emigrants eager to make their way to the West Coast. James Bell, a twenty-two year old from Tennessee, was a member of the group, and he recorded in his diary his impressions of life on the trail.

Source: *Southwestern Historical Quarterly*, Vol. XXXV, 1932, pp. 211-237.

June 3. Left San Antonio at 9 o'clock P.M., rode ten miles, encamped near some Mexican carts, in company with Mr. John James on our route to California. Lost my mule by carelessness. Let every prairie traveler make the safety of his mule of the first importance. . . .

June 6. Tuesday. Heavy fog last night, cloudy this morning. Traveled about nine miles, came up in front and found an hombre skinning three rattlesnakes. When I inquired the use he would put the skins to, he told me that by stretching the skin on the cantle of the saddle no harm would come to my posteriors, *i.e.*, no gall or sore; also by putting a piece of the skin between the lining and hat that I never could have the headache. The hombre took the fat out of the snakes and divided with those who had faith in its virtues; it is good for wounds of various kinds. The Mexican gave me a very large snakeskin when we arrived in camp, which was early, only nine miles to the next water hole; having time I stretched it tightly on the cantle, covering it entirely, and used the end for covering the horn.

Evening. Killed a beef, being in want of fresh meat — it would astonish a regular-bred butcher to see with what dispatch three Mexicans can rope, kill, and have a beef cut into ropes. The beef is first thrown down by means of rope, then stuck, not struck, on the head. The head is turned to one side, which holds the beef in the proper position, one side is skinned, the skinned side is allowed to turn up; half of the beef is dissected, the entrails then taken out, the ribs are left whole and roasted before the fire, the other half and head is made into ropes and exposed on a line in the sun until jerked. There is an old Comanche Indian in the train. He has all the peculiarities of his race — light tread, high cheekbones, restless eye, and an eager desire to see blood. When the beef was being made into ropes, he drew a twelve-inch butcher knife and pitched in with an energy which told me plainly that the sight of blood was rather to his habit than otherwise. . . .

June 11. Sunday morning. The next station we pass is the Las Moras and is beautifully situated on one of the clearest streams of water I have ever seen. We had a fine bath in cool waters. The balance of the streams I have seen in this part of the state seem to be of a volcanic nature and are warm, but the water when cooled is very good and resembles the Mississippi water.

12. Monday. I visited the Las Moras and found two young men of my acquaintance from San Antonio. The companies have two very good gardens there, and the gentleman — knowing how travelers on the plains suffer for want of vegetables — gave us some cucumbers, beets, parsnips, lettuce, parsley, etc. There were some Lipan Indians in camp begging for *carna* [meat] and seemed to be very friendly. Their business at the station was to have a talk with some of the other tribes, to arrange some little matters of difference. They are miserably poor and only the shadow of their former greatness, but still endeavor to keep up appearances by painting their faces various colors. Both sexes dress so much alike that without one is accustomed to them . . . it is difficult to distinguish the male from the female. We left camp about the usual time, traveled about ten miles, arrived at the Pedro Pinto, a very pretty little stream. Our cattle were somewhat restless during the night and came very near stampeding twice. . . .

Saturday. Cloudy. Men all around the fire looking on and waiting with impatience for breakfast. Several sick men in camp but not dangerously so. There are three men in camp: one Mexican, one American, and one German, who are perfectly worthless and it would be a godsend if the Indians would kill them. Some of the men have very little thrift and take no care whatever of their health, have no thought for the next hour, and are content to let others do what they should do themselves.

We have one poor fellow (German or Pole) who seems to be deranged on the subject of honor, and imagines everyone is trying to insult him. He will probably be sent back when we meet the San Antonio mail. . . .

21. Having been in camp about two days, resting the cattle for a forty-mile travel without water, we left camp about 4 o'clock, traveled twelve miles to camp, found no water. Day passed off pleasantly. The night would have been equally so had it not have been that most of the men had only [an] hour's rest; the noise of changing guard frequently keeps one awake.

22. Left camp about daylight, filled our vessels with . . . water, which held 100 gallons, passed a cross, made of two rough pieces [of] wood tied across, to commemorate the death of some Mexican.

We passed through a [prairie] dog town; not very extensive, however. We did not see any of the inhabitants; when we get into the country where they are more plenty, I will endeavor to give a description. Found about ten barrels of water scattered around in pockets. This gave the cattle a mouth washing each.

The men are anxiously awaiting dinner, for we have had comparatively little for two meals past, it being advisable as not creating so much thirst as a full meal.

At 12 o'clock divide the train. I was left with the wagons as an escort with ten others; arrived in camp at 3 o'clock in the morning; the cattle arrived some three hours earlier. I withstood the fatigue of about twenty hours on muleback — much better than I expected. Camp at Howards Springs. Travelers make this a resting place, consequently *some persons* are here all the time, or nearly so.

Made thirty miles. This is a matter of necessity as there is not a particle of water on the route of thirty miles.

23. In camp all day resting the cattle. During the night suspicioned the presence of Indians. After examining, all became easy again.

24. In camp, expect to start at 3 o'clock. The cattle are in good order, the men are in fine humor for going about fifteen miles. My health is good, good appetite, and could eat a peck of fruit, vegetables, etc.

Shall procure a quantity for the trip when I get to El Paso del Norte.

Left camp at 3 o'clock; made about twelve or fifteen miles at 9 o'clock without water; been traveling in Rio Diablo Canyon for ten days; got out this evening. Mountain scenery the same — entirely surrounded with broken mountains where if a man should get lost he should at once come to the conclusion to die with thirst or be killed by the Indians. The sunset this evening just as we got on the plain is such as I have never seen before; the whole heavens are one entire picture of their glory, or I might say the entire canopy is one sunset.

25. Left camp early. After about ten miles we entered the canyon again — previous to entering the canyon we passed through a large dog town, about four miles in circumference. The grass is cropped close around the town; as we passed through, a number of the inhabitants popped their heads just above the edge of the holes, barked a few times, and disappeared. Several were killed. When cooked, their meat resembles squirrel meat. The claws are sharp and always uncovered for the purpose of digging; the tail like a dog, hair between a gray and fox squirrel; the head resembles the Chihuahua dog with his ears cropped; are about the size of a grown fox squirrel.

The mountains on either side the canyon are not so irregular as those we passed a few days ago. Reach Live Oak Creek at 2 o'clock and are encamped for the night. Made seventeen miles. By the by, this *is* Sunday. No matter, it is all the same to us, we work as much on Sabbath as on weekdays. Not one-half the men know how long we have been out.

There is a fall of six feet in Live Oak Creek, several of us are going bathing now. Returning I found an oblong pile of stones. At one end found the inscription "Amanda Lewis, 1852." I read . . . it aloud when one of the young men present spoke with astonishment. He was acquainted with the person in Mississippi. She was a mother of a large family. How desolate must have been the husband and children when they performed the last sad rites over their loved mother — when with mournful feelings they turned away knowing that *then* they beheld the last of her whom they had ever looked up to with love and veneration.

In this vast expanse of hill and plain when by mere chance I came upon this grave, a feeling of desolation and insignificance came over me, and I felt content in my ignorance of the wondrous creation of earth. The spot where this woman is buried probably could not be found in one year's search, for in 1852 this portion of Texas was outside of all civilization.

Night is now approaching and the serious business of the trip is about to commence — that of standing guard and a possibility of an attack from the Indians. . . .

29. Yesterday, my attention was called to a heap of stones which seemed to have been broken for macadamizing purposes — had seen several similar heaps on different days previous. Upon inquiry and examination, found a hollow in the center two feet square and two deep with marks of fire on the stones. I can come to no other conclusion but that these places were or are now used to offer up sacrifices in time of battle or at a death.

The history of the Indians who inhabit this country could not but be very interesting; and an exploration geologically would no doubt develop inexhaustible mines of gold, silver, copper, and iron. . . .

30. Left camp half an hour after sunrise, made some twelve or fifteen miles. At 12 o'clock encamped on a water hole, the smell of which gave strong indications of iron.

Have just washed my face — the first time in two days. Forget when I combed my head last, about once a week is quite a luxury; am looking forward to our camping time this evening, with great impatience, for then — just think of it — I'll have a plunge into the water! and clean linen!

won't it be glorious; may take cold from opening the pores and clearing the dirt off the skin. If anyone could see the men together it could be sworn they were all millers — so dusty.

My hands and face and breast are a beautiful brown, something near a light mulatto color. The boys at home used to tell me that if my skin were not so fair I would readily be taken for a mulatto. I intend to school myself to bear the yoke of patience and meekness, for when I arrive in California it will be a Herculean task for me to attempt to fight everyone who will call me "Boy!" . . .

July 3. We will in a few days commence the "one hundred miles" without water; then is the time when the men and cattle will be sorely tried.

The crow is scarce here; the raven and Mexican buzzard fill up the complement of the feathered tribe, with the exception of a few small birds. We see the turkey occasionally, but at this season they are unfit to eat.

There is a confounded locust near me on a bush buzzing away, so that I can scarcely have the patience to write. The sound is more metalliclike than the locust in Tennessee, and creates an unpleasant buzzing in the ear, like the rushing of blood to the head.

Probably you would like to have some idea of my manner of sleeping, personal appearance, etc. I find the blue coat to be perfectly superfluous and generally carry it tied behind the saddle, pants in my boots; both boots and pants begin to have rather a shocking bad appearance, for after eating (having left my handkerchiefs at home), I use the pants for wiping my knife and hands on. In riding, the bosom of my check shirt works open, and along down the center of my breast is a brown stripe like the stripe on a black Dutchman's back. My nose and ears and neck are undergoing the scaling process until I look as scaly about the face and gills as a buffalo fish. My riding outfit consists of — on either side of the horn is a rope and canteen, behind the cantle is my tin cup and iron spoon, while occasionally there is to be found a dead rabbit hung by the neck waiting to be devoured. And when we expect to travel over dinner time, a slab of jerked beef finds itself flapping against the side of the mule.

My bed is made with the over and Indian rubber coat next the ground, saddle at the head, horse blanket on the saddle to make it soft, bed blanket over all, and myself on top of that; sometimes, to luxuriate a little, I pull off my boots and hat. When it rains I roll up into a ball like a porcupine and spread the gum coat over me. I like to sleep in the open air, for when I get up in the morning my sleep has been refreshing and comfortable. . . .

4. There is probably not one American in camp who does not remember today with different feelings from those of other days. We have no means of celebrating this day except by recollection of the past celebrations that we have witnessed in our youthful days. The mind will naturally go back seventy-eight years, and look with pride and veneration upon the deed which created a nation.

The portrait of Benjamin Franklin came particularly to my mind, and I could almost see his kind, fatherly, and philosophical-looking face as he stood in Congress Hall at the signing of the Declaration. . . .

5. Smith reports a fight, some forty miles ahead, Mr. Erskine had with the Indians; they stole three head oxen. Erskine retaliated by killing six Indians and taking ten horses. He was foolish to follow them into a canyon, where, with additional forces, the Indians turned on him and compelled him to retreat. If the yellowbellies should attack us, doubtless they would have a warm reception. All the men are well armed. The only thing lacking is more horses.

By the by, on the 4th I ate a piece of prairie dog. They are better than the jackass rabbit, the name might not suit some, but I don't mind such little things. Killed a beef, cut some steaks from the forequarter; as beef does not eat well when fresh killed, will save some until tomorrow. . . .

7. Friday we make a start to go through the Wild Rose Pass; the *majordomo* of the Mexicans tells me that *Puerto del Mustanga Rosa* is the Mexican interpretation of Wild Rose Pass. I am satisfied this is not correct. This man from his place ought to be the most intelligent man in their party. The poor ignorant fellow cannot tell the meaning of the simplest word; so far as I have seen of the Mexicans they are miserably ignorant, just one grade above the Indians.

This pass is considered the most dangerous on the route. Unfortunately we got behind Franklin and Dean, and were nearly the whole day in making ten miles. It is a wild country, and ten Indians could give a large party great trouble. The wild rose grows here in great profusion, from whence the name; this is not the proper season, it is as yet too cool in this altitude.

Separated at the head of the canyon, there being two roads to the head of the Limpia; at the head of the canyon found good water and grass.

None but a poet could appreciate this evening; the rising moon, the setting sun, the calm sensation the clear sky and smooth, verdant prairie gives, all combine to make it the most pleasant and delightful camp we have had during the trip.

The low mountains which surround us are just far enough to keep the eye from wearying with the desert waste, while the rich coloring of the sky, combined with the whole landscape, make anyone who has "music in the soul" wish to be a painter, and any painter wish for the power to copy it.

Around us are thousands of dogs who singly appear, give a few barks, and slip into their underground houses.

8. *Saturday*. The sun comes up clear this morning; will be comfortable day, breeze blowing. Three men are gone out ahead to find water so, if possible, to cut off a portion of the "hundred-mile" stretch. We will encamp here during the day. Ten mules and horses are kept under saddle all the time to be ready for the redskins. Some of the men are engaged digging out dogs.

Mr. James and myself went to a point on the mountain to watch for a signal within one hour to sunset; passed over two and one-half miles to gain the point. About the time stated a light smoke ascended from a mountain twenty miles distant. This was the signal for water. We answered by a similar smoke, so the men could tell at what time we would start and arrive. . . .

9. *Sunday again*. We have not had the promised sermon from the reverend gentleman. . . . Well, we are not particularly in need of spiritual food, but I could sit down and listen with patience to the greatest *ass* who had ever been *called*. . . .

13. *Thursday*. 12 o'clock, we had first meal, being without food — except dry bread — some eighteen hours; when we examined the provisions, found everything contrary to what was ordered. The cooks, previous to leaving our carts behind, did not prepare any coffee, bread, salt, pepper; you may guess the cooks would have been in a bad way had they been with us.

I have had very little sleep in the last few days and expect to have about half as much until Saturday morning at 2 o'clock. We will travel steadily until then. At that time we will behold the Rio Grande, the first running stream for some weeks.

Mother, look at these leaves, how dirty, and you can imagine how dirty my hands are. I expect to get on some clean clothes in a few days, also to have the luxury of washing my face and hands. Water can be appreciated in this country. Leave camp at 3 o'clock.

Traveled all night; lost some stock; one ox fought the drivers although he was not able to travel; it was truly dangerous to urge him forward; driving cattle when they are almost perishing for water looks like punishing the animals for amusement, but they are compelled to go forward or die.

14. Friday. The mail from San Antonio came in about 10 o'clock. Saw Capt. S. Eilman and several other acquaintances; learned that nothing of interest had occurred in San Antonio. I expected to receive some way mail, but was disappointed. I certainly shall not be so again, cause why, I will not expect anything.

There is a government station here, probably some forty or fifty men. We met a party from this place, scouting, about forty miles back; Indian rumors are as frequent as ever. I would be better able to believe them could I see a few Indians occasionally.

Mr. James arrived in camp three hours ahead of the carts. He seemed very cool when informed of the loss of seventy-five head of cattle the night before; the cause was the guard went to sleep, and the cattle broke for the nearest water, instinct learns them where it is, and when very thirsty they can smell water five miles. . . .

Arrived in camp, or rather near the Rio Grande, at daybreak; the last part of the train came in three hours after. Lost some animals during the night, some dying and some straying off for water. The majority of dead cattle are nearest the river.

It is now near 4 o'clock Saturday and I have had a piece of cornbread as big as my fist with half cup of cold coffee, and half gallon water with two drinks of *good brandy*. This is the extent of my eating in twenty-four hours. Well, we shall see what we shall see. . . .

15. Saturday. This would be a very pleasant day but for the immense quantity of decaying animal matter which covers the ground — the smell of which counteracts the pleasing sensation of the cool breeze from the south.

At sundown, I am going down to the Rio Grande del Norte to take a bath, not to take the dirt off but to get the fever out of my system caused from exhaustion.

The river . . . at this season of the year is very full, fifty yards wide, rapid, deep, and turbulent; the banks indicate continual washing in; the dry season the water scarcely runs. This I will not swear to; the old travelers on this route say so. The other bank is the *great* (?) state of Mexico. . . .

16. Sunday. Some hunters from the other camp brought in the largest white tailed deer I have ever seen; he was very old and so confounded tough that a square inch would have been sufficient for breakfast, dinner, and supper. I commenced on a mouthful, found it was no go, but thought perseverance would master it, as I had been told that perseverance would conquer anything; and I am able to say that, if no one else has, *I* have found an exception to the rule. If Goodyear and Day could see a piece of this venison they would immediately discover a new article to add to their great quantity of manufactures; that is India rubber meat for prairie travelers, and recommend it as being more easily masticated, as well as more economical. I tried to jerk some of the confounded stuff, in the Indian fashion, but the flies were so bad, was compelled to give it over; smoke and fire would not keep them off.

I could now enjoy the comfort of a home with great *gusto.*

Have been reviewing this diary, and am almost induced to destroy it. From El Paso to California I will write a better one, or none at all. Will move camp this evening; been here near the water to let the cattle fill up and get the fever out of their systems. We now move to grass. . . .

18. One of the Mexicans whom we discharged two days ago came into camp this morning, begging for something to eat. The poor devil was out all night in the storm. We gave him something to eat, with a warning to not return or loaf about camp under penalty of being whipped out.

The air is cool and pleasant this morning, with a prospect of a fine day. The Rio Grande is still rising; it washed the dam from the mouth of the little well I dug for the purpose of settling and cooling water, and disappointed me in a good drink.

The Mexicans, at breakfast, were discussing whether they would be considered white people or not in California. One settled the discussion by saying they would be considered Negroes and whistled about, called Jack! as is the custom among the Southern states.

19. Mr. James, a few of the men, and some of the cattle came in this morning, still encamped at the place where we first struck the Rio Grande. Three men left, returned to Eagle Springs this evening to join those who are behind. They intend to scout for some six days. We leave in a few hours to travel six miles up the river.

20. Left camp early, made six or eight miles to camp, passed a portion of the day in lounging about, eat some — what the Mexicans call — Mexican strawberry. These are nothing more than a species of prickly pear; the inside of the pear resembles the strawberry; it is the most delicious of the species I have tasted. Last night I was kept from sleep by the mosquitoes — they annoyed and bit me beyond all patience.

21. Friday. We will remain here all day. One of our men brought in a buffalo fish, which he shot in the backwater of the Rio Grande. He reports any quantity, the men in the other party killed four or five. I have not examined any yet, to see whether they contain an unhealthy quantity of fat. . . .

22. Saturday. Left camp at 7 o'clock. On the road I gathered some fine pears. I am falling in love with this fruit; it is generally condemned by those who travel this road and said to be unhealthy. I am under the impression that those who refuse to eat it were never used to any kind of fruit or vegetables and have been brought up on bacon, coffee, corn bread. . . .

Went to the river to water my mule. Killed an animal that somewhat resembled a medium-sized rat. It had very long and fine fur, tail twice as long as the body, mouth and teeth like a squirrel, only nearer the throat a pocket on each side the mouth lined in the inside with fur — this I suppose to carry the young in. And what is most remarkable is the hind legs are about three times the length of the fore ones, giving it the appearance of a kangaroo; in fact, by some in camp it is called the kangaroo rat. I skinned it on account of its oddity and beautiful fur. The little fellow was very fat and would no doubt been very good to eat.

Made seven or eight miles to camp on the bank of the Rio Grande; encamped there, were two wagons and one ambulance. This party is a portion of one who left eastern Texas for the purpose of mining near El Paso. They divided there, some going to California, the balance returning home by this route.

During the night a Mexican robbed the owner of $200. This he did by breaking open his chest. I, last night, caught one man asleep on guard, reported him, and had his pistols taken away while asleep; poor fellow, I hated to inform on him, but necessity required it. . . .

23. Sunday. At noon we encamped opposite a Mexican town, or *rancho.* About one dozen men came over, bringing new onions as large as my fist, eggs, chickens, and mescal liquor; we bought everything except the liquor, which they would not sell but gave to us. This liquor has a taste between whiskey and brandy, and considerable intoxicating power. Not one of these men have on pantaloons; but a few have white cotton drawers about one yard wide at the bottom, some have on a cotton shirt, just long enough to be decent, some have simply a cloth around the waist. They seem to be a happy race and don't care a fig for the superfluities of life. Corn is here worth $1 per bushel. These Mexicans present several different colors of skin — the different grades between the Castilian and Indian; our Mexicans are enjoying themselves in social converse with the others, relating the news, gossip, the rumors picked up along the road. . . .

Made two miles to camp, where we found good grass. The Mexican town we left is San Ignacio. The men were very anxious to encamp near the town so as to go to the fandango at night. One Mexican was very particular to dress in his best suit — fancy pants, red flannel overshirt, and the regular Mexican hat, the material of which is like the old-fashioned fire bucket, and nearly as heavy — it astonishes me how they can bear the enormous weight on the head; the crown part is too small for any head except a small boy's. This together with the enormous head of hair which they wear would make it unbearable for anyone except a Mexican.

24. Monday. Left camp early with a prospect of a fine but warm day. Made ten miles to camp for dinner — which is on the old channel of the Rio Grande. Have had very good water for a few days past from the lagoons of the Rio. This when cool is as good as the best cistern water. My canteen is worth $5 to me, the only thing to regret is that it keeps the water so cool that everyone runs to me for a drink; consequently, when I want a drink, my canteen is out.

Today passed a *rancho* on the opposite side. The country here begins to give some evidence of civilization. Occasionally we pass a cornfield, which is without any fencing; the crop seems to be very backward and not near so far advanced as at San Antonio. About 10 o'clock in the morning we came to the small town of San Elizario. I should have mentioned that we arrived in a small town about daylight, a few miles back of San Elizario; there we bought some apples from off the trees. They would be considered worse than common in a regular

apple country but here — half green as they are — I eat about one dozen with great gusto.

I did not inquire to what saint this town is dedicated but I imagine it ought to be Saint Diablo; for I honestly believe his majesty had a hand in laying it out. It was with difficulty we could get through, owing to the crookedness of the streets, the mud puddles and hills; we finally got through, however, and I suppose not one of our men but what left with a curse and blessing on his lips; a curse because we got into it, and a blessing because we got out. One of the men was sent ahead with the ambulance and I went along. During the day we lost our way twice, and, one time, in crossing the old bed of the Rio Grande, our lead mules were swimming. We came very near turning the ambulance over in deep water, and it was only by mere accident I did not get a good ducking.

The soil around these settlements is of a good quality; light, sandy, and river bottom; it is watered entirely by irrigation. Watermelons and muskmelons are now ripe, have had some few grapes, although generally they will not be ripe for about two weeks. Apples and pears will be full ripe in a short time; we have good green corn for dinner every day. Upon inquiry, I learn the corn is about the last crop planted here, this is the reason why it appears so backward.

I have upon invitation taken up my lodging with Dr. Giddings at a Mexican house; we have the food cooked up in Mexican style, that is, onions and pepper mixed with everything. After living on camp diet for nearly two months, this food agrees with me very well.

The houses in this country are built entirely of adobe, with the cement roofs. The confounded people have never learned the art of ventilation, but seem to make their houses as airtight as possible; only having enough openings for light and entrance.

The room where I am now writing has a window and door on one side and these open on a court where the evening and noon sun shines with all its power. The houses are generally built in the form of a hollow square.

Wheat yields a good crop, and mills in the vicinity make as fine flour as could be desired. Geo. Craig has a threshing machine running, but it does not work well; the wheat is not bearded and it has to be run through twice to get all the grain out.

I learn that there are immense vineyards on the Mexican side which yield a large revenue to the owners. This country is destined at some day to become of importance to the United States. There is no wholesale trade carried on between the two countries at this point — cause why — the tariff amounts to prohibition.

64.

Henry David Thoreau: Where I Lived, and What I Lived For

Walden, one of the half dozen most famous American books, is the record of two years (1845-1847) spent by Thoreau in solitude at Walden Pond, just outside Concord, Massachusetts. On a tract of land owned by Emerson, Thoreau built a log cabin that was to be his home and in which he attempted to live deliberately and "simply." It was no hermit's seclusion, for Thoreau was in frequent contact with his family and friends. But it was a life apart, with opportunities for study, meditation, and spiritual growth. The book that grew out of the experience was written several years later and was published in August 1854. Reprinted here is the celebrated second chapter.

Source: *Walden; or, Life in the Woods,* Boston, 1893, pp. 128-155.

At a certain season of our life we are accustomed to consider every spot as the possible site of a house. I have thus surveyed the country on every side within a dozen miles of where I live. In imagination I have bought all the farms in succession, for all were to be bought, and I knew their price. I walked over each farmer's premises, tasted his wild apples, discoursed on husbandry with him, took his farm at his price, at any price, mortgaging it to him in my mind; even put a higher price on it, took everything but a deed of it, took his word for his deed, for I dearly love to talk, cultivated it, and him too to some extent, I trust, and withdrew when I had enjoyed it long enough, leaving him to carry it on. This experience entitled me to be regarded as a sort of real estate broker by my friends. Wherever I sat, there I might live, and the landscape radiated from me accordingly.

What is a house but a *sedes,* a seat? — better if a country seat. I discovered many a site for a house not likely to be soon improved, which some might have thought too far from the village, but to my eyes the village was too far from it. Well, there I might live, I said; and there I did live, for an hour, a summer and a winter life; saw how I could let the years run off, buffet the winter through, and see the spring come in. The future inhabitants of this region, wherever they may place their houses, may be sure that they have been anticipated. An afternoon sufficed to lay out the land into orchard, woodlot, and pasture, and to decide what fine oaks or pines should be left to stand before the door, and whence each blasted tree could be seen to the best advantage; and then I let it lie, fallow perchance, for a man is rich in proportion to the number of things which he can afford to let alone.

My imagination carried me so far that I even had the refusal of several farms — the refusal was all I wanted — but I never got my fingers burned by actual possession. The nearest that I came to actual possession was when I bought the Hollowell place, and had begun to sort my seeds, and collected materials with which to make a wheelbarrow to carry it on or off with; but before the owner gave me a deed of it, his wife — every man has such a wife — changed her mind and wished to keep it, and he offered me ten dollars to release him. Now, to speak the truth, I had but ten cents in the world, and it surpassed my arithmetic to tell if I was that man who had ten cents, or who had a farm, or ten dollars, or all together. However, I let him keep the ten dollars, and the farm, too, for I had carried it far enough; or rather, to be generous, I sold him the farm for just what I gave for it, and, as he was not a rich man, made him a present of ten dollars, and still had my ten cents, and seeds, and materials for a wheelbarrow left. I found thus that I had been a rich man without any damage to my poverty. But I retained the landscape, and I have since annually carried off what it yielded without a wheelbarrow. With respect to landscapes,

I am monarch of all I *survey*,
My right there is none to dispute.

I have frequently seen a poet withdraw, having enjoyed the most valuable part of a farm, while the crusty farmer supposed that he had got a few wild apples only. Why, the owner does not know it for many years when a poet has put his farm in rhyme, the most admirable kind of invisible fence, has fairly impounded it, milked it, skimmed it, and got all the cream, and left the farmer only the skimmed milk.

The real attractions of the Hollowell farm, to me, were: its complete retirement, being about two miles from the village, half a mile from the nearest neighbor, and separated from the highway by a broad field; its bounding on the river, which the owner said protected it by its fogs from frosts in the spring, though that was nothing to me; the gray color and ruinous state of the house and barn, and the dilapidated fences, which put such an interval between me and the last occupant; the hollow and lichencovered apple trees, gnawed by rabbits, showing what kind of neighbors I should have; but above all, the recollection I had of it from my earliest voyages up the river, when the house was concealed behind a dense grove of red maples, through which I heard the house-dog bark. I was in haste to buy it, before the proprietor finished getting out some rocks, cutting down the hollow apple trees, and grubbing up some young birches which had sprung up in the pasture, or, in short, had made any more of his improvements. To enjoy these advantages I was ready to carry it on; like Atlas, to take the world on my shoulders — I never heard what compensation he received for that — and do all those things which had no other motive or excuse but that I might pay for it and be unmolested in my possession of it; for I knew all the while that it would yield the most abundant crop of the kind I wanted if I could only afford to let it alone. But it turned out as I have said.

All that I could say, then, with respect to farming on a large scale — I have always cultivated a garden — was that I had had my seeds ready. Many think that seeds improve with age. I have no doubt that time discriminates between the good and the bad; and when at last I shall plant, I shall be less likely to be disappointed. But I would say to my fellows, once for all, As long as possible live free and uncommitted. It makes but little difference whether you are committed to a farm or the county jail.

Old Cato, whose "De Re Rusticâ" is my "Cultivator," says — and the only translation I have seen makes sheer nonsense of the passage — "When you think of getting a farm turn it thus in your mind, not to buy greedily; nor spare your pains to look at it, and do not think it enough to go round it once. The oftener you go there the more it will please you, if it is good." I think I shall not buy greedily but go round and round it as long as I live, and be buried in it first, that it may please me the more at last.

THE PRESENT WAS MY NEXT EXPERIMENT of this kind, which I purpose to describe more at length, for convenience, putting the experience of two years into one. As I have said, I do not propose to write an ode to dejection, but to brag as lustily as chanticleer in the morning, standing on his roost, if only to wake my neighbors up.

When first I took up my abode in the woods, that is, began to spend my nights as well as days there, which, by accident was on Independence Day, on the Fourth of July, 1845, my house was not finished for winter, but was merely a defense against the rain, without plastering or chimney, the walls being of rough weather-stained boards, with wide chinks, which made it cool at night. The upright white hewn studs and freshly planed door and window casings gave it a clean and airy look, especially in the morning, when its timbers were saturated with dew, so that I fancied that by noon some sweet gum would exude from them. To my imagination it retained throughout the day more or less of this auroral character, reminding me of a certain house on a mountain which I had visited a year before. This was an airy and unplastered cabin, fit to entertain a traveling god, and where a goddess might trail her garments. The winds which passed over my dwelling were such as sweep over the ridges of mountains, bearing the broken strains, or celestial parts only, of terrestrial music. The morning wind forever blows, the poem of creation is uninterrupted; but few are the ears that hear it. Olympus is but the outside of the earth everywhere.

The only house I had been the owner of before, if I except a boat, was a tent, which I used occasionally when making excursions in the summer, and this is still rolled up in my garret; but the boat, after passing from hand to hand, has gone down the stream of time. With this more substantial shelter about me, I had made some progress toward settling in the world. This frame, so slightly clad, was a sort of crystallization around me, and reacted on the builder. It was suggestive somewhat as a picture in outlines. I did not need to go outdoors to take the air, for the atmosphere within had lost none of its freshness. It was not so much within-doors as behind a door where I sat, even in the rainiest weather. The Harivansa says, "An abode without birds is like a meat without seasoning." Such was not my abode, for I found myself suddenly neighbor to the birds; not by having imprisoned one but having caged myself near them. I was not only nearer to some of those which commonly frequent the garden and the orchard but to those wilder and more thrilling songsters of the forest which never, or rarely, serenade a villager: the wood thrush, the veery, the scarlet tanager, the field sparrow, the whippoorwill, and many others.

I was seated by the shore of a small pond, about a mile and a half south of the village of Concord and somewhat higher than it, in the midst of an extensive wood between that town and Lincoln, and about two miles south of that our only field known to fame, Concord Battle Ground; but I was so low in the woods that the opposite shore, half a mile off, like the rest, covered with wood, was my most distant horizon. For the first week, whenever I looked out on the pond it impressed me like a tarn high up on the side of a mountain, its bottom far above the surface of other lakes, and, as the sun arose, I saw it throwing off its nightly clothing of mist, and here and there, by degrees, its soft ripples or its smooth reflecting surface was revealed, while the mists, like ghosts, were stealthily withdrawing in every direction into the woods, as at the breaking up of some nocturnal conventicle. The very dew seemed to hang upon the trees later into the day than usual, as on the sides of mountains.

This small lake was of most value as a neighbor in the intervals of a gentle rainstorm in August, when both air and water being perfectly still, but the sky overcast, midafternoon had all the serenity of evening, and the wood thrush sang around, and was heard from shore to shore. A lake like this is never smoother than at such a time; and the clear portion of the air above it being shallow and darkened by clouds, the water, full of light and reflections, becomes a lower heaven itself so much the more important. From a hilltop nearby, where the wood had been recently cut off, there was a pleasing vista southward across the pond, through a wide indentation in the hills which form the shore there, where their opposite sides sloping toward each other suggested a stream flowing out in that direction through a wooded valley, but stream there was none. That way I looked between and over the near green hills to some distant and higher ones in the horizon, tinged with blue. Indeed, by standing on tiptoe I could catch a glimpse of some of the peaks of the still bluer and more distant mountain ranges in the northwest, those true-blue coins from heaven's own

mint, and also of some portion of the village. But in other directions, even from this point, I could not see over or beyond the woods which surrounded me. It is well to have some water in your neighborhood, to give buoyancy to and float the earth. One value even of the smallest well is that when you look into it you see that earth is not continent but insular. This is as important as that it keeps butter cool. When I looked across the pond from this peak toward the Sudbury meadows, which in time of flood I distinguished elevated perhaps by a mirage in their seething valley, like a coin in a basin, all the earth beyond the pond appeared like a thin crust insulated and floated even by this small sheet of intervening water, and I was reminded that this on which I dwelt was but *dry land*.

Though the view from my door was still more contracted, I did not feel crowded or confined in the least. There was pasture enough for my imagination. The low shrub oak plateau to which the opposite shore arose stretched away toward the prairies of the West and the steppes of Tartary, affording ample room for all the roving families of men. "There are none happy in the world but beings who enjoy freely a vast horizon," said Damodara, when his herds required new and larger pastures.

Both place and time were changed, and I dwelt nearer to those parts of the universe and to those eras in history which had most attracted me. Where I lived was as far off as many a region viewed nightly by astronomers. We are wont to imagine rare and delectable places in some remote and more celestial corner of the system, behind the constellation of Cassiopeia's Chair, far from noise and disturbance. I discovered that my house actually had its site in such a withdrawn, but forever new and unprofaned, part of the universe. If it were worth the while to settle in those parts near to the Pleiades or the Hyades, to Aldebaran or Altair, then I was really there, or at an equal remoteness from the life which I had left behind, dwindled and twinkling with as fine a ray to my nearest neighbor, and to be seen only in moonless nights by him. Such was that part of creation where I had squatted;

> There was a shepherd that did live,
>   And held his thoughts as high
> As were the mounts whereon his flocks
>   Did hourly feed him by.

What should we think of the shepherd's life if his flocks always wandered to higher pastures than his thoughts?

Every morning was a cheerful invitation to make my life of equal simplicity, and I may say innocence, with Nature herself. I have been as sincere a worshiper of Aurora as the Greeks. I got up early and bathed in the pond; that was a religious exercise, and one of the best things which I did. They say that characters were engraven on the bathing tub of King Tchingthang to this effect: "Renew thyself completely each day; do it again, and again, and forever again." I can understand that. Morning brings back the heroic ages. I was as much affected by the faint hum of a mosquito making its invisible and unimaginable tour through my apartment at earliest dawn, when I was sitting with door and windows open, as I could be by any trumpet that ever sang of fame. It was Homer's requiem; itself an Iliad and Odyssey in the air, singing its own wrath and wanderings. There was something cosmical about it; a standing advertisement, till forbidden, of the everlasting vigor and fertility of the world.

The morning, which is the most memorable season of the day, is the awakening hour. Then there is least somnolence in us; and for an hour, at least, some part of us awakes which slumbers all the rest of the day and night. Little is to be expected of that day, if it can be called a day, to which we are not awakened by our genius but by the mechanical nudgings of some servitor, are not awakened by our own newly-acquired force and aspirations from within, accompanied by the undulations of celestial music, instead of factory bells, and a fragrance filling the air — to a higher life than we fell asleep from; and thus the darkness bear its fruit, and prove itself to be good, no less than the light. That man who does not believe that each day contains an earlier, more sacred, and auroral hour than he has yet profaned, has despaired of life, and is pursuing a descending and darkening way. After a partial cessation of his sensuous life, the soul of man, or its organs rather, are reinvigorated each day, and his genius tries again what noble life it can make.

All memorable events, I should say, transpire in morning time and in a morning atmosphere. The Vedas say, "All intelligences awake with the morning." Poetry and art, and the fairest and most memorable of the actions of men, date from such an hour. All poets and heroes, like Memnon, are the children of Aurora, and emit their music at sunrise. To him whose elastic and vigorous thought keeps pace with the sun, the day is a perpetual morning. It matters not what the clocks say or the attitudes and labors of men. Morning is when I am awake and there is a dawn in me. Moral reform is the effort to throw off sleep. Why is it that men give so poor an account of their day if they have not been slumbering? They are not such poor calculators. If they had not been overcome with drowsiness, they would have performed something. The millions are awake enough for physical labor; but only one in a million is awake enough for effective intellectual exertion, only one in a hundred millions to a poetic or divine life. To be awake is to be alive. I have never yet met a man who was quite awake. How could I have looked him in the face?

We must learn to reawaken and keep ourselves awake, not by mechanical aids but by an infinite expectation of the dawn, which does not forsake us in our soundest sleep. I know of no more encouraging fact than the unquestionable ability of man to elevate his life by a conscious endeavor. It is something to be able to paint a particular picture, or to carve a statue, and so to make a few objects beautiful; but it is far more glorious to carve and paint the very atmosphere and medium through which we look, which morally we can do. To affect the quality of the day, that is the highest of arts. Every man is tasked to make his life, even in its details, worthy of the contemplation of his most elevated and critical hour. If we refused, or rather used up, such paltry information as we get, the oracles would distinctly inform us how this might be done.

I went to the woods because I wished to live deliberately, to front only the essential facts of life, and see if I could not learn what it had to teach, and not, when I came to die, discover that I had not lived. I did not wish to live what was not life, living is so dear; nor did I wish to practise resignation, unless it was quite necessary. I wanted to live deep and suck out all the marrow of life, to live so sturdily and Spartan-like as to put to rout all that was not life, to cut a broad swath and shave close, to drive life into a corner, and reduce it to its lowest terms, and, if it proved to be mean, why then to get the whole and genuine meanness of it, and publish its meanness to the world; or if it were sublime, to know it by experience and be able to give a true account of it in my next excursion. For most men, it appears to me, are in a strange uncertainty about it, whether it is of the devil or of God, and have *somewhat hastily* concluded that it is the chief end of man here to "glorify God and enjoy Him forever."

Still we live meanly, like ants; though the fable tells us that we were long ago changed into men; like pygmies we fight with cranes; it is error upon error, and clout upon clout, and our best virtue has for its occasion a superfluous and evitable wretchedness. Our life is frittered away by detail.

An honest man has hardly need to count more than his ten fingers, or in extreme cases he may add his ten toes, and lump the rest. Simplicity, simplicity, simplicity! I say, let your affairs be as two or three, and not a hundred or a thousand; instead of a million count half a dozen, and keep your accounts on your thumbnail. In the midst of this chopping sea of civilized life, such are the clouds and storms and quicksands and thousand-and-one items to be allowed for, that a man has to live, if he would not founder and go to the bottom and not make his port at all, by dead reckoning, and he must be a great calculator indeed who succeeds. Simplify, simplify. Instead of three meals a day, if it be necessary eat but one; instead of a hundred dishes, five; and reduce other things in proportion. Our life is like a German confederacy, made up of petty states, with its boundary forever fluctuating, so that even a German cannot tell you how it is bounded at any moment. The nation itself, with all its so-called internal improvements, which, by the way are all external and superficial, is just such an unwieldy and overgrown establishment, cluttered with furniture and tripped up by its own traps, ruined by luxury and heedless expense, by want of calculation and a worthy aim, as the million households in the land; and the only cure for it as for them is in a rigid economy, a stern and more than Spartan simplicity of life and elevation of purpose. It lives too fast.

Men think that it is essential that the *nation* have commerce, and export ice, and talk through a telegraph, and ride thirty miles an hour, without a doubt, whether *they* do or not; but whether we should live like baboons or like men, is a little uncertain. If we do not get out sleepers, and forge rails, and devote days and nights to the work, but go to tinkering upon our *lives* to improve *them*, who will build railroads? And if railroads are not built, how shall we get to heaven in season? But if we stay at home and mind our business, who will want railroads? We do not ride on the railroad; it rides upon us. Did you ever think what those sleepers are that underlie the railroad? Each one is a man, an Irishman, or a Yankee man. The rails are laid on them, and they are covered with sand, and the cars run smoothly over them. They are sound sleepers, I assure you. And every few years a new lot is laid down and run over; so that, if some have the pleasure of riding on a rail, others have the misfortune to be ridden upon. And when they run over a man that is walking in his sleep, a supernumerary sleeper in the wrong position, and wake him up, they suddenly stop the cars, and make a hue and cry about it, as if this were an exception. I am glad to know that it takes a gang of men for every five miles to keep the sleepers down and level in their beds as it is, for this is a sign that they may sometime get up again.

Why should we live with such hurry and waste of life? We are determined to be starved before we are hungry. Men say that a stitch in time saves nine, and so they take a thousand stitches today to save nine tomorrow. As for *work,* we haven't any of any consequence. We have the Saint Vitus' dance, and cannot possibly keep our heads still. If I should only give a few pulls at the parish bellrope, as for a fire, that is, without setting the bell, there is hardly a man on his farm in the outskirts of Concord, notwithstanding that press of engagements which was his excuse so many times this morning, nor a boy, nor a woman, I might almost say, but would forsake all and follow that sound, not mainly to save property from the flames but, if we will confess the truth, much more to see it burn, since burn it must, and we, be it known, did not set it on fire — or to see it put out, and have a hand in it, if that is done as handsomely; yes, even if it were the parish church itself.

Hardly a man takes a half-hour's nap after dinner, but when he wakes he holds up his head and asks, "What's the news?" as if the rest of mankind had stood his sentinels. Some give directions to be waked every half-hour, doubtless for no other purpose; and then to pay for it, they tell what they have dreamed. After a night's sleep the news is as indispensable as the breakfast. "Pray, tell me anything new that has happened to a man anywhere on this globe," and he reads it over his coffee and rolls, that a man has had his eyes gouged out this morning on the Wachito River; never dreaming the while that he lives in the dark unfathomed mammoth cave of this world, and has but the rudiment of an eye himself.

For my part, I could easily do without the post office. I think that there are very few important communications made through it. To speak critically, I never received more than one or two letters in my life — I wrote this some years ago — that were worth the postage. The penny-post is, commonly, an institution through which you seriously offer a man that penny for his thoughts which is so often safely offered in jest. And I am sure that I never read any memorable news in a newspaper. If we read of one man robbed, or murdered, or killed by accident, or one house burned, or one vessel wrecked, or one steamboat blown up, or one cow run over on the Western Railroad, or one mad dog killed, or one lot of grasshoppers in the winter, we never need read of another. One is enough. If you are acquainted with the principle, what do you care for a myriad instances and applications?

To a philosopher all *news,* as it is called, is gossip, and they who edit and read it are old women over their tea. Yet not a few are greedy after this gossip. There was such a rush, as I hear, the other day at one of the offices to learn the foreign news by the last arrival, that several large squares of plate glass belonging to the establishment were broken by the pressure — news which I seriously think a ready wit might write a twelve-month or twelve years beforehand with sufficient accuracy. As for Spain, for instance, if you know how to throw in Don Carlos and the Infanta, and Don Pedro and Seville and Granada, from time to time in the right proportions — they may have changed the names a little since I saw the papers — and serve up a bullfight when other entertainments fail, it will be true to the letter, and give us as good an idea of the exact state or ruin of things in Spain as the most succinct and lucid reports under this head in the newspapers; and as for England, almost the last significant scrap of news from that quarter was the Revolution of 1649; and if you have learned the history of her crops for an average year, you never need attend to that thing again, unless your speculations are of a merely pecuniary character. If one may judge who rarely looks into the newspapers, nothing new does ever happen in foreign parts, a French Revolution not excepted.

What news! how much more important to know what that is which was never old! Kieou-he-yu (great dignitary of the state of Wei) sent a man to Khoung-tseu to know his news. Khoung-tseu caused the messenger to be seated near him, and questioned him in these terms: "What is your master doing?" The messenger answered with respect: "My master desires to diminish the number of his faults, but he cannot come to the end of them." The messenger being gone, the philosopher remarked: "What a worthy messenger! What a worthy messenger!" The preacher, instead of vexing the ears of drowsy farmers on their day of rest at the end of the week — for Sunday is the fit conclusion of an ill-spent week, and not the fresh and brave beginning of a new one — with this one other draggle-tail of a sermon, should shout with thundering voice, "Pause! Avast! Why so seeming fast, but deadly slow?"

Shams and delusions are esteemed for soundest truths, while reality is fabulous. If men would steadily observe realities only, and not allow themselves to be deluded, life, to compare it with such things as we know, would be like a fairy tale and the Arabian Night's Entertainments. If we respected only what is inevitable and has a right to be, music and poetry would resound along the streets. When we are unhurried and wise, we perceive that only great and worthy things have any permanent and absolute existence — that petty fears and petty pleasures are but the shadow of the reality. This is always exhilarating and sublime. By closing the eyes and slumbering, and consenting to be deceived by shows, men establish and confirm their daily life of routine and habit everywhere, which still is built on purely illusory foundations. Children, who play life, discern its true law and relations more clearly than men, who fail to live it worthily, but who think that they are wiser by experience, that is, by failure. I have read in a Hindu book, that "there was a king's son, who, being expelled in infancy from his native city, was brought up by a forester, and, growing up to maturity in that state, imagined himself to belong to the barbarous race with which he lived. One of his father's ministers having discovered him, revealed to him what he was, and the misconception of his character was removed, and he knew himself to be a prince. So soul," continues the Hindu philosopher, "from the circumstances in which it is placed, mistakes its own character, until the truth is revealed to it by some holy teacher, and then it knows itself to be *Brahma.*"

I perceive that we inhabitants of New England live this mean life that we do because our vision does not penetrate the surface of things. We think that that *is* which *appears* to be. If a man should walk through this town and see only the reality, where, think you, would the "Mill-dam" go to? If he should give us an account of the realities he beheld there, we should not recognize the place in his description. Look at a meetinghouse, or a courthouse, or a jail, or a shop, or a dwelling-house, and say what that thing really is before a true gaze, and they would all go to pieces in your account of them. Men esteem truth remote, in the outskirts of the system, behind the farthest star, before Adam and after the last man. In eternity there is indeed something true and sublime. But all these times and places and occasions are now and here. God Himself culminates in the present moment, and will never be more divine in the lapse of all the ages. And we are enabled to apprehend at all what is sublime and noble only by the perpetual instilling and drenching of the reality that surrounds us. The universe constantly and obediently answers to our conceptions; whether we travel fast or slow, the track is laid for us. Let us spend our lives in conceiving then. The poet or the artist never yet had so fair and noble a design but some of his posterity at least could accomplish it.

Let us spend one day as deliberately as Nature, and not be thrown off the track by every nutshell and mosquito's wing that falls on the rails. Let us rise early and fast, or break fast, gently and without perturbation; let company come and let company go, let the bells ring and the children cry — determined to make a day of it. Why should we knock under and go with the stream? Let us not be upset and overwhelmed in that terrible rapid and whirlpool called a dinner, situated in the meridian shallows. Weather this danger and you are safe, for the rest of the way is downhill. With unrelaxed nerves, with morning vigor, sail by it, looking another way, tied to the mast like Ulysses. If the engine whistles, let it whistle till it is hoarse for its pains. If the bell rings, why should we run? We will consider what kind of music they are like.

Let us settle ourselves, and work and wedge our feet downward through the mud and slush of opinion, and prejudice, and tradition, and delusion, and appearance, that alluvion which covers the globe, through Paris and London, through New York and Boston and Concord, through church and state, through poetry and philosophy and religion, till we come to a hard bottom and rocks in place, which we can call *reality,* and say, This is, and no mistake; and then begin, having a *point d'appui,* below freshet and frost and fire, a place where you might found a wall or a state, or set a lamp post safely, or perhaps a gauge, not a Nilometer but a Realometer, that future ages might know how deep a freshet of shams and appearances had gathered from time to time. If you stand right fronting and face to face to a fact, you will see the sun glimmer on both its surfaces, as if it were a scimitar, and feel its sweet edge dividing you through the heart and marrow, and so you will happily conclude your mortal career. Be it life or death, we crave only reality. If we are really dying, let us hear the rattle in our throats and feel cold in the extremities; if we are alive, let us go about our business.

Time is but the stream I go a-fishing in. I drink at it; but while I drink I see the sandy bottom and detect how shallow it is. Its thin current slides away, but eternity remains. I would drink deeper; fish in the sky, whose bottom is pebbly with stars. I cannot count one. I know not the first letter of the alphabet. I have always been regretting that I was not as wise as the day I was born. The intellect is a cleaver; it discerns and rifts its way into the secret of things. I do not wish to be any more busy with my hands than is necessary. My head is hands and feet. I feel all my best faculties concentrated in it. My instinct tells me that my head is an organ for burrowing, as some creatures use their snout and forepaws, and with it I would mine and burrow my way through these hills. I think that the richest vein is somewhere hereabouts; so by the divining rod and thin rising vapors I judge; and here I will begin to mine.

The Woodsawyer's Nooning, 1853; photograph by George N. Barnard

AMERICAN IMAGES

In spite of rapid industrialization and attendant urban growth, the United States was still an agricultural country in 1850. Over 80 percent of the population depended directly or indirectly on the agricultural economy. This was most apparent in the Midwest and South where even the cities grew and prospered on the trade and commerce that agriculture produced. In the South cotton and the plantation system had reached such a dominant position that the tiny minority of the population who were plantation owners controlled the economy.

In the Midwest, mechanized equipment, like McCormick's reaper, made large acreages possible, while improved transportation to markets made this kind of farming profitable. A settled way of life was developing that was far removed from the harsh pioneer existence of only a generation earlier. Back East, farmers were turning their efforts to supplying the needs of the cities for fresh food, meat, and dairy products. Potato and poultry farms were developed on Long Island and stock breeding became a central concern at New England fairs.

Fairfield County Agricultural Society's plowing match at Bridgeport, Conn., 1852

CORN PLANTER. *at 10. Mo²*

Bred by and the property of J. M. Sherwood, Auburn, N. Y., calved 27th December, 1853.

Got by 3d, Duke of Cambridge, 5941.
Dam Lady Sale 2d, by Earl of Chatham, 10176.
Gr dam Lady Sale, by Genl. Sale, 8099.
Gr gr Clara, by Napier, 6238.
Gr gr gr dam Maid of Orleans, by Mamaluke, 2258.
Gr gr gr gr dam Helena, by Waterloo, 2816.
Gr gr gr gr gr dam Moss Rose, by Barron, 58.
Gr gr gr gr gr gr dam Angelina, by Phenomonon, 491.
Gr gr gr gr gr gr gr dam Anna Boleyn, by Favorite, 252.
Gr gr gr gr gr gr gr gr dam Princess, by Favorite, 252.
Gr gr gr gr gr gr gr gr gr dam (Bred by R. Collins,) by Favorite, 252.
Gr gr gr gr gr gr gr gr gr gr dam by Hubbuck, 319.
Gr gr gr,gr gr gr gr gr gr gr gr dam by Snoden's Bull, 612.
Gr gr gr gr gr gr gr gr gr gr gr dam by Masterman's Bull, 422.
Gr gr gr gr gr gr gr gr gr gr gr gr dam by Harrison's Bull, 669.
Gr gr gr gr gr gr gr gr gr gr gr gr gr dam bought of Mr. Pickering, of Sedgefield Hall, by Mr. Hall.

Fairs, local and statewide, were an established institution in the East. Prize stock were bought and sold and manufacturers displayed their equipment, but already the practical purposes of the fair were being submerged in carnival spirit. There were races, and side-show amusements, competitions, and judging in everything from pies to livestock. By the 1850s, the tradition had spread to the Midwest.

Advertisement for prize bull showing his champion heritage

J. M. Thompson, builder and proprietor of the Glen House, first of the White Mountain hotels; photograph taken in Portland, Me., about 1850

(Above) A farmer and his ox team at a livestock competition; (right) a mechanical thresher on exhibit by the manufacturer; (below) a man and his bull, probably a prize-winner at a fair in 1855

(Above) State Street at Buffalo Street in Rochester, N.Y., 1851; photograph by Edward T. Whitney; (below) ruins of the American Hotel, Buffalo, N.Y., 1850; photograph by McDonnell

(Above) Daguerreotype view of Baltimore, Md., from Federal Hill, about 1851; (below) group at Niagara Falls; daguerreotype by Platt D. Babbitt, about 1855

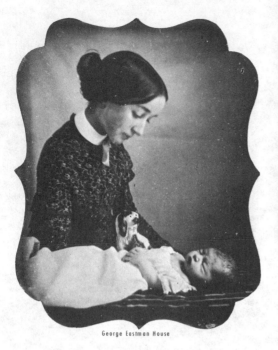

(Left) Mother and new-born child, 1850; (above) "The Hobby Horse" by an unknown artist, c. 1840

(Left) Daguerreotype of a mother with her children; (below) young widow; daguerreotype from the late 1840s

(Above) Agrippa Hull, Lafayette's valet during the Revolution, was a free citizen of Stockbridge, Massachusetts, until his death in 1848; (right) Dr. Jesse K. Smith, artist unknown

(Below) Capt. John Gass, born in 1765, moved to Wisconsin from Kentucky. Photographed at 90; (right) Shabbona (1775-1859), Potawatomi chief, warned whites of Black Hawk's plans and lived peacefully in Grundy Co., Illinois

By the 1850s the paddle-wheel steamboat had become a symbol of the exciting era of economic expansion in the Midwest. The Mississippi was filled with these craft and the cities along the river were booming. St. Louis prospered as an outfitting point for migrants going west and as the commercial outlet for surrounding farms and mines. The city's population doubled in the decade before 1860 to over 150,000. Memphis and Natchez shipped huge cargoes of cotton downriver to New Orleans. To the north, at the head of navigation on the Mississippi, the twin cities of Minneapolis and St. Paul were established to serve the nearby lumber and mining industries.

(Top) Indian tepees at Bridge Square in Minneapolis, Minn., 1854, from a daguerreotype; (right) St. Paul, Minn., in 1855; lithograph from a painting by S. Holmes Andres; (bottom) the levee at St. Paul, 1859

OPPOSITE PAGE: (Top) View of St. Louis from Lucas Place, late 1850s; lithograph by E. Saches; (center) dozens of little steamboats docked at St. Louis in 1850 before the advent of the highboats; (bottom) St. Louis levee in 1853

"The Plantation" by an unknown American artist, about 1825

Much of the commerce of the Midwest moved southward down the Mississippi to New Orleans. To this traffic was added cotton from the plantations along the river. New Orleans was the outlet to Europe or the East for most of the Mississippi Valley, and had a population of 168,000 in 1860, almost equal to that of Boston. Commercial advantage and rapid growth brought changes in the traditional Creole character of the city. Descendents of the French and Spanish settlers lived apart and were no longer dominant, although Mardis Gras and the wrought-iron balconies remain.

(Left) Slave nurse Jane holding infant son of Col. Harvey Walter, Holly Springs, Miss., 1858; (right) Mardi Gras king in New Orleans, 1857

COTTON PRESSING IN LOUISIANA

(Top) Slaves pressing cotton in Louisiana; wood engraving from ''Ballou's,'' 1856; (right) cotton-loading in upper Louisiana where there are bluffs along the Mississippi River; engraving from ''Ballou's''; (bottom) bird's eye view of New Orleans, 1851; lithograph by J. Bachman

University of Michigan, 1854; (below) Henry Tappan; (bottom) Browning Seminary, Marion, Indiana, was typical of private schools for girls, where music and practical skills were emphasized

Prior to 1850, higher education in the Midwest was entirely in the hands of numerous private colleges of uneven quality. A few "normal schools" for the training of teachers had been established and several states had, on paper, elaborate plans for public education from elementary to college levels. But it was not until the University of Michigan was reorganized, after 1852, that the idea of the state university as the capstone of the public education system became a reality. Henry Tappan, first president of the University, undertook to make the faltering state school into an institution of the first rank. The BS degree was introduced, professional schools organized, and graduate programs established.

1855

65.

Philip Schaff: The Emergence of an American Character

Swiss-born church historian Philip Schaff was engaged in study for a German professorship when he was summoned in 1843 to the Mercersburg, Pennsylvania, seminary of the German Reformed Church. In his years there Schaff established a worldwide reputation as a theologian and historian, and became genuinely American in his outlook, especially in his efforts to unite German theology and American scholarship. Schaff's book, America, *a portion of which is reprinted here, grew out of lectures he gave to German audiences on a sabbatical trip to Europe in 1854. His fellow theologians were especially interested in having their former colleague explain the United States to them.*

Source: America, A Sketch of the Political, Social, and Religious Character of the United States of North America, New York, 1855, pp. 52-67, 256-260.

National Character and Social Life

THE UNITED STATES PRESENT, in the first place, a wonderful mixture of all nations under Heaven. A tour through them is in some sense a tour through the world, and therefore one of the most interesting and instructive journeys one can make, who would see the confused motions of the living present, rather than the rich treasures of the dead past; though of the latter, Italy, for example, that flower-crowned mausoleum of history, affords infinitely more. In America, English, Scotch, Irish, Germans of all provinces, Swiss, Dutch, French, Spaniards, Italians, Swedes, Norwegians, Poles, Magyars, with their well-known national virtues and weaknesses, have peaceably settled down together in political and social equality.

And to these representatives of European nations are added the red aborigines of the country, who are constantly retreating farther into the forests and prairies of the West; and, in spite of all attempts to Christianize and civilize them, are steadily approaching the tragical fate of self-extermination by intestine wars, contagious diseases, and the poison of rum. Then the black sons of Africa, rejoicing in the childlike cheerfulness of their nature, and even in freedom bowing instinctively before the superiority of the whites. Lastly, the yellow immigrants from the Celestial Empire, attracted by the gold of California, and bringing with them their oblong eyes, their quiet disposition and mechanical culture, their industry, avarice, and filthy habits. . . .

But now what is most remarkable is that over this confused diversity there broods after all a higher unity, and that in this chaos of peoples the traces of a specifically American national character may be discerned. Those who find in the United States only the faint echo of European nationalities, and so feel obliged to deny that country an independent future in history, are very much mistaken. Whoever treads the soil of the New World with open eyes perceives at once a thoroughly fresh and energetic national life, which instantly takes up and assimilates all foreign elements, excepting only the African and the Chinese. The American's digestive power is really astonishing. How many thousands and millions of Europeans has his stomach already received! And yet he has only grown firmer and healthier thereby. . . .

The American has the same organizing talent, the same self-control, the same practical energy, the same business faculty as the Englishman. His spirit of enterprise is still stronger, and not rarely degenerates even into foolhardiness and the most reckless disregard of human life, fearfully manifest in the countless conflagrations in cities and disasters on steamboats and railroads.

The American, I grant, has less solidity than the much older Englishman. But he makes up for this in vivacity, elasticity, and capacity for improvement. The Englishman, too, is shut up on his island; the American moves on a great continent and between two oceans. The former has not yet been able to assimilate to itself the Celtic Irishman in his immediate neighborhood, nor thoroughly to redress his grievances; the latter at once infuses into the immigrant the common feeling of the American. . . .

The English national character itself is, like the English language, confessedly the result of an organic combination of the British-Celtic, the Anglo-Saxon, or Germanic, and the Norman-French nationalities; the Anglo-Saxon, however, plainly forming the proper stem upon which the Norman was grafted in the twelfth century; as, in fact, the fundamental elements of the English language, all the words for the most essential relations of human life, are of German origin.

A similar process of national amalgamation is now also going on before our eyes in America; but peacefully, under more favorable conditions, and on a far grander scale than ever before in the history of the world. America is *the grave of all European nationalities;* but a *Phoenix grave,* from which they shall rise to new life and new activity in a new and essentially Anglo-Germanic form.

The English influence, of course, predominates in America, not only in language but also in the whole social life; but it is greatly modified, partly by influences from continental Europe, partly by the political institutions of America itself. The farther west and the newer the country, the more unformed and changeable is the state of society; and on the frontiers and in uncultivated regions, the rudest state of nature sometimes appears. In California, for example, with all its gold, I would not live for any price. Everything there is still in chaotic confusion; though even in this state the indestructible Anglo-American sense of law and order already shows itself energetically among the people. Lately, for example, the authorities being too cowardly to do their duty, the people took the punishment of certain offenders into their own hands, and executed "lynch law" upon them. In the larger states of the West, however, and especially in the East and South, we find well-ordered, respectable, and cultivated society.

The interior arrangements of a house commonly afford everything that the Englishman denotes by the untranslatable word "comfort" — carpets in the rooms, on the stairs, and in the hall; a parlor with sofas, piano, cushioned rocking chairs, a center table covered with illustrated works, the latest ladies' journals, etc. After the English plan, each family occupies a house by itself, which, at least in the smaller cities and towns, has generally a garden attached. Many of the larger cities even, as New Haven and Cleveland, are charmingly arranged, almost every house having an enclosed green in front, planted with trees and flowers, so that the streets present the delightful aspect of a garden promenade. The smaller towns are, in general, much handsomer, the streets wider and straighter, the houses more inviting and convenient than in Europe. And in the principal cities, New York, Philadelphia, Boston, Baltimore, Washington, Cincinnati, New Orleans, all European luxury is making only too rapid and perilous progress. Had not New York so many churches and Christian societies, and so strictly kept Sundays, it might already be called a second Paris, which it will soon be also in point of population.

In the lead of this luxury stand sometimes the most disgusting forms of a mushroom aristocracy, which rests upon nothing but the dust of gold. These American fops and quack-aristocrats, who, void of all true nobility, have no sense for anything but outward. show, are not rarely met, to our shame, in European capitals and watering places, striving to outdo the polite world in vanity and folly. I heard but yesterday, for example, that the son of a New York merchant prince in the Berne Highlands, where everybody goes on foot, if possible, to enjoy and admire, *con amore*, the sublimity of the mountain scenery, was driving around everywhere with two horses, to show the English lords and Russian nobles right visibly his pecuniary superiority.

It is characteristic that the two largest and most princely mansions in New York and Philadelphia were built by quacks (Dr. Townsend and Dr. Jayne) out of the proceeds of their sarsaparilla. Whether the enormous increases of luxury and worldly pomp and splendor will gradually undermine the republic, whose proper foundation is the patriarchal style of simplicity and honesty, time must tell. At any rate the flourishing commerce and growing wealth of the country involves great danger of a bottomless materialism and worldliness; and I see in Christianity alone the powerful corrective, which has thus far saved the higher intellectual and moral interests, and which will secure to them in future the predominance over the "almighty dollar." It is a remarkable fact, however, that wealth hardly continues to the third generation in the states, and that all this artificial aristocracy soon runs out. The middle classes are there, more than in any other country, the proper bone and sinew of society, and always restore the equilibrium.

Social life in America is in some respects freer, in others stiffer, than in Europe. Much that is not at all offensive there is rudeness to the European; and the American, in turn, is greatly scandalized with things which in the Old World are innocent customs. It were unjust and pedantic to make such mere externals the standard of judgment respecting the people. The old proverb here holds true: So many countries, so many customs. So highly and liberally cultivated society, as is found for instance here in Berlin, where, to speak without flattery, one may spend every evening in the most stimulating and agreeable conversation, with ladies as well as with gentlemen, on matters of science and art and all the higher affairs of life, is, I grant, very rarely met with in America. Female education especially is, in general, very superficial there, valued more for outward show than for inward solidity; and in many companies of which, judging from appearance, one would expect better things, you sometimes hear for a whole evening hardly anything but the flattest and most insufferable gossip about the weather, the fashions, and the latest projects of marriage.

On the other hand, however, there is more of a kind of medium cultivation than in Europe, where accomplishment is aristocratic or confined to certain classes. The United States is the country for average intelligence, average morality, and average piety. Republican institutions, as may even be observed to some extent in Switzerland, tend to level away social distinctions. In America, while there are not so many towering heights of culture, there is, on the other hand, no such widespread and degrading ignorance as in the masses of Europe. There, almost everyone tries to become a gentleman or a lady; that is, to attain the English ideal of outward and inward intellectual and moral culture, so far as his circumstances and position allow. Almost every man has some routine, at least outwardly; he can represent something; he reads gazettes and newspapers; knows how to talk sensibly about the general affairs of his country; and can, if necessary, make a speech; and generally turn his knowledge to good, practical account.

The Yankee especially — that is, the New Englander — has a natural business genius and can undertake anything. He can begin and make a fortune easier with one idea than a German can with ten. His mottoes are: "Help yourself," and "Go ahead." He early becomes independent, and even in youth learns to push through all possible difficulties. Hence the Jews hardly play any part in America; they find their masters in the Yankees. It must not be thought, however, that these descendants of the old Puritans are made only of shrewd, selfish calculation. It would be the greatest injustice to take the famous Barnum, the prince of humbug, as the only type of the "universal Yankee nation." They are generally liberal, conscientious, temperate, strictly moral, religiously inclined, friends of liberal education,

and ardent philanthropists. The six northeastern states, included under the name of New England, especially Massachusetts and Connecticut, are still, in regard to culture and Christianity, the garden of America.

Domestic life in the United States may be described as, on an average, well-regulated and happy. The number of illegitimate births is perhaps proportionally less than in any other country. Divorces are very rare, and are made by the laws far more difficult than, for example, in Prussia. This is the good effect of the laws of old England, which has practically made divorce almost impossible by requiring for it an act of Parliament and therefore an enormous outlay of money. True, the American family life is not characterized by so much deep good-nature, and warm, overflowing heartiness as the German. But instead of this the element of mutual respect predominates. Husband and wife, parents and children stand more independently toward one another, in a respectful dignity, and thus avoid many collisions. When the partners speak of each other in the third person, it is not commonly by the familiar names: my husband, my wife, but by the family name with Mr. or Mrs. prefixed, or by the official title. In fact, even in direct address, the wife not unfrequently gives her husband his title of Doctor, Professor, etc., particularly in company.

The American's profound respect for the female sex is well known. This old Germanic trait, celebrated so early by Tacitus, has most fully developed itself in the Anglo-Saxon race under the influence of Christianity, and is very favorable to domestic and public morality. Whoever is acquainted with family life in England knows how high and dignified a position woman holds there, and how much is comprehended in the term "lady." America goes yet a step further. It is sometimes called woman's paradise. I take it, indeed, that this earthly life is a paradise neither for ladies nor for gentlemen, but for both a purgatory, to purify them for Heaven. It is a fact, however, that in the United States woman is exempt from all hard labor (except perhaps among the immigrants, who keep their foreign customs, and in new settlements, say in Texas, or Wisconsin, or Oregon, where circumstances demand the strength of all hands); that she can travel unattended, from one end of the vast country to another, without being molested in the least; that in the steamboats, the great hotels, and public places, she finds her own saloons, sometimes extremely elegant, and all possible conveniences, and has the precedence in every company.

It is characteristic, also, that in America one must address a mixed audience, not as "Gentlemen and Ladies," as in all other languages, but in the reverse order, as "Ladies and Gentlemen." Of course this respect for woman requires monogamy as its indispensable groundwork; and it is one main reason why the Mormons, who are charged, you are aware, with polygamy, are so hated there, and have been banished even by force from the territory of the organized states. They will never make many proselytes among the Americans, and they are accordingly now directing their missionary efforts almost entirely abroad.

The crown of the American family life, and one of the strongest proofs of the power of Christianity over the people, is table prayer, which is almost universal; and daily family worship, which is the rule at least in religious circles, and is proportionally more frequent there than in any other country, except perhaps, England and Scotland. The ultimate effects of this pious custom on children and children's children are incalculable; and it must go well with a people where the father feels it his duty and his joy to gather the members of his household every morning around the Holy Scriptures, as their daily bread of life, and to bow with them before the throne of the Almighty, and implore His blessing on the labors of the day. . . .

The Significance of North America for the Future Development of the Kingdom of God

The United States of North America — whose citizens are called *Americans* in an emphatic sense, because the bearers of the historical life and progress of the whole Western Hemisphere — are a wonder in the annals of the human race. Their development, in its rapidity and gigantic proportions, far outstrips all former experience, and their significance for the future mocks the boldest calculation. Though not a hundred years old, they have become already, by natural force of expansion, one of the mightiest empires of the civilized world, with the control of one entire continent and two oceans, and spread, in the most peaceful manner, the meshes of their influence over Europe, Asia, and Africa. And yet their history up to this time is only a faint prelude of what is to come; and the Americans of the 20th century will look upon the present age of their country with feelings akin to those with which modern Europeans regard the exodus of the threshold of the Middle Ages.

The "Young Giant" has not yet, so to speak, sown all his wild oats, and along with many heroic deeds, commits also some wanton and extravagant pranks, which prove, however, the exuberant vigor of his youthful powers. Providence, who creates nothing in vain, has there made physical preparations on the grandest scale, and formed an immeasurable territory, containing the most fruitful soil, the most valuable mineral treasures, and the most favorable means of commercial intercourse as a tempting asylum for all European nations, churches, and sects, who, there freed from the fetters of antiquated institutions, amid circumstances and conditions altogether new, and with renovated energies, swarm and jostle each other, and yet, in an incredibly short space of time are molded by the process into one powerful nationality. While Europe had first to work her way up out of heathen barbarism, America, without earning it, has appropriated the civilization and church history of 2,000 years as an inheritance, and already put out at the highest rate of interest for the benefit of after generations.

For, these Americans have not the least desire to rest on the laurels of the past and comfortably enjoy the present; they are full of ambition and national pride, and firmly resolved to soar above the Old World. They are a people of the boldest enterprise and untiring progress — restlessness and agitation personified. Even when seated, they push themselves to and fro on their rocking chairs; they live in a state of perpetual excitement in their business, their politics, and their religion, and remind one of the storm-lashed sea, which here

Seethes and bubbles and hisses and roars,
As when fire with water is commixed
   and contending
— it never will rest, nor from travail
   be free,
Like a sea that is laboring the birth of
   a sea.

They are excellently characterized by the expressions, "Help yourself" and "Go ahead," which are never out of their mouths. It is also a very significant fact that they have invented the magnetic telegraph, or at least perfected it, and are far advanced in the useful arts. For there the car of the world's history moves swifter on the pinions of steam and electricity, and "the days become shortened."

The grandest destiny is evidently reserved for such a people. We can and must, it is true, find fault with many things in them and their institutions: slavery, the lust of conquest, the worship of Mammon, the rage for speculation, political and religious fanaticism and party spirit, boundless temerity, boasting, quackery, and — to use the American word for it — humbug, as well as other weaknesses and dangers that are

moreover wanting to no country in Europe.

But we must not overlook the healthy, vital energies that continually react against these diseases: the moral, yea, Puritanical earnestness of the American character, its patriotism and noble love of liberty in connection with deep-rooted reverence for the law of God and authority; its clear, practical understanding; its talent for organization; its inclination for improvement in every sphere; its fresh enthusiasm for great plans and schemes of moral reform; and its willingness to make sacrifices for the promotion of God's kingdom and every good work. The acquisition of riches is to them only a help toward higher spiritual and moral ends; the gain derived from the inexhaustible physical resources of their glorious country only the material groundwork toward the furtherance of civilization.

They wrestle with the most colossal projects. The deepest meaning and aim of their political institutions are to actualize the idea of *universal* sovereignty, the education of every individual for intellectual and moral self-government and thus for true freedom. They wish to make culture, which in Europe is everywhere aristocratic and confined to a comparatively small portion of society, the common property of the people, and train up if possible every youth as a gentleman and every girl as a lady. And in the six states of New England, at least, they have attained this object in a higher degree than any country in the Old World, England and Scotland not even excepted.

In short, if anywhere in the wide world a new page of universal history has been unfolded and a new fountain opened, fraught [loaded] with incalculable curses or blessings for future generations, it is in the republic of the United States with her star-spangled banner. Either humanity has no earthly future and everything is tending to destruction, or this future lies — I say not exclusively, but mainly — in America, according to the victorious march of history, with the sun from East to West.

66.

David Christy: The Kingdom of Cotton

David Christy, although not a Southerner or a strong advocate of slavery, published in 1855 one of the most popular defenses of the Southern slave system, Cotton Is King. *In the work, portions of which follow, Christy portrayed the slave system as but one element in a vast interrelated network of agriculture, commerce, and industry that functioned under the rule of "King Cotton" to the mutual benefit of North and South. While he did at one or two points refer to slavery as an "evil," Christy's true feelings are indicated by the fact that in 1860 he sold the rights to the book to E. N. Elliott for inclusion in a collection of pro-slavery arguments.*

Source: *Cotton Is King, and Pro-Slavery Arguments,* E. N. Elliott, ed., Augusta, Ga., 1860, pp. 55-60, 215-219.

THE INSTITUTION OF SLAVERY, at this moment, gives indications of a vitality that was never anticipated by its friends or foes. Its enemies often supposed it about ready to expire from the wounds they had inflicted, when in truth it had taken two steps in advance while they had taken twice the number in an opposite direction. In each successive conflict its assailants have been weakened, while its dominion has been extended.

This has arisen from causes too generally overlooked. Slavery is not an isolated system but is so mingled with the business of the world that it derives facilities from the most innocent transactions. Capital and labor in Europe and America are largely employed in the manufacture of cotton. These goods, to a great extent, may be seen freighting every vessel from Christian nations that traverses the seas of the globe; and filling the warehouses and shelves of the merchants over two-thirds of the world. By the industry, skill, and enterprise employed in the manufacture of cotton, mankind are better clothed; their comfort better promoted; general industry more highly stimulated; commerce more widely extend-

ed; and civilization more rapidly advanced than in any preceding age.

To the superficial observer, all the agencies based upon the sale and manufacture of cotton seem to be legitimately engaged in promoting human happiness; and he, doubtless, feels like invoking Heaven's choicest blessings upon them. When he sees the stockholders in the cotton corporations receiving their dividends; the operatives, their wages; the merchants, their profits; and civilized people everywhere clothed comfortably in cottons, he cannot refrain from exclaiming: "The lines have fallen unto them in pleasant places; yea, they have a goodly heritage!"

But turn a moment to the source whence the raw cotton, the basis of these operations, is obtained, and observe the aspect of things in that direction. When the statistics on the subject are examined, it appears that nine-tenths of the cotton consumed in the Christian world is the product of the slave labor of the United States. It is this monopoly that has given to slavery its commercial value; and, while this monopoly is retained, the institution will continue to extend itself wherever it can find room to spread. He who looks for any other result must expect that nations, which for centuries have waged war to extend their commerce, will now abandon that means of aggrandizement and bankrupt themselves to force the abolition of American slavery!

This is not all. The economical value of slavery as an agency for supplying the means of extending manufactures and commerce has long been understood by statesmen. The discovery of the power of steam and the inventions in machinery for preparing and manufacturing cotton revealed the important fact that a single island, having the monopoly secured to itself, could supply the world with clothing. Great Britain attempted to gain this monopoly; and to prevent other countries from rivaling her, she long prohibited all emigration of skillful mechanics from the kingdom, as well as all exports of machinery. As country after country was opened to her commerce, the markets for her manufactures were extended and the demand for the raw material increased. The benefits of this enlarged commerce of the world were not confined to a single nation but mutually enjoyed by all.

As each had products to sell peculiar to itself, the advantages often gained by one were no detriment to the others. The principal articles demanded by this increasing commerce have been coffee, sugar, and cotton, in the production of which slave labor has greatly predominated. Since the enlargement of manufactures, cotton has entered more extensively into commerce than coffee and sugar, though the demand for all three has advanced with the greatest rapidity. England could only become a great commercial nation through the agency of her manufactures. She was the best supplied of all the nations with the necessary capital, skill, labor, and fuel to extend her commerce by this means. But for the raw material to supply her manufactories, she was dependent upon other countries.

The planters of the United States were the most favorably situated for the cultivation of cotton; and while Great Britain was aiming at monopolizing its manufacture, they attempted to monopolize the markets for that staple. This led to a fusion of interests between them and the British manufacturers; and to the adoption of principles in political economy, which, if rendered effective, would promote the interests of this coalition. With the advantages possessed by the English manufacturers, "free trade" would render all other nations subservient to their interests; and, so far as their operations should be increased, just so far would the demand for American cotton be extended. The details of the success of the parties to this combination, and the opposition they have had to encounter, are left to be noticed more fully hereafter. To the cotton planters, the copartnership has been eminently advantageous.

How far the other agricultural interests of the United States are promoted by extending the cultivation of cotton may be inferred from the census returns of 1850 and the *Congressional Reports on Commerce and Navigation* for 1854. Cotton and tobacco only are largely exported. The production of sugar does not yet equal our consumption of the article, and we import, chiefly from slave-labor countries, 445,445,680 lbs. to make up the deficiency. But of cotton and tobacco, we export more than *two-thirds* of the amount produced; while of other products of the agriculturists, less than the *one forty-sixth* part is exported. Foreign nations generally can grow their provisions, but cannot grow their tobacco and cotton. Our surplus provisions, not exported, go to the villages, towns, and cities to feed the mechanics, manufacturers, merchants, professional men, and others; or to the cotton and sugar districts of the South to feed the planters and their slaves.

The increase of mechanics and manufacturers at the North and the expansion of slavery at the South, therefore, augment the markets for provisions and promote the prosperity of the farmer. As the mechanical population increases, the implements of industry and articles of furniture are multiplied, so that both farmer and planter can be supplied with them on easier terms. As foreign nations open their markets to cotton fabrics, increased demands for the raw material are made. As new grazing and grain-growing states are developed and teem with their surplus productions, the mechanic is benefited; and the planter, relieved from food-raising, can employ his slaves more extensively upon cotton. It is thus that our exports are increased, our foreign commerce advanced, the home markets of the mechanic and farmer extended, and the wealth of the nation promoted. It is thus, also, that the free labor of the country finds remunerating markets for its products — though at the expense of serving as an efficient auxiliary in the extension of slavery!

But more: So speedily are new grain-growing states springing up; so vast is the territory owned by the United States ready for settlement; and so enormous will soon be the amount of products demanding profitable markets, that the national government has been seeking new outlets for them upon our own continent, to which, alone, they can be advantageously transported. That such outlets, when our vast possessions westward are brought under cultivation, will be an imperious necessity is known to every statesman. The farmers of these new states, after the example of those of the older sections of the country, will demand a market for their products. This can be furnished only by the extension of slavery; by the acquisition of more tropical territory; by opening the ports of Brazil and other South American countries to the admission of our provisions; by their free importation into European countries; or by a vast enlargement of domestic manufactures, to the exclusion of foreign goods from the country.

Look at this question as it now stands, and then judge of what it must be twenty years hence. The class of products under consideration, in the whole country, in 1853, were valued at $1,551,176,490; of which there were exported to foreign countries to the value of only $33,809,126. The planter will not assent to any check upon the foreign imports of the country for the benefit of the farmer. This demands the adoption of vigorous measures to secure a market for his products by some of the other modes stated; hence the orders of our executive, in 1851, for the exploration of the valley of the Amazon; the efforts, in 1854, to obtain a treaty with Brazil for the free navigation of that immense river; the negotiations for a military foothold in Santo Domingo; and the determination to acquire Cuba. . . .

IN CONCLUDING OUR LABORS, there is little need of extended observation. The work of emancipation in our country was checked and the extension of slavery promoted: first, by the neglect of the free colored people to improve the advantages afforded them; second, by the increasing value imparted to slave labor; third, by the mistaken policy into which the English and American Abolitionists have fallen. Whatever reasons might now be offered for emancipation, from an improvement of our free colored people, is far more than counterbalanced by its failure in the West Indies, and the constantly increasing value of the labor of the slave. If, when the planters had only a moiety of the markets for cotton, the value of slavery was such as to arrest emancipation, how must the obstacles be increased now, when they have the monopoly of the markets of the world? And, besides all this, a more deadly blow than has been given by all other causes combined is now leveled at Negro freedom from a quarter the least suspected. The failure of the Canadian immigrants to improve the privileges afforded them under British law proves, conclusively, that the true laws of progress for the African race do not consist in a mere escape from slavery.

We propose not to speak of remedies for slavery. That we leave to others. Thus far this very perplexing question has baffled all human wisdom. Either some radical defect must have existed in the measures devised for its removal, or the time has not yet come for successfully assailing the institution. Our work is completed in the delineation we have given of its varied relations to our agricultural, commercial, and social interests. As the monopoly of the culture of cotton imparts to slavery its economical value, the system will continue as long as this monopoly is maintained. Slave-labor products have now become necessities of human life to the extent of more than half the commercial articles supplied to the Christian world. Even free labor itself is made largely subservient to slavery, and vitally interested in its perpetuation and extension.

Can this condition of things be changed? It may be reasonably doubted whether anything efficient can be speedily accomplished; not because there is lack of territory where freemen may be employed in tropical cultivation, as all Western and Central Africa, nearly, is adapted to this purpose; not because intelligent free labor, under proper incentives, is less productive than slave labor; but because freemen, whose constitutions are adapted to tropical climates, will not avail themselves of the opportunity offered for commencing such an enterprise.

King Cotton cares not whether he employs slaves or freemen. It is the *cotton*, not the *slaves*, upon which his throne is based. Let freemen do his work as well, and he will not object to the change. The efforts of his most powerful ally, Great Britain, to promote that object have already cost her people many hundreds of millions of dollars, with total failure as a reward for her zeal; and she is now compelled to resort to the expedient of employing the slave labor of Africa to meet the necessities of her manufacturers. One-sixth of the colored people of the United States are free; but they shun the cotton regions, and have been instructed to detest emigration to Liberia. Their improvement has not been such as was anticipated; and their more rapid advancement cannot be expected while they remain in the country.

The free colored people of the British West Indies can no longer be relied on to furnish tropical products, for they are resting contented in a state of almost savage indolence; and the introduction of coolie labor has become indispensable as a means of saving the islands from ruin, as well as of forcing the Negro into habits of industry. Haiti is not in a more promising condition; and even if it were, its population and territory are too limited to enable it to meet the increasing demand. His Majesty, King Cotton, therefore, is forced to continue the employment of his slaves; and by their toil is riding on, conquering and to conquer! He receives no check from the cries of the oppressed, while the citizens of the world are dragging forward his chariot and shouting aloud his praise!

King Cotton is a profound statesman and knows what measures will best sustain his throne. He is an acute mental philosopher, acquainted with the secret springs of human action, and accurately perceives who can best promote his aims. He has no evidence that colored men can grow his cotton except in the capacity of slaves. Thus far, all experiments made to increase the production of cotton by emancipating the slaves employed in its cultivation have been a total failure. It is his policy, therefore, to defeat all schemes of emancipation. To do this, he stirs up such agitations as lure his enemies into measures that will do him no injury. The venal politician is always at his call and assumes the form of saint or sinner, as the service may demand.

Nor does he overlook the enthusiast, engaged in quixotic endeavors for the relief of suffering humanity, but influences him to advocate measures which tend to tighten instead of loosening the bands of slavery. Or, if he cannot be seduced into the support of such schemes, he is beguiled into efforts that waste his strength on objects the most impracticable; so that slavery receives no damage from the exuberance of his philanthropy. But should such a one, perceiving the futility of his labors and the evils of his course, make an attempt to avert the consequences; while he is doing this, some new recruit, pushed forward into his former place, charges him with lukewarmness or pro-slavery sentiments, destroys his influence with the public, keeps alive the delusions, and sustains the supremacy of King Cotton in the world.

In speaking of the economical connections of slavery with the other material interests of the world, we have called it a *tripartite alliance*. It is more than this. It is *quadruple*. Its structure includes four parties, arranged thus: the Western Agriculturists; the Southern Planters; the English Manufacturers; and the American Abolitionists! By this arrangement, the Abolitionists do not stand in direct contact with slavery; they imagine, therefore, that they have clean hands and pure hearts so far as sustaining the system is concerned. But they, no less than their allies, aid in promoting the interests of slavery. Their sympathies are with England on the slavery question, and they very naturally incline to agree with her on other points.

She advocates "free trade" as essential to her manufactures and commerce; and they do the same, not waiting to inquire into its bearings upon American slavery. We refer now to the people, not to their leaders, whose integrity we choose not to endorse. The free trade and protective systems, in their bearings upon slavery, are so well understood that no man of general reading, especially an editor, or member of Congress, who professes antislavery sentiments at the same time advocating "free trade," will ever convince men of intelligence, pretend what he may, that he is not either woefully perverted in his judgment or emphatically a "doughface" in disguise! En-

gland, we were about to say, is in alliance with the cotton planter, to whose prosperity free trade is indispensable. Abolitionism is in alliance with England. All three of these parties, then, agree in their support of the "free trade" policy. It needed but the aid of the Western farmer, therefore, to give permanency to this principle. His adhesion has been given, the *quadruple alliance* has been perfected, and slavery and free trade *nationalized!*

Slavery, thus entrenched in the midst of such powerful allies, and without competition in tropical cultivation, has become the sole reliance of King Cotton. Lest the sources of his aggrandizement should be assailed, we can well imagine him as being engaged constantly in devising new questions of agitation to divert the public from all attempts to abandon free trade and restore the protective policy. He now finds an ample source of security, in this respect, in agitating the question of slavery extension. This exciting topic, as we have said, serves to keep politicians of the Abolition school at the North in his constant employ. But for the agitation of this subject, few of these men would succeed in obtaining the suffrages of the people.

Wedded to England's "free trade" policy, their votes in Congress, on all questions affecting the tariff, are always in perfect harmony with Southern interests and work no mischief to the system of slavery. If Kansas comes into the Union as a slave state, he is secure in the political power it will give him in Congress; but if it is received as a free state, it will still be tributary to him as a source from whence to draw provisions to feed his slaves. Nor does it matter much which way the controversy is decided, so long as all agree not to disturb slavery in the states where it is already established by law. Could King Cotton be assured that this position will not be abandoned, he would care little about slavery in Kansas; but he knows full well that the public sentiment in the North is adverse to the system, and that the present race of politicians may readily be displaced by others who will pledge themselves to its overthrow in all the states of the Union. Hence he wills to retain the power over the question in his own hands.

The crisis now upon the country, as a consequence of slavery having become dominant, demands that the highest wisdom should be brought to the management of national affairs. Slavery, nationalized, can now be managed only as a national concern. It can now be abolished only with the consent of those who sustain it. Their assent can be gained only by employing other agents to meet the wants it now supplies. It must be superseded, then, if at all, by means that will not injuriously affect the interests of commerce and agriculture, to which it is now so important an auxiliary. None other will be accepted for a moment by the slaveholder.

To supply the existing demand for tropical products, except by the present mode, is impossible. To make the change is not the work of a day, nor of a generation. Should the influx of foreigners continue, such a change may, one day, be possible. But to effect the transition from slavery to freedom on principles that will be acceptable to the parties who control the question; to devise and successfully sustain such measures as will produce this result must be left to statesmen of broader views and loftier conceptions than are to be found among those at present engaged in this great controversy.

67.

William S. Tyler: The College and the Church

The prominent role played by religious sects in American higher education produced two distinct movements in the nineteenth century. Some educators, fearing that religious affiliation was a drawback to academic pursuits, urged the establishment of state universities. The churches, on the other hand, strove to outdo each other in the number of colleges each could sponsor. The following essay by Professor William S. Tyler of Amherst College summarizes the arguments for church affiliated schools. The essay was first published in 1855 by the Society for the Promotion of Collegiate and Theological Education at the West, which coordinated appeals for funds and distributed financial contributions among sectarian schools.

Source: *Prayer for Colleges*, New York, 1855, pp. 102-120.

Schools and colleges, wherever they exist, almost without exception, owe their origin to the church. Christianity is, in its very nature, friendly to learning. It is a religion, not of forms and of ceremonies but of the mind and heart. It saves men, not by outward means and appliances but by the inward workings of the truth and the Spirit of God in their souls. Knowledge is, therefore, essential to holiness and salvation. Its ministry is a teaching and preaching ministry, not a mere officiating and manipulating priesthood. Its sacred books contain not only the most stirring truths and the most commanding motives but the choicest specimens of history, poetry, and philosophy the world has ever seen; and those, too, originally communicated in a foreign language, and for this reason, as well as many others, requiring prolonged study and extensive knowledge in order to their full understanding and appreciation. Christianity produces an inquiring, observing, thinking, and intelligent laity. It demands a reading, studying, reflecting, and learned ministry.

The first ministers of the gospel were taught immediately by Christ, and were, moreover, constantly under the especial divine teaching of the Holy Spirit. They, therefore, stood in little need of human learning. Yet one of the apostles, and one who exceeded all the others in his labors and usefulness, was taught in the best Jewish and gentile schools of Jerusalem and Tarsus. And no sooner were the miraculous gifts, which signalized the first establishment of Christianity, withdrawn, than the churches began to found colleges and theological schools at Jerusalem and Alexandria, and the other principal cities, for the especial purpose of raising up a pious and learned ministry who should be able, not only to preach the truth to its friends but also to defend it from the assaults of its adversaries.

And though, during the Middle Ages, learning everywhere suffered a disastrous eclipse, yet what light there was shone from the schools in the monasteries, which were established by such enlightened and pious princes as Charlemagne and Alfred, chiefly for the elevation of the clergy, and which gradually grew up into universities. As this eclipse passed off slowly and universities began to appear in Italy, in France, in England, they were established and fostered by the church, and chiefly for the better education of the clergy. Oxford and Cambridge were founded, and in the course of time enriched with princely endowments for this express purpose. Zeal for religion conspired with love of learning, and college after college was added to those ancient and venerable universities, chiefly for the charitable education of intelligent young men for the service of the church.

The necessity for a well-educated ministry of the gospel has never been so generally and powerfully felt anywhere else as in our own country; and this feeling has been the leading motive in the establishment of by far the larger part of American colleges. "Dreading to leave an illiterate ministry to the churches, when our ministers shall lie in the dust" — such is the language in which the founders of Harvard College describe their own motives in that farseeing and self-denying enterprise which they undertook just as soon as they had provided comfortable houses for themselves and selected convenient places for the worship of God. And sixty years later, Cotton Mather says: "Our fathers saw that without a college to train an able and learned ministry, the church in New England must have been less than a business of an age — must soon have come to nothing." *Pro Christo et Ecclesia* — for Christ and the Church — is to this day the motto of Harvard College, though sadly fallen, alas! from the truth as it is in Jesus.

Yale College . . . was founded by ministers. It was also founded chiefly for the education of ministers for the colony of Connecticut. It originated, as they tell us, in their sincere regard and zeal for upholding the Protestant religion by a succession of learned and orthodox men.

"Princeton College was founded by the Synod of New York for the purpose of supplying the church with learned and able preachers of the Word." And its paramount religious design and spirit are well expressed in the language of President Witherspoon: "Cursed be all that learning that is contrary to the cross of Christ; cursed be all that learning that is not coincident with the cross of Christ; cursed be all that learning that is not subservient to the cross of Christ."

"Dartmouth College was originated in the warmest spirit, and established in the most elevated principles of Christian piety."

Amherst College grew out of a charity school, which was established for the education of indigent young men for the ministerial and the missionary work. It was born of the prayers and baptized with the tears of holy men; and, as in the early history of Harvard, the colonists contributed of their deep poverty, "one bringing a piece of cotton stuff, valued at 9s; another, a pewter pot of the same value; a third, a fruit dish, a spoon, and a large and small saltcellar"; so, in the founding of Amherst College, the friends of learning and religion in the vicinity brought in the materials and built up the walls with their own hands, while those at a distance gave in money, or the fruit of their labors, whatever they could spare which might conduce to the endowment of the institution and the maintenance of its officers and students. Such self-denials and sacrifices as were made by the founders of these, and, indeed, most of our colleges, could have proceeded only from religious motives — only from hearts overflowing with love to Christ and His church. Amherst College was one of the *earliest* institutions that grew up under the influence of the foreign missionary enterprise and the new impulse which was thus given to all benevolent efforts; and it is, in its character and history, a type of a new class of colleges which have sprung up, particularly in the new states, and which may be called emphatically, both as regards their origin and influence, missionary colleges.

"Western Reserve College was founded by domestic missionaries and designed to furnish pastors for the infant churches on the Reserve. Illinois College originated in the union of two independent movements; the one emanating from home missionary operations in Illinois, the other from a Society of Inquiry respecting Missions at Yale College. The site of Wabash College was dedicated to God in prayer by its founders kneeling upon the snow in the primeval forest. Marietta College was founded mainly to meet demands for competent teachers and ministers of the gospel."

In fact, nearly all of those institutions which have lived and prospered and exerted a decided influence, even in our literary and political history, were established by evangelical Christians; and have been taught, for the most part, by evangelical ministers, with a direct and special reference to supplying these churches, and the country and the world, with a learned and pious evangelical ministry. Institutions established by worldly men for mere worldly objects have not prospered. Infidelity or irreligion or no religion may have founded them, but it could not sustain them; and it has been found necessary to transfer them to the hands of religious guardians and teachers in order to save them from utter extinction. They have been planned by the wisdom of political sages, and fostered by the wealth and power of the state, but they could not be well managed and governed without the sanction of religion. They have not won the confidence of parents and guardians, for even irreligious parents do not generally want their children educated in infidelity or impiety; and Christianity, though hated in itself, has been welcomed as a necessary means. Though excluded by statutes and constitutions, it has, sooner or later, been admitted to a practical and controlling influence.

The history of the University of Virginia, the University of South Carolina, Transylvania University, Dickinson College, Girard College, and, to some extent, Harvard College, had we time to give it, would furnish a satisfactory demonstration of these statements. Baptists and Methodists, Congregationalists and Presbyterians — all the evangelical Protestant sects have their prosperous literary institutions in almost every state of the Union; but infidelity has yet to make its first successful enterprise of this sort; and state policy, state patronage, exclusive of religious influence, cannot show a single flourishing college from the Atlantic and the Great Lakes to the Pacific and the Gulf of Mexico.

These are remarkable facts, especially when considered in connection with the voluntary system and the entire civil and religious liberty of the American people. A wealthy and powerful establishment — a church wedded to the state and enriched by state patronage through successive centuries — we might well suppose, could secure such results. A rich and lordly hierarchy, lording it over the consciences and the estates of the whole people, we should think, might build religious colleges by scores in every part of the country, or might subsidize existing literary institutions and make them subservient to their views of religion. But that the free, voluntary movements of so many different denominations of Christians should have reared 120 colleges in different parts of these United States — many of them in the very infancy of the states, or provinces, and all within little more than 200 years after the first settlement of the country; and furnished them with such a succession of learned and pious teachers, and brought them so completely under the controlling influence of a practical Christianity — this is truly remarkable.

It shows that Christianity, with all its divisions and corruptions, still possesses a vital energy, and is still guided and guarded by Him who has all wisdom and all power. It shows that the church is still self-denying in her spirit and far-reaching in her plans; for nothing but self-denying charity and far-reaching sagacity will plant colleges in a new country, when there is a present demand for the necessaries of life rather than for high mental culture. It shows that there is a natural and mutual affinity between religion and learning; that each alternately seeks the alliance and support of the other, while both are left to the freest action and development. It shows that the American people are imbued with a deep, practical conviction that the college was in its origin, and is in its nature, a religious institution; and must be so if it would realize its proper literary and political ends. Above all, it proves, as we cannot but believe, and would acknowledge with devout gratitude, that the providence of God has watched over our beloved country in all its history and guarded it against the dangers to which a youthful and free people are most exposed, as if He intended, in spite of adverse agencies, to preserve this goodly land as a heritage for Himself.

The college, then, is the daughter of the church, cherished by her with all a mother's love and care and self-denial. Has the daughter done anything in return for the mother? Surely she were an unnatural child if she has made no return of filial love and service to her to whom she owes all that she has and all that she is, even to her very existence.

Is it nothing to the church that the system of popular education, the preparation of textbooks, the examination and direction of teachers, and, to so great an extent, the education of the teachers themselves is in the hands of men who have been trained by Christian scholars in Christian colleges? Is it a small thing for the church that colleges established by herself and conducted by her ablest and best men give tone, in so great a measure, to the literature of the country, and control the reading of the people, not only in books of history and philosophy, and poetry and belles-lettres, but in those magazines and newspapers which now occupy more and more the pens of our most thoughtful, learned, and elegant writers?

Is it of little or no consequence to the church that men educated at Christian colleges have, to so great an extent, filled the office of presidents, and governors, and judges, and other civil magistrates in our country, and are also extending their influence everyday more widely among the people through the popularization of learning, and those countless applications of science to common life, which are pouring wealth into the bosom of the church for her enterprises of benevolence? Is it nothing to the church that so many of our lawyers and physicians, and other men of influence in the community, have been taught in college to recognize the divine origin of Christianity, to respect the institutions of religion, and to carry more or less of Christian principles and a Christian spirit with them into the higher walks of life?

These are some of the indirect contributions of colleges to the church. Now let us look at some more direct returns of revenue which she has received from her investments in colleges. Let us see how well they accomplish the more immediate and more prominent object, which the church contemplated in their establishment.

The ministry of this country has been an educated ministry from the first. The earliest ministers in the colonies were of course educated abroad; but soon there rose up schools of the prophets in the wilderness, and the churches looked, nor looked in vain, to Harvard, and Yale, and Nassau Hall for pastors to feed them with knowledge and understanding. A minister without a thorough college education would scarcely have been tolerated among the Pilgrim fathers, or their descendants for a hundred years after them. Sects have since sprung up that for a time eschewed learning and listened to rant from the pulpit, while they looked in vain for inspiration. But as they have grown older and wiser, even these sects have fallen in with the spirit of the country and the age, and now they, too, demand a learned as well as pious ministry; now they yield to none in their zeal and liberality for the establishment of colleges and theological seminaries.

The clerical, far beyond either of the other so-called *learned professions,* is actually composed of men of thorough classical education. Half-educated fledglings are fluttering and tumbling into the practice of law and medicine more frequently now, perhaps, than at any former period of our history. But never before was there a smaller relative proportion of uneducated clergymen; never before was the standard of clerical education and attainment so high and so imperative on all who would enter the sacred office. It never has been, and is never likely to be, the doctrine of the churches in America that ministers can be qualified to interpret the sacred oracles without a thorough knowledge of the original languages, or that they can teach the wisdom of God to their fellow-men without being masters of human knowledge. . . .

American missions to the heathen had their birth in a little circle of devoted young men whose prayers have hallowed the rooms and the very fields about Williams College, and whose example has blessed the nations in every quarter of the globe. The precise locality where Samuel J. Mills and his associates consecrated themselves to a missionary life, we are happy to learn, has been recently identified, and it is to be purchased and set apart as a perpetual memorial of that sacred epoch in the history of the church. A higher monument would mark this place, were monuments any measure of the importance of the events which they commemorate, than rises from any battlefield in the New or the Old World; and Christians, if they had the spirit of Christ and of Christian missions, would go on pilgrimages, not to Bunker Hill or Waterloo but to "the Haystack," near Williams College. The sacred flame which first began to burn there has been kept alive on the same and similar altars.

American missionaries have not only been graduates of American colleges but, with few exceptions, they consecrated themselves to the missionary work while they dwelt in college walls. Facts show that very few decide to become missionaries after leaving college. "From Dartmouth College have gone out twenty-four missionaries to foreign countries; from Amherst, so recently established, thirty-six; from Williams, thirty-three; from Middlebury, twenty-four." The colleges stand in a no less sacred relation to the cause of home missions. In 1850, Amherst had as many as fifty home missionaries in the field.

The men for all our benevolent enterprises must come from the colleges, and will carry through life very much of the character and spirit they had when in college. Students give more money for benevolent objects, in proportion to their means, than almost any other community. This may not be so with all colleges and higher seminaries, but we know it is so in more than one. We have seen the poor student throw his last quarter into the contribution box, saying (with a sublime faith, not perhaps to be imitated by all, but worthy of universal admiration), "There is all the money I have in the world. I will have that safe."

But money is the smallest contribution which is made by students in college to the cause of Christian charity. They have first given themselves to the Lord and to His work, wherever and whatever it may be. With a faith like that of Abraham, they have been willing to leave their country, not knowing whither they go, while with a love like that of Christ, they have offered up themselves on the altar of reconciliation between God and their fellowmen.

The commencement of the new era of benevolence — the era of missionary and Bible and tract and education societies — was marked by the establishment of an unusual number, we might almost say, a new kind of colleges; and they in turn have sustained and furthered the various forms of associated benevolence with unwonted zeal and devotion. At the same time (to their honor be it said, as well as in truth and justice), some of the older institutions have caught not a little of the new spirit, and lavished the accumulated treasures of their wisdom and their influence in the support of those moral and religious enterprises which are the glory of the age.

Those revivals of religion which so illustrate and bless our times have prevailed in colleges with greater frequency and power than in any other communities; and who can calculate the good influences, direct and indirect, which revivals in colleges have exerted on the churches? How many minis-

ters and magistrates, professional men and men of influence have there been born into the kingdom of Christ; and how many more reconverted, so that, like Peter, they could strengthen their brethren? How many, while members of college, have caught the spirit of revivals and of missions, and carried it home to the church to which they belong, and, with the characteristic ardor and *strength of young men* in a course of education, diffused it through the place of their nativity? And when such men have been settled in the ministry, their own churches have been revival churches and missionary churches; the life of the communities around them and the light of this dark world. It has been estimated that one revival of religion, which took place in Yale College under the presidency of Dr. Dwight, raised up ministers who were instrumental of the conversion of 50,000 souls in one generation.

Thus, it appears that marked eras in the history of the church have usually been marked eras in the history of colleges, from the establishment of the first seminary in the early Christian church to the foundation of the last college in our Western wilderness. The progress of the churches has been *registered*, so to speak, and their attainments have been secured and perpetuated by the colleges, while in turn, every new wave of thought and tide of feeling in the colleges has had its corresponding wave and tide in the churches. The stream will not permanently rise higher than the fountain. The fountain determines the quality as well as the height of the stream.

The college and the church are alternately or mutually fountain and stream. More frequently the impulse originates in the college. It was so in the Reformation. It was so with the Oxford heresy. The Unitarian defection in New England originated perhaps with the churches, or rather with their pastors, but it has been perpetuated by Harvard College. The tide rose in the churches till it burst open the gates and inundated the college, but now it has turned and is flowing back, more gradually, but not less powerfully, and even more effectively, from the college into the churches and the community.

Let all our colleges become like Harvard, and Unitarianism would overflow the country. Or let them become such schools of infidelity as Jefferson and Girard would fain have established; and, unless they are abandoned and their gates closed, the next generation will forsake the religion of their fathers, and the churches will be deserted by the people. Or let our ministers and men of influence be uneducated or half educated, and errors and heresies will spring up like thorns and briars in a neglected field; for it is men who are untaught in history (especially the history of doctrines), and undisciplined in their mental and moral faculties, whose minds have been the hotbeds of theological error in every age of the church. To pray for the colleges, then, is to pray for the churches, for an educated and devoted ministry, for a pure and Protestant Christianity, for foreign and home missions, for evangelical revivals of religion; in a word, for churches that shall live and work and propagate a sound faith, lively hope, and impartial charity through the world.

68.

Massachusetts Personal Liberty Act

One of the most controversial acts of the Compromise of 1850 was the Fugitive Slave Law, which placed fugitive slave cases under the exclusive jurisdiction of the federal courts. Many Northern states passed personal liberty laws designed to prevent its enforcement. The following Massachusetts Personal Liberty Act of May 21, 1855, was passed after the infamous fugitive slave "trial" of Anthony Burns at Boston. Section 14 of the Act was aimed at Judge E. G. Loring, who had returned Burns to slavery. The Massachusetts legislature attempted to justify the Act in a resolution of April 6, 1855: "Inasmuch as there is neither any power granted . . . in the Constitution of the United States for the enactment of any law of Congress for the return of alleged fugitive slaves, nor any prohibition . . . to the States against the passage of laws upon that subject . . . the fugitive slave act is a direct violation of the tenth article of amendments to the Constitution of the United States, which declares that 'the powers not delegated to the United States by the Constitution, nor prohibited by it to the States, are reserved to the States. . . .'"

Source: *Acts and Resolves Passed by the General Court of Massachusetts in the Years 1854-5*, Boston, 1855, pp. 924-929.

An Act to Protect the Rights and Liberties of the People of the Commonwealth of Massachusetts.

Be it enacted by the Senate and House of Representatives, in General Court assembled, and by the authority of the same, as follows:

Section 1. All the provisions of the "act further to protect personal liberty," passed the 24th day of March, in the year 1843, shall apply to the act of Congress, approved

Sept. 18, in the year 1850, entitled "An act to amend, and supplementary to, the act entitled 'An act respecting fugitives from justice and persons escaping from the service of their masters.' "

Section 2. The meaning of the 111th Chapter of the Revised Statutes is hereby declared to be that every person imprisoned or restrained of his liberty is entitled, as of right and of course, to the writ of habeas corpus, except in the cases mentioned in the 2nd Section of that chapter.

Section 3. The writ of habeas corpus may be issued by the Supreme Judicial Court, the Court of Common Pleas, by any justice's court or police court of any town or city, by any court of record, or by any justice of either of said courts, or by any judge of probate; and it may be issued by any justice of the peace if no magistrate above named is known to said justice of the peace to be within five miles of the place where the party is imprisoned or restrained, and it shall be returnable before the Supreme Judicial Court, or any one of the justices thereof, whether the court may be in session or not, and in termtime or vacation.

Section 4. The Supreme Judicial Court, or any justice of said court before whom the writ of habeas corpus shall be made returnable, shall, on the application of any party to the proceeding, order a trial by jury as to any facts stated in the return of the officer, or as to any facts alleged, if it shall appear by the return of the officer or otherwise that the person whose restraint or imprisonment is in question is claimed to be held to service or labor in another state, and to have escaped from such service or labor, and may admit said person to bail in a sum not exceeding $2,000. In such case, issue may be joined by a general denial of the facts alleged, the plea may be not guilty, and the jury shall have the right to return a general verdict, and the same discretion as juries have in the trial of criminal cases; and the finding of a verdict of not

guilty shall be final and conclusive. . . . .

Section 6. If any claimant shall appear to demand the custody or possession of the person for whose benefit such writ is sued out, such claimant shall state in writing the facts on which he relies, with precision and certainty; and neither the claimant of the alleged fugitive, nor any person interested in his alleged obligation to service or labor, nor the alleged fugitive, shall be permitted to testify at the trial of the issue; and no confessions, admissions, or declarations of the alleged fugitive against himself shall be given in evidence. Upon every question of fact involved in the issue, the burden of proof shall be on the claimant, and the facts alleged and necessary to be established must be proved by the testimony of at least two credible witnesses or other legal evidence equivalent thereto, and by the rules of evidence known and secured by the common law; and no *ex parte* deposition or affidavit shall be received in proof in behalf of the claimant, and no presumption shall arise in favor of the claimant from any proof that the alleged fugitive or any of his ancestors had been actually held as a slave, without proof that such holding was legal.

Section 7. If any person shall remove from the limits of this Commonwealth, or shall assist in removing therefrom, or shall come into the Commonwealth with the intention of removing or of assisting in the removing therefrom, or shall procure or assist in procuring to be so removed, any person being in the peace thereof who is not "held to service or labor" by the "party" making "claim," or who has not "escaped" from the "party" making "claim," or whose "service or labor" is not "due" to the "party" making "claim," within the meaning of those words in the Constitution of the United States, on the pretense that such person is so held or has so escaped, or that his "service or labor" is so "due," or with the intent to subject him to such "service or labor," he shall be punished by a fine not less than $1,000, nor more than $5,000, and by imprisonment in the state prison not less than one, nor more than five, years. . . .

Section 9. No person, while holding any office of honor, trust, or emolument under the laws of this Commonwealth, shall in any capacity issue any warrant or other process, or grant any certificate, under or by virtue of an act of Congress, approved Feb. 12, 1793, entitled "An act respecting fugitives from justice and persons escaping from the service of their masters"; or under or by virtue of an act of Congress, approved Sept. 18, 1850, entitled "An act to amend . . ."; or shall in any capacity serve any such warrant or other process.

Section 10. Any person who shall grant any certificate under or by virtue of the acts of Congress mentioned in the preceding section shall be deemed to have resigned any commission from the Commonwealth which he may possess, his office shall be deemed vacant, and he shall be forever thereafter ineligible to any office of trust, honor, or emolument under the laws of this Commonwealth.

Section 11. Any person who shall act as counsel or attorney for any claimant of any alleged fugitive from service or labor, under or by virtue of the acts of Congress mentioned in the 9th Section of this act, shall be deemed to have resigned any commission from the Commonwealth that he may possess, and he shall be thereafter incapacitated from appearing as counsel or attorney in the courts of this Commonwealth. . . .

Section 13. No person who holds any office under the laws of the United States which qualifies him to issue any warrant or other process, or to grant any certificate under the acts of Congress named in the 9th Section of this act, or to serve the same, shall, at the same time, hold any office of honor, trust, or emolument under the laws of this Commonwealth.

Section 14. Any person holding any judi-cial office under the constitution or laws of this Commonwealth who shall continue, for ten days after the passage of this act, to hold the office of United States commissioner, or any office under the laws of the United States which qualifies him to issue any warrant or other process, or grant any certificate under the acts of Congress named in the 9th Section of this act, shall be deemed to have violated good behavior, to have given reason for the loss of public confidence, and furnished sufficient ground either for impeachment or for removal by address.

Section 15. Any sheriff, deputy sheriff, jailer, coroner, constable, or other officer of this Commonwealth, or the police of any city or town, or any district, county, city, or town officer, or any officer or other member of the volunteer militia of this Commonwealth who shall hereafter arrest, imprison, detain or return, or aid in arresting . . . any person for the reason that he is claimed or adjudged to be a fugitive from service or labor, shall be punished by fine not less than $1,000, and not exceeding $2,000, and by imprisonment in the state prison for not less than one, nor more than two, years.

Section 16. The volunteer militia of this Commonwealth shall not act in any manner in the seizure, detention, or rendition of any person for the reason that he is claimed or adjudged to be a fugitive from service or labor. Any member of the same who shall offend against the provisions of this section shall be punished by fine not less than $1,000, and not exceeding $2,000, and by imprisonment in the state prison for not less than one, nor more than two, years.

Section 17. The governor, by and with the advice and consent of the council, shall appoint, in every county, one or more commissioners learned in the law, whose duty it shall be, in their respective counties, when any person in this state is arrested or seized, or in danger of being arrested or seized as a fugitive from service or labor, on being informed thereof, diligently and faithfully to use all lawful means to protect, defend, and secure to such alleged fugitive a fair and impartial trial by jury and the benefits of the provisions of this act; and any attorney whose services are desired by the alleged fugitive may also act as counsel in the case.

Section 18. The commissioners shall defray all expenses of witnesses, clerks' fees, and officers' fees, and other expenses which may be incurred in the protection and defense of any person seized or arrested as a fugitive from service or labor; and the same, together with the reasonable charges of the commissioners for their services as attorneys and counsel in the case, shall be paid by the state treasurer, on a warrant to be issued by the governor.

Section 19. No jail, prison, or other place of confinement belonging to, or used by, either the Commonwealth of Massachusetts or any county therein, shall be used for the detention or imprisonment of any person accused or convicted of any offense created by either of the said acts of Congress mentioned in the 9th Section of this act, or accused or convicted of obstructing or resisting any process, warrant, or order issued under either of said acts, or of rescuing or attempting to rescue any person arrested or detained under any of the provisions of either of said acts nor for the imprisonment of any person arrested on *mesne* process, or on execution in any suit for damages or penalties accruing, or being claimed to accrue, in consequence of any aid rendered to any escaping fugitive from service or labor.

69.

FRITHJOF MEIDELL: The Birth and Growth of a Railroad Town

The boom times of the 1850s, precipitated by the California "gold rush" of 1849, were sustained by the growth of the railroads from 8,000 miles of track in 1850 to more than 30,000 miles in 1860. All along the new railroad lines towns sprang up so quickly that one wit predicted that all of America would be covered by towns, leaving no land left to farm. Frithjof Meidell, a Norwegian immigrant, wrote the following letter to his family from Springfield, Illinois, on August 7, 1855, describing how the railroad, land speculators, and eager new settlers were developing the West.

Source: *Norwegian-American Studies and Records*, Vol. IX, Northfield, Minn., 1936, pp. 48-53.

Dear Mother:

I received Hansine's letter a couple of days ago, and I was indeed glad to hear that all of you are getting along so well. The same is true of Christian and me; both of us are feeling fine. I have tried many a ruse to get him to write home, but all in vain. A real porker, that fellow! You must thank Hansine ever so much for her letter. It was very interesting. I sent her a letter about two months ago by a man from Arendal who was returning home. Likely she has received it by now. I must admit that I felt quite flattered by her praise of my epistles, and least of all did I expect that Ditmar would find anything in them worthy of printer's ink. But there you see: do not judge a tramp by his rags.

How pleased I should be if I could only secure copies of *Aftenbladet* [Norwegian newspaper] from time to time. Could not this be arranged? In the Norwegian paper *Emigranten*, which is published in Wisconsin, I find many articles from *Aftenbladet*. In the same paper I also see that you now have both railroad and telegraph. Hurrah for old Norway!

How is the railroad getting along? Here in America it is the railroads that build up the whole country. Because of them the farmers get wider markets and higher prices for their products. They seem to put new life into everything. Even the old apple woman sets off at a dogtrot when she hears that whistle to sell her apples to the passengers. Every ten miles along the railways there are stations, which soon grow up into towns. "Soon," did I say? I should have said "immediately," because it is really remarkable how rapidly the stations are transformed into little towns. I can but compare it with the building of Aladdin's castle by means of his wonderful lamp, only that things move still faster here, where it is not necessary to sit and rub a rusty old oil lantern. Here you can buy houses all ready to be placed on the freight car, and in half a day's time they can be nailed together.

Since I have nothing else to write about this time, I shall attempt to describe how these towns spring up. First — that is, after the two old log houses that stand one on each side of the tracks — first, I say, the railroad company builds a depot. Next, a speculator buys the surrounding 100 acres and lays it out in lots, streets, and a marketplace. Then he graces the prospective town with the name of an early President or a famous general — or his own name —

holds an auction, and realizes many hundred percent on his investment.

A young wagonmaker who has just completed his apprenticeship hears about the station, that it is beautifully located in a rich farming country, is blessed with good water, and, most important of all, that it has no wagonmaker. Making a hasty decision, he buys the barest necessities for setting up in his profession, hurries off to the place, rents one of the old log houses, and is soon at work. One absolute necessity he still lacks, however: a sign, of course, which is the most important part of a man's equipment here in America. The next day he hears that there is a tramp painter aboard the train; he gets him off, puts him to work, and the very next day the farmers are surprised to see a monstrous sign straddling the roof of the old log house.

The sign is an immediate success, for the farmers rush to the shop and order wagons, wheels, and the like. The poor man is overwhelmed with more work than he can handle for ever so long. He is about to regret that sign notion of his, but suddenly he has another idea. He accepts every order, and no sooner are the customers away than he seizes his pen and writes to the editors of three different newspapers that three good apprentices can secure steady work with high wages in the "flourishing town of L." Within two days he has help enough, and the work goes "like a song."

The train stops again, and off steps a blacksmith who went broke in one of the larger towns. He saunters over to the wagonmaker's shop as unconcerned as if he only wished to light his cigar. In a casual way he inquires about the neighborhood and wonders what its prospects are, without indicating that he intends to settle there — by no means! But the wagoner, with his keen Yankee nose, soon smells a rat and starts boosting the place with all his might. This inspires the smith with ecstasy; he starts jumping around and making sledgehammer motions with his arms. Off he goes and rents the other log house and nails a horseshoe over the door as a sign. The horseshoe, to be sure, cannot be seen any great distance, but the smith has a remedy for this, and he starts to hammer and pound away at his anvil so that the farmers for miles around can hear the echoes. They immediately flock to his door, and there is work enough for the blacksmith.

Within a short week, a carpenter, a tailor, and a shoemaker also arrive in town. The wagoner orders a house from the carpenter and rents the second story to the tailor and the shoemaker. Soon the blacksmith also builds a house, and things progress with giant strides toward the bigger and better.

Again the train stops. This time two young fellows jump off, look around, and go over to have a chat with the blacksmith. One of them is a doctor, the other a lawyer. Both of them rent rooms from the blacksmith and start business.

Once more the locomotive stops. But — what's this getting off? Be patient! Just let it come closer. It is nothing more nor less than a mustachioed, velvet-frocked German with an old, overworked hurdy-gurdy strapped to his back. On the hurdy-gurdy perches a measly little monkey dressed in red. The German goes over to the blacksmith shop and begins to crank his music box while the monkey smokes tobacco, dances a polka, and grinds coffee. But the German receives no encouragement for his art, nor does the monkey — except some rusty nails which the smith tosses to him. The artist realizes that his audience is very unappreciative, and the poor man's face is overcast with sorrow.

Then he looks about inquiringly as if searching for something and steps up to the doctor to ask if there is a restaurant in town. On receiving a negative reply, his face brightens again; and, after a short conversation with the the doctor and lawyer, he steams off with the next train and jumps off at the first big town, where he sells his hurdy-gurdy and monkey and buys a barrel of whiskey, another barrel of biscuits, two large cheeses, tobacco, cigars, and sausages — miles of them. Thereupon he engages a painter to make an appropriate sign, and in three days he is back again in the new town. Now he rents the blacksmith's old log house and rigs it up as a shop. Soon the sign swings over the door, the whiskey barrel is half empty, and the sausages are dispatched by the yard.

But how could it be otherwise? Our clever German calls them *egyptische Bratwürste*, an irresistible name, *nicht wahr?* And what of the sign? *Polz tausend noch einmal.* In the center rests a large barrel adorned with the magic word *Lagerbier*. On one side of the barrel is a large cheese and on the other a necklace of sausages. Between these German Valhalla delicacies we read in large yellow letters, *Wirtschafthaus zur deutschen Republik* [Restaurant of the German Republic] *bei Carl Klor.* Fortune smiles upon the German innkeeper.

His best customers are the railroad workers, most of whom are Irishmen. They discovered the shop one Sunday afternoon while it was closed. But, fortunately, two Germans in the crowd were attracted by the sign and interpreted its mysteries to the Irishmen, who at once burst into frenzies of joy and started to dance about to the accompaniment of war whoops. Then they stuck their thumbs into their mouths and pulled them out with popping sounds like the uncorking of bottles, after which they hammered at the door. The German immediately opened both his mouth and his door and began murdering the English language and tapping whiskey. He is now well on his way to becoming a capitalist, because these fellows have tremendous capacities and swallow a quart of firewater without batting an eye.

I believe I must have mentioned them before. They consist mostly of the worst riffraff of Europe, to whom America is a promised land where you earn a dollar a day and are not hanged for stealing. When these roughnecks get together it is a pretty dull party unless there are a couple of fights and someone gets a good hiding. As you go along a railway under construction, it is easy to detect the places where they have had their frolics by the torn-up sod, the tufts of hair, the broken bottles, pipes, pants' buttons, blood, and so forth, which they have left behind them. I imagine that if the most brutish hog in the world could express himself he would do it something like these fellows.

But to get back to my town again. The German, the blacksmith, and the tailor do a rushing business. The train stops again, and this time it is a printer who makes his appearance. He gets in touch with the doctor and lawyer; an old printing press is for sale in the next town; they buy it, and with this new event we can really say that the town has "arrived." Some little trouble there is, to be sure, concerning the political affiliations of the paper, because it develops that the lawyer is a Democrat, the doctor an Abolitionist, and the printer a Whig. But a compromise is soon reached and the paper announces itself as "independent." The lawyer volunteers to write the editorials, while the doctor promises a wealth of death announcements, and the German and the blacksmith undertake to fill the rest of the paper with advertisements.

Within a few years the town is very large. The wagonmaker owns practically half of it. The German deals only in wholesale. The lawyer is mayor of the town, and the blacksmith does nothing but smoke cigars, for he is now a man of affluence.

70.

California Negroes Appeal for Legal Equality

California entered the Union in 1850 as a free state, but the Negroes among its citizenry suffered legal, economic, and social restrictions oppressive enough to bring about a state convention to review their grievances. After a meeting on November 20-22, 1855, in the Colored Methodist Church of Sacramento, the Negroes issued a series of resolutions and the following address to the people of California. Despite their eagerness for legal equality, the convention shunned identification with the Abolitionist cause and even rejected a proposal that a report of the meeting be sent to William Lloyd Garrison's Liberator *or to Frederick Douglass'* North Star.

Source: *Proceedings of the First State Convention of the Colored Citizens of the State of California,* Sacramento, 1855, pp. 26-27.

THE COLORED CITIZENS of this commonwealth would respectfully represent before you their state and condition; and they respectfully ask a candid and careful investigation of facts in relation to their true character.

Our population numbers about 6,000 persons, who own capital to the amount of near $3 million. This has been accumulated by our own industry since we migrated to the shores of the Pacific.

Most of us were born upon your soil; reared up under the influence of your institutions; become familiar with your manners and customs; acquired most of your habits; and adopted your policies. We yield allegiance to no other country save this. With all her faults we love her still.

Our forefathers were among the first who took up arms and fought side by side with yours; poured out their blood freely in the struggle for American independence. They fought, as they had every reason to suppose, the good fight of liberty until it finally triumphed.

In the War of 1812, in which you achieved independence and glory upon the seas, the colored men were also among the foremost to engage in the conflict, rendering efficient service in behalf of their common country. Through a long series of years have we been always ready to lay down our lives for the commonweal, in defense of the national honor. On the other hand, instead of treating us as good and loyal citizens, you have treated us as aliens; sought to degrade us in all the walks of life; proscribed us in church and state as an ignorant and debased class, unworthy the sympathy and regard of men. Without examining into our true character, you have allowed yourselves to become bitterly prejudiced against us. When we have spoken of the wrongs inflicted upon us, you have turned a deaf ear to our representations and entreaties, or spurned us from you.

We again call upon you to regard our condition in the state of California. We point with pride to the general character we maintain in your midst, for integrity, industry, and thrift. You have been wont to multiply our vices and never to see our virtues. You call upon us to pay enormous taxes to support government, at the same time you deny us the protection you extend to others; the security for life and property. You require us to be good citizens, while seeking to degrade us. You ask why we are not more intelligent. You receive our money to educate your children, and then refuse to admit our children into the common schools. You have enacted a law excluding our testimony in the courts of justice of this state in cases of proceedings wherein white persons are parties; thus openly encouraging and countenancing the vicious and dishonest to take advantage of us; a law which, while it does not advantage you, is a great wrong to us. At the same time, you freely admit the evidence of men in your midst who are ignorant of the first principles of your government — who know not the alphabet. Many colored men, who have been educated in your first colleges, are not allowed to testify! And wherefore? Our Divine Father has created us with a darker complexion.

People of California! We entreat you to repeal that unjust law. We ask it in the name of humanity, in the enlightened age in which we live, because of the odium it reflects upon you as a free and powerful people; we ask you to remove it from your civil code; we ask it that our homes and firesides may be protected; we ask it that our just earnings as laborers may be secured to us, and none offered impunity in withholding from us our just hire; that justice may be meted out to all without respect to complexion; the guilty punished; the innocent protected; the shield of wise and wholesome and equal laws extended over all in your great state; upon her mountains, in her valleys and deep ravines; by her winding streams. May your state be a model, even to the elder sister states, in respect of your just laws; may your growth, prosperity, and happiness be bounded only by time and immortality.

71.

Arkansas Resolutions on the Kansas-Nebraska Act

The Kansas-Nebraska Act, passed in May 1854, repealed the Missouri Compromise of 1820 and thereby made slavery theoretically possible in all territories. Reaction to the act in the North was immediate and hostile. Southern states reacted with more reserve, for it was generally acknowledged that slavery was not economically feasible in the new territories. Southern statements about the Kansas-Nebraska Act were likely to be reactions to Northern denunciations. Such is the case with the following set of resolutions of the Arkansas legislature, passed on February 9, 1855. Most of the animus is directed against Ohio, a state marked by Abolitionist sentiment and also active in the "underground railroad."

Source: 33 Congress, 2 Session, House Miscellaneous Document No. 26.

Whereas the right of property in slaves is expressly recognized by the Constitution of the United States and is, by virtue of such recognition, guaranteed against unfriendly action on behalf of the general government. *And whereas* each state of the Union, by the fact of being a party to the federal compact, is also a party to the recognition and guarantee aforesaid. *And whereas* the citizens of each state are, in consequence of such citizenship, under the most sacred obligation to conform to the terms and tenor of the compact to which their state is a party: Therefore —

1. *Be it resolved by the General Assembly of the State of Arkansas,* that the legislation of Congress repealing the misnamed "compromise" of 1820, and asserting the doctrine of noninterference with slavery, alike in states and territories, is in strict accordance with the Constitution, and in itself just and expedient, and is for these reasons cordially approved by the people of Arkansas.

2. *Resolved,* that the opposition of Northern states to the legislation above mentioned is at war with the letter and spirit of the Constitution, is grossly violative of plighted faith, and is a traitorous blow aimed at the rights of the South and the perpetuity of the Union.

3. *Resolved,* that the citizens of the state of Ohio have pursued a course peculiarly unjust and odious in their fanatical hostility to institutions for which they are not responsible, in their encouragement of known felons, and endorsement of repeated and shameless violations of law and decency, and in their establishment of Abolition presses, and circulation of incendiary documents, urging a servile population to bloodshed and rapine. And by reason of the premises, it is the duty and the interest of the people of Arkansas to discontinue all social and commercial relations with the citizens of said state, and the same is hereby earnestly recommended as a punishment of past outrages and a preventive of further aggressions.

"Wall Street half past two o'clock"; painting by H. Cafferty of the Panic of 1857

BOOM AND PANIC

In the 1850s investment in industry, in railroads in particular, grew at a frenzied pace. Total invested capital tripled in the ten years from 1850 to 1860, reaching $1,150,000,000. Railroad mileage increased from 9,000 to 30,000. The first line reached Chicago in 1854. By 1860, 15 lines converged on the city and the first railroad bridge had been built across the Mississippi. Such rapid growth led inevitably to speculation in stocks and real estate. More construction was undertaken than the economy could support and a succession of minor financial panics shook Wall Street. The Panic of 1857 was the most severe, causing a brief period of general unemployment.

(Top) "Stocks Up"; (bottom) "Stocks Down"; both lithographs by N. Currier, 1849

Run on the Seamen's Bank during the Panic of 1857

The infectious self-confidence of the period made the sale of stocks a favored means of raising capital for a venture. The frequent failure of unsound enterprises hardly dampened the gambler's spirit on Wall Street. At times the nation's capital was so overextended in investments that brought little immediate return that the failure of a single large lending institution could precipitate a general panic.

Railroad construction stimulated a number of related heavy industries. Iron and steel mills sprang up in western Pennsylvania and other areas where coal and ore were obtainable at low prices.

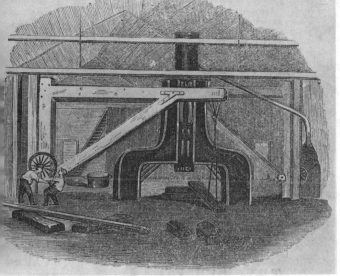

(Left) Steam-powered trip hammer; (center left) blast furnace.
Both engravings from Gleason's
magazine, 1854; (center right)
view of a factory in Glens Falls,
N.Y.; (bottom) factory in Pomp-
ton, N.J., in 1854; photograph
made from a waxed paper negative

(Above) New England mill, about 1850; (below left) weaving room in Mechanic's Mill, Fall River, Mass.; (below right) Pacific Cotton Mills in Lawrence, Mass.

(Above) Boott Cotton Mills, Lowell, Mass.; (right) title page from "The Lowell Offering" which was written and published by the girls who worked in the Lowell Mills; (bottom) Middlesex Woolen Mill in Lowell

The famed Lowell Mills of Massachusetts were an outstanding example of the effects of fierce competition in an unstable economy. Lowell was begun with the high-minded purpose of proving that the wretched conditions among English workers were not a necessary by-product of industrialization. The original workers were New England girls of "good family." They were housed in the company town, were provided with a library and a variety of "uplifting" activities. But the Panic of 1857 and vigorous competition from less idealistic producers forced the Lowell Mills to adopt the long hours and cheap immigrant labor general in the industry.

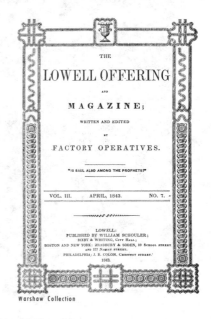

THE

LOWELL OFFERING

AND

MAGAZINE;

WRITTEN AND EDITED

BY

FACTORY OPERATIVES.

"IS SAUL ALSO AMONG THE PROPHETS?"

VOL. III.   APRIL, 1843.   NO. 7.

LOWELL:
PUBLISHED BY WILLIAM SCHOULER;
BIXBY & WHITING, CITY HALL.;
BOSTON AND NEW YORK: BRADBURY & SODEN, 10 School Street
AND 127 Nassau Street.
PHILADELPHIA: J. R. COLON, Chestnut Street.
1843.

Frank Fraprie Collection

Baldwin Locomotive Works

(Above) Daguerreotype of the locomotive "Hoosac" owned by Fitchburg Railroad; (left) drawing of a typical Baldwin passenger locomotive of 1853; (below) Baldwin locomotive photographed in Philadelphia in the late 1850s

Lightfoot Collection

Stereograph showing locomotive on the top of the suspension bridge at Niagara, N.Y.

Railroads involved huge investments of capital with no promise of quick returns. Before the trains could run, right-of-ways had to be purchased, roadbeds constructed, and rails laid. Engines and rolling stock had to be bought. To speed the process and cut costs large crews of immigrant laborers were hired at low wages. Little attention was paid to safety and wrecks were frequent. But the railroads' promise was so great that speculation in railroad stocks dominated markets across the country and attracted the interest of British investors.

(Center) "The Signs"; cartoon from "The New Mirror" showing early railroad competition; (right) train wreck near Pawtucket, R.I., in August 1853; daguerreotype by L. Wright was the first to record such an event

"The Great Exhibition of 1851"; in reference to America's imitation of the Crystal Palace show

(Left) "Yacht 'America' leaving Boston harbor"; painting by James E. Buttersworth; (below) the Collins fleet of New York and Liverpool, American mail steamers, 1854

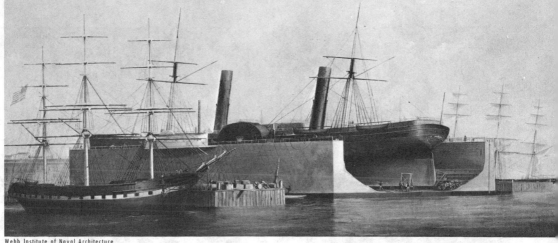

Balance Dry Dock in Brooklyn built by William Webb in 1854; Webb's ship "Ocean Monarch" is in the center

After decades of unparalleled advantage in international competition, the American merchant marine entered a period of slow decline in the 1850s. Steamboats had been improved and were competitive on the trans-Atlantic run by 1848. Americans were reluctant to shift to steam and did not have the industrial capacity to produce the large iron frames and huge boilers that steamers required. Donald McKay's clippers, the ultimate in sailing design, merely delayed the American conversion to steam. The clippers were unchallenged on the long runs to California and China for a decade, but by the late 1850s most new orders were going to steamship builders.

(Right) Daguerreotype of a sailor, taken about 1855; (below) daguerreotype view of Donald McKay's yards in East Boston, 1855, by Southworth and Hawes

(Above) Donald McKay, portrait made about 1855 by Southworth and Hawes in Boston; (right) clipper in drydock about the same time; McKay's "Great Republic" was the largest clipper ever built, but she burned in 1853 without ever going to sea

1856

72.

An Appeal to Southerners to Settle Kansas

Kansas found itself the focal point of a massive struggle over the extension of slavery after the enactment in 1854 of the Kansas-Nebraska Bill that allowed the two territories to decide whether they should be organized as free or slave territories by popular sovereignty. A referendum on the issue was called for October 1856. Abolitionists urged citizens of the Northern states to settle Kansas so that the election could be won in favor of organization as a free territory. The South adopted similar tactics. The appeal, which is reprinted here, was issued by the leaders of the Lafayette (Missouri) Emigration Society.

Source: *De Bow's Review*, May 1856: "Kansas Matters — Appeal to the South."

To the People of the South:

On the undersigned, managers of the "Lafayette Emigration Society," has devolved the important duty of calling the attention of the people of the slaveholding states to the absolute necessity of immediate action on their part in relation to the settlement of Kansas Territory. The crisis is at hand. Prompt and decisive measures must be adopted, or farewell to Southern rights and independence.

The Western counties of Missouri have, for the last two years, been heavily taxed, both in money and time, in fighting the battles of the South. Lafayette County alone has expended more than $100,000 in money, and as much, or more, in time. Up to this time, the border counties of Missouri have upheld and maintained the rights and interests of the South in this struggle, unassisted and unsuccessfully. But the Abolitionists, staking their all upon the Kansas issue, and hesitating at no means, fair or foul, are moving heaven and earth to render that beautiful territory not only a free state, so-called, but a den of Negro thieves and "higher law" incendiaries.

Missouri, we feel confident, has done her duty and will still be found ready and willing to do all she can, fairly and honorably, for the maintenance of the integrity of the South. But the time has come when she can no longer stand up, single-handed, the lone champion of the South, against the myrmidons of the entire North. It requires no great foresight to perceive that if the "higher law" men succeed in this crusade, it will be but the commencement of a war upon the institutions of the South, which will continue until slavery shall cease to exist in any of the states or the Union is dissolved.

How, then, shall these impending evils be avoided? The answer is obvious. *Settle the territory with emigrants from the South.* The population of the territory at this time is about equal — as many pro-slavery settlers as Abolitionists; but the fanatics have emissaries in all the free states — in almost every village — and by misrepresentation and falsehood are engaged in collecting money and enlisting men to tyrannize over the South. Is it in the nature of Southern men to submit without resistance, to look to the North for their laws and institutions? We do not believe it!

If, then, the South is influenced by a spirit of self-respect and independence, *let societies be formed to assist emigrants.* Those who cannot emigrate can contribute money to assist those who can. We have such societies in Missouri and we can induce more people to emigrate than we are able to support. If the whole South would adopt this system, we would succeed; Kansas would be a slave state and the slavery agitation would cease. If we permit the North to make an abolition state of Kansas, the whole South must submit to be governed by the North. Will the South help us?

The great struggle will come off at the next election, in October 1856, and unless the South can at that time maintain her ground, all will be lost. We repeat it, the crisis has arrived. The time has come for action — *bold, determined action;* words will no longer do any good; we must have men in Kansas, and that too by tens of thousands. A few will not answer. If we should need 10,000, and lack one of that number, all will count nothing. Let all,

then, who can come, do so at once. Those who cannot come must give their money to help others to come. There are hundreds of thousands of broad acres of rich land, worth from $5 to $20 per acre, open to settlement and preemption, at $1.25 per acre.

Let, then, the farmer come and bring his slaves with him. There are now 1,000 slaves in Kansas whose presence there strengthens our cause. Shall we allow these rich lands and this beautiful country to be overrun by our Abolition enemies? We know of a surety that they have emissaries and spies in almost every town, village, and city in the South, watching our movements and tampering with our slaves. Let us, then, be vigilant and active in the cause; we must maintain our ground. The loss of Kansas to the South will be the death knell of our dear Union.

Missouri has done nobly thus far in overcoming the thousands who have been sent out by Abolition aid societies; we cannot hold out much longer unless the whole South will come to the rescue. We need men; we need money; send us both, and that quickly. Do not delay; come as individuals, come in companies, come by thousands.

Our hearts have been made glad by the late arrival of large companies from South Carolina and Alabama. They have responded promptly to our call for help. The noble Buford is already endeared to our hearts; we love him; we will fight for him, and die for him and his companions. Who will follow his noble example! We tell you now, and tell you frankly, that unless you come quickly, and come by thousands, we are gone. The elections once lost, we are lost forever. Then farewell to our Southern cause, and farewell to our glorious Union. We repeat the cry, "Come over and help us."

73.

CHARLES SUMNER: The Crime Against Kansas

*The Kansas-Nebraska Act made of Kansas a battleground for all the old animosities
over the issue of slavery. Northerners opposed the act because it repealed the
Missouri Compromise and threatened to extend the geographic limits of slavery;
Southerners objected to the principle of popular sovereignty and charged that Kansas
would become "a den of Negro thieves and . . . incendiaries." In response to pro-slavery
activity in Kansas, Charles Sumner of Massachusetts delivered an attack on the slave
interest in a speech before the Senate on May 19 and 20, 1856. The speech stirred such
strong emotion in Southerners that two days later Representative Preston S. Brooks of
South Carolina entered the Senate chamber and gave Sumner a vicious beating with a
cane, from which he did not recover for several years.*

Source: *Globe, App.,* 34 Cong., 1 Sess., pp. 529-544.

IT BELONGS TO ME NOW, in the first place, to expose the Crime Against Kansas in its origin and extent. Logically this is the beginning of the argument. I say crime, and deliberately adopt this strongest term as better than any other denoting the consummate transgression. I would go further if language could further go. It is the *crime of crimes* — surpassing far the old *crimen majestatis* [crime against a sovereign power], pursued with vengeance by the laws of Rome, and containing all other crimes, as the greater contains the less. I do not go too far when I call it the *crime against nature,* from which the soul recoils and which language refuses to describe. . . .

Sir, the Nebraska Bill was in every respect a swindle. It was a swindle by the South of the North. It was, on the part of those who had already completely enjoyed their share of the Missouri Compromise, a swindle of those whose share was yet absolutely untouched; and the plea of unconstitutionality set up — like the plea of usury after the borrowed money has been enjoyed — did not make it less a swindle. Urged as a bill of peace, it was a swindle of the whole country. Urged as opening the doors to slave masters with their slaves, it was a swindle of the asserted doctrine of popular sovereignty. Urged as sanctioning popular sovereignty, it was a swindle of the asserted rights of slave masters. It was a swindle of a broad territory, thus cheated of protection against slavery. It was a swindle of a great cause, early espoused by Washington, Franklin, and Jefferson, surrounded by the best fathers of the republic. Sir, it was a swindle of God-given inalienable rights. Turn it over; look at it on all sides, and it is everywhere a swindle; and if the word I now employ has not the authority of classical usage, it has, on this occasion, the indubitable authority of fitness. No other word will adequately express the mingled meanness and wickedness of the cheat.

Its character was still further apparent in the general structure of the bill. Amid overflowing professions of regard for the sovereignty of the people in the territory, they were despoiled of every essential privilege of sovereignty. They were not allowed to choose their governor, secretary, chief justice, associate justices, attorney, or marshal, all of whom are sent from Washington; nor were they allowed to regulate the salaries of any of these functionaries, or the daily allowance of the legislative body, or even the pay of the clerks and doorkeepers; but they were left free to adopt slavery.

And this was called popular sovereignty! Time does not allow, nor does the occasion require that I should stop to dwell on this transparent device to cover a transcendent wrong. Suffice it to say that slavery is in itself an arrogant denial of human rights, and by no human reason can the power to establish such a wrong be placed among the attributes of any just sovereignty. In refusing it such a place I do not deny popular rights, but uphold them; I do not restrain popular rights, but extend them. And, sir, to this conclusion you must yet come unless deaf, not only to the admonitions of political justice but also to the genius of our own Constitution under which, when properly interpreted, no valid claim for slavery can be set up anywhere in the national territory.

The senator from Michigan [Mr. Cass] may say, in response to the senator from Mississippi [Mr. Brown], that slavery cannot go into the territory under the Constitution without legislative introduction; and permit me to add, in response to both, that slavery cannot go there at all. *Nothing can come out of nothing;* and there is absolutely nothing in the Constitution out of which slavery can be derived, while there are provisions which, when properly interpreted, make its existence anywhere within the exclusive national jurisdiction impossible. . . .

Mr. President, men are wisely presumed to intend the natural consequences of their conduct, and to seek what their acts seem to promote. Now the Nebraska Bill, on its very face, openly cleared the way for slavery, and it is not wrong to presume that its originators intended the natural consequences of such an act, and sought in this way to extend slavery. Of course they did. And this is the first stage in the Crime Against Kansas. . . .

Then was conceived the consummation of the Crime Against Kansas. What could not be accomplished peaceably was to be accomplished forcibly. The reptile monster, that could not be quietly and securely hatched there, was to be pushed full-grown into the territory. All efforts were now given to the dismal work of forcing slavery on free soil. In flagrant derogation of the very popular sovereignty, whose name helped to impose this bill upon the country, the atrocious object was not distinctly avowed. And the avowal has been followed by the act. Slavery has been forcibly introduced into Kansas and placed under the formal safeguards of pretended law. . . .

Five several times and more have these invaders entered Kansas in armed array, and thus five several times and more have they trampled upon the organic law of the territory. But these extraordinary expeditions are simply the extraordinary witnesses to successive uninterrupted violence. They stand out conspicuous, but not alone. The spirit of evil, in which they had their origin, was wakeful and incessant. From the beginning, it hung upon the skirts of this interesting territory, harrowing its peace, disturbing its prosperity, and keeping its inhabitants under the painful alarms of war. Thus was all security of person, of property, and of labor overthrown; and when I urge this incontrovertible fact, I set forth a wrong which is small only by the side of the giant wrong for the consummation of which all this was done.

Sir, what is man — what is government — without security; in the absence of which nor man nor government can proceed in development or enjoy the fruits of existence? Without security, civilization is cramped and dwarfed. Without security, there can be no true freedom. Nor shall I say too much when I declare that security, guarded of course by its offspring, freedom, is the true end and aim of government. Of this indispensable boon the people of Kansas have thus far been despoiled — absolutely, totally. All this is aggravated by the nature of their pursuits, rendering them peculiarly sensitive to interruption, and at the same time attesting their innocence.

They are for the most part engaged in the cultivation of the soil, which from time immemorial has been the sweet employment of undisturbed industry. Contented in the returns of bounteous nature and the shade of his own trees, the husbandman is not aggressive. Accustomed to produce and not to destroy, he is essentially peaceful, unless his home is invaded, when his arm derives vigor from the soil he treads and his soul inspiration from the heavens beneath whose canopy he daily toils. And such are the people of Kansas, whose security has been overthrown.

Scenes from which civilization averts her countenance have been a part of their daily life. The border incursions, which, in barbarous ages or barbarous lands, have fretted and harried an exposed people, have been here renewed, with this peculiarity, that our border robbers do not simply levy blackmail and drive off a few cattle like those who acted under the inspiration of the Douglas of other days; that they do not seize a few persons and sweep them away into captivity, like the African slave traders whom we brand as pirates; but that they commit a succession of acts in which all border sorrows and all African wrongs are revived together on American soil, and which, for the time being, annuls all protection of all kinds and enslaves the whole territory.

Private griefs mingle their poignancy with public wrongs. I do not dwell on the anxieties which families have undergone, exposed to sudden assault and obliged to lie down to rest with the alarms of war ringing in their ears, not knowing that another day might be spared to them. Throughout this bitter winter, with the thermometer at 30° below zero, the citizens of Lawrence have been constrained to sleep under arms, with sentinels treading their constant watch against surprise. . . .

Charles Sumner

As every point in a widespread horizon radiates from a common center, so everything said or done in this vast circle of crime radiates from the *one idea*, that Kansas, at all hazards, must be made a slave state. In all the manifold wickednesses that have occurred, and in every successive invasion, this *one idea* has been ever present, as the Satanic tempter — the motive power — the *causing cause*.

To accomplish this result, three things were attempted: first, by outrages of all kinds to drive the friends of freedom already there out of the territory; second, to deter others from coming; and, third, to obtain the complete control of the government. The process of driving out, and also of deterring, has failed. On the contrary, the friends of freedom there became more fixed in their resolves to stay and fight the battle which they had never sought, but from which they disdained to retreat; while the friends of freedom elsewhere were more aroused to the duty of timely succors, by men and munitions of just self-defense.

But, while defeated in the first two processes proposed, the conspirators succeeded in the last. By the violence already portrayed at the election of March 30, when the polls were occupied by the armed hordes from Missouri, they imposed a legislature upon the territory, and thus, under the iron mask of law, established a usurpation not less complete than any in history. . . .

Mark, sir, three different legislative enactments which constitute part of this work. First, according to one act, all who deny, by spoken or written word, "the right of persons to hold slaves in this territory" are denounced as felons, to be punished by imprisonment at hard labor for a term not less than two years; it may be for life. And to show the extravagance of this injustice, it has been well put by the senator from Vermont [Mr. Collamer] that should the senator from Michigan [Mr. Cass], who believes that slavery cannot exist in a territory unless introduced by express legislative acts, venture there with his moderate opinions, his doom must be that of a felon! To this extent are the great liberties of speech and of the press subverted.

Second, by another act, entitled "An act concerning attorneys-at-law," no person can practise as an attorney unless he *shall obtain a license* from the territorial courts, which, of course, a tyrannical discretion will be free to deny; and after obtaining such license he is constrained to take an oath, not only "to support" the Constitution of the United States but also "to support and sustain" — mark here the reduplication — the Territorial Act and the Fugitive Slave Bill, thus erecting a test for the function of the bar calculated to exclude citizens who honestly regard that latter legislative enormity as unfit to be obeyed.

And third, by another act, entitled "An act concerning jurors," all persons "conscientiously opposed to holding slaves," or "not admitting the right to hold slaves in the territory," are excluded from the jury on every question, civil or criminal, arising out of asserted slave property; while, in all cases, the summoning of the jury is left without one word of restraint to "the marshal, sheriff, or other officer," who are thus free to pack it according to their tyrannical discretion.

For the ready enforcement of all statutes against human freedom, the President had already furnished a powerful quota of officers in the governor, chief justice, judges, secretary, attorney, and marshal. The legislature completed this part of the work by constituting, in each county, a board of commissioners, composed of two persons, associated with the probate judge, whose duty it is "to appoint a county treasurer, coroner, justices of the peace, constables, and *all* other officers provided for by law," and then proceeded to the choice of this very board; thus delegating and diffusing their usurped power, and tyrannically imposing upon the territory a crowd of officers, in whose appointment the people have had no voice, directly or indirectly.

And still the final, inexorable work remained. A legislature, renovated in both branches, could not assemble until 1858, so that, during this long, intermediate period, this whole system must continue in the likeness of law, unless overturned by the federal government, or, in default of such interposition, by a generous uprising of an oppressed people. But it was necessary to guard against the possibility of change, even tardily, at a future election; and this was done by two different acts; under the first of which, all who will not take the oath to support the Fugitive Slave Bill are excluded from the elective franchise; and under the second of which, all others are entitled to vote who shall tender a tax of $1 to the sheriff on the day of election; thus, by provision of territorial law, disfranchising all opposed to slavery, and at the same time opening the door to the votes of the invaders by an unconstitutional shibboleth, excluding from the polls the mass of actual settlers, and by making the franchise depend upon a petty tax only, admitting to the polls the mass of borderers from Missouri. Thus, by tyrannical forethought, the usurpation not only fortified all that it did but assumed a *self-perpetuating* energy.

Thus was the Crime consummated. Slav-

Engraving showing the attack on Sumner on the floor of the Senate, 1856; from "Leslie's Illustrated Newspaper"

ery now stands erect, clanking its chains on the territory of Kansas, surrounded by a code of death, and trampling upon all cherished liberties, whether of speech, the press, the bar, the trial by jury, or the electoral franchise. And, sir, all this has been done, not merely to introduce a wrong which in itself is a denial of all rights, and in dread of which a mother has lately taken the life of her offspring; not merely, as has been sometimes said, to protect slavery in Missouri, since it is futile for this state to complain of freedom on the side of Kansas when freedom exists without complaint on the side of Iowa and also on the side of Illinois; but it has been done for the sake of political power, in order to bring two new slaveholding senators upon this floor and thus to fortify in the national government the desperate chances of a waning oligarchy.

As the ship, voyaging on pleasant summer seas, is assailed by a pirate crew and robbed for the sake of its doubloons and dollars — so is this beautiful territory now assailed in its peace and prosperity, and robbed in order to wrest its political power to the side of slavery. Even now the black flag of the land pirates from Missouri waves at the masthead; in their laws you hear the pirate yell and see the flash of the pirate knife; while, incredible to relate, the President, gathering the slave power at his back, testifies a pirate sympathy.

Sir, all this was done in the name of popular sovereignty. And this is the close of the tragedy. Popular sovereignty, which, when truly understood, is a fountain of just power, has ended in popular slavery; not merely in the subjection of the unhappy African race but of this proud Caucasian blood which you boast. The profession with which you began, of *All by the People,* has been lost in the wretched reality of *Nothing for the People.* Popular sovereignty, in whose deceitful name plighted faith was broken and an ancient landmark of freedom was overturned, now lifts itself before us, like sin, in the terrible picture of Milton —

That seemed a woman to the waist, and
    fair;
But ended foul in many a scaly fold,
Voluminous and vast! a serpent armed
With mortal sting: about her middle
    round
A cry of hell-hounds never ceasing barked
With wide Cerberian mouths full loud
    and rung
A hideous peal: yet, when they list,
    would creep,
If aught disturbed their noise, into her
    womb,
And kennel there; yet there still barked,
    and howled
Within, unseen.

The image is complete at all points; and, with this exposure, I take my leave of the Crime Against Kansas.

74.

THEODORE PARKER: The Present Crisis in American Affairs

Theodore Parker was noted among the members of the New England intellectual community for the vigor and persistence of his attacks on slavery. As pastor of the Twenty-Eighth Congregational Society of Boston, Parker drew thousands to his fiery sermons on slavery's "retrogressive" influence on American life, and on the need for a "progressive" revolt against the system. On May 7, 1856, he delivered the address reprinted in part below. It was subtitled, "The Slave-Holders' Attempt to Wrench the Territories from the Working People, and to Spread Bondage Over all the Land."

Source: *The Collected Works of Theodore Parker,* Frances P. Cobbe, ed., Vol. VI, London, 1864, pp. 240-286.

Oh! ill for him who, bettering not with
   time,
  Corrupts the strength of heaven-
    descended will,
And ever weaker grows through acted
   crime,
Or seeming-genial venial fault —
  Recurring and suggesting still!
He seems as one whose footsteps halt —
  Toiling in immeasurable sand,
  And o'er a weary, sultry land,
Far beneath a blazing vault,
  Sown in a wrinkle of the monstrous
   bill,
The city sparkles like a grain of salt.

America has now come to such a pass that a small misstep may plunge us into lasting misery. Any other and older nation would be timidly conscious of the peril; but we, both so confident of destined triumph and so wonted to success, forecast only victory, and so heed none of all this danger. Who knows what is before us? By way of warning for the future, look at the events in the last six years.

1. In the spring of 1850 came the discussions on the Fugitive Slave Bill and the program of practical atheism; for it was taught, as well in the Senate as the pulpits, that the American government was amenable to no natural laws of God, but its own momentary caprice might take the place of the eternal reason. "The Union is in danger" was the affected cry. Violent speeches filled the land, and officers of the government uttered such threats against the people of the North as only Austrian and Russian ears were wont to hear. Even "discussion was to cease." That year, the principle was sown whence measures have since sprung forth, an evil blade from evil seed.

2. The next spring, 1851, kidnapping went on in all the North. Kane ruled in Philadelphia, Rynders in New York. Boston opened her arms to the stealers of men, who barked in her streets and howled about the "Cradle of Liberty," the hiding place of

her ancient power. All the municipal authority of the town was delivered up to the kidnappers. Faneuil Hall was crammed with citizen-soldiers, volunteers in men stealing, eager for their "Glorious first essay in war." Visible chains of iron were proudly stretched round the courthouse. The supreme judges of Massachusetts crouched their loins beneath that yoke of bondage and went under to their own place, wherein they broke down the several laws they were sworn and paid to keep. They gave up Thomas Sims to his tormentors. On the 19th of April, the seventy-sixth anniversary of the first battle of the Revolution, the city of Hancock and Adams thrust one of her innocent citizens into a slave prison at Savannah, giving his back to the scourge and his neck to the everlasting yoke.

3. In the spring of 1854 came the discussions on the Kansas-Nebraska Bill; the attempt to extend bondage into the new territory just opening its arms to the industrious North; the legislative effort to rob the Northern laborer thereof, and give the spoils to Southern slaveholders. Then came the second kidnapping at Boston: a judge of probate stole a defenseless man and made him a slave. The old volunteer soldiers put on their regimentals again to steal another victim. But they were not quite strong enough alone; so the United States troops of the line were called out to aid the work of protecting the orphan. It was the first time I ever saw soldiers enforcing the decisions of a New England judge of probate; the first time I ever saw the United States soldiers in any service. This was characteristic work for a democratic army! Hireling soldiers, mostly Irishmen — sober that day, at least till noon — in the public square loaded their cannon, charged their muskets, fixed their bayonets, and made ready to butcher the citizens soon as a slaveholder should bid them strike a Northern neck. The spectacle was prophetic.

4. Now, in 1856, New England men migrate to Kansas, taking their wives, their babies, and their cradles. The old Bible goes also on that pilgrimage; it never fails the sons of the Puritans. But the fathers are not yet dead; "E'en in our ashes live their wonted fires." Sharp's rifle goes as missionary in that same troop; an indispensable missionary — an apostle to the gentiles — whose bodily presence is not weak, nor his speech contemptible, in Missouri. All the parties go armed. Like the father, the Pilgrim son is also a Puritan, and both trusts in God and keeps his powder dry.

A company went from Boston a few days ago, a few of my own friends and parishioners among them. There were some five-and-forty persons, part women and children. Twenty Sharp's rifles answered to their names, not to speak of other weapons. The ablest minister in the United States stirs up the "Plymouth Church" to contribute firearms to this new mission; and a spirit, noble as Davenport's and Hooker's, pushes off from New England, again to found a New Haven in the wilderness. The bones of the regicide sleep in Connecticut; but the revolutionary soul of fire flames forth in new processions of the Holy Ghost.

In 1656, when Boston sent out her colonists, they took matchlocks and snaphances to fend off the red savage of the wilderness; in 1756, they needed weapons against the French enemy; but, in 1856, the dreadful tools of war are to protect their children from the white border ruffians whom the President of the United States invites to burn the new settlements, to scalp and kill.

In 1850, we heard only the threat of arms; in 1851, we saw the volunteer muskets in the kidnapper's hand; in 1854, he put the United States cannon in battery; in 1856, he arms the savage Missourians. But now, also, there are tools of death in the people's hand. It is high time. When the people are sheep, the government is always a wolf. What will the next step be? Mr. Cushing says, "I know what is requisite; but it is *means that I cannot suggest!*" Who knows what *coup d'état* is getting ready? Surely affairs cannot remain long in this condition.

To understand this present emergency, you must go a long ways back, and look a little carefully at what lies deep down in the foundation of states.

The welfare of a nation consists in these three things; namely: first, possession of material comfort, things of use and beauty; second, enjoyment of all the natural rights of body and spirit; and, third, the development of the natural faculties of body and spirit in their harmonious order, securing the possession of freedom, intelligence, morality, philanthropy, and piety. It ought to be the aim of a nation to obtain these three things in the highest possible degree, and to extend them to all persons therein. That nation has the most welfare which is the furthest advanced in the possession of these three things.

Next, the progress of a nation consists in two things: first, in the increasing development of the natural faculties of body and spirit — intellectual, moral, affectional, and religious — with the consequent increasing enjoyment thereof; and, second, in the increasing acquisition of power over the material world, making it yield use and beauty, an increase of material comfort and elegance. Progress is increase of human welfare for each and for all. That is the most progressive nation which advances fastest in this development of human faculties and the consequent acquisition of material power. There is no limit to this progress.

That is the superior nation which, by nature, has the greatest amount of bodily and spiritual faculties and, by education, has developed them to the highest degree of human culture, and, consequently, is capacious of the greatest amount of power over the material world, to turn it into use and beauty, and so of the greatest amount of universal welfare for all and each. The superior nation is capable of most rapid progress; for the advance of man goes on with accelerated velocity; the further he has gone, the faster he goes.

The disposition in mankind to acquire this increase of human development and material power I will call the instinct of progress. It exists in different degrees in various nations and races: some are easily content with a small amount thereof, and so advance but slowly; others desire the most of both, and press continually forward.

Of all races, the Caucasian has hitherto shown the most of this instinct of progress, and, though perhaps the youngest of all, has advanced furthest in the development of the human faculties and in the acquisition of power over the material world; it has already won the most welfare and now makes the swiftest progress.

Of the various families of the Caucasian race, the Teutonic, embracing all the Germanic people kindred to our own, is now the most remarkable for this instinct of progress. Accordingly, in the last 400 years, all the great new steps of peaceful Caucasian development have been first taken by the Teutonic people, who now bear the same relation to the world's progress that the Greeks did 1,000 years before Christ, the Romans 800 years later, and the romanized Celts of France at a day yet more recent.

Of the Teutons, the Anglo-Saxons, or that portion thereof settled in the Northern states of America, have got the furthest forward in certain important forms of welfare, and now advance the most rapidly in their general progress. With no class of capitalists or scholars equal to the men of great estates and great learning in Europe, the whole mass of the people have yet attained the greatest material comfort, enjoyment of natural rights, and development of the human faculties. They feel most powerfully the general instinct of progress and advance swiftest to future welfare and development. Here the bulk of the population is Anglo-Saxon; but this powerful blood has been enriched by additions from diverse other sources — Teutonic and Celtic.

The great forces, which in the last 400 years have most powerfully and obviously helped this welfare and progress, may be reduced to two marked tendencies, which I will sum up in the form of ideas, and name the one Christianity and the other democracy.

By Christianity I mean that form of religion which consists of piety, the love of God and morality, the keeping of His laws. That is not the Christianity of the Christian Church, nor of any sect; it is the ideal religion which the human race has been groping after, if happily we might find it. It is yet only an ideal, actual in no society.

By democracy I mean government over all the people by all the people and for the sake of all. Of course, it is government according to the natural law of God, by justice, the point common to each man and all men, to each nation and all mankind, to the human race and to God. In a democracy, the people reign with sovereign power; their elected servants govern with delegated trust. There is national unity of action, represented by law; this makes the nation one, a whole; it is the centripetal force of society. But there is also individual variety of action, represented by the personal freedom of the people who ultimately make the laws; this makes John, John, and not James, the individual, a free person, discrete from all other men; this is the centrifugal force of society, which counteracts the excessive solidification that would else go on. Thus, by justice, the one and the many are balanced together, as the centripetal and centrifugal forces in the solar system.

This is not the democracy of the parties, but it is that ideal government, the reign of righteousness, the kingdom of justice, which all noble hearts long for and labor to produce, the ideal whereunto mankind slowly draws near. No nation has yet come so close to it as the people of some of the Northern states, who are yet far beneath ideals of government now known, that are yet themselves vastly inferior to others which mankind shall one day voyage after, discover, and annex to human possession.

In this democracy, and the tendency toward it, two things come to all; namely, labor and government.

Labor for material comfort, the means of use and beauty, is the duty of all, and not less the right, and practically the lot, of all; so there is no privilege for any where each has his whole natural right. Accordingly, there is no permanent and vicariously idle class, born merely to enjoy and not create, who live by the unpurchased toil of others; and, accordingly, there is no permanent and vicariously working class, born merely to create and not enjoy, who toil only for others. There is mutuality of earning and enjoying: none is compelled to work vicariously for another, none allowed to rob others of the natural fruit of their toil. Of course, each works at such calling as his nature demands: on the *mare liberum*, the open sea of human industry, every personal bark sails whither it may, and with such freight and swiftness as it will or can.

Government, in social and political affairs, is the right of all, not less their duty, and practically the lot of each. So there is no privilege in politics, no lordly class born to command and not obey, no slavish class born to serve and not command: there is mutuality of command and obedience. And as there is no compulsory vicarious work, but each takes part in the labor of all and has his share in the enjoyment thereof; so there is no vicarious government, but each takes part in the making of laws and in obedience thereunto.

Such is the ideal democracy, nowhere made actual.

75.

Settlers' Songs

The great Westward movement that has characterized American national development reached its height in the middle years of the nineteenth century. Settlers crossed first the Appalachians, then the Mississippi River and the Great Plains, and finally went over the Rockies to the other ocean. Some dropped out along the way. In the Kansas and Nebraska territories — destined to become the focal point of mounting tensions between North and South — early settlers found no woodlands to provide lumber for cabins, so they built houses of sod, as described in "Little Old Sod Shanty." Others urged their daughters to avoid this hard life and warned them not to marry "Kansas Boys."

Source: Allen, pp. 104-107.

❦ THE LITTLE OLD SOD SHANTY

I am looking rather seedy now while holding down my claim,
And my victuals are not always served the best;
And the mice play shyly round me as I nestle down to rest
In the little old sod shanty on my claim.
Oh, the hinges are of leather and the windows have no glass,
And the board roof lets the howling blizzard in;
And I hear the hungry coyote as he slinks up through the grass
Round the little old sod shanty on my claim.

When I left my Eastern home, a bachelor so gay,
To try to win my way to health and fame,
I never thought I'd come to burning twisted hay
In the little old sod shanty on my claim.
But I rather like the novelty of living in this way,
Though my bill of fare is always rather tame;
And I'm happy as a clam on the land of Uncle Sam
In the little old sod shanty on my claim.

My clothes are plastered o'er with mud, I'm looking like a fright,
And everything is scattered round the room;
Yet I wouldn't give the freedom that I have out in the West
For the comfort of the Eastern man's old home.
Still I wish some kind-hearted girl would pity on me take,
And relieve me from the mess that I am in;
The angel, how I'd bless her, if this her home she'd make
In the little old sod shanty on my claim.

We would make our fortunes on the prairies of the West
Just as happy as two lovers we'd remain;
We'd forget the trials and troubles we endured at the first
On the little old sod shanty on my claim.
And if fate would bless us with now and then an heir,
To cheer our hearts with honest pride and fame;
Oh, then we'd be contented for the toil that we had spent
In the little old sod shanty we call home.

KANSAS BOYS

Come, all young girls, pay attention to my noise,
Don't fall in love with the Kansas boys.
For if you do, your portion it will be,
Johnny cake and antelope and sassafras tea.

They'll take you out on the jet black hill,
Take you there so much against your will,
Leave you there to perish on the plains,
For that is the way with the Kansas range.

Some live in a cabin with a huge log wall,
Nary a window in it at all,
Sandstone chimney and a puncheon floor,
Clapboard roof and a button door.

When they get hungry and go to make bread,
They kindle a fire as high as your head,
Rake around the ashes and in the bread they throw:
The name they give it is "doughboy's dough."

When they go to milk, they milk in a gourd,
Have it in the corner and cover with a board,
Some get plenty and some get none,
That is the way with the Kansas run.

When they go to meeting, the clothes that they wear
Is an old brown coat all picked and bare,
An old white hat more rim than crown,
A pair of cotton socks they wore the week around.

When they go to farming you needn't be alarmed,
In February they plant their corn;
The way they tend it I'll tell you now,
With a Texas pony and a grasshopper plow.

When they go a-fishing they take along a worm,
Put it on the hook just to see it squirm,
The first thing they say when they get a bite
Is, "I caught a fish as big as Johnny White."

When they go courting they take along a chair,
The first thing they say is, "Has your daddy killed a bear?"
The second thing they say when they sit down
Is, "Madam, your Johnny cake is baking brown."

76.

Christopher C. Andrews: Economic Advantages of the Frontier

As settlers moved into Missouri and Iowa, the Mississippi Valley frontier shifted northward to the wilderness of Minnesota. The territory was officially opened in 1837, when the United States secured the land between the Mississippi and St. Croix rivers as well as a portion of northern Wisconsin from the Sioux and Chippewa Indians. Trappers and lumbermen were the first to enter, and they discouraged farmers from settling land that might be used for logging or for tracking game. But the farmers came, partially because the lumber and trapping camps were creating a demand for the farmers' crops. Two years after Christopher Andrews wrote the following observation on the area in 1856, Minnesota became a state, entering the Union with a population of almost 170,000.

Source: *Minnesota and Dacotah: In Letters Descriptive of a Tour Through the North-West,* 2nd edition, Washington, 1857, pp. 114-134.

I DESIRE . . . TO SAY SOMETHING about the pioneer and life on the frontier. And by pioneer I mean the true pioneer who comes into the West to labor and to share the vicissitudes of new settlements; not the adventurer, who would repine at toil and gather where he has not sown.

As I have looked abroad upon the vast domain of the West beyond the dim Missouri, or in the immediate valley of the Mississippi, I have wondered at the contrast presented between the comparatively small number who penetrate to the frontier and that great throng of men who toil hard for a temporary livelihood in the populous towns and cities of the Union. And I have thought if this latter class were at all mindful of the opportunities for gain and independence which the new territories afforded, they would soon abandon — in a great measure at least — their crowded alleys in the city, and aspire to cultivators and owners of the soil. Why there has not been a greater emigration from cities I cannot imagine, unless it is owing to a misapprehension of Western life. Either it is this, or the pioneer is possessed of a very superior degree of energy.

It has been said that the frontier man always keeps on the frontier; that he continues to emigrate as fast as the country around him becomes settled. There is a class that do so. Not, however, for the cause which has been sometimes humorously assigned — that civilization was inconvenient to them — but because good opportunities arise to dispose of the farms they have already improved; and because a further emigration secures them cheaper lands. The story of the pioneer who was disturbed by society when his nearest neighbor lived fifteen miles off, even if it be true, fails to give the correct reason for the migratory life of this class of men.

It almost always happens that wherever we go somebody else has preceded us. Accident or enterprise has led someone to surpass us. Many of the most useful pioneers of this country have been attracted hither by the accounts given of its advantages by some one of their friends who had previously located himself here. Ask a man why he comes, and he says a neighbor of his, or a son, or a brother has been in the territory for so many months, and he likes it so well I concluded to come also. A very respectable gentleman from Maine, a shipowner and a man of wealth, who came up on the boat with me to St. Paul, said his son-in-law was in the territory, and he had another son at home who was bound to come, and, if his wife was willing, he believed the whole family would come. Indeed, the excellent state of society in the territory is to be attributed very much to the fact that parents have followed after their children.

It is pretty obvious too why men will leave poor farms in New England and good farms in Ohio to try their fortunes here. The farmer in New England, it may be in New Hampshire, hears that the soil of Minnesota is rich and free from rocks, that there are other favorable resources, and a salubrious climate such as he has been accustomed to. He concludes that it is best to sell out the place he has and try plowing where there are no rocks to obstruct him. The farmer of Ohio does not expect to find better soil than he leaves; but his inducements are that he can sell his land at $40 or $50 an acre, and preempt as good in Minnesota for $1.25 an acre. This operation leaves him a surplus fund, and he becomes a more opulent man, with better means to adorn his farm and to educate his children.

Those who contemplate coming West to engage in agricultural employment should leave their families, if families they have, behind till they have selected a location and erected some kind of a habitation; provided, however, they have no particular friend whose hospitality they can avail themselves of till their preliminary arrangements are effected. It will require three months, I judge, for a man to select a good claim (a quarter section being 160 acres), and fence and plow a part of it and to erect thereon a cabin. There is never a want of land to preempt in a new country. The settler can always get an original claim or buy out the claim of another very cheap, near some other settlers.

The liberal policy of our government in regard to the disposal of public lands is peculiarly beneficial to the settler. The latter has the first chance. He can go on to a quarter section which may be worth $15 an acre, and preempt it before it is surveyed, and finally obtain it for $1.25 an acre. Whereas the speculator must wait till the land is surveyed and advertised for sale; and then he can get only what has not been preempted, and at a price which it brings at auction, not less than $1.25 an acre. Then what land is not sold at public sale is open to private entry at $1.25 an acre. It is such land that bounty warrants are located on. Thus it is seen the pioneer has the first choice. Why, I have walked over land up here that would now bring from $10 to

$20 an acre if it was in the market, and which any settler can preempt and get for $1.25 an acre.

I am strongly tempted to turn farmer myself, and go out and build me a cabin. The speculation would be a good one. But to acquire a title by preemption I must dwell on the soil and prove that I have erected a dwelling and made other improvements. In other words, before a man (or any head of a family) can get a patent, he must satisfy the land officers that he is a dweller in good faith on the soil. It is often the case, indeed, that men get a title by preemption who never intend to live on their quarter section. But they do it by fraud. They have a sort of mental reservation, I suppose, when they take the requisite oaths. In this way many valuable claims are taken up and held along from month to month, or from year to year, by mock improvements.

A pretender will make just improvements enough to hinder the actual settler from locating on the claim, or will sell out to him at a good profit. A good deal of money is made by these fictitious claimants. It is rather hard to prevent it, too, inasmuch as it is difficult to disprove that a man intends some time to have a permanent home, or, in fact, that his claim is not his legal residence, though his usual abiding place is somewhere else.

Nothing could be more delightful than for a party of young men who desire to farm to come out together early in the spring and aid each other in preempting land in the same neighborhood. The preemptor has to pay about $5 in the way of fees before he gets through the entire process of securing a title. It is a popular error (much like the opinion that a man cannot swear to what he sees through glass) that improvements of a certain value, say $50, are required to be made, or that a certain number of acres must be cultivated. All that is required, however, is evidence that the party has built a house fit to live in, and

has in good faith proceeded to cultivate the soil. . . .

Let us assume now that the settler has got his house up, either a frame house or of logs, with a part of his farm fenced; and that he has filed his application for preemption at the land office in the district in which he resides. Let us suppose further that he is passing his first autumn here. His house, if he is a man of limited means, has but two rooms, and they are both on the basement story. He has just shelter enough for his stock, but none for his hay, which is stacked nearby. The probability is that he lives in the vicinity of some clear stream or copious spring, and has not, therefore, needed to dig a well. The whole establishment, one would think, who was accustomed to the Eastern style of living, betrayed downright poverty.

But let us stop a moment; this is the home of a pioneer. He has been industrious, and everything about him exhibits forethought. There is a cornfield all fenced in with tamarack poles. It is paved over with pumpkins (for pumpkins flourish wonderfully in Minnesota), and contains twenty acres of ripe corn, which, allowing thirty-five bushels to an acre, is worth, at 90 cents per bushel, the sum of $630. There are three acres of potatoes, of the very best quality, containing 300 bushels, which, at 50 cents a bushel, are worth $150. Here then, off of two crops, he gets $780, and I make a moderate estimate at that. Next year he will add to this a crop of oats or wheat.

The true pioneer is a model farmer. He lays out his work two weeks in advance. Every evening finds him further ahead. If there is a rainy day, he knows what to set himself about. He lays his plans in a systematic manner and carries them into execution with energy. He is a true pioneer, and therefore he is not an idle man, nor a loafer, nor a weak, addle-headed tippler. Go into his house, and, though you do not see elegance, you can yet behold intelligence, and neatness, and sweet domestic bliss.

The life of the pioneer is not exposed to such hardships and delays as retarded the fortunes of the settlers in the older states. They had to clear forests; here the land is ready for the plow. And though "there is society where none intrude," yet he is not by any means beyond the boundaries of good neighborhood. In many cases, however, he has left his dearest friends far away in his native village, where his affections still linger. He has to endure painful separations and to forgo those many comforts which spring from frequent meetings under the parental roof and frequent converse with the most attractive scenes of youth. But to compensate for these things he can feel that the labor of the pioneer, aside from its pecuniary advantage to himself, is of service to the state and a helpmate to succeeding generations. . . .

I SHALL TRY to answer some questions which I imagine might be put by different classes of men who are interested in this part of the West. . . .

The most available locations are now a considerable distance above St. Paul. The valley of the St. Peter's is pretty much taken up; and so of the valley of the Mississippi for a distance of fifteen miles on either side to a point 100 miles above St. Paul. One of the land officers at Minneapolis informed me that there were good preemption claims to be had 15 miles west, that being as far as the country was thickly settled.

One of the finest regions now unoccupied that I know of, not to except even the country on the Crow Wing River, is the land bordering on Otter Tail Lake. For 40 miles all round that lake the land is splendid. More than a dozen disinterested eyewitnesses have described that region to me in the most glowing terms. In beauty, in fertility, and in the various collateral resources which make a farming country desirable, it is not surpassed. It lies south of the picturesque highlands, or *hauteurs des terres,* and about midway between the sources of the Crow Wing and North Red Rivers. From this town the distance to it is 60 miles. The lake itself is 40 miles long and 5 miles in width. The water is clear and deep, and abounds with whitefish that are famous for their delicious flavor. . . .

But let me say to the speculator that he need not covet any of these broad acres. There is little chance for him. Before that land can be bought at public sale or by mere purchasers at private sale, it will, I feel sure, be entirely occupied by actual settlers. And so it ought to be. The good of the territory is promoted by that beneficent policy of our public land laws which gives the actual settler the first and best chance to acquire a title by preemption.

Speculators have located a great many land warrants in Minnesota. Some have been located on lakes, some on swamps, some on excellent land. Of course the owner who, as a general thing, is a nonresident, leaves his land idle for something to "turn up" to make it profitable. There it stands, doing no good, but on the contrary is an encumbrance to the settler, who has to travel over and beyond it without meeting the face of a neighbor in its vicinity. The policy of new states is to tax nonresident landholders at a high rate. When the territory becomes a state and is obliged to raise a revenue, some of these fellows outside who, to use a phrase common up here, have plastered the country over with land warrants, will have to keep a lookout for the tax gatherer. Now I do not mean to discourage moneyed men from investing in Minnesota lands. I do not wish to raise any bugbears, but simply to let them know that hoarding up large tracts of land without making improvements, and leaving it to increase in value by the toil and energy of the pioneer, is a way of doing things which is not popular with the actual settler.

But there is a great deal of money to be made by judicious investments in land.

Buying large tracts of land I believe to be the least profitable speculation, unless, indeed, the purchaser knows exactly what he is buying and is on hand at the public sale to get the benefit of a second choice. I say second choice, because the preemptor has had the first choice long ago, and it may be before the land was surveyed. What I would recommend to speculators is to purchase in some good town sites. Buy in two or three, and if one or two happen to be failures, the profits on the other will enable you to bear the loss. I know of a man who invested $6,000 at St. Paul six years ago. He has sold over $30,000 worth of the land, and has as much more left. This is but an ordinary instance. The advantage of buying lots in a town arises from the rapid rise of the value of the land, the ready market, and withal the moderate prices at which they can be procured during the early part of its history.

To such persons as have a desire to come West, and are not inclined to be farmers, and who have not capital enough to engage in mercantile business, there is sufficient employment. A new country always opens up avenues of successful business for every industrious man and woman; more kinds even than I could well enumerate. Every branch of mechanics needs workmen of all grades; from the boy who planes the rough boards to the head workman. Teaming affords good employment for young men the year round. The same may be said of the sawmills. A great deal of building is going on constantly; and those who have good trades get $2.50 per day. I am speaking, of course, of the territory in general.

One of the most profitable kinds of miscellaneous business is surveying. This art requires the services of large numbers; not only to survey the public lands but town sites and the lands of private individuals. Labor is very high everywhere in the West, whether done by men, women, or children; even the boys, not fourteen years old, who clean the knives and forks on the steamboats, get $20 a month and *are found*. But the best of it all is that, when a man earns a few dollars, he can easily invest it in a piece of land and double his money in three months, perhaps in one month. . . .

I have now a young man in my mind who came to a town ten miles this side of St. Paul, six months ago, with $500. He commenced trading, and has already, by good investments and the profits of his business, doubled his money. Everything that one can eat or wear brings a high price, or as high as it does in any part of the West. The number of visitors and emigrants is so large that the productions of the territory are utterly inadequate to supply the market. Therefore, large quantities of provisions have to be brought up the river from the lower towns. At Swan River, 100 miles this side of St. Paul, pork is worth $35. . . . Board for laboring men must be about $4 a week. For transient guests at Crow Wing it is $1 a day.

I have heard it said that money is scarce. It is possible. It certainly commands a high premium; but the reason is that there are such splendid opportunities to make fortunes by building and buying and selling city lots. A man intends that the rent of a house or store shall pay for its construction in three years. The profits of adventure justify a man in paying high interest. If a man has money enough to buy a pair of horses and a wagon, he can defy the world. These are illustrations to show why one is induced to pay interest. I do not think, however, money is "tight." I never saw people so free with their money, or appear to have it in so great abundance.

There is one drawback which this territory has in common with the greater part of the West, and, in fact, of the civilized world. It is not only a drawback but a nuisance anywhere. I mean drinking or whiskey shops. The greater proportion of the settlers are temperate men, I am sure; but in almost every village there are places where the meanest kind of intoxicating liquor is sold. There are some who sell liquor to the Indians. But such business is universally considered as the most degraded that a mean man can be guilty of. It is filthy to see men staggering about under the influence of bad whiskey, or of any kind of whiskey. He who sends a young husband to his new cabin home intoxicated, to mortify and torment his family; or who sells liquor to uneducated Indians, that they may fight and murder, must have his conscience — if he has any at all — cased over with sole leather. Mr. [John B.] Gough is needed in the West.

Minnesota is not behind in education. Ever since Governor Slade of Vermont brought some bright young schoolmistresses up to St. Paul (in 1849), common school education has been diffusing its precious influences. The government wisely sets apart two sections of land — the 16th and 36th — in every township for school purposes. A township is six miles square, and the two sections thus reserved in each township comprise 1,280 acres. Other territories have the same provision. This affords a very good fund for educational uses, or rather it is a great aid to the exertions of the people. There are some flourishing institutions of learning in the territory. But the greatest institution, after all, in the country — the surest protection of our liberties and our laws — is the *free school*.

77.

Constitution of the Vigilantes of San Francisco

Corrupt public officials and an influx of criminals during the 1849 Gold Rush combined to create such a state of lawlessness in California that private citizens took law enforcement into their own hands through the formation of "vigilance committees." The first vigilante group banded together in 1851 against the "Sydney ducks," a gang of riffraff from Australia that was suspected of setting several fires that menaced the city of San Francisco. The second group, known as the Vigilance Committee of 1856, and formed under the guidance of the prominent businessman William Coleman, drew up the following constitution and rules of order. Vigilante justice was not an unusual phenomenon in the West at the time, but the San Francisco committees were conspicuous for their dignity and self-restraint.

Source: *The Works of Hubert Howe Bancroft*, Vol. XXXVII, San Francisco, 1887, pp. 111-113.

Whereas, it has become apparent to the citizens of San Francisco that there is no security for life and property, either under the regulations of society as it at present exists or under the laws as now administered; and that, by the association together of bad characters, our ballot boxes have been stolen and others substituted, or stuffed with votes that were never polled, and thereby our elections nullified, our dearest rights violated, and no other method left by which the will of the people can be manifested:

Therefore, the citizens whose names are hereunto attached do unite themselves into an association for the maintenance of the peace and good order of society, the prevention and punishment of crime, the preservation of our lives and property, and to insure that our ballot boxes shall hereafter express the actual and unforged will of the majority of our citizens.

And we do bind ourselves, each unto the other, by a solemn oath, to do and perform every just and lawful act for the maintenance of law and order, and to sustain the law when faithfully and properly administered. But we are determined that no thief, burglar, incendiary, assassin, ballot-box stuffer, or other disturber of the peace shall escape punishment, either by the quibbles of the law, the insecurity of prisons, the carelessness or corruption of the police, or a laxity of those who pretend to administer justice. And to secure the objects of this association, we do hereby agree:

1. That the name and style of this association shall be the Committee of Vigilance, for the protection of the ballot box, the lives, liberty, and property of the citizens and residents of San Francisco.

2. That there shall be rooms for the deliberations of the Committee, at which there shall be some one or more members of the Committee, appointed for that purpose, in constant attendance, at all hours of the day and night, to receive the report of any member of the association, or of any other person or persons whatsoever, of any act of violence done to the person or property of any citizen of San Francisco; and if, in the judgment of the member or members of the Committee present, it be such an act as justifies or demands the interference of this Committee, either in aiding in the execution of the laws, or the prompt and summary punishment of the offender, the Committee shall be at once assembled for the purpose of taking such action as the majority of them, when assembled, shall determine upon.

3. That it shall be the duty of any member or members of the Committee on duty at the committee rooms, whenever a general assembly of the Committee is deemed necessary, to cause a call to be made in such a manner as shall be found advisable.

4. *That whereas* an Executive Committee has been chosen by the General Committee, it shall be the duty of said Executive Committee to deliberate and act upon all important questions and decide upon the measures necessary to carry out the objects for which this association was formed.

5. *That whereas* this Committee has been formed into subdivisions, the Executive Committee shall have the power to call, when they shall so determine, upon a Board of Delegates, to consist of three representatives from each division, to confer with them upon matters of vital importance.

6. That all matters of detail and government shall be embraced in a code of by-laws.

7. That the action of this body shall be entirely and vigorously free from all consideration of, or participation in, the merits or demerits, or opinion or acts, of any or all sects, political parties, or sectional divisions in the community; and every class of orderly citizens, of whatever sect, party, or nativity, may become members of this body. No discussion of political, sectional, or sectarian subjects shall be allowed in the rooms of the association.

8. That no persons accused before this body shall be punished until after fair and impartial trial and conviction.

9. That whenever the General Committee has assembled for deliberation, the decision of the majority, upon any question that may be submitted to them by the Executive Committee, shall be binding upon the whole; *provided*, nevertheless, that when the delegates are deliberating upon the punishment to be awarded to any criminals, no vote inflicting the death penalty shall be binding unless passed by two-thirds of those present and entitled to vote.

10. That all good citizens shall be eligible for admission to this body, under such reg-

ulations as may be prescribed by a committee on qualifications; and if any unworthy persons gain admission, they shall on due proof be expelled.

And believing ourselves to be executors of the will of the majority of our citizens, we do pledge our sacred honor to defend and sustain each other in carrying out the determined action of this Committee, at the hazard of our lives and fortunes.

78.

W. H. Wallace *et al.*: Martial Law in the Washington Territory

Shortly after Isaac Stevens was named governor of the Washington Territory in 1853, he began to negotiate treaties with the Indians to secure more land for the white settlers. Indian dissatisfaction with the terms of these treaties led to a revolt in which the Indians initially defeated the regular army troops. They were subdued only after Governor Stevens called up a militia of a thousand volunteers. When certain settlers accused of being sympathetic toward the Indians sought the protection of the courts, Stevens declared a state of martial law, closed the courts, and arrested the chief justice. The following report of the governor's actions was published May 1856.

Source: *A Brief Notice of the Recent Outrages Committed by Isaac I. Stevens, Governor of Washington Territory*, Olympia, Wash., May 17, 1856, pp. 3-16.

IN THE LATTER PART of the month of March 1856, Lion A. Smith, Charles Wren, Henry Smith, John McLeod, John McField, Henry Murry, and ——— Wilson, American citizens, residents of the county of Pierce and territory of Washington, were arrested upon their several land claims in that county by a detachment of volunteers under orders of Isaac I. Stevens, governor of said territory, without process of law, and without any complaint or affidavit being lodged against them charging them with the commission of any offense against the law. They were taken by a guard to the town of Olympia, the capital of the territory, detained there overnight, and then sent in custody of a guard to the U.S. Military Post at Fort Steilacoom, with a *written* request of Governor Stevens to Lieutenant Colonel Casey, U.S. Army, commanding that post, to retain said prisoners in *close confinement*, upon a charge of *treason*.

In the early part of April, William H. Wallace and Frank Clark, attorneys-at-law, of counsel for said prisoners, started for Penn's Cove, Whidby's Island, a distance of 100 miles, the residence of Hon. F. A. Chenoweth, U.S. district judge of the 3rd judicial district of Washington Territory, to make application for the writ of habeas corpus, to test the legality of such imprisonment. The governor, having learned of this mission of justice and mercy, issued a proc-lamation, *without seal*, bearing date April 3, 1856, and in the following language:

> *Whereas,* in the prosecution of the Indian war, circumstances have existed affording such grave cause of suspicion that certain evil-disposed persons of Pierce County have given aid and comfort to the enemy, as that they have been placed under arrest and ordered to be tried by a military commission: *And whereas,* efforts are now being made to withdraw, by civil process, these persons from purview of the said commission:
>
> *Therefore,* as the war is now being actively prosecuted throughout nearly the whole of the said county, and great injury to the public and the plans of the campaign be frustrated if the alleged designs of these persons be not arrested; I, Isaac I. Stevens, governor of the territory of Washington, do hereby proclaim MARTIAL LAW over the said county of Pierce, and do by these presents suspend for the time being, and till further notice, the functions of all civil officers in said county.
>
> Given under my hand at Olympia, this 3rd day of April, 1856, and the year of Independence of the United States the eightieth.
>
> ISAAC I. STEVENS

ON BEING APPRISED of this proclamation, Colonel Casey informed the governor that, notwithstanding its issue, were a writ of habeas corpus served upon him, he would feel compelled to obey its mandates; upon this, the governor removed said prisoners again to Olympia, *out of the county,* where he pretended to hold them by the martial law he had proclaimed. In the meantime, His Honor, Judge Chenoweth, had issued a writ of habeas corpus, and unaware of the existence of the proclamation. It is not our purpose to criticize the *intention* of the governor, to defeat the service of a writ *after* the arrest of parties, defying, as it does, the wholesome spirit of that section of the Constitution which prohibits the enactment of *ex post facto* laws; for we have learned, to our mortification, that constitutions are nothing, law is idle, the *will* of the governor is *supreme.*

But we do boldly maintain the position that if his proclamation of martial law was based upon public necessity, urgently demanded for the public welfare, the great *writ of right* still stood exempt from its reach and paramount to its operation. Truth compels us, however, to deny that the proclamation was necessary, and we need only refer to the document itself to sustain our position. The preamble to said proclamation recites that "the suspected parties were in custody," their evil designs, had they any, had been thwarted, and they were now in a position that they could no longer "frustrate the campaign." Nor does it appear that any effort was made to rescue the prisoners by force; nothing is alleged, save that, by counsel, they attempted to secure what the national Constitution guarantees to every citizen.

The writ of habeas corpus issued by order of Judge Chenoweth never was served, because the prisoners had been transferred by Governor Stevens out of Judge Chenoweth's district.

Nothing further was done until the first Monday in May 1856, when, by a law of this territory, the term of the District Court for the county of Pierce was to be held. We quote from the statement made by the bar of that district, the detail of the outrages committed by the executive during that week:

> The United States judge assigned to this judicial district, being detained at home by severe illness at the time when, by law, the term of the District Court was to be held, the Hon. Edward Lander, chief justice of this territory, who resides in the adjoining district, at the special written request of Hon. Judge Chenoweth, undertook to hold said court; and on Monday, the 5th May inst., arrived at Steilacoom and opened the court in due form; having been informed, however,

on his way to the court by Lieut. Col. B. F. Shaw, commanding a volunteer force under authority of the governor of this territory, that if he attempted to hold said court he would be forcibly prevented. Judge Lander, in order to prevent a collision between executive and judicial authority, suggested that he would simply open and adjourn the court until Wednesday, that the governor might be advised to withdraw his proclamation.

About three days previous to opening court, Colonel Shaw, commanding the volunteer forces, who had received written instructions from Governor Stevens to enforce martial law until further orders, being directed at the same time to inform him immediately if in his opinion it was no longer necessary, had written by express to the governor stating that no occasion existed in the county for its continuance, informing him that important business was to be transacted before the court, and recommended that, in consequence, the proclamation be abrogated. Judge Lander, now, himself, wrote to Governor Stevens informing him of the course he had taken; that there were important causes to be tried before the court, one of which, the suit of the *U.S. v. The Former Collector of Puget Sound*, ought to be tried; that there was imminent danger of a collision between the civil authorities and the military, and recommending that martial law be at once abrogated, especially as the present condition of the county seemed not to require it.

In reply, Governor Stevens, on the 6th inst., while declining to withdraw his proclamation, suggested that Judge Lander adjourn his court to the first Monday in June, and informed him that he had examined the law and found no difficulty in his adjourning from any time to the next term of court.

Upon the receipt of this information, Judge Lander, having done his duty as a citizen in endeavoring to prevent the expected collision, proceeded to fulfill those of his judicial office by opening court at the appointed time, accompanied by the clerk, U.S. deputy marshal, and sheriff; he went to the courthouse, opened the court by proclamation in usual form, and caused the grand jury to be impaneled

and sworn. During this time, a company of volunteers (many of them citizens of Oregon, although enrolled in this territory) drawn from Clark County, on the Columbia River, entered the courtroom with loaded rifles and drew up without the bar; another company was kept in reserve without to assist them if necessary.

Judge Lander then directed the deputy marshal to prevent the entry of any armed men within the bar, but the commanding officer, having announced that he acted under orders from Governor Stevens, directed his men to arrest the judge and clerk. In obedience to the order, they entered the bar, the deputy marshal being unable to prevent it, and arrested the judge in his seat; the judge stating that he only succumbed to force, and declined calling upon the *posse comitatus* [power of the county] because he wished to avoid bloodshed. Judge Lander and the clerk, J. M. Chapman, were then removed by the military from the courthouse, and on the same day taken out of the county and carried to Olympia. The records of the court, which were at first seized, were subsequently returned to the deputy clerk.

During this time, the citizens present, though manifesting a deep feeling of indignation at the transaction, refrained from any disorderly or violent acts. The conduct of Judge Lander was, throughout, dignified, firm, and worthy of his high position, and was, we are satisfied, dictated only by a strict sense of duty.

ON REACHING OLYMPIA, the chief justice and clerk were not placed in confinement, though the former was not officially notified of his release till the 9th inst., and the clerk on the 10th inst.

On Monday, the 12th of May, the District Court of the 2nd judicial district commenced, over which Chief Justice Lander presides, and he proceeded to the discharge of that duty.

During that day, John McLeod, Henry Smith, and John McField, three of the parties arrested in Pierce County, petitioned the judge, at chambers, for a writ of habeas corpus to be directed to Isaac I. Stevens, Governor, etc., to bring them and their fellow prisoners before the chief justice, at chambers, on Wednesday ensuing. This writ was placed in the hands of the U.S. marshal and duly served the same day at 7 P.M. *Under cover of that night*, proclamations of martial law over the county of Thurston were posted up, and here is a copy of the remarkable instrument.

PROCLAMATION

Whereas, in the prosecution of the existing Indian war, it became necessary, for the reasons set forth in the proclamation of the governor of the territory of Washington, of the 3rd of April, to proclaim martial law in and through Pierce County, in said territory: *And whereas*, the same efforts are now being made in the county of Thurston by the issue of the writ of habeus corpus to take from the purview of the military commission, which is ordered to convene on the 20th inst., certain persons charged with giving aid and comfort to the enemy: *And whereas*, an overruling public necessity leaves no alternative but to persist in that trial in order that the military operations be not rendered abortive and the lives of the citizens needlessly sacrificed:

Therefore, I, Isaac I. Stevens, governor of the territory of Washington, do by these presents proclaim *martial law* in and throughout the county of Thurston, and do call upon all good citizens to see that *martial law* is enforced.

Given under my hand at Olympia, this 13th day of May, in the year of our Lord 1856, and the year of Independence the eightieth.

ISAAC I. STEVENS

On the morning of the 13th May, a company of volunteers rode into town, armed and equipped as the law directs, with no other motive than, as is supposed, *to help "good citizens see that martial law be enforced,"* and to remove a *portion of the prisoners* out of the county of Thurston. A cannon was drawn up in front of the court-

Library of Congress

Isaac Ingalls Stevens, governor of Washington Territory who declared martial law in 1856

house. On this day, the governor did not attempt to interrupt the court, though his "guards" were seated in front of the *executive office*, and paraded occasionally up and down the pavement before the building wherein the court was held.

Wednesday, May 14. At the time for the return of the writ, the governor was respectfully notified that the judge was at chambers and prepared to receive his returns to the writ of habeas corpus. Refusing to come, he pleaded to the marshal that martial law had been proclaimed, and it suspended process. Petitioners' counsel then asked for a rule returnable the next day . . . upon the governor, to show cause why an attachment should not issue for contempt.

Thursday, May 15, 1 P.M. The governor failing to appear and make return to the writ, on motion of petitioners' counsel, rule made absolute, and a writ of attachment issued to bring Isaac I. Stevens before the Hon. Edward Lander, chief justice, to answer for a contempt in refusing to make return to the writ of habeas corpus. The governor *forcibly resisted* the service of this writ, and dispatched a company of volunteers (from the territory of Oregon), commanded by Capt. Bluford Miller, to the house wherein Judge Lander was sitting at chambers, and the marshal, being ordered to keep the room clear of armed men, was compelled to lock the door. While the marshal was engaged in making a return to the writ, and the judge in making the order for an alias writ of attachment, Captain Miller called upon the judge to *surrender.*

In the meantime, the house was surrounded by armed men. The counsel engaged inside could distinctly hear the men cocking their rifles. The judge in this trying moment remained firm, cool, and dispassionate; and, finally, the door was forced open by the soldiers, the room was filled with armed men, and the chief justice, together with Elwood Evans, acting clerk of the U.S. District Court of the 2nd judicial district, was seized and taken down to the executive office.

In the presence of a large crowd, Chief Justice Lander was offered his liberty on condition of his "giving his honor that he would not hold any court or issue any further process until the proclamation of martial law was revoked." This offer was made by Captain Miller, who stated that he did it by the instruction of the governor. Justice to Judge Lander requires that we should give his dignified and manly reply: "Tell Governor Stevens for me that I will not promise not to do what the law requires at my hand; say to him that I will do my whole duty, and I trust he will do his as well."

On this answer he was taken into custody and carried out to Camp Montgomery, out of the county of Thurston, out of his judicial district, pending a regular term of court — the grand jury being yet in session, important cases undisposed of, and much un-

finished business on the docket — making the second time which Governor Stevens has interrupted the courts, and *kidnapped* the court and its clerk. The clerk was then unconditionally released.

The above is a plain, unvarnished statement of the facts of the case, and on them we base the following charges against Governor Stevens, with our reasons for so doing:

I. *He has violated his oath of office, which* inter alia [among other things], *was to support the Constitution of the United States.*

1. In this, that he has attempted to suspend the writ of habeas corpus, which, by said Constitution can only be suspended by Congress, and then only in cases of invasion and rebellion, when the public safety require it. —— *Vide Cons. U.S. Art. i. Sec. 9.*

2. In this, that he has arrested citizens and deprived them of their liberty without process of law. —— *Vide Cons. U.S. Art. v. Amendments.*

3. In this, that he has held persons to answer for an infamous and capital crime without any complaint or charge being preferred against them, and without a presentment or indictment of a grand jury being made. —— *Vide Cons. of U.S. Art. v. Amendments.*

4. In this, that he has broken into houses of citizens without the issue of any warrant therefor, and seized persons and taken them into custody. —— *Vide Cons. U.S. Art. iv. Amendments.*

5. In this, that he has deprived American citizens of the right of trial by jury of the district wherein the alleged crime was committed, and created a court of his own not known to or recognized by the law. —— *Vide Cons. U.S. Art. iii. Sec. 2; il Art. vi. Amendments.*

6. In this, that he has charged men with committing *treason*, which is only cognizable by a United States court, and ordered their trial by a tribunal of his own creation. —— *Vide Cons. U.S. Art. iii. Sec. 3.*

7. In this, that he has defied and abrogated the supreme law of the land, rendered null and void the Constitution of the United States, and erected a military despotism with nothing to guide it but his own will. —— *Vide Cons. U.S. Art. vi.*

II. *He has acted in violation of the organic act creating the territory of Washington.*

1. In this, that he has suspended the writ of habeas corpus. [*See Ordinance of 1787,* which, by act of Congress, bearing date August 14, 1848, entitled "An act to establish the territorial government of Oregon," was extended in its application to what is now Washington Territory, and reaffirmed in the organic act of this territory.]

2. In this, that he has deprived citizens of their liberty and property without process of law, and without compensation. —— *Ibid.*

3. In this, that he has deprived citizens of the territory of a right of trial by jury. —— *Ibid.*

III. *He has violated and set at defiance the laws of Washington Territory.*

1. In this, that he has suspended and interrupted the terms of the district courts of the counties of Pierce and Thurston. —— *Vide "An act to define the judicial district of Washington Territory," Laws W.T., 1854, p. 448.*

2. In this, that he has held in custody persons not charged with any offense and without a complaint filed. —— *Vide Crim. Prac. Laws W.T., Ses. 1854, Passim.*

3. In this, that he has violated the provision of law whereby "every person restrained of his liberty, under any pretense whatever, may prosecute a writ of habeas corpus to inquire into the causes of the restraint." —— *Vide Sec. 434 "Of an act to regulate the practice in civil actions," p. 212, Laws W.T., Ses. 1854. . . .*

THE GREAT JEFFERSON frequently declared himself upon this subject. He was in favor "of the eternal and unremitting force of the habeas corpus laws." On another occasion, he inquires, "Why suspend the writ of habeas corpus in insurrections and rebellions? If the public safety requires that the government should have a man imprisoned on less probable testimony in those, than other emergencies, let him be taken and tried, *retaken* and *retried,* while the necessity continues, only giving him redress against the government for damages." And now stands out the glaring fact to the world that never, till the instance we now record, has the writ been suspended.

One instance occurs, the Burr Rebellion, when the suspension was asked for and the U.S. House of Representatives, though asked to pass said bill by no less a personage than the immortal Jefferson, refused so to do by the overwhelming vote of 113 to 19, and that too on a motion *to reject the bill. . . .*

SUCH THEN IS THE VIEW we take of the gross outrage committed in attempting to suspend the writ of habeas corpus, and we can arrive at no other conclusion than that the governor is a usurper, a tyrant, and a despot.

The plea of ignorance in this case cannot avail him from these charges. *Ignorantia legis neminem excusat* [ignorance of the law excuses no one]. We assert that it was his duty to know principles at the basis of our free institutions. A school boy could not fail to know them, and for a *governor* to be so *ignorant* is at once to acknowledge his unfitness for so high a position.

Again, we charge him with culpable ignorance in asserting his determination to try, by a military commission, American citizens, either on a charge of giving *aid and comfort to the enemy* (defined by the Constitution and laws of the United States to be *treason*), or as his *vindication,* dated May 10, which . . . terms them *spies.* We accept the issue as tendered by that *vindication . . .* as corroborating all the material averments made by the bar in their statement, published May 7. . . . The governor in this vindication places himself in an unfortunate dilemma. Should he *"persist in this trial"* of these men for giving *aid* and *comfort,* the parties must be cleared on a plea to the jurisdiction, and the governor himself takes these men *"out of the purview of the military commission,"* a court we do not understand, how composed we know not, by what authority convened we cannot learn. It seems to be a "pet" of the governor, being recited in every document coming from the executive office and exhibited to the world.

If the charge made by the governor be *treason,* then we assert he becomes the *evil-disposed* person who would take his victims out of that purview. For though the Constitution may be *obsolete* in this territory, it cannot be forgotten that it does clearly establish the tribunal by which such offenses *must* be tried, and guarantees to the party charged therewith a trial by a jury of *twelve of his peers* from the district wherein the overt act was committed, if such district be legally defined. We therefore maintain that Pierce County, in the 3rd judicial district, was the proper venue of said action, and we charge upon Governor Stevens that if he had evidence of the guilt of these men, and broke up by force the only tribunal capable of trying them and thus prevented their just punishment, he is guilty of a gross dereliction of duty, requiring the utmost censure; and so far as the effects thereof are concerned, cannot claim to be much better than an *"accessory after the fact."* . . .

We may be permitted to sum up the grievances to which the people of this territory have been subjected by the acts of its present executive. In doing so we cannot fail to observe the peculiar similarity of them with several of the grievances recited as good cause for redress when George III imposed them on the Thirteen Colonies.

Was it true in 1776, as Jefferson wrote, "when a long train of abuses and usurpations, pursuing invariably the same object, evinces a design to reduce them under absolute despotism, it is their right, it is their duty" to repudiate such government? Can an American deny the sacred justice of that war which was waged, among other reasons, because a despot "deprived us in many cases, of the benefits of trial by jury; obstructed the administration of justice; erected a multitude of new offices; and called hither swarms of officers to harass our people and eat out their substance, affected to render the military independent of and superior to the civil power; took away our charters (and what better charter than the right to habeas corpus); abolished our most valuable laws; and altered fundamentally the form of our government?"

Has eighty years growth and vigor, secured by the maintenance of the truths of that sublime instrument, taught us, the descendants of those great missionaries of civil and constitutional freedom, that the people have no rights, that absolutism and despotism are again to prevail, and everything peculiar to American institutions at once be blotted from our national character?

In conclusion, a sense of duty we own to Chief Justice Edward Lander, who has twice been taken into that most offensive of all styles of arrest, that of being forced to yield in the exercise of his judicial functions to an armed force, prompts us again to tender our sympathies. He has done everything he could to maintain the supremacy of the law and the dignity of the bench. Yielding only when overwhelmed by the soldiery of the executive, his last judicial acts have been to order the punishment due to such outlaws for their contempt in invading the halls of justice, to protest firmly against the despotism of a petty military tyrant *whose day is now.* We fearlessly make the issue on this great question, and we implore the national government to redress our grievances and shield us from the despotism under which we live. Our courts are powerless;

private rights are at an end; the constitution is subverted; civil process is paralyzed; to ask for process guaranteed us by law is cause for arrest; the highest judicial functionary of our territory is now a prisoner because he dared to issue a writ of habeas corpus at the petition of five of Governor Stevens' victims.

Can this document better end than by as-serting to the world that our territory is now in such a condition that soldiers are not needed to fight an enemy, but their leisure is devoted to interrupting courts of justice, becoming jailers to judges and clerks thereof, who but perform their legitimate public duty. Such is the "great OVERRULING PUBLIC NECESSITY" *justifying the proclamation of martial law.*

79.

ANONYMOUS: The Progress of the Americans in the Art of Writing

Nineteenth-century concern with the development of a distinctively American literature received continual emphasis in the North American Review. *Founded in Boston in 1815 as a quarterly journal of literature, history, and criticism, it claimed the talents of such distinguished Americans as Edward Everett, James Russell Lowell, Jared Sparks, and Henry Adams. Its contributors produced much good literary criticism and hoped to develop standards for American literature. The following discussion of American writing is an abridgement of a review of* A Cyclopaedia of American Literature, *by Evert A. and George L. Duykinck.*

Source: *North American Review,* April 1856.

AMERICAN LITERATURE has been too exclusively regarded at the extremes of ignorant contempt and indiscriminate laudation. The sneers of British reviewers thirty years ago found their counterpart, at a subsequent period in the patriotic complacency of native critics; and if the censure was illiberal and unjust, the praise was extravagant. Sydney Smith was not far from right in declaring that, while Americans as a people were remarkably sensible, they had produced no great original minds in the field of letters; for the exceptions were so few, and their scope so limited, that this general statement was, when made, apparently warranted. The present time, indeed, offers abundant material to refute such a charge.

In history, romance, rhetoric, criticism, and poetry, we can now boast of native authors whose merit is recognized abroad as well as at home; and there is no department of science or taste which has not been signally illustrated on this side of the water. Indeed, to an experienced and thoughtful observer, the number of gifted minds devoted to such pursuits, and the amount as well as the quality of their productions seem creditable to the intellectual activity and the noble emulation of the country, when it is remembered that the spirit of our national life is the reverse of contemplative, that trade and politics inevitably absorb the mental energy of a very large proportion of our citizens, and that no international copyright law baffles the competition of British authors.

When Dugald Stewart published his *Dissertation on the Progress of Metaphysical and Ethical Philosophy,* in 1824, he wrote:

> The rapid progress which the Americans have lately made in the art of writing has been remarked by various critics, and it is certainly a very important fact in the history of their literature. Their state papers were, indeed, always distinguished by a strain of animated and vigorous eloquence; but as most of them were composed on the spur of the occasion, their authors had little time to bestow on the niceties, or even upon the purity, of diction. An attention to these is the slow offspring of learned leisure and of the diligent study of the best models. This, I presume, was Gray's meaning when he said, "Good writing not only requires great parts, but the very best of those parts," a maxim which, if true, would point out the state of the public taste with respect to style as the surest test among any people of the general improvement which their intellectual powers have received; and which, when applied to our transatlantic brethren, would justify sanguine expectations of the attainments of the rising generation.

We are not of those who can discover in a few popular effusions or books that make a sensation the basis of a national literature. Because Brockden Brown describes the yellow fever in Philadelphia with a vivid horror of detail not unworthy of some of Boccaccio's and Defoe's plague pictures; because Patrick Henry made a speech whose effective eloquence roused a state to arms, or Hamilton drafted a state paper that would do credit to Burke; because Freneau's Indian Boy charmed Scott, and Mrs.

Brooks's Zophiel won the praise of Southey; because Wirt wrote essays as good as some in the *Spectator,* Wilde, a pathetic lyric which has been translated into all languages, Poe, a most ingenious bit of somber versification, Sprague, an unsurpassed poem in heroic pentameters, and Mrs. Stowe, a melodramatic story so picturesquely exhibiting certain phases of Southern slavery as to stir up all England to the speculative rescue; because of these and many other recognized successes, great and small, transient and memorable, in the vast realm of thought and expression, we do not infer the realization of that great and enduring crown of glory, a distinct, individual, potent, and noble literature.

But what we deduce from such mental phenomena is simply the perpetuity, in our branch of the Anglo-Saxon race, of that aptitude for letters, that innate capacity for manly, graceful, true, and picturesque writing, which is an inheritance from the parent stock, the natural endowment of a people eminent for reflective, humane, free utterance, heretofore mainly exhibited in the pulpit, the forum, and the newspaper, but, under favorable auspices, certain to find the more permanent and elaborate shape of books which will become endeared heirlooms of national thought; nay, which every year more and more assume this artistic form, and, as this *Cyclopaedia* clearly proves, are continually increasing in variety, finish, and worth.

For special departments of writing, indeed, we find evidence of a peculiar fitness of the national mind. Among the clergy, from the beginning, there is obvious either a powerful logic or a fresh and sweet tone of religious sentiment, the best written expression of which will compare favorably with that of any class of divines. Their discourses often combine the elegance of the French pulpit oratory in the time of Louis XIV with the rugged fervor of those brave preachers whose memory is kept green by

Dr. South's bold ethics and Tillotson's classic diction. No modern travelers have excelled the Americans in the clear, reliable, and pleasant record of their impressions. Their facility of adaptation makes them less prejudiced and more genial reporters of foreign experience than the natives of older and more conventional communities. In political writing the exigencies of our history created a class of authors and speakers remarkable for bold good sense, lucidness of statement, and unparalleled practical discretion. The Declaration of Independence, *The Federalist,* the constitutional debates, the speeches and writings of Washington, Jefferson, Adams, Hamilton, Marshall, Dickinson, Livingston, and subsequently of Ames, Clinton, Webster, Clay, and Calhoun, constitute an armory of republican weapons and a mine of political wisdom.

When Spenser dedicated, in 1590, the early cantos of *The Faerie Queene* to Elizabeth, the inscription ran thus, "by the grace of God, Queen of England, France, Ireland, and Virginia." It may be conjectured that this is the earliest association of the New World with the literature of the Old; and it is, at once, a true and a delightful illustration of our claim to the noble heritage of English literature, and the inevitable subsequent dependence of the colonies upon the parent fountain. America, indeed, began her career under the auspices of English scholars. She was never destitute of a learned clergy, from the arrival of the first immigrants. It is with the lives of these men, who exercised so marked an influence over the infant colonies, that this *Cyclopaedia of American Literature* appropriately commences. The Cottons, Wards, Hookers, and other educated colonists left a high position at home, and brought with them books and learning — hence the early development of the New England mind and the establishment of Harvard College. As might be imagined, Latin verses and translations from the classics — the literary mania of the ep-

och — were the first fruits of the Tree of Knowledge when transplanted to the Western wilderness, followed, from the religious exigencies of time and place, by the *Bay Psalm Book,* the first book printed in America.

Edwards was born at the commencement of Queen Anne's golden era, and his abstruse work, in its earnest metaphysical logic, offers no greater contrast to the lighter graces of Addison, the brilliant couplets of Pope, and the worldly tact of Congreve than does the state of society in America at the same era offer to that in England, the latter in the flush of Marlborough's victories, and the triumph of the most artificial period of British literature, the former absorbed in laying the foundations of popular education and waging the battles of religious zeal. It was to a book of Defoe's that Franklin ascribed his first impulse to systematic intellectual activity, and the author of Robinson Crusoe died when the future American philosopher had reached his twenty-fifth year. There was a remarkable similarity in the tone of their minds — indomitable application, affinity with popular needs and aspirations, a disdain of ornament in the use of language, and a prescient intelligence as to the means of social and economical progress.

Timothy Dwight was a contemporary of Cowper, and Joel Barlow of Goldsmith; and when we compare the standard merit and the household fame of the English with the obscurity that has attended the cisatlantic bards, we can find some apology for the incredulous sneer that formerly greeted American literary pretensions abroad. Subsequently appeared that glorious constellation of modern poets, the pure and fresh worship of nature by Wordsworth, the impassioned vividness of Byron, the metrical heroism of Campbell, the graphic pictures of Crabbe, the tasteful finish of Rogers, the lyric sweetness of Moore, and the spirited verses of Scott — which grand and varied outburst of song found, on this side of the water, a beautiful indeed, but then neither a various nor a many-voiced echo from the new-strung lyres of Percival, Halleck, Drake, and Bryant. The contrast was so palpable between the profuse and splendid offering to the Muses there and their scanty honors here that only an extravagant and sensitive patriot could rationally object to the reviewer's honest query, "Who reads an American book?"

One of the earliest American scholars to recognize the future interest that would attach to such memorials as are garnered in the first volume of this work was Joseph Stevens Buckminster. Fully aware of the limited intellectual triumphs of the country at the beginning of the century, he yet, with the prescience of genius, anticipated the growth of the national mind, from the inspiration which unrivaled scenery, free institutions, and popular education would at length yield to gifted Americans. . . .

Liberal and philosophic readers in Europe will find that we are not so indifferent to learning, nor so barbarous in taste, as the superficial among their critics have made them believe. They will perceive what a spirit of free inquiry, what a love of books, and what a facility of expression are bred by popular institutions; how genuine a sympathy with nature has inspired our best poets; how wisely eloquent are our gifted statesmen; what keen appreciation our critics manifest; what refinements of style and freshness of conception have been here displayed in fiction, travels, and didactic writing; and, especially, how universal is the appetite for knowledge and the impulse to intellectual endeavor. . . .

Books are not the luxury in America which they continue to be in England; journals are universally read; the modern British poets are more familiar to our people than they are to their own countrymen; the contributions to periodical literature of Carlyle, Macaulay, De Quincey, and other famous English essayists were first collected here; and for some years past an American reputation has been cherished as the award of "a kind of living posterity" by popular English authors, notwithstanding their just chafing under the piratical system of reprints. These and many other illustrations of the reading habits of our people indicate an unparalleled degree of general intelligence, secured by our educational system, cheap journalism, popular lectures, and social equality; and will tend to explain the remarkable diffusion of average literary talent of which the work before us is a memorable exposition.

The mutual action and reaction of the New and the Old World are, indeed, traceable from the inception to the present hour of our intellectual progress. In consequence of this influence, in all the agencies which directly affect popular culture, a superior facility and greater results are acknowledged to have crowned our labors. Thus, in educational manuals, juvenile books, the diffusion of knowledge through cheap periodicals, and other methods of general enlightenment, we have the advantage; while in the sources of higher mental discipline and erudition, our continuous and incalculable obligation to Europe is equally evident.

From the administration of the most learned of New York's colonial governors, Bishop Burnet's son, to the revolutionary times when Burke's eloquent pleas associated his fame with our nascent republic, and from that period to the era when John Neal imported Bentham's speculations, and Brownson advocated Cousin's philosophy, the whole course of American study has tended to the cosmopolitan spirit which now marks the actual life of our large cities.

The individuality of our written productions lies, therefore, more in tone than in design; in the characteristic assimilation rather than in the creative originality of the materials of literary art. Chiefly in pictures of nature, in widespread general intelligence, in political disquisition, and in free self-assertion have the records of the national mind a peculiar flavor and emphasis. The honor accorded to those who have faithfully labored in the field of science and letters, and the testimony given to a more noble class of writings than the trashy novels and ephemera which fill the advertising columns of our journals, are among the claims of the *Cyclopaedia* as a representative book, fitted to vindicate our standard of attainment and industry both at home and abroad.

If, as impartial critics, we should point out any defect in the general execution of the work, considered in a historical view, it would be in the somewhat too amiable and scholarly drift of the whole, and particularly in the mild record of those religious and political animosities which made the lives of our fathers a battle, and found vehement expression in their speeches and writings. The personalities, fierce assaults, and salient reprisals which the debates, the sermons, the newspapers, and the correspondence of our earlier annals disclose are here reproduced with as little reference to the bitter and vindictive spirit of the times as possible; the picture is mellowed in the retrospect, and we scarcely imagine the polemic and partisan rage that so inflamed the hearts of our ancestors. Perhaps it was wise and justifiable thus to merge in a genial and progressive view the unruly elements whence flows the now tranquil stream of the nation's intellectual life; and to the majority of readers, whatever may be their creeds, it is probably an added recommendation of a work like the present that it revives no old feuds and relates with comparative indifference the dissensions of the past.

If there is one among the select intelligences of the revolutionary era who may be justly considered as a representative mind, it is Franklin. . . . His scientific achievements and his patriotism doubtless originated his reputation abroad and at home; but his maxims, letters, autobiography, use of language, and philosophy of life were eminently characteristic of New England, and, thus regarded, there never was an intellectual pioneer whose ideal was so thoroughly based upon use and so little cognizant of beauty. Science, indeed, might anticipate new and brilliant triumphs from such a votary, but poetry folded her wings in despair, and philosophy could find no scope, under his material wisdom, except for domestic economy and prudential aphorisms. A mind so devoted to fact, so imprisoned in the actual, so keen and determined in the pursuit of material well-being, so cautious, shrewd, and intent upon making the best of things as they are, was undoubtedly adapted to the wants of a young country. . . .

The brave pioneers of the American church, such men as Hooker and Davenport, initiated a severe but wholesome discipline. Roger Williams, by his teachings and example, reconciled the strictest faith with practical toleration. John Eliot, by his patient ministry among the Indians, won the title of their apostle. Cotton Mather bequeathed a most richly characteristic story of New England colonial life, the unfailing resource of the modern historian. Jonathan Edwards was and is the great metaphysical expositor of Protestant theology. The wit of Byles is a vivid local tradition. The character of Dr. Emmons is still cited with reverent affection. Bishop White's devotional services hallowed the memory of those discussions — than which none in history are more pregnant with great results — which led to American independence. John Woolman was such a rare specimen of Quakerism that he was beloved of Elia and is the idol of Whittier. Dwight was one of the earliest of New England travelers and bards who gave elaborate record to their impressions. Blair, Chauncy, Brainerd, Mayhew, Stiles, Linn, Belknap, Miller, Mason, and others continue to indicate the true landmarks of our civilization by the effects of their ministry at the altar, the shrines of learning, and the fireside. . . .

It is pleasant to note the early advent of a class of men who have always appeared to us at once the most precious and the least appreciated ornaments of our race; men who love knowledge for its own sake, cultivate intimate relations with nature, retain the simplicity of youth, are devoted seekers, benign, candid, and simple in their tastes — in a word, what we understand by the generic term philosophers. Whether as naturalists, moralists, rhymers, patriots, a certain truthful, kindly, and unambitious character places them in strong contrast to the soldier, the statesman, and the professional man. Their position is less clearly defined, their spirit more disinterested. Of a tendency rather scientific than political, however far apart in renown and success, they are associated by mutual labors, kindred tastes, and, as is amply manifested in this chronicle, by frequent correspondence. Some of them are identified with invaluable discoveries, others with original speculations, and not a few with great practical devotion to the social welfare.

The most charming episodes in this work refer to these philosophers. At their head, in some aspects of his complex character, stands Benjamin Franklin, and they are admirably represented in Philadelphia by William Logan, John Bartram, Rittenhouse, and Dr. Rush; and in New York by Cadwallader Colden and Dr. Samuel L. Mitchill. In the same general category may be included Benjamin Thompson, afterward Count Rumford, John Winthrop of Harvard, Crevecoeur, and Hugh Williamson. Jefferson partook largely of this character, and so did Francis Hopkinson.

Attention has been diligently bestowed by our authors upon historical gleanings; and they have presented to us some curious specimens of primitive annals, such as the records of Capt. John Smith and Benjamin Church; while the data preserved by Peters, Prince, Ramsay, Belknap, Thacher, Graydon, Minot, and others have been better known and of more extended service. . . . There are . . . the accounts of Samuel Peters and of Parke, the translator of Horace, of the printers Keimer and Rivington, of Lindley Murray, the primitive grammarian, of Byrd, the Virginia "man of pleasure and literature," of Dennie, the pioneer of periodicals, of Weems, the gossiping biographer of Washington, of Hannah Adams, the first of our female authors, of Dunlap, the annalist of stage and studio, of Brockden Brown, the earliest American novelist, and others whose isolated struggles abound in original, quaint, and suggestive traits both of the romance and the reality of authorship.

There are also Joseph Green, Royal Tyler, Mather Byles, and R. T. Paine, Jr., the recognized wits of their day, whose sayings and doings are prolific of the humorous. Sullivan's *Letters on Public Characters* and Wirt's *Essays* reflect in genial tints the social characteristics of that period, as they dwelt upon the memory of a later generation. Nor are the poetic remains of the colonial and revolutionary times devoid of permanent literary value. The ballad literature, at once the most fugitive and the most significant, has been wisely embodied apart, and forms a curious study.

We have, likewise, Anne Bradstreet, Peter Folger, Wigglesworth, Aquila Rose, Mercy Warren, and Godfrey to illustrate the verse of earlier days, culminating in Philip Freneau, the bard of the Revolution, of whose life and poems we have here a most interesting and satisfactory account. Trumbull, Dwight, Phillis Wheatley, Barlow, and Alsop succeed; and the more feeling and polished rhymes of Clifton appropriately end this early flight of our unfledged Muse. . . .

From Paulding's first book to the foundation of the Astor Library, we have a long and regularly increasing array of names, many of them of established reputation, identified with every department of literature, together with a new and important cluster of universities and associations which have been established to meet the growing intellectual wants of a rapidly extended country.

The improvement in style, the advent of fresh bards whose artistic verse evinces a higher standard of taste, for elegant historians, aesthetic critics, novelists who describe native scenery and manners, and, interspersed with these, that "mob of gentlemen who write with ease" which marks an era of prosperous national life, all yield a rich contrast to the erudite, quaint, and more occasional writing of a previous epoch. Indeed, with the progress of their work, the authors seem embarrassed by the number and variety of literary aspirants. The record of each successive writer is curtailed for want of space; authors increase in number and books in interest; and the temptation to linger over favorite names and cherished productions grows stronger as the list draws to a close. The mention of still-living writers adds to the interest as to the delicacy of the task; and the flowers of poesy, romance, and genial speculation become, at last, so numerous and inviting that the old fallow ground is transformed into a garden, whose choicest fruits are the familiar pride and luxury of the present hour.

We renew our acquaintance with *The Sketch Book* and *The Idle Man,* with *Hadad* and "Thanatopsis," "Marco Bozzaris" and *The Spy,* Channing's *Essays* and *The Scarlet Letter,* Webster's oratory and Holmes's wit, the beautiful Scripture paraphrases of Willis and the early critiques of Everett; the example of scholars like Walsh, Verplanck, and Legaré, of genial local sketchers like Flint and Kennedy, of fresh and adventurous travelers, such as Melville and Taylor, Mackenzie and Hall, Hoffman and Sanderson,

opens new and charming vistas in the prospect; Sparks reproduces the most interesting documentary annals of the Revolution, and Wheaton gains a European reputation for his *Treatise on International Law;* a galaxy of female writers sheds pure light from the firmament of mind; standard works, like those of Prescott, Bancroft, and Ticknor, impart a certain permanent dignity to the roll of native authors; a new order of pulpit orators arises; and the casual but finished writings of professional men, to whom authorship is only an accomplishment, multiply, so that we are at length bewildered by the number and the merit of literary aspirants, and find ample cause for national felicitation and hope in the scope and the quality of our more recent literature.

De Tocqueville, one of the few commentators on American life and institutions who have drawn broad philosophical inferences, predicted that our literature would be marked by "untutored and rude vigor of thought," and that the object of our writers would be "to stir the passions more than to charm the taste." This voluminous repertory of the past and actual intellectual life of the country falsifies his prophecy. New England, the most prolific nursery of authors, and for a long period the "Mecca of the mind" in America, has been, and is, more remarkable for the number of its disciplined scholars and finished writers than on account of any original and impassioned native literature. The occasional addresses, reviews, lectures, travels, and other incidental products of the pen in that latitude are chiefly memorable for the familiarity they indicate with the best English classics, for the purity of their moral sentiment, and the elegance of their style. They do more credit to the literary culture and the conservative taste of that enterprising and educated section than to its mental independence or local and social inspiration.

The only writer who has bravely tried the traditions and primitive character of

New England in the crucible of analytical imagination is Hawthorne, and his "boldness and vigor" are chastened by remarkable finish of execution. Dana early adventured in the field of ideal sentiment, tragic emotion, and psychological criticism, but was too soon, though quite naturally, discouraged by the inadequate pecuniary returns for labors too intense and artistic to be sustained alone by the praise of the judicious few. Boston claims historians second to none of the same tongue in patient research, refined collocation of words, good sense, and picturesque narrative; some of her critics exhibit an Addisonian grace and a pure insight; and not a few of her preachers have left behind them homilies of unrivaled beauty and eloquence. In rhetorical skill in scholarly illustrations, in ready and excellent discourse, the average performance has been all that the most highly cultured society can demand. But these efforts have been occasional — the temporary displays of acquisition and talent mainly devoted to professional or official toil.

The same distrust of success which, at an earlier day, chilled the nascent fervor of those richly endowed for authorship, on account of its limited rewards and the extreme deference for English models and critics, has been perpetuated by the free competition open to transatlantic writers. The demand of the literary market for native fruits has therefore been limited, while there has been casually manifest abundant evidence of ability in every department. A singular feature in this program or chart of American literature, accordingly, is the number of youthful aspirants whose devotion to the Muse and to letters has been as transient as it was full of promise; and the remarkable versatility with which men of acknowledged literary aptitude, and even decided genius, have turned aside to more practical or profitable avocations. . . .

Until within a very few years literature with us has scarcely risen to the dignity of a profession. American writers usually become so through a remarkably strong native impulse, or by accidental circumstances. The pen has been a most precarious resource, unless in the service of journalism. It is, therefore, as the chart of a people's intellectual development, of the growth of mental activity in the direction of literature, and of the results of popular education that this work attracts the philosopher. We behold those primal needs of a young nation, religion and politics, at first absorbing the best minds, and gradually expanding into more artistic forms as the refinements of life increase and the resources of civilization are multiplied. . . .

What of erudition or talent the American possessed was called into service by the exigencies of the time. With a material prosperity to achieve, a boundless wilderness to subjugate, a vast political system to organize, a positive sphere of active labor and love to fill, he could but snatch a casual hour to "behold the serene countenance of truth in the still air of delightful studies," to record his travels, indite a poem for the *fête* of his *alma mater*, finish up a speech to sway the electors, pen an essay for the columns of his favorite journal, or, perchance, hymn the joys and griefs of his domestic experience. And yet, with these disadvantages, in the midst of external hindrance and ceaseless activity, how much of true, manly, efficient, and characteristic intellectual life has been realized, the work which we have now reviewed authentically and gracefully declares.

400

80.

Walt Whitman: Letter to Emerson

When Walt Whitman's Leaves of Grass *first appeared in 1855, Whitman, who had himself set type for the volume, personally promoted it by publishing his own anonymous reviews of the work. The book did not sell, however, and professional critics either ignored it or issued blasts like the review in the* Boston Intelligencer *that dubbed the work "a heterogeneous mass of bombast, egotism, vulgarity, and nonsense." The first word of praise came from Ralph Waldo Emerson, who wrote to Whitman on July 21, 1855, that* Leaves of Grass *was "the most extraordinary piece of wit and wisdom that America has yet contributed." Emerson later qualified his praise in a May 1856 letter to Thomas Carlyle calling the work "a nondescript monster which yet had terrible eyes and buffalo strength, and was indisputably American." Whitman nonetheless seized upon Emerson's testimonial; he arranged to have the letter published in the* New York Tribune, *and when the second edition of* Leaves of Grass *appeared in June 1856, its back cover bore in a gold script the quotation: "I greet you at the beginning of a great career. R. W. Emerson." In an appendix to that edition Whitman reprinted the whole of Emerson's letter with the following reply.*

Source: *Leaves of Grass*, Brooklyn, 1856, pp. 346-358.

HERE ARE THIRTY-TWO POEMS, which I send you, dear friend and master, not having found how I could satisfy myself with sending any usual acknowledgment of your letter. The first edition, on which you mailed me that till now unanswered letter, was twelve poems. I printed 1,000 copies, and they readily sold; these thirty-two poems I stereotype, to print several thousand copies of. I much enjoy making poems. Other work I have set for myself to do, to meet people and The States face to face, to confront them with an American rude tongue; but the work of my life is making poems. I keep on till I make 100, and then several hundred — perhaps 1,000. The way is clear to me. A few years, and the average annual call for my poems is 10,000 or 20,000 copies — more, quite likely. Why should I hurry or compromise? In poems or in speeches I say the word or two that has got to be said, adhere to the body, step with the countless common footsteps, and remind every man and woman of something.

Master, I am a man who has perfect faith. Master, we have not come through centuries, caste, heroisms, fables, to halt in this land today. Or I think it is to collect a tenfold impetus that any halt is made. As nature, inexorable, onward, resistless, impassive amid the threats and screams of disputants, so America. Let all defer. Let all attend respectfully the leisure of These States, their politics, poems, literature, manners, and their freehanded modes of training their own offspring. Their own comes, just matured, certain, numerous and capable enough, with egotistical tongues, with sinewed wrists; seizing openly what belongs to them. They resume personality, too long left out of mind. Their shadows are projected in employments, in books, in the cities, in trade; their feet are on the flights of the steps of the Capitol; they dilate, a larger, brawnier, more candid, more democratic, lawless, positive native to The States, sweet-bodied, completer, dauntless, flowing, masterful, beard-faced, new race of men.

Swiftly, on limitless foundations, the United States, too, are founding a literature. It is all as well done, in my opinion, as could be practicable. Each element here is in condition. Every day I go among the people of Manhattan Island, Brooklyn, and other cities, and among the young men, to discover the spirit of them, and to refresh myself. These are to be attended to; I am myself more drawn here than to those authors, publishers, importations, reprints, and so forth. I pass coolly through those, understanding them perfectly well, and that they do the indispensable service, outside of men like me, which nothing else could do. In poems, the young men of The States shall be represented, for they outrival the best of the rest of the earth.

The lists of ready-made literature which America inherits by the mighty inheritance of the English language — all the rich repertoire of traditions, poems, histories, metaphysics, plays, classics, translations, have made, and still continue, magnificent preparations for that other signified literature, to be our own, to be electric, fresh, lusty, to express the full-sized body, male and female — to give the modern meanings of things, to grow up beautiful, lasting, commensurate with America, with all the passions of home, with the inimitable sympathies of having been boys and girls together, and of parents who were with our parents.

What else can happen to The States, even in their own despite? That huge English flow, so sweet so undeniable, has done incalculable good here, and is to be spoken of for its own sake with generous praise and with gratitude. Yet the price The States have had to lie under for the same has not been a small price. Payment prevails; a nation can never take the issues of the needs of other nations for nothing. America, grandest of lands in the theory of its politics, in popular reading, in hospitality, breadth, animal beauty, cities, ships, machines, money, credit, collapses quick as lightning at the repeated, admonishing, stern words. Where are any mental expressions from you, beyond what you have copied or stolen? Where the born throngs of poets, literates, orators, you promised? Will you but tag after other nations?

They struggled long for their literature, painfully working their way, some with deficient languages, some with priestcraft, some in the endeavor just to live; yet achieved for their times, works, poems, perhaps the only solid consolation left to them through ages afterward of shame and decay. You are young, have the perfectest of dialects, a free press, a free government, the world forwarding its best to be with you. As justice has been strictly done to you, from this hour do strict justice to yourself. Strangle the singers who will not sing you loud and strong. Open the doors of The West. Call for new great masters to comprehend new arts, new perfections, new wants. Submit to the most robust bard till he remedy your barrenness. Then you will not need to adopt the heirs of others; you will have true heirs, begotten of yourself, blooded with your own blood.

With composure I see such propositions, seeing more and more every day of the answers that serve. Expressions do not yet serve, for sufficient reasons; but that is getting ready, beyond what the earth has hitherto known, to take home the expressions

The Granger Collection

Walt Whitman; engraved frontispiece by Samuel Hollyer to the first edition of "Leaves of Grass"

when they come, and to identify them with the populace of The States, which is the schooling cheaply procured by any outlay any number of years. Such schooling The States extract from the swarms of reprints, and from the current authors and editors. Such service and extract are done after enormous, reckless, free modes, characteristic of The States. Here are to be attained results never elsewhere thought possible; the modes are very grand too. The instincts of the American people are all perfect and tend to make heroes. It is a rare thing in a man here to understand The States.

All current nourishments to literature serve. Of authors and editors I do not know how many there are in The States, but there are thousands, each one building his or her step to the stairs by which giants shall mount. Of the twenty-four modern mammoth two-double, three-double, and four-double cylinder presses now in the world, printing by steam, twenty-one of them are in These States. The 12,000 large and small shops for dispensing books and newspapers; the same number of public li-

braries, any one of which has all the reading wanted to equip a man or woman for American reading; the 3,000 different newspapers, the nutriment of the imperfect ones coming in just as usefully as any; the story papers, various, full of strong-flavored romances, widely circulated; the one-cent and two-cent journals, the political ones, no matter what side; the weeklies in the country, the sporting and pictorial papers, the monthly magazines, with plentiful imported feed; the sentimental novels, numberless copies of them; the low-priced flaring tales, adventures, biographies; all are prophetic; all waft rapidly on. I see that they swell wide, for reasons. I am not troubled at the movement of them, but greatly pleased. I see plying shuttles, the active ephemeral myriads of books also, faithfully weaving the garments of a generation of men, and a generation of women, they do not perceive or know.

What a progress popular reading and writing has made in fifty years! What a progress fifty years hence! The time is at hand when inherent literature will be a main part of These States, as general and real as steampower, iron, corn, beef, fish. First-rate American persons are to be supplied. Our perennial materials for fresh thoughts, histories, poems, music, orations, religions, recitations, amusements, will then not be disregarded, any more than our perennial fields, mines, rivers, seas. Certain things are established and are immovable; in those things millions of years stand justified. The mothers and fathers of whom modern centuries have come have not existed for nothing; they too had brains and hearts. Of course all literature, in all nations and years, will share marked attributes in common, as we all, of all ages, share the common human attributes. America is to be kept coarse and broad. What is to be done is to withdraw from precedents, and be directed to men and women — also to The States in their federalness; for the union of the parts of the body is not more necessary to their life than the union of These States is to their life.

A profound person can easily know more of the people than they know of themselves. Always waiting untold in the souls of the armies of common people is stuff better than anything that can possibly appear in the leadership of the same. That gives final verdicts. In every department of These States, he who travels with a coterie, or with selected persons, or with imitators, or with infidels, or with the owners of slaves, or with that which is ashamed of the body of man, or with that which is ashamed of the body of woman, or with anything less than the bravest and the openest, travels straight for the slopes of dissolution. The genius of all foreign literature is clipped and cut small, compared to our genius, and is essentially insulting to our usages, and to the organic compacts of These States. Old forms, old poems, majestic and proper in their own lands, here in this land are exiles; the air here is very strong. Much that stands well and has a little enough place provided for it in the small scales of European kingdoms, empires, and the like, here stands haggard, dwarfed, ludicrous, or has no place little enough provided for it. Authorities, poems, models, laws, names, imported into America, are useful to America today to destroy them, and so move disencumbered to great works, great days.

Just so long, in our country or any country, as no revolutionists advance, and are backed by the people, sweeping off the swarms of routine representatives, officers in power, book-makers, teachers, ecclesiastics, politicians, just so long, I perceive, do they who are in power fairly represent that country, and remain of use, probably of very great use. To supersede them, when it is the pleasure of These States, full provision is made; and I say the time has arrived to use it with a strong hand. Here also the souls of the armies have not only overtaken the souls of the officers but passed on, and left the souls of the officers behind out of sight many weeks' journey; and the souls of the armies now go *en masse* without officers. Here also formulas, glosses, blanks, minutiae, are choking the throats of the spokesmen to death. Those things most listened for, certainly those are the things least said.

There is not a single history of the world. There is not one of America, or of the organic compacts of These States, or of Washington, or of Jefferson, nor of language, nor any dictionary of the English language. There is no great author; every one has demeaned himself to some etiquette or some impotence. There is no manhood or life-power in poems; there are shoats and geldings more like. Or literature will be dressed up, a fine gentleman, distasteful to our instinct, foreign to our soil. Its neck bends right and left wherever it goes. Its costumes and jewelry prove how little it knows Nature. Its flesh is soft; it shows less and less of the indefinable hard something that is Nature. Where is any thing but the shaved Nature of synods and schools? Where is a savage and luxuriant man? Where is an overseer? In lives, in poems, in codes of law, in Congress, in tuitions, theaters, conversations, argumentations, not a single head lifts itself clean out, with proof that it is their master, and has subordinated them to itself, and is ready to try their superiors.

None believes in These States, boldly illustrating them in himself. Not a man faces round at the rest with terrible negative voice, refusing all terms to be bought off from his own eyesight, or from the soul that he is, or from friendship, or from the body that he is, or from the soil and sea. To creeds, literature, art, the army, the navy, the executive, life is hardly proposed, but the sick and dying are proposed to cure the sick and dying. The churches are one vast lie; the people do not believe them, and they do not believe themselves; the priests are continually telling what they know well enough is not so, and keeping back what they know is so. The spectacle is a pitiful one. I think there can never be again upon the festive earth more bad-disordered persons deliberately taking seats, as of late in These States, at the heads of the public tables — such corpses' eyes for judges — such a rascal and thief in the presidency.

Up to the present, as helps best, the people, like a lot of large boys, have no determined tastes, are quite unaware of the grandeur of themselves, and of their destiny, and of their immense strides, accept with voracity whatever is presented them in novels, histories, newspapers, poems, schools, lectures, everything. Pretty soon, through these and other means, their development makes the fiber that is capable of itself and will assume determined tastes. The young men will be clear what they want and will have it. They will follow none except him whose spirit leads them in the like spirit with themselves. Any such man will be welcome as the flowers of May. Others will be put out without ceremony.

How much is there, anyhow, to the young men of These States, in a parcel of helpless dandies, who can neither fight, work, shoot, ride, run, command — some of them devout, some quite insane, some castrated — all second-hand, or third-, fourth-, or fifth-hand — waited upon by waiters, putting not this land first but always other lands first, talking of art, doing the most ridiculous things for fear of being called ridiculous, smirking and skipping along, continually taking off their hats; no one behaving, dressing, writing, talking, loving out of any natural and manly tastes of his own but each one looking cautiously to see how the rest behave, dress, write, talk, love; pressing the noses of dead books upon themselves and upon their country; favoring no poets, philosophers, literates here, but doglike danglers at the heels of the poets, philosophers, literates of enemies' lands; favoring mental expressions, models of gentlemen and ladies, social habitudes in These States, to grow up in sneaking defiance of the popular substratums of The States?

Of course, they and the likes of them can never justify the strong poems of America. Of course, no feed of theirs is to stop and be made welcome to muscle the bodies, male and female, for Manhattan Island, Brooklyn, Boston, Worcester, Hartford, Portland, Montreal, Detroit, Buffalo, Cleveland, Milwaukee, St. Louis, Indianapolis, Chicago, Cincinnati, Iowa City, Philadelphia, Baltimore, Raleigh, Savannah, Charleston, Mobile, New Orleans, Galveston, Brownsville, San Francisco, Havana, and a thousand equal cities, present and to come. Of course, what they and the likes of them have been used for draws toward its close, after which they will all be discharged, and not one of them will ever be heard of anymore.

America, having duly conceived, bears out of herself offspring of her own to do the workmanship wanted. To freedom, to strength, to poems, to personal greatness, it is never permitted to rest, not a generation or part of a generation. To be ripe beyond further increase is to prepare to die. The architects of These States laid their foundations and passed to further spheres. What they laid is a work done; as much more remains. Now are needed other architects, whose duty is not less difficult but perhaps more difficult. Each age forever needs architects. America is not finished, perhaps never will be; now America is a divine true sketch. There are Thirty-Two States sketched — the population 30 million. In a few years there will be Fifty States. Again in a few years there will be A Hundred States, the population hundreds of millions, the freshest and freest of men. Of course such men stand to nothing less than the freshest and freest expression.

Poets here, literates here, are to rest on organic different bases from other countries; not a class set apart, circling only in the circle themselves, modest and pretty, desperately scratching for rhymes, pallid with white paper, shut off, aware of the old pictures and traditions of the race, but unaware of the actual race around them — not breeding in and in among each other till they all have the scrofula. Lands of ensemble, bards of ensemble! Walking freely out from the old traditions, as our politics has walked out, American poets and literates recognize nothing behind them superior to what is present with them — recognize with joy the sturdy living forms of the men and women of These States, the divinity of sex, the perfect eligibility of the female with the male, all The States, liberty and equality, real articles, the different trades, mechanics, the young fellows of Manhattan Island, customs, instincts, slang, Wisconsin, Georgia, the noble Southern heart, the hot blood, the spirit that will be nothing less than master, the filibuster spirit, the Western man, native-born perceptions, the eye for forms, the perfect models of made things, the wild smack of freedom, California, money, electric telegraphs, free trade, iron and the iron mines — recognize without demur those splendid resistless black poems, the steamships of the seaboard states, and those other resistless splendid poems, the locomotives, followed through the interior states by trains of railroad cars.

A word remains to be said, as of one ever present, not yet permitted to be acknowledged, discarded or made dumb by literature, and the results apparent. To the lack of an avowed, empowered, unabashed development of sex (the only salvation for the same) and to the fact of speakers and writers fraudulently assuming as always dead what everyone knows to be always alive, is attributable the remarkable non-personality and indistinctness of modern productions in books, art, talk; also that in the scanned lives of men and women most of them appear to have been for some time past of the neuter gender; and also the stinging fact that in orthodox society today, if the dresses were changed, the men might easily pass for women and the women for men.

Infidelism usurps most with fetid, polite face; among the rest infidelism about sex. By silence or obedience the pens of savants, poets, historians, biographers, and the rest have long connived at the filthy law, and books enslaved to it, that what makes the manhood of a man, that sex, womanhood, maternity, desires, lusty animations, organs, acts, are unmentionable and to be ashamed of, to be driven to skulk out of literature with whatever belongs to them. This filthy law has to be repealed; it stands in the way of great reforms. Of women just as much as men, it is the interest that there should not be infidelism about sex but perfect faith. Women in These States approach the day of that organic equality with men, without which, I see, men cannot have organic equality among themselves. This empty dish, gallantry, will then be filled with something. This tepid wash, this diluted deferential love, as in songs, fictions, and so forth, is enough to make a man vomit; as to manly friendship, everywhere observed in The States, there is not the first breath of it to be observed in print.

I say that the body of a man or woman, the main matter, is so far quite unexpressed in poems; but that the body is to be expressed, and sex is. Of bards for These States, if it come to a question, it is whether they shall celebrate in poems the eternal decency of the amativeness of Nature, the motherhood of all, or whether they shall be the bards of the fashionable delusion of the inherent nastiness of sex, and of the feeble and querulous modesty of deprivation. This is important in poems, because the whole of the other expressions of a nation are but flanges out of its great poems. To me, henceforth, that theory of anything, no matter what, stagnates in its vitals, cowardly and rotten, while it cannot publicly accept and publicly name, with specific words, the things on which all existence, all souls, all realization, all decency, all health, all that is worth being here for, all of women and of man, all beauty, all purity, all sweetness, all friendship, all strength, all life, all immortality depend. The courageous soul, for a year or two to come, may be proved by faith in sex and by disdaining concessions.

To poets and literates — to every woman and man, today or any day — the conditions of the present, needs, dangers, prejudices, and the like, are the perfect conditions on which we are here, and the conditions for wording the future with undissuadable words. These States, receivers of the stamina of past ages and lands, initiate the outlines of repayment a thousandfold. They fetch the American great masters, waited for by old worlds and new, who accept evil as well as good, ignorance as well as erudition, black as soon as white, foreign-born materials as well as home-born, reject none, force discrepancies into range, surround the whole, concentrate them on present periods and places, show the application to each and anyone's body and soul, and show the true use of precedents. Always America will be agitated and turbulent. This day it is taking shape, not to be less so but to be more so, stormily, capriciously, on native principles, with such vast proportions of parts! As for me, I love screaming, wrestling, boiling hot days.

Of course, we shall have a national character, an identity. As it ought to be, and as soon as it ought to be, it will be. That, with much else, takes care of itself, is a result, and the cause of greater results. With Ohio, Illinois, Missouri, Oregon; with the states around the Mexican sea; with cheerfully welcomed immigrants from Europe, Asia, Africa; with Connecticut, Vermont, New Hampshire, Rhode Island; with all varied interests, facts, beliefs, parties, genesis; there is being fused a determined character, fit for the broadest use for the freewomen and freemen of The States, accomplished and to be accomplished, without any exception whatever — each indeed free, each idiomatic, as becomes live states and men, but each adhering to one enclosing general form of politics, manners, talk, personal style, as the plenteous varieties of the race adhere to one physical form. Such character is the brain and spine to all, including literature, including poems. Such character, strong, limber, just, openmouthed, American-blooded, full of pride, full of ease, of passionate friendliness, is to stand compact upon that vast basis of the supremacy of individuality — that new moral American continent without which, I see, the physical continent remained incomplete, maybe a carcass, a bloat — that newer America, answering face to face with The States, with ever satisfying and ever unsurveyable seas and shores.

Those shores you found. I say you have led The States there — have led me there. I say that none has ever done, or ever can do, a greater deed for The States than your deed. Others may line out the lines, build cities, work mines, break up farms; it is yours to have been the original true Captain who put to sea, intuitive, positive, rendering the first report, to be told less by any report, and more by the mariners of a thousand bays, in each tack of their arriving and departing, many years after you.

Receive, dear master, these statements and assurances through me, for all the young men, and for an earnest that we know none before you, but the best following you; and that we demand to take your name into our keeping, and that we understand what you have indicated, and find the same indicated in ourselves, and that we will stick to it and enlarge upon it through These States.

81.

Walt Whitman: Wicked Architecture

The rapidly growing metropolitan areas became, by the middle of the century, prime targets for reform. Government, the church, the press, and novelists sought to expose the ills of city life. Walt Whitman spent most of his early life in and around New York City. For a time he assisted his father in building houses there, and he frequently lodged in boardinghouses, where he received "one of my best experiences and deepest lessons in human nature behind the scenes." In the following essay, published a year after Leaves of Grass *appeared, Whitman described some of the problems of urban life and proposed a new concept in housing, similar to modern apartment buildings, as more conducive to normal family life.*

Source: *Life Illustrated,* July 19, 1856.

Not wicked in carelessness of material construction, like the crumbly structures sometimes run up in our city by mercenary builders, that prove deathtraps to the inmates; nor in purpose, like an Inquisition or a panel thief's haunt; but in the unrighteous spirit of ostentation that unconsciously directs it, and in the manifold and frightful social evils flowing from it.

It may not at first appear that the architecture of New York has any very distinct connection with anything good or evil. But there *is* a connection, and one startlingly close and efficient. The domestic architecture — the dwelling house architecture — of the city (for our Architectural Wickedness exists mainly there), even though perhaps not absolutely in itself the efficient cause of evil, is the most striking type of that condition of social morals which is the fertile hotbed for evils the most enormous.

A house to live in is the third great necessity; food and clothing only being before it. And, furthermore, it is in some sense true that a man is not a whole and complete man unless he *owns* a house and the ground it stands on. Men are created owners of the earth. Each was intended to possess his piece of it; and however the modifications of civilized life have covered this truth, or changed the present phase of it, it is still indicated by the universal instinctive desire for landed property, and by the fuller sense of independent manhood which comes from the possession of it.

In New York, closed in by rivers, pressing desperately toward the business center at its southern end, and characterized by an unparalleled fierceness in money chasing, land is dear. This, of course, makes the possession of it a basis for an increased ostentation of it; for the dearer a thing is, the more pride in showing it, and wonder in staring at it.

Next; ways of thinking, throughout society, are more or less formed on the patterns set by the rich. And, accordingly, it may be stated, as a general principle, that in New York City, among all ranks except the poorest, there is a habit of occupying houses outrageously and absurdly too expensive, whether in prime cost or in rent, for the resources of the occupant. The wealthy began by building such houses for themselves. Then they, as landowners, or builders as speculators, went on to build blocks and ranges of similar edifices to lease to people of less wealth; and these again were not slow to hire them on the great American principle, that I am as good as anybody; which, however, is unfortunately taken to include this: that I may therefore have whatever anybody else has, *whether I can afford it or not.*

This ambitious folly, however, is operative only among the better classes. The great mass of the poor live in insufficient tenements, because the competition on the narrow island for dwelling places is so keen that dwellings, both "cheap and nasty," to use an expressive late English Saxonism, pay large rents; and if the landlords get their rent, what matter whether the house be a house or a sty? And the poor tenants, knowing that landlords can always find occupants, and consequently not being able to coerce improvement by threatening to remove, must live in such dens as they may. What too many of those dens are, the reports of the Legislative Tenement Committee, now engaged in examining the leased dwelling houses occupied by our city poor, most impressively show; but with this branch of the subject we have not now to deal.

In no other city in the whole world does rent occupy so large a proportion of expenses as in New York; in no other city in the world would so many years' income be required from the man of whatsoever pecuniary and social standing to purchase for himself a piece of ground and a house, whereon and wherein to live.

London is the most expensive capital in Europe. From it economical Englishmen flee to the continental cities, large and small, to live in equal comfort at less expense. Rents in London are from one-half to one-fourth of New York rates. A house

corresponding with our "first-class brownstone front English basement" tenements, on a twenty-five foot lot, renting for $2,000, may be had in London for about £200; roughly, $1,000. A "second-class" house may here rent for $800 to $1,200. The corresponding house in London costs but about $500. A very large number of houses are rented in New York for from $600 to $800, say at an average of $700. In London such houses would be rented at about $200.

"Twenty years' purchase," that is, the total of rent for twenty years, is in London considered a fair rate for valuing the house and lot; so that one-twentieth of the value, or 5 percent on it, is paid for rent. In New York, twelve and ten years' rent would buy many houses; that is, 8 or 10 *percent* on the value is paid for rent.

Such is a succinct statement, illustrated by statistics and comparison, of our domestic architectural habits in New York City. Next comes the development of those consequences of them which make us call it Wicked Architecture.

They may be stated in brief and in mass as, *Difficulty of Marriage and Settlement in Life.* Mr. Brown, we will suppose, is a substantial, well-to-do old gentleman. His house is a four-story one, if you please, brownstone front, and all that sort of thing.

Mrs. Brown tells her daughters, "Now, girls, it's all very well to have a loving husband, and to love him; but it's a great deal better to have substantial comfort and a sufficient pecuniary income. Have a good husband and love him, if possible; but marry well, at any rate. That's sound common sense; I've lived longer than you have; and I know better what's flummery and what isn't."

The girls are well prepared by their city training for such advice as that, and they take it.

A worthy young clerk or just-established junior partner, perhaps a thriving mechanic,

even — if it be not a profane presumption!
— asks leave of old Brown to seek one of
his daughters in marriage.

Mr. Brown. "Mr. Driver, you are doubtless a very excellent young man. But can
you maintain Melinda Ann in the style to
which she has been accustomed?"

Driver rather confusedly begins to talk
about present narrow circumstances, good
prospects, future wealth, earnest devotion,
etc.

Mr. Brown. "Yes, yes. I know. But it appears to me, young man, that you'd a little
better wait awhile until you are certain of
this position. As a friend, Mr. Driver," etc.

Driver leaves. This specimen (from actual
life, by the way) abundantly expresses the
state of expectation on the one hand, and
the necessary hesitation on the part of all
but the already rich on the other, to which
we refer. Illogical old Brown! Did you begin at the large end of the horn? You
would have been wiser to remember the
pride with which you and Mrs. B. stood
within the first little two-story whole house
that you rented; the cheap struggling year
through which you crawled like a caterpillar
up to the riches that now gild you so
grandly!

Well. Very large numbers of young men,
some of no principle and some of a little,
well-intentioned enough, but not fortified
very strongly against fierce temptations,
stand in this relation to the maidens from
among whom they should select their
wives.

Either they marry, or they do not. If not,
they at best live single and imperfect lives,
losing the healthy, beautifying power which
God intended them to find in the family
relations, isolated units in a world whose
essence is association. But if they are not
strong enough for that, facts show that in
great numbers they lose the very nucleus
and essence of all usefulness and power —
purity of soul — and, degrading themselves
by submission under the tyranny of ignoble

lusts, fall into one or the other of two states
— or into both of them — of which we
can here say but very little; in brief, into
the practice of haunting those abodes which
are the gates of hell, or into an illegitimate
and unblessed association with some one
woman, necessarily of coarse and impure
mind, or low character and social standing,
and of downward tendency in every channel
of life.

The mothers who send beloved sons into
the city to live would feel little hope and
much and painful fear could they know
how large a proportion of the businessmen
and active male population of the city generally, under the age of twenty-five years,
are either in the constant practice of visiting
houses of ill-fame or are living in a quasi-
household with a kept mistress. Upon this
point we cannot enlarge. Suffice it to say
that there is no man of *general* and *thorough*
acquaintance in New York who cannot
point out, if he chooses, five, or ten, or
twenty young men, almost — and perhaps
quite — to his personal knowledge so cir-
cumstanced!

But suppose that, in spite of all, our
young friends marry. They cannot afford a
house. And, consequently, as the little girl
aptly said when asked where her parents
lived, "They don't *live;* they *board.*"

Few are aware of the extent of boardinghouse life in New York. Whole neighborhoods of boardinghouses now stand, for instance, around St. John's Park, in Houston
and Bleecker Streets, in many other localities formerly as aristocratic as "Fifth Ave-
noodledom." Thousands of young or
"moderately well-off" people, absolutely
unable to find the right residence for them,
hire a house quite too large, and eke out
the rent by subletting one, two, three, or
more rooms, or entire floors, to such lodgers as they can find. This custom prevails
everywhere. Fifth Avenue, Fourteenth
Street, from river to river, Twenty-second
and Twenty-third Streets, and, indeed,

nearly every other respectable portion of the city are dotted with houses thus portioned off. Judicious and extensively informed observers estimate the proportion of dwelling houses which are either professedly boardinghouses or in which one or more rooms are thus sublet to "one or two respectable young gentlemen," "a married couple without encumbrance," etc., as seven out of every ten. Counting in this class of residences those hotels which are occupied mostly by permanent boarders, it is probable that nearer three-quarters than two-thirds of all the adult inhabitants of New York City, of the middle and wealthy classes, live in boardinghouses.

What is this boardinghouse life? Simply a place to keep a man's trunk and his wife while he is at work, and where he has breakfast, tea, and sleeping room. All day long, these thousands and thousands of wives, many of them with their children, are left alone, without responsibility, with little or no employment; they may read or study, probably with a master, and, if so, under the inevitable risks of such avocations; they spin street yarns in Broadway; shop; dine at Taylor's or Thompson's; make calls; talk scandal; sleep. There is no chance for the gathering of the wretched husband's family. There is no chance for the development of the unhappy wife into a mature and noble woman, the

> Perfect being, nobly planned,
> To warn, to comfort, to command

of the poet. Listlessness, emptiness; sloth; nerves; dyspepsia; flirtations; prodigality; vain show; perhaps — often, might we not say? — immorality, nay, infamy. These are the accomplishments which the boardinghouse life most tends to develop.

We must hasten. Of whatever remedies are applicable to this state of things, many are too profound and remote even to be stated in a newspaper article. That which we shall mention — we can do little more — is one which combines the recommendation of practicability and profit. It is simply the erection of tenement houses, so arranged that each floor is a complete, isolated habitation by itself. There are already a few such buildings, and they are eagerly sought for. In London they have been introduced within the last few years and meet with great favor. By the arrangement of two tenements on each floor, space is given for a well, which will afford light and ventilation to the midmost of the tier of rooms; and the two end apartments may be used for the social daylight uses of the family.

Such tenements as these, judiciously located and handsomely finished, could be rented at reasonable rates; would restore to many of these wretched "married bachelors" a place for their household goods, a home and a hearth of their own, if not forever, at least in independent separation for the time being; would furnish the unoccupied mind and listless bodies of their wives with the stimulus and responsibilities which they need, and which God meant for them; and last — and least — yet most necessary of all, could, as may be demonstrated, yield a remunerative percentage on the investment of the capitalist.

Perhaps we may add that if any persons desire further information in this matter of tenement homes, it shall be given as far as practicable upon application at the office of this paper.

Man's capacities have never been measured; nor are we to judge of what he can do by any precedents, so little has been tried.

HENRY DAVID THOREAU, *Walden*, 1854

82.

George William Curtis: The Duty of the American Scholar

*After a successful career as author and traveler, George William Curtis turned his
attention to public affairs. The lecture reprinted below, "The Duty of the American
Scholar to Politics and the Times," may be called the keynote address of his new
involvement in civic life. He took the duties of citizenship seriously and urged his
hearers to accept the responsibilities that a democratic society entailed. Curtis
himself became involved in most of the reform movements of his time: antislavery,
women's rights, labor problems, and civil service reform. The address, which was
delivered August 5, 1856, was certainly motivated in part by the sectional conflicts of
the decade and the preoccupation with them of Curtis' friends.*

Source: *Orations and Addresses of George William Curtis,* Charles Eliot Norton, ed.,
New York, 1894, Vol. I, pp. 3-35.

Gentlemen, the scholar is the representative of thought among men, and his duty to society is the effort to introduce thought and the sense of justice into human affairs. He was not made a scholar to satisfy the newspapers or the parish beadles, but to serve God and man. While other men pursue what is expedient and watch with alarm the flickering of the funds, he is to pursue the truth and watch the eternal law of justice.

But if this be true of the scholar in general, how peculiarly is it true of the American scholar, who, as a citizen of a republic, has not only an influence by his word and example, but, by his vote, a direct agency upon public affairs. In a republic which decides questions involving the national welfare by a majority of voices, whoever refuses to vote is a traitor to his own cause, whatever that cause may be; and if any scholar will not vote, nor have an opinion upon great public measures because that would be to mix himself with politics, but contents himself with vague declamation about freedom in general, knowing that the enemies of freedom always use its name, then that scholar is a traitor to liberty, and degrades his order by justifying the reproach that the scholar is a pusillanimous trimmer.

The American scholar, gentlemen, has duties to politics in general; and he has, consequently, duties in every political crisis in his country. What his duties are in this crisis of our national affairs I shall now tell you as plainly as I can. The times are grave, and they demand sober speech. To us young men the future of this country is entrusted. What names does history love, and every honest man revere? The names of those who gave their youth and strength to the cause which is waiting for us to serve it. . . .

The object of human government is human liberty. Laws restrain the encroachment of the individual upon society in order that all individuals may be secured the freest play of their powers. This is because the end of society is the improvement of the individual and the development of the race. Liberty is, therefore, the condition of human progress, and consequently that is the best government which gives to men the largest liberty, and constantly modifies itself in the interest of freedom.

The laws of society, indeed, deprive men of liberty, and even of life, but only when by crime they have become injurious to society. The deprivation of the life or liberty of the individual under other circumstances is the outrage of those rights which are instinctively perceived by every man, but are beyond argument or proof.

Human slavery annihilates the conditions of human progress. Its necessary result is the destruction of humanity; and this not only directly by its effect upon the slave, but indirectly by its effect upon the master. In the one it destroys the self-respect which is the basis of manhood, and is thus a capital crime against humanity. In the other it fosters pride, indolence, luxury, and licentiousness, which equally imbrute the human being. Therefore, in the slave states there is no literature, no art, no progressive civilization. Manners are fantastic and fierce; brute force supplants moral principle; freedom of speech is suppressed, because the natural speech of man condemns slavery; a sensitive vanity is called honor, and cowardly swagger, chivalry; respect for woman is destroyed by universal licentiousness; lazy indifference is called gallantry, and an impudent familiarity, cordiality. To supply by a travesty of courage the want of manly honor, men deliberately shoot those who expose their falsehoods. Therefore they go armed with knives and pistols, for it is a cardinal article of a code of false honor that it is possible for a bully to insult a gentleman.

Founded upon crime — for by no other word can man-stealing be characterized —

the prosperity of such a people is at the mercy of an indignant justice. Hence a slave society has the characteristics of wandering tribes which rob, and live, therefore, insecure in the shadow of impending vengeance. There is nothing admirable in such a society but what its spirit condemns; there is nothing permanent in it but decay. Against nature, against reason, against the human instinct, against the divine law, the institution of human slavery is the most dreadful that philosophy contemplates or the imagination conceives. Certainly, some individual slaveholders are good men, but the mass of men are never better than their institutions and certainly some slaves are better fed and lodged than some free laborers, but so are many horses better fed and lodged than some free laborers. Is, therefore, a laborer to abdicate his manhood and become a horse? . . .

As American citizens, we are called upon to fight that battle [for liberty] by resisting the extension of the institution which I have described. The advocacy of the area of its extension is not a whim of the slave power but is based upon the absolute necessities of the system. An institution which is mentally and morally pernicious cannot be economically advantageous. To suppose so is to accuse God of putting a premium upon sin. The system of slave labor by demoralizing the population and exhausting the soil absolutely demands expansion.

Of this economical fact there can be no doubt. The state of Virginia, for instance, has a finer climate, richer and cheaper soils, with less expensive means of developing their wealth than Pennsylvania, or New York, or Massachusetts. At the Revolution, Virginia had twice the population of Pennsylvania, much more disposable capital, and the best facilities for external commerce and internal communication. In 1850, the cash value of farms in Pennsylvania was $25 an acre; in Virginia, $8 an acre. In New Jersey, with a soil inferior to that of Virginia, the average value of farming land is $44 an acre. Governor Johnson, late governor of Virginia, says that at a period not very remote her trade exceeded that of all New England, and Norfolk surpassed New York in the extent of her shipping. At the Revolution, the commerce of Virginia was four times that of New York. In 1853, the imports into New York were $180 million and into Virginia less than $400,000. Lands in Virginia capable of producing twenty-five to thirty bushels of wheat to the acre, and only twenty-four hours by rail from New York, are to be had for a fortieth of the price of similar lands in New York itself.

Virginia is a Northern slave state, but a senator from Alabama, the most southern of the slave states, confesses of his own home:

> A country in its infancy, where fifty years ago scarce a forest tree had been felled by the pioneer, is already exhibiting the painful signs of senility and decay apparent in Virginia and the Carolinas.

These are specimens of the statistics which are to be found in books that any man can read. All the travelers tell the same story. They find fat slaves and a starved and exhausted soil. Desolation, like a miasma, broods upon the land.

Extension of area is therefore vital to the system, and we shall find that the political power of slavery in the United States has been constantly directed to the acquisition of territory. . . .

Do you ask me our duty as scholars? Gentlemen, thought, which the scholar represents, is life and liberty. There is no intellectual or moral life without liberty. Therefore, as a man must breathe and see before he can study, the scholar must have liberty, first of all; and as the American scholar is a man and has a voice in his own government, so his interest in political affairs must precede all others. He must build his house before he can live in it. He must be a perpetual inspiration of freedom in politics. He must recognize that the intelligent exercise of political rights which is a privilege in a monarchy is a duty in a republic. If it clash with his ease, his retirement, his taste, his study, let it clash, but let him do his duty. The course of events is incessant, and when the good deed is slighted, the bad deed is done.

Young scholars, young Americans, young men, we are all called upon to do a great duty. Nobody is released from it. It is a work to be done by hard strokes, and everywhere. I see a rising enthusiasm, but enthusiasm is not an election; and I hear cheers from the heart, but cheers are not votes. Every man must labor with his neighbor — in the street, at the plough, at the bench, early and late, at home and abroad. Generally we are concerned, in elections, with the measures of government. This time it is with the essential principle of government itself. Therefore there must be no doubt about our leader. He must not prevaricate, or stand in the fog, or use terms to court popular favor which every demagogue and traitor has always used. If he says he favors the interest of the whole country, let him frankly say whether he thinks the interest of the whole country demands the extension of slavery. If he declares for the Union, let him say whether he means a Union for freedom or for slavery. If he swear by the Constitution, let him state, so that the humblest free laborer can hear and understand, whether he believes the Constitution means to prefer slave labor to free labor in the national representation of the territories. Ask him as an honest man, in a great crisis, if he be for the Union, the Constitution, and slavery extension, or for "*Liberty* and union, now and forever, one and inseparable."

Scholars, you would like to loiter in the pleasant paths of study. Every man loves his ease — loves to please his taste. But into how many homes along this lovely valley came the news of Lexington and Bunker

Hill eighty years ago; and young men like us, studious, fond of leisure, young lovers, young husbands, young brothers, and sons, knew that they must forsake the wooded hillside, the river meadows golden with harvest, the twilight walk along the river, the summer Sunday in the old church, parents, wife, child, mistress, and go away to uncertain war. Putnam heard the call at his plough, and turned to go without waiting. Wooster heard it and obeyed.

Not less lovely in those days was this peaceful valley, not less soft this summer air. Life was as dear, and love as beautiful, to those young men as to us who stand upon their graves. But because they were so dear and beautiful those men went out bravely to fight for them and fall. Through these very streets they marched, who never returned. They fell and were buried; but they can never die. Not sweeter are the flowers that make your valley fair, not greener are the pines that give your river its name, than the memory of the brave men who died for freedom. And yet no victim of those days, sleeping under the green sod of Connecticut, is more truly a martyr of liberty than every murdered man whose bones lie bleaching in this summer sun upon the silent plains of Kansas.

Gentlemen, while we read history we make history. Because our fathers fought in this great cause, we must not hope to escape fighting. Because 2,000 years ago Leonidas stood against Xerxes, we must not suppose that Xerxes was slain, nor, thank God! that Leonidas is not immortal. Every great crisis of human history is a pass of Thermopylae, and there is always a Leonidas and his 300 to die in it, if they cannot conquer. And so long as liberty has one martyr, so long as one drop of blood is poured out for her, so long from that single drop of bloody sweat of the agony of humanity shall spring hosts as countless as the forest leaves and mighty as the sea.

Brothers! the call has come to us. I bring it to you in these calm retreats. I summon you to the great fight of freedom. I call upon you to say with your voices, whenever the occasion offers, and with your votes when the day comes, that upon these fertile fields of Kansas, in the very heart of the continent, the upas tree of slavery, dripping death dews upon national prosperity and upon free labor, shall never be planted. I call upon you to plant there the palm of peace, the vine and the olive of a Christian civilization. I call upon you to determine whether this great experiment of human freedom, which has been the scorn of despotism, shall, by its failure, be also our sin and shame. I call upon you to defend the hope of the world.

The voice of our brothers who are bleeding, no less than of our fathers who bled, summons us to this battle. Shall the children of unborn generations, clustering over that vast Western empire, rise up and call us blessed or cursed? Here are our Marathon and Lexington; here are our heroic fields. The hearts of all good men beat with us. The fight is fierce — the issue is with God. But God is good.

In this enlightened age there are few, I believe, but what will acknowledge that slavery as an institution is a moral and political evil in any country. It is useless to expatiate on its disadvantages. I think it, however, a greater evil to the white than to the black race, and while my feelings are strongly enlisted in behalf of the latter, my sympathies are more strong for the former.

ROBERT E. LEE, letter to his wife, Dec. 27, 1856

Daguerreotype of Henry Clay

THE LAST COMPROMISE

Congressional action in 1850 marked the end of an era with the passage of the last great compromise designed to avert what more and more partisans, both Northern and Southern, were characterizing as the "irrepressible conflict." Webster and Calhoun were 68 years old; Henry Clay, active in national politics for thirty years, was 73. Clay, the "Great Compromiser," sought to stem the tides with a plan that would admit California to the Union as a free state, but would pacify the South by requiring rigorous enforcement of the fugitive slave laws. New Mexico and Utah would decide for themselves on freedom or slavery (popular sovereignty). The Compromise of 1850, opposed by President Taylor, was supported by his successor, Millard Fillmore, and be-

came law. Clay, supported by Webster, had deferred the Civil War for ten years. Calhoun, a bitter opponent of the Compromise, died while fighting it. The Southern Convention he had called for convened only after his death, and did little but pass resolutions.

The Fugitive Slave Law raised bitter opposition among Abolitionists and traffic on the Underground Railway boomed. Webster was execrated by the antislavery groups. The popular sovereignty applied to New Mexico and Utah led inexorably to the blood-stained struggle over Kansas and Nebraska a few years later. The Southern quest for new slave territories led to attempts by private interests to take over Cuba and other Latin areas.

Read and Ponder
THE
FUGITIVE SLAVE LAW!

Which disregards all the ordinary securities of PERSONAL LIBERTY, which tramples on the Constitution, by its denial of the sacred rights of Trial by Jury, *Habeas Corpus*, and Appeal, and which enacts, that the Cardinal Virtues of Christianity shall be considered, in the eye of the law, as CRIMES, punishable with the severest penalties,—*Fines and Imprisonment.*

Freemen of *Massachusetts*, REMEMBER, That Samuel A. Elliott of Boston, voted for this law, that Millard Filmore, our whig President *approved* it and the Whig Journals of Massachusetts sustain them in this iniquity.

Broadside announcing the enactment of the Fugitive Slave Law, September 1850

Thomas Hart Benton opposed 1850 Compromise

Webster; Southworth and Hawes daguerreotype

"Conquering Prejudice"; lithograph criticizing Webster's support of the Fugitive Slave Law

PREAMBLE AND RESOLUTIONS

OF

THE SOUTHERN CONVENTION.

SOUTHERN CONVENTION,
November ~~OCTOBER~~ 18th, 1850.

Notes from the convention called by Calhoun to protest the Compromise of 1850

(Above left) Howell Cobb, Southern congressman who supported the Union and the Compromise; (above right) Robert B. Rhett, called the "father of secession"; (below) "Black and White Slaves"; political caricature of the 1840s

Daguerreotype of Caesar, allegedly the last slave held in New York, 1850

Thomas Sims, slave who was captured in Boston and forced to return to Georgia, 1851

View of the crowds outside Boston courthouse during Sims's trial as a fugitive slave

(Above) Fillmore, President after Taylor's death; (below) William C. Marcy, secretary of state

Franklin Pierce; (below) execution of Americans captured in abortive attempt to stir up a revolution against Spanish rule in Cuba

"U.S. Japan Fleet, Commo. Perry Carrying the 'Gospel of God' to the Heathen, 1853"

American commercial expansion scored a great achievement in 1854 with the signing of a Japanese-American treaty. Matthew Calbraith Perry cleared away Japan's traditional isolation with the threat of force from his frigates. First reaching Japan in 1853, he had insisted, despite diplomatic refusal, on delivering a "demand" for diplomatic relations. This act was to open Japan to Western ideas of progress. Perry became a hero to America, and was regarded as the outstanding authority on the Orient.

(Above) Japanese watercolor of Perry; (left) daguerreotype of Perry about 1852

Townsend Harris, consul-general to Japan, 1855, negotiated first Japanese-American treaties

Japanese watercolor of one of the ships in Perry's fleet in harbor

The steam railway along the seacoast of Yokohama built by Perry's expedition

FREE STATE
CONVENTION!

All persons who are favorable to a union of effort, and a permanent organization of all the Free State elements of Kansas Territory, and who wish to secure upon the broadest platform the co-operation of all who agree upon this point, are requested to meet at their several places of holding elections, in their respective districts on the 25th of August, instant, at one o'clock, P. M., and appoint five delegates to each representative to which they were entitled in the Legislative Assembly, who shall meet in general Convention at

Kansas State Historical Society

Broadside calling for convention to organize Kansas Territory as a free state, 1855

The Compromise of 1850 bore bitter fruit in the struggle over the status of slavery in Kansas. Emigrant armies from the North and the South colonized the territory, each striving to control its destiny. Strong-arm methods prevailed: John Brown's Pottawatomi raid was but one expression of the terrorist tactics used by both sides. Rev. Henry Ward Beecher raised funds in the North; much of the money went to purchase Sharps' rifles, thereafter known as Beecher's Bibles. The Free-Soil Party eventually won, and Kansas became a free state in 1861.

(Left) Daguerreotype of John Brown; (below) a Free State battery in 1856, typical of the militant measures used in the North-South struggle for control of this territory

Boston Athenaeum
Kansas State Historical Society

Dr. John Doy (seated) with the group that rescued him from jail in St. Joseph, Mo.

Constitutional Convention in Kansas Territory, December 1855; from "Leslie's Illustrated Newspaper"

Peace convention at Fort Scott, Kan., one of several clashes during the 1850s

"The Great Republican Reform Party calling on their candidate"; lithograph pertaining to the 1856 election. John C. Fremont is at right

Museum of the City of New York, Harry T. Peters Coll.

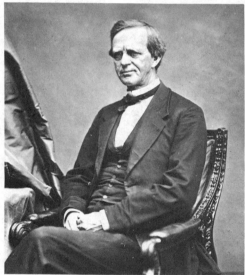

Library of Congress

James Buchanan, a Democrat, won the election of 1856 on a platform supporting previous compromise solutions to "the slavery question." Both the Whigs and the Know-Nothings nominated Millard Fillmore. Most noteworthy was the success of the new Republican Party, with John C. Fremont as candidate. The Republican platform, upholding Congressional control over slavery in the territories and favoring a free Kansas, drew nearly one-third of the votes. Called "Black Republican" by Southerners, the party's emergence further polarized political opinion.

Three elements coming together in the Republican Party: (left) Lyman Trumbull, Free-Soiler; Orville Browning, conservative Whig (below left); Charles Sumner, antislavery spokesman

Library of Congress

Library of Congress

Buchanan and his Cabinet, 1856

A SERVICEABLE GARMENT.
OR REVERIE OF A BACHELOR.

Buchanan admires his old coat, formerly a "fashionable Federal coat," now patched and turned into a "Democratic Garment." The Cuba patch refers to Buchanan's role in the "Ostend Manifesto" controversy. In 1854, while ambassador to Britain, Buchanan had joined in a recommendation that Cuba was indispensable to the existence of slavery and should be bought or taken from Spain

Fremont, led by Horace Greeley and other radical newspapermen, has come to a halt before the "Union Tollgate"; hope for compromise was still strong

Frederick Douglass

Sojourner Truth, escaped slave who became a popular speaker for the Abolitionist movement

The Dred Scott decision of the Supreme Court, handed down in 1857, led to a hardening of pro- and antislavery positions. Associate Justice John McLean dissented on the decision. Meanwhile, powerful Negro voices were being raised in the antislavery chorus — notably those of Frederick Douglass and Sojourner Truth.

Dred Scott, Negro slave who sued unsuccessfully for his liberty after living in a free state

John McLean dissented in Dred Scott decision

83.

John A. Engelhard: Southern Education for Southerners

Dissension between North and South over the slavery issue had become so pronounced by the mid-1850s that Southerners who dared endorse the new Republican Party quickly became objects of public censure. Benjamin S. Hedrick, a Southerner by birth and a professor of chemistry at the University of North Carolina, suffered such censure for his endorsement of the 1856 Republican presidential candidate, John C. Frémont. The following letter denouncing Hedrick for that action was written by John Engelhard, a student in the University of North Carolina law school. Hedrick's reply to the letter increased public feeling against him and when he refused to resign his university post, the board of trustees dismissed him. Engelhard's letter, which appeared in a North Carolina paper, was signed "An Alumnus."

Source: *North Carolina Standard*, September 27, 1856.

WE HAVE NOTICED with pleasure that Southern fathers are beginning to feel the necessity of educating their sons south of Mason and Dixon's Line. The catalogues of Yale and other Northern armories of Sharpe's rifles have but few (shame upon those few) Southern names. The importance of emancipating our young men from the baneful influences of the North — and nowhere is this influence more zealously exerted and powerfully felt than in Northern colleges and under black Republican teachers — has taken firm hold on our people; and we notice, with a high degree of gratitude to Bishop Polk of Louisiana, that the clergy and the church are in a fair way of taking concerted measures for more fully bringing about an object so much desired. We have every reason to believe that unless the course of the North very materially changes — and we are forced to say we see no immediate chance for such a result — there will be inaugurated at the South a system of education congenial to our institutions.

We are proud of such names as Harvard and Yale; and feel that such benefactors of the human race should be held in everlasting remembrance by a grateful country. But their laudable objects are being frustrated by the fanatics that have obtained possession of the government of the schools their charity has founded, for the benefit equally of the slave owner and the slave hirer. At the former, the South is insulted by the dismissal of an instructor for performing his constitutional duty as judge; and at the latter the Southern young men see their professors and fellow students, in the name of the college — nay, of the very class of which they are members — buying *religious rifles* to shoot their own brothers that may be seeking honorable and profitable employment in Kansas. These colleges have been turned from their legitimate channels and been perverted into strongholds of fanaticism; and from being great links of union between all parts of our country, have become hothouses for the nature of artificial statesmen of the Garrisonian school and manufactories of "bleeding Kansas" tragedies.

Then, when our fathers and guardians see such a state of things, it is not to be wondered at that our Southern colleges are so largely attended and Southern seminaries of all grades full to overflowing.

The cause is palpable; a determination to free ourselves from Northern thraldom and stop the revenue accruing to their Abolition treasuries from the labor of Southern slaves. It is a praiseworthy object; and we glory to see this great reaction in the proportionate numbers of Northern and Southern schools.

But the question occurs — Are we entirely rid of Northern influence in the South? Can North Carolina tell the world that her seminaries of learning are free from the corrupting influences of black Republicanism, and Southerners can receive Southern education unmixed with instructions hostile to the feelings and opinions their parents have instilled into them? Nay, can the trustees of our own state university invite pupils to the institution under their charge with the assurance that this mainstream of education contains no deadly poison at its fountainhead? Can boys be taken from Northern colleges and transferred to our university with perfect security?

We have been led to these considerations, Messrs. Editors, by an article headed "Frémont in the South" in a late issue of the *Standard,* and more particularly the following closing paragraph:

If there be Frémont men among us, let them be silenced or required to leave. The expression of black Republican opinions in our midst is incompatible with our honor and safety as a people. If at all necessary we shall refer to this matter again. Let our schools and seminaries of learning be scrutinized; and if black Republicans be found in them let them be driven out. That man is neither a fit nor a safe instructor of our young men, who even inclines to Frémont and black Republicanism.

We were very much gratified to notice this article in your paper at this particular time; for we have been reliably informed that a professor at our state university is an open and avowed supporter of Frémont, and declares his willingness — nay, his desire — to support the black Republican ticket; and the want of a Frémont electoral ticket in North Carolina is the only barrier to this Southern professor from carrying out his patriotic wishes. Is he a fit or safe instructor for our young men?

If our information be entirely correct in regard to the political tendencies and Frémont bias of this professor, ought he not to be "required to leave," at least dismissed from a situation where his poisonous influence is so powerful and his teachings so antagonistical to the "honor and safety" of the university and the state? Where is the creative power? To them we appeal. Have they no restrictive clause in the selection of instructors or limiting code in regard to their actions?

If the trustees or faculty have no powers in regard to the matter in question, we think it a fit object of early legislation at the next meeting of our General Assembly. This ought and must be looked to. We must have certain security, under existing relations of North with South, that at state universities at least we will have no cankerworm preying at the very vitals of Southern institutions.

Upon what ground can a Southern instructor relying for his support upon Southern money, selected to impart healthy instruction to the sons of Southern slave owners, and indebted for his situation to a Southern state, excuse his support to Frémont with a platform which eschews the fathers of his pupils and the state from whose university he received his station and from whose treasury he supports his family?

Does he tell the young men that he is in favor of a man for the presidency, nominated by men whom their fathers could not nor would not sit in convention with; placed upon a platform hostile to their every interest; its separate planks put together by the vilest Southern haters of the North, upon which all the isms of Yankeedom find aid and comfort; whose cabinet, in the event of his election, would be composed of such men as Speaker Banks, who is willing to "let the Union slide"; and Mr. "Niagara" Burlingame, who demands an "antislavery Bible and an antislavery God"; whose orators belch forth vile slanders upon the South under flags whose venomous folds reveal but sixteen stars, and whose torch-light processions do not "march under the flag nor keep step to the music of the Union"? Does he read the following extract taken from his candidate's letter accepting the nomination: "I am opposed to slavery in the abstract and upon principle, sustained and made habitual by long-settled convictions"? Are these the doctrines he advocates to young men, two-thirds of whose property consists in slaves?

It cannot be denied by any person cogni-zant of college influences that each professor has his quota of friends and admirers among the students, and their minds are to a certain degree, upon general subjects, merely daguerrotypes of his opinions. This is natural. The student is young, and the instructors are placed over them, *in loco parentis*, to guide them correctly; and the young graduate leaves with opinions molded by his instructors that will cling to him through life.

We ask, are we correctly informed concerning the political inclination and expressed opinions of this professor? If not, we hope to be corrected; and if we are, we call upon the proper authorities to take action for the sake of the prosperity of our alma mater and the good of the state.

84.

JOHN P. SANDERSON: Adverse Views on Foreign Immigration

The prospect of a better life lured a quarter of a million immigrants to the United States in the period between the Revolution and the War of 1812. The number steadily increased up until the 1840s in response to expanding industry, new territorial acquisitions, and the construction of railroads. In the single decade between 1850 and 1860 over 2,500,000 new settlers entered America. In addition to problems of adjustment to a new country and new customs, immigrants flooded the labor market and bred slums in the cities. While some Americans proposed better education, improved housing, and adequate job training as solutions, others reacted by urging restrictions on immigration. In the following selection from a book published in 1856, John P. Sanderson analyzed the social problems created by immigrants and urged such restrictive policies by the government.

Source: *Republican Landmarks: The Views and Opinions of American Statesmen on Foreign Immigration*, Philadelphia, 1856, pp. 26-41, 334-340.

THE PUBLISHED CENSUS RETURNS of 1850 are lamentably deficient in detailed information on the subject of paupers and convicts. We learn from it, however, that the amount of public means expended within the year preceding 1850 for the support of paupers was $2,954,806; and the number of paupers supported within the same year, in whole or part, was 134,972, of which number *over one-half were foreigners*, there being 66,434 native-born, and *68,538 of foreign birth*. It thus appears that of the 2,244,625 foreign-born population in the United States at that time, 1 of at least every 33 was a pauper, supported at the public expense, while of the 19,979,563 native-born, including the free colored and those returned as of unknown birth, only 1 of every 300 was thus a charge on the public. . . .

OTHER SIMILAR STATISTICS might be adduced, all showing the same state of things in different sections of the country; but the following extract from a recent letter of Jeremiah Clemens, late United States senator from Alabama, will suffice:

By reference to the annual report of the governors of the Alms-House, I find there were in the New York Alms-House during the year 1853, 2,198 inmates; of these only 535 were natives and 1,663 foreigners, supported at the expense of the city. And now I propose to use on our side the argument of our opponents, that there are only 3 million foreigners to 20 million natives. According to that ratio, there ought to be about 7 natives to 1 foreigner in the Alms-House; whereas we find more than 3 foreigners to 1 native. No wonder that a people who are taxed to support such a body of paupers should be the first to set about devising means to get rid of them. Let us pursue the record: In the Bellevue Hospital, in the same city, there were 702 Americans, 4,134 foreigners; now the proportion rises to nearly 6 to 1. There were of outdoor poor, that is, persons who had some place to sleep but nothing to eat and nothing to make a fire, 957 native adults and 1,044 children; 3,131 foreign adults and 5,229 foreign children, or children born of foreign parents. This number were relieved during the year with money. Of those relieved with fuel, there were 1,248 adult Americans and 1,810 children; 10,355 adult foreigners and 17,857 children. But the record is not yet complete — let us turn to the statistics of crime. In the city prisons there were during the year 6,102 Americans, 22,229 foreigners. I pass on to an abode even more gloomy than that of the prison cell and call your attention to those whom God in His wisdom has seen fit to deprive of the light of reason. In the lunatic asylum, there were admitted, from the year 1847 to 1853, 779 Americans, 2,381 foreigners. For the year 1853 there were 94 Americans, 393 foreigners. These tables might be made more complete by adding organ grinders, strolling mendicants, and professional beggars; but of these I have no reliable data, and therefore pass them with the single remark that I have never seen a native American who belonged to either class.

These figures are far more conclusive than any language could be to prove the necessity of arresting the tide of immigration. Let every American impress them deeply upon his memory: 42,369 foreign paupers and invalids, 2,381 lunatics, and 22,229 criminals taxing the industry and blighting the prosperity of a single city. In that list of crimes is embraced murder, rape, arson, robbery, perjury; everything which is damning to the character of the individual, and everything which is dangerous to society.

CRIME HAS ALSO BEEN enormously increased by immigration. According to *De Bow's Census Compendium*, the whole number of criminals convicted within the year preceding that the census of 1850 was taken in all the states but California, was 26,679, of which number 12,988 were natives and 13,691 *were foreigners,* being 1 conviction out of every 1,580 of the native, and 1 out of about every 165 of the foreign population in the United States at that time. In the *free* states there were 10,832 natives and 12,789 foreign convictions, and in the *slave* states there were 2,166 natives and 1,902 foreigners. . . .

INTEMPERANCE IS UNDOUBTEDLY ONE of the great causes of crime. . . . Who, then, are those generally engaged in selling liquor, and who thus contribute to the increase of crime? A large majority are foreigners, and, though accurate statistical information cannot be had on the subject, there is sufficient to be had to justify the assertion. According to a report of the marshal of the city of Boston in 1853, there were then 1,300 places in that city where liquor was sold, of which but 490 were kept by Americans, and the remainder by foreigners, of whom 900 were Irish and 110 German and Swedes. We have no similar statistical information in relation to New York, Philadelphia, Baltimore, and other cities and large towns; but, if obtained, there remains not a reasonable doubt it would present a like state of facts.

But, it will be inquired, "What of it, if it be so? Do you mean by these general declarations to ascribe all the evils of vice and crime to the liquor sellers, and to condemn all as being engaged in a business which should be prohibited by law?" It is not necessary here to make a categorical answer to such an interrogatory. Suffice it to say that the groggeries, which are mainly the cause of the prevailing vice of intemperance, should be prohibited, and that these are chiefly kept by foreigners, while the Americans engaged in the business are keepers of respectable hotels and houses of entertainment, which are so conducted as to be in a great degree exempt from the charge of contributing to the increase of pauperism and crime. It is the groggeries, many of which sell liquor without license, that are responsible for the pauperism and crime in our country, that make widows and orphans and contribute to increase juvenile vagrancy and delinquency; and these, it is safe to aver, are chiefly kept by foreigners. . . .

AMERICA FOR AMERICANS is a demand not based upon narrow sectarianism or mere party predilections. It is no new doctrine; it has been avowed and maintained in all ages and in all countries, so long as the people remained true to their country and had a respect for and pride in their nationality; it rests upon the love of home and of country, and involves not only a natural right but a solemn and imperative duty which birthright alone can impose. Who that will not adopt the language of the poet and cordially agree that:

There's not a spot on this wide peopled earth
So dear to the heart as the land of our birth;
And the home of our childhood! the beautiful spot,
Which memory retains when all else is forgot.

Why, then, should it be deemed illiberal, unkind, and unjust in Americans to feel a devotion to their country and an interest in its institutions which induces a desire on their part to rule America? Have not other free nations claimed and exercised the same prerogative? . . .

The Americans are but discharging a duty they owe to the land of their birth, equally due to the memory of their revolutionary ancestors and to their own posterity, when they set to work to purify the body politic from disease which threatens destruction to the country and to the institutions committed to their guardianship by their forefathers. What is the malady that afflicts us; what the evil they have set about to remedy? In one generation we have attained a growth exceeding that of any other nation; our flag floats in every sea and is everywhere honored and respected; while our institutions are the theme of admiration throughout the civilized world; and yet we are obliged to struggle to maintain our distinct nationality at home.

Millions of the oppressed in other lands resort hither to enjoy the blessings of freedom, and, in our contact with those who thus seek refuge from tyranny, our system has been inoculated with the decayed matter of the worn-out, corrupt, and dying systems of the Old World, which renders it necessary to purify ourselves and lop off the fungus. And are Americans to be blamed for this? Surely no one can assert the affirmative and satisfactorily maintain it. Say what we will, there exists such an evil in the country. The people know and feel it. The gross abuses of the hospitality extended to those of foreign birth, and the outrageous violations of our laws, and infringements upon our rights by foreigners coming among us — incited thereto, it must be with sorrow and shame confessed, by demagogues and knavish politicians in our own country — has been for a long while an alarming and growing evil in our elections, until at length it has become intolerable.

It is notorious that the grossest frauds have been practised on our naturalization laws, and that thousands and tens of thousands have every year deposited votes in the ballot box who could not only not read them and knew nothing of the nature of the business in which they were engaged but who had not been six months in the country and, in many cases, hardly six days. By such influences, by the destruction of ballot boxes and by forcibly preventing native-born citizens from coming to the polls, the foreign element has at times carried the elections in our cities and towns, and thereby controlled states and the Union! The power thus wielded has led to the most disgraceful subserviency to the foreign element on the part of our native demagogues, and wholesale bargaining and traffic has been the result.

It is in the horror and disgust of such a state of things that the American movement has had its origin and that has given a healthful tone to public sentiment in regard to the evil under which the country has labored. The people have become aroused to the danger and have accordingly determined to guard against it by placing the power of ruling only into the hands of those in whose devotion to the country they feel they may have confidence.

The right of Americans to prescribe terms of admission into the country, as well as to prescribe terms to be admitted to citizenship, or to refuse either or both, is a power which has been and continues to be exercised by all governments. It was so among the Jews, the Greeks, and the Romans, in ancient times, and continues so in England, France, and all other countries of modern times; and it is so, in a general sense, in the United States. Congress has control over the subject. The Constitution has confided to it the power of passing laws regulating naturalization, and if it should so change the law as to require twenty-one years' residence before citizenship could be conferred, or should wholly repeal all laws on the subject, without providing any new process by which aliens could be made citizens, no one could have any well-founded ground of complaint.

To become a citizen is not a right which an alien can command, but a privilege which may be conceded and afforded, or withheld and refused; and, so long as no attempt be made to interfere with any existing right of citizenship, and that is not at all likely ever to be attempted, there can be nothing to justify the cry of persecution. Those who have acquired the rights and privileges of citizens are entirely beyond the reach of legislation; they are invested with all the dignity of citizenship, which no power except they, by their own conduct, can take from them. Their rights are sacred and cannot be infringed. The alteration or entire repeal of the naturalization laws cannot, therefore, affect the rights and privileges of naturalized citizens. No war is made against them. Why, then, should naturalized citizens feel different in regard to the matter than native-born citizens? Being sworn citizens of the United States, it does not accord with their obligations to regard themselves as a distinct class and to feel aggrieved at legislation as a reflection upon them, when it is intended for the equal benefit of all who have a claim to American citizenship. They have no right, as good citizens, to regard themselves in any other light than Americans, and they lessen the dignity of citizenship by thinking of themselves as aliens still, and bestowing all their care and sympathy upon those of kindred birth who do not enjoy the rights of citizenship.

The manner in which Congress shall exercise the power given to it by the Constitution, in relation to the naturalization of aliens, should have no other object in view than the public good; and, if circumstances which have transpired and the experience of the past unite in dictating the propriety of lengthening the period of residence preliminary to the investiture of the rights of citizenship, or the entire cessation of conferring those rights upon those who shall hereafter migrate into the country, it is the duty, as well as it should be deemed the pleasure, of naturalized as well as native citizens, to sustain and uphold such a policy. It is a fallacy to argue that an extension of the period beyond that now required to become a citizen, or an entire refusal to naturalize, would be a proscription of men on account of "the accident of birth." As well might the unfortunate youth who struggles against the adverse circumstances of poverty claim as a right to appropriate to himself a portion of the estate of his rich neighbor, and, on being denied his claim, arraign him for proscribing him on account of "the accident of birth." Place of birth may be an accident; it undoubtedly is so, humanly speaking; but so is, in the same sense, being born at all, or being born under favorable instead of adverse circumstances; and yet these accidents constantly affect human rights and privileges, and the common sense of mankind admits the propriety of their doing so, nor has it ever yet called in question the wisdom and beneficence of the Creator in so ordaining the affairs of man.

The time and circumstances of birth and death are quite as much accidents as the place of birth, and yet these are the great controllers of the rights of property. Why, then, may not place of birth also, in a measure, control the rights of citizenship? None but Scotch Socialists, French Red Republicans, German Rationalists, or American Clootzes have ever yet denounced the laws controlling property, and which allow the accidents of birth to fall so frequently between men and fortune; and why then complain about "proscribing men on account of the accident of birth"? There is nothing in the rights of citizenship to exempt it from the influence of accidents which constantly affect other rights; and the assumed fact that there is an inherent right in every man to a full participation in the government of every country in which he may choose to take up his residence has never been either recognized or acknowledged by any government on earth and cannot be conceded by our own without involving the admission that our whole system is founded upon erroneous principles and needs reformation.

Our Constitution contains many restrictions upon the rights of the people, though its Preamble declares it to have been their own act. It requires the President to be a native-born citizen, or one who was a citizen at the time of its adoption, and to be of a certain age; and, annexing those qualifications, the people cannot disregard them and elect whom they choose. It requires, also, certain qualifications as prerequisites to hold a seat in the Senate or House of Representatives, which the people cannot disregard in their exercise of the elective franchise. So in regard to the qualifications of electors. These are prescribed by the state constitutions, and consist in a certain period of residence in the state, county, city, borough, township, or precinct, payment of tax, etc., all of which, if the argument now advanced be correct, would have to be abolished to relieve our system from the imputation of proscribing men on account of the accident of birth, residence, age, etc. Carrying the argument out, where would it lead to? According to its theory, all restrictions would be proscriptive, and there could not consistently be a condition of any kind annexed to enable an alien to become a citizen.

Common sense revolts at a doctrine which would lead to such conclusions, and its utter absurdity is made manifest by even those who arraign the American movement as proscriptive in its character.

The admission of foreigners to citizenship is not an inherent right they can claim *nolens volens* [willy-nilly] but involves a question of expediency which it is in the power of Congress to determine. It may abolish all naturalization laws, or it may annex such conditions to become a citizen as the public good may seem to demand; and, however onerous these may be made, they cannot be justly denounced as proscriptive in their character. If it can, as it has, fix a period of five years' residence to enable an alien to become a citizen, it can, if the good of the country demands it, extend the period to twenty-one years, or withdraw the power and authority from courts to naturalize at all. Grant the power to impose a condition of any kind, and no one denies that, and the whole argument of those who assail the American theory as proscriptive falls to the ground.

Thus a Democratic meeting, held this summer in Daviess County, Kentucky, unintentionally and unconsciously surrendered the whole argument against the movement, and conceded the expediency and propriety of it, by adopting the following resolve, in substance, that "the foreigner cannot consistently with reason and right be deprived of a voice in our government, and at the same time be taxed to support the same," but that "the naturalization laws should be so altered as to lengthen his time of probation, that he may become more thoroughly imbued with the principles and spirit of our institutions!" Such an admission concedes the whole argument and contradicts the charge of proscription, leaving but one question to be determined, and that is: Is any extension of time long enough, and, if so, to what period should it be extended?

As to the question of taxing foreigners without conferring upon them the right of voting, the argument used by the Daviess County Democracy is plausible, but is nevertheless a sophism which will not bear the test of scrutiny. If it be sound, then foreigners ought not to be taxed while they are here on probation, and should not be called on to contribute to the support of government until they have a voice in its management; and yet they are taxed as soon as they take up a permanent residence in a state, and it is right and proper that they should be. And why? Because there exists no necessary connection between taxation and the right of suffrage. The correct idea of taxation is that it is the price paid for the protection afforded by government to person and property. Hence the property of widows, maids, and minors is taxed; and why ought that of aliens, who enjoy the same protection, be exempt?

There is then nothing in the Constitution obligating Congress to any specific mode of action with regard to foreigners, nor anything in Americanism which implies or conveys personal or invidious reproach against any citizen, whether of foreign or native birth. No such distinctions are sought to be created. The movement only recognizes and seeks to enforce such distinctions as the law of self-preservation and the true principles of our government have already established. It has been argued that a policy carried out, such as Americans now seek to establish, would create in our country a class corresponding with that of the helots of ancient Sparta — a degraded caste whose presence would be dangerous to society. This is, however, a far-fetched argument and entitled to no great consideration. The history of civilized states negatives the assumption, reason repudiates it, and our Constitution which requires a naturalization law at all denies it. Our own experience proves to us that the denial of the right of suffrage does not necessarily produce such a class. It is not so in the District of Columbia, whose inhabitants have not the right of voting for President.

Nor are the unnaturalized foreigners in our midst, while serving their probation, more degraded than after their naturalization. There exists not the least analogy between their condition and that of the helots of Sparta. They are in the enjoyment of all the rights of property and the protection of their persons, character, privileges, and freedom, with no mark of distinction against them but as to the right of suffrage, and that voluntarily assumed by them. In determining to change their homes, they had to decide between their native lands, where they are not allowed to vote (for neither the Irish, German, Frenchman, nor Scotchman can be said to enjoy the elective franchise), and our own country, where they may, after a residence of a certain period, or may not vote, which depends upon the policy pursued by the government.

They come with a full knowledge that their admission to full citizenship depends upon the action and policy of our government; and to say that they will become more degraded here, if the right of suffrage be withheld from them, than they were in their native land, though they never enjoyed it there, is simply to utter a ridiculous absurdity which is unsustained by history and contradicted by our own personal experience. Washington, Franklin, Sherman, Jay, Hamilton, Madison, and the other framers of the Constitution could have had no such fears, or they would not have inserted a provision in the Constitution requiring aliens to be naturalized at all. Had they supposed that there lurked danger in requiring foreigners to remain some years on probation before becoming citizens, they would have provided for their immediate admission to all the rights and privileges of the government.

85.

FREEMAN HUNT: Business Success

By the mid-1850s American society was well on the way to producing the class of conspicuously wealthy capitalists — the Morgans, the Carnegies, the Vanderbilts — who came to dominate the era Mark Twain called "the Gilded Age." Freeman Hunt endeavored to give commerce a dignified image and a guiding rationale through his Merchants' Magazine, *founded in 1828 as the first periodical devoted wholly to commerce. He also penned such other works as the biographical* Lives of American Merchants *and* Worth and Wealth. *The latter volume, from which the following selections are taken, appeared in 1856.*

Source: *Worth and Wealth: A Collection of Maxims, Morals and Miscellanies for Merchants and Men of Business*, New York, 1856, pp. 103-105, 120-123, 503-504.

A MAN OF BUSINESS should be able to fix his attention on details and be ready to give every kind of argument a hearing. This will not encumber him, for he must have been practised beforehand in the exercise of his intellect and be strong in principles. One man collects materials together and there they remain, a shapeless heap; another, possessed of method, can arrange what he has collected; but such a man as I would describe, by the aid of principles, goes farther, and builds with his materials.

He should be courageous. The courage, however, required in civil affairs is that which belongs rather to the able commander than the mere soldier. But any kind of courage is serviceable.

Besides a stout heart, he should have a patient temperament and a vigorous but disciplined imagination; and then he will plan boldly and, with large extent of view, execute calmly, and not be stretching out his hand for things not yet within his grasp. He will let opportunities grow before his eyes until they are ripe to be seized. He will think steadily over possible failure in order to provide a remedy or a retreat. There will be the strength of repose about him.

He must have a deep sense of responsibility. He must believe in the power and vitality of truth, and in all he does or says should be anxious to express as much truth as possible.

His feeling of responsibility and love of truth will almost inevitably endow him with diligence, accuracy, and discreetness: those commonplace requisites for a good man of business, without which all the rest may never come to be "translated into action."

ALMOST EVERY MERCHANT has been rich, or at least prosperous, at some point of his life; and if he is poor now, he can see very well how he might have avoided the disaster which overthrew his hopes. He will probably see that his misfortunes arose from neglecting some of the following rules:

Be industrious. Everybody knows that industry is the fundamental virtue in the man of business. But it is not every sort of industry which tends to wealth. Many men work hard to do a great deal of business and, after all, make less money than they would if they did less. Industry should be expended in seeing to all the details of business, in the careful finishing up of each separate undertaking, and in the maintenance of such a system as will keep everything under control.

Be economical. This rule, also, is familiar to everybody. Economy is a virtue to be practised every hour in a great city. It is to be practised in pence as much as in pounds. A shilling a day saved amounts to an estate in the course of a life. Economy is especially important in the outset of life, until the foundations of an estate are laid. Many men are poor all their days because, when their necessary expenses were small, they did not seize the opportunity to save a small capital, which would have changed their fortunes for the whole of their lives.

Stick to the business in which you are regularly employed. Let speculators make their thousands in a year or day; mind your own regular trade, never turning from it to the right hand or the left. If you are a merchant, a professional man, or a mechanic, never buy lots or stocks unless you have surplus money which you wish to invest. Your own business you understand as well as other men; but other people's business you do not understand. Let your business be some one which is useful to the community. All such occupations possess the elements of profits in themselves, while mere speculation has no such element.

Never take great hazards. Such hazards are seldom well balanced by the prospects of profit; and if they were, the habit of mind which is induced is unfavorable, and generally the result is bad. To keep what you have should be the first rule; to get what you can fairly, the second.

Do not be in a hurry to get rich. Gradual gains are the only natural gains, and they who are in haste to be rich break over sound rules, fall into temptations and distress of various sorts, and generally fail of their object. There is no use in getting rich suddenly. The man who keeps his business under his control and saves something from year to year is always rich. At any rate, he possesses the highest enjoyment which riches are able to afford.

Never do business for the sake of doing it and being counted a great merchant. There is often more money to be made by a small business than a large one; and that business will in the end be most respectable which is most successful. Do not get deeply in debt; but so manage as always, if possible, to have your financial position easy, so that you can turn any way you please.

Do not love money extravagantly. We speak here merely with reference to getting rich. In morals, the inordinate love of money is one of the most degrading vices. But the extravagant desire of accumulation induces an eagerness, many times, which is imprudent and so misses its object from too much haste to grasp it.

Freeman Hunt, engraving from a photograph

SUCCESS IN LIFE mainly depends upon perseverance. When a man has determined to follow a certain line of business, he must at the same time resolve to persevere until success crowns his efforts. He must never be cast down by the difficulties which may beset his path, for whoever conquers difficulty conquers a weakness of his own frail nature likewise. How many men have commenced business under the most favorable auspices, and yet, when a cloud has momentarily overshadowed their path, have lost all command over themselves and fled before the temporary gloom instead of persevering on until the cloud has been dispersed and sunshine once more smiled upon their efforts. Others, more fickle, have thought their business, in some minor departments, unworthy of their perseverance and energy, and, forgetting the golden maxim that "whatever is worth doing is worth doing well," have ceased to persevere in small matters, until sloth has entered deeply into their minds and their whole business greatly neglected.

We are too apt to attribute success in business to good fortune instead of great perseverance. This is a great evil and should be eschewed, as it leads many to suppose that Dame Fortune will do that for them which they are unwilling to do for themselves.

The history of every great success in business is the history of great perseverance. By perseverance the mind is strengthened and invigorated, and the difficulty that once seemed so formidable is a second time surmounted with ease and confidence.

Energy and great perseverance are never thrown away on a good cause or left unrewarded; and to every man of business, perseverance should be his motto, and then he may look with confidence to fortune as his reward.

"I'M BUT A GATHERER AND DISTRIBUTOR of other men's stuff," said Isaac Walton. This would have constituted him a merchant, although he had traded, like Daniel Dowlas, in small wares down to wooden nutmegs. The poorest peddler is an itinerant merchant; and since man is the only trading animal on earth, he is bound to qualify himself *thoroughly* for whatever branch he embraces. As an accomplished linguist is familiar with foreign characters, using them only in the tongue to which they belong, so an individual, with a sound mercantile education, when addressing another, cautiously employs the technical terms known to his correspondent. Errors arising from neglect of this rule have frequently occurred, which we will illustrate by a story from a contemporary which may not be generally known: A brewer once employed a brickmaker to manufacture a quantity of bricks, the latter having agreed, wrote for two or three loads of "Spanish" — the technical term for ashes or laystal stuff to mix with clay, instead of which he received from the brewer a dozen hogsheads of molasses!

Such want of knowledge is likely to produce serious delay. In the above instance it only incited merriment; but it plainly shows that a thorough businessman is familiar with the general peculiarities of other trades as well as his own. He is posted up in manufacturers' prices, the best markets for barter, rate of duties, etc. A mind well stored with essential data is not likely to be alarmed at the deceptions published by speculatories in daily journals; it only perceives the laws that regulate supply and demand, as all fluctuations are considered matters of course.

We might dilate on this subject on two accounts, deprecating those unprincipled newsmongers who pander to stockjobbers, and lamenting the superficial instruction too many of our traffickers receive, which is painfully evident when rogues can raise panics with impunity — each one more alarming than the last — until our poor novices "lose the sense of action," like a certain visionary who remained transfixed in a sepulchral vault, all night dreading to move, under the supposition that something supernatural pulled his gown tail, which had hitched on a hook. The terrors of imagination, like a fog cloud, magnify every danger.

Judgment — good common sense — is the motive power that raises a utilitarian to the summit of success. During the smoke of battle, skillful generals direct the motions of their army with the same dexterity as they would shift draftsmen on a checker board, because they are versed in mathematics, and every position on the field presents a problem, which is familiar with Euclid's disciplinarians. Thus are merchants schooled in the game of life, and no "weak invention of the enemy" can discompose their equanimity.

The diurnal, methodical routine continues, whether public banks expand or contract, and their best friend — capital — is treated as a friend. They know well how to invest a surplus capital and where a good mercantile security is to be found — want of such necessary knowledge too often occasions sad embarrassment. Of fixed or floating capital, the latter is most profitable; the former is too fluctuating and precarious, arising from rents or interest, while "all commodities, the entire cost of which is replaced out of the current income, are floating capital. The former are stationary, yielding only income, and slow of transfer; the latter are constantly circulating."

The mutations of traffic render it important that a reserve fund should be convertible into cash at any time. How many men have been ruined by making advances on growing crops, vaguely anticipating the profits or produce that has to pass through a manufacturing process before it is marketable. Innumerable cases might be cited of errors in judgment committed by mercantile men, from not having been rigidly trained "in the way they should go." A visionary boasted of having driven a nail into the sky, and another replied, "But I clenched it." An ignoramus drives at random, but one who is regularly disciplined will, by judicious management, fix what an unskilled neighbor fails in.

THERE IS A CLASS OF MEN whose patronage of art has been princely in its munificence, as their wealth has equaled that of princes, whose interests have become a chief concern of statesmen and have involved the issues of peace and war; whose affairs afford a leading subject of the legislation of states and fill the largest space in the volumes of modern jurists. This class has produced men who have combined a vast comprehensiveness with a most minute grasp of details, and whose force of mind and will in other situations would have commanded armies and ruled states. They are men whose plans and combinations take in every continent, and the islands and the waters of every sea; whose pursuits, though peaceful, occupy people enough to fill armies and man navies; who have placed science and invention under contribution and made use of their most ingenious instruments and marvelous discoveries in aid of their enterprises; who are covering continents with railroads and oceans with steamships; who can boast the magnificence of the Medici and the philanthropy of Gresham and of Amos Lawrence; and whose zeal for science and zeal for philanthropy have penetrated to the highest latitude of the Arctic seas ever reached by civilized man in the ships of Grinnell.

Modern scholars have seen the important bearing of the history of commerce upon the history of the world; have seen, rather — as who, in this most commercial of all eras, can fail to see — how large a chapter it forms in the history of the world, although crowded out of the space it ought to fill by the wars and crimes which destroy what it creates. Hume was among the first to call attention to this branch of historical inquiry, and Heeren has investigated with much learning the commerce of the ancients. If we were in possession of lives of the great merchants of antiquity, what light would they not throw upon the origin of states, the foundations of cities, and inventions and discoveries of which we now do not even know the dates?

Trade planted Tyre, Carthage, Marseilles, London, and all the Ionic colonies of Greece. Plato was for a while a merchant; Herodotus, they say, was a merchant. Trade was honorable at Athens, as among all nations of original and vigorous thought; when we find discredit attached to it, it is among nations of a secondary and less original civilization, like the Romans.

But if commerce forms so large a chapter in the history of the world, what would the history of America be if commerce and men of commerce were left out? Trade discovered America in the vessels of adventurers, seeking new channels to the old marts of India; trade planted the American colonies and made them flourish, even in New England, say what we please about Plymouth Rock; our colonial growth was the growth of trade; revolution and independence were the results of measures of trade and commercial legislation, although they undoubtedly involved the first principles of free government. The history of the country, its politics and policy, has ever since turned chiefly upon questions of trade and of finance, sailor's rights, protection, banks, and cotton.

I trust a good deal to common fame, as we all must. If a man has good corn, or woods, or boards, or pigs to sell, or can make better chairs or knives, crucibles or church organs than anybody else, you will find a broad, hard-beaten road to his house, though it be in the woods.

RALPH WALDO EMERSON, *Journal*, 1855

1857

86.

ROGER B. TANEY: *Dred Scott v. Sandford*

*By the mid-1850s there existed a widespread feeling that the slavery question, which
Congress had been unable to resolve, should be dealt with by the courts; and
President Buchanan, in his inaugural address (March 4, 1857), made reference to
a coming decision that he hoped all would be able to abide by. Two days later, on
March 6, the Supreme Court handed down its ruling in* Dred Scott v. Sandford, *a
case as famous as any in its history. Dred Scott, a Negro slave, had been taken by
his master to Illinois, where slavery had been forbidden by the Ordinance of 1787,
and to the Wisconsin Territory, where it was illegal by the Missouri Compromise,
and had remained on free soil during most of the period from 1834 to 1838. In 1846
he had sued for his liberty in a Missouri court, holding that he had become free
because of his stay in free territory. The case involved three important issues:
(1) whether Scott was a citizen of Missouri and thus able to sue in a federal court;
(2) whether his sojourn in free territory had made him legally a free man; and
(3) the constitutionality of the Missouri Compromise. Each of the judges handed
down a separate opinion, although that of Chief Justice Taney is customarily cited
for the majority. In effect, the majority ruling held that Scott (and hence all slaves
or their descendants) was not a citizen; that his status in free territory did not
affect his status in Missouri, where slavery was legal; and that the Missouri
Compromise was unconstitutional under the Fifth Amendment. The decision was
eventually nullified by the Thirteenth and Fourteenth Amendments.*

Source: 19 Howard 393.

MR. CHIEF JUSTICE TANEY delivered the
opinion of the Court. . . .

The question is simply this: Can a Negro,
whose ancestors were imported into this
country and sold as slaves, become a member of the political community formed and
brought into existence by the Constitution
of the United States, and as such become
entitled to all the rights and privileges and
immunities, guaranteed by that instrument
to the citizen? One of which rights is the
privilege of suing in a court of the United
States in the cases specified in the Constitution.

It will be observed that the plea applies
to that class of persons only whose ances-

tors were Negroes of the African race and imported into this country, and sold and held as slaves. The only matter in issue before the Court, therefore, is whether the descendants of such slaves, when they shall be emancipated, or who are born of parents who had become free before their birth, are citizens of a state in the sense in which the word "citizen" is used in the Constitution of the United States. And this being the only matter in dispute on the pleadings, the Court must be understood as speaking in this opinion of that class only; that is, of those persons who are the descendants of Africans who were imported into this country and sold as slaves. . . .

In discussing this question, we must not confound the rights of citizenship which a state may confer within its own limits and the rights of citizenship as a member of the Union. It does not by any means follow, because he has all the rights and privileges of a citizen of a state, that he must be a citizen of the United States. He may have all of the rights and privileges of the citizen of a state and yet not be entitled to the rights and privileges of a citizen in any other state. . . .

It is true, every person, and every class and description of persons who were at the time of the adoption of the Constitution recognized as citizens in the several states, became also citizens of this new political body; but none other; it was formed by them and for them and their posterity, but for no one else. And the personal rights and privileges guaranteed to citizens of this new sovereignty were intended to embrace those only who were then members of the several state communities or who should afterward by birthright or otherwise become members, according to the provisions of the Constitution and the principles on which it was founded. It was the union of those who were at that time members of distinct and separate political communities into one political family, whose power, for certain specified purposes, was to extend over the whole territory of the United States. And it gave to each citizen rights and privileges outside of his state which he did not before possess, and placed him in every other state upon a perfect equality with its own citizens as to rights of person and rights of property — it made him a citizen of the United States.

It becomes necessary, therefore, to determine who were citizens of the several states when the Constitution was adopted. And, in order to do this, we must recur to the governments and institutions of the thirteen colonies when they separated from Great Britain and formed new sovereignties and took their places in the family of independent nations. We must inquire who, at that time, were recognized as the people or citizens of a state, whose rights and liberties had been outraged by the English government; and who declared their independence and assumed the powers of government to defend their rights by force of arms.

In the opinion of the Court, the legislation and histories of the times, and the language used in the Declaration of Independence, show that neither the class of persons who had been imported as slaves nor their descendants, whether they had become free or not, were then acknowledged as a part of the people nor intended to be included in the general words used in that memorable instrument.

It is difficult at this day to realize the state of public opinion in relation to that unfortunate race which prevailed in the civilized and enlightened portions of the world at the time of the Declaration of Independence and when the Constitution of the United States was framed and adopted. But the public history of every European nation displays it in a manner too plain to be mistaken.

They had for more than a century before been regarded as beings of an inferior order and altogether unfit to associate with the white race, either in social or political relations; and so far inferior that they had no rights which the white man was bound to respect; and that the Negro might justly and lawfully be reduced to slavery for his benefit. He was bought and sold and treated as an ordinary article of merchandise and traffic whenever a profit could be made by it. This opinion was at that time fixed and universal in the civilized portion of the white race. It was regarded as an axiom in morals as well as in politics, which no one thought of disputing, or supposed to be open to dispute; and men in every grade and position in society daily and habitually acted upon it in their private pursuits, as well as in matters of public concern, without doubting for a moment the correctness of this opinion. . . .

The language of the Declaration of Independence is equally conclusive. It begins by declaring that

When, in the course of human events, it becomes necessary for one people to dissolve the political bands which have connected them with another, and to assume among the powers of the earth the separate and equal station to which the laws of nature and nature's God entitle them, a decent respect for the opinions of mankind requires that they should declare the causes which impel them to the separation.

It then proceeds to say:

We hold these truths to be self-evident: that all men are created equal; that they are endowed by their Creator with certain unalienable rights; that among them is life, liberty, and the pursuit of happiness; that to secure these rights, governments are instituted, deriving their just powers from the consent of the governed.

The general words above quoted would seem to embrace the whole human family, and if they were used in a similar instrument at this day would be so understood. But it is too clear for dispute that the en-slaved African race were not intended to be included and formed no part of the people who framed and adopted this Declaration; for if the language, as understood in that day, would embrace them, the conduct of the distinguished men who framed the Declaration of Independence would have been utterly and flagrantly inconsistent with the principles they asserted; and instead of the sympathy of mankind, to which they so confidently appealed, they would have deserved and received universal rebuke and reprobation.

Yet the men who framed this Declaration were great men — high in literary acquirements, high in their sense of honor and incapable of asserting principles inconsistent with those on which they were acting. They perfectly understood the meaning of the language they used and how it would be understood by others; and they knew that it would not in any part of the civilized world be supposed to embrace the Negro race, which, by common consent, had been excluded from civilized governments and the family of nations and doomed to slavery. They spoke and acted according to the then established doctrines and principles and in the ordinary language of the day, and no one misunderstood them. The unhappy black race were separated from the white by indelible marks, and laws long before established, and were never thought of or spoken of except as property and when the claims of the owner or the profit of the trader were supposed to need protection.

This state of public opinion had undergone no change when the Constitution was adopted, as is equally evident from its provisions and language.

The brief Preamble sets forth by whom it was formed, for what purposes, and for whose benefit and protection. It declares that it is formed by the *people* of the United States; that is to say, by those who were members of the different political communities in the several states; and its great object is declared to be to secure the blessings of liberty to themselves and their posterity. It speaks in general terms of the *people* of the United States and of *citizens* of the several states when it is providing for the exercise of the powers granted or the privileges secured to the citizen. It does not define what description of persons are intended to be included under these terms, or who shall be regarded as a citizen and one of the people. It uses them as terms so well understood that no further description or definition was necessary.

But there are two clauses in the Constitution which point directly and specifically to the Negro race as a separate class of persons and show clearly that they were not regarded as a portion of the people or citizens of the government then formed.

One of these clauses reserves to each of the thirteen states the right to import slaves until the year 1808, if it thinks proper. And the importation which it thus sanctions was unquestionably of persons of the race of which we are speaking, as the traffic in slaves in the United States had always been confined to them. And by the other provision the states pledge themselves to each other to maintain the right of property of the master by delivering up to him any slave who may have escaped from his service and be found within their respective territories.

By the first above mentioned clause, therefore, the right to purchase and hold this property is directly sanctioned and authorized for twenty years by the people who framed the Constitution. And by the second, they pledge themselves to maintain and uphold the right of the master in the manner specified, as long as the government they then formed should endure. And these two provisions show, conclusively, that neither the description of persons therein referred to nor their descendants were embraced in any of the other provisions of the Constitution; for certainly these two clauses

were not intended to confer on them or their posterity the blessings of liberty or any of the personal rights so carefully provided for the citizen. . . .

Undoubtedly, a person may be a citizen, that is, a member of the community who form the sovereignty, although he exercises no share of the political power and is incapacitated from holding particular offices. Women and minors, who form a part of the political family, cannot vote; and when a property qualification is required to vote or hold a particular office, those who have not the necessary qualification cannot vote or hold the office, yet they are citizens.

So, too, a person may be entitled to vote by the law of the state who is not a citizen even of the state itself. And in some of the states of the Union foreigners not naturalized are allowed to vote. And the state may give the right to free Negroes and mulattoes, but that does not make them citizens of the state, and still less of the United States. And the provision in the Constitution giving privileges and immunities in other states does not apply to them.

Neither does it apply to a person who, being the citizen of a state, migrates to another state; for then he becomes subject to the laws of the state in which he lives and he is no longer a citizen of the state from which he removed. And the state in which he resides may then, unquestionably, determine his *status* or condition and place him among the class of persons who are not recognized as citizens but belong to an inferior and subject race; and may deny him the privileges and immunities enjoyed by its citizens.

But so far as mere rights of person are concerned, the provision in question is confined to citizens of a state who are temporarily in another state without taking up their residence there. It gives them no political rights in the state as to voting or holding office, or in any other respect; for a citizen of one state has no right to participate

Roger B. Taney, chief justice of the Supreme Court which decided against Dred Scott

in the government of another. But if he ranks as a citizen in the state to which he belongs, within the meaning of the Constitution of the United States, then, whenever he goes into another state, the Constitution clothes him, as to the rights of person, with all the privileges and immunities which belong to citizens of the state.

And if persons of the African race are citizens of a state, and of the United States, they would be entitled to all of these privileges and immunities in every state, and the state could not restrict them; for they would hold these privileges and immunities under the paramount authority of the federal government, and its courts would be bound to maintain and enforce them, the Constitution and laws of the state to the contrary notwithstanding. And if the states could limit or restrict them, or place the party in an inferior grade, this clause of the Constitution would be unmeaning and could have no operation; and would give no rights to the citizen when in another state. He would have none but what the state itself chose to allow him.

This is evidently not the construction or meaning of the clause in question. It guarantees rights to the citizen, and the state cannot withhold them. And these rights are of a character and would lead to consequences which make it absolutely certain that the African race were not included under the name of citizens of a state and were not in the contemplation of the framers of the Constitution when these privileges and immunities were provided for the protection of the citizen in other states. . . .

No one, we presume, supposes that any change in public opinion or feeling in relation to this unfortunate race, in the civilized nations of Europe or in this country, should induce the Court to give to the words of the Constitution a more liberal construction in their favor than they were intended to bear when the instrument was framed and adopted. Such an argument would be altogether inadmissible in any tribunal called on to interpret it. If any of its provisions are deemed unjust, there is a mode prescribed in the instrument itself by which it may be amended; but, while it remains unaltered, it must be construed now as it was understood at the time of its adoption.

It is not only the same in words but the same in meaning and delegates, the same powers to the government and reserves, and secures the same rights and privileges to the citizen; and, as long as it continues to exist in its present form, it speaks not only in the same words but with the same meaning and intent with which it spoke when it came from the hands of its framers and was voted on and adopted by the people of the United States. Any other rule of construction would abrogate the judicial character of this Court and make it the mere reflex of the popular opinion or passion of the day. This Court was not created by the Constitution for such purposes. Higher and graver trusts have been confided to it and it must not falter in the path of duty.

What the construction was at that time,

we think, can hardly admit of doubt. We have the language of the Declaration of Independence and of the Articles of Confederation, in addition to the plain words of the Constitution itself; we have the legislation of the different states before, about the time, and since the Constitution was adopted, we have the legislation of Congress, from the time of its adoption to a recent period; and we have the constant and uniform action of the Executive Department, all concurring together and leading to the same result. And, if anything in relation to the construction of the Constitution can be regarded as settled, it is that which we now give to the word "citizen" and the word "people."

And upon a full and careful consideration of the subject, the Court is of opinion that, upon the facts stated in the plea in abatement, Dred Scott was not a citizen of Missouri within the meaning of the Constitution of the United States and not entitled as such to sue in its courts, and, consequently, that the Circuit Court had no jurisdiction of the case and that the judgment on the plea in abatement is erroneous. . . .

The case before us still more strongly imposes upon this Court the duty of examining whether the court below has not committed an error in taking jurisdiction and giving a judgment for costs in favor of the defendant; for, in *Capron* v. *Van Noorden*, the judgment was reversed because it did *not appear* that the parties were citizens of different states. They might or might not be. But in this case it *does appear* that the plaintiff was born a slave; and if the facts upon which he relies have not made him free, then it appears affirmatively on the record that he is not a citizen, and consequently his suit against Sandford was not a suit between citizens of different states, and the court had no authority to pass any judgment between the parties. The suit ought, in this view of it, to have been dismissed by the Circuit Court, and its judg-

ment in favor of Sandford is erroneous and must be reversed.

It is true that the result either way, by dismissal or by a judgment for the defendant, makes very little, if any, difference in a pecuniary or personal point of view to either party. But the fact that the result would be very nearly the same to the parties in either form of judgment would not justify this Court in sanctioning an error in the judgment which is patent on the record, and which, if sanctioned, might be drawn into precedent and lead to serious mischief and injustice in some future suit.

We proceed . . . to inquire whether the facts relied on by the plaintiff entitled him to his freedom. . . .

In considering this part of the controversy, two questions arise: (1) Was he, together with his family, free in Missouri by reason of the stay in the territory of the United States hereinbefore mentioned? and (2) If they were not, is Scott himself free by reason of his removal to Rock Island, in the state of Illinois, as stated in the above admissions?

We proceed to examine the first question. The act of Congress upon which the plaintiff relies declares that slavery and involuntary servitude, except as a punishment for crime, shall be forever prohibited in all that part of the territory ceded by France, under the name of Louisiana, which lies north of 36°30′ north latitude and not included within the limits of Missouri. And the difficulty which meets us at the threshold of this part of the inquiry is whether Congress was authorized to pass this law under any of the powers granted to it by the Constitution; for, if the authority is not given by that instrument, it is the duty of this Court to declare it void and inoperative and incapable of conferring freedom upon anyone who is held as a slave under the laws of any one of the states.

The counsel for the plaintiff has laid much stress upon that article in the Constitution which confers on Congress the power "to dispose of and make all needful rules and regulations respecting the territory or other property belonging to the United States"; but, in the judgment of the Court, that provision has no bearing on the present controversy, and the power there given, whatever it may be, is confined, and was intended to be confined, to the territory which at that time belonged to, or was claimed by, the United States and was within their boundaries as settled by the treaty with Great Britain, and can have no influence upon a territory afterward acquired from a foreign government. It was a special provision for a known and particular territory, and to meet a present emergency, and nothing more. . . .

This brings us to examine by what provision of the Constitution the present federal government, under its delegated and restricted powers, is authorized to acquire territory outside of the original limits of the United States, and what powers it may exercise therein over the person or property of a citizen of the United States while it remains a territory and until it shall be admitted as one of the states of the Union.

There is certainly no power given by the Constitution to the federal government to establish or maintain colonies bordering on the United States or at a distance, to be ruled and governed at its own pleasure; nor to enlarge its territorial limits in any way, except by the admission of new states. That power is plainly given; and if a new state is admitted, it needs no further legislation by Congress, because the Constitution itself defines the relative rights and powers and duties of the state, and the citizens of the state, and the federal government. But no power is given to acquire a territory to be held and governed permanently in that character.

And indeed the power exercised by Congress to acquire territory and establish a government there, according to its own un-

limited discretion, was viewed with great jealousy by the leading statesmen of the day. And in *The Federalist* (No. 38), written by Mr. Madison, he speaks of the acquisition of the Northwestern Territory by the confederated states, by the cession from Virginia, and the establishment of a government there, as an exercise of power not warranted by the Articles of Confederation and dangerous to the liberties of the people. And he urges the adoption of the Constitution as a security and safeguard against such an exercise of power.

We do not mean, however, to question the power of Congress in this respect. The power to expand the territory of the United States by the admission of new states is plainly given; and in the construction of this power by all the departments of the government, it has been held to authorize the acquisition of territory, not fit for admission at the time but to be admitted as soon as its population and situation would entitle it to admission. It is acquired to become a state and not to be held as a colony and governed by Congress with absolute authority; and, as the propriety of admitting a new state is committed to the sound discretion of Congress, the power to acquire territory for that purpose, to be held by the United States until it is in a suitable condition to become a state upon an equal footing with the other states, must rest upon the same discretion.

It is a question for the political department of the government and not the judicial; and whatever the political department of the government shall recognize as within the limits of the United States, the judicial department is also bound to recognize and to administer in it the laws of the United States, so far as they apply, and to maintain in the territory the authority and rights of the government, and also the personal rights and rights of property of individual citizens as secured by the Constitution. All we mean to say on this point is that, as there is no express regulation in the Constitution defining the power which the general government may exercise over the person or property of a citizen in a territory thus acquired, the Court must necessarily look to the provisions and principles of the Constitution and its distribution of powers for the rules and principles by which its decision must be governed.

Taking this rule to guide us, it may be safely assumed that citizens of the United States who migrate to a territory belonging to the people of the United States cannot be ruled as mere colonists, dependent upon the will of the general government, and to be governed by any laws it may think proper to impose. The principle upon which our governments rest, and upon which alone they continue to exist, is the union of states, sovereign and independent within their own limits in their internal and domestic concerns, and bound together as one people by a general government, possessing certain enumerated and restricted powers, delegated to it by the people of the several states, and exercising supreme authority within the scope of the powers granted to it, throughout the dominion of the United States.

A power, therefore, in the general government to obtain and hold colonies and dependent territories over which they might legislate, without restriction, would be inconsistent with its own existence in its present form. Whatever it acquires, it acquires for the benefit of the people of the several states who created it. It is their trustee acting for them and charged with the duty of promoting the interests of the whole people of the Union in the exercise of the powers specifically granted. . . .

But the power of Congress over the person or property of a citizen can never be a mere discretionary power under our Constitution and form of government. The powers of the government and the rights and privileges of the citizen are regulated and plainly defined by the Constitution itself.

And, when the territory becomes a part of the United States, the federal government enters into possession in the character impressed upon it by those who created it. It enters upon it with its powers over the citizen strictly defined and limited by the Constitution, from which it derives its own existence and by virtue of which alone it continues to exist and act as a government and sovereignty. It has no power of any kind beyond it; and it cannot, when it enters a territory of the United States, put off its character and assume discretionary or despotic powers which the Constitution has denied to it. It cannot create for itself a new character separated from the citizens of the United States and the duties it owes them under the provisions of the Constitution. The territory being a part of the United States, the government and the citizen both enter it under the authority of the Constitution, with their respective rights defined and marked out; and the federal government can exercise no power over his person or property beyond what that instrument confers, nor lawfully deny any right which it has reserved.

A reference to a few of the provisions of the Constitution will illustrate this proposition.

For example, no one, we presume, will contend that Congress can make any law in a territory respecting the establishment of religion, or the free exercise thereof, or abridging the freedom of speech or of the press, or the right of the people of the territory peaceably to assemble, and to petition the government for the redress of grievances. Nor can Congress deny to the people the right to keep and bear arms, nor the right to trial by jury, nor compel anyone to be a witness against himself in a criminal proceeding.

These powers, and others, in relation to rights of person, which it is not necessary here to enumerate, are, in express and positive terms, denied to the general government; and the rights of private property have been guarded with equal care. Thus the rights of property are united with the rights of person and placed on the same ground by the Fifth Amendment to the Constitution, which provides that no person shall be deprived of life, liberty, and property without due process of law. And an act of Congress which deprives a citizen of the United States of his liberty or property, merely because he came himself or brought his property into a particular territory of the United States, and who had committed no offense against the laws, could hardly be dignified with the name of due process of law.

So, too, it will hardly be contended that Congress could by law quarter a soldier in a house in a territory without the consent of the owner, in time of peace, nor in time of war, but in a manner prescribed by law. Nor could they by law forfeit the property of a citizen in a territory who was convicted of treason for a longer period than the life of the person convicted; nor take private property for public use without just compensation.

The powers over person and property of which we speak are not only not granted to Congress but are in express terms denied, and they are forbidden to exercise them. And this prohibition is not confined to the states, but the words are general and extend to the whole territory over which the Constitution gives it power to legislate, including those portions of it remaining under territorial government as well as that covered by states. It is a total absence of power everywhere within the dominion of the United States and places the citizens of a territory, so far as these rights are concerned, on the same footing with citizens of the states and guards them as firmly and plainly against any inroads which the general government might attempt under the plea of implied or incidental powers. And if Congress itself cannot do this — if it is be-

yond the powers conferred on the federal government — it will be admitted, we presume, that it could not authorize a territorial government to exercise them. It could confer no power on any local government established by its authority to violate the provisions of the Constitution.

It seems, however, to be supposed that there is a difference between property in a slave and other property and that different rules may be applied to it in expounding the Constitution of the United States. And the laws and usages of nations and the writings of eminent jurists upon the relation of master and slave and their mutual rights and duties, and the powers which governments may exercise over it, have been dwelt upon in the argument.

But, in considering the question before us, it must be borne in mind that there is no law of nations standing between the people of the United States and their government and interfering with their relation to each other. The powers of the government and the rights of the citizen under it are positive and practical regulations plainly written down. The people of the United States have delegated to it certain enumerated powers and forbidden it to exercise others. It has no power over the person or property of a citizen but what the citizens of the United States have granted. And no laws or usages of other nations, or reasoning of statesmen or jurists upon the relations of master and slave, can enlarge the powers of the government or take from the citizens the rights they have reserved. And if the Constitution recognizes the right of property of the master in a slave, and makes no distinction between that description of property and other property owned by a citizen, no tribunal, acting under the authority of the United States, whether it be legislative, executive, or judicial, has a right to draw such a distinction or deny to it the benefit of the provisions and guarantees which have been provided for the protection of private property against the encroachments of the government.

Now, as we have already said in an earlier part of this opinion, upon a different point, the right of property in a slave is distinctly and expressly affirmed in the Constitution. The right to traffic in it, like an ordinary article of merchandise and property, was guaranteed to the citizens of the United States, in every state that might desire it, for twenty years. And the government in express terms is pledged to protect it in all future time if the slave escapes from his owner. This is done in plain words — too plain to be misunderstood. And no word can be found in the Constitution which gives Congress a greater power over slave property or which entitles property of that kind to less protection than property of any other description. The only power conferred is the power coupled with the duty of guarding and protecting the owner in his rights.

Upon these considerations it is the opinion of the Court that the act of Congress which prohibited a citizen from holding and owning property of this kind in the territory of the United States north of the line therein mentioned is not warranted by the Constitution and is therefore void; and that neither Dred Scott himself, nor any of his family, were made free by being carried into this territory; even if they had been carried there by the owner with the intention of becoming a permanent resident.

We have so far examined the case as it stands under the Constitution of the United States and the powers thereby delegated to the federal government.

But there is another point in the case which depends on state power and state law. And it is contended, on the part of the plaintiff, that he is made free by being taken to Rock Island, in the state of Illinois, independently of his residence in the territory of the United States; and, being so made free, he was not again reduced to a state of slavery by being brought back to Missouri.

Our notice of this part of the case will be very brief, for the principle on which it depends was decided in this Court, upon much consideration, in the case of *Strader et al.* v. *Graham*. . . . In that case, the slaves had been taken from Kentucky to Ohio, with the consent of the owner, and afterward brought back to Kentucky. And this Court held that their status or condition, as free or slave, depended upon the laws of Kentucky, when they were brought back into that state, and not of Ohio; and that this Court had no jurisdiction to revise the judgment of a state court upon its own laws. This was the point directly before the Court, and the decision that this Court had not jurisdiction turned upon it, as will be seen by the report of the case.

So in this case. As Scott was a slave when taken into the state of Illinois by his owner, and was there held as such, and brought back in that character, his status, as free or slave, depended on the laws of Missouri and not of Illinois.

It has, however, been urged in the argument, that by the laws of Missouri he was free on his return, and that this case, therefore, cannot be governed by the case of *Strader et al.* v. *Graham*, where it appeared, by the laws of Kentucky, that the plaintiffs continued to be slaves on their return from Ohio. But whatever doubts or opinions may, at one time, have been entertained upon this subject, we are satisfied, upon a careful examination of all the cases decided in the state courts of Missouri referred to, that it is now firmly settled by the decisions of the highest court in the state that Scott and his family, upon their return, were not free, but were, by the laws of Missouri, the property of the defendant; and that the Circuit Court of the United States had no jurisdiction when by the laws of the state, the plaintiff was a slave and not a citizen.

87.

Negro Protest Over the Dred Scott Decision

The response by free Negroes to the Dred Scott decision was swift and angry. They objected vehemently to the Supreme Court's ruling that Negro slaves and the freed descendants of slaves could not claim citizenship or bring suit in court; that a Negro could not claim the status of a freeman by virtue of residence in a free state; and that the Missouri Compromise of 1820 was unconstitutional because Congress had no authority to exclude slavery from the territories. The following resolutions of protest delivered by Robert Purvis and Charles L. Remond to a Negro meeting at Israel Church, Philadelphia, on April 3, 1857, are typical of Negro reaction to Dred Scott v. Sandford.

Source: *Liberator*, April 10, 1857.

Resolutions by ROBERT PURVIS:

Whereas, the Supreme Court of the United States has decided in the case of Dred Scott that *people of African descent are not and cannot be citizens of the United States, and cannot sue in any of the United States courts;* and, *Whereas,* the Court, in rendering its decision, has declared that:

this unfortunate class have, with the civilized and enlightened portion of the world, for more than a century, been regarded as being of an inferior order and unfit associates for the white race, either socially or politically, having no rights which white men are bound to respect;

and, *Whereas,* this Supreme Court is the constitutionally approved tribunal to determine all such questions; therefore,

Resolved, that this atrocious decision furnishes final confirmation of the already well-known fact that, under the Constitution and government of the United States, the colored people are nothing and can be nothing but an alien, disfranchised, and degraded class.

Resolved, that to attempt, as some do, to

prove that there is no support given to slavery in the Constitution and essential structure of the American government is to argue against reason and common sense, to ignore history, and shut our eyes against palpable facts; and that while it may suit white men, who do not feel the iron heel, to please themselves with such theories, it ill becomes the man of color, whose daily experience refutes the absurdity, to indulge in any such idle fantasies.

Resolved, that to persist in supporting a government which holds and exercises the power, as distinctly set forth by a tribunal from which there is no appeal, to trample a class underfoot as an inferior and degraded race, is on the part of the colored man at once the height of folly and the depth of pusillanimity.

Resolved, that no allegiance is due from any man, or any class of men, to a government founded and administered in iniquity, and that the only duty the colored man owes to a Constitution under which he is declared to be an inferior and degraded being, having no rights which white men are bound to respect, is to denounce and repudiate it, and to do what he can by all proper means to bring it into contempt.

Resolutions by C. L. REMOND:

Resolved, that though many of our fathers and some of us have, in time past, exercised the right of American citizenship, this was when a better spirit pervaded the land, and when the patriotic services of colored men in the defense of the country were fresh in the minds of the people; but that the power to oppress us lurked all the time in the Constitution, only waiting to be developed; and that now, when it suits the slave oligarchy to assert that power, we are made to feel its grinding weight.

Resolved, that what little remains to us of political rights in individual states, we hold, as we conceive, only by sufferance; and that

when it suits the purposes of the slave power to do so, they will command their obedient, doughfaced allies at the North to take these rights away from us and leave us no more place under the state government than we have under the federal.

Resolved, that we rejoice that slaveholding despotism lays its ruthless hand, not only on the humble black man but on the proud Northern white man; and our hope is that when our white fellow slaves in these so-called free states see that they are alike subject with us to the slave oligarchy, the difference in our servitude being only in degree, they will make common cause with us, and that, throwing off the yoke and striking for impartial liberty, they will join with us in our efforts to recover the long lost boon of freedom.

88.

Ohio Resolution on the Dred Scott Decision

The Supreme Court decision in Dred Scott v. Sandford *gave the South everything it could hope for short of a wholesale endorsement of slavery, but it aroused a storm of protest in the North. Most Northerners refused to accept the Court's ruling against Negro citizenship and its denial of congressional authority over the territories, and many Northerners charged that the Court was prejudiced because five of the justices who decided with the majority were Southerners and all seven of the majority were Democrats. Despite the Court's decision, Republicans continued to demand that slavery be excluded from the territories. The following resolution, adopted by the Ohio legislature on April 17, 1857, is typical of reactions in Northern states.*

Source: *Acts of a General Nature and Local Laws and Joint Resolutions Passed by the 52nd General Assembly of the State of Ohio: at its 2nd Session,* Vol. LIV, Columbus, 1857, p. 301.

Resolved by the General Assembly of the State of Ohio:

1. That this General Assembly has observed with regret that, in the opinion lately pronounced by Chief Justice Taney in be-

half of a majority of the Supreme Court of the United States in the case of Dred Scott against J. H. Sanford, occasion has been taken to promulgate extrajudicially certain doctrines concerning slavery, not less contradictory to well-known facts of history than repugnant to the plain provisions of the Constitution and subversive to the rights of freemen and free states.

2. That in the judgment of this General Assembly, every free person born within the limits of any state of this Union is a citizen thereof, and to deny to such person the right of suing in the courts of the United States, in those cases where that right is guaranteed by the Constitution to all citizens of the United States, is a palpable and unwarrantable violation of that sacred instrument.

3. That the doctrine announced by the chief justice, in behalf of a majority of the Court, that the federal Constitution regards slaves as mere property and protects the claims of masters to slaves, to the same extent and in the same manner as the rights of owners in property, foreshadows, if it does not include the doctrine, that masters may hold slaves as property within the limits of free states during temporary visits or for purposes of transit, to the practical consequences of which doctrine no free state can submit with honor.

4. That the doctrine also announced in behalf of a majority of the Court that there exists no power in the general government to exclude slavery from the territories of the United States subverts the spirit of the Constitution, annuls the just authority of the people of the United States over their own territories, and contradicts the uniform practice of the government.

5. That the General Assembly, in behalf of the people of Ohio, hereby solemnly protest against these doctrines as destructive of personal liberty, of states' rights, of constitutional obligations, and of the Union; and, so protesting, further declares its unalterable convictions that in the Declaration of Independence the fathers of the republic intended to assert the indestructible and equal rights of all men, without any exception or reservation whatever, to life, liberty, and the pursuit of happiness; and in the Constitution by the comprehensive guaranty that no person shall be deprived of life, liberty, or property, without due process of law, designed to secure these rights against all invasion by the federal government, and to make the establishment of slavery outside of slave states a constitutional impossibility.

Resolved, that the governor be requested to transmit a copy of the foregoing resolutions to the President of the United States, to the governors of the several states respectively, and to each senator and representative of Ohio in Congress.

The pressure of public opinion is like the pressure of the atmosphere; you can't see it — but, all the same, it is sixteen pounds to the square inch.
JAMES RUSSELL LOWELL, interview with Julian Hawthorne

89.

ROBERT J. WALKER: Address to the People of Kansas

Robert J. Walker had a distinguished political career, serving the nation both in the Senate and in the Cabinet, and it is likely that he envisioned himself in the White House. As a supporter of Buchanan in the 1856 election, Walker was rewarded with the governorship of the Kansas Territory, a position, however, that he held only from May to December 1857. Although Walker was from Mississippi, his position on slavery was moderate at a time when it did not pay Democrats to be so, and to enunciate, as he did in his inaugural address of May 27, 1857, the old view that slavery had natural boundaries was to anger the South and lose administration support and thus his post as governor.

Source: John Gihon, *History of Kansas*, Philadelphia, 1857, pp. 328-348.

UPON LOOKING AT THE LOCATION of Kansas, equidistant from north to south, and from the Atlantic to the Pacific, I find, that, within reasonable boundaries, she would be the central state of the American Union. On the north lies the Nebraska Territory, soon to become a state; on the south, the great and fertile Southwestern Indian Territory, soon, I hope, to become a state also. To the boundary of Kansas run nearly all the railroads of Missouri, while westward, northward, and southward these routes, continued through Kansas, would connect her directly with Puget Sound, the mouth of the Oregon River, and San Francisco. The southern boundary of Kansas is but 500 miles from the Gulf of Mexico, and the same railroad through the great Southwestern Indian Territory and Texas would connect her with New Orleans, with Galveston, with all the roads of Arkansas, and through Texas to San Francisco and other points upon the Pacific; northward and eastward our lines would connect with the roads of Iowa, Illinois, Wisconsin, Nebraska, Minnesota, and the lakes of the North.

It is the people of Kansas who in forming their state constitution are to declare the terms on which they propose to enter the Union. Congress cannot compel the people of a territory to enter the Union as a state, or change, without their consent, the constitution framed by the people. Congress, it is true, may for constitutional reasons refuse admission, but the state alone, in forming her constitution, can prescribe the terms on which she will enter the Union. This power of the people of a territory in forming a state constitution is one of vital importance, especially in the states carved out of the public domain. Nearly all the lands of Kansas are public lands, and most of them are occupied by Indian tribes. These lands are the property of the federal government, but their right is exclusively that of a proprietor, carrying with it no political power.

Although the states cannot tax the constitutional functions of the federal government, they may assess its real estate within the limits of the state. Thus, although a state cannot tax the federal mint or custom-houses, yet it may tax the ground on which they stand, unless exempted by state authority. Such is the well-settled doctrine of the

Supreme Court of the United States. In 1838 Judge McLean, of the Supreme Court of the United States, made the following decision:

It is true the United States held the proprietary right under the act of cession, and also the right of sovereignty, until the state government was established; but the mere proprietary right, if it exist, gives no right of sovereignty. The United States may own land within a state, but political jurisdiction does not follow this ownership. Where jurisdiction is necessary, as for forts and arsenals, a cession of it is obtained from the state. Even the lands of the United States within the state are exempted from taxation by compact.

By the recent decision of the Supreme Court of the United States, so justly favorable to the rights and interest of the new states, especially those formed out of the territory acquired, like Kansas, since the adoption of the Constitution, it is clear that the ownership of the public lands of such territory is viewed by the court exclusively as a proprietary right, carrying with it no political power or right of eminent domain, and affecting in no way the exercise of any of the sovereign attributes of state authority. When Kansas becomes a state, with all the attributes of state sovereignty coextensive with her limits, among these must be the taxing power, which is an inherent element of state authority. I do not dispute the title of the government to the public lands of Kansas, but I do say that this right is that of an owner only, and that, when Kansas becomes a state, the public lands are subject to taxation by state authority, like those of any individual proprietor, unless that power is relinquished by the state in the ordinance, assuming the form of a compact, by which the state is admitted into the Union.

This relinquishment of the taxing power as to the public lands, so important to the general government, and which has heretofore been exacted by Congress on their own terms from all the new states, is deeply injurious to the state, depriving her almost entirely of the principal recourse of a new state by taxation to support her government. Now that this question is conclusively settled by the Supreme Court of the United States, as a consequence of their recent decision, it is proper for the state, in making this relinquishment of the right to tax the public lands, to annex the conditions on which she consents to such exemption. This should be done in the constitution upon terms just to Kansas and to the federal government.

Should Kansas relinquish the right of taxing the public lands for equivalent, she should, in my judgment, although sustained by irresistible conclusions from the decision of the Supreme Court of the United States, and sound constitutional views of state rights, place the question in its strongest form by asking nothing more than has been granted to the other new states, including the grants for education, railroads, etc. She will thus give the highest proof that she is not governed by sordid views, and that she means to exact nothing from Congress that is unjust or unusual.

I cannot too earnestly impress upon you the necessity of removing the slavery agitation from the halls of Congress and presidential conflicts. It is conceded that Congress has no power to interfere with slavery in the states where it exists; and if it can now be established, as is clearly the doctrine of the Constitution, that Congress has no authority to interfere with the people of a territory on this subject, in forming a state constitution, the question must be removed from congressional and presidential elections.

This is the principle affirmed by Congress in the act organizing this territory, ratified by the people of the United States in the recent election, and maintained by the late decision of the Supreme Court of the United States. If this principle can be carried into successful operation in Kansas — that her people shall determine what shall be her social institutions — the slavery question must be withdrawn from the halls of Congress, and from our presidential conflicts, and the safety of the Union be placed beyond all peril. Whereas, if the principle should be defeated here, the slavery agitation must be renewed in all elections throughout the country, with increasing bitterness, until it shall eventually overthrow the government.

It is this agitation which, to European powers, presents the only hope of subverting our free institutions, and, as a consequence, destroying the principle of self-government throughout the world. It is this hope that has already inflicted deep injury upon our country, exciting monarchical or despotic interference with our domestic as well as foreign affairs, and inducing their interposition, not only in our elections but in diplomatic intercourse, to arrest our progress, to limit our influence and power, depriving us of great advantages in peaceful territorial expansion, as well as in trade with the nations of the world.

Indeed, when I reflect upon the hostile position of the European press during the recent election, and their exulting predictions of the dissolution of our Union as a consequence of the triumph of a sectional candidate, I cannot doubt that the peaceful and permanent establishment of these principles, now being subjected to their final test in Kansas, will terminate European opposition to all those measures which must so much increase our commerce, furnish new markets for our products and fabrics, and, by conservative, peaceful progress, carry our flag and the empire of our Constitution into new and adjacent regions indispensable as a part of the Union to our welfare and security, adding coffee, sugar, and other articles to our staple exports while greatly reducing their price to the consumer.

Nor is it only in our foreign intercourse that peace will be preserved and our prosperity advanced by the accepted fact of the permanence of our government, based upon the peaceful settlement of this question in Kansas, but at home the same sentiment will awaken renewed confidence in the stability of our institutions, give a new impulse to all our industry, and carry us onward in a career of progress and prosperity exceeding even our most sanguine expectations; a new movement of European capital will flow in upon us for permanent investment, and a new exodus of the European masses, aided by the preemption principle, carry westward the advancing column of American states in one unbroken phalanx to the Pacific.

And let me ask you, what possible good has been accomplished by agitating in Congress and in presidential conflicts the slavery question? Has it emancipated a single slave, or improved their condition? Has it made a single state free where slavery otherwise would have existed? Has it accelerated the disappearance of slavery from the more northern of the slaveholding states, or accomplished any practical good whatever? No, my fellow citizens, nothing but unmitigated evil has already ensued, with disasters still more fearful impending for the future, as a consequence of this agitation.

There is a law more powerful than the legislation of man — more potent than passion or prejudice — that must ultimately determine the location of slavery in this country; it is the isothermal line; it is the law of the thermometer, of latitude or altitude, regulating climate, labor, and productions, and, as a consequence, profit and loss. Thus, even upon the mountain heights of the tropics, slavery can no more exist than in northern latitudes, because it is unprofitable, being unsuited to the constitution of that sable race transplanted here from the equatorial heats of Africa.

Why is it that in the Union slavery recedes from the North and progresses South? It is this same great climatic law now operating for or against slavery in Kansas. If, on the elevated plains of Kansas, stretching to the base of our American Alps, the Rocky Mountains, and including their eastern crest crowned with perpetual snow, from which sweep over her open prairies those chilling blasts, reducing the average range of the thermometer here to a temperature nearly as low as that of New England, should render slavery unprofitable here, because unsuited to the tropical constitution of the Negro race, the law above referred to must ultimately determine that question here, and can no more be controlled by the legislation of man than any other moral or physical law of the Almighty.

Especially must this law operate with irresistible force in this country, where the number of slaves is limited, and cannot be increased by importation, where many millions of acres of sugar and cotton lands are still uncultivated, and, from the ever augmenting demand exceeding the supply, the price of those great staples has nearly doubled, demanding vastly more slave labor for their production.

If, from the operation of these causes, slavery should not exist here, I trust it by no means follows that Kansas should become a state controlled by the treason and fanaticism of abolition. She has, in any event, certain constitutional duties to perform to her sister states, and especially to her immediate neighbor, the slaveholding state of Missouri. Through that great state, by rivers and railroads, must flow, to a great extent, our trade and intercourse, our imports and exports. Our entire eastern front is upon her border; from Missouri come a great number of her citizens; even the farms of the two states are cut up by the line of state boundary, part in Kansas, part in Missouri; her citizens meet us in daily intercourse; and that Kansas should become hostile to Missouri, an asylum for her fugitive slaves, or a propagandist of abolition treason, would be alike inexpedient and unjust, and fatal to the continuance of the American Union. In any event, then, I trust that the constitution of Kansas will contain such clauses as will forever secure to the state of Missouri the faithful performance of all constitutional guarantees, not only by federal but by state authority, and the supremacy within our limits of the authority of the Supreme Court of the United States on all constitutional questions be firmly established. . . .

Is it not infinitely better that slavery should be abolished or established in Kansas, rather than that we should become slaves and not permitted to govern ourselves? Is the absence or existence of slavery in Kansas paramount to the great questions of state sovereignty, of self-government, and of the Union? Is the sable African alone entitled to your sympathy and consideration, even if he were happier as a freeman than as a slave, either here or in Santo Domingo, or the British West Indies or Spanish America, where the emancipated slave has receded to barbarism, and approaches the lowest point in the descending scale of moral, physical, and intellectual degradation? Have our white brethren of the great American and European race no claims upon our attention? Have they no rights or interests entitled to regard and protection? Shall the destiny of the African in Kansas exclude all considerations connected with our own happiness and prosperity? And is it for the handful of that race now in Kansas, or that may be hereafter introduced, that we should subvert the Union and the great principles of self-government and state sovereignty, and imbrue our hands in the blood of our countrymen! Important as this African question may be in Kansas, and which it is your solemn right to determine, it sinks into insignificance compared with the perpetuity of the Union and the final successful establishment of the principles of state sovereignty and free government.

If patriotism, if devotion to the Constitution and love of the Union, should not induce the minority to yield to the majority on this question, let them reflect that in no event can the minority successfully determine this question permanently, and that in no contingency will Congress admit Kansas as a slave or free state unless a majority of the people of Kansas shall first have fairly and freely decided this question for themselves by a direct vote on the adoption of the constitution, excluding all fraud or violence. The minority, in resisting the will of the majority, may involve Kansas again in civil war; they may bring upon her reproach and obloquy, and destroy her progress and prosperity; they may keep her for years out of the Union, and, in the whirlwind of agitation, sweep away the government itself; but Kansas never can be brought into the Union with or without slavery except by a previous solemn decision, fully, freely, and fairly made by a majority of her people in voting for or against the adoption of her state constitution.

Why, then, should this just, peaceful, and constitutional mode of settlement meet with opposition from any quarter? Is Kansas willing to destroy her own hopes of prosperity merely that she may afford political capital to any party and perpetuate the agitation of slavery throughout the Union? Is she to become a mere theme for agitators in other states, the theater on which they shall perform the bloody drama of treason and disunion? Does she want to see the solemn acts of Congress, the decision of the people of the Union in the recent election, the legislative, executive, and judicial authorities of the country all overthrown, and revolution and civil war inaugurated throughout her limits? Does she want to be "bleeding Kansas" for the benefit of political agitators, within or out of her limits; or does she prefer the peaceful and quiet arbitrament of this question for herself? What benefit will the great body of the people of Kansas derive from these agitations? They may, for a brief period, give consequence and power to political leaders and agitators, but it is at the expense of the happiness and welfare of the great body of the people of this territory.

Those who oppose slavery in Kansas do not base their opposition upon any philanthropic principles or any sympathy for the African race; for, in their so-called constitution, framed at Topeka, they deem that entire race so inferior and degraded as to exclude them all forever from Kansas, whether they be bond or free, thus depriving them of all rights here, and denying even that they can be citizens of the United States; for, if they are citizens, they could not constitutionally be exiled or excluded from Kansas. Yet such a clause, inserted in the Topeka constitution, was submitted by that convention for the vote of the people, and ratified here by an overwhelming majority of the antislavery party. This party here, therefore, has, in the most positive manner, affirmed the constitutionality of that portion of the recent decision of the Supreme Court of the United States declaring that Africans are not citizens of the United States.

This is the more important, inasmuch as this Topeka constitution was ratified, with this clause inserted, by the entire Republican Party in Congress, thus distinctly affirming the recent decision of the Supreme Court of the Union that Africans are not citizens of the United States; for, if citizens, they may be elected to all offices, state and national, including the presidency itself; they must be placed upon a basis of perfect equality with the whites, serve with them in the militia, on the bench, the legislature, the jury box, vote in all elections, meet us in social intercourse, and intermarry freely with the whites. This doctrine of the perfect equality of the white with the black, in all respects whatsoever, social and political, clearly follows from the position that Africans are citizens of the United States.

Nor is the Supreme Court of the Union less clearly vindicated by the position now assumed here by the published creed of this party, that the people of Kansas, in forming their state constitution (and not Congress), must decide this question of slavery for themselves. Having thus sustained the Court on both the controverted points decided by that tribunal, it is hoped they will not approve the anarchical and revolutionary proceedings in other states, expunging the Supreme Court from our system by depriving it of the great power for which it was created, of expounding the Constitution. If that be done, we have in fact no unity of government or fundamental law, but just as many ever varying constitutions as passion, prejudice, and local interests may from time to time prescribe in the thirty-one states of the Union.

I have endeavored heretofore faintly to foreshadow the wonderful prosperity which would follow at once in Kansas the peaceful and final settlement of this question. But, if it should be in the power of agitators to prevent such a result, nothing but ruin will pervade our territory. Confidence will expire, and law and order will be subverted. Anarchy and civil war will be reinaugurated among us. All property will greatly depreciate in value. Even the best farms will become almost worthless. Our towns and cities will sink into decay. Emigration into our territory will cease. A mournful train of returning settlers, with ruined hopes and blasted fortunes, will leave our borders. All who have purchased property at present prices will be sacrificed, and Kansas will be marked by universal ruin and desolation.

Nor will the mischief be arrested here. It will extend into every other state. Despots will exult over the failure here of the great principles of self-government and the approaching downfall of our confederacy. The pillars of the Union will rock upon their base, and we may close the next presidential conflict amid the scattered fragments of the Constitution of our once happy and united people. The banner of the stars and stripes, the emblem of our country's glory, will be rent by contending factions. We shall no longer have a country. The friends of human liberty in other realms will shrink despairing from the conflict. Despotic power

will resume its sway throughout the world, and man will have tried in vain the last experiment of self-government. The architects of our country's ruin, the assassins of her peace and prosperity, will share the same common ruin of all our race. They will meet, while living, the bitter curses of a ruined people, while history will record as their only epitaph: *These were the destroyers of the American Union, of the liberties of their country and of the world.*

But I do not despair of the republic. My hope is in the patriotism and intelligence of the people; in their love of country, of liberty, and of the Union. Especially is my confidence unbounded in the hardy pioneers and settlers of the West. It was such settlers of a new state, devoted to the Constitution and the Union, whom I long represented in the Senate of the United States, and whose rights and interests it was my pride and pleasure there, as well as in the Treasury Department, to protect and advocate. It was men like these whose rifles drove back the invader from the plains of Orleans and planted the stars and stripes upon the victorious field of Mexico. These are the men whom gold cannot corrupt nor foes intimidate. From their towns and villages, from their farms and cottages, spread over the beautiful prairies of Kansas, they will come forward now in defense of the Constitution and the Union.

These are the glorious legacy they received from our fathers, and they will transmit to their children the priceless heritage. Before the peaceful power of their suffrage this dangerous sectional agitation will disappear, and peace and prosperity once more reign throughout our borders. In the hearts of this noble band of patriotic settlers the love of their country and of the Union is inextinguishable. . . .

My reliance also is unshaken upon the same overruling Providence which has carried us triumphantly through so many perils and conflicts, which has lifted us to a height of power and prosperity unexampled in history, and, if we shall maintain the Constitution and the Union, points us to a future more glorious and sublime than mind can conceive or pen describe. The march of our country's destiny, like that of His first chosen people, is marked by the footprints of the steps of God. The Constitution and the Union are "the cloud by day, and the pillar of fire by night" which will carry us safely under His guidance through the wilderness and bitter waters into the promised and overextending fields of our country's glory. It is His hand which beckons us onward in the pathway of peaceful progress and expansion, of power and renown, until our continent, in the distant future, shall be covered by the folds of the American banner, and, instructed by our example, all the nations of the world, through many trials and sacrifices, shall establish the great principles of our constitutional confederacy of free and sovereign states.

90.

Abraham Lincoln: The Dred Scott Decision and the Declaration of Independence

The Dred Scott decision of March 1857 dealt a severe blow to Republican efforts to prevent the expansion of slavery. As the leading Republican in Illinois, Abraham Lincoln felt bound to oppose Democrats like Stephen A. Douglas, who upheld the Court's decision. Lincoln took his stand in the following speech delivered at Springfield, Illinois, June 26, 1857, a full year before his campaign against Douglas for the U.S. Senate.

Source: Nicolay-Hay, II, pp. 315-339.

AND NOW AS TO THE DRED SCOTT DECISION. That decision declares two propositions: first, that a Negro cannot sue in the United States courts; and, second, that Congress cannot prohibit slavery in the territories. It was made by a divided Court, dividing differently on the different points. Judge Douglas does not discuss the merits of the decision, and in that respect I shall follow his example, believing I could no more improve on McLean and Curtis than he could on Taney.

He denounces all who question the correctness of that decision as offering violent resistance to it. But who resists it? Who has, in spite of the decision, declared Dred Scott free and resisted the authority of his master over him?

Judicial decisions have two uses: first, to absolutely determine the case decided; and, second, to indicate to the public how other similar cases will be decided when they arise. For the latter use, they are called "precedents" and "authorities."

We believe as much as Judge Douglas (perhaps more) in obedience to, and respect for, the judicial department of government. We think its decisions on constitutional questions, when fully settled, should control not only the particular cases decided but the general policy of the country, subject to be disturbed only by amendments of the Constitution as provided in that instrument itself. More than this would be revolution. But we think the Dred Scott decision is erroneous. We know the Court that made it has often overruled its own decisions, and we shall do what we can to have it to overrule this. We offer no resistance to it.

Judicial decisions are of greater or less authority as precedents according to circumstances. That this should be so accords both with common sense and the customary understanding of the legal profession.

If this important decision had been made by the unanimous concurrence of the judges, and without any apparent partisan bias, and in accordance with legal public expectation, and with the steady practice of the departments throughout our history, and had been in no part based on assumed historical facts which are not really true; or, if wanting in some of these, it has been before the Court more than once, and had there been affirmed and reaffirmed through a course of years, it then might be, perhaps would be, factious, nay, even revolutionary, not to acquiesce in it as a precedent.

But when, as is true, we find it wanting in all these claims to the public confidence, it is not resistance, it is not factious, it is not even disrespectful, to treat it as not having yet quite established a settled doctrine for the country. But Judge Douglas considers this view awful. Hear him:

> The courts are the tribunals prescribed by the Constitution and created by the authority of the people to determine, expound, and enforce the law. Hence, whoever resists the final decision of the highest judicial tribunal aims a deadly blow at our whole republican system of government — a blow which, if successful, would place all our rights and liberties at the mercy of passion, anarchy, and violence. I repeat, therefore, that if resistance to the decisions of the Supreme Court of the United States, in a matter like the points decided in the Dred Scott case, clearly within their jurisdiction as defined by the Constitution, shall be forced upon the country as a political issue, it will become a distinct and naked issue between the friends and enemies of the Constitution — the friends and the enemies of the supremacy of the laws.

Why, this same Supreme Court once decided a national bank to be constitutional; but General Jackson, as President of the United States, disregarded the decision and vetoed a bill for a recharter, partly on constitutional ground, declaring that each public functionary must support the Constitution "as he understands it." But hear the general's own words. Here they are, taken from his veto message:

> It is maintained by the advocates of the bank that its constitutionality, in all its features, ought to be considered as settled by precedent and by the decision of the Supreme Court. To this conclusion I cannot assent. Mere precedent is a dangerous source of authority and should not be regarded as deciding questions of constitutional power, except where the acquiescence of the people and the states can be considered as well settled. So far from this being the case on this subject, an argument against the bank might be based on precedent. One Congress, in 1791, decided in favor of a bank; another, in 1811, decided against it. One Congress, in 1815, decided against a bank; another, in 1816, decided in its favor. Prior to the present Congress, therefore, the precedents drawn from that source were equal. If we resort to the states, the expressions of legislative, judicial, and executive opinions against the bank have been probably to those in its favor as four to one. There is nothing in precedent, therefore, which, if its authority were admitted, ought to weigh in favor of the act before me.

I drop the quotations merely to remark that all there ever was in the way of precedent up to the Dred Scott decision, on the points therein decided, had been against that decision. But hear General Jackson further:

> If the opinion of the Supreme Court covered the whole ground of this act, it ought not to control the coordinate authorities of this government. The Congress, the Executive, and the Court must, each for itself, be guided by its own opinion of the Constitution. Each public officer who takes an oath to support the

Constitution swears that he will support it as he understands it and not as it is understood by others.

Again and again have I heard Judge Douglas denounce that bank decision and applaud General Jackson for disregarding it. It would be interesting for him to look over his recent speech and see how exactly his fierce philippics against us for resisting Supreme Court decisions fall upon his own head. It will call to mind a long and fierce political war in this country, upon an issue which, in his own language, and, of course, in his own changeless estimation, was "a distinct issue between the friends and the enemies of the Constitution," and in which war he fought in the ranks of the enemies of the Constitution.

I have said, in substance, that the Dred Scott decision was in part based on assumed historical facts which were not really true, and I ought not to leave the subject without giving some reasons for saying this; I therefore give an instance or two which I think fully sustain me. Chief Justice Taney, in delivering the opinion of the majority of the Court, insists at great length that Negroes were no part of the people who made, or for whom was made, the Declaration of Independence or the Constitution of the United States.

On the contrary, Judge Curtis, in his dissenting opinion, shows that in five of the then thirteen states — to wit, New Hampshire, Massachusetts, New York, New Jersey, and North Carolina — free Negroes were voters and in proportion to their numbers had the same part in making the Constitution that the white people had. He shows this with so much particularity as to leave no doubt of its truth; and as a sort of conclusion on that point holds the following language:

> The Constitution was ordained and established by the people of the United States through the action, in each state, of those persons who were qualified by its laws to act thereon in behalf of them-

Library of Congress

Lincoln, ambrotype by Samuel Alschuler, 1858

selves and all other citizens of the state. In some of the states, as we have seen, colored persons were among those qualified by law to act on the subject. These colored persons were not only included in the body of "the people of the United States" by whom the Constitution was ordained and established; but in at least five of the states they had the power to act, and doubtless did act, by their suffrages, upon the question of its adoption.

Again, Chief Justice Taney says:

> It is difficult at this day to realize the state of public opinion in relation to that unfortunate race which prevailed in the civilized and enlightened portions of the world at the time of the Declaration of Independence and when the Constitution of the United States was framed and adopted.

And, again, after quoting from the Declaration, he says:

> The general words above quoted would seem to embrace the whole human family, and if they were used in a similar instrument at this day would be so understood.

In these the Chief Justice does not directly assert but plainly assumes as a fact that the public estimate of the black man is more favorable now than it was in the days of the Revolution. This assumption is a mistake. In some trifling particulars the condition of that race has been ameliorated; but, as a whole, in this country, the change between then and now is decidedly the other way; and their ultimate destiny has never appeared so hopeless as in the last three or four years. In two of the five states — New Jersey and North Carolina — that then gave the free Negro the right of voting, the right has since been taken away, and in a third — New York — it has been greatly abridged; while it has not been extended, so far as I know, to a single additional state, though the number of the states has more than doubled.

In those days, as I understand, masters could, at their own pleasure, emancipate their slaves; but, since then, such legal restraints have been made upon emancipation as to amount almost to prohibition. In those days, legislatures held the unquestioned power to abolish slavery in their respective states, but now it is becoming quite fashionable for state constitutions to withhold that power from the legislatures. In those days, by common consent, the spread of the black man's bondage to the new countries was prohibited, but now Congress decides that it will not continue the prohibition, and the Supreme Court decides that it could not if it would. In those days, our Declaration of Independence was held sacred by all and thought to include all; but now, to aid in making the bondage of the Negro universal and eternal, it is assailed and sneered at and construed, and hawked at and torn, till, if its framers could rise from their graves, they could not at all recognize it.

All the powers of earth seem rapidly combining against him. Mammon is after him, ambition follows, philosophy follows, and the theology of the day is fast joining the cry. They have him in his prison house; they have searched his person and left no prying instrument with him. One after another they have closed the heavy iron doors upon him; and now they have him, as it were, bolted in with a lock of a hundred keys, which can never be unlocked without the concurrence of every key — the keys in the hands of a hundred different men, and they scattered to a hundred different and distant places; and they stand musing as to what invention, in all the dominions of mind and matter, can be produced to make the impossibility of his escape more complete than it is.

It is grossly incorrect to say or assume that the public estimate of the Negro is more favorable now than it was at the origin of the government.

Three years and a half ago Judge Douglas brought forward his famous Nebraska bill. The country was at once in a blaze. He scorned all opposition and carried it through Congress. Since then he has seen himself superseded in a presidential nomination by one endorsing the general doctrine of his measure but at the same time standing clear of the odium of its untimely agitation and its gross breach of national faith; and he has seen that successful rival constitutionally elected, not by the strength of friends but by the division of adversaries, being in a popular minority of nearly 400,000 votes. He has seen his chief aids in his own state, Shields and Richardson, politically speaking, successively tried, convicted, and executed for an offense not their own, but his. And now he sees his own case standing next on the docket for trial.

There is a natural disgust in the minds of nearly all white people at the idea of an indiscriminate amalgamation of the white and black races; and Judge Douglas evidently is basing his chief hope upon the chances of his being able to appropriate the benefit of this disgust to himself. If he can, by much drumming and repeating, fasten the odium of that idea upon his adversaries, he thinks he can struggle through the storm. He therefore clings to this hope, as a drowning man to the last plank. He makes an occasion for lugging it in from the opposition of the Dred Scott decision. He finds the Republicans insisting that the Declaration of Independence includes *all* men, black as well as white, and forthwith he boldly denies that it includes Negroes at all, and proceeds to argue gravely that all who contend it does do so only because they want to vote, and eat, and sleep, and marry with Negroes! He will have it that they cannot be consistent else.

Now I protest against the counterfeit logic which concludes that, because I do not want a black woman for a slave, I must necessarily want her for a wife. I need not have her for either. I can just leave her alone. In some respects she certainly is not my equal; but in her natural right to eat the bread she earns with her own hands without asking leave of anyone else, she is my equal and the equal of all others.

Chief Justice Taney, in his opinion in the Dred Scott case, admits that the language of the Declaration is broad enough to include the whole human family, but he and Judge Douglas argue that the authors of that instrument did not intend to include Negroes by the fact that they did not at once actually place them on an equality with the whites. Now this grave argument comes to just nothing at all, by the other fact that they did not at once, or ever afterward, actually place all white people on an equality with one another. And this is the staple argument of both the chief justice and the senator for doing this obvious violence to the plain, unmistakable language of the Declaration.

I think the authors of that notable instrument intended to include *all* men, but they did not intend to declare all men equal *in all respects*. They did not mean to say all were equal in color, size, intellect, moral developments, or social capacity. They defined with tolerable distinctness in what respects they did consider all men created equal — equal with "certain inalienable rights, among which are life, liberty, and the pursuit of happiness." This they said, and this they meant. They did not mean to assert the obvious untruth that all were then actually enjoying that equality, nor yet that they were about to confer it immediately upon them. In fact, they had no power to confer such a boon. They meant simply to declare the right, so that enforcement of it might follow as fast as circumstances should permit.

They meant to set up a standard maxim for free society which should be familiar to all and revered by all; constantly looked to, constantly labored for, and even though never perfectly attained, constantly approximated, and thereby constantly spreading and deepening its influence and augmenting the happiness and value of life to all people of all colors everywhere. The assertion that "all men are created equal" was of no practical use in effecting our separation from Great Britain; and it was placed in the Declaration not for that but for future use. Its authors meant it to be — as, thank God, it is now proving itself — a stumbling block to all those who in aftertimes might seek to turn a free people back into the hateful paths of despotism. They knew the proneness of prosperity to breed tyrants, and they meant, when such should reappear in this fair land and commence their vocation, they should find left for them at least one hard nut to crack.

I have now briefly expressed my view of the meaning and object of that part of the Declaration of Independence which declares that "all men are created equal."

Now let us hear Judge Douglas' view of the same subject, as I find it in the printed report of his late speech. Here it is:

> No man can vindicate the character, motives, and conduct of the signers of the Declaration of Independence except upon the hypothesis that they referred to the white race alone, and not to the African, when they declared all men to have been created equal; that they were speaking of British subjects on this continent being equal to British subjects born and residing in Great Britain; that they were entitled to the same inalienable rights, and among them were enumerated life, liberty, and the pursuit of happiness. The Declaration was adopted for the purpose of justifying the colonists in the eyes of the civilized world in withdrawing their allegiance from the British Crown and dissolving their connection with the mother country.

My good friends, read that carefully over some leisure hour and ponder well upon it; see what a mere wreck — mangled ruin — it makes of our once glorious Declaration.

"They were speaking of British subjects on this continent being equal to British subjects born and residing in Great Britain!" Why, according to this, not only Negroes but white people outside of Great Britain and America were not spoken of in that instrument. The English, Irish, and Scotch, along with white Americans, were included, to be sure, but the French, Germans, and other white people of the world are all gone to pot along with the judge's inferior races!

I had thought the Declaration promised something better than the condition of British subjects; but no, it only meant that we should be equal to them in their own oppressed and unequal condition. According to that, it gave no promise that, having kicked off the king and lords of Great Britain, we should not at once be saddled with a king and lords of our own.

I had thought the Declaration contemplated the progressive improvement in the condition of all men everywhere; but no, it merely "was adopted for the purpose of justifying the colonists in the eyes of the civilized world in withdrawing their allegiance from the British Crown and dissolving their connection with the mother country." Why, that object having been effected some eighty years ago, the Declaration is of no practical use now: mere rubbish, old wadding left to rot on the battlefield after the victory is won.

I understand you are preparing to celebrate the "Fourth" tomorrow week. What for? The doings of that day had no reference to the present; and quite half of you are not even descendants of those who were referred to at that day. But I suppose you will celebrate and will even go as far as to read the Declaration. Suppose, after you read it once in the old-fashioned way, you read it once more with Judge Douglas' version. It will then run thus: "We hold these truths to be self-evident: that all British subjects who were on this continent eighty-one years ago were created equal to all British subjects born and then residing in Great Britain."

And now I appeal to all — to Democrats as well as others — are you really willing that the Declaration shall thus be frittered away — thus left no more, at most, than an interesting memorial of the dead past — thus shorn of its vitality and practical value and left without the germ or even the suggestion of the individual rights of man in it?

But Judge Douglas is especially horrified at the thought of the mixing of blood by the white and black races. Agreed for once; a thousand times agreed. There are white men enough to marry all the white women, and black men enough to marry all the black women; and so let them be married. On this point we fully agree with the judge, and when he shall show that his policy is better adapted to prevent amalgamation than ours, we shall drop ours and adopt his.

Let us see. In 1850 there were in the United States 405,751 mulattoes. Very few of these are the offspring of whites and free blacks; nearly all have sprung from black slaves and white masters.

A separation of the races is the only perfect preventive of amalgamation; but, as an immediate separation is impossible, the next best thing is to keep them apart where they are not already together. If white and black people never get together in Kansas, they will never mix blood in Kansas. That is at least one self-evident truth. A few free colored persons may get into the free states, in any event; but their number is too insignificant to amount to much in the way of mixing blood. In 1850 there were in the free states 56,649 mulattoes; but for the most part they were not born there; they came from the slave states, ready made up. In the same year the slave states had 348,874 mulattoes, all of home production. The proportion of free mulattoes to free blacks — the only colored classes in the free states — is much greater in the slave than in the free states. It is worthy of note, too, that among the free states those which make the colored man the nearest equal to the white have proportionably the fewest mulattoes, the least of amalgamation. In New Hampshire, the state which goes farthest toward equality between the races, there are just 184 mulattoes, while there are in Virginia — how many do you think? — 79,775, being 23,126 more than in all the free states together.

These statistics show that slavery is the greatest source of amalgamation, and next to it, not the elevation, but the degradation of the free blacks. Yet Judge Douglas dreads the slightest restraints on the spread of slavery, and the slightest human recognition of the Negro, as tending horribly to amalgamation.

The very Dred Scott case affords a strong test as to which party most favors amalgamation, the Republicans or the dear Union-saving Democracy. Dred Scott, his wife, and two daughters were all involved in the suit. We desired the Court to have held that they were citizens so far at least as to entitle them to a hearing as to whether they were free or not; and then, also, that they were in fact and in law really free. Could we have had our way, the chances of these black girls ever mixing their blood with that of white people would have been diminished at least to the extent that it could not have been without their consent. But Judge Douglas is delighted to have them decided to be slaves and not human enough to have a hearing, even if they were free, and thus left subject to the forced concubinage of their masters and liable to become the mothers of mulattoes in spite of themselves: the very state of case that produces nine-tenths of all the mulattoes — all the mixing of blood in the nation.

Of course, I state this case as an illustration only, not meaning to say or intimate that the master of Dred Scott and his family, or any more than a percentage of masters generally, are inclined to exercise this particular power which they hold over their female slaves.

I have said that the separation of the races is the only perfect preventive of amalgamation. I have no right to say all the members of the Republican Party are in favor of this, nor to say that as a party they are in favor of it. There is nothing in their platform directly on the subject. But I can say a very large proportion of its members are for it and that the chief plank in their platform — opposition to the spread of slavery — is most favorable to that separation.

Such separation, if ever effected at all, must be effected by colonization; and no political party, as such, is now doing anything directly for colonization. Party operations at present only favor or retard civilization incidentally. The enterprise is a difficult one; but "where there is a will there is a way," and what colonization needs most is a hearty will. Will springs from the two elements of moral sense and self-interest. Let us be brought to believe it is morally right, and at the same time favorable to, or at least not against, our interest to transfer the African to his native clime, and we shall find a way to do it, however great the task may be. The children of Israel, to such numbers as to include 400,000 fighting men, went out of Egyptian bondage in a body.

How differently the respective courses of the Democratic and Republican parties incidentally bear on the question of forming a will — a public sentiment — for colonization is easy to see. The Republicans inculcate, with whatever of ability they can, that the Negro is a man, that his bondage is cruelly wrong, and that the field of his oppression ought not to be enlarged. The Democrats deny his manhood; deny, or dwarf to insignificance, the wrong of his bondage; so far as possible, crush all sympathy for him, and cultivate and excite hatred and disgust against him; compliment themselves as Union-savers for doing so; and call the indefinite outspreading of his bondage "a sacred right of self-government."

The plainest print cannot be read through a gold eagle; and it will be ever hard to find many men who will send a slave to Liberia, and pay his passage, while they can send him to a new country — Kansas, for instance — and sell him for $1,500, and the rise.

91.

Edmund Ruffin: Advantages of Independence for the Slaveholding States

Edmund Ruffin was a Virginia planter who spent the greater part of his adult life in researching and developing means of agricultural improvement. Politically, he was an advocate of states' rights and a strong defender of slavery. For many years before the Civil War, he was convinced of the merits of secession. In 1860 Ruffin published Anticipations of the Future, *which set forth his dream of an independent South built on the slave system of labor. He fired the first shot against Fort Sumter and in 1865, when the Confederacy collapsed, he took his own life. The selection below is taken from a series of five articles that appeared, under the title "Consequences of Abolition Agitation," during the last seven months of 1857.*

Source: *De Bow's Review,* June, September, October, November, and December 1857.

THE PRESENT CONTEST between the Northern and Southern states, in regard to Negro slavery, has been growing in violence for a long time. It was begun with the iniquitous aggression of attempting to exclude Missouri from the Union as a slaveholding state, and in the successful exaction of the Missouri Compromise, in relation to which, both the general enforcement and exceptional violation of its principle by the North have been exercised and varied, the more to wrong and injure the Southern states.

But it has been only since the (falsely so-called) compromise enactments of 1850 that

Abolition has been hastening toward its object with gigantic strides; and also that the South has been partially roused from its sleep of fancied security. Unfortunate it has been that this sleep had not been effectually shaken off thirty years sooner, and every means then used for defense that was abundantly possessed by the South at that time. If, when the Missouri Compromise was submitted to, the proposed restrictions had been resisted by the South at all hazards, there would have been no further trouble about slavery. And if the fanaticism (or, more truly, the unholy grasping for political power) of the North had then been so unyielding as to permit a separation of the United States, the Southern portion would now have double of their present wealth and power — and the Northern states would not have attained half of their present greatness and wealth, which have been built upon the tribute exacted from the South by legislative policy. But no separation would have been produced.

If, at the time of the Missouri Compromise, the Northern members and states had been firmly resisted, they would have drawn back, and the spirit of political Abolition would have been crushed in the bud. The sincere Abolitionists, who are actuated by what they deem moral and religious considerations, are but the simple and deluded tools of the hypocrites and knaves who are using them to further their own objects of personal ambition and political power.

Without looking even as far as twenty years into the future of the effects of the Northern crusade against Southern slavery, let us see what might have been the speedy consequences if the contingency had occurred, which was so near occurring, of an Abolitionist being elected President — he being the candidate of the Northern states only, and on the Abolition question and principle. It is true that a more conciliatory policy would probably have been adopted at first, because the victorious party would not have risked the driving their conquered opponents to desperate and revolutionary measures of resistance. But it is fair to suppose that a party so fanatical, greedy, and unscrupulous would have used every means to reach its object that could be used safely and successfully.

Let us, then, see what means, and all claimed as constitutional by the North, could be used by an Abolitionist administration of the government of the United States. If elected, it would have been supported by a majority of the people of the states and of the House of Representatives. It would not have required much time or management (by corruption or other influences) for the President to have also at his command a majority of the Senate — representing states that were already his supporters. Then, the President, with a majority of both houses of Congress, might adopt any or all of the following measures, to weaken and destroy the institution of slavery:

The first and greatest measure is already openly avowed by the Abolitionists and the majority of every Northern state as their designed policy and plan of action hereafter. This is to admit into the Union no new territories as slaveholding states. This alone, even if nothing else is done, will soon increase the nonslaveholding states to three-fourths of the whole, so that the Constitution can be changed and slavery abolished. But, in advance of the consummation of this great and effectual measure, various other auxiliary means might be used to hasten the end, as thus:

Each of the largest nonslaveholding states might be divided by act of Congress, so as to make two states of each, and so have four Abolition senators in place of two.

Every office and emolument in the gift of the federal government might be bestowed on Abolitionists only, and in all the Southern states on Northern Abolitionists, until corruption and fear, or despair, should induce conversions or professions and acts of Abolitionism in Southerners as offering the only road to office or gain.

The zealous and active exertions of all these many thousands of government officials and employees, down to the lowest laborers on any government work, would be counted on and secured to operate against the institution of slavery and the interests of slaveholders. This open, unassailable, and powerful influence would be added to and serve to increase a hundredfold the existing secret influence and concealed operations of the many Abolition agents, male and female, lay and clerical, who, in various ostensible business employments, have long been operating on our slaves, often under the hospitable shelter of our own roofs and as our pretended friends.

Every military and naval officer hereafter to be appointed might be an Abolitionist; and all now commissioned and not Abolitionists might be dismissed from service on other pretexts, or otherwise not entrusted with any command.

The various lands held by the federal government for forts, dockyards, arsenals, lighthouses, etc., in the South and every national ship in Southern waters would be made places of secure refuge for fugitive and even rebellious slaves, and secure positions for any other incendiary action.

The District of Columbia would be made nonslaveholding by law, and soon in sentiment. It would be openly and entirely what it is already partially (by Northern and government influence), ground, within the Southern and slaveholding territory, where the enemies of the South have the greatest facilities for their most effectual and dangerous action. Already under the protecting shield of the federal government and its administration, at a former time, the agents of the Abolitionists have been able there to effect more injury to slaveholders, and with more of impunity, than anywhere, even in the Abolition states.

The removal of slaves by sales from states where they were in excessive numbers to other states or new territories where they were most deficient would (as long threatened) be forbidden by an early law under the complete supremacy of a Northern administration. This alone would prevent the making of any new slaveholding states in the small extent of the remaining territory in which climate does not forbid slavery; while the increase of slaves in the old states, from which they would have no sufficient outlet, would render them an unprofitable burden and a dangerous nuisance to the whites. The condition of the slaves would thereby be made much worse in regard to their own happiness, and the institution of slavery would be hastened toward its doomed extinction.

Some of these measures might require that liberal mode of construing the federal Constitution, which is general at the North, and especially on this subject. But even the strict construction of that instrument might be conformed to, literally, and yet an Abolition administration, in a little more time, can as effectually extinguish the institution of slavery and the prosperity and existence of the Southern states as independent communities.

Such might have been, and, to great extent, such would have been the earlier or later effects and operation of an Abolitionist's election to presidential office. Such, and with more sure and extended operation, will be the effects of the future election, by a much stronger constituency, of a Seward or some other Northern Abolitionist, or of another Southern renegade and traitor of more ability than the one who was lately raised so nearly to the height of his ambition, only to be let fall and sink in an abyss of contempt.

Will the Southern states wait for the completion of these surely coming results, or will they take the warning so plainly to be read in their enemies' acts and avowals and save themselves from the impending ruin? The fast-growing strength of the Abolition Party and the signal success of that party in the next presidential election may cause every Southerner to regret that its candidate was not elected in the recent contest, when the South was relatively stronger for defense than it will ever be hereafter.

In such a contingency as we have just now barely escaped, the election of a President by Abolition and sectional votes, there will remain no chance for the slaveholding states to preserve their property and their political rights, unless by another declaration of independence of, and separation from a despotic party, whose wrongful and oppressive acts have already far exceeded, and threaten to exceed much more in future, all the acts of actual and prospective oppression of our mother country, against which our free and patiotic fathers revolted — preferring a struggle for freedom, with all the certain disasters and incalculable dangers of a war with a nation of tenfold their power, to submission to unjust oppression.

We, the sons of those fathers, eulogize and glorify their act of separation from the previous glorious and happy union of these colonies with their mother country. Their act of separation and disunion we deem a noble and patriotic devotion to freedom, worthy of all praise. We, the children of those fathers, in maudlin love of and devotion to a union with those who were formerly deemed our brethren but now are our most malignant and dangerous enemies, have submitted to oppression and wrong incalculably greater than ever England inflicted, or thought of inflicting on her colonies. And, still, many of the South continue to recommend patience and endurance and submission to every wrong and evil rather than the evil of disunion!

If Frémont had been elected, the consequences would have been so manifestly and highly dangerous to the rights and the safety of the slaveholding states that they would scarcely have waited to be completely shackled, and powerless for defense, before they would have seceded or separated

from the victorious and hostile states of the present Confederacy. It is proposed here to inquire what would have been the results of such separation, and especially to consider the question of the danger of war, which it is so generally believed would necessarily ensue between the separated communities, and the results of any war.

If the necessity was manifest to the people of the South, there would be no obstacle to their deliberate action and no probability of opposition by the Northern states, nor by the then remaining fragment or shadow of the federal government of the previous Confederacy. The legislatures of the offended states would call conventions, and these conventions would declare their separation and independence, and, by subsequent acts, make a new confederation. If all the fifteen slaveholding states united in this action, they would be far stronger, at home and for repelling invasion, than would be the Northern states as invaders. Even if but five or six adjacent Southern states alone seceded, no remaining power of the federal government, or of all the Northern states, could conquer or coerce the seceders.

But, contrary as is the opinion to that which generally prevails, I maintain that such act of secession would offer no inducement or occasion for war; and that there would be no war, as the immediate or direct result of secession or separation.

The malignant hostility of feeling that is even now entertained by the Abolition Party, and perhaps by a majority of the Northern people, toward those of the South is not here overlooked or underrated. If they could, by merely willing it, they would ruin us, even while united with them under one government — and still more readily if we were separated. If the mere wish of Abolitionists could effect the destruction of our system of Negro slavery, even by the destruction of the entire white population of the South, I would fear that consummation would not be a remote event.

But *to will* and *to do* are very different

things. And even Northern fanaticism (to say nothing of Northern self-interest and avarice) would be glad to forgo these gratifications if they were to be purchased only at the cost, to the North, of hundreds of millions of dollars and hundreds of thousands of lives. Even if admitting what is so arrogantly and falsely claimed by the North, that it could conquer and desolate the South, any such victory would be scarcely less ruinous to the conquerors than the conquered.

But there would be no such war and no movement toward it, because war could not subserve or advance any interest of the North. It is unnecessary to maintain the like proposition in regard to the South inasmuch as it is universally admitted. No one, of either side, has ever asserted or supposed that the South would assail or make war upon the North in consequence of their separation. Whether this peaceful disposition is ascribed to a greater sense of justice, or to the weakness, or the timidity of the Southern people, all concur in the belief that the South would desire peace and would avoid war, unless necessary for defense. Then, passing by this contingency, deemed impossible by all parties, we have only to examine the supposed inducements for offensive war and attack by the North on the South.

"But," it is urged by many among ourselves, "even if the North refrained from making war, still it would retain the direction of the federal government, and exercise its rights and remaining power — and also hold possession of the seat of government, the Army and Navy, the fortifications, and the public lands. How could the public property be divided peaceably? And, without resorting to war to enforce our right to a fair share, would not all be necessarily lost to the South?" I answer that, even if admitting all these premises, still there would be no need and no advantage for the South to seek justice through war — and no benefit to the North would be gained by with-

holding our just dues, either by war or in peace.

Nations, in modern days, do not often go to war and never in advance of negotiation, to recover debts or to settle pecuniary accounts and obligations. There are other means, in many cases, to induce, and even constrain, nations to render justice; and, luckily, in our case, the means available for the South would be of the most cogent influence. . . .

Even if the result of separation to the South was, indeed, the loss of every value named above (except the few spots of Southern ground heretofore ceded to the federal government, and which would necessarily go finally to the states in which they were situated), the South would still gain by separation much more than it would lose by this great spoliation. As to the Army, it would, probably, like the present federal government, cease to exist as soon as the Union was dissolved.

The public buildings, fortifications, and Navy, and all other material values held by the government of the Union, and the annual revenue, have been mainly (at least two-thirds of the whole) acquired from the contributions of the Southern states — while the larger proportion of all disbursements of government, and pecuniary bounties and benefits of all kinds, have as regularly gone to enrich the Northern people. If, then, this regular and very unequal apportionment of the burdens and bounties of government were stopped, as it would be by separation, the South would gain more in retaining, for the future, its own resources for its own benefit, than the actual pecuniary value to the South, in the Union, of its share of all the present national property. And these retained resources, within a few years, would amount to a fund sufficient to more than replace the forfeited values of Army, Navy, and all the public edifices.

As to the public lands, vast as is their extent and enormous their value, the South has already been virtually deprived of them. No Southerner can safely remove with his slaves to any new territory. They were thus unjustly and illegally shut out from the rich fields and richer mines of California by the action of the North and the federal government. The conquest of Mexico was achieved by men and money supplied (as of all other contributions) in much the larger proportion by the Southern states. By their much larger expenditure of both blood and treasure, California and New Mexico were acquired. Yet the people of the South, as slaveholders, were excluded from the territory; and Southern men have had no access to or benefit from the rich mines and lands of California, that were not as open to, and equally enjoyed by, the semi-barbarians of China and the Sandwich Islands, the former convicts of Australia, and the needy and desperate outcasts, invited by these benefits, from every foreign land.

A like virtual exclusion of slaveholders will be effected hereafter as to every other new territory. And even from the sales of public lands and through the federal Treasury, it can scarcely be expected that any considerable benefit will hereafter accrue to the South or serve to lessen its greater share of the burden of taxation; for nearly all the resources from the public lands have, in latter years, been squandered by Congress, and mainly to benefit Northern men and Northern interests. So little revenue from the public lands will hereafter reach the Treasury that the amount will probably not more than defray the great expenses of the land surveys and sales, and the much greater expenses incurred in governing and protecting the new territories.

If the gigantic and much urged and favorite scheme of either one or three railroads to the Pacific Ocean should be adopted by Congress (as seems probable), all the net proceeds of future sales of public lands, and that amount doubled by additional grants from other funds of the government, will not suffice to construct and to keep in use this work of unexampled magnitude and unheard of national folly or extravagance.

According to these views, the entire loss to the South and, at once, of all the public property would be no greater damage than the former and present and prospective unjust apportionment of contributions and disbursements. Still, this is no reason why, in the event of separation, the South should submit to lose its just rights in the common public property. And in this respect, the independent South would be more able to obtain redress for spoliation, or to save something out of the general wreck of the present public property, than will be possible if remaining united to and governed by the stronger Northern states.

As a separate power, wronged by spoliation, the South would negotiate for redress, calmly and peaceably. And, if necessary, until redress was obtained and an acceptable composition made, a prohibition should be enacted against the introduction or sale of all Northern commodities and the employment of any Northern vessels in the Southern states. These peaceful means would soon produce satisfactory redress or, otherwise, ample retaliation for any amount of previous injury. These measures would be far more potent than war, and yet entirely peaceful, and such as could not be opposed or countervailed, or even complained of, by the Northern states.

WHEN ASSUMING an independent political existence, and afterwards, every consideration of self-interest will cause the Southern Confederacy to desire to have peace, amity, and also free trade with the Northern states, if true and real amity can subsist. And the best possible relation also for the North would be amity (and, as a necessary condition, the refraining from all the now-existing causes of exasperation) and trade as nearly free as may be with the South. But, whether with a moderate tariff of duties, for revenue only, or with no duties, Northern vessels and imports, in the Southern Confederacy, would at best stand only on equal footing with those of all other foreign countries. The Northern states and their commerce and manufactures and shipping would be deprived of all their former advantages by which Northern interests gained monopoly prices and profits, and which were paid for by the South.

No more protecting duties for Northern manufactures; no more fishing bounties (in which $10 million have been already paid, mostly from Southern taxation, and received exclusively by the Northern navigation interests); no more bounties to Collins' or other lines of Northern steamers, also mainly paid by Southern taxes, and by which policy of the federal government the last remnant of direct trade with Europe has been taken away from the Southern states. This new commercial condition of the North, though equal to that of all other nations, would be bad enough compared to the former and present system, by which so much of unjust and iniquitous gain has been made at the expense and to the great detriment of the Southern states. But, by resort to war, whether of arms or of tariffs, even the benefit of free or of equally burdened trade would be lost to the North, if not also all commercial intercourse with the South.

The separation of the Northern and Southern states by secession of the latter would, by the very act of dismemberment, put an end to the present Confederation and its government. But, probably, the Northern remnant will claim to be still the "United States," and to have authority to administer the government for all, as well as to hold to the national domain and all other public property. In this case, the South has the full means for redress, in commercial restrictions, as has been already stated.

But suppose that these measures were ineffectual for redress for any cause whatever, and that the South had to suffer the spoliation without compensation. There would

still be, and mainly because of this act of spoliation, consequences for the old Northern states (the leaders and main actors in the Abolition movement) much worse than yielding the unjustly held spoils, by agreeing to a just and fair division of the national property. The new Northwestern and Pacific states and territories, within which would lie all the public lands to be embraced in the great Northern section, would never agree to share the domain in proportion to population with the old Northern states. Each new state and the squatters on each new territory would claim and would hold all the vacant land within their respective boundaries. Then the old Northeastern states will have robbed the South, only that the Northwestern and Pacific states and territories may secure all the most valuable spoil.

This will not be the only evil of vast importance to the old Northern states. When the separation of the present Union has been consummated, there will no longer remain to Northern men any political object or gain for which to agitate the slavery or Aboliton questions. The Sewards and Hales and Wilsons, no longer kept down by Southern intellect and patriotism, would be the established leaders and rulers of the Northern Confederacy, and they could gain nothing more by denouncing slavery or contending against slaveholders. It would then be seen that the Abolition question had been agitated only for political effect and benefit to the prime agitators; and when such agitation could no longer serve their interest, the alleged sin and horrors of slavery in the Southern Confederacy would be as little noticed by Abolitionists as has been always the case in regard to Cuba and Brazil.

Certainly the condition of the slaves in those countries was far more wretched and more strongly calling for the sympathy of philanthropists than in these Southern states. Moreover, the illegal African slave trade, of the most cruel and murderous character (and with many of the slave vessels fitted out in Northern cities and by Northern capital), continued to add to the number of slaves and, by such additions, to increase the sufferings of all. These worst evils and sufferings incident to the worst condition of African slavery and the forbidden slave trade certainly were, and are, as much worthy of the attention of moral reformers and philanthropic Abolitionists as the more humane treatment and comfortable condition of slaves in these Southern states. Yet scarcely have the Northern Abolitionists noticed the horrors of Cuban or Brazilian slavery, while all their denunciations and hostility have been reserved for the milder slavery in the Southern states. This, if alone, ought to have shown, in advance, how false and hypocritical has been the pretense of this Abolition Party being influenced by considerations of humanity or benevolence — by morality or religion.

Separation of political connection will be the certain end of all actual and injurious Abolition agitation. The newspapers of the North, after separation, and public speakers, both lay and clerical, may continue to denounce the iniquity of slavery and the atrocious acts of slaveholders. So are we denounced and abused in Canadian papers and speeches, and in British newspapers and reviews. But, as in these latter cases, there has never been sufficient inducement for attempting more active or practical interference with our rights and property, so neither will there be with the people of the Northern states when no political gain can be made or sought by aid of such interference. Then the Abolition agitation by politicians will die for want of object and aliment; and the deluded people of the North will then recover their lost sanity on this subject.

When this change shall have occurred and the now prevailing delusion is at an end, the people of the new Northwestern states,

who are especially connected with the South in bonds of trade by the Mississippi and who have no such ties with New England, will see their error in following the fanatical course of the latter to the end of separation from the Southern states, their natural allies and best customers. It will be found by them a source of great inconvenience and loss to have no trade with the Southern states, or a taxed trade in time of peace, though the passage of the Mississippi to the ocean or to foreign ports would be still open to their vessels and freights. And if the North should force war on the South, then, of course, the navigation of the Lower Mississippi will be no longer open to the use of any portion of the hostile country.

This would be ruinous to the Northwestern states. And on this ground, even without the anticipated difficulty growing out of the contest for the public lands, these Northwestern states, on the upper waters of the Mississippi, would soon secede from the Northeastern and Atlantic states and make a separate community, and also would make a separate peace — if not seek to be reunited to the Southern states. This abandonment by this vast and fertile region would leave the Northeastern states in a much more weak and hopeless condition than previously.

And as early, or perhaps earlier, there will be another secession from the first Northern Confederacy, by California, Oregon, Utah, and all the other territory of the present United States lying on the Pacific slope. This separation will take place as soon as the residents of the Pacific states and territories shall deem the measure more beneficial to their interest than to enjoy the bounties and have the protection of the present federal government, and the consummation will only be hastened and hurried by the previous separation of the slaveholding from the nonslaveholding states. And even under the present state of things, if such a separation were to take place, and if the parties would maintain perfect free trade with each other after their separation (as while under one government), it would be no evil to the other portion of the present Union, and especially to the Southern states, if all the Pacific territory would at once declare its independence and secede from the United States.

The Southern people, from the first possession, have been unjustly excluded from their equal rights to California. They will never receive either the value of an acre of land or an ounce of gold from this part of the public domain. And the only pecuniary interest that will accrue to the South (if not to the United States) from the possession of the territory on the Pacific slope, will be the Southern (and much larger) share of the cost of its government, maintenance, and improvement in time of peace, and the incalculably greater cost of its military and naval defense in time of war. It would be far better for the South that the Pacific states and territories should secede at once, and even if without conditions or amicable arrangement, before we shall have to incur our legal share of the enormous cost of constructing one or more railroads to the Pacific, or of defending the Pacific Coast from a foreign enemy and naval power.

Already King Brigham Young is the despotic and secure ruler of the virtually independent Mormon people and country, to which the government and people of the United States pay tribute, (in defraying the expenses of its territorial government, etc.) and over which, or its ruler, the general government dares not attempt to exercise any coercive control.

While such elements of division, if not of strife, would operate to separate the nonslaveholding states into at least three portions, the slaveholding states would have common interests and unity of opinion and principles as to matters of general policy. United in a confederacy, they would possess enough of territory, population, and wealth for an independent community — strong enough for defense in arms against any single power whatever — and of more than double the absolute strength of all the thirteen colonies when they revolted from and defied in arms their mother country, then one of the most powerful nations of the world.

But a guarantee of safe defense, and almost of immunity from war, would be found in the important fact that this Southern Confederacy would supply nearly all the cotton for the factories and the consumption of both Europe and America. The only nations of both hemispheres that could be dreaded as foes would incur far more injury from being shut out by war from the needed supply of our cotton than would be compensated by any possible amount of military success.

The revenue and resources of the Southern states, heretofore contributed mainly to aid Northern interests, foster Northern industry and trade, and increase Northern wealth and power, would thenceforward be retained and used to sustain and build up our own commerce and cities and general prosperity. In twenty-five or thirty years our population and wealth will be doubled, and the value of our products and their demand by the commercial world will be increased in still greater proportion. There will probably be no community of more vigorous and healthy growth, or with better prospects of stable prosperity. With the aid of our own annual profits of industry and capital, and the encouragement that the new condition and demands of the Southern states will create, manufactures and navigation and commerce will increase rapidly, even if the growth was stimulated and maintained by Southern resources only.

But in advance of this natural and slower growth, these branches of industry, and the men to carry them on, and the capital to sustain them, will be transplanted to any amount that may be desired and permitted from the Northern to the Southern states, as soon as they shall have become separate political communities. Plenty of manufacturing capital, and also of capitalists and laborers, and plenty of ships and sailors, will come to obtain the benefits of an establishment in the South. There would be nothing more wanting for this speedy and extensive transference of capital, industry, and also of (at least) professed allegiance than the sure and simple operation of greatly reduced employment and profits in the Northern states, and the great increase of both in the independent and flourishing Southern Confederacy — then just beginning to use its own funds and resources to build up and sustain their own cities, manufactures, and navigation.

92.

GEORGE FITZHUGH: Slaves Without Masters

Two years after the publication of his first major work on slavery, Sociology for the South, *George Fitzhugh traveled north to lecture at Harvard and Yale. There he met Harriet Beecher Stowe and other Abolitionists, whose views prompted Fitzhugh to embark on a second major defense of the Southern slave system. In 1857 he published* Cannibals All! or, Slaves Without Masters, *a chapter of which is reprinted here. Fitzhugh's works were distinctive in defending slavery as a positive good, rather than being apologies for the weaknesses of the system. His denunciation of Northern society as a system that professed liberty for all while reducing the white workers to the level of "slaves without masters" was an integral part of his defense of the patriarchal organization of the slaveholding South.*

Source: *Cannibals All! or, Slaves Without Masters,* Richmond, Va., 1857, Ch. 1: "The Universal Trade."

WE ARE, ALL, NORTH AND SOUTH, engaged in the white slave trade, and he who succeeds best is esteemed most respectable. It is far more cruel than the black slave trade, because it exacts more of its slaves, and neither protects nor governs them. We boast that it exacts more when we say, "that the *profits* made from employing free labor are greater than those from slave labor." The profits made from free labor are the amount of the products of such labor which the employer, by means of the command which capital or skill gives him, takes away, exacts, or "exploitates" from the free laborer. The profits of slave labor are that portion of the products of such labor which the power of the master enables him to appropriate. These profits are less, because the master allows the slave to retain a larger share of the results of his own labor than do the employers of free labor.

But we not only boast that the white slave trade is more exacting and fraudulent (in fact, though not in intention) than black slavery but we also boast that it is more cruel, in leaving the laborer to take care of himself and family out of the pittance which skill or capital have allowed him to retain. When the day's labor is ended, he is free, but is overburdened with the cares of family and household, which make his freedom an empty and delusive mockery. But his employer is really free and may enjoy the profits made by others' labor, without a care or a trouble as to their well-being. The Negro slave is free, too, when the labors of the day are over, and free in mind as well as body; for the master provides food, raiment, house, fuel, and everything else necessary to the physical well-being of himself and family. The master's labors commence just when the slave's end. No wonder men should prefer white slavery to capital, to Negro slavery, since it is more profitable and is free from all the cares and labors of black slaveholding.

Now, reader, if you wish to know yourself — to "descant on your own deformity" — read on. But if you would cherish self-conceit, self-esteem, or self-appreciation, throw down our book; for we will dispel illusions which have promoted your happiness, and show you that what you have considered and practised as virtue is little better than moral cannibalism. But you will find yourself in numerous and respectable company; for all good and respectable people are "cannibals all," who do not labor, or who are successfully trying to live without labor, on the unrequited labor of other people; while low, bad, and disreputable people are those who labor to support themselves and to support said respectable people besides.

Throwing the Negro slaves out of the account, and society is divided in Christendom into four classes: the rich, or independent respectable people, who live well and labor not at all; the professional and skillful respectable people, who do a little light work for enormous wages; the poor, hardworking people, who support everybody and starve themselves; and the poor thieves, swindlers, and sturdy beggars, who live like gentlemen, without labor, on the labor of other people. The gentlemen exploitate, which, being done on a large scale and requiring a great many victims, is highly respectable, while the rogues and beggars take

so little from others that they fare little better than those who labor.

But, reader, we do not wish to fire into the flock. "Thou art the man!" You are a cannibal! and if a successful one, pride yourself on the number of your victims, quite as much as any Fiji chieftain who breakfasts, dines, and sups on human flesh. And your conscience smites you if you have failed to succeed, quite as much as his when he returns from an unsuccessful foray.

Probably you are a lawyer, or a merchant, or a doctor, who have made by your business $50,000, and retired to live on your capital. But, mark! not to spend your capital. That would be vulgar, disreputable, criminal. That would be to live by your own labor; for your capital is your amassed labor. That would be to do as common workingmen do; for they take the pittance which their employers leave them to live on. They live by labor; for they exchange the results of their own labor for the products of other people's labor. It is, no doubt, an honest, vulgar way of living; but not at all a respectable way.

The respectable way of living is to make other people work for you and to pay them nothing for so doing, and to have no concern about them after their work is done. Hence, white slaveholding is much more respectable than Negro slavery, for the master works nearly as hard for the Negro as he for the master. But you, my virtuous, respectable reader, exact $3,000 per annum from white labor (for your income is the product of white labor) and make not one cent of return in any form. You retain your capital and never labor, and yet live in luxury on the labor of others. Capital commands labor as the master does the slave. Neither pays for labor; but the master permits the slave to retain a larger allowance from the proceeds of his own labor, and hence "free labor is cheaper than slave labor."

You, with the command over labor which

your capital gives you, are a slave owner; a master without the obligations of a master. They who work for you, who create your income, are slaves without the rights of slaves. Slaves without a master! While you were engaged in amassing your capital, in seeking to become independent, you were in the white slave trade. To become independent is to be able to make other people support you without being obliged to labor for *them*. Now, what man in society is not seeking to attain this situation? He who attains it is a slave owner in the worst sense. He who is in pursuit of it is engaged in the slave trade.

You, reader, belong to the one or other class. The men without property, in free society, are theoretically in a worse condition than slaves. Practically, their condition corresponds with this theory, as history and statistics everywhere demonstrate. The capitalists, in free society, live in ten times the luxury and show that Southern masters do, because the slaves to capital work harder and cost less than Negro slaves.

The Negro slaves of the South are the happiest and, in some sense, the freest people in the world. The children and the aged and infirm work not at all and yet have all the comforts and necessaries of life provided for them. They enjoy liberty, because they are oppressed neither by care nor labor. The women do little hard work and are protected from the despotism of their husbands by their masters. The Negro men and stout boys work, on the average, in good weather, not more than nine hours a day. The balance of their time is spent in perfect abandon. Besides, they have their Sabbaths and holidays. White men, with so much of license and liberty, would die of ennui; but Negroes luxuriate in corporeal and mental repose. With their faces upturned to the sun, they can sleep at any hour; and quiet sleep is the greatest of human enjoyments. "Blessed be the man who invented sleep." 'Tis happiness in itself, and re-

sults from contentment with the present and confident assurance of the future.

We do not know whether free laborers ever sleep. They are fools to do so; for, while they sleep, the wily and watchful capitalist is devising means to ensnare and exploitate them. The free laborer must work or starve. He is more of a slave than the Negro, because he works longer and harder for less allowance than the slave, and has no holiday, because the cares of life with him begin when its labors end. He has no liberty and not a single right. We know, 'tis often said, air and water are common property, which all have equal right to participate and enjoy; but this is utterly false. The appropriation of the lands carries with it the appropriation of all on or above the lands — *usque ad caelum, aut ad inferos* [up to the sky or down to the depths]. A man cannot breathe the air without a place to breathe it from, and all places are appropriated. All water is private property "to the middle of the stream," except the ocean, and that is not fit to drink.

Free laborers have not a thousandth part of the rights and liberties of Negro slaves. Indeed, they have not a single right or a single liberty, unless it be the right or liberty to die. But the reader may think that he and other capitalists and employers are freer than Negro slaves. Your capital would soon vanish if you dared indulge in the liberty and abandon of Negroes. You hold your wealth and position by the tenure of constant watchfulness, care, and circumspection. You never labor; but you are never free.

Where a few own the soil, they have unlimited power over the balance of society, until domestic slavery comes in to compel them to permit this balance of society to draw a sufficient and comfortable living from *terra mater*. Free society asserts the right of a few to the earth; slavery maintains that it belongs, in different degrees, to all.

But, reader, well may you follow the

slave trade. It is the only trade worth following, and slaves the only property worth owning. All other is worthless, a mere *caput mortuum* [deadhead], except insofar as it vests the owner with the power to command the labors of others: to enslave them. Give you a palace, 10,000 acres of land, sumptuous clothes, equipage and every other luxury; and, with your artificial wants, you are poorer than Robinson Crusoe or the lowest workingman if you have no slaves to capital or domestic slaves. Your capital will not bring you an income of a cent, nor supply one of your wants, without labor. Labor is indispensable to give value to property, and if you owned everything else and did not own labor, you would be poor. But $50,000 means, and is, $50,000 worth of slaves. You can command, without touching on that capital, $3,000 worth of labor per annum. You could do no more were you to buy slaves with it, and then you would be cumbered with the cares of governing and providing for them. You are a slaveholder now, to the amount of $50,000, with all the advantages and none of the cares and responsibilities of a master.

"Property in man" is what all are struggling to obtain. Why should they not be obliged to take care of man, their property, as they do their horses and their hounds, their cattle and their sheep? Now, under the delusive name of liberty, you work him "from morn to dewy eve," from infancy to old age; then turn him out to starve. You treat your horses and hounds better. Capital is a cruel master. The free slave trade, the commonest yet the cruelest of trades.

93.

J. W. Fowler: Plantation Management

In a debate as heated as the one that raged for twenty years about slavery, it is not surprising to find that both sides were prone to exaggerations and inaccuracies. The pro-slavery arguments have long been discredited, but the Abolitionist view, that it was common practice to mistreat, underfeed, and overwork slaves, is not correct either. That such treatment at least was not universal is attested by the following rules for the management of a cotton plantation in Coahoma County, Mississippi. The instructions were given to his overseers in 1857 by J. W. Fowler, owner of the plantation.

Source: Commons, I, pp. 112-113.

THE HEALTH, HAPPINESS, good discipline, and obedience; good, sufficient, and comfortable clothing; a sufficiency of good, wholesome, and nutritious food for both man and beast being indispensably necessary to successful planting, as well as for reasonable dividends for the amount of capital invested, without saying anything about the master's duty to his dependents, to himself and his God, I do hereby establish the following rules and regulations for the management of my prairie plantation, and require an observance of the same by any and all overseers I may at any time have in charge thereof to wit:

Punishment must never be cruel or abusive, for it is absolutely mean and unmanly to whip a Negro from mere passion or malice, and any man who can do this is entirely unworthy and unfit to have control of either man or beast.

My Negroes are permitted to come to me with their complaints and grievances and in no instance shall they be punished for so doing. On examination, should I find they have been cruelly treated, it shall be considered a good and sufficient cause for the immediate discharge of the overseer.

Prove and show by your conduct toward the Negroes that you feel a kind and considerate regard for them. Never cruelly punish or overwork them, never require them to do what they cannot reasonably accomplish or otherwise abuse them, but seek to render their situation as comfortable and contented as possible.

See that their necessities are supplied, that their food and clothing be good and sufficient, their houses comfortable; and be kind and attentive to them in sickness and old age.

See that the Negroes are regularly fed and that their food be wholesome, nutritious, and well cooked.

See that they keep themselves well cleaned. At least once a week (especially during summer) inspect their houses and see that they have been swept clean; examine their bedding and see that they are occasionally well aired; their clothes mended, and everything attended to that conduces to their health, comfort, and happiness.

94.

HINTON R. HELPER: Slavery and the Deficiency of Commerce in the South

In addition to those opponents of slavery in the years preceding the Civil War who attacked it on moral and ethical grounds were others, like Hinton Helper, who regarded slavery as an economic evil. Helper, a nonslaveholder from North Carolina and one of the few Southern Abolitionists, saw in slavery the cause of the "shame, poverty, ignorance, tyranny and imbecility" of Southern society. In The Impending Crisis (1857), *he encouraged the small nonslaveholding farmers to "strike for freedom" by overthrowing the plantation aristocracy. The book was welcomed by Northern Abolitionists and sixty-eight Republican congressmen sponsored a fund to distribute it as a propaganda piece. The following chapter from* The Impending Crisis *is representative of Helper's economic arguments against slavery.*

Source: *The Impending Crisis of the South: How to Meet It*, New York, 1857, Ch. 9: "Commercial Cities — Southern Commerce."

OUR THEME IS A CITY — a great Southern importing, exporting, and manufacturing city, to be located at some point or part on the coast of the Carolinas, Georgia, or Virginia, where we can carry on active commerce, buy, sell, fabricate, receive the profits which accrue from the exchange of our own commodities, open facilities for direct communication with foreign countries, and establish all those collateral sources of wealth, utility, and adornment, which are the usual concomitants of a metropolis, and which add so very materially to the interest and importance of a nation. Without a city of this kind, the South can never develop her commercial resources nor attain to that eminent position to which those vast resources would otherwise exalt her.

According to calculations based upon reasonable estimates, it is owing to the lack of a great commercial city in the South that we are now annually drained of more than $120 million! We should, however, take into consideration the negative loss as well as the positive. Especially should we think of the influx of emigrants, of the visits of strangers and cosmopolites, of the patronage to hotels and public halls, of the profits of travel and transportation, of the emoluments of foreign and domestic trade, and of numerous other advantages which have their origin exclusively in wealthy, enterprising, and densely populated cities.

Nothing is more evident than the fact that our people have never entertained a proper opinion of the importance of home cities. Blindly, and greatly to our own injury, we have contributed hundreds of millions of dollars toward the erection of mammoth cities at the North, while our own magnificent bays and harbors have been most shamefully disregarded and neglected. Now, instead of carrying all our money to New York, Philadelphia, Boston, and Cincinnati, suppose we had kept it on the south side of Mason and Dixon's Line — as we would have done had it not been for slavery — and had disbursed it in the upbuilding of Norfolk, Beaufort, Charleston, or Savannah, how much richer, better, greater, would the South have been today! How much larger and more intelligent would have been our population. How many hundred thousand natives of the South would now be thriving at home, instead of adding to the wealth and political power of other parts of the Union.

How much greater would be the number and length of our railroads, canals, turnpikes, and telegraphs. How much greater would be the extent and diversity of our manufactures. How much greater would be the grandeur, and how much larger would be the number of our churches, theaters, schools, colleges, lyceums, banks, hotels, stores, and private dwellings. How many more clippers and steamships would we have sailing on the ocean; how vastly more reputable would we be abroad; how infinitely more respectable, progressive, and happy would we be at home.

That we may learn something of the importance of cities in general, let us look for a moment at the great capitals of the world. What would England be without London? What would France be without Paris? What would Turkey be without Constantinople? Or, to come nearer home, what would Maryland be without Baltimore? What would Louisiana be without New Orleans? What would South Carolina be without Charleston? Do we ever think of these countries or states without thinking of their cities also? . . .

Every metropolis may be regarded as the nucleus or epitome of the country in which it is situated; and the more prominent features and characteristics of a country, particularly of the people of a country, are almost always to be seen within the limits of its capital city. Almost invariably do we find the bulk of the floating funds, the best talent, and the most vigorous energies of a nation concentrated in its chief cities; and does not this concentration of wealth, energy, and talent conduce, in an extraordinary degree, to the growth and prosperity of the nation? Unquestionably. Wealth develops wealth, energy develops energy, talent develops talent. What, then, must be the condition of those countries which do not possess the means or facilities of centralizing their material forces, their energies, and their talents? Are they not destined to occupy an inferior rank among the nations of the earth? Let the South answer.

And now let us ask, and we would put the question particularly to Southern merchants, what do we so much need as a great Southern metropolis? Merchants of the South, slaveholders! You are the avaricious assassinators of your country! You are the channels through which more than $120 million are annually drained from the South and conveyed to the North. You are daily engaged in the unmanly and unpatriotic work of impoverishing the land of your birth. You are constantly enfeebling our resources and rendering us more and more tributary to distant parts of the nation. Your conduct is reprehensible, base, criminal.

Whether Southern merchants ever think of the numerous ways in which they contribute to the aggrandizement of the North, while at the same time they enervate and dishonor the South, has for many years, with us, been a matter of more than ordinary conjecture. If, as it would seem, they have never yet thought of the subject, it is certainly desirable that they should exercise their minds upon it at once. Let them scrutinize the workings of Southern money after it passes north of Mason and Dixon's Line. Let them consider how much they pay to Northern railroads and hotels, how much to Northern merchants and shopkeepers, how much to Northern shippers and insurers, how much to Northern theaters, newspapers, and periodicals. Let them also consider what disposition is made of it after it is lodged in the hands of the North. Is not the greater part of it paid out to Northern manufacturers, mechanics, and laborers for the very articles which are purchased at the North; and, to the extent that this is done, are not Northern manufacturers, mechanics, and laborers directly countenanced

and encouraged, while, at the same time, Southern manufacturers, mechanics, and laborers are indirectly abased, depressed, and disabled?

It is, however, a matter of impossibility, on these small pages, to notice or enumerate all the methods in which the money we deposit in the North is made to operate against us; suffice it to say that it is circulated and expended there among all classes of the people to the injury and impoverishment of almost every individual in the South. And, yet, our cousins of the North are not by any means blameworthy for availing themselves of the advantages which we have voluntarily yielded to them. They have shown their wisdom in growing great at our expense, and we have shown our folly in allowing them to do so. Southern merchants, slaveholders, and slave breeders should be the objects of our censure; they have desolated and impoverished the South; they are now making merchandise of the vitals of their country; patriotism is a word nowhere recorded in their vocabulary; town, city, country — they care for neither; with them, self is always paramount to every other consideration. . . .

In this age of the world, commerce is an indispensable element of national greatness. Without commerce we can have no great cities, and without great cities we can have no reliable tenure of distinct nationality. Commerce is the forerunner of wealth and population; and it is mainly these that make invincible the power of undying states. . . .

How it is, in this enlightened age, that men of ordinary intelligence can be so far led into error as to suppose that commerce, or any other noble enterprise, can be established and successfully prosecuted under the dominion of slavery, is, to us, one of the most inexplicable of mysteries. "Commercial" conventions, composed of the self-titled lordlings of slavery — generals, colonels, majors, captains, etc. — may act out their annual programs of farcical nonsense from now until doomsday; but they will never add one iota to the material, moral, or mental interests of the South — never can, until their ebony idol shall have been utterly demolished. . . .

It is a remarkable fact, but one not at all surprising to those whose philosophy leads them to think aright, that Baltimore and St. Louis, the two most prosperous cities in the slave states, have fewer slaves in proportion to the aggregate population than any other city or cities in the South. While the entire population of the former is now estimated at 250,000, and that of the latter at 140,000 — making a grand total of 390,000 in the two cities — less than 6,000 of this latter number are slaves; indeed, neither city is cursed with half the number of 6,000.

In 1850, there were only 2,946 slaves in Baltimore and 2,656 in St. Louis — total in the two cities, 5,602 — and, in both places, thank Heaven, this heathenish class of the population was rapidly decreasing. The census of 1860 will, in all probability, show that the two cities are entirely exempt from slaves and slavery; and that of 1870 will, we prayerfully hope, show that the United States at large, at that time, will have been wholly redeemed from the unspeakable curse of human bondage.

What about Southern commerce? Is it not almost entirely tributary to the commerce of the North? Are we not dependent on New York, Philadelphia, Boston, and Cincinnati for nearly every article of merchandise, whether foreign or domestic? Where are our ships, our mariners, our naval architects? Alas! echo answers, where?

Reader! would you understand how abjectly slaveholders themselves are enslaved to the products of Northern industry? If you would, fix your mind on a Southern "gentleman" — a slave breeder and human-flesh monger, who professes to be a Christian! Observe the routine of his daily life. See him rise in the morning from a Northern bed and clothe himself in Northern apparel; see him walk across the floor on a Northern carpet, and perform his ablutions out of a Northern ewer and basin. See him uncover a box of Northern powders, and cleanse his teeth with a Northern brush; see him reflecting his physiognomy in a Northern mirror, and arranging his hair with a Northern comb. See him dosing himself with the medicaments of Northern quacks, and perfuming his handkerchief with Northern cologne. See him referring to the time in a Northern watch, and glancing at the news in a Northern gazette. See him and his family sitting in Northern chairs, and singing and praying from Northern books. See him at the breakfast table, saying grace over a Northern plate, eating with Northern cutlery, and drinking from Northern utensils. See him charmed with the melody of a Northern piano, or musing over the pages of a Northern novel. See him riding to his neighbor's in a Northern carriage, or furrowing his lands with a Northern plow. See him lighting his cigar with a Northern match, and flogging his Negroes with a Northern lash. See him with Northern pen and ink, writing letters on Northern paper, and sending them away in Northern envelopes, sealed with Northern wax, and impressed with a Northern stamp.

Perhaps our Southern "gentleman" is a merchant; if so, see him at his store, making an unpatriotic use of his time in the miserable traffic of Northern gimcracks and haberdashery; see him when you will, where you will, he is ever surrounded with the industrial products of those whom, in the criminal inconsistency of his heart, he execrates as enemies, yet treats as friends. His labors, his talents, his influence are all for the North and not for the South; for the stability of slavery, and for the sake of his own personal aggrandizement, he is willing to sacrifice the dearest interests of his country.

As we see our ruinous system of commerce exemplified in the family of our Southern "gentleman," so we may see it exemplified, to a greater or lesser degree, in almost every other family throughout the length and breadth of the slaveholding states. We are all constantly buying, and selling, and wearing, and using Northern merchandise, at a double expense to both ourselves and our neighbors. If we but look at ourselves attentively, we shall find that we are all clothed *cap à pie* [head to foot] in Northern habiliments. Our hats, our caps, our cravats, our coats, our vests, our pants, our gloves, our boots, our shoes, our undergarments — all come from the North; whence, too, Southern ladies procure all their bonnets, plumes, and flowers; dresses, shawls, and scarves; frills, ribbons, and ruffles; cuffs, capes, and collars.

True it is that the South has wonderful powers of endurance and recuperation; but she cannot forever support the reckless prodigality of her sons. We are all spendthrifts; some of us should become financiers. We must learn to take care of our money; we should withhold it from the North and open avenues for its circulation at home. We should not run to New York, to Philadelphia, to Boston, to Cincinnati, or to any other Northern city every time we want a shoestring or a bedstead, a fishhook or a handsaw, a toothpick or a cotton gin.

In ease and luxury we have been lolling long enough; we should now bestir ourselves and keep pace with the progress of the age. We must expand our energies and acquire habits of enterprise and industry; we should arouse ourselves from the couch of lassitude and inure our minds to thought and our bodies to action. We must begin to feed on a more substantial diet than that of pro-slavery politics; we should leave off our siestas and postmeridian naps and employ our time in profitable vocations. Before us

there is a vast work to be accomplished — a work which has been accumulating on our hands for many years. It is no less a work than that of infusing the spirit of liberty into all our systems of commerce, agriculture, manufactures, government, literature, and religion. Oligarchal despotism must be overthrown; slavery must be abolished.

For the purpose of showing how absolutely Southern "gentlemen," particularly slaveholding merchants, are lost to all sense of true honor and patriotism, we will here introduce an extract from an article which appeared more than three years ago in one of the editorial columns of the leading daily newspaper of the city of New York. It is in these words:

> Southern merchants do indeed keep away from New York for the reason that they can't pay their debts; there is no doubt that if the jobbers of this city had not trusted Southern traders for the past three years, they would be a great deal better off than they are. . . . Already our trade with Canada is becoming as promising, sure, and profitable, as our trade with the South is uncertain, riskful, and annoying.

Now, by any body of men not utterly debased by the influences of slavery, this language would have been construed into an invitation to stay at home. But do Southern merchants stay at home? Do they build up Southern commerce? No! Off they post to the North as regularly as the seasons, spring and fall, come round, and there, like cringing sycophants, flatter, beg, and scheme, for favors which they have no money to command.

The better classes of merchants, and indeed of all other people at the North, as elsewhere, have too much genuine respect for themselves to wish to have any dealings whatever with those who make merchandise of human beings. Limited as is our acquaintance in the city of New York, we know one firm there, a large wholesale house, that makes it an invariable rule never to sell goods to a merchant from the slave states except for cash. Being well acquainted with the partners, we asked one of them, on one occasion, why he refused to trust slave-driving merchants. "Because," said he, "they are too long-winded and uncertain; when we credit them, they occasion us more loss and bother than their trade is worth." Nonslaveholders of the South! Recollect that slavery is the only impediment to your progress and prosperity, that it stands diametrically opposed to all needful reforms, that it seeks to sacrifice you entirely for the benefit of others, and that it is the one great and only cause of dishonor to your country. Will you not abolish it? May Heaven help you to do your duty!

95.

Henry J. Gardner: New England Nativism

The development of nativist political movements in the United States after the 1830s was enhanced by popular resentment of Catholics and immigrants. The most successful of these parties, the American Party — dubbed "Know-Nothings" because members were sworn to secrecy and answered all questions with "I know nothing about it" — attracted a large membership at the time of the Kansas-Nebraska Act, when many voters hesitated to support either the pro-slavery Democrats or the antislavery Republicans. The American Party's victories in New England and the border states in 1854 and 1855 nourished hopes that it might win the 1856 presidential election, but the slavery issue divided party ranks so severely that its candidate, Millard Fillmore, carried only Maryland. In his inaugural address of January 9, 1857, reprinted here in part, Governor Henry Gardner of Massachusetts blamed the defeat on the immigrant vote.

Source: *Acts and Resolves Passed by the General Court of Massachusetts in The Years 1856-7*, Boston, 1857, pp. 705-733.

Our nation has just passed through another presidential contest under circumstances which would have imperiled the existence of any other government on the globe; and yet, so admirably harmonious are the workings of our system, and so readily obedient are our people to the will of the majority, that a stranger among us would hardly have supposed so momentous an event had transpired as the struggles between antagonistic theories concerning the administration of our government, which, though nominally for the term of four years, nevertheless may tell upon its policy and destiny for generations. And though nowhere was the result so great a disappointment to so large a proportion of our citizens as in Massachusetts, and nowhere was the real magnitude of the issue more fully appreciated, and hopes of a different termination more earnestly indulged, yet here, with a firm reliance on the ultimate triumph of the great principles we cherish, our people acquiesce in the result in the proper spirit of our institutions. Yet, though as patriots and good citizens we submit to the will of the majority, it is not only our right but our duty to examine thoroughly the causes which produced so unfavorable a result — a result not only prejudicial, we fear, to the cause of freedom but portending evil to the integrity of our Union — and to strive, as far as we may, legally, justly and honorably, to remove them for the future.

The issue involved in this great struggle was declared to be, both while it was pending and since its termination, directly or more remotely, not only whether freedom or slavery should be established in the territory of Kansas but whether foreign nations should be absorbed, and Cuba, Mexico, and Central America annexed to our southern borders; not only whether the powers of the executive and the legislation of Congress should be prostituted to the establishment of serfdom in latitudes once free but also whether the extension of the area of slavery by diplomacy, by conquest, and by purchase was not to be, and to continue to be, the established policy of our government.

Although it was freely asserted and widely believed that the question of freedom or slavery in Kansas would hinge upon the result of this election, and although, had it terminated in a different manner, the probability of her early admission into the Union as a free state would have been materially strengthened, yet recent developments give strong hopes that the present chief executive officer of that territory, in contradistinction to his predecessor, will administer the laws fairly and impartially, will protect the actual settlers in their just rights, and will resist the intrusion of nonresidents for illegal purposes. Such are the convictions of those on the spot most capable of judging and most effectively aiding in the accomplishment of these desired purposes. If so, the energy of our citizens in the race of colonization, aided by the individual and associated cooperation of the intellectual influence and material resources of the people of the North, will certainly outstrip the more sluggish tide of Southern emigration and insure the triumph of free territory in the approaching state of Kansas; a result glorious in itself, and still more so as it renders impotent the violation of a national compact and an illegal invasion by people of another state for the avowed purpose of overawing and outnumbering the suffrages of rightful citizens, accompanied with inhuman and barbarous murders and all the atrocities of actual and desperate warfare.

Still, so far as the decision of the presidential election is final, so far as the action of the present is inevitably developed in immeasurable and incomprehensible consequences and influences on the future, and so far as a step has been taken which it may require a generation to retrace, our citizens have the bitter assurance of knowing that that decision has been made, that action fixed, and that step taken by the casting votes of aliens born, aliens unnaturalized, and aliens entirely ignorant of our institutions and grossly callous to the vast interests involved in this stupendous issue.

While this horde of foreign-born voters has thus stricken down a noble cause, which appealed to the moral sentiment and enlightened patriotism of our country, it only affords another confirmation of a fact which our whole history establishes, that the foreign vote, with hardly an exception, always has been and, in the nature of things, ever will and must be attracted to that party which, under high-sounding generalities on the abstract rights of man, always practically cooperates with slavery at the South, and banishes from its platform the moral questions and nobler instincts and more enlightened sentiments of the age.

All classes of aliens, both high and low, are absorbed, with few exceptions, into this extreme and self-styled progressive party, by laws of the human mind as inevitable as they are constant. . . .

With these prepossessions the foreigner lands upon our shores and irresistibly attaches himself to the party bearing this name he has been taught to worship. So it has been, and so it ever will be. And it is this alien body which has decided in the past many of our great national elections, and, in the future, unless checked, is destined to thwart many of the noblest movements which New England, cooperating with the New England sentiments — morality and education — diffused through the great West, may undertake in behalf of freedom, humanity, and the nobler spirit of the century.

It was the deadening influence of this body which counteracted the great Northern uprising of the last national election. For wherever New England sentiments, New England education, and New England morality, by reason of state colonization from the indigenous and unmixed population of these six states, were diffused and predominated, there, without an exception, the cause of free territory triumphed. And not only foreign ignorance and vice but German rationalism, the infidelity of southern Europe, and the Godless philosophy so prevalent among her educated men and better citizens bear an instinctive antagonism to the moral sentiment and practical Christianity which underlaid the movement involved in this presidential contest, and which will underlie all conservative attempts to develop and carry out the genuine American spirit of our republican institutions. . . .

Born and brought up under totally dissimilar principles of government and accustomed to be led by the clannish influences which surround them rather than by enlightened individual responsibility, aliens are unfitted to appreciate or rightly use the great trust, in the exercise of which they are unwisely permitted to participate. While we would grant them, and defend them in, the enjoyment of their religious belief, in the worship of the Supreme Arbiter of all our destinies, according to their customs or their preferences, yet, in considering the propriety of voluntarily granting or withholding, for a suitable period, the exercise of those functions that constitute our own political privileges and birthright, we may properly, and should necessarily, remember that the class of aliens, to whom we specially refer, are blindly attached to a religious faith whose cardinal principle is implicit obedience to its temporal head — and that temporal head a foreign potentate — which forbids independence of action and the right of private judgment; which claims not only the power to inflict temporal ills on those who dare question its infallibility but also to entail future and eternal vengeance; whose prelates notoriously coerce politically as well as spiritually its followers; and which arrogates to itself, and actually exerts, a potent and malign political influence at war with the teachings of our Constitution and the essence of our government.

It matters not to the true patriot — to the thinking statesman — whether at any particular election they vote as he deems right or not; their power is the same, the danger of its influence is as great, in which way soever it may for the time be exercised.

Witnessing this vast influence for evil, which is continually swollen by accessions from the Old World, and seeing, year after year, the manifold dangers which not only threaten the future but are pernicious to the present, it seems strange that all who value the exhortations of the fathers of our country, the teachings of past history, or the repeated warnings of the present do not unite to counteract this acknowledged danger. Our faith in a righteous cause, our trust in an overruling Providence, and the consciousness of the approval of our own judgments, as well as of the approbation of many of the wisest and best of our fellow citizens, should constrain us to unremitted efforts and assure us of ultimate success.

This purpose cannot properly be deemed intolerant or oppressive, for it is not proposed to interfere in any way with any rights, whatsoever, already acquired and at present existing. Everyone now entitled to exercise the elective franchise or to hold office is to be, and should be, protected in those rights. It is merely desired to establish a legislative compact with the incoming race, that if they choose hereafter to make their home within our borders, they may do so, freely participating in our gratuitous educational privileges, protected by our laws, defended by our government, elevated by our republican institutions, but subject to the sole condition that they shall take no part in the selection of our rulers or the administration of our government until they are fitted by experience to understand its workings and appreciate its blessings.

Not only our own interests but theirs also necessitate this policy; the perpetuity of our political system demands it; the progress of humanity requires it; the teachings of our early statesmen inculcate it; the experience of our own lives teaches it; and our judgment, duty, and patriotism all point to it as a primal, inevitable, and absolute obligation.

96.

"Cape Cod Chantey"

Steam-powered vessels date from the early nineteenth century, but the invention of this new means of ocean transportation did not spell the immediate end of the age of sail. The longer the voyage, the more coal had to be carried, and since coal is a heavy and relatively inefficient fuel it remained economically advantageous to use sails on runs around the Horn, to Australia, and to China. The following chantey reflects the popularity of the Australia run, which remained the monopoly of sailing ships until oil-powered vessels came into general use at the beginning of the twentieth century. The sleds made of codfish heads were a delightful fabrication, but it was true enough that combs were made out of codfish bones as well as from the cartilage of the great whales that were the other leading industry of Cape Cod and the Massachusetts coastal towns.

♫ CAPE COD CHANTEY

Cape Cod girls they have no combs,
  Heave away, heave away!
They comb their hair with codfish bones,
  We are bound for Australia!

Cape Cod boys they have no sleds,
  Heave away, heave away!
They slide downhill on codfish heads,
  We are bound for Australia!

Chorus:
Heave away, my bully, bully boys,
  Heave away, heave away!
Heave away, and don't you make a noise,
  We are bound for Australia!

97.

Rhode Island Child Labor Law

The deleterious effects of physical labor on the health, education, and life expectancy of children did not escape the attention of social reformers of the nineteenth century. Child labor laws, such as the following Rhode Island Statute of 1857, and compulsory school laws attest to the changing social attitude. But the laws were easily evaded, carried insignificant penalties, and were frequently challenged in the courts as unconstitutional. It would be many decades before state laws would deal adequately with these matters.

Source: *The Revised Statutes of the State of Rhode Island and Providence Plantations,* Providence, 1857, pp. 326-330.

Section 1. Every minor, within the age of twenty-one years, may be bound by deed as a servant and apprentice by his father, and in case of his decease by his mother, when sole, or being within the age of fourteen years, by his guardian legally appointed.

Section 2. The minor, if fourteen years of age and having no such parent, may, of his voluntary accord, with the approbation of his guardian or, in case of no such guardian, by and with the approbation of the town council of the town where such minor belongs or resides, bind himself by deed as an apprentice or servant.

Section 3. Females may be bound or bind themselves as aforesaid, to the age of eighteen years, or to the time of their marriage within that age, and males to the age of twenty-one years. . . .

Section 20. No covenant of apprenticeship entered into by any minor, his parent, or guardian for the purpose of such minor's becoming or being instructed in any trade or mystery, and made to any master, the wife of such master, or to the executors, administrators, or assigns of such master, shall be binding on such minor, parent, or guardian after the decease of the master;

but on the death of such master the said contract shall be deemed void from that time; and in any such case any minor may be bound out anew, in manner as is hereinbefore directed.

Section 21. No minor under the age of twelve years shall be employed in or about any manufacturing establishment, in any manufacturing process, or in any labor incident to a manufacturing process.

Section 22. No minor under the age of fifteen years shall be employed in any manufacturing establishment in this state, unless such minor shall have attended school for a term of at least three months in the year next preceding the time when such minor shall be so employed; and no such minor shall be so employed for more than nine months in any one calendar year.

Section 23. No minor who has attained the age of twelve years, and is under the age of fifteen years, shall be employed in any manufacturing establishment more than eleven hours in any one day, nor before 5 o'clock in the morning, nor after half-past 7 o'clock in the evening.

Section 24. Any owner, employer, or agent of a manufacturing establishment who shall knowingly and willfully employ any minor, and any parent or guardian who shall permit or consent to the employment of his or her minor child or ward, contrary to the provisions of the next three preceding sections of this chapter shall be liable to a penalty of $20 for each offense, to be recovered by complaint and warrant before any justice of the peace in the town in which such child shall reside, or in which the manufacturing establishment in which such child shall have been employed shall be situated, one-half thereof to the use of the complainant and the other half thereof to the use of the district school of the district in which such manufacturing establishment shall be situated; or, if in the city of Providence, to the use of the public schools of said city. . . .

Section 26. Labor performed in any manufacturing establishment and all mechanical labor during the period of ten hours in any one day shall be considered a legal day's work, unless otherwise agreed by the parties to the contract for the same.

98.

Report on Higher Education in New York

Decades of discussion by educators like Francis Wayland, F. A. P. Barnard, Henry Tappan, and Andrew D. White aroused public interest in the establishment of a modern American university patterned after the great universities of England, France, and Germany. Educational leaders envisioned the true university as an institution free from sectarian limitations, where the most brilliant scholars might be gathered to advance knowledge and at the same time to meet the needs of the greater number of citizens. The New York Board of Regents, which was established in 1784 and was authorized to establish secondary schools and colleges, appointed a committee of five in March 1856 "to inquire into the practicability and expediency of establishing a university of active instruction." A report, a portion of which follows, urging such an institution was submitted the following April. It was almost a hundred years (1948), however, before the State University of New York was established by the legislature.

Source: *Report of the Select Committee of the Regents of the University, of the State of New-York*, Albany, 1857.

THE SELECT COMMITTEE to which was referred the following resolution —

Resolved, that it be referred to a select committee of five to inquire and report whether it be practicable and expedient for the regents to organize and maintain the University of the State of New York as an active university of instruction — respectfully submit the following report:

Public instruction looks to the good of the state. Its immediate subjects are indeed the individuals who are to be taught, but the good of the state is the real purpose and the ultimate end of the system . . . so in organizing a complete system of educational arrangements, its purpose should be to secure the greatest amount of those national advantages which education confers upon a people. We are not . . . to be deterred or diverted from the best course, because some individuals must inevitably derive greater advantages than others. . . .

In a nation constituted like ours, all the elements of usefulness, strength, and glory rest in the individual citizen. The state has no strength or resources except in the number, intelligence, virtue, productive power, and property of the citizens. The whole purpose of the government is to increase all these things. . . .

What we need, then, is not simply schools for the purpose of instructing children "in the lower branches of education, such as reading their native language with propriety, and so much of writing and arithmetic as to enable them to transact business with each other." These are necessary, not for what they are but for what is to come after them. It is not these simple elements, taught to children, which the state wants for its protection, preservation, power, and glory, but that education and cultivation that give the world assurance of a man. All his faculties must be sharpened; all his powers strengthened; his resources multiplied; his whole man developed and invigorated: this is the want of the nation. . . .

It is believed that we can in no manner meet the wants of the nation so soon or so well as by establishing universities, to give unity, coherence, and system to modes of teaching; and nowhere else than in universities, perhaps, can we expect to find that stimulating rivalry, that atmosphere of free investigation and profound learning, and that strength from mutual support which are so necessary to great enterprises of literary and scientific progress, bringing less of pecuniary profit than of glory; and it is only from a university, properly constituted and governed by right influences, that can fall those seeds which spring up in subordinate schools and institutions, and give life and vigor and steady growth to national industry and honor. . . .

Columbia College, incorporated in 1754, was for a long period the only seminary of higher education in this state. It was suspended by the Revolutionary War; but immediately after the peace of 1783, it was again in operation. Among the first acts of the state government in 1784 was one to give it its present name and to regulate its affairs, and, in the same statute, to institute a university. They gave to a university corporate existence and perpetual succession, and placed its interests in the keeping of a Board of Regents, to be organized and developed as they in their wisdom might provide, as time and progress should develop the demands of the future. . . .

The title of the act ["An act for granting certain privileges to Kings College, for altering the name and charter thereof, and erecting a university within this state"], the first sentence of the 1st Section, and the 4th Section show that the whole purpose of the act was to institute a university different from and of a higher grade and wider extent than the colleges, and one whose proper function should be the promotion of literature and the advancement of useful knowledge; instituted by the legislature at that time, but to be organized and managed by the regents at some future time. . . .

It is now seventy-three years, about three-quarters of a century, since the regents of the university were incorporated, with their highest and characteristic function, the promotion of literature and the advancement of useful knowledge through the agency of a university. We are the successors of the first Board of Regents, and we keep the records of their acts. They have performed a large amount of exceedingly useful labor; but for the promotion of literature and the advancement of useful knowledge, if they have done anything, let it be set forth in their vindication. Have they not always slumbered on that portion of their interesting and important duty? What is it to promote literature and to advance useful knowledge? Is it to keep up, without even the show of actual personal inspection, the routine of elementary instruction, which is the object of our common schools, academies, and colleges? . . .

If the regents, seventy years ago, had interpreted their powers and duties in the manner apparently intended by the law, and had devoted as much zeal and ability to the development of a university as was devoted to the establishment of the common school system by those who had that in charge, how easy, with the vantage ground of their position and purpose, to have made themselves felt affirmatively in the legislation of the state on the subject of higher education, and to have secured at least a provision that a reasonable percentage of all the moneys raised for the purpose of education should be placed at accumulation, for the purpose of supporting a university sufficient for the wants and worthy of the power and wealth of the state. If only that had been done, and the Board had slept quietly on, we should now have a fund in hand sufficient for several universities.

The past is gone, but the future is before us. Shall we not begin now? What shall be said of us and our successors, three-quarters of a century hence, when this state shall have grown in wealth and power as it has for the last seventy-five years? Shall it be said that we only turned in our bed and slept more soundly on the other side; or shall it be said that we began in earnest the neglected labor?

99.

Slums and Tenant Housing in New York

Although the latter half of the nineteenth century is usually singled out as the significant period of growth for cities in America, the trend toward urbanization was already well under way by 1850. In the single decade, 1850-1860, the population of the United States grew by 36 percent, but the population of cities increased by 75.4 percent. This enormous influx into urban centers created many problems, none more serious than that of housing. Among the first exhaustive studies of this problem is the following report of a select committee of the New York state legislature, published March 9, 1857, as the result of a house-to-house survey of slum areas in New York.

Source: *Report of the Select Committee Appointed to Examine Into the Condition of Tenant Houses in New-York and Brooklyn*, New York State Assembly Document 205, March 9, 1857.

"GREAT CITIES," IT HAS BEEN SAID, "are great sores," but why they should necessarily be such excrescences upon the body of created things is a subject for legitimate inquiry. Man is gregarious in his nature, yearning for neighborhood and companionship. Benevolent theorists in all ages have not failed to picture their symmetric civic structures in which noble cities, brilliant with all the luxuries of refined architecture and lovely with all the contrivances of well-directed wealth, made up the foreground; and even Sacred Writ, in its exalted ideas of futurity, has coupled the forms of earthly splendor with the more spiritual excellences of a New Jerusalem. It might, then, be conjectured that cities ought not to be invariably doomed to association with all that is vile and repulsive in worldly habitation, but that, on the contrary, they may and should be the abodes of intelligent comfort, if not of intellectual and moral beatitude. Indeed, if desolate nature, with its isolation from all appliances requisite for the necessities of civilized man, be symbolical of savage or barbarous life, surely its extreme opposite, if measured by an ascending scale of progressive comfort, ought to be sought in a society where the accessibility of every means of human enjoyment amounts almost to commonness; where merchantry brings its lavish treasures, art her priceless products, luxury its profusion, and industry its unnumbered fruits.

Yet here, in reality, where pleasure wreathes perennial flowers, and magnificence runs wild with varied forms; here, in sad refutation of utopian speculation . . . the tenant house . . . rises in squalid deformity, to mock civilization with its foul malaria, its poison-breeding influences, its death-dealing associations. . . .

There is offered, through this very distinctiveness of the tenant-house system, a means of ameliorating the conditions of our poorer fellow beings, of directing their physical habits and improving their moral nature. The tenant house, with its pariah inhabitants, presents a field of missionary labor which, beginning at material necessities, may extend its influence to higher wants, in educational and religious points of view.

The tenant house is the offspring of municipal neglect as well as of its primary causes, overpopulation and destitution. As a city grows in commerce and demands new localities for traffic and manufacture, the store and workshop encroach upon the dwelling house and dispossess its occupants. At first the habitations of citizens are removed to a limited distance, because, with an industrious population, time is money, and neighborhood of residence and business secures both economy and convenience. The merchant and master, then, find it for their interest to dwell in the vicinity of their active operations; and so, likewise, do the mechanic, laborer, and all dependent on business life. It is at this stage of a community's growth that proper regulations and restrictions, looking to the ultimate well-being of the city, are of paramount necessity. . . . Had the evils which now appall us been prevented or checked in their earlier manifestation by wise and simple laws, the city of New York would now exhibit more gratifying bills of health, more general social comfort and prosperity, and less, far less, expenditure for the support of pauperism and of crime.

But legislation interposed not in its proper season, and hence the system of tenant-house leasing was soon begotten of the wants of poverty. As our wharves became crowded with warehouses and encompassed with bustle and noise, the wealthier citizens, who peopled old "Knickerbocker" mansions near the bay, transferred their residence to streets beyond the din; compensating for remoteness from their countinghouses by the advantages of increased quiet and luxury. Their habitations then passed into the hands, on the one side, of boardinghouse keepers, on the other, of real estate agents; and here, in its beginning, the tenant house became a real blessing to that class of industrious poor whose small earnings limited their expenses and whose employment in workshops, stores, or about the wharves and thoroughfares rendered a near residence of much importance. At this period rents were moderate, and a mechanic with family could hire two or more comfortable and even commodious apartments in a house once occupied by wealthy people for less than half what he is now obliged to pay for narrow and unhealthy quarters.

This state of tenantry comfort did not, however, continue long; for the rapid march of improvement speedily enhanced the value of property in the lower wards of the city, and, as this took place, rents rose and accommodations decreased in the same proportion. At first the better class of tenants submitted to retain their single floors, or two and three rooms, at the onerous rates, but this rendered them poorer, and those who were able to do so followed the example of former proprietors and emigrated to the upper wards. The spacious dwelling houses then fell before improvements, or languished for a season, as tenant houses of the type which is now the prevailing evil of our city; that is to say, their large rooms were partitioned into several smaller ones (without regard to proper light or ventilation), the rates of rent being lower in proportion to space or height from the street; and they soon became filled, from cellar to garret, with a class of tenantry living from hand to mouth, loose in morals, improvident in habits, degraded or squalid as beggary itself. . . .

Blocks were rented of real estate owners, or purchased on time, or taken in charge at a percentage, and held for underletting to applicants with no ready money and precarious means of livelihood. To such unfortunates it was not difficult to dictate terms or furnish habitations, for to them the mere sufferance of tenancy might appear like benevolence on the part of house owners. To this class, then, entire blocks of buildings, worn out in other service, were let in hundreds of subdivided apartments, and rates of rent were established, as well as seasons and modes of payment, which, while affording the wretched tenantry some sort of shelter within their scanty means, secured at the same time prompt payment of weekly dues, and an aggregate of profit from the whole barracks (risks and losses taken into account) of twice or thrice the amount which a legitimate lease of the building to one occupant would bring if granted for business purposes at the usual rate of real estate interest.

As no caretaking of premises could be expected from the majority of this class of tenants collected, or rather herded together, thus indiscriminately, the charges for occu-

pancy by the month or week were fixed at a rate which not only covered all risks, and secured exorbitant interest on investment, but left wide margin for damage and abuse, allowing the buildings to decay or fall to pieces as rapidly as constant occupancy would permit. It is true that stipulations were usually made to secure the property from wanton or willful demolition by tenants, and provisos to guard against accumulation of filth or insure precautions against accidents by fire were generally indicated in the terms of contract, but no stringent regulations on the part of landlords, no provisions for the maintenance of health, and no convenience for securing neatness, cleanliness, ventilation, or general order and comfort in the establishment, were ever dreamed of in connection with the tenant-house system, as it spreads its localities from year to year. . . .

In this stage of tenancy, the evils of a system which crowds hundreds of human beings into quarters inferior in comfort and accommodation to the pens of our cattle appear in flagrant distinctness. . . . Poverty, as we have seen it in New York, is wedded to despair, and its offspring is vengeance. It is a shape that sickens the heart with disgust and chills the blood with horror. . . .

We could tell of one room, 12 feet by 12, in which were five resident families comprising twenty persons, of both sexes and all ages, with only two beds, without partition or screen, or chair or table; and all dependent for their support upon the sale of chips gleaned from the streets, at 4 cents a basket; of another apartment, still smaller and still more destitute, inhabited by a man, a woman, two girls, and a boy, who were supported by permitting the room to be used as a rendezvous by abandoned women of the street; of another, an attic room, 7 feet by 5, containing scarcely an article of furniture but a bed, on which lay a fine-looking man in a raging fever, without medicine, drink, or suitable food, his toil-worn wife engaged in cleaning the dirt from the floor, and his little child asleep on a bundle of rags in the corner; of another of the same dimensions, in which we found, seated on low boxes around a candle placed on a keg, a woman and her eldest daughter (the latter a girl of fifteen, and, as we were told, a prostitute), sewing on shirts, for the making of which they were paid 4 cents apiece, and even at that price, out of which they had to support two small children, they could not get a supply of work; of another room, about as large, occupied by a street ragpicker and his family, the income of whose industry was about $8 per month; of another apartment, scarce larger (into which we were drawn by the screams of a wife beaten by her drunken husband), containing no article of furniture whatever; of another, warmed only by a tin pail of lighter charcoal placed in the center of the floor, over which a blind man bent, endeavoring to warm himself, while three or four men and women were quarreling around him, and in one corner lay the body of a woman who had died the day before of disease, her orphan children sleeping near on a pile of rags; of another room, from which a short time before twenty persons, sick with fever, had been taken to the hospital to die. But why extend the catalog? . . .

RECONSTRUCTED TENANT HOUSES

These consist mainly of a series of contiguous buildings, of a combination of apartments adapted or reconstructed for tenant purposes, within the walls of some large house or public building. Of this class (proceeding from the lower point of New York City) we came, first, to one of inferior dimensions, but with its full proportion of wretchedness, the entrance of which is at 16 Washington Street, in the First Ward. This is a three-story building (owned by an Irish woman residing in Pearl Street), accessible through a narrow door and steep stairway, ascending over a stable wherein an express company's horses are kept.

The dilapidation of this entire building is extreme; its rickety floors shook under the tread, and portions of the wall, black and mildewed, were continually breaking off, while nearly every vestige of mortar had disappeared from some of the rooms, leaving only smoke-discolored lathing, through which thick moisture was constantly oozing. A poor woman who occupied an apartment on the second floor complained that this last discomfort was incessant. "The ould ceiling," she said, "is ould as meself, and it's full uv the *dhrop* it is," *i.e.*, it was soaked with water that entered through the broken roof whenever it rained. Indeed, the committee were assured (and from appearances the fact could not be doubted) that in wet weather the upper floors of this ruinous habitation were completely flooded, and the poor occupants were obliged to move their drenched beds from spot to spot as the dropping became too troublesome to permit sleep.

In the rear of this building was another of the same height (three stories), and with a ground floor of 100 feet in length to 16 deep, connecting with the street by two narrow alleys. The decay and dilapidation of the premises was only equaled by the filth of the inhabitants. The number of tenants in both houses was reported as seventy, all Irish. In the front section the rent varied from $2 to $6 per month; in the rear from $6 to $8; rooms dark, narrow, and ill ventilated. The price for an apartment, with two small closets answering for bedrooms, was $7 per month. The lessee of the premises, who underlet, and was responsible to the proprietor, informed the committee that he paid $1,456 per annum, including taxes. . . .

In a cellar beneath, rooms were "to let." The first floor was used by the lessee as a sailors' lodging house, the accommodation of which consisted of bunks, arranged one above another like a ship's lockers. The upper floors were occupied by Irish families, to the height of the garret, which was reached by a kind of ladder. Under the broken and leaky roof, three families were crouching, one of which (a woman and child) paid $3 per month for a portion of the miserable garret; the woman had been obliged to sell her bedstead to meet the rent and slept with her baby on the floor. The total rent collected from tenants in this house (18 by 30 feet, and three stories) was $90 per month.

At 46 Trinity Place (Third Ward), in rear of Trinity Church and overlooked by the stained windows of that beautiful edifice, was a tenant house which had been altered from a school building; in this house there were fourteen families — in all, seventy-six persons — each tenement comprising a room 12 by 14 feet in area, with two bedrooms, or rather closets, where neither light nor air penetrated. Some of the families inhabiting these premises kept lodgers at 1s. per night. One widow-woman had nine men boarding with her, dwelling in the one dining room and two bedrooms. . . .

In Mulberry Street, near the "Five Points" (Sixth Ward), the committee examined a large tenant house in a very dilapidated condition. It had been reconstructed, through its interior, from an old wooden church once used by the Baptists and adapted to occupancy in the most careless manner. The sewer connection serving for the premises was a four-inch pipe, wholly inadequate to the necessary uses of such a conduit. In this establishment there were 85 apartments, containing more than 100 families and comprising 310 persons. In the basement, entered by shattered steps, the depth below the street level was measured by the committee, and ascertained to be 5 feet, 2 inches. In these vaults, families were dwelling and paying $3 per month for their damp and sickly quarters. On the fifth floor of this structure, $4.50 per month was paid for apartments.

The entire fabric is cased and cramped, and the walls, floors, and roofing of such inflammable materials that, in case of fire in any portion, it would be impossible to arrest its spread. Should such a calamity take place at night, it is more than probable that scores of the unfortunate inmates would perish ere they could find egress through the narrow doors and passages. . . .

At No. 17 Baxter Street, the committee penetrated through an alley passage, where the black mud was two inches deep; [at the] . . . rear of these premises was a collection of sheds built of rough boards, each containing four dark rooms, rent, $3 per month, inhabited by poor people who subsisted by the sale of spearmint, which they grew in boxes on the roof and disposed of to hotels and barrooms, a fact which suggested that certain fashionable beverages in vogue might be traced back for their constituents to the malaria and filth of the Five Point tenant houses. The average rent of rooms in this locality, where are many houses of the same description, is $4 per month. . . .

In this connection it may be mentioned that rear buildings and their surroundings present, in general, the most repulsive features of the tenant-house system. As business has increased upon the streets, the buildings located favorably for stores have been converted to the use of trade, and the area comprised in the distance intervening, from square to square, generally filled with wooden structures, has been seized upon by the tenant-house speculator. Sometimes a dozen narrow and dark apartments in a single house, but often a collection of moldy walls, covering a space of from 40 to 200 feet square, with cramped, miserable apartments, scarce fit for dog kennels, may be discovered in the rear of some busy factory in our lower wards, or seen from the windows of a hotel, or overlooked from the roof of a marble store. To reach these stumbling and squalid rookeries, the visitor must sometimes penetrate a labyrinth of alleys, behind horse stables, blacksmiths' forges, and, inevitably, beside cheap groggeries, till he finds himself in a dim close, thick with mephitic gases, and nauseous from the effluvia of decaying matter and pools of stagnant water.

THE RAGPICKING AND BONE-GATHERING TENANTS

At No. 88 Sheriff Street, a rambling row of wooden tenements called "Ragpickers' Paradise" was inspected by the committee. The locality was infected for squares around by the effluvia of putrefying flesh, from numberless bone-boiling places, and bags of filthy rags stored in the cellars and sheds. "Ragpickers' Paradise" is inhabited entirely by Germans, who dwell in small rooms, in almost fabulous gregariousness, surrounded by scores of dogs and canopied by myriads of rags fluttering from lines crossing their filthy yards, where bones of dead animals and noisome collections of every kind were reeking with pestiferous smells. One establishment (which is devoted to the same purpose, situated on Third Street, and owned by a former member of our state senate) contains more than fifty families. Though extreme squalor is apparent to a visitor, the Germans inhabiting these localities appear to be thrifty, and, in their way, comfortable.

It is said that habits of economy and constant application to their wretched business enable nearly all, sooner or later, to accumulate sufficient funds to enable them to migrate to the West. We were told of a colony of 300 of these people who occupied a single basement, living on offal and scraps, and who saved money enough to purchase a township on one of the Western prairies. Nevertheless, their means of livelihood, degraded as it is, is likewise exceedingly precarious, especially in severe winters when snowstorms, covering the ground, hide the rags, shreds of paper, etc., on the sale of which they subsist. In such seasons the children are sent out to sweep crossings or beg, and many of the most adroit practitioners on public charity are found among these urchins, who are generally marked by a precocity and cunning which render them, too often, adepts in vice at the tenderest ages.

The presence and customs of the bone-gathering tenants were made known to the committee through other senses besides that of vision. In the yards, where ferocious-looking dogs greeted the visitors with threatening demonstrations, a number of bags of bones, just brought thither from slaughterhouses, with decaying flesh clinging to them, saluted our nostrils with noxious effluvia. These bones were to be boiled on the premises, and their stench, mingled with the fetid exhalations from wet rags, was to be sent abroad over the neighborhood, thence to ascend and be carried by the wind, with all the deadly particles, to the chambers of sick people and the parlors of wealthy residents upon other avenues. On the wooden piazzas, and choking up the narrow entries, were bags and baskets of calves' heads, offensive with putrid portions of the jowls and bones in every stage of decomposition.

The class of tenants above mentioned, i.e., ragpicking and bone gathering, have a sort of internal polity by means of which they preserve an amicable understanding, though competing in the same miserable business. For the purpose of their daily life the city is districted or partitioned into streets and neighborhoods, certain individuals or families being allowed their distinct fields, over the boundaries of which they must not pass to trespass on another's. The colonies sally out at daybreak with their baskets and pokers, disperse to their respective precincts, and pursue their work with more or less success throughout the day. On their return, the baskets, bags, and carts (for some aspire to the convenience of a dogcart) are emptied into a common heap. Then, from the bones and scraps of meat, certain portions are selected wherewith to prepare soups and ragouts. The rags are separated from the bones and sorted, washed, and dried; the bones, after everything that may serve for food has been scraped from them, are boiled, after which rags and bones are sold — the former to adjacent shopkeepers who live by the traffic, at about 2 cents per pound, and the latter for 30 cents per bushel.

When it is recollected that the process of washing filthy rags, collected from the gutters, sinks, hospital yards, and every vile locality imaginable, is conducted in the single apartment used for cooking, eating, sleeping, and general living purposes by the tenants (sometimes a dozen in one room), where furthermore, bone boiling, with its odors, is a constant concomitant; and where, to these horrible practices, are superadded the personal filth, stagnant water, fixed air, and confined, dark, and damp holes, all characteristic of the tenant-house system, such as witnessed by the committee in every variety, it is no wonder that these unfortunate people are yearly decimated; it is not strange that the cholera and other epidemics have, as we are told, made frightful havoc among them in past years.

100.

Lewis Cass: Trade with China Under Suitable Guarantees

American interest in the Far East developed slowly despite possibilities for lucrative trade. The United States first appointed a consular agent to China in 1786, but it was fifty-seven years before a diplomatic mission finally concluded a commercial treaty with the government of China. When the Taiping Rebellion hindered enforcement of the treaty, the United States was urged to join Great Britain and France in an aggressive policy toward China. The American government rejected the proposal, but in the following letter of instructions of May 10, 1857, Secretary of State Lewis Cass advised Envoy William B. Reed to work for "peaceful cooperation" with France and Great Britain. The treaty subsequently negotiated by Reed served as the basis of American policy in China for ten years.

Source: 36 Congress, 1 Session, Senate Executive Document No. 30, pp. 6-11.

I HAVE ALREADY ANNOUNCED to you your appointment as envoy extraordinary and minister plenipotentiary from the United States to China, and I am now to furnish you, for your guidance, with the general views of the President upon the subjects connected with your mission.

Many of these views are contained in the communication of April 10 last, from this department, to Lord Napier, the British minister, of which a copy accompanies this letter, and to which your attention is specially directed. You will also receive, herewith, copies of several communications from Lord Napier, and of dispatches from the British government to some of its officers, which disclose the purposes of that government in China, and the measures by which it expects to accomplish them. As to these objects and measures, there seems to be an entire unanimity of sentiment and action between Great Britain and France, extending even to armed cooperation, and you will find from the papers annexed that the United States have been invited to join the alliance and to participate in its hostile movements.

The reasons of the President for declining this participation are sufficiently stated in the communication to the British minister already referred to, together with his opinions as to the extent to which the United States may fairly cooperate with the allied powers in China.

The objects which it is understood the allies seek to accomplish by treaty stipulations are:

1. To procure from the Chinese government a recognition of the right of other powers to have accredited ministers at the court of Peking, to be received by the emperor, and to be in communication with the authorities charged with the foreign affairs of the Empire.

2. An extension of commercial intercourse with China, which is now restricted to five ports enumerated in the treaty.

3. A reduction of the tariff of duties levied upon domestic produce in its transit from the interior to the coast, as the amount now imposed is said to be a violation of the treaty. On this subject you will be able to ascertain the true state of the alleged grievance when you reach China, and to act accordingly.

4. A stipulation for religious freedom to all foreigners in China.

5. An arrangement for the suppression of piracy.

6. Provision for extending the benefits of the proposed treaty to all the other civilized powers of the earth.

These objects are recognized by the President as just and expedient, and, so far as you can do so by peaceful cooperation, he expects that you will aid in their accomplishment. In conformity with this policy, you will communicate frankly with the British and French ministers upon all the points of common interest, so that it may be distinctly understood that the three nations are equally influenced by a determination to obtain justice, and by a desire to procure treaty arrangements for the extension and more adequate protection of their commercial intercourse with China. But on your side these efforts must be confined to firm representations, appealing to the justice and policy of the Chinese authorities, and leaving to your own government to determine upon the course to be adopted should your representations be fruitless.

Special reference is made to your communication with the ministers of Great Britain and France, not only from our common interest with those nations in the trade of China, and in the means suggested for its extension, but because they alone among the great powers of the world have diplomatic representatives at Canton. It is understood, however, that Russia, which has long been represented in China by missionaries of religion, has attempted recently to secure the reception there of an accredited minister, and you may possibly find this purpose accomplished when you reach your destination. In that event, there is no good reason why you should not have the same friendly relations with the Russian envoy as with the representatives of Great Britain and France.

You are authorized, therefore, to communicate with him as far as practicable upon all subjects of mutual concern, and should his disposition prove favorable, as it is believed it will, his cooperation may be highly advantageous in promoting the objects of your mission. This cooperation is to be expected, moreover, with the greater confidence, because there is nothing in the policy of the United States with respect to China which is not quite consistent with the pacific relations which are understood to exist between that Empire and Russia.

This country, you will constantly bear in mind, is not at war with the government of China, nor does it seek to enter that Empire for any other purposes than those of lawful commerce, and for the protection of the lives and property of its citizens. The whole nature and policy of our government must necessarily confine our action within these limits and deprive us of all motives either for territorial aggrandizement or the acquisition of political power in that distant region.

During the hostilities which now exist in China, we may be able to avail ourself of this fortunate position, not only for the benefit of our countrymen who reside there, or who have extensive interests there of a commercial character, but in order to facilitate also the general objects sought to be accomplished by a revision of the existing treaties. It is possible, even, that it may be employed with advantage as a means of communication between the belligerent parties, and tend in this way to the termination of the war. You will, therefore, not fail to let it be known to the Chinese authorities that we are no party to the existing hostilities and have no intention to interfere in their political concerns or to gain a foothold in their country.

We go there to engage in trade, but under suitable guarantees for its protection. The extension of our commercial intercourse must be the work of individual enterprise, and to this element of our national character we may safely leave it. With the domestic institutions of China we have no political concern, and to attempt a forcible interference with them would not only be unjust in itself but might defeat the very object desired. Fortunately, however, commerce itself is one of the most powerful means of civilization and national improvement.

By coming into peaceful contact with men of other regions and other races, with different habits and greater knowledge, the jealous system of seclusion which has so long separated China from the rest of the world will gradually give way, and with increased intercourse will come those meliorations in the moral and physical condition of its people which the Christian and the philanthropist have so long and so ardently desired. . . .

By the copy which accompanies this paper of the instructions of the secretary of the Navy to the commanding officer of our Chinese squadron, you will perceive that our forces in that quarter have been increased, and that their movements have been placed, as far as possible, within your control. The armed steamer *Minnesota* has been specially assigned for your accommodation, not only on your passage to China but during your residence there; and the commander of the squadron has also been authorized to charter a small steamer "for the purpose of ascending rivers or entering ports inaccessible to the other vessels of his squadron." It is hoped that these instructions will enable you to have the cordial cooperation of our naval forces for the purposes of your mission. On the other hand, I am persuaded that I only anticipate your own views when I suggest to you the importance of cultivating the most friendly relations with the officers of the squadron, and especially of maintaining the most unreserved intercourse with its commander.

101.

Oliver Wendell Holmes: "Ode for a Social Meeting"

Oliver Wendell Holmes, whose writings and personality reflected the highly cultivated New England society into which he was born, delighted readers with a sparkling wit that gave a human quality to his social criticism. In 1857 Holmes and other members of the Cambridge, Massachusetts, "Saturday Club" launched the Atlantic Monthly *magazine, and Holmes's "Autocrat of the Breakfast-Table," which appeared monthly, quickly became one of the* Atlantic's *most popular features. The urbanity and humor of this "table talk" did not conceal the fact that Holmes was often sharply critical — witness the following jab at teetotalers.*

Source: *Atlantic Monthly,* December 1857.

Here is a little poem I sent a short time since to a committee for a certain celebration. I understood that it was to be a festive and convivial occasion, and ordered myself accordingly. It seems the president of the day was what is called a "teetotaler." I received a note from him in the following words, containing the copy subjoined, with the emendations annexed to it.

Dear Sir:

    Your poem gives good satisfaction to the committee. The sentiments expressed with reference to liquor are not, however, those generally entertained by this community. I have therefore consulted the clergyman of this place, who has made some slight changes, which he thinks will remove all objections, and keep the valuable portions of the poem. Please to inform me of your charge for said poem. Our means are limited, etc., etc., etc.   Yours with respect.

Here it is — with the *Slight Alterations!*

Come! fill a fresh bumper, for why should we go

         logwood
While the ~~nectar~~ still reddens our cups as they flow?

         decoction
Pour out the ~~rich juices~~ still bright with the sun,

                        dye-stuff
Till o'er the brimmed crystal the ~~rubies~~ shall run.

         half-ripened apples
The ~~purple-globed clusters~~ their life-dews have bled;

                     taste   *sugar of lead*
How sweet is the ~~breath~~ of the ~~fragrance they shed!~~

                 rank poisons
For summer's ~~last roses~~ lie hid in the

    wines!!!
    ~~wines~~

                     stable-boys smoking
That were garnered by ~~maidens who~~

         long-nines.
    ~~laughed thro' the vines.~~

         scowl   *howl*   *scoff*
Then a ~~smile,~~ and a ~~glass,~~ and a ~~toast,~~

         sneer,
    and a ~~cheer,~~

         strychnine and whiskey and ratsbane and
For all the ~~good wine, and we've some of~~

    beer
    ~~it here!~~
In cellar, in pantry, in attic, in hall,

Down, down with the tyrant that masters us all!

~~Long live the gay servant that laughs for us all!~~

102.

COUNT GUROWSKI: Virtues of the American Mind

European interest in American political and social institutions drew many travelers and journalists to this country in the nineteenth century. One of the most perceptive reports on American life and character was Count Adam de Gurowski's America and Europe *(1857). Gurowski came to the United States in 1849 after fleeing Poland for his part in the rebellion against Russia. He traveled widely in America before joining the State Department as a translator during the Civil War. The latter experience led Gurowski to publish his more widely known* Diary, *in which he attacked the North's conduct of the war. This work fell short of the objectivity he attained in* America and Europe, *from which the following chapter on "The American Mind" is taken.*

Source: *America and Europe*, New York, 1857, pp. 333-348.

THE GENUINE AMERICAN MIND is the sum of various components, intuitive as well as objective in their source and in their operations. Various inward and external combinations, events, and conjunctures have added to the English substratum new, diversified, spiritual, and so to say, corporeal terms and substances. . . . The contending forces in the American mind manifest themselves in various ways and in efforts for asserting individuality, originality, and an independent mode of perception. Nevertheless the substratum maintains its ground, yielding slowly and stubbornly to the pressure of the elements which accumulate upon it. In the oscillations produced by this struggle originate those contrasts which mark more or less distinctly the intellectual manifestations.

The American mind tends preeminently toward the objective, at times, however, being given to the subjective, even to abstract speculation. It is singularly impulsive and receptive, seizes eagerly upon the most antagonistic objects, and embraces them with considerable elasticity. Expansive, and at times daring, it is less disciplined and subdued by routine than is the case with the English mind. Hitherto the American mind has not reached the elevated standpoint of an absolute, intuitive individuality. Stimulated by the fullness and vigor of intuitiveness, but open to the breathing influences of outward nature, to the ever freshly pouring combinations of events, the mind ascends slowly, step by step, into the expanding region of normal self-consciousness. It is inquisitive, analytic, dismembering, and still eager often to discover, to comprehend a general law, to accept general formulas and axioms, and to submit to them. It grapples willingly with difficulties, but is not, however, always enduring or patient enough to overcome and subdue them, above all when the difficulties are founded in merely abstract, speculative combinations. Evoked to self-conscious activity, the American mind was thrown at the start into a stern and rough medium, and cut off from the motherland; it was obliged to direct all its intensity to struggles with nature, with destructive matter, was forced to choose and decide swiftly, to act, and not to remain in musing contemplation.

Immediate practical results are more attractive for the American mind, although not exclusively, than the charms of imagination. In its intellectual, positive turn, it yields easily to the pressure of outward events and combinations. Intellect finds more food, more stimulus in externalities, and therefore it overpowers the spirit, the imagination, as well as the tendency to abstract, interior contemplation. Of great mobility, expansive but not deep, the American mind as yet seems unable to seize thoroughly and penetrate deeply into the infinity of intuitive ideas, engrossed as it has hitherto been by sensations. The social condition, the primitive state of nature, opening uninterruptedly her wider and wider circles before the Americans, challenge and attract the intellectual powers, carry away the activity into one general, explorative, mechanical, commercial current. But, then, even a certain inborn elasticity redeems and saves it from utter degradation. And so, notwithstanding this seemingly all-absorbing commercial propensity, the mind of the people at large does not become eaten up or narrowed, as is the case, for example, with the immense majority of the various commercial classes in Europe. The so-called petty shopkeeper spirit does not prevail in America to the same extent as in most of the European parent countries.

Excitability, omnipotent in the American character, scarcely affects the activity of mind. The keen internal perception of the object strongly resists excitability or nervousness and dispels the mist that has been aroused. If the Americans do not resist but yield to the current of excitement, it is more from want of independence than from want of a sound, internal, mental judgment. Comparatively rapid and comprehensive in assimilation and combination — far more so than the English — the American mind seems to be indifferent to method; at the same time, by a striking contrast, the intellect is disciplined by it in most of its mechanical dealings with the realm of matter.

Though not absolutely rigorous in its operations, the American mind is earnest, giving fixity and ballast, and forming a counterpoise to the often febrile unrest of character.

The various peculiarities of the American mind, the outbursts of its originality and independence, are manifested more generally and freely in the people at large, in its promptings and impulses, than in those which are commonly considered as the representative minds, the literary stars, or any other exponents of the spiritual or imaginative faculties. Among the people, likewise, as, for example, among that of New England, that of the West gushes out and is domestic — the rich vein of humor, which constitutes a trait of originality distinct from the English humor and from that of other European nations.

Taken in the whole, in its substance, the American mind is eminently a progressive one. If it is as yet comparatively deficient in absolute philosophical comprehensiveness, if it assiduously elaborates the special and the single, by this process it gathers and prepares materials to become coordinated and then fused together. The eternal spirit which watches over the progress and the development of mankind alternately evokes to prominent activity the various powers and attributes of the mind, bringing them into full play and making them preponderate, the one over another, according to the given conditions and necessities. Observing in mankind the march of mental culture, there is clearly perceptible an alternated but uninterrupted putting out and holding back of the various mental powers, the intuitive and the intellectual playing into each other.

This assimilation and fusion at the given moment of the life of individuals, as of a whole people, constitute a complete real progress and civilization. Almost every mental and intellectual phenomenon corresponds to a philosophical and social claim of our being, and solutions are obtained by their harmonious interweaving. Then again new problems arise, requiring new combinations and fresh efforts. Exclusive idealism and exclusive positivism bear the mark of onesidedness and uniformity, and are not virtually progressive. A wheel can stand still, can turn backward, but its normal function is to move onward, and carry onward all its composing atoms. So it is with the mind; it embraces subject and object and moves on, because movement and progress are the sole conditions of life and of development; they alone are creative. . . .

As soon as independence was asserted by the nation, the activity of mind became evoked in all directions; poetry and literature began to be a domestic American product. Lyrical poetry preeminently pours out abundantly, in powerful streams and often full of grace, freshness, and charm. The lyric productions of acknowledged American poets, men and women, as well as many accidental effusions, can fairly stand beside, and some above the lyricism of other nations. Many of the little fiery or graceful poems that have been evoked by events of national domestic character bear the mark of originality.

Generally, however, their literature, with its poetical and ephemeral creations, is not original in conception, not stamped with individuality to the same degree as are the life of the people and its political institutions. Emancipated as a nation, the Americans remain mentally, by their literary productions, in the colonial dependence upon England. They have outstripped the Old World in most of the productions of intellect, in mechanical arts and inventions, impressing on them, to a certain degree, the stamp of originality; *per contra* in literature, they with difficulty take an independent start. Many are the natural as well as the conventional reasons and causes which account for the phenomenon, that in reality there does not exist — a few productions excepted, as,

for example, Longfellow's *Evangeline* — an original American literature but only an imitation, or a continuation of the English literature. Hitherto literature seems rather to be engrafted on than to sprout out of the vitality of the nation.

It may be considered as trivial, and in itself not worth mentioning, but nevertheless a regret presses on one's mind, that with such countlessly accumulated elements for originality in every direction, no new language could have been created in America. When the Latin world succumbed, out of its linguistic ruins emerged the Italian, the Spanish, the Portuguese, the Provençal, and the French idioms; the two last (the Provençal through minstrels) contributing again, with the Latin and Saxon, to shape out the English. All these offshoots of the Latin developed themselves, to a certain degree, independently. The parturition was difficult and its process took centuries. Dante complained of not having a literary national language; but he became the godfather of the idiom used by the people, lifted it up, and purified it, and the Tuscan was created. By the formation of the above-named sprouts from the Latin, new agencies for the expansion of the inborn productivity of the human mind were brought forth, and the world endowed with new characteristic literatures, reflecting the mental, the imaginative, the social peculiarities of those various nations. Such newly formed languages are generally richer in words than is their matrix; but they are poorer in grammatical forms.

The English colonists in America, although immersed in a new world of intuitions as well as of facts, impressions, emotions, but neither politically nor mentally severed from the mother country, did not attempt to assert a social, and still less a literary independence. They were not yet *a people*; and it is only in a people, in its distinct, independent existence, that the urgings for self-consciousness in mental, social, and literary creations are revealed. They dared not to overstep the authority or, what very likely they believed, the propriety of the English language, and increase irreverently, by new linguistic combinations and creations, the original parent stock. They unconsciously submitted therein to the all-powerful authority of the masters, using old names for daily newly appearing mental and material phenomena.

Languages, those great arteries of mental vitality, repose not on authorities — they were not taught by any primitive creator or inventor — but their creative essence and force are in the people, and a distinct language is the cardinal assertion of independence. Hitherto, all the great nations of mighty and lasting historical significance have had a distinct language. The American nation appears the first on the social and political horizon, as yet deprived of this symbol of individuality. Independence must exist within, in the thought, and then it becomes asserted outwardly, in all the intellectual, social, and physical or material manifestations of an independent people.

An innate relation exists between thinking and speaking; and the completeness and fullness of this relation reveals and points out, in the crowd of nations, the historical people. To speak an original, one's own language, is to have an original, individual manner of thinking, instead of borrowing other people's comprehensions, ideas, and utterances. To speak an original language is to have independent, individual intuition and conception; because to speak is to manifest the inner thought. Language is the manifestation of the *geist* [spirit] which animates man. Freedom is the characteristic and the element as well as the attribute of the spirit, in contrast to nature or matter.

Language is the fullest utterance of the spirit; it pours out from the intuitive freedom and evidences that freedom is man's destiny. The development of the spirit and of language generally traverse identical

stages, both being manifestations of virtual individuality. The spirit and the language are the highest and purest essences of man's mental activity. Language has to answer to the demands of the mind; it is therefore ever-living and ever-moving, and not made once in time, to last for all eternities. Language ought to keep pace with the expansion of an onward, striving people. Words break out from the inward man, and their generator is life, and not dictionaries and authorities. A people in the condition of normal and healthy growth and development, extending its faculties of comprehension, increasing its multifarious mental productions, expanding its aspirations, multiplying its mental and material wants, and the means and resources for their satisfaction — such a people must unavoidably want new expressions and it creates them. Such words are the spontaneous revelations of the immanent spirit. The substratum of the American people, in its unrelenting activity, makes use of such creative force.

This people moves on a separate, almost limitless orbit, and develops its individuality among the new mental and physical phenomena therein encountered. The people is not disturbed by models or traditional authorities but creates new words for new ideas, conceptions, objects, emotions, and bestows on them the right of citizenship. Already many of the same words and expressions have different meanings in America and in England. The vocabulary of Americanisms forms a thick volume. The Americanisms will increase, will become sifted; and from the lips of the people, they will indubitably pass into books, in spite of their so-called barbarism, and become used by refined literators [litterateurs]. Their origin, the power creating them, are the same as were those of all preexistent languages and words that are now sustained by authorities and included in dictionaries.

The American literators, being brought up and nursed on English models, entertain for these authorities the most filial deference. They look up to them, rather than to the living fountain within themselves and in the people. They are less daring than the people amidst whom they move, and who attempt continually to rival old models, to surpass them, to strike in every direction an independent vein, dissimilar to the English. The highest aim of literators is to imitate, to approach those examples, to remain within the boundaries traced by those whom they recognize as their masters, to win their approbation.

The majority, above all, of the elder, leading literators, almost in all branches, who publish their labors, count upon the circulation in America, but turn nevertheless their mind toward England, wherefrom they are anxious to receive the supreme consecration, the knightly accolade. England is for them the supreme judge of the correctness and purity of the language, of the form, the style. This pupil-like deference to that distant authority must influence and cramp the spontaneity of their mind, of their imagination, always on the alert not to commit a breach upon the proprieties of conventional or established English rules; not to be self-relying, young; not to use words or images, not to introduce forms, unknown in dictionaries and in time-honored authorities.

The Americans of all nations at any time upon the earth have probably the fullest poetical nature. The United States themselves are essentially the greatest poem.

WALT WHITMAN, Preface to *Leaves of Grass*

Index of Authors

*The numbers in brackets
indicate selection numbers
in this volume*

Crisis of the South: How to Meet It (1857), one of the few Southern protests against slavery, and later several bitter anti-Negro tracts, such as *Nojoque* (1867). [94]

HOLMES, OLIVER WENDELL (Aug. 29, 1809-Oct. 7, 1894), physician, poet, and humorist. Professor of anatomy (1838-40) at Dartmouth College and (1847-82) at Harvard Medical School; wrote humorous works (*The Autocrat of the Breakfast-Table*, 1857), poetry ("Old Ironsides," "The Chambered Nautilus," "The Wonderful One-Hoss Shay"), biographies *Ralph Waldo Emerson*, 1885), and hymns ("Lord of all being! throned afar"). [101] See also Author Index, Vols. 9, 11.

HUNT, FREEMAN (March 21, 1804-March 2, 1858), publisher and editor. Writer for the *Boston Daily Traveller*; with John Putnam published *Juvenile Miscellany*, the *Jackson Republican*, and the *Ladies' Magazine*; published and edited (c. 1840-58) the *Merchants' Magazine and Commercial Review*. [85]

JONES, JAMES C. (June 7, 1809-Oct. 29, 1859), public official. Governor of Tennessee (1841-45); U.S. senator (1851-57). [30]

LINCOLN, ABRAHAM (Feb. 12, 1809-April 15, 1865), lawyer and statesman. Sixteenth President of the United States (1861-65); U.S. representative from Illinois (1847-49); defeated in senatorial campaign (1858) by Stephen A. Douglas; issued the Emancipation Proclamation (Jan. 1, 1863); delivered dedicatory address at Gettysburg National Cemetery (Nov. 19, 1863); assassinated by John Wilkes Booth, a fanatical actor, only five days after Lee's surrender to Grant at Appomattox Court House. [58, 59, 90] See also Author Index, Vols. 6, 9.

MANN, HORACE (May 4, 1796-Aug. 2, 1859), educator. First secretary (1837-48) of the Massachusetts Board of Education; revolutionized public school organization and teaching methods; established (1839) the first state teachers college; U.S. representative (1848-53); president (1853-59) of Antioch College. [2] See also Author Index, Vols. 6, 7.

MEIDELL, FRITHJOF (?-1864), Norwegian immigrant. Described life in the American West in letters published in the Norwegian newspaper *Aftenbladet*. [69]

MELVILLE, HERMAN (Aug. 1, 1819-Sept. 28, 1891), novelist. Sailed on the whaling ship *Acushnet* (1841-42); jumped ship at the Marquesas Islands; sailed on the Australian whaler *Lucy Ann* but left her at Papeete (1842); seaman on the frigate *United States* (1843-44); wrote stories based on his experiences: *Typee* (1846), *Moby-Dick* (1851), *The Piazza Tales* (1856), *Billy Budd* (1892). [17] See also Author Index, Vols. 9, 10.

OLMSTED, FREDERICK LAW (April 27, 1822-Aug. 28, 1903), landscape architect. Designed Central Park, New York City; developed the grounds of the Capitol, Washington, D.C., the campus of Leland Stanford University, and the south Chicago lakefront; wrote *Journeys and Explorations in the Cotton Kingdom* (1861). [49] See also Author Index, Vol. 10.

PARKER, THEODORE (Aug. 24, 1810-May 10, 1860), Unitarian clergyman and social reformer. Minister (from 1845) of the liberal "Congregational Society" of Boston; antislavery agitator; member of the secret committee to aid John Brown's raid on Harpers Ferry. [22, 74] See also Author Index, Vol. 7.

PULSZKY, FRANCIS (1814-1897) and THERESA (fl. 1848-1853), Hungarian political activists and writers. Accompanied Lajos Kossuth, exiled Hungarian political leader, to U.S. (1852); described their trip in *White, Red, Black* (1853). [45]

RUFFIN, EDMUND (Jan. 5, 1794-June 18, 1865), agriculturalist and author. Founded and edited (1833-43) *Farmer's Register* to encourage scientific farming; wrote *Anticipations of the Future* (1860) in favor of slavery and an independent South; as a member of the Confederate Palmetto Guard volunteers, fired the first shot against Fort Sumter (April 12, 1861). [91]

SANDERSON, JOHN P. (fl. 1856), writer. Author of *The Views and Opinions of American Statesmen on Foreign Immigration* (1856). [84]

SCHAFF, PHILIP (Jan. 1, 1819-Oct. 20, 1893), theologian and church historian. Professor of church history and biblical

nor of Kansas Territory (1857-58); U.S. financial agent in Europe (1863-64). [89] See also Author Index, Vol. 7.

WALLACE, W. H. (fl. 1856), lawyer. Wrote *A Brief Notice of the Recent Outrages Committed by Isaac I. Stevens, Governor of Washington Territory* (1856). [78]

WAYLAND, FRANCIS (March 11, 1796-Sept. 30, 1865), Baptist clergyman and educator. President (1827-55) of Brown University, where he liberalized curriculum and enlarged the school; wrote *Thoughts on the Present Collegiate System in the United States* (1842) and *Report to the Corporation of Brown University* (1850) on educational reform. [13] See also Author Index, Vol. 7.

WEBSTER, DANIEL (Jan. 18, 1782-Oct. 24, 1852), lawyer, orator, and statesman. U.S. representative from New Hampshire (1813-17) and from Massachusetts (1823-27); U.S. senator from Massachusetts (1827-41, 1845-50); secretary of state (1841-43) under Tyler and (1850-52) under Fillmore. [4, 21] See also Author Index, Vols. 4, 5, 6, 7.

WHITMAN, WALT (May 31, 1819-March 26, 1892), poet, schoolteacher, and journalist. Edited (1846-48) the *Brooklyn Eagle* and wrote (1848) for the *New Orleans Crescent;* hospital nurse (1862-64) in Washington, D.C.; clerk in U.S. Department of the Interior (1865), but dismissed by the secretary of the interior because of the "licentiousness" of his poetry; wrote *Leaves of Grass* (1855 and nine later revisions), *Drum-Taps* (1865), *Democratic Vistas* (1871). [80, 81] See also Author Index, Vols. 7, 9, 10, 11.

WHITTIER, JOHN GREENLEAF (Dec. 17, 1807-Sept. 7, 1892), poet, journalist, Abolitionist, and humanitarian. Editor (1830-32) of the *New England Weekly Review;* wrote *Justice and Expediency* and poems in behalf of the Abolitionist cause; also wrote religious works and poems of New England, including "Snow-Bound" (1866). [5, 53] See also Author Index, Vols. 6, 7, 9.